The

CURSE OF IGNORANCE

A History of Mankind

The

CURSE OF IGNORANCE

A History of Mankind

From primitive times to the end of the
Second World War

BY

ARTHUR FINDLAY

IN TWO VOLUMES

"Ignorance is the curse of God.   Knowledge is the wing wherewith
we fly to heaven."—SHAKESPEARE

VOLUME TWO

THE HEADQUARTERS PUBLISHING CO. LTD.
5 Alexandria Road, West Ealing,
London, W13 0NP.

First Impression	1947
Second Impression	1947
Third Impression	1948
Fourth Impression	1948
Fifth Impression	1956
Sixth Impression	1963
Seventh Impression	1993

Arthur Findlay was the first to give a scientific explanation of death and the hereafter. This he did in his famous book On the Edge of the Etheric, and translated into 18 foreign languages. He was the first to make the etheric world comprehensible in terms of vibrations, and this he did in The Rock of Truth and The Unfolding Universe. He was the first to trace the origin of all world religions to psychic phenomena, and show that all religious beliefs, rituals and ceremonials had a psychic origin. This he did in The Psychic Stream. In The Curse of Ignorance he is the first to write world history from the psychic angle of thought, and this presents the past from a completely new and different aspect.

THE SPIRITUALISTS' NATIONAL UNION was left the copyright to all of Arthur Findlay's books, with the request to keep the titles in print. The SNU is the largest Spiritualist Church organisation in the UK. The SNU also owns the Arthur Findlay College at Stansted Hall.

The SNU is based at Redwoods, Stansted Hall, Stansted Mountfitchet, Essex, CM24 8UD.

All of the Arthur Findlay books are now published by one of the foremost publishers in the psychic sphere:-
THE HEADQUARTERS PUBLISHING COMPANY LIMITED.
Booksellers, publishers of books and two Spiritualists' monthly magazines "TWO WORLDS" and "HERE AND THERE".
5 Alexandria Road, West Ealing, London, W13 0NP.

THE ANN THOMPSON FUND The publishers are indebted to the Ann Thompson Fund for providing an interest free loan that enabled us to bring these two important volumes back into print. Hylton Thompson established the Ann Thompson fund in memory of his first wife, for the advancement of psychic science.

THE SERIES   ISBN 0 947823 32 8
VOLUME 2   ISBN 0 947823 34 4

Printed and bound in Great Britain

ARTHUR FINDLAY'S BOOKS

THE CURSE OF IGNORANCE Arthur Findlay took seven years to finish this two volume work. It covers troubles that have beset mankind in the past and present. Past follies and achievements are recorded, acting as a guide and signpost to present and future generations. Only after reading these volumes will you realise the revolution in thought this work stands for.
VOL 1 ISBN 0 947828 33 6   VOL 2 ISBN 0 947828 34 4

THE PSYCHIC STREAM This book traces the origin of all world religions to psychic phenomena, and shows that all religious beliefs, rituals and ceremonials had a psychic origin.
ISBN 0 947828 31 X

ON THE EDGE OF THE ETHERIC Is the spirit world real and tangible? Do its inhabitants retain their individuality? Is it true that spirit people eat? What is the afterlife like? Do animals survive? All these questions are answered.   ISBN 0 9723 05 0

THE UNFOLDING UNIVERSE Arthur Findlay writes of a new era 'The days of faith are passing and the day of knowledge has arrived. Creeds, dogmas, ceremonials and rites must fade away in the light of the new knowledge.'   ISBN 0 947828I3 1

THE ROCK OF TRUTH It is not the social side of the Church's work that this book attacks, but orthodox Christianity as preached from nearly every pulpit in Christendom, and it is this which affects the great majority of the people.   ISBN 0 947823 04 1

LOOKING BACK Is Arthur Findlay's story. A truly remarkable, important and absorbing volume detailing the life, times and beliefs of one of the world's finest ever Spiritualists. ISBN 0 847823 17 4

THE WAY OF LIFE 'If I could only describe to you the lovely walks we have sometimes. There is no waste and no decay. The flowers just fade away. You never see them decay, and then fresh ones come in their place.' So said a woman who died and returned to tell of her continued existence.   ISBN 0 947823 06 9

WHERE TWO WORLDS MEET This book tells of nineteen seances Arthur Findlay attended with famous Glasgow direct voice medium John Sloan. All these literally hundreds of spirit communicators spoke. An expert stenographer took down everything said by the so-called dead.   ISBN 0 947823 07 7

THE HEADQUARTERS PUBLISHING CO.LTD.
5 ALEXANDRIA ROAD, WEST EALING,
LONDON W13 ONP

To understand the theme of this book the First Volume should be read before the Second Volume.

The dates given against the names of Emperors, Kings, Popes and Presidents refer to the year they commenced to rule and the year they gave up office, either by death, resignation, or because their term of office expired. The dates given after the names of Prime Ministers refer to their period of office. All other dates following personal names relate to the year of birth and the year of death. The dates below the heading of each chapter refer to the earliest and latest dates mentioned so far as they relate to the period under review.

CONTENTS

CONTENTS

SECOND VOLUME

CHAPTER XII.

CHRISTIAN CIVILISATION.
(1377-1610.)

Introduction. (1) *The Catholic Church Splits in Two.*
(2) *England Suffers from a Long and Savage Civil War.*
(3) *Britain During the Reformation.* (4) *The Effect of
the Apostolic Church on the Reformation.* (5) *Britain and
Ireland after the Reformation.*

By now it will be clearly realised that the past story of
mankind consists of his efforts in seeking nourishment, as well as satisfaction for his body, and comfort
for his undying mind. Our ancestors have given as
much thought to the things pertaining to their welfare
hereafter as to their conditions on earth. Every one
of us is potentially an etheric man or woman, clothed
in a garb of flesh for the time he or she lives on earth,
but that does not mean that when the garment of
flesh is discarded we are no longer real and solid,
and of the same appearance as on earth, any physical
deficiencies or defects being rectified.

The etheric duplicate body cannot be destroyed or
damaged, and its tangibility, reality and solidity come
about because after death we inhabit a world composed
of substance made up of the same quantity or frequency
of vibrations as makes up our etheric body. Knowledge of these vital facts comes from the study of
psychic science, which is overthrowing all the age-old
superstitions of every religion. There are no gods and

devils in the other world, its inhabitants being men and women like ourselves who are both good and bad, wise and stupid, grave and gay, just as they are here on earth.

Likewise revelation consists of their communications by various and different means with us here on earth; in fact everything the theologians have termed supernatural is natural, and all their mysteries are now mysteries no longer. This means that supernatural religion, having no basis of truth, is false, and that the only religion which is true is the one which accepts nature's laws, and builds up a philosophy on experience and observation. This more rational and wider outlook will come with increased knowledge, combined with greater wisdom, and so save future generations from repeating the mistakes, the follies, the cruelties and the intolerance which have so smeared the pages of history down the ages.

If we are sufficiently informed, if our minds are clear, logical and free from all religious prejudices, we are now able to grasp the most extraordinary fact in human experience, one which is so far-reaching that it touches every phase of life from the time of primitive man to our own times. All supernatural religious endeavour is, and always has been, misdirected effort, because we enter the other world at death just as naturally as we entered this one at birth. Birth needs no special passport, and, just as the newly born child is welcomed here, so are we welcomed in the other world, where our character, not our religious beliefs and observances, determines the people who will be our friends and companions.

When this simple, but nevertheless stupendous,

fact is once firmly appreciated, we realise the vast amount of misdirected effort and wealth which has been, and still is, expended on something quite unnecessary. This applies to all supernatural religions, but to most readers of this book the beliefs and observances of the Christian faith are best known. As explained in Chapter VII, these are founded on a natural, though rare, event, namely an other-world man being seen after death.

The circumstances of his deification have therein been explained, but all that followed was quite superfluous, and, this being so, the Christian Church has always been, and still is, maintained on a false assumption, a fact which explains its dishonesty, folly and depravity. For sixteen hundred years it has occupied the time and energies of millions of priests, creating mystery where there was no mystery. Millions of people have been employed in producing for the needs of these parasites, and vast wealth has been wasted in first erecting, and then maintaining, churches, theolological colleges and houses for their requirements, all to no purpose if the people had been free from the curse of ignorance.

It is now apparent to those possessed with modern knowledge that the Christian Church was a quite unnecessary institution. Now we know that its claim to be the medium between the two worlds is not only false, but that it, and its beliefs, have nothing whatever to do with our salvation or the obtaining of our desires from supernatural beings. No such organisation is necessary to ensure our happiness in the other world, as there our happiness depends upon ourselves. On arrival there we shall be met and welcomed by our friends who have preceded us, but after that we must make our own conditions, and each one lead the life he or she prefers. We can become good or bad citizens of our new abode, we can be happy or miserable, useful or useless, according to our taste, as there full liberty is granted to all to do as they please, provided they keep within the accepted laws.

How natural and rational all this is, and yet the stupendous fact remains that, in consequence of ignorance, this other-world order of life has had the most baneful effect on mankind on earth. Its natural interaction with earth has produced numerous and fantastic religions, the one which has influenced most readers of this book being caused by a Jew, who died a painful death, being seen after death by one or more of his contemporaries. The seeing of this man from the other world has produced much of the recorded history from that time to this, and now we are about to read of further great events and tragedies which were the outcome of this rare but quite natural event.

If knowledge instead of ignorance had reigned, the numerous religions everywhere throughout the world would never have come into being. They evolved because mankind mistook what we today call psychic phenomena for something unnatural, to which the name "supernatural" was given. Supernatural religions began and developed, because mankind imagined the men and women of the other world to be unnatural beings, to whom he gave the name of gods and devils, but, if it had been known in these far-off days that the other world is a natural place, its inhabitants being the same men and women who had lived and died on earth, what a stupendous difference this would have made to history!

If it had been realised that these other-world men and women had no control over nature's laws, and are as much subject to them as we are on earth, they would never have been prayed to and worshipped. If it had been known that those other-world people were only interested in this world because they once lived here, and because those who had recently made the change still had friends and relations living on earth, they would never have been feared. Consequently there would have been no misdirected wealth and effort expended for the purpose of attempting to secure their help and friendship, in order to obtain our needs and comforts here, and what is called our salvation hereafter.

When these momentous facts are remembered, we better realise the enormous mountain of misdirected energy which has been employed in religious observances, for no valid purpose whatever except to give comfort to the ignorant. To those who know the truth, it will be realised how much better and happier the world would be today if all this misplaced wealth and effort had been used for improving our minds, our characters, our health and our surroundings on earth, and so raising humanity to a higher level of thought and action.

Let these vital facts, which have been stressed since this chapter opened, remain with the reader of this book as he thinks back over what he has already read, and reads on to the end, because the misdirected effort was accompanied by an intolerance which brought about intense misery. This followed from the cruelty and suffering which came from those who denied to others the right to hold beliefs relating to the other world which were different from their own. Whenever we worship error instead of truth, misery and suffering are our companions. Truly in religion we find the curse of ignorance hanging as heavily over mankind as in any other phase of life, and if only everyone would forsake the unreal supernatural, and adopt a realistic natural outlook on life, how much wealth and misplaced energy would be saved, to be available for much nobler purposes.

Man has been so ignorant of the constitution of the substance which makes up the universe, that it is not surprising he was quite unaware of the true nature of all there is within his own surroundings. He knew little about his own visible environment, and much less about the etheric world, which, to its inhabitants, is as real and solid as is this earth. Not until he invented instruments did he discover that the two worlds could be similar, and differ only in the intensity of their vibrations. Yet instinctively he believed that there was something surrounding him which was real but of a different density, and that when the change called death took place he would experience this other environment.

So he anticipated the change, and tried to prepare himself for it, elaborating and pondering over mystical theological doctrines which have both helped and hindered him on his road through life to death, quite unaware that these were unnecessary for his future happiness. Nevertheless all this wasted and mistaken effort in no way alters the fact that he is the same man after death as he was before it, with the same individuality, the same character, the same personality, and the same qualities and vices as he had on earth. It is the mind which is the man, and that is all-important, the etheric body, in which it functions, being but a garment. Ignorant of his rightful position in the cosmos, religion helps him to face death, but supernatural religion does not help him after death, because sooner or later he will have to shed the errors he acquired on earth, and adopt a philosophy in accordance with the natural laws which govern the etheric world in which he will find himself.

If we wish to attain happiness hereafter we must cultivate the qualities on earth which make for happiness, and all experience shows that unselfishness produces happiness and selfishness unhappiness. On this basis the ethical code has developed from small beginnings, and even today it is not yet complete. Organised or orthodox religion, under any name, is a system produced by priests to satisfy the ignorant about their life after death, an ever-present fear with those who lack the knowledge of nature's laws. The priests have soothed the people with their own-made medicine, greatly to their personal profit and worldly advancement, but this theological mixture must never be confused with ethics, which solely relate to our conduct one towards another.

All religions recognise an ethical code, but pass it by in favour of the belief in doctrine and dogma. The people were, and many still are, too backward morally to recognise ethics as essential to the happiness and well-being of the race, though they could appreciate the dogma the priests told them they must believe, as it related to each one personally. A child can more easily believe a story to be true than it can be unselfish, kind, just and compassionate. So, when the priests told our childlike ancestors the story of a substitute being punished in Palestine many years ago, and that they were now saved from their sins, if only they believed that this was so, they did believe, and received the comfort which this belief brought to them.

Ethics have therefore occupied only a small part of religious experience. This comes from the fact that religion relates to the emotions, to one's own feelings, and is not concerned with others, except that the intense believer does his utmost to make others believe the same as he does for their own eternal happiness. Thus ignorance leads to intolerance, and intolerance to misery.

So far we have read of the effort of the Church to secure adherents for its own material aggrandizement, but some Christians were genuinely concerned over the salvation, as it is called, of those whom they thought had wandered from the true path. Some of the intolerance, about which we have read, is due to this, and now we come to the time when the division of Christian opinion widens perceptibly, to the accompaniment of increased intolerance, which, in those days of cruelty, meant intensified persecution.

Every religion depends on belief, and the distinction between one religion and another is in belief, as each has different theological dogmas, whereas ethics are the same throughout the world. Each religion has taught that belief in its own special interpretation of the things appertaining to the hereafter was all that mattered, and thus a Church organisation was maintained and the priests were supreme. This form of rule suited the people during their infancy, but their characters suffered as a result because ethics were quite neglected. What one believed, and not what one did, was thought to be pleasing in the sight of God, and our religious teaching is still based on the principle that only the orthodox theological belief satisfies the powers who rule in heaven. When this fact is carefully considered, and all prejudice, due to early training, is put aside, the explanation will be discovered for the deplorable condition into which the Christian Church had fallen at the time we have now reached.

With printing came reading, and with reading greater enlightenment followed. Though the Church persecuted and murdered any they found reading the Bible in their mother tongue, differences in the interpretation of its teaching increased, the reason being that, when the priests produced the Christian creeds and doctrines in the 4th and 5th centuries, they quite ignored the fact that everything they decided could be contradicted by other passages in the Bible. One has only to read the sayings attributed to Jesus, and those claimed to have been written by Paul, to realise that Paul, and not Jesus, was the authority for the creeds and dogmas. These, we imagine, would have been meaningless and even repulsive to him who is reported as going about doing good, and denouncing the priests and orthodoxy of his time.

If we look back over the pages we have read, from the time of the inception of the Christian Church, we find that its difficulties have always come from the fact that its foundations are rotten, as it was founded on fraud and violence. Its creeds, doctrines and dogmas are based on theological speculation, which quite ignores truth and honesty. From the time the Apostle Paul felt influenced to write as he did, because he thought that Jesus, in the other world, was directing him, onwards to the year when Christian belief was fixed at Nicaea, we find that facts were quite neglected and imaginative fancy given free rein. The endeavour was not to propagate that which was true, but that which appealed to an ignorant emotional people, the consequence being that the crazy erection called Christianity arose out of Paganism and Judaism, to give satisfaction to the multitude burdened with their sins.

To find an easy way out, and ease their consciences, the people relied for their salvation on the death of the age-old scapegoat, now given a new name, as the masses had neither the intelligence, nor the desire, to follow the advice of the Greek philosophers and work out their own salvation by good deeds and kind thoughts. Moreover, they were cursed by the ancient theological belief, propounded by all religions, that man is a fallen being, impregnated by original sin, and that only by some religious observance could he find salvation. Now we know that theology was utterly mistaken, and that, instead of this being so, man is an evolving being, and by his own endeavour can reach to heights to which no amount of religious teaching will ever raise him.

"Everyone is born in sin," trumpet the clergy, many still preaching, especially in Roman Catholic countries, that "Every unbaptised infant is damned," but all are unanimous that "Only Christ and his

Church can save you." The claims and assertions which run through the entire Anglican Prayer Book are so embracing that everyone is involved. They have, moreover, been preached to such effect that no one can estimate the vastness of the wealth which has been passed over to the Church by simple-minded ignorant people, who believed the tale that only by accepting its creeds, and performing its ceremonies, could they be cleansed from the taint of sin. If ignorance did not hang like a cloud over Christendom in our own times, the clerical profession would be so discredited by now that it would have no place within an honest intelligent community.

Smothered under this tremendous error, weak, ignorant humanity gladly passed over the burden of "original sin" to a saviour, but, like "Christian" in *The Pilgrim's Progress*, life continued hard and difficult, even after they had rid themselves of this cumbersome load. This theological belief in a saviour helps the believer to die happily, but not to live wisely, and, although everyone in Christendom was sure of salvation hereafter, few knew the right way to live on earth. That was beyond their understanding and comprehension, as to know this requires knowledge of the past, and the sense to profit by experience, to do which they were mentally incapable.

With education quite neglected, ignorance of these essentials was profound. Like little children they lived by theological instruction or dogma, and accepted without question all their ignorant pedantic doctrinaires told them to believe. As these beliefs were not based on facts the time came when, by the discovery of printing, reading produced new thoughts and ideas. These caused men to wonder and to think, not on the falsity of all they had been taught, but on its interpretation. Then, when knowledge was slight, Christian theology was only doubted by the very few, the questioning which arose being concerned only with what was then believed to have been accretions, for which successive popes were held to be responsible. No one suggested that ethics should replace dogma, and, in consequence, creeds continued to take the place of deeds.

So we now enter a new phase of religious history when Christians, debating furiously as to what is true, rush onwards to moral and social destruction, because they had no sound, solid or truthful basis for their beliefs and ideology.

Dogmas separate but ethics unite the race, and this means that religion, based on dogma, is unethical. Moreover, as supernatural religion is the outcome of an incorrect interpretation of natural law, it can achieve no good purpose, and never will unite humanity in one brotherhood intent on righteous living. Religious leaders from all over the world do not meet to discuss plans for the ethical improvement of the race; in fact the leaders of one religion are often not on speaking terms with those of other religions. Each religion claims that it came into being as a direct revelation from heaven, all unbelievers being damned, whereas ethics make no such claim, as they embrace the entire human race, having come into being through experience. They are the common property of all mankind, and require no religious organisation for their protection or cultivation.

We must always bear the foregoing facts in mind,

as the time in history we have now reached requires clear thinking. A few changes were made by the reformers in some of the dogmas, and in Church government, but nothing was done to stimulate the cultivation of character or improve the ethical standard of Europe. Those who broke away from the old-established authority were no better men and women ethically than those from whom they parted, the mental change that took place only relating to the interpretation of certain old beliefs.

The decisions made at the Council of Nicaea were in no way upset, and the Nicene Creed remained unassailed by any of the reformers. Consequently Catholic doctrine, the name given to the Christian beliefs which were established at Nicaea, remained as much the heritage of the Protestants as of those who continued true to the Pope at Rome, to whom the name Roman Catholics was now given to distinguish them from the Protestant Catholics.

(1) THE CATHOLIC CHURCH SPLITS IN TWO.

Let us try in imagination to picture Europe at this period. If we could be transported back in time, to experience the way the people lived, it would seem to us to be mad indeed, and as if we had become inmates of an asylum. Continual confessions to a priest, frequent absolutions, on the one hand, and on the other excommunications and the most dreadful curses laid by the Church on the people it disliked. Church services, prayers, penances, and almost every other day a holy day, were the people's recreation. For every sin there was a pardon, for every evil deed absolution, and poor boys were set aside to be whipped for the misdeeds of the children of the rich. Such was Christian justice, its saviour being "the whipping-boy" who had been punished for the wickedness of mankind. Nothing was too wicked to be pardoned, if the Church could secure additional income.

Around the local church revolved the lives of the people, it being their hospital, clinic, school and club, the priest, by his prayers, acting as doctor and, by his sermons, as schoolmaster, the church being the only social centre of the district. Everything that happened found its explanation in the church, which was the channel through which God, by way of the priest, ruled the world. Consequently religious devotions occupied a large part of the lives of the people, all their sorrows, diseases and misfortunes being capable of alleviation by prayer, but no intelligent thought was given to procuring happiness, comfort, good health and security by rational means. To think themselves out of their troubles was quite beyond the mentality of these times, the saving of their souls from hell, by means of religious observances, being as far as they could reach.

Nothing was too fantastic for the people to accept, pictures of unbelievers roasting in hell being prominent in every church, and, in the Confessional Box, each one delivered himself or herself over into the power of the priest, who, with the intimate knowledge he thus obtained of every one in his parish, had a hold over his flock from childhood to old age. A few mumbled Latin words of absolution meant more than virtue and honour, and to reach heaven and avoid hell, by means of continual purification up to the last gasp, was the predominant thought of everyone. Consequently the thumb-mark of hell smears every page of Christian history, the fear it caused being used by the priests to increase the wealth and power of the Church, and keep the people ignorant and servile, because all knowledge was sinful and to think for oneself meant eternal damnation.

Emphasis has already been laid on the fact that the pliable mind of a child can be so moulded that the impressions planted in it in childhood become fixed ideas as strong as iron. So far, by this means, the Christian Church had been very successful in retaining the unswerving support of the people, but the invention of printing greatly increased the reading of the Bible, from which some made new interpretations of hitherto accepted doctrines. Others noted the difference between the simplicity of the Apostolic age and the wealth and luxurious living of the clergy, and drew their own conclusions.

Martin Luther (1483–1546) was one of those who were influenced to make protest on the methods pursued by the Pope to raise money, but to read of his mental agony, when he began to form opinions contrary to those he had been taught as a child and youth, proves what a powerful influence early instruction has on our lives for either good or evil. In these days only a strong and independent thinker could break the chains of his mental bondage, but, after much travail and distress, he succeeded in reaching the decision that the Church was not infallible, and that salvation came from faith and not by clerical absolution, the outcome of which conclusions is now the subject of our story.

In the year 1517 an event, which then seemed of only local importance, started a series of repercussions which split the Church in two. In this year at Wittenberg in Germany, Luther, the son of a slate-cutter, and now Professor of Theology at this town's university, fastened upon the church door his famous ninety-five arguments against the Church selling indulgences, the latest method the Pope, and his cardinals, had devised to raise money for building the new great Church of St. Peter's at Rome.[1] This church was intended as a further fruitful addition to the papal money-making business, as it would attract many pilgrims to Rome whose money the Church authorities would cunningly obtain by their now well-tested methods of defrauding the simple-minded.

The ignorant German people had been told that for each indulgence purchased, Pope Julius II (1503–1513) would secure the release of the soul of a friend or relation from purgatory. Christian civilisation in those days was in the lowest depths of depravity, and Julius, its chief corner-stone, was a man accused of immorality and unnatural vice, a quite unscrupulous prelate, debased in mind and foul of tongue, besides being the master of every type of cruelty. His successor, Leo X (1513–1521), was an equally vile character, he being likewise a sodomist, besides being a murderer and the patron of everything indecent

[1] St. Peter's today contains a Post Office, owned by the Vatican, which issues its own postage stamps, a shop where relics, souvenirs, postcards, etc., can be bought, a statue of Jupiter labelled Saint Peter, whose right toe is nearly kissed off, the so-called tomb of Saint Peter, and nearby his foot-prints, besides numerous places where the faithful, in exchange for payment, can place candles, flowers, etc. Money-boxes are everywhere for the offerings of the numerous visitors who visit it each day.

that happened in Rome.   Moreover, he was a blatant liar, unscrupulous and dishonest in all he said and did. Nevertheless he was the traditional mouthpiece of God, and the representative of Christ on earth, and as such he declared that the death of Jesus had bequeathed to the Church an inexhaustible supply of merit which the Pope could dispose of as he pleased.

Consequently he promised that those who bought indulgences would not only have their wickedness forgiven, but have them expunged from existence, by being entirely erased from "the Lamb's Book of Life".[1]   To this state of degradation the Christian Church had reduced morality in Europe.   Divine pardon could be secured in return for money.   God would forgive all, provided the Pope obtained the cash!

There was nothing distinctively novel in Luther's protest against this interpretation of religion by the priests of the Christian Church, because Wycliffe, Huss, and others, had already publicly denounced their behaviour without obtaining any reform.   These earlier heralds of a reformed Christianity had not the soil suitable for their seed, and consequently it did not develop.   Before an intellectual movement can succeed the conditions necessary for its growth must be present, and, when Luther struck, the right time had come, as the political state of Europe made it impossible for the Church to receive support from

[1] A modern version of this method of raising money is to be found in a circular dated 1st March, 1944, and issued by the Roman Catholic Archbishop of Winnipeg during the Second World War to the wives and parents of Canadian Roman Catholics in the army.   This document stated that for the payment of 40 dollars the Church will "guarantee, should he be killed, that he will go at once to his maker, to be with him for all eternity".

either Spain, France or Germany, one or other in the past always coming to her aid in time of trouble.

Dissatisfaction at its doings certainly prevailed throughout Christendom, and, with the coming of Luther on the scene as a reformer, revolt spread in Germany. However, the Emperor Charles V (1519–1558), the most powerful monarch of the 16th century, a man who was neither a statesman, a soldier, nor even cultured, was so busy elsewhere attending to the affairs of his vast empire that he could not suppress what was to him an outrageous attack on the Holy Mother Church. Then it was that his Spanish possessions in South America were yearly growing in size, a rebellion had to be quelled in Spain, the Turks were threatening Vienna, and France was his bitter enemy, even allying herself with the infidel Turks and the Protestants in Germany so as to make conditions for the Emperor more difficult.

This great contest between France and the Holy Roman Empire dominated everything during the reign of Charles V, and France supported everyone who was an enemy of the Empire, even when this meant going contrary to the policy of the Church. So, while suppressing heresy at home, she supported it abroad, and to this bitter rivalry between France and the Empire we can trace one reason why it was possible for the revolt from the Church to spread over a large part of Germany without a determined attempt being made to have it suppressed. The other reason was the defeat of Hungary by the Turks, these two factors enabling the reform movement to take root and grow into a strong endeavour before the chief ruler of Europe, fearful of the invading

Turks, had the opportunity to wage war against it. When he did move the chance had passed, as by then it was too strong to destroy, but it only survived after many bloody battles and endless persecution and torture proved incapable of uprooting it.

The success of Luther's reform movement lay in his strong character and fanatical faith and courage, which inspired many to believe that not only Church reform would follow from his attack, but also that the people would obtain a greater measure of influence in their political life. Besides dissatisfaction about their religion the German people aspired to freer, wider and better social conditions, and many rallied round Luther in the hope that a reformed religion would in time bring about an improved social system for the good of all.

Germany, moreover, was not a nation, but a country divided into over three hundred different states, some of which, especially Saxony, supported the new movement. Their reason for so doing was not wholly altruistic, as, along with the desire for a reformed religion, went the craving to seize as much as possible of the Church's vast ill-gotten wealth, and such an opportunity, when a religious reason could be found, was not to be lightly overlooked.

The mild, peace-loving, devout Frederick, Elector of Saxony, had higher motives, and gave the new movement the encouragement needed to carry it over the dangerous early stages. He protected Luther in his castle at Wartburg where the reformer translated the Bible into German, a work which did as much to preserve the uniformity of the German language as the English Authorised Version of 1611 did to preserve that of the English language. Here the foundation was laid of the Lutheran Church, the University of Wittenberg becoming the exponent of Lutheran theology, moulded and mellowed by Philip Melanchthon, the gentle scholar, who produced the first elementary work on Christian beliefs as seen by the German reformer. To Wittenberg came divines from the University of Cambridge, to return home with these new ideas which converted many English people to the Protestant faith, and raised an obscure fenland town to the position it has since maintained as the centre of Protestant theology.

Luther was neither a profound theologian nor a philosopher. He did not believe in liberty or freedom of thought, in enquiry, discussion, toleration or scientific progress. Faith to him was everything and reasoned thought nothing.[1] He was a reactionary in everything pertaining to increased knowledge, social progress, and religion, as to him all knowledge was contained in the Scriptures, which were the only guide to mankind during his sojourn between the cradle and the grave. Because the Bible gave no support to indulgences he attacked this method of securing salvation, but because Paul propounded salvation by faith he made this the foundation of his belief. As, however, the Word of God contained nothing in favour of education, social welfare, humanitarianism, a higher standard of life for the down-trodden peasants, toleration of other people's

[1] Like Saint Augustine, whom he so admired, Luther hated reason, and in one of his sermons he thundered against the people using their reason, telling his hearers to throw spit in the face of reason, because she was the devil's whore, rotten with itch and leprosy, who ought to be kept in the privy.

opinions, and political or religious liberty, he had no use for such ideas, and vehemently opposed all who had.

Jews, heretics, erring priests, and the poor German peasants, struggling for improved living conditions, received his violent curses and savage abuse. He was a typical German, violent, harsh and cruel, yet at times tender and kind; coarse but fond of music, filled with over-confidence, ruthlessly overbearing, and yet experiencing paroxysms of contrition. Morally he, and his leading clerical supporters, were no better than many of the popes whose lives they denounced, as, to further their cause, they urged Philip of Hesse to cast off his lawful wife and marry another because polygamy was sanctioned in the Bible. Fearing criticism, Luther urged that this be done secretly, and that the second marriage be concealed by telling "a great bold lie for the good of the Christian Church", a method which did not appeal to the more honest Philip, whose enthusiasm for Lutheranism was so damped that he crossed over and gave his support to the cause of the Holy Father, thus producing the first split in the Protestant ranks.

In 1520 the Pope excommunicated Luther, but the reformer burned the Bull containing this proclamation in the market square at Wittenberg, together with the volumes of the Canon Law, which it will be remembered first of all came into being as the Theodosian Code. He was summoned to attend the Diet of Worms at which Charles V presided, and there he faced his enemies. Next he was placed under the ban of the Empire, and then it was that the Elector of Saxony took him in disguise to his castle, as both the Pope and the Emperor had laid their plans for his capture. In 1522 another Diet was called at Nuremberg, but the Emperor was too busy to attend, and, instead of banning Luther, it formulated on this occasion a series of grievances against the Pope.

The German peasants now looked to Luther to redress their grievances, as they were no better than serfs to a prosperous upper and middle class. To make their demands better understood they drew up twelve articles containing the reforms they demanded, which included freedom from their feudal serfdom, the abolition of tithes, and instruction in the contents of the Bible. Civil war followed in 1524, and terrible atrocities were committed on both sides, especially by the authorities in their attempt to suppress the agrarian reform movement. Luther, alarmed at the turn events had taken, and fearing that it would interfere with his own theological reform movement, threw his influence against the peasants, and thundered against them with his characteristic vehemence and ferocity, going so far as to incite the nobles to crush the rising by any means, no matter how cruel. As a forerunner of the Nazi outlook on life, and true to the German mentality, which puts ruthlessness before all else, he wrote:—

Damned be love into the abyss of hell, if it is maintained to the damage of faith. . . . It is better that tyrants should sin a hundred times against the people than that the people should sin once against the tyrants. . . . The ass wants to be thrashed, the mob to be governed by force.

Luther's denunciation of all who stood in his way revolted those possessed of any decency and humane feelings, but, to this predecessor of Bismarck and Hitler, democracy, or anything savouring of the people having any rights, was a snare of the devil. Consequently the Lutheran Church ranged itself against the people, and, like the Church from which it had parted, became associated with the ruler, always ready, if it were in its interests, to do his will. The Lutheran clergy made no attempt to see the people's point of view, or to hear and adjust their real grievances, which were so apparent, and whose demands were so reasonable.

Instead of so doing they supported and encouraged savage barbarities against them, and reduced the German peasantry to such a state of weakness that their position became inferior to that of any other like class in Europe. That the Lutherans should have supported the tyrannical rulers and landlords as they did, and sided so violently against the poor and needy, is a blot against the Lutheran Church which can never be expunged. Again we have clear evidence that theology cares nothing for humanitarianism, social progress or reform, being only interested in speculating about the god or gods of its own creation, and the observance of its narrow doctrines, which have always led to quarrels and misery. Whatever stood in the way of these speculations being accepted was always ruthlessly brushed aside.

The peasant movement failed, and these poor down-trodden people never forgave Luther for his cruelty and active hostility. He thus lost their support, but he obtained the help of those with whom he sided, becoming dependent on the aristocracy, intent on their own selfish interests, who were against all social reform, a state of affairs which was characteristic of the reformed religion so long as its clergy retained the power.

His movement, however, had one good effect, because it established another authority for Christianity besides the Pope.　The Bible, as interpreted by Luther, was the basis of his idea of Christianity, and the Bible, as interpreted by the Pope, remained his idea of Christianity.　When there was only one interpretation of Scripture there was no room for other opinions, but, when one body of Christians accepted Luther's interpretation, and another that of the Pope, there was obviously room for a third, as supplied by Calvin. This led to a fourth, and so on until ultimately, in the 19th century, religious freedom of opinion was secured after much persecution by whichever side was in power.

In 1529, at the Diet of Speier, it was decided that the Roman Catholic form of worship was to be allowed in those states which had adopted the Lutheran form of Christianity, but the reformers objected in these words: "We hereby protest to you that we cannot and may not concur therein but hold the resolution null and not binding."　From this amendment came the word "Protestantism," a queer name for a religion which had originated in a difference of opinion about the selling of indulgences, and not from any protest against the Christian beliefs and dogmas, or their unethical consequences.

Protestants, from this time onwards, became just as intolerant as those who were now called Roman Catholics, and, when they had the power, equally cruel. Consequently the religious struggle became more brutal and fiercer than ever, the next three centuries witnessing the slaughter, torture, imprisonment and banishment of many millions of innocent and decent men and women. Verily the transforming of Jesus into the Christ, the true into the false, the natural into the supernatural, brought discord and not peace to the world.

As the kings and princes of those countries which became Protestant took the place of the Pope as head of the Church of their country, international Christianity perished, its place being taken by a national Church in each Protestant country. These national Churches became just as intolerant, and determined to protect from heresy their form of religious thought, as was the Roman Catholic Church. Long and bitter was the struggle between these new established Churches and the Protestants who would not accept their authority. The cruelties inflicted by established Protestantism on the Nonconformist Protestants were just as terrible as any perpetrated by the Roman Catholics on the Protestants, because the latter followed the methods of the former without pity or restraint.

Another evil which followed the Reformation was the division it made between the nations and individuals. Catholic Christendom became divided nationally between two brands of Christians who bitterly hated each other, but socially the division was just as marked and equally bitter. Roman Catholics and Protestants ceased to be friends, and the children of the former would not marry those of the latter and vice-versa—"Be ye not unequally yoked together with unbelievers" (2 *Corinthians* vi, 14) being quoted by both sides. Protestants likewise grouped themselves according to their sects, Anglicans, Calvinists and Lutherans only marrying amongst themselves and having little social intercourse one with another. Even today such unnatural conditions exist, and they are all the outcome of ignorance, a misinterpretation of the life hereafter and the powers governing the universe.

At the inception of the reform movement the Roman Catholics were in the majority, having both the power and the wealth behind them, and Charles V struck deeply at the Netherlands, a small country, and the least able to resist. Declaring that he owed to God a sacred debt to cleanse this land of the foul stain of heresy, he established there the Inquisition in 1522. Nevertheless he failed to break the courage and endurance of these hardy people, who maintained that they, like Charles, were still Christians, two victims at Antwerp, to prove this, repeating the Nicene Creed, and singing the Te Deum when being led to the stake. Thus did thirty thousand men and women perish in the Netherlands during the reign of this Holy Roman emperor, because they held some theological opinions that differed from those set down by the orthodox Church, which, to bring them back from their erring way, supplied Charles with the men and the money to carry out the bloody work. So diabolical were the things done to the Netherlanders that Froude, the historian, remarks, "The blackest ogre in a negro fetish is a benevolent angel in comparison with these fiends" who perpetrated these abominations.

In 1530 Luther set out his doctrines in a statement known as The Confession of Augsburg, and this consolidated the new form of Christianity, but by now Charles V had found the time to take seriously this new movement in Germany, and he vehemently denounced it, threatening with punishment all who would not return to the original Catholic Church. This brought into being The League of Schmalkalden, consisting of all the German Protestant states, for the defence of their new beliefs, but thirteen years passed before the Emperor moved his army against them, because the Turks were steadily approaching Germany up the Danube, and he could not contemplate civil war at home.

To understand the position of the Emperor we must go back to the year 1526, when the Turks secured their notable victory at the Battle of Mohacs, which opened up to them the vast plains of Hungary. Truly Christian civilisation was in greater peril than ever before, as the Infidel was striking at the heart of Europe, then a cauldron of bitter religious factions. Finally in 1552 Henry II of France, a Roman Catholic, yet allied to the Turks, promised to help the Protestants if they would aid him to get the bishoprics of Metz, Toul and Verdun, and, moreover, the Emperor's brother Ferdinand was claiming the inheritance of the Hapsburg Empire, which Charles wished to pass down to his son Philip.

Within these twenty-six years Charles had conducted a successful campaign against the Turks in Africa, and in 1535 captured Tunis. Moreover, he had been at war with France, off and on, for twenty-three years (1521–1544), during which time five separate bloody campaigns had been fought, to end in him being still master of Lombardy and the Kingdom of Naples.

During his reign Charles had thus one distraction after another to deflect him from his aim to rid his empire of Protestantism, and only in 1544, having made peace with France, was he able to concentrate his attention on the extermination of the German heretics.

By now Württemberg, Baden, Hesse, Saxony and Brandenburg had definitely declared themselves as Protestant, and, as Charles was less anxious about the Turkish invasion, he collected a large army the following year and marched against the rebels, now without their leader, because just before the conflict began Luther died. Some states yielded without a struggle, and the rest were defeated in 1547 at Mühlberg on the Elbe. A Diet was then called at Augsburg, when the Roman Catholic form of Christianity was once again reiterated, but, though certain concessions were made, the Protestants refused to accept its findings.

Such then was the position after the first Diet of Augsburg, when the Protestants, encouraged by the promise of renewed help from France, rallied, and, without even a conflict, reasserted their position in Germany. Maurice of Saxony, the unscrupulous Protestant leader, thus secured a bloodless victory, Charles decamping to Innsbruck, and thence to Italy, rather than face the resuscitated Protestant army. Charles now decided to strike at France for helping to bring about his humiliation, but he was defeated at Metz (1553), an event which led to his retirement to a monastery, his son Philip II succeeding him.

By his passing from the scene, the first stage of the

Reformation closes with the Peace of Augsburg in 1555, when it was agreed (1) that all attempts to force the Roman Catholic form of religion on all the German people be abandoned, and (2) that each state in future would be responsible for the religion within its own territory. As toleration was not expected it was agreed (1) that the Roman Catholics in the Protestant states should move into Roman Catholic states, (2) that the Protestants be moved into Protestant states, that (3) no other forms of religious belief would be tolerated in Germany, and (4) that "the confession of the subject was to be dependent on that of the territorial lord".

Now that the shackles of the orthodox Catholic Church were broken in Germany, an opportunity was offered for a different religious outlook to be expressed in a way as never before. No matter what these recurring Diets decided, they could not stem the tide of new ideas which were surging up in men's minds. After being kept in bondage for over a thousand years, some minds in Europe now felt free to roam and wander upon hitherto unfamiliar paths.

Many in disgust had thrown over the old Church which they had been taught to look upon as their only religious leader, and, as they required some guide, they put the Bible in its place, an unfortunate decision because this book, or rather this miscellaneous series of historical, legal, prophetical and mystical writings, was never produced for such a purpose. Covering as it does the history of a thousand years of a barbarous oriental tribe, and ending with many of the Pagan mystical beliefs under new names, the religious reformers of the 16th century had now ample scope to make new interpretations, which they believed were more in conformity with the Scriptures than those hitherto taught by the Church.

Anyone can produce without difficulty a Biblical text in support of every variety of belief, and it is not surprising that the Protestants quickly divided into diverse sects as other leaders arose who took different views from those expressed by Luther. Moreover, as everyone was under the curse of ignorance, intolerance reigned supreme. Few people, if any, in those days could tolerate other people having different opinions from their own, and nearly everyone thought that everyone else should think as he thought. Force, and not reasoned argument, was the only method then employed to produce this desired uniformity of thought, and, in consequence, torture, and every possible cruelty, was used by those who had the power to do so.

What is termed the Peace of Augsburg, which decreed that only Roman Catholicism and Lutheranism were to be the religions of Germany, brought about the disastrous Thirty Years' War, of which we shall be reading in the next chapter. The reason for this terrible conflict was because another type of Christianity, produced by a law student of the name of Calvin, forced itself into Germany from Geneva. Yet another brand was also spreading, which had been invented by Zwingli, the most genial, gifted and democratic of all the reformers, who began his reform movement from Zurich. He obtained a large following in Switzerland, and, like Luther, attracted his followers by attacking the sale of indulgences.

For a time Zwingli (1484–1531) kept in step with

Luther, but serious differences arose on the subject of Church government and the Eucharist, which latter, like the Trinity, has been the cause of endless disputes, sects and divisions in the Church. The origin of these two fundamentals has already been considered in earlier chapters, and can be traced back to primitive religious beliefs. The Eucharist, for example, to the offering of the etheric duplicate body of the sacrificed victim as food to the gods, and the Trinity to the fact that man is made up of a physical body, its etheric duplicate, and mind. From this psychic origin the priests produced theological and mystical beliefs which in time evolved out of Paganism into Christianity, to cause endless differences of opinion.

The orthodox Christian belief is that Jesus, in some undefined way, enters the Eucharist bread and wine and is thus partaken of by the communicant. This constituted the ancient primitive belief that by eating the victim sacrificed on the altar, the communicant was fortified and strengthened by what the Greeks called his "mana." This idea, in Christian times, found expression in the word "transubstantiation," which had definite scriptural support from the record of The Last Supper, now accepted by scholars as a late addition derived from Pagan sources. The verses read as follows:—

And as they were eating, Jesus took bread, and blessed it, and brake it, and gave it to the disciples, and said, Take, eat, this is my body. And he took the cup, and gave thanks, and gave it to them, saying, Drink ye all of it. For this is my blood of the new testament, which is shed for many for the remission of sins. (*Matthew* xxvi, 26-28.)

This is quite clear and unequivocal, but it is on this very subject that Protestants differ so widely from their Roman Catholic and Greek Orthodox brethren. The Bible was now available in the German language, and here was a point of doctrine on which Christians differed in their interpretation. The Christian Church hitherto had accepted the injunction literally, but now we have come to the time when there was a definite cleavage of opinion, so wide that no council could close it. The corruption in the Church brought about the Reformation, and the Reformation opened to discussion this hitherto accepted doctrine. On this rock the Catholic Church split in two, to bring about the second great disruption in the Christian Church, as it will be remembered that in the 11th century the Church had divided into the Eastern and Western Churches on the question of the definition of the Trinity.

Luther rejected the orthodox belief about transubstantiation, and believed that the bread and wine of the Eucharist were unchanged by the mystical formula uttered by the priest, but for long he was mystified how to explain the presence of the body and blood of Jesus in the Sacrament. Then he came across something written by William of Ockham in the 14th century which he seized upon as the answer to the riddle. Jesus survived death, the English sage argued, in a body which could occupy the same space as matter, or otherwise he could not have entered a room as an etheric man when the door was closed. This is precisely what our present-day knowledge of vibrations makes understandable, but to apply his theory he went on to argue that, this being so, what we would today call the etheric body of Jesus enters the bread and the wine and is partaken of by the communicant.

As iron can contain heat, so consecration of the elements affected them as fire did iron, and this Luther called Consubstantiation, which, as we have already read, is just another name for the old savage cannibalistic idea that the sacrificed victim's body and blood contain his "mana", which fortifies the communicant. Zwingli rejected Luther's theory, after a conference lasting four days, and, when he put out his hand to say "Good-bye", Luther refused to shake hands because Zwingli held the opinion that the body and blood of Jesus were not present in the sacrament. Luther quoted again and again, against this opinion, the words from Matthew's gospel, "This is my body" and "This is my blood", and explained his interpretation of them. Neither would yield, and so these two short sentences were the cause of the first split on doctrine which occurred amongst the Protestants, amidst fierce denunciations by Luther of Zwingli, who, he declared, was an enemy of the truth, a heretic and a rationalist.

In truth Zwingli was mentally far in advance of the Protestants of his time, because he was sufficiently intelligent to appreciate the greatness of the Greek and Roman philosophers, who were as much anathema to the Protestants as they were to the Roman Catholics. In his treatise on Providence he placed Socrates, Plato and Seneca on a level with Moses and Paul, and greatly in advance of many of the saints worshipped by Christians. For this heresy he was denounced by both branches of the Church, to such effect that his

teaching did not make the headway it would have
done.   The Protestants, in their own way, were just
as reactionary as the Church they had left.   Nevertheless he lit a lamp which, with increasing strength,
has radiated light from his day to this for the good
of all Christendom.

Still another opinion was to be put forward as to
the meaning of Christianity, the orthodox Catholics
meanwhile looking on with delight at all the disputing
and quarrelling which followed those who broke
away from the mother Church.   John Cauvin, known
to us as Calvin (1509–1564), who was first a priest and
then a law student, became converted to the new
outlook, and this made it necessary for him to leave
France to avoid persecution.   He was studious,
polite, refined, and, as the son of a Picardy notary,
accustomed to mix in the best French society, his
manners being the antithesis of those displayed
by his contemporary Luther, the coarse and harsh
German reformer.

At Basel he wrote his book *Institutes of the Christian
Religion*, and finally settled at Geneva, then a Protestant
city.   Here he gradually assumed the power of a
pope, and became the leader of another reform
movement which he clearly defined to represent
(1) a complete separation of the Church from the State,
(2) a new form of Church government under the
direction of ministers and laymen, and (3) a strict
moral discipline.   Calvinism accepted the doctrine of
predestination, and believed that the Eucharist service
was a necessary means of sanctification and grace,
though it denied any miraculous change in the bread
and wine.

This new doctrine made the division in the ranks of the Protestants more pronounced, as the Lutherans would not accept it, but it spread widely in Germany, to have far-reaching consequences, as we shall discover. Calvinistic intolerance was just as pronounced as Lutheran and Roman Catholic, and when Servetus (1511–1553), the Spanish physician, took refuge in Geneva, in consequence of his opposition to the Roman Catholic Church in Spain, he was arrested and burned there on the instigation of Calvin, the reason being that each defined the Holy Trinity differently. This fierceness in Calvinism made it a great driving force, so much so that its fanatical adherents aroused a devotion and enthusiasm for its doctrines far and away beyond anything reached by the Lutherans. It nearly drove the Roman Catholic Church out of France, it gave to the Puritans of England, and the Presbyterians of Scotland, their determination never to submit to the Episcopalian form of Christianity, and it transformed Holland into a free republic.

Calvin, who was a classical scholar, translated the Bible into French, and this, besides stabilising the language, had a great influence on many of the people, who came to be known as Huguenots. Nevertheless Calvinism is a cold, dour, cruel, merciless religion, which took all pleasure and happiness out of life, and reduced the individual to a creature of fate, whose God, according to Robert Burns, "sends ane to heaven and ten to hell a' for his glory". The Calvinistic Sabbath, the doctrine of predestination, and the salvation only of the elect, produced a gaunt unimaginative inartistic sect, from whom all joy of living was sucked out by a crude and narrow theology. Intolerance flourishes in such an atmosphere, as it regards hell as an open furnace which swallows all but orthodox Calvinists, who are the elect and predestined to be saved.

While the Protestants were active in propagating their new doctrines, some of the Roman Catholic laity were by no means idle. Many realised the canker which, over the centuries, had eaten out everything tending to righteousness within their vast money-making organisation. They realised, moreover, the danger to which it was threatened from the Protestant movement, and a fresh effort was made, just as is being done today by leading Protestant ecclesiastics, to make the Church appear to stand for high ideals, a purpose for which it was never founded, and which is quite lacking in its constitution.

In 1545 Charles V succeeded in forcing Pope Paul III to call a council of European Roman Catholic leaders, and the city of Trent in Italy was chosen as its meeting-place. Previous popes had refused to consider the idea, but the danger which now threatened the Church enabled Charles to secure his desire, though the reactionary Paul plotted for war and the extermination of all heretics. Italian bishops predominated, and on them the Pope relied to make certain that the abuses continued and his power was in no way curtailed.

The Council of Trent sat for eighteen years, off and on, but the aim of Charles to force reforms on the Holy See was not realised, in fact the Council strengthened the policy of the reactionaries. A legate of the Pope presided at all gatherings, and nothing could be proposed to which he did not agree. An attempt to find a basis of compromise between the Roman Catholics and the Protestants dismally failed. Tradition, supplemented by the Latin Vulgate translation of the Hebrew Scriptures, the Gospels and Epistles, as translated and edited by the fanatical, unscrupulous Jerome, was claimed to be the final authority for the Christian faith. Luther's doctrine of justification by faith, outside the mother Church, was rejected, and all Protestant arguments on this and other subjects were contemptuously pushed aside.

Nothing was said at the Council about justice, mercy, kindness, tolerance, honesty, the common brotherhood of man, or the joining together of all Christendom into one united front for the furtherance of righteousness and the combat of everything evil. However, time was found to debate on the question as to whether women had souls or not, the resolution in favour being carried by only three votes. The only part of the Sermon on the Mount which interested the Christians of those days was that relating to the chopping off of hands and the gouging out of eyes (*Matthew* v, 29), to which the Holy Inquisition was actively attending when not at work driving out devils from the bodies of victims chained to the stake.

What a chance the Church missed of scrapping its ancient constitution, and, instead of being the propagator of a primitive superstition, becoming the champion of righteousness and welcoming into its fold all good men and women who had as their aim the welfare of humanity. Such an eminently sane and sensible idea never received a moment's consideration from men trained from youth upwards in theological colleges. To them the entire human race lived under

the sin of Adam, "For as in Adam all die, even so in
Christ shall all be made alive." (1 *Corinthians* xv, 22.)
For their salvation from this curse brought on mankind by Adam, the Church was founded to celebrate
the Eucharist and the ceremony of baptism, teach the
creeds, dogmas and doctrines, and perform the other
rites and ceremonies, all of which, if duly observed
and believed, removed the curse.

Thus only could the people be saved, their conduct
being of little importance, as a victim had already
suffered for their sins. Ethics consequently never
received any consideration, education and social
improvement being passed by, because the Church
knew all there was to teach, and everyone was in the
place God intended him to occupy, salvation from hell
being of much greater importance than social welfare.
Death and the hereafter dominated the thoughts of our
ancestors, to the exclusion of social progress. Instead
of discarding all its man-made theological speculations which were causing such bitter strife, the
Council of Trent again emphasised the fact that the
Pope was the final authority upon everything, and
thus his powers were strengthened in every department of Church government. Moreover, it was
decided that all theological disputes must end, that no
union with Protestantism was possible, and that the
Church must present a strong, united, disciplined front
against all who criticised its beliefs and methods.
By such decisions the Council of Trent prepared the
Roman Catholics for the coming struggle, which was
to drench Europe in rivers of blood over the next
two hundred years.

Most of northern Europe had by now accepted the

Protestant belief in one form or another, part of Switzerland from 1524 onwards, Germany (excluding the Roman Catholic states) from 1526, Sweden from 1528, England from 1532, Norway and Denmark from 1538, Scotland from 1560 and Holland from 1572, including those lands bordering the eastern coast of the Baltic Sea. The effect of this change on England and Scotland will be considered further on in this chapter, but here something must be said of those lands in Europe which suffered greatly through the attempt made by the orthodox Catholic Church to prevent any secession from the hitherto accepted faith.

The rule of Charles V, the Emperor, was not a success in Germany, but his reign as Charles I, King of Spain, was filled with triumphs. In Spain he reigned supreme, his great expedition against the Moslems in North Africa having crushed their power in Tunis. Improved government had been introduced into the American colonies, considerable additions had been made to his power and dominions, and the free use of the Holy Inquisition in Spain and Italy had stamped out all freedom of thought, only to have the opposite effect in the Netherlands.

When he abdicated, his son Philip II (1556–1598) inherited a great and prosperous kingdom which, however, did not include the Hapsburg territories in Central Europe. These had passed to Ferdinand, the Emperor's brother, and over them he ruled with the active support of the Roman Catholic Church. Philip commenced his reign with supreme power and vast possessions. His greatest successes were the defeat of the Turkish fleet in 1571 at the Battle of Lepanto, in the Gulf of Corinth, a victory which had such far-reaching effects. Then, in 1580, when the Portuguese throne became vacant on the death of Henry, he conquered Portugal, too weak to resist after a long period of persecution by the Holy Inquisition, which had left the oppressed people quite indifferent as to what happened to them. Thus he became King of Portugal, with all her vast territories in Brazil and her trading centres in India, but his attempt to add England and France to his dominions was frustrated by the British navy, and the French army under Henry of Navarre.

Philip II, a man with a cold, uncongenial, unhappy temperament, was as devout a Roman Catholic as his father, and gave much of his time and thought to rid his great Empire of Protestant heresy. The policy of this solemn, laborious, narrow-minded man was to suppress by force and torture all freedom and progress, and from Madrid he directed his energies with this end in view, especially against his subjects in the Netherlands, who were imbued with the growing desire for greater freedom and the reformed Christian faith. Here, in this prosperous delta of the Scheldt and the Rhine, great and flourishing cities, Bruges, Ghent, Antwerp, Amsterdam and Rotterdam had developed a thriving sea-borne trade which yielded to Spain a greater revenue than it obtained from all its new world possessions. They had sullenly resisted the harsh rule of Charles, but when Philip, his son, attempted to exercise the same authority as he adopted in Spain they rebelled.

The Netherlanders wanted one of their own nobles, preferably Count Egmont, or William of Nassau, called the Prince of Orange, and also better known as William the Silent and William of Orange, as Philip's representative, but, instead, he made Margaret of Parma, his half sister, Governor of the Netherlands. The seventeen states, comprising the Netherlands, objected, and matters came to a crisis when he attempted to crush out the Protestant movement by sending the fiendishly cruel Duke of Alva, in 1567, with a large army to accomplish what he could not do by negotiation. Count Egmont, and Count Hoorn another of the great Dutch leaders, were executed, William of Orange saving himself from the same fate by flight. A Council was set up, which came to be known as the Council of Blood, for the punishment of all treason and heresy, and for six years a reign of terror swept the land, the Inquisition doing its deadly work as thoroughly as elsewhere throughout Christendom.

By the year 1572 the country was in revolt against the weight of new taxation, and the provinces of Holland and Zeeland, calling William of Orange to their aid, declared war on Spain. Thus the War of Independence began, which lasted for forty years, during which time Spain poured out so much of her substance that it greatly contributed to her final downfall. The Netherlanders maintained their control of the sea, and this greatly helped in their final victory, but it was a long and bloody struggle, fought mainly behind city walls, as they were no match for the Spaniards in the open, the sieges of Haarlem, Alkmaar and Leyden being epic but tragic events when the inhabitants suffered terrible hardships. The dykes, on critical occasions, were cut, the land was flooded, but,

behind the suffering and carnage, William, their great
leader, never lost courage. With sustained resolution
and patient temper he guided his people on to victory.

The Spaniards gained their victories, but the determined Netherlanders would never admit defeat.
Finally the Spanish army revolted because of lack of
pay, and spread over the country, plundering everywhere, but twenty thousand fresh troops, under the
Duke of Parma, the greatest general of his time,
inflicted such a severe defeat on the Netherlanders at
Gembloux in 1578 that he secured the return to Spain
of the southern provinces. This battle decided that
the Netherlands would in future pursue two different
political and religious paths; it split the low countries
into two, Protestant Holland in the north, and what
was to become Roman Catholic Belgium in the south.

William, bitterly disappointed at the loss of the
southern provinces, was now entirely dependent on
the Protestant northern states, which formed themselves (1579) into the Union of Utrecht. As such they
continued the struggle under the declaration that when
a king grinds down his people, and treats them as
slaves, his lands are forfeited and another takes his
place. This declaration, in after years, echoed through
France, England and America, as it was the first
proclamation by the people that unjust and intolerant
rule would not be accepted.

Here it is of interest to recall the reason why the
poor hardy Dutch were able to keep control of the sea,
and receive the supplies which sustained them until
final victory. They outfought the great Spanish
Empire at sea, and won, just as did the British some
years later, and the explanation of both victories is

because Spain, though then the strongest land power in Europe, was largely a Mediterranean sea power. There her seamen were trained by keeping down pirates, and fighting the Turks. In the decisive sea battle of Lepanto she smashed the Turkish navy, but seventeen years later was completely defeated when she came up against a much smaller British fleet in the English Channel.

Her seamen were trained in the ancient Mediterranean method of sea warfare, the galley, moved by oars, dashing in and grappling with the enemy, the issue being decided by a hand-to-hand struggle when the soldiers swarmed across to the enemy vessels. The method had not changed since Greek and Roman days, and this meant that when Spain met the Dutch and British at sea she lacked the experience to counter their different tactics, which were to destroy the cumbrous galleons by sailing in amongst them and sinking them with cannon-ball, or setting them on fire.

The Spaniards, trained in head-on galley fighting, had no special means of defending their ponderous ocean-going galleons against the easily manœuvred little ships which assailed them. They could not rise above the galley mentality, and, in the narrow waters of the North Sea and English Channel, their ships made good targets to an enemy who could slip out of safe bases, attack swiftly, and return to safety. So the great galleons, crowded with soldiers, were quite unable to grapple with the enemy, strike him down, and finish the struggle by hand-to-hand fighting, as happened in the smoother waters of the Mediterranean.

Consequently Spain, the owner of so much of

South America, was never master of the seas, and the Dutch, hard pressed on land, could sail the ocean until, by a series of favourable events, the tide slowly turned in their favour, though too late for William to experience, as he was assassinated in 1584 by an agent of the Spanish government. The creator of modern Holland, the greatest statesman of his time, thus died before his task was accomplished, and so did not live to see his small country rise to a position in world affairs far beyond the size of her population. Her cities became important commercial centres, Amsterdam, Rotterdam, Leyden, Dordrecht, Delft and the Hague exercising a powerful influence on the finance, trade and culture of Europe, as well as in the East Indies, where factories were established, the first Dutch East India Company being formed in 1601.

Holland secured her independence because of the wide dispersal of the Spanish forces throughout the Empire, the English army that landed in Holland being unable greatly to affect the issue. With the men at his disposal the Duke of Parma was expected to do too much. The army he had collected for the invasion of England was used, after the defeat of the Armada, to promote the Spanish interests in France instead of attacking Holland, and the Duke died with none of his tasks accomplished. The loss of this great military leader, and Spain's overwhelming defeat by the English at sea, marks the beginning of the decline of Spanish power, and from now onwards her fortunes waned, Holland and England forming an alliance against her.

Maurice, the son of William, a man of greater military skill than his father, now took command, and finally decisively defeated the Spaniards in open battle at Turnhout in 1597. Thus ended this long and bloody war for independence, during which over 100,000 sturdy Netherlanders fell in battle, or were cruelly murdered while fighting for their liberty. Since those days the House of Orange has served Holland with devotion and ability, helped by the guidance of able statesmen, the most outstanding being John van Oldenbarnveldt, who, for thirty-two years (1586–1618), steered the ship of state with great wisdom. From now onwards the Dutch took their full share in the arts and sciences of Europe, though, like other people, they passed through periods of intolerance, the Calvinists persecuting, excluding from office and exiling all those who differed from them.

Calvinism soon gained a strong hold in France, one reason being that Calvin was a Frenchman who wrote in the language the literate French could read. The nobles, and through them the peasants, were influenced by his teaching, but the former, in many cases, took up the new movement more in the hope of embarrassing the King and securing some of the rich plunder in the form of Church land and wealth. Paris remained true to the orthodox faith, but elsewhere, especially in the south and west, the Protestant outlook made great headway, though nowhere were its adherents sufficiently strong to secure freedom for the public expression of their belief. Between these two forms of belief stood an intellectual class, led by men like Rabelais and Montaigne, who advocated more reliance on the individual's own reason, and a greater concentration on humanitarianism and ethical conduct.

When Henry II of France was killed by accident at a tournament in 1559, his wife Catherine de Medici, a debased creature, was left with a young family, none of whom could aspire to the throne for some years. She became the Regent, but there were other claimants. Anthony, King of Navarre, and Louis, Prince of Condé, who espoused Calvinism for political reasons, were the Protestant aspirants, while, on the Roman Catholic side, the Duke of Guise, with fifteen bishoprics in his family, and the owner of vast estates, was the most prominent.

When Francis, the son of Henry II, grew up he married Mary Stuart, and they became King and Queen of France in 1559, but their reign was short and marred by religious conflict. He, a lifelong invalid, died the following year, and was succeeded by the neurotic Charles IX (1560–1574), during whose reign efforts were made to bring about peace between the Roman Catholics and Protestants. One of the few men then in Europe who believed in toleration was the Chancellor, L'Hôpital, who issued an edict permitting the adherents to the reformed faith to worship within certain limits, but this did not satisfy the Protestants, who inflamed the passions of the Roman Catholics by destroying churches, images and sacred relics.

The fire of a disastrous civil war was, however, lit by the Roman Catholics, when the Duke of Guise, with some soldiers, dispersed a Calvinist service in the small town of Vassy in 1562, a large number of the congregation being killed. This act is known as the Massacre of Vassy, and from now onwards for thirty years persecution and strife rent the country. Families were divided against one another, and towns and villages were at deadly grips. Misery, poverty, cruelty and suffering reduced France materially and mentally to such a low level that the social conditions which prevailed had seldom ever been worse. Roman Catholics and Protestants fought one another without decisive results, and the Lutherans, to show their hatred of Calvinism, sent soldiers from Germany to fight with the Roman Catholics against the French Protestants.

Catherine de Medici played throughout a reactionary part, as her influence was always for uniformity in religion. Anthony of Navarre, the Prince of Condé, and Admiral Coligny, a man of high purpose, led the Protestants, receiving help from England and Switzerland, while the Roman Catholics received support from Spain. Many important indecisive battles were fought, during which time both Guise and Condé were killed, and then the Peace of St. Germain (1570) brought a truce which gave the Protestants freedom to worship as they pleased, besides entry on equal terms with Roman Catholics to the universities and public services.

Coligny and the King, moreover, decided on an alliance with England, and an attempt was made to persuade Queen Elizabeth to marry Henry, the King's brother. The marriage fell through, but the alliance was concluded. Henry of Navarre was encouraged to marry Margaret of Valois, the King's sister, and, when this was accomplished, France became once more politically united, and ready to send troops to help the oppressed Netherlands against Spain, which she wished to humiliate and curb from gaining a further grip on Europe. The fear of Spain doubtless influenced the King in making these decisions, which united, and staunched the wounds of a bleeding, France, but his policy was only to end in failure because of one of the most insane and despicable incidents in all history.

Catherine de Medici, fearing war between a strong united Spain and a France disunited by religion, decided that the split in the Christian Church could best be mended by massacring all the Protestants in France. This, to the criminally minded, is always a solution of most difficulties; kill your opponent, and then you have everything your own way. One can understand how unbalanced minds could conceive of this drastic way of solving religious and political differences, but she was as normal as anyone else of those days, as were also the priests and conspirators who worked along with her.

On 24th August, 1572, St. Bartholomew's Day, Catherine de Medici, Henry, the King's brother, the Duke of Guise, and other leading authorities in Paris, with the consent of the King, carried out a wholesale massacre of the French Protestants in the capital and elsewhere. Some historians place the number slaughtered in cold blood at 70,000, but, whatever the number was, it was sufficiently large to make the massacre one of the worst and foulest in the long black record of religious persecution. The Protestants, now roused to fury, and bitter because of the death of Coligny, who was one of the victims, rose in a body to defend their lives and liberties. Consequently war between the Roman Catholics and Protestants broke out afresh, to last for a year, when peace returned by the Protestants obtaining the right to worship as they pleased.

The massacre caused great jubilation amongst the Roman Catholics everywhere in France, many a zealot taking the opportunity to secure a victim or mutilate his corpse. Coligny's head was sent to the licentious Pope Gregory XIII, who, in return, sent the King a golden rose and ordered a special medal to be struck to commemorate the occasion. Rejoicings took place throughout the land, banquets were held, and the Te Deum was sung in all the churches. "Christian principles", "Christian ethics", "Christian justice", "Christian brotherhood", "Christian ideals" and so on, about which we hear so much in our own times, are anchored on nothing solid, the orthodox of past times considering themselves the possessors of all the virtues, a mistake which has been so often repeated since then. Ethics cannot pertain to supernatural religion, because it is founded on error, and its exclusiveness debars the entire human race, these two facts alone being contrary to the fundamental basis on which rests the ethical code.

Fortunately Germany escaped a similar massacre as the one France experienced, though Pope Pius V did his best to bring this about after failing to get the Roman Catholics in Britain to rise against the Protestants and murder Queen Elizabeth. His attempt to force the Emperor Maximilian II (1564–1576) to exterminate the German Protestants, and rid the land of the pestilent heretics, received a blunt refusal, the Emperor declining to be guilty of such a crime. Likewise he refused the demand of the German Protestants to persecute the Roman Catholics, his policy, he declared, being to allow everyone to believe as his conscience thought right.

This good man has the honourable position of being one of the first European rulers, since Christianity first darkened this earth, to refuse to persecute anyone for his opinions, and the reason was because he was not a Christian, and did not worship the Christian god who punished unbelievers in eternal hell. He was not afraid of the Christian hell for himself or anyone else, and was blessed with sufficient intelligence to renounce the evil superstition, and not be guided by either Roman or Protestant Catholic priests, refusing, moreover, the Sacrament on his deathbed. Tolerant, humane, just and attractive, this imperial sinner has received little praise from Christian historians, because he was rational enough to decline to subscribe to their debased ideology.

In the 16th century, as had been the case since Christianity came into being, and as it was up to last century, Christian principles relating to toleration in religion were guided by the following Scriptural texts :—

It is more profitable for thee that one of thy members should perish and not that thy whole body be cast into hell. (*Matthew* v, 29.)

Fear him which is able to destroy both soul and body in hell. (*Matthew* x, 28.)

If thy hand offend thee, cut it off; it is better for thee to enter into life maimed than having two hands to go into hell, into the fire that never shall be quenched. (*Mark* ix, 43.)

If any man . . . hate not his father and mother, and wife and children, and brethren and sisters, yea, and his own life also, he cannot be my disciple. (*Luke* xiv, 26.)

But those mine enemies, which would not that I should

reign over them, bring hither and slay them before me. (*Luke* xix, 27.)

He that believeth not shall be damned. (*Mark* xvi, 16.)

If any man love not the Lord Jesus Christ let him be anathema maranatha (everlastingly cursed by God). (1 *Corinthians* xvi, 22.)

The foregoing are only a few of the sacred injunctions against toleration, and in favour of torture, to be found in the Bible, the cutting off of hands and ears, the putting out of eyes, the maiming of the body so that "thy members should perish and not that thy whole body be cast into hell" being the Christian justification for torture. These divine warnings, and the Psalmist's uncompromising utterances against unbelievers, were dinned into our ignorant ancestors by both Roman Catholic and Protestant clergy in their sermons. Consequently they honestly believed that they were pleasing God by perpetrating every possible atrocity on every one who differed from them, every Christian considering himself a true disciple and a shining light of his Saviour, who had told him so to behave towards all unbelievers.

The cause of the massacre of Saint Bartholomew consequently lay in ignorance, which gave those who planned and executed it a mistaken idea of God and the future life. This ignorance can be directly traced to the tragic decisions made at Nicaea in 325. Their effects have already been plain, and will become more pronounced from now onwards. The Christian fanatics wanted France to be united, and free from what they considered was a mental canker eating into the belief in the true and only means of salvation. The orthodox were intense believers in the Christian religion "as received by the Christian Church from the Holy Spirit acting for Christ in heaven", and everyone firmly believed that they were numbered with the elect and destined for heaven, the unfortunate unorthodox and heathen having only misery as their future portion.

Few gave thought to the injustice of this verdict, those who did so being told that it was a divine mystery into which none dared to enquire. Religion, then as always, was a theological maze to the thoughtful, to become ever more so as reading increased. The word "mystery" is always applied to something unknown, but, when the mystery is solved, it ceases to be a mystery. To the ignorant everything is mysterious, but, as ignorance gives place to knowledge, mysteries fade away. So few there be who realise that they are ignorant, in fact they are ignorant that they are ignorant, and, because of this, their minds are constantly screened from the light of knowledge. They live in a narrow vale of ideas shut out from contact with other minds, ignorance keeping them from understanding other opinions, and the fact that divergence of opinion is essential because every mind is different. Intolerance therefore follows, and this causes frenzy and hatred, from which comes cruelty, to be followed by misery.

Only by removing ignorance and increasing wisdom can mankind be freed from the cause which creates so much unhappiness and suffering, but Christian civilisation knew nothing of this fundamental truth. It was quite satisfied with what is called the only revelation that has ever come to man from God, which disclosed a way of salvation quite apart from ethics and morality. Nature's law that as one sows one reaps, was ignored, and both Roman Catholics and Protestants continued to follow the path of ignorance, whichever side being the stronger oppressing and persecuting the other.

Protestantism in those days was of young and tender growth and the weakest power in France, the consequence being that the Roman Catholics were the aggressors and the Protestants the victims, but the events which followed somewhat improved their position. On the death of Charles IX in 1574, Henry, the King's brother, became king as Henry III (1574–1589), the Protestants now being led by Henry of Navarre, the heir to the throne. Against them was the Catholic League, formed for the purpose of extirpating heresy and excluding all Protestants from the throne. It received so much support from the people that its leader, the Duke of Guise, became a national hero, so much so that the King, fearing he would be replaced, murdered him.

The result was far different from what he expected, as he so raised the Roman Catholics against him that he was forced to join up with the Protestants. He now spoke honeyed words to the orthodox Catholics, reminding them (1) of their common Christian brotherhood, (2) their belief in the same creeds, (3) their common Saviour, and (4) their union in Christ, phrases which came strangely from one of the leaders of the Saint Bartholomew massacre. The army of the Catholic League could not, however, prevent the combined forces of Henry III and the Protestants from marching on Paris, but, before they captured the city, the King was assassinated by a Dominican monk.

Henry of Navarre, the first of the Bourbons, proclaimed himself King Henry IV (1589–1610), but, as the royal army melted away, he had to abandon the siege of Paris and resume his fight for the throne. He won important battles, and again gradually became strong enough to besiege Paris, which was on the point of surrender, when Philip II of Spain, realising that many of the French Roman Catholics would rather be ruled by Spain than by a Protestant king, sent an army from the Netherlands to relieve the city. The Protestant leader was forced to abandon the siege and turn his forces against the invaders, but the Spaniards withdrew, to again, by the same tactics, prevent him from capturing Rouen.

This terrible civil war might have lasted for years had Henry of Navarre not decided that the simplest way to secure the throne was to become a Roman Catholic. So he renounced his Protestant convictions, and went to Mass in 1593. When it is remembered that both sides believed the same creed, acknowledged the same God, and worshipped the same Christ, the change over was not one of any great difficulty, as, except for the orthodox Catholic belief in transubstantiation, and that the Pope is head of the Church, there is little of importance between Protestant and Catholic Christianity. France acclaimed Henry with enthusiasm, and the Catholic League welcomed him as a hero. Paris, the last to acknowledge him, finally opened its gates and he rode in amid great rejoicings. The Pope granted him absolution, and Henry began his difficult reign.

France in places was in a state of barbarism, many large districts were out of cultivation, and the country, after thirty years of civil war, was bankrupt. So the new king, though he had no serious opposition, had a difficult task to bring the country back to prosperity, but, with the help of Sully, his chief minister of State, who was a Protestant, order was finally brought out of chaos. Sully was a man of great ability and high integrity, his policy being to stimulate agriculture and set in being the construction of roads and canals. The King encouraged industry, and it was during his reign that the silk-worm was introduced into France.

To satisfy his former Protestant supporters, who were resentful at his conduct, he issued the famous Edict of Nantes in 1598, which gave the Protestants in France a much better position than they enjoyed elsewhere in Europe. Never before had such toleration been shown in Christendom, and, so long as this lasted, France was happy and prosperous. Unfortunately, neither the Roman Catholics nor the Protestants believed in, nor even understood, the meaning of toleration, and before a hundred years had passed this great Charter of Liberty was withdrawn.

The Jesuits gave the new king much trouble. They tried to murder him, and he expelled them for a brief period. Again he angered them when he had completed his plans to break in pieces the Roman Catholic Hapsburg Empire, with the assistance of the German Protestants. · In consequence he was assassinated in 1610, at the instigation of the Jesuits, who in those days commended murder to secure their ends, these zealous fanatics being prepared to adopt any method which furthered the power and glory of the Pope and his Church.

The Society of Jesus, whose members are known

as Jesuits, was founded by Ignatius of Loyola (1491-1556), now a saint in heaven. He was a tough, illiterate, but gallant Spanish nobleman, with many love affairs to his credit, who, after a dangerous illness, decided to become a Knight of Christ, renounce earthly love, and give it instead to the Mother of God. After many vigils, much fasting, penance and self-torture he went on a pilgrimage to the Holy Land, to be ordained as a priest on his return home in 1538.

He was then able to realise his ambition to establish a great aggressive Roman Catholic missionary order to carry the Gospel far and wide. It was constituted somewhat after the pattern of the Salvation Army, with a general in supreme command, to whom the Pope came first and all else last. Its members recognised no other authority, and if the Pope said "white was black, then black it was" They paid no taxes, and considered themselves above the law of the land in which they lived, only the advancement of the Church being their policy. Consequently a Jesuit confessor was always available to advise and help all Roman Catholic rulers, the Protestant monarchs, on the other hand, being the object of their hatred and intrigue for the purpose of undermining their authority.

Missionaries were sent to China, India and North and South America, and theological schools were established throughout Christendom. The Jesuits attacked the abuses in the Church, and it was greatly due to the enthusiasm with which they inspired the Roman Catholics in France that the Protestant movement failed to succeed in its endeavour to make France a Protestant country. Elsewhere they stopped the flood of Protestantism in Germany and Poland, but in England their efforts were less successful, as there they were expelled or put to death.

So France remained Roman Catholic, and, in the following century, the murdering, torturing, deportation and persecution of the Protestants recommenced, to continue well on into the 18th century. Then Voltaire, by his exposure of the Church and its priests, brought it to an end, but this valiant fight for liberty will be told later on. With the death of Henry IV we come to the beginning of the 17th century, and for a time we must leave Europe to consider what has been taking place across the Channel.

(2) ENGLAND SUFFERS FROM A LONG AND SAVAGE CIVIL WAR.

In the previous chapter we reached the period in English history when a foundation had been laid for both parliamentary government and secular education. Then England was at the height of her power in France, her victories there having greatly heightened the prestige of the English throne throughout Europe. When Richard II (1377–1399) became king, England was realising her strength and weakness in trade and commerce, so much so that she was beginning to experiment in what was to become in the centuries ahead a very controversial economic question, namely protection or free trade. Attempts at one or the other had so far been tried without a decision being reached as to which was best, and now we find that navigation laws were passed excluding foreign vessels from English ports. This exclusive policy failed because there were not enough English ships to meet the demand, a deficiency which was not met until the 17th century.

Richard succeeded his grandfather Edward III in 1377, because his father, Edward the Black Prince, had died the previous year. He was only ten years of age, and, as his four uncles all aspired to the Regency, a provisional government by a council was formed. The war with France had by now turned against England, the Black Death had created a shortage of labour, and legislation to fix prices and wages at the level prevailing before this terrible visitation had proved ineffective. In 1381 the peasants revolted because of their hard conditions, while bands of lawless adventurers, home from devastating France, were wandering far and wide, living on what they could steal.

England had made herself responsible for the government of Ireland in 1166, but little had been done, and now, after the King of Scotland had attempted to become King of Ireland, the English awoke to the fact that Irish legislation was a problem which awaited solution. Laws were therefore passed for the purpose of strengthening English authority, and all absentee English landlords were instructed to return to Ireland.

Such were the problems facing the English during the reign of the brave but foolish and vindictive Richard, to which must be added the ferment caused by Wycliffe and the Lollards in their attacks on the Church. This story, and the account of the peasants' revolt led by Wat Tyler and John Ball, the pioneers in England of the movement to secure the rights of the common man, have already been told. After occupying London, and killing the reactionary Simon Sudbury, the Archbishop of Canterbury, the mob dispersed and the rising was everywhere cruelly suppressed. The peasants failed· to secure their demands, and a century·was to pass before the prevailing system of bondage, and the lack of legal rights, finally passed away, but the villeins never forgot the way they were massacred when they rebelled. They became so sullen and hostile that gradually the landowners were glad to receive rents for their houses and lands in place of unwilling service.

At the other end of the social scale, the great nobles, dissatisfied with the King's tyrannical methods, planned and plotted against him, finally to dethrone him, but before they succeeded he executed or banished the leaders, made peace with France, and went off to Ireland to deal with pressing problems. During his absence Henry of Lancaster, his cousin, whom he had banished, returned and led a revolt against him, which was so successful that when. Richard arrived home he found nearly everyone his enemy. He surrendered in 1399 and Parliament deposed him.

Henry of Lancaster became Henry IV (1399–1413), and now we are approaching the time picturesquely called the Wars of the Roses, when England suffered from conditions similar to those she had imposed on France. Parliament supported Henry, who was an able man, but he was so selfish that he made many enemies during his reign of fourteen years. One who overthrows a king, and takes his place, must always be ready to face the same experience. It is a dangerous precedent, and the usurper is not for long established before others are ready and willing to do the same to him when opportunity offers. England was soon to suffer from an unstable throne, and when the head is removed the body quickly decays.

Apart from a successful war against the Welsh, who were prevented, by the Battle of Shrewsbury in 1403, from receiving help from the Percys of Northumberland, most of the King's concern during his reign was to combat bitter intrigues at court, and satisfy the Church which was out for the blood of the heretics. Persecution became general after the passing of the statute of 1401, which authorised the burning of all who did not conform to orthodox Christianity, but, though there was reaction in religion, progress took place politically as Parliament gained further control, particularly of finance, and secured the power to initiate all legislation within this sphere.

Moreover legal education, in place of theological instruction, advanced in the 15th century, so much so that when Henry V (1413–1422) succeeded his father Henry IV, associations of lawyers—the first learned laymen—had acquired inns, the name given to the town houses of noblemen, in which to assemble and discuss law, a union which conferred on the members the right to plead in court. This gleam of intelligent progress was, however, overshadowed by ignorance, which is for ever staining the pages of history, and in this case the trouble came about because Henry V married Katherine of France, an alliance which led England into the blackest period of her history.

The story has already been told of how Henry V reopened the war with France, and, by great skill, won the Battle of Agincourt. Civil war in France followed, and Henry marched on Paris, where he made himself Regent, as the French king, Charles VI, was insane and quite unfit to govern. Henry should have known something of the law of heredity, and the danger of marrying the daughter of this imbecile monarch, but, love being blind, his affections doubtless overcame his reason.

Katherine's son became Henry VI, and unfortunately inherited his French grandfather's mental weakness, a calamity which brought disaster to England. Agincourt was a dearly bought victory. The misspent reign of Henry V brought misery to both France and England, his sense of duty urging him to humble France abroad and exterminate the Lollards at home. He died the year after his son's birth, but, had he lived a few months longer, many interesting events might have followed, because the French had agreed to him being their king on the death of Charles, their weak-minded sovereign. Henry, however, died in 1422, within two years of his entry into Paris, and Charles, whom he would have succeeded, died only two months later.

When only nine months old Henry VI (1422–1461) began his long and unhappy reign. A long regency was inevitable, and his uncle John, Duke of Bedford, took over the position with the title of Protector. His rule was efficient, and the war with France continued to proceed for a time successfully, much booty finding its way across the Channel to England. Then, as already recorded, Joan of Arc changed the scene, and, from this time onwards, the charm which victories and loot had produced on

England vanished, to the accompaniment of sordid intrigues for power. As time passed the King grew up and married Margaret of Anjou. He was a man of fine character, too good and kind to meet his nobles on their own ground, in fact a hopeless king for the times. The meek cannot inherit the earth if they are surrounded by the unscrupulous, and this was the position at the English court in those days.

Consequently the King exercised little influence, and Cardinal Beaufort, the King's great-uncle, and the Duke of Gloucester, the King's uncle, struggled for power during the time the Protector, the Duke of Bedford, was directing operations in France. When defeat followed victory, confusion came to England, and the treacherous Duke of Suffolk, who had become the King's chief adviser on the deaths of Beaufort and Gloucester, was impeached and murdered on his flight to France. That was the price he paid for his incapacity, as on him was put the blame for the disasters in France.

Jack Cade then led a popular revolt, composed chiefly of men of Kent, because the people greatly resented the way things had been managed in France, the source for so many years of much rich loot, and the hunting-ground for numerous English adventurers. Cade occupied London, executed certain unpopular officials, and the King fled, to return when the rebel was slain and his revolt crushed. This episode is interesting, as it is the first record of the people in England expressing their opinion on foreign policy, their evolution from bondage to freedom having now begun.

In 1453 the trouble in England began in earnest, because in that year the French expelled the English from all their domains except Calais, and Henry became mentally unfitted for his position. The mistake made by his father in marrying the insane French king's daughter, after his successful war in France, was now apparent, and England was to suffer the consequences. A regent was necessary, as an heir to the throne had just been born, following Henry's marriage to Margaret of Anjou. If this son had not arrived, Richard, Duke of York, the great-grandson of Edward III, would have been heir to the throne. Richard was an energetic capable man of immense wealth, and the possessor of numerous retainers always ready to fight for him. To many he seemed the very man to be king in these dark and difficult times, especially as he had the support of the Nevilles, and the powerful Earl of Warwick—to become known as the King-maker—with all their immense possessions and thousands of retainers.

Thus was the stage set for the Wars of the Roses, called by this name because the badge of the Duke of York was a white rose and that of the Lancasters, who were the supporters of the insane king, was a red rose. The struggle, which began as a protest against a mentally weak king and his ministers, who were considered to be incompetent, developed into a ferocious civil war for possession of the crown by Richard of York, who, as we have read, had been its heir up to the moment of the birth of a son to Henry VI and his wife, Margaret of Anjou. Treachery was common throughout this terrible conflict, no quarter was given, prisoners were massacred, and all the degradation that the war in France had produced on the soldier came to the surface.

The weak-minded king did not count, but Richard of York had to meet the resistance of an infuriated queen, intent on maintaining the heritage of her infant son. She assembled her forces, battles were won and lost, until finally she encountered Richard at Wakefield, where he was slain, his severed head, with a paper crown, grimly adorning one of the gates of York. Unfortunately this was not the end, and his popular, handsome but self-indulgent son Edward continued the struggle, which was decided after terrible slaughter at Towton near York in 1461, when his army was victorious, a decisive gain which made him King Edward IV.

Edward IV (1461–1483) had won the throne by the help of the Earl of Warwick, but this did not end the conflict. The King and Warwick now quarrelled over the King's marriage to Elizabeth Woodville, and the King-maker, who wanted an alliance with the sister of Louis XI of France, went over to the Lancastrians, allying himself with the former Queen, Margaret of Anjou. He obtained help from Louis, and, after each side had secured its victories and defeats, Edward IV was driven from the throne, and found refuge in Flanders. So, for the second time in this fierce conflict, Henry VI was again king, but Edward IV would not admit defeat, and, with the help he received from Charles the Bold of Burgundy, he returned to England and attacked the forces of the Earl of Warwick.

At Barnet (1471) Warwick was defeated and slain, and a month later the same fate befell the army of Queen Margaret, to be followed by the death of her son and husband, the insane king. All the nobles who had supported the House of Lancaster were murdered when found, and few of the old aristocracy survived, the consequence being that for the next twelve years Edward reigned in comparative peace. He died in 1483 at the age of forty from the effects of a depraved and vicious life, leaving two sons, the eldest being only twelve years old.

This boy, who became Edward V, was left by his father under the care of his uncle Richard, Duke of Gloucester, who became Lord Protector, an able, ambitious, cruel and unscrupulous man with a shameful record of lies, intrigues and murder. He immediately imprisoned the boy king and his brother in the Tower, murdered them both, and then took the title of Richard III (1483–1485). This was the signal for a new struggle, as Henry Tudor, Earl of Richmond, who was descended from John of Gaunt, son of Edward III, raised the standard of rebellion.

War and murder had so reduced the claimants before him that he had now a rightful claim to the throne, and at Bosworth, near Leicester, in 1485, his forces met the army of Richard III, when the blood-stained king was defeated and killed after a reign of only two years. This newcomer Henry Tudor, of Welsh descent, and intent on restoring peace to a stricken land, was a man of great ability and foresight, strong but just, besides having a remarkable grasp of foreign policy, finance and trade. He became king as Henry VII, and established the House of Tudor, which was to give England kings and queens for the next 118 years, who were to figure prominently during her rise to the position of a world power, and carry her through the political and religious upheavals of the years ahead.

So ended the disastrous feud between the representatives of the houses of Lancaster and York, a struggle which cost 100,000 lives and lasted for thirty years. Its long-time effect was to break the power of the nobles, and bring to an end the feudalism which had chained nearly all but the priests and nobles to the daily drudgery on the land, from dawn to sunset, without a gleam of brightness in their lives. The immediate effect was to leave England impoverished, poor and miserable.

Morality and justice were never lower, disorder was never greater, and at no time in France, Spain or Italy at their worst were scenes of greater violence witnessed than during this black period of England's history. Though the war was confined to the nobles and their retainers, and agriculture and trade continued with little interruption, neither villein, craftsman nor tradesman taking part in it, England sank morally, mentally and materially to the lowest depths. She had sown her evil deeds in France, which she had ravaged and devastated, and she had reaped the whirlwind by bringing into her own royal house the insanity which had afflicted her victim's monarch. England certainly garnered in sorrow what she had planted in France.

Again we ask, why will men fight and suffer to advance the interests of their masters, who fling them aside when they have no further use for them? One can understand how the spirit of adventure, for the sake of achievement, can rouse enthusiasm for a cause and enable men to suffer and die for its attainment.

Many have suffered for the sake of discovery, but they represent only a minute fraction of those who have endured the agony of wounds and died on the battle-field for something from which they gained nothing. No soldier benefited from this futile controversy between ambitious nobles fighting for and against the throne, and the entire country was left scarred and bleeding.

What happened then has happened from early times up to our own day. What German or Italian soldier would have been the gainer if these two countries had won the Second World War? The power and wealth would have been retained by the Nazi and Fascist chiefs, but the ordinary individual, who risked all, left home, wife, children and employment to live a life of great discomfort, hard discipline and danger, would have been no better off. What gullible dolts and simpletons men are to allow themselves to be duped and doped by false promises, which the study of the past shows to have been always illusive. More would have been won by each man remaining at his ordinary productive work than he could possibly have gained from the loot stolen from ravished lands, even if he lived to be fortunate enough to discover something which he could keep or send home. Helmets and leather belts are about all the booty that soldiers nowadays are allowed to keep.

When armies were composed of voluntary adventurers, who kept what they stole, it is possible to understand how a small proportion of the population, the riff-raff, who could not settle down to honest work, preferred the freedom of army life to that of serfdom. They had no home ties, no honour, no morality, and they liked the life of freebooters on land and pirates at sea. Now things are vastly different, as fighting has become compulsory, a modern form of the Press Gang, called Conscription, forcing all young and middle-aged men to fight and kill, to leave home, wife and children, and exchange freedom and comfort for discipline and discomfort. They leave freedom for servitude, and good money-making work for a dangerous uncomfortable life with miserable pay. Why is such folly possible?

Many such questions could be asked. Why, for instance, do aggressive nations rush into war gladly, a feature of all wars, and imagine quick and easily won booty, only soon to regret their folly and long for peace? Why do the people so honour the soldier, the destroyer of life and wealth, and pass by the engineer, the producer of wealth and comfort? Why are our hero soldiers well known and remembered, and our great constructors so little known? Why is Napoleon, a master destroyer, known by name to everyone, but the builder of the Forth Bridge, one of the greatest engineering feats of all time, known only to the few? Why are the greatest honours, and the most numerous decorations, reserved for those who have been trained to destroy, while those who have made the greatest contribution to the world's wealth, comfort and happiness are so often passed over, few knowing even their names?

We must alter our sense of values, and appreciate more what is good and less that which is evil. Moreover, we must grow more quickly out of the childish mentality which so many retain until middle age, and this can only come about by education and increased wisdom. If we study children playing on the sea-shore, building and then destroying one another's sand castles, fighting and quarrelling over this and that, we realise that they just represent the human family well on into middle age, after which we become mature, more rational in our thoughts and actions—in other words wiser.

It is this childishness in so many, when they are supposed to be grown up, that causes so much unnecessary trouble to everyone. Like children, they accept what they are told because they lack both know-ledge and wisdom. Some are easily led into evil ways by those who are unscrupulous and forceful in char-acter, some love a fight for its excitement, and many lack, from childish want of appreciation of the feelings of both humans and animals, the sense of kindness and consideration for others which is so necessary for our peace and happiness. This want of individuality, this weakness of character in individuals, is likewise the characteristic of nations, made up of individuals, who are led into war by the most forceful personalities, just as children are led into mischief, but with good leaders the people can equally well be led into the path of peace, progress and happiness.

In our time the leaders led the Germans, Italians and Japanese into war against those who desired peace, and who, in self-defence, had to fight for self-preser-vation, but it was not so very long ago that men of similar mentality led France, Spain, Britain, and other countries of the world, into war against those who wished peace. This lack of individual thinking can only be cured by mental development, and when this comes about we shall cease being children, not at middle age, but when we pass the adolescence stage. When that happens a new chapter will open in the history of the human race.

Why did men work as vassals for an overlord in the years gone by? Because they were too weak to act alone, and the overlord could always find men whom he armed, paid and fed well, to keep his serfs from rebellion. By union came strength, and the time came when the Trade Unions, composed of the workers, fought for the individual worker, and gave to each and all the support required to secure justice for service rendered. When will the men of every land join themselves into an anti-aggression union pledged only to defend their country, but never to invade a neighbouring land and kill its people?

No one man, or group of men, can decide for themselves when ordered to attack in war, as those who urge them on shoot all who disobey. Only the union of men of each nation can determine the fate of each and all, and only it can say to aggressive leaders: "No, never again. For thousands of years the people have fought for knaves like you, suffered for tyrants like you, and died for scoundrels like you. Only thugs like you have obtained the glory, the honour and the plunder. Now we know that promises coming from ruffians like you are false, as we are no longer ignorant and history is our guide. Now we know that all the plunder won, even if equally divided, could never compensate us for what we lose from leaving our present profitable work. We shall now live for our country and not die for it. Never again, is our answer." When that time comes, everywhere war will cease, just as slavery, serfdom, filth, plague, squalor and general degradation came to an end in Europe as the people advanced in intelligence.

It is difficult for us to realise the depth of depravity in which the people of Britain, and throughout all Christendom, lived during the period called the Middle Ages. The great majority were serfs, working several days a week for their overlord in exchange for the hovel in which they lived, and the strip of land that went with it. If they did not work hard for the time stipulated they were thrashed by the bailiff. Then, when skilled craftsmen were erecting wonderful cathedrals by serf labour, street processions consisted of people following men holding aloft the heads of those who had been beheaded, and also the congenital organs of men who had been put to death after being castrated. That cruel emblem, the crucifix, received general veneration, and all knelt and prayed as companies of filthy priests passed down the street with it at their head.

The death rate was appalling, as plague and disease swept off the people, whose average duration of life was only twenty years, as compared with fifty years in our day. No house, not even the king's castle, had more than one living-room, and the vermin-covered people, their faces pitted with the effects of smallpox, their bodies the abode of lice which spread typhus, lived in wattle hovels, in perpetual smoke, lacking windows and chimneys, and always surrounded by soot and dirt. The first house with a chimney was built in Britain in 1420, after which coal was used with wood, but, in the previous century, a man was hanged in London for burning coal in his house because the fumes which came from it stifled the occupiers.

Toil from morning to night, with few enjoyments,

comprised the lives of the great majority of the people, while the feudal lords fought each other, or hunted game. In England 30,000 priests and monks, out of a population of 2,500,000, lived on what comfort and luxuries there were, while the people had to eat kale, salt meat, and coarse bread, with teeth no better than tusks. Both men and women wore gowns down to their feet. Beds consisted of straw laid on the floor. There were no sanitary conveniences, and no one used forks or spoons, even the nobles eating with their fingers and throwing on the floor what remained on their plates. Everyone blew the mucus out of their noses as do animals, and their saliva and the droppings from their food bespattered their clothes. There were no handkerchiefs, tablecloths, napkins, carpets, towels or soap, as these refinements are of comparatively recent date. Such was the social condition of Christendom which the Church did its utmost to maintain, as we shall discover as we proceed.

The first of the Tudors, Henry VII (1485–1509), married Elizabeth, only daughter of Edward IV, and thus fused the house of York with that of Lancaster, her mother Elizabeth Woodville being given the lands of Stansted Hall in Essex for life. This union brought the bloody strife between the two royal houses to an end, and gave the country a chance to recover under his firm rule.

Henry was supreme and absolute, as civil war had reduced the nobles in numbers and wealth. To strengthen his position he revived the Court of the Star Chamber, composed of his Chancellor and a few other leading officials, to deal with any unruly barons, because he was determined that never in his reign would another nobleman, like the Earl of Warwick, gather forces to fight against the throne. Ireland was treated in the same drastic way, and English law was there made compulsory, but never did he depart from his policy of mercy and justice. He did not make Ireland orderly, but better than he found it, and her Parliament was brought under the King's immediate control to be summoned only when he pleased.

Henry amassed a huge fortune from taxation, and this he put aside to enable him to hire soldiers should another rebellion occur. The Pope urged him to lead a Crusade against the Turks, but he refused because the country needed rest from foreign wars. So he pursued a peaceful policy and, by marrying his daughter Margaret to James IV of Scotland, and betrothing his son Henry to Catherine of Aragon, the devout, charitable and dignified daughter of Ferdinand and Isabella of Spain, he did what he could to secure the friendship of these two countries. The marriage of his daughter to the King of Scotland produced the most enduring results, as, because of it, the thrones of England and Scotland were united after the death of Queen Elizabeth, when their great-grandson, James VI of Scotland, became James I of England.

During the reign of Henry VII the country made industrial and economic progress, commercial treaties being made with Spain, Milan, Denmark and the Netherlands. That is one side of the picture, but England was then full of thieves and highwaymen, and there were no police. For law and order the King relied on the local Justices of the Peace, who did their work efficiently, and it was all done voluntarily and unpaid. Their task was rendered difficult by the Church shielding any ruffian who claimed sanctuary, and, besides this, it insisted on trying all criminals in holy orders, a number which was considerable in those days, because both priests and monks abounded and were subject only to the Bishop's court.

Henry's foreign policy was also directed towards peace, and he was the first English sovereign to make treaties for the express purpose of maintaining peace. The Tudors were the first to realise the folly of England attempting to dominate France, and, in consequence, her plundering adventurers took to the sea, to become the pioneers who laid the foundation of the British Empire. Instead of looting France they robbed the Spanish galleys and colonies.

As trade improved the population increased. England was then a land of open spaces, great forests, moors and fens. Her wide expanse of arable lands was tilled by scores of smallholders, and nowhere could one see a fence or a hedge. Every village had its common, its church and its manor house, and there were market towns dotted all over the country within some ten miles of each village. The middle class became ever more important, because the late civil war had so reduced the power and wealth of the nobles. On them England now relied for her salvation, and she was not disappointed.

The towns began to increase in size, and became ever more necessary to the economic life of the community. Many stately edifices, public buildings and private mansions were erected during this period, such as Westminster Abbey, Trinity College and

King's College Chapel at Cambridge. Books began to circulate as Caxton's printing press produced them in greater numbers, but England, owing to the civil war, had hardly yet felt the influence of the Renaissance. There was no toleration in religion, and the followers of Wycliffe and other heretics were persecuted, tortured and burned.

Only once did Henry engage in a foreign war, when he joined a league against France, but it was of short duration. His reign of twenty-four years brought peace and prosperity to England, but it was at the expense of the people's liberty, as he ruled through his Council, which issued ordinances that took the place of laws, his leading minister, Cardinal Morton, playing the same important part as did Cardinal Wolsey in the next reign.

Henry died in 1509, and was followed by his son, Henry VIII, whose incursions into religion left their mark on future English history. Religious beliefs are of slow growth, and never really new, each having an ancestor which goes far back into antiquity, but religious organisations came into being as the direct result of an action on the part of a ruler or outstanding man. King Asoka of India established the Buddhist Church; Vistaspa, the wealthy Persian nobleman, the Zoroastrian Church of Persia, and Constantine established the Christian Church. Luther split the Catholic Church and formed the Lutheran Church; Calvin produced the Calvinist Church, and to Henry VIII falls the credit of founding the Episcopalian Church of England. This historic episode, and his other activities, will now be recorded at greater length in the section which follows.

(3) BRITAIN DURING THE REFORMATION.

Thanks to the financial and political ability of his father, Henry VIII (1509–1547), at the age of eighteen, succeeded to a despotic throne, a well-filled treasury, and a land prospering from its period of peace. He had the benefit of the help and loyalty of a priest of outstanding ability, as Thomas Wolsey (1471–1530), the son of an Ipswich farmer, devoted his life to the increase of his royal master's influence.

Wolsey became Archbishop of York in 1514, and Chancellor a year later, but, although he became a Cardinal, he never attained his ambition of being elected Pope, though he was prepared to give 100,000 ducats for the office. He cared nothing for progress or reform, his craving being for power, and, besides being Chancellor and Archbishop, he was Abbot of St. Albans and bishop of six dioceses, one being the fabulously rich See of Durham, all of which he sadly neglected. Moreover, he obtained for his natural son four arch-deaconries, a deanery, five prebends and two rectories.

Here indeed was a Prince of the Church, a man who treated both nobles and gentlemen as dirt beneath his feet. He maintained a household of nearly a thousand persons, and marched in state with silver pillars and pole-axes borne before him. This extraordinary man, about as wealthy as his sovereign, was the last in England of the long line of clerical statesmen. He established for fourteen years a repulsive ecclesiastical tyranny, he being a despotic autocrat to whom the King gave unlimited power, glad to have such an able, industrious and loyal servant to relieve him of the task of government. By gathering all ecclesiastical power into his own hands, Wolsey so reduced the control of the Holy See over England that, without intending to do so, he paved the way for Henry's overthrow of papal authority.

Wolsey's private life was quite immoral, but, as a statesman, his policy was to make his royal master play a commanding part in the great contest for power which was then going on in Europe. His diplomatic skill proved invaluable in keeping steady the balance of power in Europe during the war between France and Spain, because he dangled the prize of England's friendship and support before the eyes of Francis I of France and Charles V, the Holy Roman Emperor, in their long-drawn-out conflict.

Henry's first European adventure was to join a Holy League of European powers against France in 1511, but the success achieved was not impressive. The Scotch, as usual, sided with France, to reap their punishment in the crushing defeat they experienced at Flodden (1513), when the flower of their army was wiped out. Peace followed, but Henry would never commit himself to an alliance with France, and finally concluded a pact with Spain. This meant another war with France in 1523, to end in an alliance with France against Spain, which was then becoming too powerful to be safe. Two years later a general European peace was concluded.

The position England occupied in those days of holding the balance of power in Europe, besides the results which followed Henry's quarrel with the Pope, and his sensational matrimonial experiences, make his reign stand out as one of particular interest. He was never the figurehead of a political or religious faction, like his son Edward VI and his daughter Mary, but always acted as a national ruler. Consequently he received the loyalty of the great majority in the country, and only slight internal strife clouded his reign. In England, as in Europe, this was a time of mental disruption when the Church was losing its previous stranglehold on kings, princes and people. Its power was passing over to monarchs, but, though its prestige had declined, its doctrines were still sincerely believed, and St. Paul's Churchyard was the place where all the heretical books were burned.

Parliament had not yet the tradition, nor even the necessary popular support, to enable it to replace the Church, and the power which the Church lost in England the throne gained. Nevertheless Parliament, during this change, was never effaced as it was in Spain and France, only overshadowed, and, in later years, it regained its power. Henry was the voice of England, and his policy was the country's policy. What he did was done in the name of England, as his rule was a dictatorship for which he alone, and not Parliament, was responsible.

Henry entered into political life, like his two great contemporaries on the Continent, Francis I and Charles V, at one of the turning periods of history. Prior to this time one Faith, one Church and one King had for centuries been the accepted form of all settled government in Europe. The Pope received his power from God, the King from the Pope, and between them, with their respective organisations, they carried on the government of each separate kingdom. Tradition is harder to break than iron, as it is a mental bond with the past, and mind is the greatest force on earth, but what makes these days memorable is the fact that the mind of Europe had now ceased to be tranquil, a mental storm was raging, and tradition was bending under the force of the gale.

Consequently Henry, like others of his time, was lifted by a wave of enthusiasm to take his share in the great mental upheaval, writing a treatise against Luther in 1521 for which Leo X, one of the many wicked popes, rewarded him with the title of Defender of the Faith. This honour quite went to his head, and from now onwards Henry believed that all his theological utterances were divinely inspired, he being now the mouthpiece of God, who had appointed him as his representative on earth. The Faith he defended was the orthodox Catholic form of Christianity, but, from that day to this, the Protestant monarchs of Britain have added this distinction to their other royal titles.

Henry lived at the time when the old order was ending, and a new one was slowly and timidly taking its place. Things were being done and said which were new and strange, and so it came about that in his reign William Tyndale (1484–1536) was driven out of England as a heretic (1524) because he commenced to translate the New Testament into the English language. He settled in Worms, where he completed this work, and then later translated the Pentateuch, but he was now a marked man and had to move from place to place to elude the plots and intrigues the Church authorities had planned for his destruction. Finally he was arrested near Brussels, found guilty of heresy and put to death by strangling, his body then being burned at the stake.

This outrageous crime is one more proof, if such be needed, that the Church was against education, and did not wish the people to learn how to read and write. It did not wish them to read the Scriptures, and thus form their own interpretation. The reformers, on the other hand, put the authority of the Scriptures in place of that of the Pope, and this meant that the knowledge of how to read became necessary. This important fact eventually gave birth to education, as appreciated by Aristotle, and as we now understand it, because when some could read and write knowledge grew, to end in general education being established in Britain and elsewhere at the close of last century. However, in the reign of Henry, we can only see a gleam of the coming day (when reading and writing would transform the thoughts and life of mankind), by the appointment of the first British Postmaster, Sir Brian Tuke, who, in 1533, was appointed to supervise the conveyance of letters both at home and abroad.

The theological universities and colleges formed the framework round which education grew, just as the theological weeds were gradually uprooted. This development was slow and difficult, the belief that the Bible contained all there was to know being always a reactionary influence, this subversive idea not being generally abandoned until the end of last century. Only then did real education commence, after centuries of opposition from Roman Catholics and many Protestants. Fortunately, in our time, theology is a discredited science, all thinking people having abandoned it as a means to explain the phenomena of nature, the consequence being that the road to knowledge has at long last been reached.

The process from theological instruction to our present-day system of education caused much suffering and discord. In spite of persecution, learning, however, advanced, and the work of Tyndale was the first step, as, until the Bible was available for study by everyone, the false claims made for it could not be challenged. Still, for three centuries to come, it held its place in the esteem of the people, but developing mind eventually revealed its human origin.

This discovery would never have been made had education not made its first halting entrance into the lives of the more intelligent of the people during the period we have now reached in the story of man's upward climb from darkness to light. From the 14th century onwards, kings, churchmen and laymen founded and endowed schools and colleges, which combined education with theological instruction, just as happened within the Roman Empire when wealthy Pagans, intent on the spread of education, established schools and colleges for purposes other than the training of men for the priesthood.

The reign of Henry VIII was thus a time when Europe, including England, was beginning to awaken from its long and profound slumber. Henry himself, influenced by the anti-clericalism of the scholarly Dutchman, Erasmus, was a rebel against Church authority, and, though no friend of the reformers, he pursued a line of his own which was quite unorthodox, to end eventually in the Reformation reaching England.

Small causes often have far-reaching consequences, and now we have reached another of the important cross-roads of history, when great changes came about from causes which then seemed to be of only minor importance.

Henry was desperately anxious to have a son, and if Catherine of Aragon had given him one and not a daughter, Mary, England might have played little or no part in the religious upheaval of those days. England today might still be, in name at least, a Roman Catholic and not a Protestant country. For eighteen years Henry's hopes of a male heir were dashed aside, as year after year Catherine produced one stillborn child after another, or children who died at birth.

No female had so far ruled England in her own right, and, with his strong sense of duty to his people, he foresaw with fear another bloody civil war when he died, and all the good work done by his father dashed to pieces. It is strange to think that the improper functioning of a woman's creative organs should have determined a great nation's destiny, and that our way of thinking and living today can be traced back to this event. Truly our lives hang on small but vital issues.

Because his loyal and devoted wife Catherine could not produce a living son, and Henry was determined to have one, a series of events followed which made England a Protestant country, the first being his decision to divorce Catherine and marry again. So he applied to Pope Clement VII to annul his marriage, but this was just something the Holy Father could not do. Here we must recall our earlier story about the army of the Emperor Charles V rebelling in Italy, devastating Rome more thoroughly than ever before in history, and capturing Clement. Consequently the Pope, now completely subservient to the Emperor, could not grant the divorce of a Spanish princess, who was the aunt of his captor, even if he had been otherwise quite willing to do so.

Henry was very wrathful, and this made him remember the constant papal interference in English national affairs. Otherwise he was a good Catholic, and not a heretic, but the trend of the times made him take a strong line against the political power of the Holy See, just as had been done in Europe by sovereigns over the previous three hundred years. He had no wish to change the doctrine or form of worship of the Church of England, but he certainly coveted the wealth of the monasteries, and made their corrupt state the excuse for their abolition and robbery. Except for this he did nothing to disturb the existing orthodox Catholic faith, and he had no sympathy with either Luther or Calvin; in fact he was so antagonistic to their opinions that he secured the enactment of the Six Articles, reaffirming the belief in transubstantiation and other doctrines in dispute, so as to prevent their heretical doctrines taking root in England. All who denied the truth of orthodox Christianity were heretics, their fate being death at the stake, and the people generally accepted this as the right and proper way to deal with all who accepted the Protestant outlook on religion.

The excuse Henry made for the divorce was because Catherine had been previously married to his

brother Arthur,[1] who had died, and, as the Pope
would not consent, he summoned Parliament, whose
members were mostly devout Roman Catholics, but
quite disloyal to His Holiness, and strongly against
the power and privilege of the Church.   This previous
marriage of Catherine to his brother evidently preyed
on Henry's mind, he allowed it to become an obsession,
and came to think that the death of his children at
birth was indeed the curse of God upon him for having
married his deceased brother's wife.   Consequently
he came to believe that he was not legally married to
Catherine, and the sooner a divorce was obtained
the better.

On its sovereign's instructions, Parliament passed
the necessary statutes to secure the independence of the
Church of England, by making the King in future
the head of the Church, and when this was done
Henry secured his divorce from Thomas Cranmer
(1489–1556), Archbishop of Canterbury, which enabled him to marry the frivolous unstable Anne
Boleyn.   Thus Henry got his way, but the unfortunate
Wolsey, who had angered the King because of his
failure to secure the assent of the Holy See to the
divorce, was deprived of the Great Seal, summoned
to London on a charge of treason, and died at Leicester
Abbey on the way.

Anne Boleyn gave Henry a daughter, Elizabeth,
but no son, and he beheaded her for infidelity and
married again.   His third attempt produced the
desired result, as Jane Seymour presented him with a

[1] Before Henry married Catherine, Pope Julius II gave him a special
dispensation in 1503, this being necessary because of the Levitical law that
"if a man shall take his brother's wife it is an unclean thing".   (*Leviticus*
xx, 21.)

son, who became Edward VI, but she died a few days after the birth of her child. Then he considered marrying the Duchess of Milan or a French princess, but the negotiations fell through, to be followed by a request to the French king that Henry might personally inspect a few princesses at Calais, a petition which was refused. Next he turned his thoughts to Germany, and the prospect of an alliance with the Lutheran states by a marriage to Anne of Cleves, a placid gentle young woman. However, when he saw her on her arrival in England he vehemently protested at the way he had been misled, because, instead of the lady being clever and beautiful, as he had been told, she was quite the reverse.

Yet he married her for political reasons, but was so repelled by her looks, when he saw her in bed, that he declared he never consummated the marriage. As day after day passed he became increasingly antagonistic towards this stranger from a foreign land, to end in first of all a separation and then a divorce. She was given the rank of a princess, and received a pension of £4000 a year besides two manor houses, attending Henry's later marriages. When she died in Mary's reign, her body was buried in Westminster Abbey with much pomp and ceremony. Henry's next wife was Catherine Howard, who was executed for infidelity, and lastly he married for the sixth time the kindly sensible Catherine Parr, who outlived him.

Henry reigned like an Eastern despot, and crushed for ever the feudalism still prevailing in Yorkshire and the barbarous Border counties. Though the power of Parliament was dormant it was not dead, but not until the Stuarts claimed to rule by divine authority did its vitality return with some vigour. After the fall of Wolsey, Sir Thomas More, a man of firm principles, became Chancellor, only to be beheaded because he would not acknowledge his master to be the head of the Church of England, the inflexible, devout John Fisher, Bishop of Rochester, and others, suffering the same fate for the same reason. Then followed the unscrupulous, audacious, but clever Thomas Cromwell (1490–1540), the son of a blacksmith, who was made Vicar-General, and given complete control over the Church, then in possession of a third of all the land in England.[1]

Under his direction the monasteries were suppressed, a small part of their vast wealth being used to found theological schools, but most of it enriched the Crown and its leading supporters, to bind them more closely to the King in his stand against the Pope. Some of it was used to build the Navy, and fortify the coast, because it was expected that the Pope, sooner or later, would influence France or Spain to attack heretical England. Many heads fell during this time of social revolution, and Cromwell, who had sent hundreds to the block, suffered the fate of his predecessors, as he was executed for treason, corruption and heresy, his pitiful appeals to the King for mercy passing by unheeded.

The tyranny of Wolsey had focused in the minds of many Englishmen the corruption of the Church, and consequently Henry had considerable public support in his decision to abolish the monasteries. This

[1] The coalfields of England were then in the possession of the Church. Much of this source of wealth was taken from it by Henry VIII, but the remnant in our own times still yields the Church of England £400,000 a year, one seventh of all the coal royalties.

event, which was brought about by the need for money as well as reform, changed the social life of England. Henry, foolishly extravagant, his money spent in pageants and masques, his treasury empty from his war with France, had to sell much of the spiritual land he confiscated to obtain the cash, and so arose the squires who became known as the landed gentry and the gentlemen of the realm. Likewise also arose the yeomen (each being addressed as "Goodman", from the Saxon Gutmahnn, meaning a farmer), who from now onwards were such a feature of the country's life. Both squires and yeomen largely replaced the power of the ecclesiastics, now that the great nobles had been so reduced by the Wars of the Roses, but, unlike the French, the English gentry made no claim to nobility, and, with their sons in trade or the professions, there was no rigid upper or lower class, as in France, with no one between.

In this way the Sovereign obtained financial relief, but, besides this he defrauded his subjects by debasing the coinage, and this raised the cost of living, already rising from the increase in the supply of silver. Unfortunately neither education nor the poor benefited from the greatest exchange of wealth so far experienced in England. Most of the roads remained impassable in winter, and for long were to remain infested with highwaymen. Instead of the people as a whole benefiting, much of the released land passed into the hands of successful lawyers and merchants, who built, within the precincts of a deer park, attractive picturesque brick manor houses, now having chimneys for the first time because of the increase in the use of coal. These were the men who became the squires and gentry of England, being always addressed as "Master". Their descendants combined landowning with the professions and trades, while the younger sons devoted their energies to making money in the towns, with which they also purchased land.

Cromwell beggared the monasteries, and in the process became a millionaire, the Cecils, the Russells, the Cavendishes and others, mostly by cheap purchases from the Crown, likewise securing princely fortunes out of the spoil. Ten thousand displaced monks, friars and nuns were given adequate pensions, and, with this way of life closed, many, in the years to come, who might have been attracted by it, turned their attention to more useful occupations.

Never before nor since has there been such a quick change-over of so much wealth, because the Church had accumulated enormous possessions since the Conquest, when the Pope and William I divided Saxon England between the Church and the Norman barons. With its enormous affluence and influence the Church did little for the good of the people, who vividly realised this, and gave it no sympathy in its distress. The abbeys and monasteries had outlived their original use, having become centres of ignorance, iniquity, sodomy and tyranny. Their inmates thrived on the produce of their vast landed possessions, giving nothing to the country in exchange, neither educating the people, ministering to them, nor raising them socially or morally.

Each abbot interpreted the law of the land in the light of the belief that Christ had delivered to the Church the keys of heaven and hell. Priests and monks were above the law, only the Pope being their authority for everything temporal and divine. As each prince of the Church had his own army of hired retainers, paid to do his bidding, the bishops and abbots were complete masters over great areas. In their palatial homes they did as they pleased, from hanging a man for eating meat on a Friday to taking land and wealth from this one and that, as it suited them. Landowners, who refused to bow to the bishops' or abbots' commands, had generally to fight against superior forces or yield, failing which they were murdered if they did not make a safe escape. Others were kidnapped and secretly shipped off to Spain, where they were either tortured and killed, or forced to end their days in some foul dungeon. Women heiresses found themselves carried off and placed in convents, their property being seized by the neighbouring abbey, it being their heir, as they were now the brides of Christ and married to the Church.

In most cases such extreme measures were unnecessary because the fear of hell, in itself, was sufficient to produce the necessary liberality. On this fear the priests traded to such effect that the Church acquired colossal power and vast possessions by promising absolution and salvation to all benefactors. Never at any time before the Christian era was such profitable use made of ignorance by a great army of unscrupulous priests, intent only on the aggrandizement of their Church, in whose wealth they directly participated.

This form of robbery, having now gone on for twelve centuries, had raised the Church of the 16th century to the height of its power and to the zenith of its wealth and influence. Morally it had sunk so low that the monasteries and convents were hot-beds of wickedness, vice and immorality, so gross that in our day we find it difficult to believe the accounts which have come down to us of what went on within these institutions scattered everywhere throughout Europe.

Besides having been centres of wickedness since the 12th century, the abbeys, monasteries and convents of 16th-century England housed the papal garrison. To Rome only they gave their allegiance, each one being the source of propaganda helpful to the enemies of England. Henry's quarrel with the Pope focused all this evil-doing as never before, and, when the Act of Supremacy of 1534 made the King supreme head of the Church, the priests were given the choice of swearing loyalty to the Throne and abjuring the Pope, or losing their heads.

The wrath of Henry towards the Pope brought terror into the homes of the clergy and admiration from the people, for so long the victims of Church tyranny.[1] In this conflict with the Church, Henry carried all before him, his popularity increased, and few of the laity regretted England's severance from

[1] Prior to the dissolution of the monasteries, Henry VIII received a petition from which we give the following extracts: In the times of your noble predecessors, craftily crept into your realm strong, puissant, counterfeit, holy, idle beggars and vagabonds, the Bishops, Abbots, Priors, Deacons, Archdeacons, Priests, Monks and Friars. And who is able to number this idle, ruinous sort which, setting all labour aside, have begged so importunately that they have gotten into their hands more than the third of all your realm? Besides this they have the tenth part of all the corn, meadow, pasture, grass, wool, colts, calves, lambs, pigs, geese, eggs and chickens. . . . Who is she that will set her hands to work to get 3*d.* a day and may have at least 20*d.* a day to sleep an hour with a friar, monk or priest? Finally the petition declares that these holy rogues should be deprived of their wealth for the benefit of the realm and be allowed to marry so that other people's wives might not be seduced.

Rome. Consequently Henry stepped peacefully into the place of the Pope, and the Protestant Church of England slowly and haltingly emerged, those not submitting to the royal will being subject to the most dreadful penalties.

This English autocratic monarch had his own opinions as to the meaning of Christianity. He it was who drew up the first Church of England articles of belief in 1536. He it was who refused to join up with the Protestants of Europe, and he it was who decided that the King of England was the Pope of England. This royal theologian set down the shape of things to come in England's religious life, executing Lutherans and Roman Catholics at his pleasure, the Cambridge divine Thomas Cranmer, a sincere bigot, advising his royal master in like manner as did the unscrupulous Eusebius his master Constantine twelve centuries earlier, when this semi-Pagan emperor produced the Christian faith at Nicaea.

Towards the end of his reign Henry was again at war with France and Scotland, capturing Boulogne, which remained English until 1550, when the French bought it back. The most interesting and far-reaching naval event of this period was the foundation of the British navy, from now onwards called the Royal Navy because it was then supported by the Crown—the British army, on the other hand, not being royal, because, as today constituted, it was a parliamentary creation at the end of the 17th century in the reign of William III. Henry constructed Woolwich and Deptford dockyards, and built forty-six battleships. Here, in Elizabeth's reign, Sir John Hawkins produced a new type of warship, low in the water and with sides pierced by many guns, a creation which caused terrible havoc to the unwieldy castellated ships of the Spanish Armada.

Henry's break with the Pope was by far the most important episode in his despotic, cruel and unsavoury career, as it opened up the way for the reformed faith to reach the people. Otherwise this would not have happened when it did, and it all came about because a foreign army mutinied in Italy! Behind the constantly changing panorama of our earthly lives is there an unchanging purpose constantly at work, or are we all the creatures of a blind fate? Here we only see the threads of the pattern from underneath, and perhaps some day, somewhere, we shall better appreciate the design from a wider and more comprehensive angle than is possible on earth.

Nature is no respecter of persons, and tyrants, like their victims, must make the change called death. So the all-powerful Henry passed on when his time came, to be succeeded by Edward VI (1547–1553), the son Jane Seymour bore him, but, as this boy was only nine years old, his uncle, the Duke of Somerset, became Protector. The Duke favoured the Protestants, Mass was abolished, the wealthy Chantries, where prayers were sung for the dead, were plundered, the Roman Catholics fiercely persecuted, while images and pictures were removed from the churches, and Henry VIII's statute of the Six Articles repealed.

Cranmer, in 1552, produced in English a new Prayer Book, and twelve years later his Forty-Two Articles of Religion were reduced to thirty-nine in number, the Church of England, largely due to his influence, approaching towards the beliefs held by the

Protestants in Europe, though it claimed continuity with the past. Furthermore, he procured a decree that a copy of the Bible, in English, be set up in every Church in a place where it could be read by those who wished to do so. Finally his last important undertaking was the revision of Church Law, in which was laid down in the strongest terms the necessity of persecution to the death of all heretics who did not conform to the reformed religion. These changes aroused bitterness amongst the Roman Catholics, but the Calvinists would have liked the Reformation to have been more drastic.

Two serious insurrections followed, which were partly religious and in part political. These were suppressed by the unscrupulous Duke of Northumberland, who succeeded the more honourable Somerset as Protector. The Duke, who led the Protestant faction, persuaded Edward to leave the throne to Lady Jane Grey, a great-granddaughter of Henry VII, so as to ensure the Protestant succession, but his real aim was probably his own advancement, as he then arranged a marriage between her and his son Guildford Dudley. Cranmer likewise became involved in this tragic episode. Anticipating a continuity of Protestant rule, he broke his promise to Henry VIII to support Mary's claim to the throne, and instead gave his allegiance to the "twelve-day queen", a miscalculation which brought about his downfall and death.

When Edward died in 1553, at the age of fifteen, many welcomed Mary (1553–1558), the daughter of Henry VIII and Catherine of Aragon, as their queen, but the reformers were dismayed, foreseeing the undoing of all their work. Her integrity is unquestioned, as whatever she did was inspired by what she judged was honourable and just, but, suffering like all her contemporaries of those days from the curse of ignorance, she was fanatically devout. Her zeal for the old religion was boundless, and she honestly believed that heresy was the most damnable sin against God and his Church on earth.

Consequently the Bible, from which the priests preached but the laity was not now allowed to read, and also the Prayer Book, were suppressed, and England made peace with Rome. The Protestant bishops lost their sees, Cranmer, the intellectual force behind the Reformation, was deposed, and Northumberland, Lady Jane Grey and her husband were executed for acting contrary to Henry's will. With them also died the leaders of the insurrection, which was directed against Mary marrying Philip of Spain.

We might well ask, why did Philip wish to marry the unattractive Mary? He certainly did not love her, and the answer is to be found by studying the map. Philip wished to protect Spanish ships sailing through the English Channel, so that they might go and come in safety from the ports of the Netherlands. There the prosperous cities supplied the wealth from which Spain drew much revenue in taxation. With England a friend the Channel bottleneck was safe, but if England were hostile she could cork the bottle and the overseas trade of the Netherlands would wither away. So Philip wanted England's friendship, and, after Mary had passed away, he would have married Elizabeth, heretic though she was. Only when Elizabethan England proved itself definitely hostile did he give up the attempt to keep on friendly terms with the land that held the key to his rich domains at the mouth of the Scheldt.

With Mary now on the throne the Pope quickly made his influence felt, and all the earlier anti-Roman Catholic legislation was annulled. His Holiness was again recognised as the head of the Church in England, and Henry's statutes, making the sovereign the head of the Church, were scrapped, the laws against the Protestants being revived. Everywhere they were persecuted, and, on the decision of the Ecclesiastical Court, under the direction of Stephen Gardiner, Bishop of Winchester and Lord Chancellor of England, three hundred perished at the stake, including Ridley, Latimer and Cranmer, three of the outstanding Protestant leaders, the latter receiving the punishment he had prescribed for others.

Other less prominent people also shared the same fate, one being the heroic Alice Benden, a poor woman who lived near Canterbury. She and her small son were imprisoned in the Archbishop's dungeon, and almost starved for nine weeks, during which time she was periodically interrogated and tortured because she refused to attend her local church, as she disliked the pre-Reformation liturgy. In June 1557 she was burned to death at the stake, while the priests and people around her sang the Te Deum and chanted prayers and the Creed.[1] Amongst the great army of martyrs this brave woman, though little known, holds a high place because of the courage

[1] The *Directorium Inquisitorum*, the Church handbook on the torture of heretics, states: "It is good that the people should assemble to witness the torture and punishment of the wicked. Heaven will afford the faithful a fuller and more prolonged vision, but even here below we can see justice done."

and fortitude she displayed to maintain her liberty to think as she considered right.

Mary's savagery, which gave her the title of "Bloody Mary", strengthened the resistance of the Protestants, and even antagonised some of her friends, so much so that her policy to make England again a Roman Catholic country failed. Under her father Henry both the orthodox and unorthodox were persecuted, under her step-brother Edward the Protestants lashed out at their former tormentors, and under her they, in turn, were made to bite the dust, but fortunately England was spared a civil war, and she did not have to go through the agonies suffered in Europe in consequence of the Reformation.

Mary's marriage to Philip of Spain increased her unpopularity, because it dragged England into the Spanish war against France, an event which ended in England losing Calais. The English, moreover, greatly resented their country being largely a vassal state of Spain, and the loss of Calais, the gateway for the wool trade into Europe, was considered to be a national humiliation. Taken all in all, Mary's home and foreign policy failed completely. Her marriage was never popular, and did not bring her happiness, her husband, who became His Most Catholic Majesty Philip II of Spain, being a cold, austere, devout man who neither loved her nor liked her country. Fortunately she had no children, as, if she had been so blessed, it is doubtful if the Reformation would have made any headway in England. She was never beloved by the people, and, after a reign of five years, her death was not greatly regretted.

Mary deeply resented the treatment of her mother

Catherine by her father, and naturally hated Anne
Boleyn. She for ever brooded on the fact that her
father's attitude towards his marriage with Catherine
made her no better than an illegitimate child. This
embittered her, and she carried her resentment to her
death. When this came about her people were so
disgusted at the persecutions and burnings of heretics
that they hailed with delight the more human and
less rigid Elizabeth (1558–1603), her step-sister, the
daughter of Henry VIII and Anne Boleyn, who
succeeded her at the age of twenty-five.

Elizabeth's mother was a Protestant, which
explains why she adopted the same faith. Few are
individualistic enough to sit down calmly and dispassionately and reason out their religious beliefs,
because these depend on where and when one is born,
and what is taught in childhood. So Elizabeth was a
Protestant for the same reason as her predecessor was a
Roman Catholic. The Roman Catholic Church had
decreed Elizabeth to be illegitimate and Mary Stuart
of Scotland the legitimate and lawful queen, but
if Elizabeth had become a Roman Catholic that would
have been forgotten. Now the Protestants persecuted
the Roman Catholics just as bitterly as the Roman
Catholics ever persecuted the Protestants. Ireland
was the happy hunting-ground for the Protestant
bigots, who treated the inhabitants of this misruled
land much as Philip II of Spain was treating the
people of the Netherlands at the same time.

Christian civilisation could not change, and the
people had to develop out of it. Christian doctrines
could not change, and only by disbelieving them
could the idea of hell for unbelievers vanish, and be

treated with the ridicule it deserves. Three centuries were to pass, however, before that happy time came, and meanwhile supernatural religion reigned supreme. Looking back from the vantage point the human mind has secured in our day, in consequence of the cultivation of knowledge through experience, observation and research, what do we make of this 16th-century world floundering in theological superstition?

Surely the futility of all the religious discord then prevailing must strike everyone who thinks, all the more so if we remember the facts and are not misled by theological fancies. These facts are (1) that men and women like ourselves inhabit the other world, (2) that they once lived on earth and went there naked when they died, (3) that clothes are provided for the new arrivals, and that they live in the other world quite naturally, much as they did on earth, their etheric bodies appearing to everyone there as real and solid, and (4) that their new abode appears to them not only as solid and real as their bodies but it rotates along with this earth. Further, (5) that on arrival there they are no better and no worse than they were on earth, as death does not change the orthodox wicked into glorified perfect saints and angels, or the unorthodox good into wicked devils. Finally (6) that their world surrounds and inter-penetrates this earth, and the journey there is the shortest on earth, because it comes about by our discarding our physical body and functioning in our etheric body, which responds to the etheric world vibrations that are all around us.

If these vital facts had been known to our ancestors, and they had known that there was nothing to fear, because they likewise would have this experience when they died, what a transformation it would have made in their religious outlook and their deeds! Moreover, what a difference it would make to countless millions today who still live in theological darkness which creates fear of the unknown!

All down the ages the men and women of the other world have been looked upon as good or evil supernatural beings, while in Christian times those who had been orthodox were called saints and angels, they having been transformed by the saving grace of faith into vaporous glorified beings, no matter how wicked they had been on earth. On the other hand, the unorthodox, no matter how good their lives had been here, were changed into wicked devils for lack of the saving power of belief in a saviour.

Presiding over the orthodox Christians, theological imagination created three principal gods and a goddess, surrounded by archangels who were for ever praising their power and glory, the realm in which they lived being a nebulous supernatural and unnatural world called heaven. Thereto went all believers in the Nicene Creed, all unbelievers being destined for the fiery abode of the chief devil, called Satan, whose army of devils was for ever trying to influence poor humanity to disbelieve in this creed which was the only passport into heaven.[1]

---

[1] It is interesting to note that this belief was held by many, although the orthodox opinion has always asserted that the dead go to hades, or purgatory, to await the last judgment, when believers and unbelievers would rise from their graves in their earth bodies to be judged and then dispatched to either hell or heaven. The Jewish and Egyptian belief in the last judgment and the resurrection has been intermixed with Greek ideas of immediate entry into heaven or hell, to such an extent that Christian eschatology is impossible to understand. It lacks all sense, logic and reason.

How was it possible for peace and harmony to reign on earth when this fantastic conception of God and the after life prevailed? What is natural was made unnatural, and what is a natural transition from one order of life to another was transformed by theologians into a ridiculous conception whereby men and women are changed into gaseous supernatural saints, angels or devils. Human destiny was determined solely by the belief or disbelief in 126 words produced by a council of ignorant priests at Nicaea, presided over by the cruel autocrat Constantine, who shortly before had murdered Licinius, his brother-in-law, a war captive, whose life he had promised to spare.

Constantine's evil deeds, his murders and cruelties, so horrified his subjects, that he had to leave Rome, never to return. What did such a scoundrel care about what is right or wrong, true or untrue? All that interested him was to put together something which all his subjects would believe, and so unify his empire. To this end he promised the Christian priests full ecclesiastical power if they would only produce a formula the majority of the clergy would accept.

On the acceptance of this creed it was believed by Christians, from his time onwards, that their salvation depended. Surely there is nothing in history to equal this absurd extravagance, which only deserves the derision of every sane person, and yet the fact remains that our ancestors believed, and many even today sincerely and devoutly believe this fiction and in the honesty and sanctity of the Church which proclaims it. When all that pertains to the other world was in the keeping of theologians and priests, to whom facts and reason mean nothing, this gigantic illusion was kept going to their great profit in power and wealth. Fortunately today a change of outlook amongst many is becoming obvious, as, by means of the psychic gifts of those sensitive people called mediums, whom the priests have always destroyed, we have now substantial facts to refute all their supernatural nonsense.

Always in the past the views of the materialist, with his negative opinions to the effect that death ends all, were brushed aside by the priests, who well knew that nearly everyone instinctively believes in an after life and fears what follows death. Against this shadowy belief, and innate fear of the unknown, the materialist can make little headway, and consequently he did little harm to supernatural religion, which is accepted by the vast majority who believe but never reason.

Now, however, students of psychic science in their thousands come forward with actual proof of their claim that those regarded in the past as supernatural gods, angels and devils are just men and women like ourselves, who live in a natural rational world, well ordered and justly governed, and have found their place and happiness there quite irrespective of their religious beliefs on earth. Thus has been burst the full-blown supernatural bubble, one of the greatest delusions in all history, and the well informed in a wondering world behold the exposure of as great an illusion as was revealed by Copernicus, when he made clear that the earth was neither the centre of the universe nor was it encircled daily by the sun.

From this new angle the orthodox religious opinions of the past and present must be regarded.

From this new aspect history must be viewed, the follies and cruelty pertaining to supernatural religion being explained as the result of ignorance of history, of biology, of our bodily construction, and of the structure of the universe, a vast network of vibrations weaving both the physical and etheric worlds together into an abode of active life and thought. Moreover, we now know that reality can exist apart from our limited physical senses, and that two things at different frequencies of vibration can occupy the same space.

With this vast panorama now before us, how narrow and limited were the beliefs of the past, how little our ancestors knew about themselves or their surroundings, the result being that like children their imagination ran wild, and the other world and its inhabitants were transformed into unreal supernatural creations existing in misty realms of childish imagination. Consequently cruelty, folly and misery followed from this simple ignorance, and at no time in history was this more apparent than during the period we are now considering.

In Elizabeth's time triumphant ignorance, under the name of the Episcopalian Church of England, commonly called the Anglican Church, was murdering, persecuting and banishing all who could not believe the doctrines contained in the Thirty-Nine Articles of Religion produced by the Protestant priests under the direction of Cranmer. The Protestants, who devoutly conducted family worship morning and evening, were naturally delighted to have Elizabeth as their queen, and, now that they had the power of the throne behind them, they proceeded to treat the Roman Catholics in just the same way as they had been treated by them when the latter had the power.

Everyone was forced, under a penalty of a fine or imprisonment for absence, to attend the local church services. The bitterness of the Roman Catholics against Elizabeth consequently became intense, especially as they considered her a bastard because her father had married her mother without first obtaining from the Pope a divorce from Catherine of Aragon, a matter which in those days was considered a terrible sin.

Mary, Queen of Scotland, in their opinion, was the rightful queen, as she was the great-granddaughter of Henry VII through his daughter Margaret, the wife of James IV of Scotland, who was her grandfather. Mary took the same view, and was continually plotting with the Roman Catholics to secure the English throne, while Elizabeth likewise intrigued with the Protestants in Scotland against Mary. The curse of religious controversy and intolerance, due to ignorance, clouded much of Elizabeth's reign, and, when it is all dispassionately examined, the principal doctrinal difference becomes focused in the way the elements at the Sacrament were vitalised. The Lutheran explanation, and the orthodox Catholic opinion, were not far apart, as has already been explained, and Cranmer was influenced by the German Lutheran clergy who visited England for the purpose of arranging for the two countries to adopt the same confession of faith.

What was much more important to the authorities of those days was the question as to whether the

Pope or the Monarch was the head of the Church, and, as only two hundred of the eight thousand English clergy chose the Pope, the change-over to Protestantism was simply and quietly effected. Consequently Christianity became a political issue in England and Protestant Europe, and those who looked on the Pope as the head of the Church were there considered more in the light of traitors than heretics.

In point of fact neither the Pope nor the King is head of the Church, if we go back to the constitution of the Apostolic Church, which was an assembly of believers in Jesus having appeared on earth after his violent and untimely death, the Church then being an organisation to unite them until his anticipated early and more permanent return. When this did not materialise the Eucharist was introduced, with all its Pagan associations, to cause endless bloodshed and unhappiness. Now, as we have read, many in disgust have separated from the corrupt retrograde Church, an event which was to usher in an era of slaughter throughout the following two hundred years. This dreadful period of suffering and misery will be better understood if we go back and trace the evolution of religion from primitive times, the lack of this knowledge, and the ignorance of man's destiny after death, having been the cause of all this terrible agony and anguish.

(4) THE EFFECT OF THE APOSTOLIC CHURCH ON THE REFORMATION.

First of all let us gather together again the basic strands which produced religion. We remember how research has discovered that every saviour-god religion can be traced back to a common origin, namely the seeing of the apparition of a sacrificed victim. If we go back farther we find that religion, all the world over, consisted of Ancestor Worship, which likewise was caused by clairvoyants seeing in their etheric bodies the men and women who had died. He who was a chief on earth became a god in heaven, until the other world became a place peopled with gods and devils according to the way they had lived on earth and behaved when they came back, the devils being those who were responsible for what we today call poltergeist haunting

These etheric beings were believed to govern the earth, bring plenty and famine, happiness and misery, good and bad health; in fact they became so much intertwined with the life of the people on earth that the medium of the tribe was set aside as a sacred instrument through whom the chief communicated with the gods. Then arose a class of men who were responsible for the care of these gifted individuals, to become known as priests, their calling being priest-craft, and their organisation a priesthood. From their psychic experiences they laid the foundation for theology, or the knowledge of the gods, but the time came when they became so debased and powerful that the medium was pushed into the background and theology took the place of the "conversations with the gods", as it was called.

An extensive and comprehensive mythology developed, consisting of stories of the doings of these other-world men and women, and this gave religious comfort to the many who imagined the hereafter as a glorified earth, and its inhabitants as either embellished or defiled beings to whom was given the comprehensive names of gods and devils. The priests became responsible for the good humour of the gods, who had to be fed on etheric food, consisting of the etheric bodies of humans and animals, and what was termed the essence of vegetation, or otherwise dire calamities would come to the people on. earth. Out of sacrifice developed the saviour-god, a sacrificial victim of the priests, who was deified because he was seen after death. Consequently it was thought that the curse of death had been broken because of his sacrifice, and he was given both gratitude and worship.

During the two thousand years preceding the beginning of the Christian era, similar conditions brought into being sixteen different saviour-god religions in various parts of the world, and, as their origin was the same, the beliefs which came to surround each saviour corresponded to those which were draped round Jesus when he became the Christ. In each case a priesthood took charge of the religion, elaborated its beliefs, and formed a Church consisting of believers who partook of the Sacrament for two reasons: (1) in memory of the saviour's death, and (2) in order to fortify themselves by eating the bread and drinking the wine the priests miraculously turned into his body and blood.

First of all the sacrificed victim was seen after death. Next a small cult developed within the prevailing religion, to separate from it and have its own churches and priesthood, the same sequence of causes and effects following when Jesus, a victim of the priests, was seen after his death, to produce a small Jesuian cult within the Jewish Church. We remember how Paul of Tarsus later grafted Jesuism on to the prevailing saviour-god beliefs, to produce a new religion, Jesus- eventually being evolved into just another Pagan Christ.

Monotheistic Judaism was thus united with polytheistic Paganism, to end in the former being almost ignored and the latter reigning supreme. This new theology became known as Christianity, and its basic beliefs, namely those surrounding its five main doctrines which it took from Paganism, have remained unchanged since the 4th century when they were fixed at the Council of Nicaea.

At the time of the Reformation many wished to go back to Apostolic simplicity in religion, but no one ever suggested the adoption of the Jesuian beliefs and the discarding of what we now know to be Paganism, the reason being that the roots of Christianity go down far too deep into the superstitions of the past for them to be lightly discarded. Tradition, like a rod of iron, holds together the ancient Pagan theology, the consequence being that in the 16th century no change was made in the beliefs surrounding baptism, confirmation, marriage, the holy communion, death and burial, salvation and damnation, heaven and hell.

If the beliefs surrounding these had been new, and fixed for the first time at Nicaea, or elsewhere, they would never have held together unbroken all these years, and it is because Christianity is no new revelation but a very old form of belief, presented under new names, that it has survived intact to this day. Christianity, as has been made clear in earlier chapters,

is Paganism consolidated under a new name, and the
functions allotted to all the different Pagan gods
became amalgamated within the framework of the
Christian heavenly hierarchy. These new names
in large measure were forced on what became Christendom, after the Christian Church obtained autocratic
power because of the fall of the Roman Empire.

It was in no way new for the Pagans, when they
became Christians, to offer up a prayer of thanks
before and after meals, to make prayers and supplications to the Father God, to baptise their infant
children, to be initiated into the Church, to be married
by a priest, to have only one wife, to sit down and
partake of a eucharist to a saviour, to be frightened
by the torment of hell, comforted by anticipating an
endless life of bliss in heaven, and to be told by the
priest at the graveside that the body would rise
again on the resurrection day. All these ceremonies
and beliefs, besides much else which is now called
Christianity, were accepted long before the Christian
era, and the converts to Christianity had only to
rename their gods to become Christians, a change
of names which had happened in the past, the
statues of their deities more than once before having
had the old names chiselled out and new ones put in
their place.

So the Pagans, who worshipped the different
saviour-gods, Mithra in Persia, Dionysus in Greece,
Osiris in Egypt, Bel in Mesopotamia, Odin (Woden)
and Thor in Germany and Scandinavia, found nothing
particularly new in Christianity when they were
converted by persuasion or force. India was not
within the Christian sphere of influence, so Krishna

still reigns as the saviour-god of the Hindus, but
Europe fell before the power and prestige of the
Christian Church, the successor of the old Roman
Empire.

When the Bible first came to be read, the composite
nature of Christianity became apparent, but, as it was
looked upon as a new revelation, its confliction with
Judaism was passed over, its Paganism not being
realised, as no one then knew what the Pagans believed.
Everyone who was not a Jew or a Christian was
considered a heathen, this being Paul's opinion, and,
as the heathen were looked upon as savages, who
worshipped gods of wood and stone, all their dead
were now believed to be suffering for their wickedness
in hell.

Little was then known about history, apart from
what the Bible told about the Hebrews and surrounding
nations, because most Roman and Greek history books
had been destroyed by the Church as heathen produc-
tions.   Nevertheless the Bible did reveal to those intelligent enough to notice it, that the Apostolic Church
was a much more simple and a much less ornate and
elaborate affair than the Church which grew out of it,
the priests having been abolished with the coming of
Jesus.   Consequently there was no place for pope,
cardinals, archbishops, bishops, or any kind of
priest, "Christ being come an High Priest" (*Hebrews*
ix, 11) he being "the one Mediator between God and
men". (1 *Timothy* ii, 5.)   The difference between the
simple duties, and the unpretentious lives, of the
ministers of the Apostolic Church, and the lives of, and
claims made by, the priests of the Christian Church,
therefore became apparent to everyone who read the

New Testament, but within the orthodox ranks the
Bible remained a closed book to all but the priests.

This radical difference between the Apostolic
Church and the Christian Church, which evolved out
of it, must be remembered, or otherwise all the
controversies about which we have read, and are
still to read, are hard to understand. The Apostolic
Church was founded on an apparition of Jesus, whereas
the Christian Church was established on the prevailing
Pagan doctrines. These doctrines, which incorporated the mystical beliefs of the Greek Mystery
religion, were gradually added to the gospel records
that were produced, in the first place, to tell the early
Jesuians something about their Lord, the original
documents telling the story of a man who went about
healing and speaking in parables, nothing supernatural
being mentioned.

As time passed and Jesus did not return to earth
as expected, the Pagan records of what happened to
their saviours after death took the place of the early
belief in his reappearance as an etheric being. The
original story, of which only fragments remain, was
consequently changed into one recording his physical
resurrection, so as not to be behind the Pagans, whose
religious beliefs comprised the story of their risen
saviour and his empty tomb.[1]

The original traditional story about Jesus, who was
probably a healing medium, in whose presence psychic
phenomena also occurred, was later amplified by
quotations from the Hebrew scriptures, and, in order
to heighten his glory, some of the wonderful deeds

---

[1] The reason why and how this happened is clearly and fully explained
in *The Psychic Stream.*

attributed to the Pagan saviour-gods were likewise ascribed to him, until finally, in the 4th century, the story we now have was fixed at the Council of Carthage in 397. This council was called after Jerome had translated, revised and altered the Gospels and Epistles to make them conform to the Christianity as believed in his day, an event which has already been recorded in Chapter VIII.

Everything developed without systematic thought—contradictions, absurdities and mystical speculations being all thrown together to become Christianity—and now, in the 16th century, the people, after freeing themselves from the authority of the Pope, which hitherto had been final, groped about in a theological maze to find a basis for the beliefs they had been taught as orthodox Christians. Differences of opinion were inevitable, and, as there was no toleration, whoever accepted opinions held by a minority was persecuted.

According to the *Acts of the Apostles*, which Christians consider· is an inspired document, the early Jesuians were convinced that they were in communication with heaven through the Holy Spirit (also called the Holy Ghost), whom they called the Divine Spirit, a name which referred to the other-world man who spoke through the medium when in trance. They held séances, when those who were mediumistic were used by those believed to be the inhabitants of the other world.

Moreover, they expected Jesus to return to them, and that the end of the world would come within their lifetime. Besides this they anticipated that all would be given psychic gifts similar to those possessed by Jesus, basing this opinion on his reported saying, "The works that I do shall he do also, and greater works than these shall he do." (*John* xiv, 12.) Besides this, a very important fact must not be overlooked, namely that they regarded Jesus as no more than "a man approved of God by miracles and wonders and signs which God did by him in the midst of you". (*Acts* ii, 22.)

When this was written "a man approved of God" was one we today call a medium, and the miracles, wonders and signs were what we now call psychic phenomena. This can be discovered by getting back to the original meaning of the words, the same words being also used in connection with other men and women of these times who were mediums and in whose presence psychic phenomena occurred.[1] The early Jesuians, believing as they did that ministers and not priests were the men ordained to conduct their services, looked only to Jesus in heaven to guide them through the Divine Spirit, who used the medium in trance to give the address during their church services. This is all made abundantly clear from the Jesuian literature of these times, about which Christians are quite ignorant, because it has not been in the interests of the clergy to inform them.

Out of this simple beginning all the priestly theological dogmas, doctrines, ceremonies, rites and beliefs developed, to end in what became known as the Christian faith in the 4th century of our era. Now, in the 16th century, we have arrived at the time when the power of the Chief Priest, who had no place whatever in the original Apostolic Church, was being

[1] In *The Psychic Stream* this subject is fully examined and made clear.

questioned, and, as the centuries pass on to the present day, we shall discover that the place the priests usurped for themselves in the 3rd and 4th centuries became ever more and more questioned and disputed.

In our own time intelligent people realise that orthodox Christianity is a travesty, a caricature, of the original belief, that the clergy never had a place in its constitution, and that the medium was originally the instrument through whom communications came from the other world. As, however, the priests had abolished and liquidated all the mediums when they obtained the power, the hereditary psychic gifts, which had so vitalised the early Jesuian communities, were now lacking in the 16th century, and no layman then knew anything about the original form of worship.

Some had only made the discovery that every Pope from the first had made claims for himself for which he had no scriptural authority. So these reformers put monarchs in place of the Pope, but they still retained a Protestant priesthood, who now set to work to translate from Latin into English the dogmas and doctrines produced by Augustine, Jerome and others, and express their opinions about each. Thus it came about that in England a committee of Protestant priests (Archbishop Parker and three bishops) solemnly sat down, under the control of the Holy Ghost, so they claimed, and put the Christian religion, as they understood it, into English in order that all could hear, if they could not understand, what Elizabeth decreed every one was now to believe, all unbelievers being considered as heretics.

Here, then, is a summary of what these priests

produced, the foundation stone of Episcopalian Christianity, to be duly approved by Parliament, ratified by Elizabeth in 1571 and become known as the Thirty-Nine Articles of Religion, three of the articles introduced by Cranmer being discarded.

(1) God consists of three persons, the Father, the Son and the Holy Ghost, who are all one God.

(2) Christ was divine, and he suffered as a sacrifice for the sins of humanity.

(3) Christ died for humanity, was buried and went down into hell.

(4) Christ rose from the grave and took again his body, with flesh and bones, with which he ascended to heaven, where he sits till he returns on the day of Judgment.

(5) The Holy Ghost is of the same substance, majesty and glory as the Father and Son.

(6) The Holy Scripture containeth all things necessary to salvation; everything outside of the scriptures is unnecessary for salvation.

(7) Jesus is the only mediator between God and Man. No Christian is free from the obedience of the Commandments.

(8) The Nicene Creed, the Athanasian Creed and the Apostles' Creed ought to be thoroughly believed.

(9) All deserve God's wrath and damnation, but there is no condemnation for believers who are baptised.

(10) Man has no power to do good works without the grace of God.

(11) Our righteousness before God comes, not by our works, but by the merit of Christ. Therefore we are justified only by faith and not by works.

(12) Good works cannot put away sin, yet they are pleasing to God.

(13) Works not springing from faith are not pleasant to God, yea rather they have the nature of sin.

(14) Doing more than duty requires cannot be taught without arrogancy and impiety.

(15) Jesus was sinless, the Lamb without spot who sacrificed himself and took away the sins of the world.

(16) Repentance is not denied to such as fall into sin after baptism.

(17) Predestination to Life is the everlasting purpose of God, to deliver from curse and damnation those whom he has chosen in Christ, to bring them to everlasting salvation.

(18) They are accursed who believe that every man shall be saved by the Law or who frame their lives according to the light of nature.

(19) The Church of Christ is a congregation of faithful men in which the Pure Word of God is preached and the Sacraments duly administered.

(20) Rites and ceremonies are lawful if approved by the Church, provided they are not contrary to God's word.

(21) Princes only may convene General Councils, but their ordinances relating to salvation have authority only if in accordance with the Holy Scripture.

(22) Purgatory, Pardons, Worshipping and adoration of Images and Relics, and Invocation of Saints are un-scriptural.

(23) It is unlawful for those not lawfully called, to preach or minister the sacraments.

(24) All public worship must be conducted in a language the people understand.

(25) Partaking of the Sacraments of Baptism and Supper of the Lord denotes a Christian and is the means of grace.

(26) The effect of Christ's ordinance is not withdrawn because of the officiating priest's wickedness.

(27) Baptism denotes difference between Christians and non-Christians and is a sign of Regeneration, as those baptised are grafted into the Church and have the promise of the forgiveness of their sins.

(28) To such as rightly, worthily and with faith receive the same, the bread is a partaking of the Body of Christ and the wine a partaking of his Blood. Transubstantiation is unscriptural. The Body of Christ is eaten in a heavenly and spiritual manner.

(29) The wicked, and such as be devoid of a lively faith, though they press the bread with their teeth, are not partakers of Christ.

(30) The cup is not to be denied to the laity.

(31) There is no other satisfaction for sin apart from the offering of Christ.

(32) It is lawful for priests to marry.

(33) All unbelievers ought to be considered by the faithful as heathen and publican.

(34) Traditions, Ceremonies and Rites may differ and be changed or abolished by those in authority.

(35) A list of Homilies is here given containing godly and wholesome doctrine.

(36) Concerns the Consecration of Bishops and Priests.

(37) The Bishop of Rome hath no jurisdiction in England. Laws of the Realm may punish Christians with death for grievous offences, and it is lawful for Christians to wear weapons and serve in wars.

(38) The Riches and Goods of Christians are not common property, but every man ought to give liberally to the poor.

(39) A Christian may swear when the magistrate requires it.

Needless to say there is not an iota of evidence for a single one of the foregoing statements, in so far as they relate to dogma and doctrine, though every Church of England priest from that day to this has sworn before God that he believes every one of these assertions. In the main they are derived from the ancient Greek Mystery Religion, of which the Greek Orthodox Church is the present-day representative. The present-day Greek churches, and their form of worship, resemble more closely than any other this pre-Christian form of mystical belief which, in the 2nd and 3rd centuries, transformed the simple Jesuian faith into a mass of theological dogma and doctrine, to become known as Christianity. This produced a civilisation composed of ignorant (Article 6), arrogant, cruel and bigoted men and women (Articles 18, 27, 33), who were just as hateful as the Nazis and Fascists of our day, and it is because no sensible person today takes these articles of religion seriously that we have become tolerant and reached the social level now prevailing.

The early Jesuians had no records of what Jesus had said or done, but tradition had passed on the impression that he wanted to reform the Jewish religion, and establish love, kindness and regeneration in place of priestly dogmas, ritual and sacrifice. So they attributed to him ethical sayings, culled from the Hebrew Scriptures, and the moralisings of the sages of the past. They, moreover, formed themselves into communistic societies, all sharing alike, so that there would be no poor or needy, and, though this was found to be impracticable, the aim they had of service to others is clear. This state of affairs did not last long, ethics became overshadowed with dogma, and, as the centuries passed, dogma became supreme and ethical standards unimportant, so much so that when the religion became standardised at Nicaea in 325, ethics were never even considered. Dogma thus replaced ethics, salvation becoming dependent on the belief in a creed, and the acceptance of the formulas produced by the priests.

No one can produce one historical fact, or natural law, to support a single one of the dogmatic opinions set out in the Thirty-Nine Articles of the Church of England and the Confession of Faith of the Church of Scotland, which makes similar assertions. They are simply and solely theological speculations which, originating in psychic phenomena, had developed in priestly minds down the ages. The priests of Elizabeth's days, in their ignorance, believed that they had apostolic authority for each of these thirty-nine beliefs, but now we know that this authority was based on the mutilated translations made by Jerome, who made himself responsible for bringing the earlier Jesuian documents into line with the paganised Christianity of his time.

Now we understand why Christianity is a religion of speculative dogma without a basis of truth, and that this made for evil and not for righteousness. So it is not surprising that the Christian era has been a period of crime, immorality, cruelty, intolerance and injustice, such as never before has cursed this earth. Ethics, righteousness, justice, truth, mercy, loving-kindness and education did not interest priests who were intent on securing the belief of their doctrines, so that they could obtain and retain the power, wealth and position of their priestly offices.

The original ethical utterances attributed to Jésus were smothered by their dogmas and doctrines, and the ignorant rabble was soothed in its wickedness by being told that if they believed that their sins had been cleansed by a saviour, all would be well for them hereafter. This was accompanied by confessions, prayers, ceremonies and ritual, which gave the priests employment, a lucrative salary, a position above the laity and power beyond imagination. The Reformation in Protestant countries only removed the authority of the Pope but not that of the clergy, who, under the new name of Protestant, continued the old beliefs and ceremonies, to the accompaniment of torture, imprisonment, death and banishment of all who did not accept what they now produced as the true Christian faith.

Each individual life is too short for it to pass judgment on the slow evolutionary process always at work, but, looking back, we can see the changes great events produce, and the Reformation was undoubtedly the prelude to freedom of religious thought, though it took three centuries to mature. In Scotland it was more thorough than in England, as, besides bringing Church government more into line with the Apostolic Church, John Knox (1505-1572), the Calvinist leader, and one of the most outstanding figures in Scottish history, started schools which educated the children of some of the poor while similar English children remained illiterate up to 1870, education only then becoming general throughout the United Kingdom.

Knox, by his vigorous preaching, made the Reformation in Scotland a movement of the people against Roman Catholicism, whereas in England the force came from the throne. He also introduced Calvinism, whereas the English sovereign, and her priestly advisers, manufactured the Anglo-Catholic type of Christianity, as represented by the doctrines of the reformed Church of England, which was managed by bishops, hence the name Episcopalian from the Greek episkopos, meaning an overseer. So Scotland became Presbyterian, with its individual churches managed by presbyters, a word which comes from the Greek presbuteros, meaning an elder, but to understand things better we must go back to the early Apostolic

Church and refresh our minds with what is reported to have happened then.

In these early Apostolic churches, up to the 3rd century, there were no priests, and they had no place in the framework of the new religion. Consequently the Presbyterians changed the name priest to minister. The first to be called a minister of the Church was Matthias (*Acts* i, 26), who was chosen by the community in which he lived, but there is no mention that he passed on this commission, or that he laid his hands upon his successor, and thus commenced the chain of hand-laying which Roman Catholic and Episcopalian priests falsely claim has proceeded in an unbroken line from Peter to this day.

By the end of the 2nd century the organisation of the various Jesuian congregations was for all practical purposes identical, because they adopted as their pattern of Church organisation that of the Roman and Greek civic senates. At the head of each church was an overseer whose function was to conduct public worship, control the church funds, and keep a watch over the manners of his flock. In conducting the worship, and in ministering to the wants of the poor, he was assisted by the deacons. The presbyters were a small body whose business it was to advise the overseer, who acted as chairman at their business meetings, and was himself a presbyter. Otherwise he had no special standing or privilege. The presbyters were chosen from among the deacons, and the overseer, or minister, was chosen from the presbyters, but all these men continued in their ordinary occupations during the week, and gave their services on Sunday or when required.

At the Sunday services the responsiblity of the minister was to lead the congregation in prayer and praise. The duty of "edifying", as it was called, was left to the one with charismata, as the Greeks termed it, which means psychic gifts (1 *Corinthians* xii, 1–10), or, as we would say today, to the one who, by clairvoyance, clauraudience, or through trance, made contact with the men and women in the etheric world. The present-day service at a Spiritualist church, which is quite devoid of creeds and dogmas, approaches more to the one held in an Apostolic church than does any other church service.

The Spiritualists are guided by what they term Seven Principles: (1) belief in an overruling power to which is given the name of God, (2) that death is the separation of the duplicate etheric body from the physical body, and that our mind, which guides us on earth, controls the etheric body after death, each of us then being the same individual as we are now, (3) that communication, under suitable conditions, is possible between this and the next order of existence, (4) that we must do to others what we wish them to do to us, (5) that each individual is his own saviour, and (6) he must reap what he sows, this being a law of nature, every cause being followed by an effect. Finally (7) that the path of progress is never closed, and there is no known end to the advancement of the individual.

The British Broadcasting Corporation will not, however, allow a Spiritualist service to be broadcast, because, as their announcement on the subject reads, it "is not within the mainstream of Christian tradition". True, a Spiritualist service is not within the mainstream of Christian tradition, as,

when the Christian Church replaced the Apostolic
Church, theology and dogma took the place of the
medium. Nevertheless it is true that such a service
corresponds more closely to what the original Jesuians
adopted, and whatever scriptural authority the priests
have for anything different was added by their predecessors of the 3rd century when they changed
Jesuism into Christianity.

The B.B.C. Religious Advisory Committee is
controlled by Christian priests, whose forerunners
turned out the mediums and took over the Church
for their own profit and aggrandizement. As the priesthood can last just so long as it can keep the people
ignorant of the truth, the public must, as long as
possible, be kept from realising what took place in the
first three Christian centuries, and that the natural and
only way to make contact with the other world is
through mediumship, the method adopted by the
early followers of Jesus.

The founder of the Christian priesthood, as we
have already read, was Cyprian. He did as much as
anyone to raise the ministers into the position of
priests, and establish the Christian priesthood in the
position it now occupies. Cyprian saw that the one
with psychic gifts, or the medium of the church, was
the focus of the entire service, and that the minister
took second place. This he resented, and so produced his scheme to give the ministers the same
authority and standing as that enjoyed by the Pagan
priests, who claimed to be the channel through whom
their gods acted.[1]

[1] *The Psychic Stream* gives all the facts about this early controversy between the priests and the mediums, and also the history of the evolution
of the Christian priesthood.

A knowledge of early Church history is required in order to realise that the Reformation was only partial, and that the reformers never returned to the original Apostolic religion, but retained Christianity, which was the creation of Paul of Tarsus, as explained in an earlier chapter. The leading reformers were mostly priests or men who, from youth upwards, had been trained in the Roman Catholic outlook on religion. Consequently they could not free themselves from theological dogma and return to the charismata, or psychic gifts, exercised in the early Church, so graphically described by the famous Roman lawyer and scholar Tertullian, in his book *De Anima*, written and published in the year 211, before the priest displaced the medium. Moreover, the Christian Church had destroyed, by burning or drowning, over a quarter of a million innocent people, most of whom in one way or another displayed charismata. As mediumship is a hereditary gift, there were consequently few mediums available to take the place intended for them in the original Apostolic Church, even if the reformers had decided that the medium must be replaced in the position then held.

The Presbyterians, apart from the dogma which they accepted in common with the Roman Catholics, Episcopalians and Lutherans, did, however, get nearer to the original form of Church management than any other of the Christian sects. If they had only thrown over the doctrines which had accumulated from the 2nd century onwards, and given charismata the place originally intended, their return to early Jesuism would have been complete. This they did not do, and, in consequence, they omitted the vital link between the two worlds which is the channel for all revelation, and the cause which brought Jesuism, the forerunner of Christianity, and all other religions, into being.

The Presbyterians certainly rejected the claims made for the priesthood by Cyprian, and their ministers moreover did not claim, as did the Roman Catholic priests, that they had the power to forgive sins. Otherwise they had the same priestly theological outlook, and vehemently preached hell and damnation for all who did not accept the Presbyterian definition of Christianity. "The new presbyter is but old priest writ large," wrote Milton in the 17th century when Presbyterianism was attempting to dominate both Scotland and England.

Every supernatural religion, whatever its name, produces its own type of god, because, as we have already discovered, man makes God in his own image. Cruel men produce a cruel god, and to know the mental development of the people at any age of the world's history all that is necessary is to study the god they worshipped. Both the Episcopalians and the Presbyterians produced the god of their own creation, and, as they were cruel and intolerant, they concentrated on the debased utterances in both the Old and New Testaments to justify their thoughts and deeds. The Christian god therefore remained, as heretofore, the product of a cruel age which burned and tortured the minority who thought differently from the majority, and only when the people advanced mentally did their god do likewise.

(5) BRITAIN AND IRELAND AFTER THE REFORMATION.

The history of Scotland from the time of Bannock-burn is that of a self-contained people, of not more than 500,000 in the 16th century, who lived poor and hardy lives. The barbaric highlanders were con-tinually raiding the more prosperous lowlands, and the border counties were for ever in a state of unrest because of gangs of marauders crossing and re-crossing the frontier. From the year 1341, when Berwick alone remained in English hands, various indecisive battles were fought between the two kingdoms, a decision only being reached in 1513 at the Battle of Flodden, which broke up the Scottish army.

Scotland, after her victory at Bannockburn (1314), was from time to time defeated but never dominated by England, and her sovereigns David II (1329–1371), Robert II (1371-1390), Robert III (1390–1406), James I (1406–1437), James II (1437–1460), James III (1460–1488), James IV (1488–1513), James V (1513–1542), Mary (1542–1567) and James VI (1567–1603) reigned supreme. David II had no children, and Robert II, the son of Walter, High Steward of Scotland, suc-ceeded as his mother was Marjory Bruce, the daughter of Robert Bruce. Robert II was the first of the house of Steward, called after his father's position, and changed to Stuart by the French because the letter W is not used in their language.

James V pleased the Roman Catholics in Scotland by marrying Madeleine, a daughter of Francis I of France, but she only lived seven months as queen. On her death he married Mary of Guise, who produced

Mary Stuart, whose son became James VI, and later James I of Great Britain on the death of Elizabeth. James V refused the request of Henry VIII to repudiate the Pope's authority, and seize the wealth of the monasteries. Henry VIII then asked him to meet him at York to discuss religious questions, and, because he refused, Henry sent an army north which defeated the Scotch at Solway Moss in 1542, after which, within a fortnight, James V died; leaving Mary Stuart as his heir. He is reported to have said that the Scottish crown "cam wi' a lass (Marjory Bruce) and that it would soon "gang wi' a lass", a forecast which came true.

The Regent, during Mary's minority, was the Earl of Arran, who favoured the Protestants and permitted the free circulation of the Bible. He supported an alliance with England, and would have agreed to Mary marrying Edward VI, but the English Protector, the Duke of Somerset, was so arrogant that the negotiations were cancelled. Somerset then determined to "put all to fire and sword" in Scotland, and, as the Scotch were beaten at Pinkie (1547), Mary was sent for safety to France, where she married the Dauphin, who later became Francis II, thus bringing about an alliance with France, greatly to the concern of the English. He died in 1560, after being King of France for only eighteen months, and Mary returned to Scotland.

In spite of persecution, and the burning of heretics, Protestantism spread throughout the land. Patrick Hamilton, the herald of the Reformation in Scotland, was burned at the stake in 1528. In 1539 five heretics were burned in Edinburgh and two in Glasgow.

Cardinal Beaton was the leader of the Roman Catholics, and in 1546 was responsible for the death by fire of George Wishart, an outstanding Protestant, and many others. Beaton was then murdered, and his murderers, together with John Knox, were sent as galley slaves to France, but this persecution fades into insignificance when compared with the one which followed a hundred years later when the Episcopalians were in power.

In France, Knox became imbued with the Protestant belief, and, escaping, returned to Scotland, where he obtained numerous converts of all ranks. Many of the nobles, foreseeing loot from the Church, joined his crusade, just as they did in Germany, France and England for the same reason. The following year Knox visited Geneva, where the influence of Calvin made a deep and lasting impression, and when he, the greatest of Calvin's disciples, returned to Scotland (1558), he delivered a sermon at Perth denouncing the Mass, an outburst which was followed by monasteries and churches being destroyed and the Roman Catholics robbed and harried.

The Scottish Roman Catholics appealed to France for help and troops arrived, to be met at Leith by warships and an army sent by Elizabeth's great statesman William Cecil, Lord Burleigh, at the request of the Scottish Protestants. Elizabeth was glad of this opportunity to break Scotland's alliance with France, as Scotland, the friend of France, was like a dagger poised to strike at the heart of England. The siege of Leith followed, but soon the French withdrew before the determined resistance of the Scotch and English, who, for the first time in history, fought against a common enemy, and not against each other.

This help, which the English then gave to Scotland, was one of the wisest acts ever performed by an English statesman. For the first time the English entered Scotland as friends and helpers, and not to ravage and destroy. No event in British history has had such far-reaching results as the Treaty of Edinburgh which followed, because it secured lowland Scotland's friendship for England, made Protestantism predominant in the Scottish Lowlands, paved the way for the union of the two countries, and broke for ever the Scottish-French alliance which was such a constant danger to the safety of England.

The Scottish Parliament now gave the Protestants the liberty for which they had been fighting, the Pope's authority was abolished, the Roman Catholic Church displaced, and Mass made illegal, all of which vitally important events can be directly traced to Knox. He, by his powerful personality, had changed lowland Scotland from a Roman Catholic to a Protestant country and, in so doing, solidified Britain in its antagonism towards the old orthodox form of Christianity.

This event had important political consequences, because, if England had stood alone against Roman Catholic Spain and France, who were determined to conquer her and force her back into what they considered was the true faith, she would have been very vulnerable if Scotland had remained Roman Catholic and retained her old alliance with France. Scotland, by becoming Protestant, probably saved Protestantism in England and perhaps throughout the world, because, if England had been conquered, the Roman Catholic Church would doubtless have triumphed everywhere in Europe, and all North America would have been at its mercy.

Mary of Guise, the mother of Mary Stuart, had acted as Regent during her daughter's absence in France. She died the same year as did Mary's husband, and the Scottish queen arrived home to find her land in the throes of a great religious upheaval. Though she feared that the Presbyterian Church would become a rival to the throne, yet she was tolerant, whereas Knox and his followers were not. She set herself to gain their confidence, but her approach was in vain, as Knox remained her enemy to the end. If, instead of denouncing her, he had tried to guide and help her, how very different everything might have been! But he had no use for women; in fact he wrote a book against them which he called *The First Blast of the Trumpet against the Monstrous Regiment of Women*, wherein he described them as the "Port and the Gate of the Devil" and "Like the Gulf of Hell". How much wiser and happier he would have been if his experience of women had been similar to that of the writer of the last chapter of the *Book of Proverbs*, who could find only praise and no blame for the women he knew.

In those days women had no rights whatever, and were regarded as no better than the chattels of men, who made use of them as they pleased, the fact that they even possessed souls being doubted by some, as will be discovered by the question being debated at the Council of Trent, an incident already recorded. On mankind their sister Eve had brought all the troubles to which flesh is heir, and they never obtained the favoured position during the Christian era as was secured by the Roman matron, a misfortune not only for themselves but also for men, who would probably have been improved by their influence.

The attitude of the Church was always against an improvement in their lot, their education being neglected; in fact, as late as last century, Pope Pius IX (1846–1878), one of the weakest and most stupid of all the Roman pontiffs, remarked that "it would be a shameful thing for a girl to know how to read and write, as she might write love letters". If that could be said so recently, how servile must have been the position of women three hundred years earlier!

Four years after her return from France, Mary married her cousin Lord Darnley, a union which produced an heir to the throne, but the marriage was unpopular with the nobility, who disliked one of their own order being above them. It was an unhappy marriage, made worse by Darnley's jealousy of Rizzio, his wife's cultured and amiable Italian secretary, who was murdered in her presence. Darnley was then murdered by his fellow conspirators (one of whom was the nefarious Earl of Bothwell) because he denied his participation in this deed.

Three months later Mary made her greatest mistake when she married Bothwell, an act which raised the nobles in rebellion and alienated the English Roman Catholics, he having just divorced his innocent wife. Bothwell fled, Mary was imprisoned in Lochleven Castle, and forced to abdicate (1567) in favour of her son, who became James VI. Then she escaped, raised an army, was defeated at Langside (1568), and fled to England, where she sought the protection of Elizabeth, who kept her in confinement for nineteen years.

Finally she was beheaded for plotting with her co-religionists to murder the English queen.

Such is the tragic story of this unfortunate woman, whose son James VI became king at twelve years of age, to become engaged a few years later in a struggle with the Presbyterian Church, which was now called the Church of Scotland. Its leader, Andrew Melville, the successor of Knox, who had died in 1572, insisted on it being independent of the Crown, to which James would not agree, as he wished to be its head. In fact he was against the Presbyterian form of worship, and in favour of his country adopting the Episcopalian method, he being desirous of a unified form of worship throughout Great Britain, which he foresaw would be his kingdom on the death of Elizabeth.

His policy succeeded until 1592, when he was forced to agree to the establishment of the Presbyterian Church, but by then Episcopacy had taken such a hold that for the next hundred years, with the support of the Stuart kings, there was a bitter and bloody struggle between it and the Presbyterians. Many thousands of Presbyterians, intent on freedom to worship as they desired, were tortured, imprisoned, banished and put to death by this great tyrannical instrument, invented by the priests in the time of Elizabeth and called the Episcopalian Church. Nowhere was the curse of organised religion more felt than in Scotland, though Ireland's ordeal came first.

England's policy towards Ireland, from the time of Henry VII, was always harshly repressive. The Irish were entirely different in race and outlook from the English. They could look back upon an ancient glory and culture, distinctive and remarkable, which was utterly destroyed by the Vikings in the 10th century, and always they longed for their own independence, which England would not consider. In 1494 the legislative authority of the English Parliament was extended to Ireland, and then, forty years later, Henry VIII, who called himself King of Ireland, pillaged the monasteries and forced upon the people his own brand of Christianity, greatly to their dislike.

Elizabeth continued this policy, being determined to force Ireland to adopt the Episcopalian form of worship, just as Spain was then trying to force the orthodox Catholic tenets on the Netherlands. Episcopacy must take the place of Roman Catholicism, she decreed, but matters reached a head when, unlike Spain, she confiscated more than 500,000 acres of land and gave them to English settlers. Rebellion followed, led by the Earl of Tyrone, and encouraged by Spain. After utterly devastating the country for ten years, during which time upwards of 15,000 Irish perished, the English army in 1584 was driven out of Ireland, which was by then no better than a bloodless corpse.

Again the English returned with a large force in 1599 to restore order in a stricken lawless land, this time under the command of the cultured handsome Earl of Essex, but at the Battle of the Curlew Hills he was decisively defeated. Tyrone now demanded home rule for Ireland and full religious liberty, a claim which Elizabeth flatly refused, terming such an idea "an insolent proposal" Essex returned home disgraced, and was later executed for leading an insurrection against the Queen's ministers but not until

1603 was the Irish rebellion crushed. Tyrone mean-time had escaped to the Continent, where he died

The Episcopalian Church was a colossal failure in Ireland, where the people did not understand English, and could not follow the service. Its Prayer Book drenched the land in blood and, as happened in England and Scotland, was the cause of the torture, death, imprisonment and banishment of many who would not accept it as their guide to worship. The Pope, with the help of Spain, took up the Irish cause, and, in consequence, Roman Catholicism, and the policy of freedom from England, went hand in hand. Every priest became England's enemy, and, from that day to this, has systematically inculcated into the minds of the Irish people that England ever was and ever will be their foe.

Elizabeth, after her defeat at the Curlew Hills, was faced with complete conquest or failure. She chose the former, Ireland being conquered and devastated, while the people were driven from their battered homes and cruelly ill-treated. For these fiendish atrocities Elizabeth earned the title of "Bloody Elizabeth", by which she is known in Ireland to this day. Spain was pursuing the same diabolical methods in the Netherlands, but never did she exceed the cruelties and brutalities which the English practised in Ireland, barbarities which laid the seed for all the troubles which were to follow between the two countries.

The Act of Supremacy placed the entire control of the Church of England in the hands of Elizabeth, who, not realising that every mind is different and thinks differently, passed the Act of Uniformity (1558)

making all forms of worship, apart from that of the Church of England, illegal. Heavy fines and imprisonment were inflicted on all who did not attend the services, but the Roman Catholics, Lutherans and Calvinists would have nothing to do with this Church created by Henry VIII and his daughter, who, like Constantine in the 4th century, had produced the type of Christianity which was best suited to the political requirements of the time.

From the time of Constantine, Christians had found it impossible to dwell harmoniously within the same temple. That which is built on fraud and error can have only evil consequences. Divisions, sects, differences, quarrelling, all of which led to abominable cruelties and suffering, naturally followed. After seven hundred years of contention the Christians built a wall down the middle of their temple, on one side of which worshipped the Catholics, and on the other the Orthodox Greeks. The Catholics then could not agree, and we have just witnessed their habitation being divided into four compartments, labelled Roman Catholic, Episcopalian, Lutheran and Calvinist.

Each denomination used separate doors, and none would participate with any of the others in the Communion Service, a state of affairs which continues to the present day, even though a banner flies from the Temple dome on which is printed "Ye are all one in Christ Jesus". (*Galatians* iii, 28.) Such is the tragedy of a religion having its beliefs based on mystical speculations which are unsupported by facts, and whose priests sold themselves to the semi-Pagan Constantine, who gave them in exchange a creed for all to believe, besides the power and position which came from his recognition of their superstition as the state religion of the Roman Empire.

Elizabeth's treatment of Mary Stuart aroused the resentment of the English Roman Catholics, and her excommunication by the Pope followed, His Holiness releasing them from obedience to their queen. Consequently they rose in rebellion, burning bibles and prayer books, and plots were hatched for her murder, to which she replied by passing severe laws against them, until finally the profession of the Roman Catholic faith was considered to be high treason. All Jesuits and Roman Catholic priests were put under sentence of death, spies and informers being encouraged by Lord Burleigh, the Himmler of these days, to denounce them, when they were heavily fined, tortured, imprisoned or put to death.

The Calvinists likewise hated Episcopacy, as they objected to bishops, vestments, ritual and images of any kind, and because Elizabeth was determined to force on the people a uniform belief, the Calvinists were also cruelly treated, severely persecuted, and some were put to death. In France the end of the 16th century witnessed the Edict of Nantes, a measure of religious toleration which did not come to Britain until the 19th century, and, although the persecution of heretics returned to France in the following century, Britain had to endure and suffer from religious persecution without respite up to within the past hundred years.

To understand better Elizabeth's position we must, however, remember that she was faced during a critical period of her reign by a bitter, unscrupulous enemy in Pope Pius V, who had vowed to bring England again under papal domination. Pius was a Dominican, and all his life he had been closely identified with the Inquisition, being at one time Inquisitor-General. He was one of its most cruel and bloodthirsty leaders, and during his long period of power its atrocities were greater than during any other time in its history. He moreover bitterly persecuted the Jews and stamped out the Reformation in Italy by killing, torturing or exiling everyone who supported it, his victims numbering many thousands. A Roman historian of the time (1568) wrote:—

At Rome some are every day burned, hanged or beheaded, all the prisons and places of confinement are filled, and they are obliged to build new ones. That large city cannot provide gaols for the number of pious persons who are continually apprehended.

Both in Spain and France the evil domination of Pius V brought slaughter and misery to the Protestants. In France, where they were strongest, he set to work to uproot the reformed faith and the measures he secured prepared the way for the massacre of Saint Bartholomew. In England he intrigued with Mary Stuart against Elizabeth, the Bull which excommunicated Elizabeth declaring her "to be cut off as the monster of iniquity from the communion of the faithful", and it released her subjects from their allegiance, who henceforth were not to recognise her as their Sovereign under threat of excommunication if they did.

He planned her murder, offered a high money reward, and promised a foremost place in heaven for all who helped in its execution. He blessed anyone "who would sheath his dagger in her breast". More-over, this wicked pontiff urged Philip II of Spain to invade England, and, when he heard that the King was not hastening his preparations he, in a furious temper, flung the dinner plates and dishes at the heads of his assembled guests, and threatened to put them where the popes put their enemies—down through the trap-door that opened from his dining-room floor into the drain which led to the Tiber.

To have this super-criminal as a bitter and deter-mined enemy, and the Roman Catholics of England as his active agents, must have brought fear to the bravest, and the courage displayed by Elizabeth, who always refused protection, reveals her to have been a woman of outstanding character. In her day tolerance in religion was unknown, and she met the Pope's chal-lenge in the only way that was then understood. She thus broke the tyrant's power over England, but how different would have been this island's history had she been cowed by his threats, and the fear of invasion, into surrendering her religious beliefs! Had she become a Roman Catholic many of her people would have followed her example, and the Reformation in England would have been stillborn.

Instead of bowing to the power of Rome and Spain, the two greatest forces of her time in Europe, she stood firm as a rock, never swerving in her religious beliefs, or in the conviction of her country's capacity to defend itself. She paid the Roman Catholics back in their own coin, and by her policy she saved Protestantism in England, and probably in Europe, a fact which from that time to the present day the Holy See has not forgotten or forgiven. This meant that the earlier totalitarian form of Catholic belief, as formulated in Rome, was now shattered, the Lutherans, the Calvinists, the Episcopalians and the Roman Catholics now sharing the power hitherto solely held by the former indivisible, infallible Catholic Church for the past twelve hundred years. Once this happened, and with the magic circle broken, the belief previously held everywhere that there could be only one kind of Christianity, that as determined by the Pope, vanished, leaving a place open for others to propound their ideas.

Consequently Europe became a seething cauldron of different religious opinions, a situation the Church had averted since the Council of Nicaea in 325 by ruthless persecution and banishment. Now, fortunately, the disruption was beyond repair, many and varied interpretations of Christianity appearing, and although Roman Catholics, Lutherans, Episcopalians and Calvinists continued when they had the power the hitherto accepted practice of persecuting and banishing all they considered heretics, the fabric of the Christian edifice had become too loosely knit together to maintain uniformity. With the end of uniformity came liberty very slowly and haltingly, three centuries having to pass before persecution and banishment ceased, during which period countless atrocities were practised in the name of Christ.

Both the Pope and Elizabeth, in their own way, fought for religious uniformity, a conflict which in the long run brought about the freedom we now enjoy. By being intolerant Elizabeth laid the foundation of toleration, by being ruthless she prepared the way for liberty, by being brave and courageous during a time of great difficulty and danger she broke the power of the greatest tyranny of all time, and made possible the age of liberty she never foresaw nor could even understand. For thus saving England, and securing to us, and much of Christendom, the liberty we now enjoy, we should be grateful to Elizabeth for the stand she bravely took against the most unscrupulous tyrant of her age.

Our present-day freedom evolved out of a period of hatred which had a terrible effect on the people's conduct one towards another, and it is difficult, even in imagination, to picture this side of English life during the reign of Elizabeth. Hatred abounded, the Anglicans, Calvinists and Roman Catholics loathing each other with a fierceness which they expressed by oaths, calling down the curse of God and the horrors of hell on everyone who held different opinions. Every one considered himself saved and one of the elect, and had grave doubts about his neighbour. Treachery and dishonesty were rampant, trust in one another being lacking, while many Roman Catholics secretly plotted for Elizabeth's death, hoping that Philip of Spain would then become their king. Towards Elizabeth, and her supporters, there was this black malignant hatred on the part of those belonging to the old orthodox faith, it being fanned to ever greater heat every time one of their co-religionists was disembowelled and then hanged, their loyalty to the Pope being as pronounced as was their disloyalty to the throne.

The other side of the picture is less repulsive, as, apart from the numerous fanatics and zealots, most of the English people pursued their quiet lives, interested in their own families and business affairs, and quite content to accept the Christianity their popular sovereign decided was best for them. Their manners were coarse and their ideas very crude, but slowly a freer and fuller life was developing for both the citizen and the peasant. There was more joy and happiness, both science and literature expanded, trade and wealth increased, and the influence of the Renaissance began to be felt for the first time in England.

When thinking of these times our thoughts inevitably concentrate on William Shakespeare (1564–1616), one of the world's greatest wonders and greatest mysteries. His father, John Shakespeare, was a leather merchant and general dealer in Stratford-on-Avon, and eventually rose to be mayor of the town. His business at first prospered, as he was energetic, ambitious and public spirited, but he lacked prudence and wisdom, so much so that by the time his eldest son William was fifteen his financial affairs had become deeply involved. Consequently he had to mortgage the sixty acres of land belonging to his wife Mary Arden, a woman of culture, refinement and good social position, her ancestors for centuries having played a leading part in Warwickshire. More than once they had filled the position of Lord Lieutenant and High Sheriff of the county, to as far back as Anglo-Saxon times, one, who was related to the royal house of Athelstane, being Sheriff of Warwickshire in the time of Edward the Confessor.

William, who had received a classical education, was attracted to the stage as a youth when his father, the mayor, entertained a company of players who had come to the town, and when the family fortunes dwindled he set off to London in 1586, at the age of twenty-two, to make his own way in life.   Here he prospered, to become, so it is thought, part owner of the Blackfriars Theatre, and here also he acted on the stage the plays he wrote.   These made him not only famous but also a prosperous man, so much so that he was able to recover the family land and support his parents in comfort for the remainder of their lives.   He was a devoted son, his mother receiving his greatest affection, and he loved his native town and the surrounding country. Sixteen crowded years in busy expanding London, with a population now nearing 200,000, had made him great and rich, but he seemed to tire of all the adulation he received.   Consequently he returned to Stratford-on-Avon in 1602 to pass the remainder of his years in peace and happiness, occupying his time in managing his landed estate with the same care, attention and ability as had brought him fame and prosperity.

Everything we read of William Shakespeare points to him being a man of simple natural tastes, of sterling character, honest to a degree, thrifty but not mean, gentle, kind, cultured, amiable, considerate and courteous, his strong character being noticeable in his sturdy independence, self-respect, business ability, and the free way he expressed himself, always exercising full liberty of thought and speech.   Like his father, who was fined because he would not go to church, William maintained a sensible indifference to the religious superstitions of the time, and so helped to raise the people to a higher and nobler level of thought.

After he settled down in London with his wife, who

was Anne Hathaway, he set about equipping himself for his life's work, reading all the books he could secure, learning French and Italian, and mixing, when possible, with the men who then crowded London from all parts of the world, remembering their conversations, which gave him useful facts for his plays. He arrived in the capital at the moment best fitted for the full development of his dramatic genius. After the gloom of Mary Tudor's reign the people responded to the greater freedom of her successor, Elizabeth, which brought a new and brighter page to England's history when drama and the arts rose in national esteem. Eager and excited audiences crowded the crude theatres from floor to ceiling, all feeling the keenest interest in life and action.

Never before, except in the days when Pericles ruled in Athens, had all the elements and conditions for dramatic talent been so fused in perfect union, the stirring world events of the times stimulating the people's minds, which had hitherto been kept in darkness. Shakespeare supplied just what was wanted, the representation of life and heroic deeds on the stage, so that the people could behold for themselves dramas akin to those wondrous tales which were the prevailing conversation of the time.

How it came about that this genial kindly man was endowed with a mind which was an intellectual ocean, that touched all shores of thought, has been made by some a quite unnecessary mystery. It may always remain a problem, but, knowing as we now do that many books were then in circulation, and that he adapted passages from Greek and Latin authors into his own poetic language, there is nothing strange or puzzling about it all, and we need not seek for another to have produced all the thoughts which were published under his name.

He was acknowledged in his own time as an outstanding dramatist and play-writer, two of his most cherished companions being the poets Drayton and Ben Jonson, who were his guests at Stratford a few days before he passed peacefully away in his fifty-second year (1616) after a short illness. The recognition of his genius did not only come from the friends he made, as in 1595 one of his sonnets was included in a book of poems, and three years later a poem was written around his name. Another author in *Wits Treasury* compared him eulogistically to former and living poets. In 1600 ninety extracts from his plays were published in a book called *England's Parnassus*, and in the same year another book, *Garden of the Muses*, published several of his works, a third book in the same year, *England's Helicon*, containing poems by Shakespeare and other poets of the time.

Twelve years after he commenced to write, he took his place amongst the leading poets and dramatists of his day, being referred to in 1600 as "Our fellow Shakespeare who puts them all down", and yet the extraordinary fact remains that he never mentioned directly in his plays the name of any of his contemporaries. He lived in stirring times when great discoveries were made on land and sea, when the world was circumnavigated by Francis Drake, when great religious wars were waged, when great painters were making their wonderful contributions to mankind, when the Armada attacked his country's shores, when the Turks were driving into Europe, when they were defeated at the great sea battle of Lepanto, when Spain was carrying fire and sword throughout the Netherlands, and England was devastating Ireland, when Mary Stuart was executed, when the massacre of Saint Bartholomew's day was followed by the Edict of Nantes, and when Henry III, King of France, was assassinated.

These, and many other outstanding events, occurred during his lifetime, which was a period of valiant deeds and adventures in far-off lands and seas, but he passed by unnoticed those who were the actors in these contemporary human dramas. At a time when the mind of man was being reborn into a new age of thought, Shakespeare mentions no living king or queen, no contemporary adventurer, no great statesman, priest, nobleman, sailor or soldier, no great discoverer, no great thinker, and no producer of those treasured pictures now deemed priceless, while Galileo, who was then exploring the heavens, was passed by unnoticed.

Amidst the great he stood alone and apart from his fellow men, on a pinnacle of his own, observing with eagle eye the deeds of mankind, his inspiration seemingly coming to him from the keen interest he took in life and the countryside. In an age when an actor was considered a vagabond, and treated as a menial, when to play a part was considered not only disgraceful but contrary to the will of God, this man produced words and phrases which have elevated, enriched and delighted the greatest minds of every land and every age. Out of a civilisation, laid barren for centuries by the grossest superstition, he produced a garden, each flower a rose which has bloomed with ever greater beauty as every year has passed.

Into finely woven phrases he compressed the knowledge of his time, gathering his ideas from all he saw and read in order to produce his many pictures of life within the framework of his own unique vocabulary. He added to and emblazoned the thoughts of others, some of his passages having been already written in other words, but, though the stones were there, he polished them afresh and made them give forth an increased lustre.

Such, then, was this freethinking humanist, whose mind ranged far and wide in its search for material to transform into poetic phrases for the stage, and produce characters which still live in imagination as he portrayed them. He lifted the human intellect above the sordid thoughts of his time, and presented men and women as thinking, sensitive human beings, loving, hating, striving, struggling, hoping, fearing; he portrayed them as the greatest products of developing mind, and not as damned sinners fit only for destruction. He was one of the greatest of pioneers, as he helped to lead the people out of the bondage of the theological age; he replaced faith by reason, and brought back to man his sense of worth and dignity which the previous centuries of servitude had all but destroyed.

Other play-writers also lived during this joyful resurgent age, this time when songs and ballads were everywhere composed and sung, when the English language reached its fullest beauty and power, and when music attained a standard never before known. Little is known about Thomas Dekker except that his plays were in great request for the stage. About his contemporary John Webster there is likewise some mystery, but his comedies were lively and humorous, and in his day he was looked upon as a poet and dramatist of the foremost rank. More is known about Thomas Nash (1564–1601), the poet, dramatist and pamphleteer who was one of the most notable literary celebrities in the brilliant last decade of Elizabeth's reign, as was also Christopher Marlowe (1564–1593), the father of English tragedy and the creator of English blank verse. Robert Greene (1560–1592) is notable for his plays, which were enlivened by comic humour and farcical fun.

During a long and laborious life Ben Jonson (1573–1637) displayed in his dramatic works a richness and breadth which surpassed most of his literary contemporaries, and George Chapman (1559–1634) is famed for his translation of the works of Homer. The pioneer of education in England was Richard Mulcaster, who, about 1580, wrote one of the best treatises on the right way to teach children and train teachers. Intellectually and socially England advanced, and was none the worse for her new form of religion, her people being well fed and clothed, the rich wearing costly attire bedecked with jewels and gold charms. In striking contrast, poverty-stricken Scotland, under Calvinism, experienced only recession and gloom, Calvinistic austerity cramping the people's vision and creative spirit, while internal feuds, restrictions and monopolies fettered them both industrially and socially.

A Calvinist home was dismal and sullen, over which hovered the devil ever waiting to catch a sinner after death, and consign him for all eternity to his ever burning lake of fire. The minds of children were deformed and dwarfed, their desires being defeated and destroyed in the process of training them "in the nurture and admonition of the Lord". Some were believed to be predestined to everlasting bliss, but the majority to eternal damnation. Along this dark fearsome road each child passed until, as a result, a harsh and dour manhood was reached, when the same austere process began again with the next generation. Life contained no laughter, no sunshine nor joy, as "the fear of God" for ever haunted these miserable creatures, ruled with a rod of iron by their ministers, who, as Buckle says in his *History of Civilisation in England*, "kept the people in worse than Egyptian bondage inasmuch as they enslaved both mind and body", by "one of the most detestible tyrannies ever seen on earth". Such was the effect of Calvinism in Scotland and Puritanism in England, up to within our own times, and it spread all over the world wherever Protestant beliefs were accepted.

The brighter side of Protestantism lay in the fact that its clergy were now permitted to marry, and thus end the scandal of their having mistresses and illegitimate children. This reform was the most important social event in Elizabeth's reign, and did much to simplify the change over to the new faith, the legitimate wife creating amongst the Protestant clergy a vested interest in the continuity of the new order. Still, it was many years before the people became accustomed to the clergy having wives, and, throughout her reign, neither Elizabeth nor her subjects cared to recognise these women socially and invite them to their homes.

Another change was the introduction of the

Puritan Sabbath, and all its rigid taboos, all joy and laughter being banished on that holy day. No altar now occupied the east of the chancel, and instead "the Lord's Table" stood in the centre of the church, while the metrical version of the Psalms, as now used in Scotland, took the place of the chanted prose. Long sermons in church (one to two hours long) and family worship twice a day, each day of the week, separated the religious life of the Protestants from that of the Roman Catholics, the Bible being worshipped by the former and the Holy Mother Church by the latter, while a fierce intolerance brooded over the land.

This was an age in England of palaces and mansions, where carpets replaced rushes, but, though fleas consequently decreased in number, sanitation was neglected, the result being that plague and disease thrived under such conditions. Sport and plays amused the less rigid amongst all classes, whether they assembled in a field, a theatre, or the courtyard of a village inn, but poverty prevailed, and was relieved by a comprehensive and well-administered Poor Law which was passed in 1601. Once again use was found for the country gentlemen, the Justices of the Peace, these men who, without payment, administered justice, fixed prices and wages and did the work done by the County and District councils in our time. They were now made responsible for collecting the Poor Rate and using the money to relieve distress, or to buy material to provide work for the robust and sturdy beggars. Nothing, however, was done for general education, and consequently 90 per cent. of the population remained illiterate, this being also the position throughout Europe.

Nevertheless wealthy laymen founded private schools, such as Uppingham and Harrow, the consequence being that the merchants in those days were well educated for the time, they being the most intelligent and sensible people in the land. The desire for increased wealth and greater comforts was their incentive towards honest trading, in contrast to the looting and destruction caused by the soldiers in war. Following many centuries of experience, the merchants of Europe had discovered that honesty is always the best policy, and that a fair exchange of goods is wiser in the long run than stealing, a vital fact which unfortunately is not yet accepted by all the world's politicians.

Local fairs had been the place up to now where exchanges had taken place, but the time had come, decided Sir Thomas Gresham (1519–1579), to erect a suitable building in the centre of London to accommodate the city merchants and financiers. Here these traders, many the younger sons of the manor house, where none were expected to live idle lives, could meet and transact their business quickly and efficiently, all the buyers and sellers being together under the same roof. This very able enlightened man, who was a London merchant, and had been Lord Mayor, was Royal Agent at Antwerp in his early life, a city then the hub of the world's trade, whence he brought the idea of an Exchange to England. So he built at his own expense the Royal Exchange, which was opened by Elizabeth in 1570, the year she broke the power of the nobles in the north of England, and at a time when the country was at the beginning of her world-wide business career.

England in those days was prosperous, and her large open spaces, unfenced and unhedged, supported great flocks of sheep that supplied the wool for her thriving cloth trade. Though poverty prevailed then, as it has always done, life to the majority had become easier because the currency, after its debasement by Henry VIII, had been stabilised, economy had replaced extravagance in state administration and prices had ceased to rise. With the seas now open everywhere for navigation, owing to the use made of the compass, English trade increased, and London took the place of Antwerp as the world's greatest seaport and commercial city, to become the business' centre of the world. What England gained the Netherlands lost, and that was the tragic consequence which befell the Flemings because of the persecution and devastation they had suffered from their Spanish overlords. So England stepped into the place of the Netherlands, and trading companies were organised, the most important being the East India Company in 1600.

Many of these were little better than associations of sea adventurers. The chance of loot and booty took daredevils to sea, and Sir Humphrey Gilbert gathered together some doughty stalwarts to colonise Newfoundland. Sir Walter Raleigh founded Virginia in 1584, and here he discovered the potato, which he brought back to Ireland and England. Sir Richard Grenville, the hero of the "Revenge" that fought fifty-three Spanish ships alone, then organised expeditions which transported the first colonists to this new-found land.

In those days men of vision were peering north to

find some way round by the Arctic sea to the east. John Davis and Sir Martin Frobisher attempted, but failed, to discover the north-west passage, but the unsuccessful attempt made by Richard Chancellor and Sir Hugh Willoughby to find the north-eastern passage to India brought about the development of trade with Russia. Sir John Hawkins worked up a lucrative trade in slaves, the unfortunate creatures being captured in Sierra Leone and taken to the Spanish colonies, to be exchanged for merchandise.

Hawkins was one of the most outstanding men of this age of great men. Pious and puritanical, he was honest at a time when honesty received little respect, and, as we have already read, it was he who built up the efficient navy which defeated the Spanish. He was a seaman of first rank, but, besides that, he was a wise and far-seeing man who advocated a policy for overthrowing the power of Spain by putting everything into the navy, and attacking the enemy on her treasure route from South America. His plan was to blockade continuously the Azores, at which the Spanish ships had to call to replenish. Thus the life-blood of Spain would be destroyed and much of her power gone.

If this policy had been adopted, and the money had been used on the navy that was employed on the army for fruitless excursions on the Continent, there might never have been an Armada, and England might have choked her enemy before she struck at her. By skilful diplomacy, Elizabeth and Burleigh had kept England out of serious trouble, whereas Hawkins, forseeing the growing power of Spain, would have acted and not talked. Nevertheless, when war did come, England was ready, because Hawkins, over the previous ten years, had seen to it that every ship was sound, modern and well provisioned.

The course of time has made romantic and glamorous this period of English history. Novelists have found many daring exploits which they have spun into thrilling stories to delight both old and young. Pirates and filibusters abounded, as, on the high seas and in the far-off newly discovered lands, there was no law and order, many a richly laden Spanish galleon being boarded, robbed, and the crew made to walk the plank. Every one who sailed the sea was a law unto himself, and, as England had then the best seamen, the best shipbuilders and the largest shipbuilding capacity of any country, her ships and daring seamen were the terror of the honest trader, whose ships were nowhere safe from capture.

Ruffians, as many of them were, yet they were brave men, because they knew that if they, in their turn, fell into Spanish hands it meant a terrible death at the hands of the Inquisition, before which many an English seaman was brought and tortured, not because he was an enemy of Spain but because he was a Protestant. Every voyage in those days involved this terrible risk, and yet these English seamen took it, well knowing that if captured with a Bible or Prayer Book on board, torture and burning at the stake would be the lot of the entire crew when brought into a Spanish port. A voyage through the Mediterranean was equally dangerous, as capture by the Turks, whose pirate crews abounded, meant the rest of one's life as a galley slave.

Life in those days was certainly coarse and brutal, and the people looked on with relish at the gruesome sight of a law-breaker being disembowelled alive. The Queen boxed the ears of her courtiers, the father thrashed his children, the craftsman his apprentice and the farmer his labourer, this way of living continuing well on into the 19th century.

Opening up the seas to trade was not done without much suffering, and many a seaman paid with his life for the widening of man's horizon. From being a small compact affair the world had become to many a place of vast extent, almost without limit, with treasure abounding for those possessed of the necessary pluck and endurance. Spain and Portugal had secured for themselves an El Dorado, and every English adventurer considered that it was right and proper to engage in any undertaking which would remove some of their gains into English pockets, Elizabeth associating herself with her subjects' enterprise and sharing in their profits. Deep and bitter as was the English hatred of the Spaniards, the detestation by English Protestants of the Pope was still more profound, and never could they forget that his predecessor, in the preceding century, had given to Spain so much of that vast new continent across the Atlantic, and entirely ignored England, to whom he had allotted nothing.

Officially Elizabeth pursued a most decorous policy both at home and abroad, her endeavour at home being to prevent a religious disruption amongst her 4,000,000 subjects, and abroad to pacify her potential enemies until the country had become united under the Anglican faith. Many, including her chief ministers, considered that she was too cautious and that the leading Protestant sovereign should meet her Roman Catholic enemies with sword unsheathed. Ultimately force took the place of diplomacy, but, during the period of peace, a few wise men foresaw increased trade and wealth from the new lands across the seas. Those who tried to discover the north-western and north-eastern passages to India and the islands of the Pacific, the Spice Islands, as they were called, were the pioneers of trade, but their efforts were frustrated by the snow and ice of the Arctic regions.

These bold adventurers were, however, quite the exception, as the majority of English seamen were pirates, whose aim in life was the theft and destruction of everything belonging to Spain, endless conflicts being fought to this end. On one occasion when Drake and Hawkins were sheltering with their five ships from a hurricane in the Mexican port of San Juan, after a successful plundering expedition, they were set upon by thirteen Spanish galleons, to escape with only two of their fleet, and a small portion of their crew, after a hard struggle.

For twenty-eight years Sir Francis Drake (1545–1595), the son of a peasant, was a great and respected buccaneer to all Englishmen, soon to be made conscious of their country's exploits overseas by Hakluyt's stirring tales of adventure, endurance and rich booty won, every attack Drake made on Spanish possessions receiving their warm approval. To his countrymen this famous pirate was "the master thief of the unknown world", and his daring deeds filled all England with delight. So much was this the case that when he arrived home in his ship the *Golden Hind* after his voyage round the world, with much booty secured from looting Spanish galleons and the Spanish possessions on the way, he was welcomed by his sovereign on his arrival at Deptford and honoured with a knighthood.

Later Drake became an admiral, to show his courage and resource in routing the Spanish Armada, but, if he had done nothing else, his circumnavigating the world (1577–1580) entitles him to fame, in spite of all his nefarious deeds. He was the first Englishman to undertake this great adventure, and the second seaman to accomplish this then dangerous enterprise. He sailed by way of South America and returned home by South Africa, thus repeating the exploit of the Magellan expedition of sixty years earlier. His ravaging of the Spanish possessions, and the many other hostile actions of English seamen, greatly angered Philip II of Spain and his subjects, and, if Philip had not been fully occupied at the time with France and the Netherlands, war would have followed sooner than it did.

The persecution of the Roman Catholics in England and Ireland further enraged the Spaniards, but not until England openly sided with their enemies did war between the two countries become inevitable. England set the light to the powder magazine when Elizabeth, in 1584, dispatched to the Netherlands an army of six thousand men under her intimate lover, the much-hated dandy, the Earl of Leicester, to help the Flemings in their fight against Spanish rule. At Zutphen the English were defeated, when Sir Philip Sidney (1554–1586), the outstanding soldier, statesman and poet, was killed.

Perhaps Philip II had hoped that the Roman Catholics would succeed in their attempt to murder Elizabeth and put Mary Stuart on the throne, but, when the Babington plot was discovered, and Mary was executed in 1587, he delayed no longer and prepared to attack. To the Spanish this decision was the opening of a great religious crusade, which received the blessing of the Pope, and in every Roman Catholic church in Europe prayers were offered up for its success. Only by a Spanish victory, to be followed by the deposition of the heretical bastard Elizabeth, and the King of Spain becoming King of England in her place, could the long outstanding differences between the two countries be satisfactorily settled. So thought the Roman Catholics everywhere, but Drake postponed the conflict for a year by sailing into Cadiz and destroying forty Spanish ships, a feat which was paralleled in the Second World War when the Royal Air Force destroyed the German invasion barges assembled at Dunkirk and Calais in 1940.

The year 1588 found everything ready for the great assault, and one mid-July morning the English on the south coast beheld a great armada of 132 ships, carrying 8000 sailors and 20,000 soldiers, sailing up the English Channel. Only 36 English vessels, besides 160 privately owned ships, were there to meet it, and prevent the execution of the enemy's plan of campaign. This was to defeat the English navy and then transport to England the army of 40,000 men, under the Duke of Parma, assembled at Dunkirk, it being expected that when the English fleet was defeated the Dutch warships, patrolling off Dunkirk, would quickly succumb.

The English navy was under the command of Lord Howard of Effingham, who was assisted by Frobisher, Hawkins and Drake, and it enjoyed one great advantage over the Spaniards. The smaller English craft could manœuvre more easily, and sail closer to the wind than the large unwieldy Spanish galleons. Moreover, by their rapid and accurate broadside gunfire, the enemy ships were much battered by the time they reached Calais. There they suffered further losses by blazing ships being sent into their midst. Off Gravelines the Spaniards were defeated, after which followed a fierce gale which drove them into the North Sea. Those that remained tried to return home by rounding the north of Scotland, but many were wrecked on the way and only fifty-three returned to Spain.

Thus was Britain saved from invasion, and all northern Europe from the return of the domination of the Pope. The victory also brought about the freedom of the Netherlands, and indirectly was the cause of the Edict of Nantes. Protestantism, where it had taken root, was now free to grow and flourish, it being helped to do so in England because, to the average Englishman, Roman Catholicism stood for Spain and the Pope, both of whom were bitterly hated.

Well can we imagine what all this meant to the Holy See, which by prayer, intrigue and money had worked for the downfall of England. Vividly can we picture there the interest and excitement when Philip's great fleet set sail to destroy Protestant England, and restore the only true Christian faith, because this would mean that when Protestantism was crushed in England, then Germany, and other strongholds, would share the same fate. What a feeling of dismay and disappointment the news of the English victory must have occasioned! Surely it must have been one of the blackest periods in the history of the Holy Catholic Church, and Drake's failure to capture Lisbon the following year did nothing to lighten it.

Seldom had Elizabeth, during her despotic reign, done anything to anger the English people, and now her popularity was at its zenith. Her subjects forgave her for her arrogance, lying, vanity and deceit, because they found that by trusting this remarkably able coarse-tongued Tudor, England had been victorious, even though they could not follow her crooked foreign policy. Her victory, in the greatest of all gambles, war, raised her to the position she has since occupied in the estimation of the public. Her success, courage and steadfastness, and not her nobility of character, made her great. She was the product of a cruel intolerant age, and this background must be remembered in passing judgment.

Throughout her reign Elizabeth was well served by her ministers Burleigh, Walsingham and Parker, to whose guidance much of her success was due. At the beginning of her rule, Spain and England were allies and at war with France, but the toleration accorded in France to the Protestants by Henry of Navarre, when he became king, and the aggressive Roman Catholicism of Spain, brought England and France together in an alliance. Now, with Spain defeated, the remainder of her reign was lived in comparative peace, and in the knowledge that her country was safe. Moreover, by the defeat of the

Turks on both land and sea, the nightmare of an Asiatic domination of Europe had lessened, and from this time onwards the Aryans, and not the Mongols, became the masters of the world, a question which was still in the balance when she came to the throne.

In 1603, Elizabeth, the last of the Tudors, died at the age of seventy after a reign of forty-five years, an era which was crowded with important events to the English people, one of these being that England during her reign had become the chief maritime power in Europe, an occurrence which was to be the making of the British Empire in the centuries ahead. During her reign the prestige of Parliament, consisting largely of country gentlemen, was higher than ever before, and then it was that the basis was laid for present-day parliamentary procedure. Within this period the population of London doubled, the feudal castles disappeared and were succeeded by manor houses with chimneys and glass windows. Local magistrates exercised such a powerful restraint on lawlessness that men ceased wearing armour to appear clothed in velvet and lace. Greater refinement, music and poetry replaced some of the coarseness of the past.

The age of Elizabeth was one of great achievement, her death being the signal for yet another notable event, as a messenger was at once dispatched to Holyrood from a Council of Ministers with a proclamation hailing James VI as King of England. At long last England and Scotland were united under one sovereign, James I of Great Britain, to the lasting benefit of both countries.

CHAPTER XIII.

CHRISTIAN CIVILISATION.
(1513–1796.)

Introduction. (1) *Germany is Devastated for Thirty Years.* (2) *France Becomes the Dominant Power in Europe.* (3) *Parliament Gradually Replaces Absolute Monarchy in Britain.* (4) *Spain Falls from Her High Position.* (5) *Russia Becomes a Great Nation.*

At the time when the Germans occupied France during the Second World War, and were murdering batches of French hostages, as reprisals for the death of German officers by unknown patriots, President Roosevelt stated that this victimisation of innocent people was revolting and a reversion to barbarism, as no one should suffer for the deed of another. When our ancestors were uncivilised, and had a crude conception of justice, they saw nothing wrong in an innocent person suffering to atone for a crime, and there are many instances of single innocent victims being killed for the crime another committed, as well as wholesale massacres of innocent people.

We now talk of this form of justice as barbaric, but when Christianity grew out of the old Pagan religions it was looked upon as right and proper. Consequently Christians borrowed from their contemporaries the belief about a saviour-god dying for the wickedness of humanity, and we have this age-old story wound round Jesus, who became known as the

Christ, the title being the Greek for the anointed one, because the victim was always first anointed with oil, so as to roast and taste better after being sacrificed on the altar.   Jesus became the theological Christ, as the result of Paul connecting the apparition he saw of him after death with what was believed of certain Pagan priestly victims of the past.   They likewise had appeared after death, to become in consequence saviour-gods, and be surrounded with the mysticism and theology of the times.   Paul sowed the seed which was tended by the theologians of those days so zealously that by the 4th century it had grown into the Christian religion as we now know it.

All the creeds and dogmas of this religion are based upon the belief that Jesus, an innocent victim, was sacrificed by Jehovah for the sins and wickedness of all believers.   On the preaching and teaching of this blasphemous and barbaric belief, all the Christian Church propagandists, from the Pope and the Archbishop of Canterbury down to the humblest minister of the gospel, earn their living and obtain their social position.   By now we have realised how great a part the Christian religion has played in shaping the history of Europe, and how the Church and its priests were active participants in everything to do with war, persecution and banishment.   They were, and still are, the representatives of a barbaric form of injustice attributed to their god, and, when this is remembered, their actions, and the state in which they kept the people, will be better understood.

Their religion is based on a primitive conception of justice, their laws reflecting this mental level, as, when religious beliefs are based upon merciless savagery, the methods of its propagandists are likewise savage, and its history is equally so. Yet, as even the greatest suffer from early upbringing, and at times give little thought to logical thinking, President Roosevelt, on another occasion, joined in the chorus of stupid politicians and crafty priests to state that the Second World War was fought to save Christianity and the Christian way of life. Could the curse of ignorance, from which we suffer, be better exemplified than in this utter lack of appreciation of history and its lessons?

All the saviour-god religions are based upon an innocent victim dying for the sins of believers, because the theologians, who produced them, considered this to be divine justice. Whoever preaches and accepts this doctrine today has the barbaric mind, and, when we remember that Christians have always accepted, and still accept, this cruel belief, we can better understand the mentality which has afflicted Christendom. Only when everyone is sufficiently informed to understand the fundamental causes which determine our lives can we advance to a higher range of thought and action, but, when we find glorified that which is evil, we can better appreciate why ignorance produces evil.

Only when everyone replaces ignorance with knowledge, and wisely follows where this knowledge leads, will our conduct be based upon ethical principles which, down the ages, have been found to give the happiness we all so ardently desire. Man imagines God in his own image, and it is around this facsimile that we are now about to witness the most devastating religious war in history, one which, for its destruction of life and property, has no equal in the annals of mankind until we come to our own times.

The 17th century opens with all Europe quarrelling about religion, and this quarrel goes on throughout the century. So far our tale of persecution has mostly concerned the murdering and torturing of heretics by Christians who were united in thought and action, but now we come to a new phase in the tragic story, because those who withdrew from the orthodox Church, and called themselves Protestants, proved themselves to be equally cruel and intolerant. The Protestants, when they had the power, now tortured and murdered the Roman Catholics, but they went one step further and killed and persecuted each other.

The 17th century abounds with this bitter religious persecution of Christians, who ill-treated one another in the name of Christ, thinking that it was pleasing to Jehovah. He, according to their inspired holy Scriptures, had outdone in cruelty anything his worshippers had ever so far attempted, not because they would not, but because they could not. Jehovah, they believed, had drowned, by means of a world-wide flood, every man, woman and child except a handful, and, if our ancestors could have done the same to all who thought differently from them, they would have done so. That was why they believed this blasphemy about God, whose thoughts and doings they imagined were like unto their own.

Germany, whose people in our time have on two occasions within a generation devastated, and brought death, starvation, misery and untold suffering to the greater part of Europe, was herself the victim of religious intolerance in the first half of the 17th century, when her population was decimated and her fair countryside laid waste. This tale of woe will now be told, as we have reached the time when all this happened.

(1) Germany is Devastated for Thirty Years.

Europe, in the opening years of the 17th century, was a boiling cauldron of religious controversy, and all that was required was someone to take the lid off, when this seething pent-up energy would be released to scorch the earth. This state of affairs recalls a similar period when Jesuism was evolving into Christianity. Then it was that some unknown person, to explain all the quarrelling and discord this was causing amongst believers, added the following to the Gospels which the priests were then cunningly altering to suit the changing outlook:—

> Think not that I have come to send peace on earth: I came not to send peace, but a sword. For I have come to set a man at variance against his father, and the daughter against her mother, and the daughter in law against her mother in law. (*Matthew* x, 34.)

Amid so much that is false in the Gospels this certainly is true. The birth of Jesus did not bring peace and goodwill amongst men, the reported forecast by an angel that it would do so (*Luke* ii, 14), having been disproved, and a religion that brings war and strife, and not peace and harmony, is a curse and not a blessing. So far the Christian record fully bears out this prediction of strife, and now we find the Lutherans and Calvinists bitterly hostile towards each other, a religious tyranny existing as great as ever prevailed before the Reformation. Where Calvinism predominated only Calvinistic Christianity could be practised, but in the Lutheran states only the Lutheran type could exist. Saxony and Brandenburg were Lutheran, whereas the Palatinate was Calvinist under the energetic direction of Frederick the Elector. In this divided Protestant Germany the Jesuits set themselves to wreck the new heretical movement, and they had as their leader Maximilian, Duke of Bavaria, who had expelled all the Protestants from his domains. In reply the Protestants formed (1608) the Evangelical Union under the direction of Frederick, and this was followed the next year by the formation of the Catholic League under Maximilian.

While the Protestants were at deadly grips with one another, and Germany was rushing onwards to chaos and disaster, the counter-reformation, planned and engineered by the Jesuits, was making headway. The ignorant multitude was ignored by these cunning zealots, because they knew that their aims could best be achieved by devoting their energies towards influencing the upper classes to their system of thought. Everyone with authority was wooed and flattered by the Jesuit priests, who, sensing the tendency of the age, patronised the culture and learning which was now appealing to the thoughtful as never before.

Spanish Jesuits spread over Germany for the purpose of founding theological schools and colleges to restore the old faith, and within ten years of the death of Luther they were in control of the Universities of Cologne, Ingolstadt, Munich, Vienna, Bonn, Mainz, Speier, and Würzburg, which became active centres of Roman Catholic propaganda. Vienna was the headquarters of their activities, and thence they spread all over Protestant and Roman Catholic Europe, the result being that Austria, the Rhineland, Bavaria and Poland were saved for the Roman Catholic faith, the latter country, which had largely espoused the Protestant cause, being won back to the old tradition within some fifty years.

Thus the Jesuits, the Lutherans and the Calvinists set the stage for a long and wasteful struggle which decided that western Europe was never to be wholly reconquered by the Christian Church with its principal seat in Rome. Christianity was now definitely split up into three main groups—the Roman Catholics, who looked to the Pope at Rome as the authority for their belief, the Protestant Catholics, who, when they had the power to do so, set up the reigning sovereign as head of the Church, and the Orthodox Russians who looked to the Patriarch of Moscow and all Russia as their religious leader. If we weigh up the comfort and consolation Christianity gave to the ignorant multitude, against the mountain of misery which was caused by its loosely defined and unethical beliefs, we realise more than ever the tragedy which came upon humanity when Greek philosophy and the enlightened Roman educational system were liquidated by the Christian Church in the 5th century, and the old Paganism, under the Christian name, was tightly fastened on Europe.

Rudolf II (1576–1612), a Hapsburg, now reigned as Holy Roman Emperor. He was brought up in Spain as a Jesuit, and became an ardent advocate of Roman Catholic domination, but insanity developed before the conflagration started, and his brother Matthias (1612–1619) reigned in his stead. He likewise was determined to return to the old idea of one Pope, one Sovereign and one Faith throughout his empire, comprising Silesia, Austria, Bohemia, Styria, Tyrol and the western part of Hungary. He had the support of Spain, whose royal house was likewise Hapsburg through the marriage of Philip, the son of the Emperor Maximilian of Austria and Mary of Burgundy, to Joanna, daughter and heiress of Ferdinand and Isabella of Spain. Thus those Hapsburg dominions which were Roman Catholic combined against the Protestant states of Germany, and, if they had remained united, Protestantism might easily have been obliterated. The story of the split which developed will be told later on, as they remained allies for the first eleven years of the war.

The trouble began in Bohemia, now part of Czechoslovakia, where, in 1618, a riot occurred in Prague, because some Protestant churches were demolished by the Roman Catholics. From this spark the whole of Europe became ablaze, the centre of the inferno being in Germany. This conflict, known as the Thirty Years' War, was the most terrible religious conflict in history, and when it was over Germany required fifty years to recover. Bohemia was mostly Lutheran, but the Calvinists took the lead in resisting Roman Catholic aggression. So, when the Emperor broke his promise and destroyed their churches, the Calvinists threw his representatives out of the windows of the castle at Prague, and deposed their fanatical Jesuit-trained King Ferdinand, who, the following year, succeeded Matthias as Holy Roman Emperor. The Bohemians offered the throne to Frederick, the young inexperienced Elector of the Palatinate (now called the

Rhineland, and then the stronghold of Calvinism), who accepted it in 1618.

His acceptance was an unfortunate decision, one which greatly angered Ferdinand, who, when Matthias died the following year (1619), and he became emperor, vowed to exterminate Protestantism from his empire. Now had come the time the authorities at the Vatican had longed and prayed for, for the past fifty years. Before long they believed there would be once again only one Church of Christ in the west, and the hated heresy would be destroyed for ever. So Pope Paul V gave his blessing and support to the Emperor, and thus began the greatest and blackest crime ever perpetrated by the Holy Catholic Church. The Holy Roman Emperor, the fanatical Ferdinand II (1619–1637), the man next to Hitler responsible for the death, mutilation and misery of the greatest number of human beings, thus made himself responsible for starting the most widespread and the fiercest of all religious wars which, during the next thirty years, reduced much of Europe to a shambles.

From now onwards Germany and Bohemia were devastated, mostly by foreign mercenary troops, with no other interest than to kill and pillage. Thence the war spread until every state from the Carpathians to the Rhine became involved. Each side raised armies composed largely of adventurers, who were out to satisfy their fleshly lusts and steal all they could, being quite indifferent as to the methods they pursued. As the struggle increased in intensity foreign powers joined in, Denmark and Sweden, to save the Protestant cause, and France to prevent the hated Hapsburgs from coming off victorious.

The Austrian imperial forces under the Count of Tilly, which included the Lutherans of Saxony, who hated the Calvinists just as much as they did the Roman Catholics, advanced into Bohemia and routed the army of Frederick (1620) near Prague. Frederick escaped to Holland, but many of his supporters, who were not so fortunate, were executed, large tracts of land were confiscated, heavy fines imposed, and thousands exiled. The devastation that went on in Bohemia for thirty years can better be realised when it is remembered that this small country's population was reduced by 2,000,000. The sufferings of Bohemia were, however, shared in like manner by her neighbour Germany, because, not long after the war started, Tilly occupied the Palatinate, the chief stronghold of Calvinism, a large part of which was transferred to Maximilian of Bavaria, the head of the Catholic League. Thus was Protestantism stamped out of Bohemia and the Rhineland.

Now Denmark became involved in the struggle, as their Protestant King Christian, who was also Duke of Holstein, gave the Protestants his support, more for the purpose of obtaining plunder from the Catholics than for the advancement of the Protestant faith, he having his eye on certain bishoprics in which he intended to place his sons. Under his able leader Mansfeld the Protestants struggled on, but, though Sweden also joined them to save the Protestant cause, and then France, to prevent the Hapsburgs from becoming too powerful, their efforts availed little. They were defeated, first by the ruthless Tilly, and then by Wallenstein, a Bohemian noble, one of the outstanding military figures of his age, who by speculation and plunder made a fortune out of war. His great position, wealth and reputation as a soldier, besides his generosity in the loot and licence he allowed his army of thieves, attracted all the scoundrels and adventurers of Europe, so much so that he gathered together a large body of ruffians, whom he paid largely from his own treasury, all being ready and willing to obey his commands.

They plundered and massacred the helpless peasantry, and all who opposed them, so successfully that no one dared to face them, but never did Wallenstein allow his men to disobey his orders. By his great wealth, and capacity as a general, he became the most powerful man in Germany. His soldiers everywhere were undefeated, so much so that for the first time since the Reformation the Emperor was the master of Germany. In 1629 the Emperor Ferdinand II issued the Edict of Restitution, which restored to the Roman Catholic Church all the lands and property seized by the Protestant Church. Though this meant that the vast wealth, formerly owned by two archbishoprics, twelve bishoprics, and numerous monasteries, would be withdrawn from the Protestants, who had in the first place stolen them from the Roman Catholics, they could do nothing but accept their fate.

The great power of Wallenstein, however, raised jealousy amongst his allies, and Maximilian, Duke of Bavaria, who feared him as much as he disliked him, persuaded the Emperor to dismiss him. Thus the Roman Catholics lost their greatest general, who withdrew from the scene in 1630, just as Gustavus Adolphus (1611–1632), King of Sweden, landed in Germany with an army to fight for the Protestant cause.

Gustavus was a devout and zealous Protestant, but he also saw his chance of obtaining control of the Baltic for Sweden, and reducing Roman Catholic Poland to subjection. He realised the danger to Sweden if the imperial troops encroached nearer to his possessions, because he well knew that the aim of the Emperor was to bring all northern Europe, which had become Protestant, within the Roman Catholic fold.

Gustavus, known as the Lion of the North, was an outstanding soldier and, as his army, which contained a large proportion of Scotchmen, was imbued by a fierce religious zeal, the Protestants for the first time had some chance of success. At first none would rally to his help in Germany, because the Protestants there were all cowed by fear. Tilly was ravaging the land, Magdeburg had been captured, and about 30,000 of its 35,000 inhabitants slaughtered. Finally sheer terror forced the Lutheran states of Brandenburg and Saxony to join with Gustavus in self-protection, as they realised that this whirlwind of devastation would overtake them also if they did not do so.

Gustavus, by greater military skill and better trained forces (each man for the first time in history being distinguished from the enemy by wearing green-and-yellow scarves), inflicted a decisive defeat on Tilly near Leipzig in 1631, and thence he marched south to attack the ecclesiastical states on the Danube, meeting with no resistance. Munich, the headquarters of the Catholic League, was captured, and Bavaria occupied. The Emperor in despair now turned for help to Wallenstein, whom he had so recently dismissed, and, after promising him complete power over the army, succeeded in securing his invaluable services. The magnetic power of his name brought thousands of men to his standard, but, on this occasion, their hopes of more plunder were disappointed, as Gustavus was victorious in a fierce and long-drawn-out battle which was fought in 1632 at Lutzen.

The victory was dearly bought, because Gustavus was killed before the battle ended, thus leaving the Protestants without a leader. Wallenstein, without an opponent, was again master of the situation, but he so angered the Emperor and the Roman Catholics by his attempt to secure a peace which would allow Christians, professing three different brands of the same religion, to live in peace and freedom, that he was removed by assassination, the deed being done at the Emperor's bidding by three Irish adventurers.

The Swedes, with no leader, now joined with the rest of the plundering gangs in robbing and massacring the people, until they were eventually rounded up at Nordlingen in 1634 and completely defeated. Again the Lutherans went over to the side of the Emperor and cast off their Swedish allies, but, as everyone was now heartily tired of the struggle, the Peace of Prague, which followed a year later, restored to the Protestants their rights and liberties, together with the lands and buildings they had taken from the Roman Catholic Church, their ownership of these being, however, limited to a period of fifty years.

Everyone now thought that the war was over, and that all could set to and repair the devastation the conflict had caused, but a Roman Catholic cardinal thought otherwise, as he saw an opportunity to seize from the weakness of his enemy every possible advantage. Richelieu, the Prime Minister of Louis XIII, and holder of the coveted Order of the Holy Ghost, now dominates the scene. He cared nothing for the upliftment of humanity, being quite indifferent to human suffering, and he was completely ignorant of everything except power politics, his overmastering passion being the increased prestige of his divinely appointed royal master, the greatness of France, and the destruction of the power then possessed by the Huguenots.

France, now anxious to cripple the Emperor's power, brought Sweden again into the struggle by liberal financial help, and reorganised the German Protestant rabble army, putting Bernard of Weimar at its head. She then declared war on Spain, the Emperor's ally, and so entered the fray with her army under the command of Condé and Turenne. Meanwhile, Torstenson, the Swedish general, had been appointed as successor to Gustavus. Thus the stage was set for a renewal of the struggle, France, Sweden and the German Protestant states being on one side. On the other were Austria, Spain, Roman Catholic Germany and Pope Urban VIII, the pontiff who persecuted Galileo and amassed a fortune of £20,000,000 by selling indulgences and the high offices of the Church.

Behind this new upheaval the powerful figure of Richelieu was always in evidence, plotting and planning so that France would obtain whatever plums the struggle could yield. For fourteen years each side strove for a decisive victory, but, though France defeated the Spanish at Rocroi in 1643, and then at Lens, peace was not reached until 1648, when the Peace of Westphalia was signed. This treaty marked the end of the Reformation period, each side remaining undefeated and much as they were before the bloody and devastating conflict began thirty years earlier.

The Roman Catholics had thus not succeeded in exterminating Protestantism, and, though south and west Germany remained Roman Catholic, the north and east continued to be Protestant. The Edict of Restitution was cancelled, and all former ecclesiastical property, to which the Roman Catholics had laid claim, was restored to the Protestants. The Treaty, however, did not establish religious freedom, as the people of each state were expected to accept the beliefs of their ruler, though, as the years passed, toleration very slowly increased, but there was still much suffering in store for those of independent mind.

Attempts were made to effect a reconciliation between the two religious opinions, especially by Gottfried Leibnitz (1646-1716), the distinguished German philosopher and mathematician, but without success. The overthrow of the Stuarts in England, and the establishment of the Protestant succession, finally convinced this man of affairs, and the other Protestant theologians working with this end in view, that a common understanding was now impossible. The reason, though then obscure, is now plain, because here we are at an important fork in the religious road which divided supernatural from natural religion. Though both roads ran close together for the next hundred years, they have tended, slowly but surely, to widen apart, the old road containing those who rely on tradition, ritual and ceremonial to satisfy their religious emotions, and the new road those who prefer to depend on reason and rational thinking to satisfy their more developed minds.

The Thirty Years' War left Germany quite disunited, the land being divided into large and small
states, numbering 343 in all, with their own independent foreign and home policy. It nearly finished
off the Holy Roman Empire, the Hapsburgs now
virtually ceasing to be rulers over the German people,
but they retained Bohemia, where all the trouble
started, and this they turned into a Roman Catholic
dependency.

This historic year of 1648, which brought peace to
a distracted Europe, also brought independence to
two small but gallant countries which for years had
fought for their independence. Spain in that year
recognised the sovereignty of Holland, and Austria
that of Switzerland. The Austrian Empire, now
shorn of its German-speaking subjects, remained
composed of a mixed lot of non-Germanic people.
France, on the other hand, regained the long-disputed
bishoprics of Metz, Toul and Verdun, and all Alsace
which was to remain a bone of contention between
Germany and France up to our own day. Sweden,
with a population of only 1,500,000, became a great
power and master of the Baltic by securing western
Pomerania and the towns of Bremen and Verden,
besides others of lesser importance.

Portugal overthrew the hated Spanish domination,
John Braganza becoming John IV, and thus she again
secured the independence she had lost sixty years
earlier. Spain was left a poor, exhausted, badly
administered country, the victim of the curse of
theological ignorance which afflicts her even to the
present day. Bohemia's population was reduced from
3,000,000 to less than 1,000,000, only 6,000 out of

30,000 villages remaining. Germany became a land of utter destitution, her population being reduced from 20,000,000 to 6,000,000.

The country districts were almost deserted, the populations of the towns much reduced, Berlin's inhabitants having declined from 24,000 to 6,000, while trade and communication were at a standstill. All art, literature and culture vanished, and the people became more like brutes than humans, cannibalism being quite common. Germany, as a force in Europe, had disappeared, and France took the opportunities which now came her way.

This is what war does. War means killing or being killed, destroying or being destroyed, besides waste of wealth, poverty, suffering and misery. Until mankind alters its outlook, and changes its sense of values, the victims of today will become the aggressors of tomorrow, because the course of history makes clear that aggression is not confined only to certain nations and not to others. Has the time not come for the human race to cease glorifying war, and, instead, devote its energies only to construction and the prolongation of life? Let us cease having our lives determined by the greatest of all gambles. Let us cease hanging up flags in churches, and elsewhere, which were captured in war; let the priests bless no more regimental flags and battleships; let the race end the display of all these time-honoured war trophies, and wipe the hateful thing from off our minds. In place of war let us make sure of the success of the United Nations Charter for the furtherance of peace, trade and international goodwill amongst all the nations of earth.

No one nation can do this, as the conversion from insanity to sanity must be world-wide. No one nation can cease honouring its soldiers who have fought for their country, especially those who have shown superb courage and self-sacrifice, because both victims and aggressors know what they suffered and endured on behalf of their native land. Let us, however, close that chapter and open a new one, wherein we cease thinking in terms of national honour and national security, considering ourselves in future as world citizens, and as being one because we all belong to the human race. Only then will it be possible to cease honouring the heroes of war, the products of that which is evil, even though individually each one displays courage and fortitude well deserving of admiration and gratitude. Although these noble qualities emerge from what is wicked, there is no virtue for that reason in continuing that which is evil, because those who display these outstanding accomplishments should be directing them for the good of humanity and not for its destruction.

Let us become really humane instead of being only human, and honour instead the real heroes, those whose deeds and thoughts advance the race still further from its animal ancestors. Let our gratitude go out to those who show courage, endurance and perseverance in achieving those things which make life happier, fuller and easier, and raise our minds to a higher level of thought. When the human race erects statues only to the outstanding men and women who have relieved suffering, to those who have brought knowledge to mankind and broken the chains of mental bondage, to the statesmen who have guarded our freedom and improved our social conditions, and to all who have added to our comfort and happiness, we shall have attained to wisdom and understanding, but not until then.

The power of leadership, which some men possess, has had a profound effect on history, and has brought both happiness and misery to mankind, the people readily following a strong character without much thought as to where he led them. How important it is that increased discernment should be shown in the future, and that by more independent critical thinking the leader be always curtailed in his powers, and never, as has happened in the past, be allowed to carry his followers forward to their impoverishment.

Increased education should some day stimulate more individualism, and less reliance on leaders, who would then come to know that only by doing what is right will they be followed, because the people, then always critical of their deeds, and with a developed ethical conscience, will have no need of them unless they keep to the straight path. With these thoughts in mind we shall now see how France fared under the leadership of three outstanding men.

(2) France Becomes the Dominant Power in Europe.

During the first half of the Thirty Years' War, civil war and a state of complete confusion prevailed in France. The States-General was moribund, and, though it assembled in 1614, it did not meet again until 1789 on the eve of the Revolution. Henry IV, better known as Henry of Navarre, was murdered in

1610, leaving a boy of nine as his successor. This child became Louis XIII (1610–1643), but, until he came of age, his mother Marie de Medici acted as Regent. Not until 1624 did affairs in France improve, and the change came about when Cardinal Richelieu (1624–1642) became chief minister of state, to remain until his death the most outstanding and influential figure of the 17th century.

Like Wolsey, in the time of Henry VIII, he devoted himself wholeheartedly to the advancement of the throne and the greatness of his country. He was a devout orthodox Catholic, but France always came first and his religion second. Because of this he was detested by the Roman Catholic hierarchy in Rome. To further the interests of France he supported the Protestants in the Thirty Years' War, but he was just as ready to turn against them if this conformed to his policy. It suited Richelieu on that occasion to support the Protestants, and it was he, a Roman Catholic cardinal, who enabled Protestantism to become firmly established and unassailable. France, he saw, could not be supreme in Europe so long as Austria and Spain were united and strong, and he made use of the great religious conflict, then waging in Germany, to strike a blow for France against her rivals.

Though weak in body he was strong in will, and his ferocious personality made the greatest tremble. His knowledge of the politics of Europe was profound, and, though quite unscrupulous, he was one of the greatest politicians and diplomatists in the annals of France. He was quite tolerant of the different beliefs of his time, but he was determined to curb the power given to the French Protestants. Under the Edict of Nantes they had the right to control the garrisons of certain towns, and to hold synods which had become independent parliaments. This gravely interfered with the authority of the King, and, to break this power, he went personally in charge of a force against La Rochelle in 1627, the chief Protestant stronghold, where the Protestants were holding out against the abolition of these excessive privileges.

The Protestants, or Huguenots, the nickname Calvinists received in France, asked England for help, but this, when sent, was beaten back and starvation forced the besieged garrison to surrender. By 1629 all the other Protestant garrisons had surrendered, and then Richelieu gave them, by the Peace of Alais, all the religious liberty the Edict of Nantes had secured for them, but no power to maintain garrisons of their own. He treated the nobles in the same thorough way, and during his long term of office he was for ever fighting to curb their claims and power.

His life was in constant danger, plots and intrigues being continually hatched against him, but, in spite of the hatred of those whose vested interests he was for ever attacking, he retained his authority and the confidence of the King. To achieve his ends he ruthlessly executed all who stood in his path, even when necessary blowing up and destroying the nobles' strongholds. He put an end to duelling, 7,000 men in Europe having been killed over the previous twenty years by this method of private warfare. Then men, who thus settled their differences, were considered to be heroes, but, as we have developed mentally since those days, we now think differently. Still further mental development will some day make everyone change their opinions about those who take part in war.

Instead of allowing the nobles to govern their districts he appointed middle-class officials, responsible only to the King, who were given the title of Intendants. Only they had the power to raise armed forces for the Crown, collect taxes and administer the law, a method which worked so well that it continued until the Revolution. All representative government was abolished, the States-General ignored, and, in its place, Richelieu called together, from time to time, the leading men whose function was only to give advice which the King was in no way bound to accept.

The King governed his realm by means of a council, which was divided into separate departments, each having its duties to perform, a method that continued until the Revolution. So it was that France, from now onwards, until the time came when this great upheaval overthrew the monarchy, was governed by the King and his ministers, the earlier more representative system being scrapped. When the people are uneducated, democratic government is impossible, and, though it may conflict with our present-day outlook to read of kings having everything in their own hands, no other method in those days was possible, political decrees and ecclesiastical dogma being the only means of managing a multitude having the minds of children.

The evolution from the tribe stage to the nation, composed of an educated intelligent population, who can fittingly use a vote, was slow and uncertain. Until the people rose to this mental level someone had to make the decisions. When the King had not the power, nor the capacity, to do so, civil war and chaos followed, because the ignorant mob just did the bidding of whichever man they looked upon as their lord and master. Ignorance is always to be found at the root of mankind's troubles and sorrows, and nowhere is this more apparent than in national organisation and direction.

The people, now that they are being educated, must try and remedy the troubles which the dictators have failed to solve. Surely some day they will find a way to improve on the past policy of British and European statesmen, which has been directed towards crippling any European nation they feared was becoming powerful. Britain, for her own safety, has led this policy, as, since the 16th century, she has feared a too-powerful Spain, then a too-powerful France, and then a too-powerful Russia. France likewise wished no continental rival, and pursued the policy up to the 19th century of keeping the German states disunited, the British, on the other hand, helping them to attain unity so as to be a check on France. One war has followed after another in consequence of this attempt to maintain the balance of power, and what we have so bitterly experienced in our time was likewise happening in the 17th century, France being then Britain's enemy, and not Germany.

Richelieu's foreign policy was just as bold as were his efforts at home, and his political career was largely occupied in weakening the power of Austria and Spain now that Germany was down and out. He supported Gustavus Adolphus and the German Protestants more to weaken his enemies than to save Protestantism, and, while the Swedish army attacked the Roman Catholics in Poland on the east, France attacked them in Spain

on the west. When, at first, the French were unsuccessful, Richelieu plotted with Portugal to create
civil war in Spain, and this brought about internal
chaos for many years. However, this outstanding
man did not live to see the end of his schemes, as he
died in 1642, his royal master, whom he had served so
well, following him into the beyond a year later.

Louis XIV (1643–1715) was only a child of five
when his father died, and his mother Anne, who before
her marriage was the Infanta of Spain, became Regent.
She appointed Cardinal Mazarin (1643–1661), as her
chief minister, a milder but more subtle and cunning
man than his predecessor, and many believed that she
married him secretly. During his term of office the
Thirty Years' War came to an end with the Peace of
Westphalia, which was his greatest triumph. He, like
his predecessor, was at constant warfare with the
nobles, who, taking advantage of the Regency, tried
to regain their lost privileges. France, financially, was
in a chaotic condition, the nobles demanding a reduction of the heavy taxation, and the people some
form of parliamentary government. What are called
the Fronde rebellions, under the direction of the Prince
of Condé and Paul de Gondi, followed, to bring
about Mazarin's retirement, and he did not return to
power until the royal authority had been restored.

France still remained at war with Spain, because
the Peace of Westphalia only related to Germany, but
she could not obtain a decisive victory. Both countries
asked for English aid, and Cromwell, in 1657, decided
to help France against Spain in the hope of securing the
Spanish colonies. English troops were landed in
France, where, in the Battle of the Dunes, they and the

French engaged the Spanish near Dunkirk, to inflict upon them a decisive defeat. England, for her help, received Dunkirk from the French, and the Treaty of the Pyrenees which followed gave France additional territory in the south, besides a great increase in her power and prestige. Germany, Austria, and now Spain, had fallen within the past ten years from their previous powerful positions, and the time had come, thought Mazarin, for a more enduring peace between Spain and France.

A marriage was therefore arranged between Louis XIV and the Spanish princess Maria Theresa. The marriage contract renounced all claims by France to Spanish territory to which she was heiress, on payment by Spain of a large dowry in cash. Spain either could not or would not pay, and this default brought about a fresh war, as we shall discover later on. Mazarin, who accumulated an immense fortune and had several illegitimate children, died in the year following this marriage, which was considered to be his great diplomatic triumph, and this made it possible for Louis to take over the powerful and rich heritage his great minister had left to him. For the next fifty-four years he ruled France alone. No Richelieu nor Mazarin helped him to guide the affairs of state, as he was convinced that God had delivered the kingdom into his keeping to curb the nobles, destroy Protestantism, and raise his country to the pinnacle of fame.

For seventy-two years this laborious unbalanced man was King of France, the longest reign of any monarch in Europe. All went well at first, a new stern discipline took the place of the past more carefree life the people had lived, but, as the years passed, disaster followed disaster, to end, after forty years of warfare, in France becoming a bloodless corpse. Louis had great military ambitions, considerable diplomatic skill, and a thorough knowledge of European politics. With his grace, dignity, and handsome appearance, he fitted in with the position he was born to fill, the most powerful monarchy that Europe had so far ever known, but, like most of his contemporaries, he was neither honest nor moral. His court was magnificent, and its brilliance dazzled every other nation into believing that only now had France discovered the right and proper way of government. Alone in England a form of parliamentary government still existed, but few believed that this would ultimately triumph and replace unlimited monarchy.

Kings, like other people, are only human, and a one-man government may succeed if the monarch is himself a great and wise statesman, but how few there have been who filled this role, the great majority being weaklings or despots, who ruled for their own ends, and not for the good of the people. It is so easy, when all-powerful, to think only of oneself and not of others. Government by the people, and for the people, has now been proved to be the best method so far discovered by an intelligent and educated community, but the inhabitants of France in those days were neither educated nor intelligent, and so they obtained the form of government for which they were mentally fitted.

Then the idea that the people of any country could govern themselves was looked upon as quite fantastic, just as ridiculous as we today would consider the possibility of a school being run by the children

without masters. In the 17th century the people of
France did not even expect their country to be run
for their own benefit, but for the glory of the monarch.
When the Duke of Burgundy, during the reign of
Louis XIV, put forward the strange suggestion that
the King existed for the good of the people, and not
the people for the good of the King, the servile courtier
to whom he made it was "delighted with the bene-
volence of the saying, but startled by its novelty, and
terrified by its boldness".

Equally strange in those days was the idea that one
nation owed another country any moral right. The
conception of law embraced only the nation, but not
the rest of mankind, and when a far-seeing Dutchman,
Huig van Groot, one of the most outstanding men of
the 17th century, produced a book *De Jure Belli et
Pacis* in the year 1625, envisaging a system of international law, combined with the suggestion of a league
of European nations to work together and keep the
peace, he put forward a proposition which was so
novel as to be incapable of being understood.

Yet he was not the first to make such a proposal,
the honour for this sensible and humane idea being
due to the wise and benevolent Henry IV of France,
who, shortly before he was murdered in 1610, proposed a European League of Nations, a Pacific
Republic as it was called, each nation being represented on a central council whose purpose was to
prevent war and maintain the peace of Europe. Thus
these two really great men laid the seed that some day
may grow into a strong and healthy plant, one which
in our day is beginning to show its strength, because
we now discriminate between just and unjust wars, a

thing which was not done until towards the end of last century.

The people during the 17th century were down-trodden and quite ignorant, only a small minority being able to read and write. The men who rose to eminence in France were few and quite exceptional, such as the three great dramatists Molière, Racine and Corneille. Like Shakespeare, Molière was a man who stands out as sublimely tolerant in an intolerant age. He had to contend against blind prejudice and cruel persecution because of his unorthodox opinions, his body being denied a decent burial when he died. Thus was he persecuted even unto death, because he kept to what was true and honest, never fearing to denounce and ridicule the prevailing wickedness, intolerance, folly and ignorance of his age.

Descartes, who was not permitted to publish his writings in France, and Pascal, were famous philosophers, Fénelon and Bossuet being outstanding theologians. Vauban was the most distinguished soldier-engineer of his time, whose genius was in great demand for warfare purposes. The Prince of Condé, better known as Condé the Great, and the Viscount of Turenne, who distinguished themselves in the Thirty Years' War, were the outstanding military leaders whose skill few in Europe could rival, and the army was well served by the Marquis of Louvois, the minister for war, who was unrivalled for his ability in equipping the troops.

By far the greatest French statesman of the century was Jean Colbert (1619–1683), the exceptionally able and energetic finance minister, who straightened out the country's tangled finances and put them on a sound but not equitable basis. He reformed the law, built a large navy, imposed an import tariff on goods manufactured abroad, encouraged colonial development, envisaging a vast French empire throughout the world, and founded trading companies to increase exports.

Nevertheless this brilliant man suffered from the prevailing delusion that only by destroying the ships and trade of other nations could the commerce of France increase. The ignorance of economics in those days was pitiful, and, though Colbert encouraged the building of ships, and the construction of canals and roads, the foundation of wealth was not understood. Wealth was then believed to consist of gold, and to be strictly limited, it not being realised that this is a false conception, and that wealth is determined by productive capacity, being potentially limitless, enough being available for everyone to secure comfort, luxuries, and all the bounties stored up by nature, if only intelligence is mingled with our labour.

Louis XIV, like many other dictators, could not rest with what had been accomplished, and, at the death of Philip IV of Spain (1665), he claimed Maria Teresa's share of the Spanish Netherlands. This he had renounced in his marriage contract in exchange for a dowry of cash down, but, as the cash had never been paid, he now felt free to claim his wife's inheritance. Spain refused and war followed, the Spanish Netherlands, now called Belgium, being quickly overrun by the French. England, Holland and Sweden, realising that this was but a step to further aggression, just as Great Britain did when Germany invaded Belgium in 1914, combined, and Louis withdrew and returned most of his conquests to Spain.

Then it was that Charles II of England secretly betrayed his own country and sided with France, as will be told in the next section.

Louis now bided his time, and when the opportunity came, in 1672, he attacked Holland, which he disliked because (1) it was a republic, (2) the Dutch were formidable trade rivals, (3) it was an asylum for religious and political exiles from France, and lastly, books were being published there which attacked his policy and character. William of Orange, who became William III of England, defended his country by cutting the dykes, and, by skilful diplomacy, secured the help of Spain, his country's old enemy, besides that of Brandenburg, and England who by then had discovered her king's treachery. France was much too strong to be resisted, and, when peace was made in 1678 at Nijmegen, she secured from Spain and Holland considerable territorial additions. With no power able to withstand him, Louis then claimed and secured overlordship of Alsace, including Strassburg, occupying Luxemburg and a portion of northern Italy.

Here we find Louis at the height of his power, the first half of his reign being a series of triumphs. It was, moreover, an age when Europe began to taste the fruits of a higher civilisation. In Holland celebrated artists flourished, in Westminster Abbey large congregations had their emotions roused by the beauty of Purcell's music, and in Italy Stradivari produced the finest violin. All kinds of useful instruments were invented, and table cutlery took the place of one's fingers. Watches, clocks, thermometers, barometers, telescopes, microscopes, wax candles and street lighting, from being novelties became necessities as the 17th century drew to a close. Newspapers, marine insurance, and cheap letter delivery now made their appearance, and champagne, tea and coffee took the place of home-brewed ale.

Yet it was a century of almost continuous war and religious persecution. Religion everywhere played a great part in the life of the people, and nowhere was it more in evidence than at the court of the dissolute Louis XIV, where corruption, intrigue, gaiety, luxury and licentiousness flourished while the poor downtrodden peasantry toiled wearily to make a bare existence. No one was more devout than the King, and, though the Pope had been told that his interference in French affairs would never be tolerated, Louis hated heresy with a fanatical hatred, and the latter part of his reign was stained by two bitter religious persecutions. One man in every fifty was a priest or a monk, and they acted for Louis as did the gestapo in Germany for Hitler, many an innocent victim being liquidated on suspicion of heresy.

With the support of the Holy See Louis stamped out Jansenism, named after Jansen, Bishop of Ypres. His theological treatise published in 1640 started a movement in the Roman Catholic Church for the purpose of revising the orthodox beliefs on the subject of salvation, predestination and grace, about which there was such a controversy between Augustine and Pelagius in the 5th century. Pascal, and other eminent men, such as Arnauld and Racine, anxious for the return of religion to the simplicity of the Apostolic Church, and disgusted with the depravity of ecclesiastical Christianity, besides the open wickedness of professing Christians, joined the movement, which was never anti-Roman Catholic nor directed against the Church.

The Pope, Innocent XI, and the King were, however, determined on its destruction, and, as they were all-powerful, its adherents were brutally liquidated, their literature publicly burned, and the reform movement faded away, all that its adherents have left to us being the epithet "Jesuitical", invented by Pascal to denote anything to do with fraud, cunning and deceit.

There still remained, however, the despised Huguenots, two million of them pursuing this unorthodox form of worship, and, where they were in the majority, exercising a bitter antagonism towards their Roman Catholic neighbours, who everywhere looked upon these heretics as servants of the devil. Why, the orthodox argued, could they not adopt a religion that was good enough for the King and his nobles, instead of having one which required black-robed ministers who taught strange precepts? Year after year the Roman Catholic Church authorities petitioned the King for the complete destruction by massacre or banishment of these devout, harmless, and particularly industrious people, whose only crime was their different interpretation of the Bible on certain points of doctrine.

In the end the orthodox secured their object, to the accompaniment of paeans of praise and thanksgiving to God for having delivered his enemies over to receive their just retribution, and Louis rose to the position of a great Christian hero, to be placed alongside the saints of the past. In 1685 he withdrew the Edict of Nantes, thus depriving the Protestants of their religious liberty. Heresy hunts took place throughout the land, and those who could not escape abroad were tortured, imprisoned and killed. Families were broken up, and 700 Protestant places of worship destroyed. A million escaped to England, Holland, Switzerland and Protestant Germany; in fact France lost by exile and massacre about 1,500,000 of her best and most loyal citizens, who, greatly to the benefit of their protectors, brought to their new homes the arts and crafts of which they were the masters. Frederick William, the Elector of Brandenburg, gave some of these refugees land and houses in Berlin, from which time the city grew and prospered.

With Roman Catholicism triumphant, France intellectually sank to lower and still lower levels, because where freedom of thought does not exist there can be no mental progress. From now onwards other influences worked against her, the first being the defeat of the Turks outside the gates of Vienna by the King of Poland in 1683. From now onwards Turkish power in Europe, which embraced what is now Yugo-Slavia, Hungary, Rumania, Bulgaria and Greece, diminished, much to the relief of Austria and the detriment of France, who for long had been their ally for the purpose of encouraging them to encroach on Austria and keep her from becoming too powerful. When the Turks were finally driven from Hungary they, France's only friends in Europe, were too crippled to be of any further assistance to her, and, with Austria free from this long-standing menace, a new turn was given to the kaleidoscope of European politics.

The Revolution in England (1688), which turned out the Roman Catholic James II, was another blow to France, because William of Orange, a Protestant, became King of Great Britain and Ireland as William III. He was no lover of France, and the British, who had disposed of one tyrant, did not look with favour on the tyranny which was going on across the Channel, especially as Louis had encouraged James II in his reactionary rule. William III, when he felt his throne in Britain to be secure, set to work to build up a European alliance against France, and, with great diplomatic skill, and the strength of the combined British and Dutch fleets behind him, which outnumbered that of France, he finally succeeded.

The turning point in Louis's victorious career had come at last when first Holland, and then Spain, Brandenburg, Denmark and Sweden joined in the union. The fugitive James II had meantime gone over to Ireland to raise an army to win back his throne, but, though many Irish out of hatred to Britain rallied round him, he was defeated at the Battle of the Boyne in 1690, and Ireland was once again subdued.

For no other reason than fear of France, the allies went to war against her, and this policy of knocking down any nation in Europe which threatened the independence of any of the others has continued to our own times, to become known as the policy of maintaining the Balance of Power. William III and his allies, however, found France to be more powerful than they expected, her frontiers being strongly defended, thanks to the work of Vauban.

In 1690, off Beachy Head, the French fleet defeated the combined British and Dutch navies, but two years later, in the Battle of La Hogue, France was defeated, and her ships so depleted that Britain felt safe against invasion. In the Netherlands, that battleground of Europe, combat after combat took place for over nine years, with France generally the victor, but finance brought the war to an end, as she became bankrupt. At the Peace of Ryswick, in 1697, France conceded some of her former gains, recognised William as King of England, and Louis promised never again to support the Stuart cause. She retained Alsace and Strassburg, and still remained the greatest military power in Europe, but her aim at European domination had suffered a severe setback.

So far France had been victorious in all her conflicts, but the real trial of strength was still to come. An extraordinary situation now loomed before the statesmen of Europe. In a small way it is one which happens every day when someone with money is about to die. All the relatives wonder how his will will determine the distribution of his wealth. At the end of the 17th century the governments of Europe were faced with this question on a world-wide scale, as a man was about to die who owned a great part of the earth.

Such was the practice of those days, that the king owned all the territory over which he ruled, and could dispose of it as he willed. Just as if the King of Great Britain could will the British Empire to whom he pleased. The people of those times, having no say in their own government, accepted this as the right and proper way to dispose of countries and the people who lived in them. Consequently, the problem facing European statesmen at the period we are considering was not new, but unusual, because of the great territories and wealth about to change hands.

What was to become of the Spanish Empire

consisting of Spain, much of Italy, Sicily, Sardinia, the Balearic Islands, the Spanish Netherlands, the Philippines, the Canary Islands, Cuba, Mexico, Florida, California, Panama, and all South America except Brazil? The disposal of this vast estate was at the discretion of a childless imbecile Charles II (1665–1700), now seen to be nearing his end, and whose only confidant was his Jesuit confessor. One of three princes had the prospect of receiving it all, or having it divided between them. These were Philip, Duke of Anjou, who was the grandson of Louis XIV; Charles, the second son of Leopold I of Austria; and Joseph Ferdinand, the Elector of Bavaria, who was a nephew of Charles II of Spain.

As this was an international problem of outstanding importance, England, France and Holland drew up a Treaty of Partition, but nothing came of it because Joseph Ferdinand of Bavaria died. This made a difficult problem almost insoluble, because Austria and Spain now announced that they would never agree to the Spanish Empire being divided. So nothing was done, and when Charles II died in 1700 it was found that his entire empire was left to Philip of Anjou, on the understanding that if he did not take the lot it was to go to Charles of Austria.

Louis XIV was now faced with agreeing to his grandson's acceptance of this great inheritance, or seeing it pass over to Austria, his bitter enemy, and no one can blame him for accepting these further heavy responsibilities. Philip of Anjou therefore became ruler of Spain and her empire as Philip V, and this led in 1702 to the War of the Spanish succession, not because Philip became King of Spain, but because

Louis now became both arrogant and aggressive, and acted as if France had taken over Spain and her empire. Once again the Netherlands seemed destined for France, and England shivered at the prospect.

To protect themselves, England, Austria and Holland were brought together into an alliance by William III of England, these countries considering themselves to be in the greatest danger. Holland was particularly so, as the Spanish Netherlands, so close to her, contained well-garrisoned and strongly fortified towns, such as Namur, Mons, Charleroi, Nieuport, Ostend and other places, names which have such a familiar ring to us all.

Both Britain and Holland, which had important trade connections with Spain and her possessions, feared that with France and Spain united they would be excluded from, or seriously handicapped in, these valuable trading centres, and Louis would give no guarantee to the contrary. Austria, on the other hand, did not want France in those parts of Italy and Sicily, now controlled by Spain, to which objection both Britain and Holland agreed, as they did not wish France to dominate the Mediterranean.

Consequently Britain, Holland and Austria entered into an agreement that (1) France and Spain were not to be allowed to unite their thrones, (2) all the commercial privileges which they enjoyed under Charles II of Spain were to be continued, (3) France was to be prevented from seizing the Spanish possessions, (4) the allies were to take possession of the Spanish Netherlands, and (5) the States of Milan, Naples and Sicily were to be taken by Austria. They had no objection to Philip becoming King of Spain, but, as

Louis would give no guarantee that this would end the problem, they were prepared to fight rather than see their fears realised.

Britain was not anxious for another war, and, if Louis had not made the first move, the alliance might never have become active. However, in the same month as his grandson entered Madrid as King of Spain, Louis replaced the Spanish garrisons in the Spanish Netherlands with French troops, and, seven months later, recognised the son of the exiled James II as King of Great Britain. This last act definitely settled British opinion, which was undecided even after the occupation by French troops of the Spanish Netherlands. Parliament voted William III the men and the money he required for the war, but he died (1702) two months before the declaration was made, leaving John Churchill, Duke of Marlborough (1650–1722), a brilliant but quite unscrupulous man, to mobilise and direct the army which was placed under his command. As a soldier he was as great as either Wellington or Cromwell, but as a statesman he surpassed them both.

Bavaria joined up with France and gave what help she could, but Spain, to begin with, did little. On the other side there was close co-operation between the allies, because Marlborough and Prince Eugène, the representative of the Emperor Leopold I, worked together in close understanding and friendship. The allies had complete control of the sea, and the war was carried on (1) in the Netherlands, where the British and Dutch attacked the Spanish possessions; (2) in Italy, where the Austrians ejected the French and Spaniards from Milan and other districts; (3) in

Bavaria, which acted as a barrier between the British and Dutch and the Austrians; (4) in Spain, and (5) in Cevennes, in south-eastern France. There, in Cevennes, the Protestants, taking advantage of the occasion, rose in insurrection against their Roman Catholic oppressors, and for a time France could do nothing to suppress the rising.

Many battles were fought, the most decisive being Blenheim in 1704, when half the French army, and Tallard its commander, were taken prisoners by the combined efforts of the British and Austrians. This great victory foiled the French advance on Vienna, and enabled the two allied armies, which had been separated by Bavaria, to join hands. Bavaria now ceased to count, and the long-held widespread idea that the French were invincible was shattered. The Spanish Netherlands, as the result of the Battle of Ramillies in 1706 and the Battle of Oudenarde in 1708, were now occupied by the British, and the final bloody conflict at Malplaquet in 1709, which cost Britain 20,000 men, completed Marlborough's great military achievements, because Louis sued for peace when the British made ready to march on Paris.

Austria had turned the French and Spanish out of Italy, the British had captured Gibraltar in 1704, and the Archduke of Austria had entered Madrid in 1706 to be proclaimed King Charles III of Spain. This event aroused the Spanish national spirit, and, after inflicting defeats on the allies, they expelled them from their territories and set Philip V once more on the throne, Barcelona and Gibraltar being all that the allies could retain.

By now the British were tired of this long bloody

war, which had cost them £50,000,000, and the Whig party, which had been responsible for its commencement and for its victorious conclusion, were turned out of office in 1710. Whenever the Tories obtained power they commenced peace negotiations, and Britain withdrew from further participation. Austria, thus isolated, was defeated at Denain, and she likewise agreed to peace negotiations. The Peace of Utrecht in 1713 completed Britain's part in the conflict, and Austria a year later made peace at Rastadt, thus bringing to an end eleven years of destruction and bloodshed, and the Spanish domination over the Netherlands and Italy.

Philip V, who founded the Spanish Bourbon dynasty, remained King of Spain and the Spanish possessions beyond the sea, on the understanding that the crowns of France and Spain would never be united. The Spanish Netherlands became the Austrian Netherlands, to become independent Belgium in 1790, this independence being guaranteed between 1831 and 1832 by France, Britain, Austria, Prussia and Russia, a treaty which was to become "a scrap of paper" to the Germans in 1914. Savoy secured Sicily, while Austria obtained the Duchy of Milan, the Kingdom of Naples and Sardinia, her rule being no less bitterly resented than was that of Spain. This subjection to foreign domination continued until the Italian War of Independence, when, in 1870, all Italy regained the sovereignty and freedom lost more than fourteen hundred years earlier when the Roman Empire collapsed.

Britain, now the greatest sea power, retained Gibraltar and Port Mahon in Minorca, as well as the recognition of her treasured and lucrative trade of catching negroes in Africa and selling them in the West Indies, besides the right to send a trading ship once a year to the Spanish colonies, a privilege which she extended by various means. France recognised the Protestant succession in Britain, expelled the Pretender, and ceded to Britain Nova Scotia, the Hudson Bay Territory, and other regions to which reference will be made later on. Battles certainly decide the fate of nations, and war, like a knife, is for ever carving this earth into pieces of different size to which we give various names, always forgetting that the human race is indivisible, having the same desires, feelings and destiny. Only when this is realised, and the people of this earth find a way to devise an unshakable unified international rule, will the destruction, suffering, death and hatred which are caused by war cease, and the blessings of peace come to a distracted world.

France was thoroughly exhausted by the war, her finances were in chaos, her prestige greatly diminished, absolute monarchy discredited, and loyalty to the Crown much weakened. Here we are at the time when the foundation stone of the French Revolution was laid, and Britain's more democratic way of life received greater sympathy from her former critics. They now realised that she had something that was well worth their consideration. So France's leading men began to think and write on the subject of greater freedom and liberty, and some came over to England to study British institutions on the spot.

Louis was now a very old man, and he had to bear not only the criticism of his people, but experience the death of his eldest son, then his eldest grandson, and lastly his great-grandson, which meant that his heir was a child of two years of age. He appointed a Council of Regency to act after his death, which occurred in 1715, but it never functioned for reasons to be related further on.

Meantime we must turn our attention elsewhere, and leave France for the present. The death of Louis marked the end of an epoch, in which France led Europe in both peace and war. It was in many respects the most important period of her history, but now that the glamour of it all had gone she quickly sank from her high position as the first power in Europe, her place being taken more and more by Great Britain, whose history must now be brought up to date from the time we left it at the death of Elizabeth.

(3) PARLIAMENT GRADUALLY REPLACES ABSOLUTE MONARCHY IN BRITAIN.

When the 17th century opened, the monarch in Britain had almost absolute power, but, as the result of the experience gained during the intervening years, the 18th century commenced with these powers largely taken over by Parliament. The 17th century for Britain was a time of struggle for political and religious emancipation, one which produced not only many great men, but also civil war and much cruelty and persecution before a certain measure of liberty and freedom of thought was secured.

So we take up our tale when James I (1603–1625), accompanied by a retinue of courtiers and adventurers, came from Edinburgh to London to rule Great Britain with very definite opinions about the rights of sovereigns. For his time he knew somewhat more than did most kings, but he greatly lacked wisdom, judgment and human sympathy, being dubbed by Henry of Navarre "The wisest fool in Christendom". Both in his home and foreign policy, and by his reckless extravagance, he not only angered his subjects but dismayed his chief minister, Sir Robert Cecil, who was a statesman. Only the Episcopalians would accept his dictum that he had been appointed by God to rule, and that to God only was he responsible. The outstanding Tudors doubtless thought the same, but they were more tactful about it, and, beside this, they gave some evidence of superior mentality and convinced the people of their ability.

Now, however, when a blundering egotist took up the divine role, conflict with Parliament was inevitable, to continue throughout the reigns which followed until the Revolution of 1688. During this period of Stuart rule, Parliament and the King were in open conflict on this question of divine kingship, to end in the victory for Parliament, and the final defeat of an idea first of all brought to Europe from the East by Alexander the Great.

Louis XIV dazzled the later Stuarts with his belief in divine majesty, and they looked upon him as the ideal monarch who was demonstrating how a nation should be governed. Parliament, James declared, was there to advise him but not to instruct him. Parliament could levy taxes but the King had the same right. Parliament had not the right to criticise, dismiss, or punish the ministers of the Crown.

Throughout his reign James and Parliament fought each other, not only on these vital principles but on his foreign policy, as he was set on being friends with Spain and marrying his son Charles to a Spanish princess.

To this plan Parliament would never agree, and before the end of his reign he saw his mistake. He was just as obstinate over the help Parliament wished to send to the Protestants in Germany, then engaged in the Thirty Years' War. Frederick, the Elector of the Palatinate, who was the husband of Elizabeth, daughter of James, asked for British help, but this James refused because he did not wish to offend Spain, and only towards the end of his reign, when he reversed his policy, were 12,000 men sent to help his son-in-law.

James, as we learned in the previous chapter, was a strong upholder of Episcopacy, and had no sympathy for the Roman Catholics, Puritans or Presbyterians. Some Roman Catholics, finding that he would not withdraw the penal laws against them, tried to blow him up when he attended Parliament in 1605. This attempt, carried out by Guy Fawkes and Robert Catesby, and known as the Gunpowder Plot, was discovered, the conspirators executed, and severe laws passed against the Roman Catholics, who were looked upon as traitors.

No Roman Catholic could now become a doctor, a lawyer, or an officer in the army or navy. The Puritans, who objected to the Church of England being governed by bishops appointed by the King, adopted more peaceful methods, as, when James informed them that he would "harry them out of the land", a number of them set sail for America in the *Mayflower* in 1620. There they hoped to find religious liberty, only to become as intolerant in their puritanical opinions as were the Episcopalians they had left at home, anyone not a member of the Puritan Church being excluded from the franchise.

The Presbyterians were treated by James in the same uncompromising way. "No bishop, no king," James declared, as "presbytery agreeth as well with monarchy as God and the Devil", and there was much more behind that remark than one imagines. The King appointed the bishops, and the bishops the priests, who from the pulpit every Sunday guided the thoughts of the people. Loyal bishops and priests meant a loyal people, and this powerful influence of the pulpit James, like Elizabeth before him, fully realised. Consequently Episcopacy was made the national form of worship in Scotland, the Presbyterian Church being displaced, though its General Assembly, Synods, and gatherings were permitted. Thus was laid the seed for a devastating persecution of the Presbyterians in the second half of the century, one which has left bitter memories even to this day.

Another seed he planted, which grew tares, was the confiscation of a large part of Ulster from the Irish Roman Catholics, and the settling thereon of English and Scottish Protestants, who, by their hatred of the Irish Roman Catholics, made all attempts to solve the Irish problem on statesmanlike lines impossible. Otherwise Home Rule for Ireland might have been practicable, and if so all Ireland might then have become a satisfied member of the British Commonwealth, instead of being divided into a minority of loyal

Protestants in the north and bitter antagonistic Roman Catholics in the south. James was wiser in his attempt to join the parliaments of Scotland and England, and remove all trade barriers between the two countries, but, as national prejudice was still strong, neither Parliament would agree to the union.

A great influence on British history was an improved translation of the Bible, in the form of the Authorised Version of 1611,[1] to which James gave his support, as therein he found the Eastern idea of the divine right of kings receiving the benediction of no less an authority than Jehovah. No higher could the King look in support of his own opinions, and he consequently had this holy book dedicated to himself as "the most High and Mighty Prince by the Grace of God, King of Great Britain, France and Ireland". Then follows about him the most ridiculous and fantastic panegyric in the English language, which is as false as is the statement that he is King of France. From that time to the present day this blatant lie has been published on the first page of the holy book, a fact which reveals the entire lack of truth and honesty in the Christian conscience.

In this age the belief in witchcraft reached its height, James being its chief supporter, even going so far as to write a book to explain how witches were to be recognised and treated. Then it was that a man in Scotland was burned to death because he was accused of producing a storm at sea for the purpose of drowning

[1] In 1881 a new translation of the Bible was made which revealed 36,191 mistakes in the version of 1611, still looked upon by many Protestant Christians as infallible and the Word of God. The Protestants overthrew the infallible Church and put in its place an infallible book.

one of the royal family; a woman was tried before Sir Matthew Hale, one of the most celebrated lawyers of the day, and found guilty of acting as a nurse to demons and causing children to vomit crooked pins. For this crime she also was burned to death. Harmless men and women were found guilty of witchcraft if they sank after being thrown into water, or if they were burned when handling hot iron. This superstition was believed from the highest to the lowest everywhere throughout Christendom, the leaders in this warfare against those so-called servants of the devil being the Church authorities. From its inception the Church waged unrelenting war against these harmless people, who, in many cases, were probably endowed with psychic gifts.

Today we call such people mediums, but, up to within the last hundred years, they were regarded with fear and horror. This ignorance was only then dissipated by the discoveries made at Hydesville in New York State, to which further reference will be made in Chapter XV. The psychic occurrences therein mentioned convinced competent investigators that the haunting of a farmer's house was caused by a man who had been murdered there five years previously, and wished to reveal the fact that he still lived and give the name of his murderer.

The two young daughters of the farmer, who were mediumistic, were found to be the channel he used to make his presence known and convey his messages. In Pagan times, and in the Apostolic Church, mediums received much honour and respect, because to the Pagans they were the revealers of the gods, and to the Jesuians they were believed to be the medium used by the Divine Spirit to guide the people until the return of Jesus to earth.

How depraved and degraded religion had become since the days when the ancient Greeks, in imagination, had fraternised with the gods by means of their romantic mythology! The delight and comfort they received from their belief that the handsome cultured benign Apollo, and the fleet-footed sport-loving Hermes, acted as liaison gods between heaven and earth can only be imagined. Religion in those days was what the word means, a binding back again of earth to heaven, and, though childish imagination pictured the men and women of the other world as gods and goddesses, they were generally considered as friendly to mankind, the immortals regarding the mortals as like unto themselves though limited by earth conditions.

The purpose of religion is to give comfort, and at no time did it give more hope and consolation to mankind than in the days when the Greek gods and goddesses were regarded as the friends and helpers of mankind. Then priestcraft had little political influence, but, whenever the priests obtained control, by the introduction of the worship of one of the Eastern saviour-gods, everything changed for the worse. Then religion, which was meant to comfort, was used to frighten the people into doing the bidding of the clergy. So, in Christian times, the mythology which had given such consolation to the Greeks and Romans was banned, heaven becoming a fantastic place far, far away, and an equally absurd hell stood open very, very near.

The closer we get to truth the happier we are in

all walks of life, and the Greeks got nearer to reality in their religion than any other people. To them heaven was very close, within our atmosphere, where lived the gods, the immortals who had once lived on earth, and had desires, frailties and qualities such as we have, their bodies and heavenly abode being real and solid. These beings had no grudge against us mortals, and came amongst us to converse with us as superman to man. That natural belief came about by the Greeks and Romans using mediums as nature intended, because through them is revealed the other world of men and women. These other-world beings were not regarded, as they were in Christian times, as either winged angels or cloven-hoofed devils, but as friends of frail humanity, always ready and willing to give what help they could to us mortals on earth.

Christianity, based on falsehood and error, altered everything for the worse and burlesqued religion, fear being as much its province as comfort, and now in the 17th century we find the climax to all the error, ignorance and folly of the past. Innocent women were regarded as mediums of grotesque devils, ever striving to hurt and torment the human race, while every natural event which we have to strive to over-come, such as illness, disease, storm and earthquake, was attributed to them. Only by their human mediums being destroyed could this devilish influence on earth be thwarted, and the people live in safety.[1] Such was the prevailing belief up to last century.

[1] Witchcraft is condemned in the Bible from beginning to end, the fate of the wizard or witch being death: "Thou shalt not suffer a witch to live" (*Exodus* xxii, 18), and their fate hereafter was hell. (*Galatians* v, 20–21.) So Christians had every reason to believe that in torturing and murdering all endowed with psychic gifts they had the sanction of their god. No other religion has such a terrible record.

In the 17th century trials of witches and wizards were numerous, seventeen people in Lancashire (1634) being tortured and put to death on the evidence of one boy. Between 1645 and 1647 hundreds perished in Suffolk and Essex. In the parish register of Glamis in Scotland the following entry, dated June 1676, exists: "Nae preaching here this Lord's Day, the minister being at Gortachy burning a witch." Volumes would be required to tell of the ignorance, stupidity and fear which led to the abominable cruelties inflicted on these once much-honoured, and at times highly gifted, people, now termed wizards and witches.

All the laws passed against witchcraft were based on the laws of Moses, but in the story entitled "Saul seeketh a witch at Endor", the word "witch" nowhere occurs. The translators added "witch" to the heading, but the text throughout refers to her as a woman, and, from what is there told of her, she was evidently a clairvoyant and clairaudient medium, a woman of noble character, refined and talented, as can be discovered by anyone who reads the story carefully. Such, then, was the mentality of the English translators, their fear of witchcraft being so intense, that this simple story of a psychic experience was made to seem something very dreadful.

Consequently we need not be surprised to learn that of the 250,000 so-called witches who perished during the age of Christian civilisation, at least some 30,000 innocent men and women were either burned, hanged or drowned in England. Greatly to the indignation of many people, Parliament in 1736 repealed the law that all witches must die, the last

victim in Scotland perishing in 1722, in Belgium in
1815 and in Germany in 1836. But for the restraining
influence of the gentry in Britain, who brought about
the repeal of the law, witches in country districts
would have been put to death well on into the 19th
century, so long did the thirst for their blood remain
unquenched amongst the ignorant people in these
parts.

Martin Luther, like everyone else in his time,
believed the most fantastic stories about witches, and
that their children were produced by the devil. He
recommended one woman to drown her child because
its father was the devil, all because what we now call
psychic phenomena occurred in her house. Such is
the prevailing ignorance in our own time on this
subject, that honest mediums are heavily fined, or
given long terms of imprisonment, for exercising their
psychic gifts, and though every attempt has been made
up to the present day to abolish this flagrant injustice,
nothing will induce the British Government to revoke
the Witchcraft and Vagrancy Acts.

So we have not yet finally emerged from the
Theological Age, which so misrepresented the activities of the men and women of the other world, called
angels and devils by the theologians, the consequence
being that we still experience the injustice this ignorance brought to mankind. Half of history is made up
of what has followed from man's theological speculations, which caused him to fear those he called devils,
and woo and cajole imaginary gods for his needs. He
lived in fear of the latter withholding their bounties,
and he feared to die because of what the devils might
do to him hereafter, but today the well-informed

realise that natural causes were, and still are, at the root of every one of his theological beliefs.

Psychic phenomena, or those supernormal things that happen in the presence of a medium, were the cause of every religious belief, of the belief in gods and devils, of all superstition, of the belief in sorcery, besides that most far-reaching of all mental conceptions, the belief in heaven and hell, including all the many weird ideas with which theology has surrounded them. What a conspicuous place all these beliefs have taken in human affairs, and what momentous consequences they have produced!

How simple, however, is the truth. Both good and bad men and women die, and live on as men and women, good and bad, wise and foolish, in another order of vibrations surrounding and interpenetrating the vibrations which we call the earth. Though the good and the bad naturally keep apart, all can, if they wish, adjust themselves to earth vibrations by means of a medium whose etheric body is not so firmly implanted in flesh as is that of most people. By so doing, they can communicate with the people of earth, besides making their presence known in various different ways. Consequently these past inhabitants of earth have been responsible for half the history of mankind, though historians have not yet recognised this potent fact, and so have robbed history of half its meaning. This book, *The Curse of Ignorance*, by making good these vital omissions, may fairly claim to be the forerunner of a new and more scientific presentation of the past story of mankind, thus giving further interest and value to important but overlooked causes which have been responsible for what we do and think today, and the kind of world in which we live.

In the time of James I no one knew anything about psychic science, man's make-up and destiny being a complete mystery, as was likewise the world and universe in which he lived. Eschatology had been quite neglected throughout the Christian era, the theologians having contributed nothing to its solution. Where ignorance reigns there is always folly and often cruelty, which come from fear, and, at the opening of the 17th century, men's minds had only developed sufficiently to wonder whether all that the theologians had taught could be true, and if there were not other paths of knowledge for man to explore.

One of the early pioneers who put science in place of theology was Sir Francis Bacon (1561–1626). He advocated that only by experience and observation could truth be discovered, and prejudice and error removed. He was the forerunner of, and guiding light to, those philosophers and scientists who followed after him, his works *Advancement of Learning*, published in 1605, and *New Atlantis* in 1607, marking a definite break with the past, and heralding the dawn of a new day which would enthrone knowledge in place of ignorance. Bacon became first of all Solicitor-General, then Attorney-General, and finally Chancellor, from which high office he was deposed and imprisoned on the charge of graft and corruption, he, like many of his predecessors, taking bribes which, however, in his case had little influence on the justice of his judgements.

In his book *New Atlantis* he advocated the foundation of a corporate body devoted to the study of science. This idea ultimately materialised in the reign of Charles II, when the Royal Society of London for Scientific Investigation was formed, an event which was to stimulate an outlook on life so revolutionary that the old way of living and thinking was entirely changed. Desirous as Bacon was to further the increase of knowledge, and important as were his works on philosophy, he was very much a product of his time, being even ignorant of things some of his contemporaries knew to be true.

All the same the intense passion of his life was to increase knowledge, but his desire to receive the rays of royal sunshine reached the height of absurdity when he dedicated his book, *Advancement of Learning*, with panegyrical effusiveness, to the superstitious and foolish James I, whom he placed before Marcus Aurelius in wisdom! Many of the things Bacon wrote were stupid, his science was crude, and his poetical verse, which he began to write when over sixty years of age, was not up to Shakespearian standard. Nevertheless there can be no doubt that a long line of thinkers, from his time onwards, have drawn inspiration from him, he being regarded as the originator of the empirical school which relied on experiment and observation in reaching conclusions.

Between 1607 and 1611 Henry Hudson, one of the most daring of explorers, sailed both north-east and north-west to try and find a passage through to Asia, but without success. In 1616, the year in which Shakespeare died, William Baffin likewise unsuccessfully attempted to discover the north-west passage to the East. Two years later Sir Walter Raleigh, a far-seeing man, who laid the foundation of the British Empire, went for a treasure hunt to Spanish Guiana, but had to return home empty-handed as the gold mine he was hoping to find was not discovered.

For thirty years this outstanding man had urged the founding of a British colony there, as a base from which to attack Spanish shipping, but nothing came of it, and England lost her chance to secure a foothold in South America. He died tragically and ingloriously, but it so happened that on this his last voyage he so angered the Spanish, with whom James wished to keep on friendly terms, that on his return home he was executed on an old charge of conspiracy against the King. Raleigh, like every other British seaman of those days, had an intense hatred towards the Spaniards. When endeavouring to find the gold mine, he wiped out an entire village without any provocation, but the days of these deeply devout Elizabethan buccaneers, out to "singe the beard of the King of Spain", were now over, he being the last.

Throughout the reign of James I a steady flow of emigrants, three-quarters of whom died as the result of the voyage, disease, starvation or exposure, left British ports for Virginia, New England and Barbadoes, and these included many banished because of their objection to Episcopacy. Those who remained were imprisoned and persecuted, two Unitarians (a sect which had retained the early Jesuian beliefs) suffering death at the stake in 1612, after which time the hanging of heretics was substituted for burning. Another century, however, was to pass before the evil deeds of the theologians were replaced by the less painful persecution of social ostracism, and meantime the devout James was gathered to his fathers and his son Charles reigned in his stead.

The Anglo-Catholic Charles I (1625–1649) began his reign badly by being ill-advised by his father's favourite, the Duke of Buckingham. Britain's participation in the Thirty Years' War, a year before the death of James, led to war with Spain, and Charles sent a fleet of ninety ships to capture Cadiz, an enterprise which ended in failure, as did also an expedition to relieve the Huguenots in La Rochelle. These two abortive ventures revealed the rottenness and corruption in high quarters, as the badly treated seamen sickened and died in thousands because of the putrid food they were given to eat, those who survived being turned adrift on their return home to live as best they could. Public feeling expressed itself in the assassination of Buckingham in 1628. Not only was he much disliked, but his influence over the King, in the early years of his reign, made Charles equally so, which unpopularity was intensified because his wife, Queen Henrietta, the daughter of Henry IV of France, was a Roman Catholic.

To this unfortunate marriage can be traced some of the causes which led to the Civil War, to her husband's execution, to the religious persecutions during the reigns of Charles II and James II, to the inglorious end of the Stuart dynasty, and to all the misfortunes this change of regime produced. The reactionary Henrietta, with her own personal agent at the Vatican, was an unwise adviser to her husband, and influenced her two sons, Charles and James, in favour of the old orthodox faith now repugnant to the majority of Englishmen, the consequences of which will be unfolded in the pages which follow.

Charles, like his father, was in constant conflict with Parliament, to end in it refusing to vote him money to carry on the State, because it had no control over its ·expenditure. However, when he commenced to imprison without trial everyone who refused to contribute when demanded, the "Petition of Right" was drawn up by two of the leading parliamentarians of the day, Pym and Wentworth. This Bill deprived the King of the right to raise money without the consent of Parliament, or to imprison anyone without just cause, but he continued on his illegal course, quite unaware that he was riding for a fall.

In religion the King was equally dictatorial and intolerant, his principal advisers being priests who occupied important positions at Court and in the affairs of state, much to the distaste of the Puritans, who now had a strong representation in Parliament, and bitterly hated William Laud, Archbishop of Canterbury, the chief supporter of the King's claim to absolute power. Laud, the ambitious son of a Reading tailor, was determined to force everyone to adopt his ritualistic form of worship, and to attend an Anglican church every Sunday, his zeal dividing the Episcopalian Church from this time onwards into what is now called High and Low Church. He, like all the Christian monarchs and high priests of the past, was set on a uniform system of worship, and justified his policy, as did his predecessors, by the words attributed to Jesus:—

And other sheep I have, which are not of this fold; them also I must bring, and they shall hear my voice, and there shall be one fold and one shepherd. (*John* x, 16.)

These words were used to justify the Inquisition and all the persecution throughout the Christian era, and Laud did no more than follow in the footsteps of his priestly predecessors. In his time there was ample scope for his activities, because Bible-reading had suggested to many other ways of worship besides the orthodox Anglican method, but, when he ordered the Lord's Table to be moved from the centre of each church to the eastern wall of the chancel, to conform with the practice of the Church of Rome, there was strong objection taken by the Puritans. Few, however, realised that the Christian Church had originally copied this eastern position from Paganism, and that it, in turn, had copied it from sun worship, because there the first rays of the rising sun struck the sacrificial victim prostrated on the altar, this being the signal for its death.

Laud insisted that the Prayer Book must be used in every church, and, as many disliked this form of worship, he hunted down both Puritans and Nonconformists with pitiless energy, his merciless spies keeping close vigilance on the devotions of the people in their homes. None could escape from this Anglo-Catholic tyranny except by emigration abroad, and, during eleven years (1629–1640), 200 emigrant ships sailed with 20,000 Englishmen for the colonies in North America.

Many who opposed the Archbishop were brought before the Star Chamber to be sentenced to heavy fines, long terms of imprisonment, or banishment, a fate which often meant ending one's life as a galley slave. Others were hanged, or had their noses slit, their ears cut off, their tongues cut out, and their eyes burned out with red-hot pokers. Some were placed on the rack, and had every bone in their body pulled out of joint, the thumb-screw, the contracting boot, and other devilish devices being freely used by this devout and zealous representative of Christ.

Christian civilisation, Christian ideals, and the Christian way of life, did not improve under the care of the Protestant Anglican Church, many of whose priests were just as cruel, intolerant and ruthless as were those who conducted the Holy Inquisition. All this was done to men and women who preferred a simpler form of service, and wished to worship God in their own way, as they did not like the ritual, the sermons, or having to repeat the prayers written by Thomas Cranmer. Because they were forced, under severe penalties, to attend the parish church, some sailed to America and founded New England, and those who remained at home eventually rebelled and overthrew the King. So it came about that this bigoted prelate, Archbishop Laud, was the cause of these two great historical events, and also of a division between the British people on the question of religion so bitter that in Scotland, where the worst persecutions prevailed, the dislike of the Episcopalian Church remains to this day.

What dreadful times these were when two brands of Christianity divided the country in two! Then families, each member a devout Bible-reader and nurtured in morning and evening family worship, as was the custom in every household, broke up and became hostile one towards another. Squires and yeoman, hitherto friendly, and both proud of their political independence, avoided each other and became bitter enemies, to such a degree that eventually they tried to kill each other on the field of battle. Neighbours ceased to know one another, and the touchstone of a good Englishman, to one side, was his belief that the King, "the Lord's anointed", could do no wrong. On the other hand, the other half of the country believed just the opposite, and that Parliament had now replaced the dictates of the King. To the former the only true Christianity was that accepted by the King, and by the latter he was regarded as falsely claiming divinity and infallibility for himself, like the Pope in Rome whom England had overthrown.

The Anglicans, who did their utmost to preserve totalitarian government and keep the people in subjection, had as their motto "No Bishop, No King", meaning that the monarchy and the Church were indivisible, but the parliamentarians, who stood for the will of the people prevailing, and not that of the King, cried out "For God and Parliament". So Anglicans would not trade with Nonconformists or Independents in religion, and they, in turn, refused to deal with any who supported the State Church.

England indeed was divided, and, as the Anglicans had the power of the throne behind them, they made all who thought differently from them to suffer intensely. Here we are in the throes of a mighty vital struggle, the outcome of which made Britain what she is today. Nevertheless before the will of the people finally prevailed there was much bloodshed, and many cruel and foolish deeds were done by both sides, each intensely believing that God was guiding it in the conflict to establish the true religion and the right form of government.

In this age, blighted by struggles over religious doctrines, there is one bright feature to record. The

Puritanical Sunday, which lasted until within the life-time of many of us, was abolished by Charles I in 1633, who was distressed to find that on Sunday no amusements were permitted. So he decreed that:—

"Our pleasure is that after the end of divine service our good people be not disturbed, letted or discouraged from any lawful recreation, such as dancing, archery, leaping, vaulting, or any other such harmless recreation, nor from having of May-games, Whitsun-ales and Morris-dances."

Oliver Cromwell stopped all that, making Sunday a day of gloom and misery, and it has taken us three hundred years to return to sanity and become human on this once Pagan holy day. The Puritans thought that by keeping the Hebrew Sabbath on the Pagan Sunday they were doing the will of Jehovah, but they did not know then that the Hebrews, after the Captivity, had adopted the Babylonian Sabatu; and attributed to Jehovah the Babylonian laws relating to this holy day.

Charles ruled for eleven years without a Parliament, and obtained money by selling monopolies, levying "ship money" at the ports,[1] and forcing landowners to accept, in exchange for money, a knighthood or go to prison, which illegal methods supplied his needs until war came with Scotland, which rose in rebellion against the enforced use of the Prayer Book. The rebellion commenced with a riot in St. Giles' Cathedral, Edinburgh, when Jennie Geddes flung her stool at the preacher, exclaiming, "Ye'l no say mass in my lug"

[1] This was the revival of an old tax on maritime districts for the purpose of obtaining money to build and keep in being a navy to resist invasion. When inland districts were taxed John Hampden refused to pay, but the High Court, and then the Appeal Court, decreed the tax to be legal and could be enforced without the consent of Parliament.

(ear). Sixteen thousand Scottish people, in 1638, signed a National Covenant binding them to resist Episcopacy, and Charles marched north with a large force as far as Berwick, where he wisely agreed to allow the Scottish Parliament, and the Presbyterian General Assembly, to settle the matter.

So ended what is called the First Bishops' War (1639), but although the Scottish Parliament and the General Assembly decided in favour of abolishing Episcopacy in Scotland, Charles refused to ratify their decision, and the following year summoned the English Parliament to vote him money for a campaign against his loyal Scottish subjects. Thus began the Second Bishops' War, which ended with the English being defeated at Newburn and the Scotch occupying Newcastle. As Charles could not find money to continue the struggle, he agreed to end the war, to which proposal the Scotch gladly consented.

Great Britain was now definitely split into two hostile camps, Episcopalians, as a rule, being on one side, the Puritans and Presbyterians being mostly on the other, which cleavage of opinion, combined with the division which existed on the question of the King's divine right to rule as he pleased, led to the civil war of 1642. Thomas Wentworth (1593–1641), a rough-tongued despotic Yorkshireman, in his early political career had been a prominent advocate of parliamentary government, but he changed over to become an ardent supporter of the King, who elevated him to the peerage as the Earl of Strafford and created him his Chief Minister. What is called the Long Parliament, because of its duration, dismissed him from office, and the King forsook his champion, permitting his execution on a charge of high treason, Archbishop Laud suffering the same fate four years later.

The death of Strafford was a delight to the people, but a mortal blow to the King, his chief political prop having now gone, and for his remaining years he lived as one from whom all vitality and honour had departed. The Ritualists regarded the bloodstained Laud as a martyr, and certainly his violent death lit a candle that kept alight the Anglo-Catholic faith, which otherwise might quite easily have died in those puritanical days, never to rise again. Such is one of the many incidents we discover in history which in later years determine our lives. Another was the continued rise in prices due to the increased flow of silver from the mines of Spanish America, a factor which made it difficult for the King to meet expenses, while, on the other hand, it enriched the merchants, the class which was becoming ever more opposed to the monarchy for religious and political reasons. Both these effects, which followed the increased supply of silver, contributed to bring about the civil war and decide its issue.

The Long Parliament was one of great historical importance, as it represented the growing determination of the people to have a greater control over the King. By taking over financial control of the State, Parliament could more effectively direct its policy and increase its authority. Consequently the Triennial Act was passed, to ensure that Parliament met once in three years, and then came legislation to the effect that Parliament could not be dissolved without its own consent. The Star Chamber was next abolished, and the devious devices of the King to raise money were made illegal.

The Episcopalians in Ireland had been persecuting the Roman Catholic Irish since the time of Elizabeth, but now the victims rose in revolt and massacred thousands of their persecutors. This slaughter had a great effect on the people of England, because it followed immediately after the unsuccessful attempt to pass the Root and Branch Bill to curb the domineering and aggressive methods of the English Episcopalians. The Puritans and Nonconformists thought that this could best be accomplished by abolishing the Anglican State Church, its bishops and its prayer book, and putting Parliament at the head of a Puritan Church. The King was to be no longer recognised as the head of the Church, but the Bill did not obtain a majority and had to be dropped. So the stage was now set for a bitter religious civil war, because the Episcopalians and the Nonconformists were each determined to have things as they wished them.

Parliamentary government in Britain was now far and away stronger than in France or elsewhere, and John Pym (1584–1643), always courageous, calm and vigilant, stands out at this time as the great champion of the rights of Parliament, he being the driving force behind the movement for greater parliamentary control. What he accomplished remained, and from now onwards Parliament retained the grip over affairs which he had so bravely won. Britain, however, had one great advantage over the Continent. She was an island, and consequently required no large standing army as did Continental monarchs, who were always able to bring a strong striking force against those who opposed their arbitrary rule. The most that Charles could do was to enter the House of Commons (1642) with an armed force, and attempt to arrest five of his chief opponents, who were fortunate to escape.

London was now too hostile a place for the misguided monarch, and he left it within a week. His rash procedure had sealed his doom, and hastened the outbreak of civil war, which lasted for three years until 1645. It was a fight by Episcopacy, and its divine king, against Calvinism, a bloody struggle for the Prayer Book, whereas in Europe Roman Catholicism, and its divine Pope, waged a ceaseless fight against all who did not accept the traditional orthodox outlook, nearly every Christian country in Europe being involved. The revolution in England was but an incident in the fight for freedom, a conflict which lasted for many years and embraced both Ireland and Scotland, two countries which suffered grievously from Episcopalian tyranny and brutality.

The Royalists, or Cavaliers, as they were called, who wore their hair in long curls, had the support of the Episcopalian Church and the Universities of Oxford and Cambridge, their two leaders being Prince Rupert, the King's nephew, and the Duke of Newcastle. On the other side were the Puritans, embracing the Presbyterians and Independents in religion, who were known as the Roundheads because they wore their hair short, and they were led by the Earl of Essex, the Earl of Manchester and two members of Parliament, Sir Thomas Fairfax and Oliver Cromwell.

Both sides consisted of men lacking in human sympathy, tolerance or charity. Puritan hated Royalist and his hatred was returned in full measure. The manners and language of both sides were coarse, the most lurid abuse and vilification being the accepted mode of conduct. Such were the men who faced each other, devout, fanatical and brutal, spitting everywhere, and without an idea of the use of a handkerchief, they being like beasts in their habits. The parliamentary forces, more like a rabble than an army, lacked training, a defect which was rectified in 1645, when Parliament set about training and equipping an army of 20,000 men, which became known as "The Ironsides", over which Fairfax was placed as commander. These men were well paid, well trained, and sincerely believed that they were fighting a holy war, with God leading them forward.

Charles, in 1642, moved from Nottingham on London, the capital being strongly Puritan and against him, but at Edgehill he was checked and retired to Oxford. If the navy had stood by the King, London could have been subdued by blockade alone, but the entire fleet supported Parliament because of the sordid conditions afloat, and the humiliation it had suffered from its enemies in consequence of the King's incompetence. Next year the royal troops were generally successful, and this continued until the King had about three-quarters of England under his control. English troops from Ireland then joined the royal standard, while a Scottish army of 20,000 men, under General Leslie, came south to help Parliament, having first of all signed the Solemn League and Covenant.

Henceforth the Scottish Presbyterians were known as Covenanters, and they helped Parliament because of its promise that England would become Presbyterian. With their help Charles was defeated at Marston Moor near York in 1644, a bloody battle in which over 4000 fell on a summer's evening, and again at

Naseby the following year, victories for the Calvinists
which virtually ended hostilities.

In Scotland the Scottish Episcopalians, under
James Graham, Marquis of Montrose, defeated the
Covenanters in their first encounter, but at Philiphaugh
in 1645 the Episcopalians were decisively defeated.
The Ironsides, whom Cromwell had now turned into
a disciplined army of sober and temperate men, then
ignored Parliament and negotiated with the King about
his restoration, but Charles, who might have won his
way back to power, refused to face facts, and instead
induced the Scotch to invade England on the promise
that he would establish Prebyterianism in England.

Had the English Parliament kept its previous
promise to reform the Church of England "according
to God's holy word", as interpreted by the Presbyterians, he would not have received this help, but
because it did not the Scotch now felt that they had
no other alternative than to accept the King's promise.
They therefore changed sides and supported their
former enemy. The Ironsides, every man of whom
had an equal say in affairs, looked on this act of Charles
bringing the Scotch in against them as treason, and
it cost him his head.

Charles gained nothing from the Scottish invasion
of England, and before the invaders were forced to
return home he, realising that the end had come,
surrendered himself to the Scottish army at Newark,
which handed him over to the English Parliament.
He escaped and was captured. Parliament was then
purged of the Presbyterians because of the support
they had given to the King, after his promise to
establish the Presbyterian faith, and what remained

became known as the "Rump" Parliament. This was the assembly that brought the King to trial for waging war against his people, but it in no way represented the nation, and his judges were all picked men who were known to be biased against him. He was condemned and executed in 1649, thus ending an attempt at absolute monarchy in an age when the British body politic was coming to life.

Hitherto monarchy had kept law and order by issuing commands which the people obeyed, a live head having ruled a comatose body, but now the bodily nerves were beginning to function. A wise head would have responded to this increased vitality, but Charles, with his mind in the past, and believing that it was God's will that the king should rule and the people obey, could not adapt himself to changed circumstances. We are now nearing the end of an age, the age when the body did not influence the head, as before the century ended a British monarch reigned who responded to Parliamentary decisions. Finally the time came when the people alone ruled themselves through their representatives in Parliament, and the king became a constitutional monarch.

During this period of bitter Protestant warfare, certain outstanding theologians, or divines as they termed themselves, set to work to amplify the Thirty-Nine Articles of Christian belief. The outcome of their work at Westminster was the famous declaration known as The Westminster Confession of Faith, which was taken over by the Scottish Presbyterian Church in 1647 as its standard of belief. The Scottish Parliament ratified it in 1649 and again in 1690. The Thirty-Nine Articles of the Church of England and The Confession of Faith contain exactly the same dogmas, doctrines and beliefs about everything from salvation to damnation, and from predestination to baptism, marriage, and the Sacrament, the only difference being in the number of words used, the former occupying about thirteen pages, whereas the latter contains thirty-three chapters each about a page in length.

When the rule of Cromwell comes to an end we arrive at a period in the long age of religious persecution which is as extraordinary as it is cruel. Fifteen years after the Confession of Faith had been accepted by the Presbyterians as their standard of belief, the Episcopalians of England and Scotland were fighting, killing, torturing, imprisoning and banishing their Presbyterian co-religionists because the latter did not wish to use the Episcopalian Prayer Book in their worship, or have bishops over their ministers. They preferred to have their churches grouped under elected presbyteries, and managed by elders instead of by bishops in charge of dioceses. We shall learn, before this chapter closes, what this was to mean in bloodshed and human suffering for twenty-nine years after the time of Cromwell, and it was not until 1689, when William III became king, that this bloody religious persecution came to an end.

Meanwile Charles I had been executed, the House of Lords abolished, and Cromwell had taken up the reins of a single-chamber Commonwealth government. The king died a hero, saint and martyr to most Episcopalians of the time, and a traitor in the eyes of the Nonconformists, but whichever way we may look back on this tragic figure, all must now agree that no man ever lost more chances to establish his throne on the goodwill of the people than did Charles.   He never grew up to be a man, he being mentally part a woman, part a priest, and he behaved like a bewildered delicate boy who was never able to take a firm grasp of affairs. For this weakness of character he was to be pitied, but that such a man should have become an autocratic king clearly reveals the dangers and evils which flowed from despotic hereditary monarchy, and how much the people have suffered from being too ignorant to rule themselves.

For ten years (1649–1658) the well-born Huntingdon squire, Oliver Cromwell, ruled Britain and Ireland by force, and, throughout his term of office as Lord Protector, he had to rely on the army to secure his authority.   A freely elected Parliament would have made a quick end to his rule, but he relied on his military successes, which had secured for him the power he wielded, and, like a Roman Emperor, he ruled the land.   He was the leader of the Puritans, who regarded the reformation of the Church of England as incomplete, and sought to abolish unscriptural and corrupt practices.   He dismissed the bishops, banned the Prayer Book, and tried to form a new national Church to include the Presbyterians and the Independents. He prohibited Episcopalian services, which were consequently held in secret, and he retained the harsh laws against the Roman Catholics.

Thousands of Royalists were banished to the colonies, to live out their lives as slaves, and, after the Restoration, this was the lot of criminals, reformers and those who dissented from the Episcopalian way of worship. It is strange to think that in these early days the growing British Empire was peopled by those who were considered unfit to live in Britain, but so it was, and consequently most colonists had their grievances against the home government. What happened under Cromwell was neither new nor strange, as this folly had been going on since the time of the intolerant James I, to be responsible for some of the bad feeling which produced the revolt of the American colonies a hundred years later.

Cromwell was tolerant for his time, and he compares favourably with other rulers who secured supreme power, but his was an age when tolerance was considered to be sinful. He did not torture or hang those in England who thought differently from him on religious questions, and his tyrannical rule was forced upon him owing to the intense bitterness of religious opinion in these times. With intense feeling he once exclaimed, "I have sought the Lord that he would rather slay me than put upon me the doing of this work." But he could not now turn back. He was sincere and honest in his endeavour to bring peace to a distracted land, though his treatment of the Irish was both harsh and cruel.

He received the support of only a minority of the people, and disaffection even in his own army had to be crushed. Open rebellion broke out in Ireland when the Anglican supporters of the monarchy joined hands with the Roman Catholics and proclaimed Charles, the son of Charles I, as their king. Cromwell crossed over to Ireland in 1649, captured their strongholds and massacred their garrisons, the slaughter being particularly thorough at Drogheda and

Wexford. So ruthless was he that Ireland was laid waste, 40,000 being banished, 9000 sent as slaves to the West Indies, while thousands died from famine, massacre or in combat. Cromwell considered all Roman Catholics to be idol-worshippers, and, like many other Christians before and after his time, justified his cruelties by quotations from the Bible,[1] such as:—

And they made them molten images . . . Therefore the Lord was angry . . . and there was none left . . . and the Lord . . . afflicted them and delivered them into the hand of spoilers until he had cast them out of his sight. (2 *Kings* xvii, 16–20.)

Historians consider that the English treatment of the Irish was even worse than that of the Spaniards towards the Netherlanders, as the Spanish never confiscated large tracts of land and removed their inhabitants. Both Cromwell and Elizabeth lit the flames of hatred in Irish minds towards England, which burned fiercely during the following centuries, and continue to do so even in our own times. Wars between nations can be and are forgotten, foes become friends, but massacres and persecutions are remembered, and ages of time are required before the stain they make is removed.

In Scotland, Charles' son, who was later to become Charles II, was welcomed because he accepted Presbyterianism, and this event took Cromwell

[1] From first to last throughout the Bible, idolaters receive pitiless condemnation, and they receive no mercy hereafter, as "idolaters shall have their part in the lake which burneth with fire and brimstone". (*Revelation* xxi, 8.) When the Christian god treated those who reverenced images in such an unjust and cruel way, it is not to be wondered that Christians were equally savage towards all they considered to be unbelievers.

north with his army where he defeated the Scots at Dunbar in 1650. Then they crowned Charles as their king at Scone and he led their army south to be defeated in 1651 at Worcester; an event which Cromwell claimed as his "crowning mercy" and led to Scotland being occupied and governed as a conquered country. Charles, their king and leader, after a dangerous ride to the south coast, disguised as a servant, escaped to France, and then Cromwell dismissed the "Rump" Parliament which had sent Charles I to trial. This was the tail end of the Long Parliament, after being purged of its Presbyterian and Royalist members, but its successor, equally unrepresentative, and known as the "Barebones" Parliament,[1] resigned after five months of existence. The next two Parliaments assembled only to be dismissed, and so the country was ruled by the army under district major-generals, Scotland, for the first time, being united with England in trade and law under a military governor, General Monk.

The people continued to be taxed without parliamentary consent, and to be imprisoned without trial, but the Jews, who had been banished, were allowed to return. All joy and gladness in life were, however, tabooed. Amusements were abolished, all theatres closed, love and affection frowned upon, adultery became a hanging matter, and the land lay under the blight of a puritanical religion which considered all laughter and happiness to be sinful.

In his foreign policy Cromwell worked successfully to stimulate the country's trade abroad. Then it

[1] It was called by this peculiar name after a prominent member who, because of the religious zeal of his parents, was fated to go through life with the name of Praise God Barebones.

was (1654) that the Anglo-Portuguese alliance was first made, which gave to English ships the facilities of the wonderful natural harbour of Lisbon, a compact which is unbroken to this day, and served a very useful purpose during the Second World War. When, however, Cromwell passed the Navigation Act, which permitted imports only in British ships, or the ships of the country from which they came, the Dutch, who were the ocean carriers of Europe, declared war in 1652.

The Dutch in those days, as they still are, were respected for their thrift, energy and commercial ability, but they were also feared as traders and because of their powerful navy. In England it was felt that the world was not large enough for both Dutch and English merchants, the former having built up the largest merchant fleet, and strongest trade connection, of any country in Europe. Capital was cheap and abundant in Holland, banking was highly developed, and shipbuilding was quick and good. The Dutch navy was efficient their sailors resolute, while England relied on the Press Gang and inefficient officers whose social position, and not their ability, secured for them their rank.

So Cromwell exposed England to serious attack by his Navigation Act, as the conflict which followed was fought at sea. The English, under Admiral Blake, were first beaten by Van Tromp off Dungeness, only to be victorious the next year when the two admirals again met off Portland and the Frisian Islands. After this victory Cromwell went to war with Spain in 1657, as an ally of France, because he felt that God now wanted him to bring down this citadel of Roman

Catholicism, but he also wished to break the Spanish trade monopoly with the West Indies and America as well as steal some more of her colonies, Jamaica having already been taken from the Spanish by the British.

Blake had previously captured the Scilly Islands and Jersey from the English Royalists, and St. Helena from the Dutch. Then he destroyed the Spanish fleet off Teneriffe, and a British army landed in France to join the French at St. Quentin. For this help Britain received Dunkirk. Pirates in the Mediterranean were destroyed by British warships, and Cromwell brought to an end the Roman Catholic persecution of the Protestants in Savoy. Britain, by the nations of Europe, was now looked upon with some fear and respect, though their kings hated her ruler, who had usurped the place of her martyred and divinely guided monarch.

At the time of his death in 1658, Cromwell had raised Britain to the height reached in Elizabethan days, monopolies at home had been abolished, and her trade was free from restrictions. So this outstanding imperialist, who had refused the crown offered him by Parliament, passed on to his son Richard a country just at the dawn of its world-wide greatness. Richard was unpopular, without his father's talents and strength of character, and he retired into private life in the following year. General Monk then assembled a freely elected Parliament, which invited Charles, the son of Charles I, to come over from Holland, where he had been in exile, and occupy the vacant throne. Promising religious toleration, he entered London in triumph and amid delirious rejoicings in 1660, an event which marks the end of the Commonwealth, when the power of Parliament was stronger than ever before.

The ablest, the most deceitful, the most dissolute and the most cunning of the Stuarts was Charles II (1660–1685), a man who did not keep his promises on reaching the throne, and strove throughout his reign to become an absolute monarch and restore the orthodox Catholic faith.   He lived the most licentious life of any British monarch.   His court was the most scandalous which the country has probably ever experienced, his numerous mistresses producing many illegitimate children, six of whom he made dukes and two duchesses.   His legitimate wife was obliged to humiliate herself and treat them with kindness and without scorn, her own childlessness making her position particularly difficult.

Charles was a tactful genial man, and his winning ways appealed to the people, who had not been happy under the Puritan regime, because they intensely disliked its military despotism.[1]   Consequently there was the natural reaction, the nobles, bishops and squires resuming the political and social leadership they had held before the Commonwealth, and, when Parliament met in 1661, it enacted four laws known as the Clarendon Code, named after the King's chief minister.   These laws, produced by feelings of bitter-

---

[1] Soldiers were ordered to enter private houses to make sure that the Sabbath was not being profaned, and that the fast days were duly observed. Even after this form of Parliamentary tyranny ceased the mental effect it produced remained, to perpetuate the Puritanical Sunday which many living today still remember with horror.

ness occasioned by the period of harsh Puritan domination, made it illegal for anyone who did not belong to the Episcopalian Church to hold a public office, or enter the professions, and the use of the Prayer Book was made compulsory.

Those who did not conform to the Episcopalian form of worship, mostly men and women of the middle or lower classes, residing in the towns, who prided themselves on their political and religious independence, were called Nonconformists, and their lives were made intolerable. Besides this they were not permitted to meet together to hold a religious meeting, and no Nonconformist minister could live within five miles of a town. Two thousands priests, a name which the Episcopalians retained, refused to use the Prayer Book and were expelled from their parishes in 1662, to become the nucleus of all those now called Dissenters.

This produced a social cleavage which has lasted up to our own time, because they were denied the education and privileges which are today considered to be due to all. From now onwards the village parish church received the special patronage of the Squire in England (and the Laird in Scotland), who occupied the most important pew, the congregation consisting mostly of his own tenants, who regarded him with awe and reverence. He secured the election of the candidate of his choice at Parliamentary elections, as no tenant farmer had then a vote, only the freehold yeoman.

Consequently the Parliaments of both Scotland and England were now strongly Episcopalian, and the persecution of both Nonconformists and Dissenters was bitter throughout the land. This persecution came from Parliament, and was distasteful to the King, but he made no protest. In Scotland it was especially severe, as there the Episcopalians, led by the fanatical James Sharp, Archbishop of St. Andrews, and his bishops, tried hard to stamp out Presbyterianism, 300 Presbyterian ministers giving up their parishes rather than be under the bishops. Persecuting Acts were then passed, one of which forbade these dissenting ministers from approaching within twenty miles of their former parishes.

Between 1661 and 1689 over 28,000 harmless loyal Scottish men and women, out of a population of 1,000,000, were ruthlessly slaughtered or tortured by the contracting boot, the thumb-screw, the rack and other diabolical methods, while many thousands were imprisoned or shipped abroad as slaves to Barbadoes and Jamaica. Many died from months of exposure on the moors, while twelve hundred were herded throughout winter and summer in the open, without any shelter, in Greyfriars Church-yard, Edinburgh. The Inquisition in Edinburgh was as active and fierce as ever it was in Europe, the Episcopalians being in no way behind the Roman Catholics in their pitiless cruelty towards all who would not subscribe to their form of Christianity.

The Killing Time, as it is still called in Scotland, was one of the most merciless periods in that bar-barous age called the Christian era, when Christian civilisation reduced the dignity of man to the level of a slave. Anyone not attending the Episcopalian Church was first tortured, then imprisoned, and finally shot or hanged, and many a Conventicle, the name given to the secret gatherings of the Presbyterians, was broken up by the soldiers, who, under the direction of John Graham of Claverhouse, scoured the lowlands of Scotland for victims on which to exercise their savagery. The Episcopalian clergy were an active gestapo force, acting as informers, and leading the soldiers to their hapless quarry, the ferocity of the persecution becoming so bitter that in self-defence the Presbyterians gathered together an untrained army which was defeated at Bothwell Bridge in 1679. A month earlier Archbishop Sharp had been murdered, both of which events just increased the slaughter until only the followers of Richard Cameron remained.

Looking back over the pages of ancient history, to those days before Christianity had come to fill men's minds with cruel hatred towards one another, to those so-called heathen times of long ago, we find few instances of this savage intolerance so noticeable in Christian civilisation, and it makes one wonder what good Christianity has done for mankind. The Greeks and Romans generally tolerated all forms of religion in their midst, and gods, of different names and in different ways, were worshipped, the people thus obtaining all the comfort they required.

Christianity was certainly no more elevating, and has given no more comfort to believers, than did these old beliefs. This being so, it is one of the great tragedies of history that Constantine ever made his bargain with the Christian priests to elevate Christianity to be the state religion of Rome, whenever they agreed on a creed which could be enforced on everyone.

Far better would it have been for the happiness of a great part of the human race if Christianity had not been raised to a position for which it was not fitted. If only it had been allowed to take an equal place with the many other supernatural religions of the time, instead of being put over them, how much unnecessary misery would have been savèd! Its strange medley of beliefs, in part Jewish but largely Pagan, clamped by force on what became Christendom, brought untold suffering and misery to mankind.

Lacking in truth and reason, its doctrines left the door wide open to many different interpretations, and no one can say today which one of its numerous sects represents the true Christian faith, because there is no such thing, its variety of beliefs having developed in a haphazard fashion out of the different theological ideas which prevailed in the lands in which it was cradled. What a curse this illogical and contradictory tangle of mystical and theological beliefs has been to humanity, and what a misfortune that they ever came into being!

Only the Christian clergy have benefited socially and financially from its existence, and in consequence they are for ever proclaiming its wonders, but never do they tell of the blight it has been on human happiness. How well it all can be compared with what has taken place in Germany and Italy within our own times. The gang in power in these two countries, and the army of officials in their pay, blazoned forth the Nazi and Fascist creed as the only one for all mankind, and liquidated everyone who thought otherwise. When history is honestly reported, and intelligently understood, the similarity between the aims and deeds of the Christian Church and those of the Nazis and Fascists will be clear to everyone who seeks truth, and is not bound by prejudice and the worship of ancient tradition.

Today, however, the people are as ignorant of the history of the Christian Church as they are of its origin, and so we find columns in our newspapers devoted to its benign influence throughout the Christian era. *The Scotsman*, in its issue of 9th October, 1941, displayed the following in bold headlines across two columns:—

BEST IN CIVILISATION.   THE FRUIT OF CHRISTIAN INFLUENCE.

and underneath followed an appeal by the Reverend Professor Donald Maclean, D.D., for "the Church re-educating her people in the fundamental elements of the faith".   Dr. Maclean followed up this remark with the blatantly false statement that "It is now admitted by unbelievers that the best in our civilisation has been the fruit of Christian influence, mediated by the Christian Church."

Living as they do in historical darkness, most people believe this priestly falsehood, little realising that the Church has always maintained a well-organised propaganda system, which is as dishonest and unscrupulous as was the one set up by Dr. Goebbels to mislead and keep in subjection his German dupes.   Its spokesmen are the clergy, whose minds are so twisted in the theological colleges they entered as youths, that truth and honesty have ceased to be regarded with respect.   Every sermon was, and still is, a propaganda talk in support of ideas which maintain them in their existing favoured positions.   Surely Dr. Maclean, as a Scottish Presbyterian Church professor, knows something about his own Church history, which records the death, suffering and persecution inflicted on the Scottish Presbyterians by the Scottish Episcopalians between 1661 and 1689—only about 250 years ago.

Because the people are so simple and ignorant, these untruthful propagandists get the respect and publicity which has always followed clerical utterances. If the clergy were judged by their past foolish and inaccurate utterances they would cease to be respected and reported, and the newspapers, instead of encouraging them by publicity, would expose their false statements. A Church which has cruelly slaughtered 25,000,000 innocent victims, who wished to believe as their consciences directed them, deserves no respect. Religious wars, instigated by the Church, caused the death of millions (16,000,000 died as the result of the Thirty Years' War), and to this vast host of victims we must add the multitude who refused to accept its teaching that kings reigned by divine right. Surely everyone who thinks must admit that such an organisation has been a curse and not a blessing to mankind. When Christianity was truly and earnestly believed, when nearly everyone openly avowed their belief in all its supernatural claims, there was no toleration, and Christendom was just one huge slave camp from the 4th century to within our own times.

Christianity has now lost its old fire and meaning, while its driving force, hell, has burned itself out, and just because this is so the Church cannot now perpetrate the foul deeds that stained its name up to the 19th century. Because of secular education we are today less cruel, bigoted and intolerant, but it would indeed be a tragedy if Dr. Maclean's desire, and that of his brother clergy, were realised, and the people were re-educated in the "fundamental elements" which were the cause of so much misery and suffering. Fortunately for us all, the black army, fighting under the banner of orthodoxy, is nearly everywhere in retreat, and Christianity is slowly slipping into the land of the shades, to keep company with all the other forgotten superstitions of the past.

In 1664 Britain captured New Amsterdam from the Dutch, naming it New York, and the following year war was declared between Holland and Britain. The British won a sea victory off Lowestoft, but two years later (1667), when peace terms were being discussed, Charles disbanded a large part of the British fleet, and the Dutch, taking advantage of the position, sailed up the Thames and Medway, destroyed shipping at Chatham, and blockaded London. This was a fleeting triumph, and when peace was signed the same year Britain retained New York. Then followed the signing of a Triple Alliance, comprising Britain, Holland and Sweden, for the purpose of checking French aggression in Europe.

At the time when Parliament was allying Britain with Holland, Charles, who was a much abler, subtler man than the mere trifler he appeared to his courtiers and the people, formed a secret council, a cabal, the precursor of the present-day Cabinet. Then he dismissed his Chancellor, Lord Clarendon, the persecutor of the Puritans, Presbyterians and Nonconformists, because he had sold Dunkirk to the French. This Cabal approved of a secret treaty made by Charles with Louis XIV, by which Charles promised to support the French against the Dutch for an annual subsidy. This secret Treaty of Dover, as it is called, committed Charles to re-establish Roman Catholicism in Britain with the aid of troops and money sent by Louis. It was the most treasonable act of any English king, and base treachery against the Dutch, but such are the depths to which supernatural religion can drag down an individual, every virtue being cast aside if only his beliefs prevail.

To prepare the way for the re-establishment of the orthodox Catholic faith in Britain, Charles issued the Declaration of Indulgence, suspending the penal laws against both Roman Catholics and Nonconformists, but Parliament compelled the King to withdraw it, and passed in its place the Test Act of 1673. This forced everyone serving under the Crown to take the Sacrament according to the rites of the Church of England, and to deny the doctrine of transubstantiation. Hundreds of Roman Catholics resigned from the army, navy and civil services, including the King's brother, the Duke of York, who was Lord High Admiral of the Fleet, a position he filled with considerable ability.

So as to receive from Louis his annual subsidy, Charles, without consulting Parliament, forced on another war with the Dutch, but nothing of importance happened except an indecisive naval engagement. Then, in 1673, the Cabal broke up, and the Earl of Danby became Chief Minister. His principal claim to fame was the arranging of a marriage between Mary, the daughter of the Duke of York (later James II), and William of Orange, who, after her father was dethroned, became Queen, and her husband King William III of Great Britain.

Louis XIV was anxious to keep the British Parliament from assembling, as he knew that its sympathies lay with the Protestant Dutch. So he continued to supply Charles with the money he required, and this made it unnecessary for Charles to call Parliament to vote supplies, but the marriage of William of Orange and Mary so angered Louis that he revealed to Parliament the secret treaty he had made with Charles. Danby was made the scapegoat and imprisoned in the Tower, a wave of fear and hatred against the Roman Catholics rising to dangerous heights.

The religious fervour of the times can best be realised by the disclosure of a Roman Catholic plot in 1678, which proved to be a mare's-nest. An evil and debased character, Titus Oates, an Anglican priest, reported that he had discovered a Roman Catholic plot, the purpose of which was to obtain help from France to murder Charles and make his brother James, an avowed Roman Catholic, the King. The people, frenzied with fear, turned on the Roman Catholics, and a number of innocent people were killed, sentenced to death or imprisoned. Seven years later, when the excitement had abated, Oates was discovered to have fabricated his evidence, and he was made to stand in the pillory, undergo grievous torture, and then imprisonment for three and a half years.

During this time of religious delirium a prominent figure holds the stage. He was Anthony Ashley Cooper, for a time Lord Chancellor, and first Earl of Shaftesbury (1621–1683), who led the Whigs and championed the Protestant cause on all occasions, particularly the Presbyterian sect, of which he was the spokesman. Consequently he had been the enemy of Cromwell, and was now the enemy of the Anglicans, whom he hated for their intolerance. Later he became the bitter enemy of the King, who dismissed him from office because he opposed the legislation against the Nonconformists and Presbyterians, which permitted only Anglicans to hold municipal office, enforced the use of the Prayer Book, and made Nonconformist meetings illegal.

Shaftesbury's zeal for the cause he made his own led him to encourage the belief in the already mentioned Roman Catholic plot, and he found Parliament willing to support his counter-measure. Consequently an Act was passed excluding Roman Catholics from sitting in either the upper or lower houses of Parliament, but, much to his disappointment, the House of Commons made the proviso that the Duke of York be excepted. Many a speech did he make warning the nation of the dangers ahead if the Roman Catholics obtained any power, and in Anglicanism he saw the thin end of the wedge, which he took every opportunity to blunt. He it was who secured the passage of the invaluable Act of Habeas Corpus (1679), which made it necessary for the prisoner to be charged with his offence within twenty-four hours of his arrest. His championship of the Duke of Monmouth, the King's Protestant illegitimate son, as the successor to the throne, led to his arrest for high treason, but he escaped to Holland disguised as a Presbyterian minister. How vastly different British history would have been from now onwards if his policy had succeeded without strife or civil war !

Religion in those days, as ever before, determined

not only the lives of the people but the political outlook. The gods, the men and women of the other world, then looked upon as supernatural beings, on whom the fate of everyone and everything depended, made also the two political parties of Great Britain. In those days there was the Court Party, mostly made up of the Anglicans, who hated all Non-Anglicans and believed that their persecution was God's will, and the Country Party, mostly consisting of Nonconformists and Presbyterians.

The Anglicans, who were much the more intolerant, were nicknamed Tories, a name given to the Irish outlaws, and the Nonconformists, who were more liberal minded, were called Whigs, the popular name for the Scottish Covenanters, appellations which remained the Party labels until the 19th century. So Britain's party system is based on the Christian religion, which, in turn, came into being because of a ghost, seen in Palestine, being turned into a god. Just another of the many ways supernatural religion has made history, or, to put it another way, because stupid humanity imagined the men and women of the other world to be gods, angels or devils, history has taken the course it has. Indeed, how true it is that the world we pass to at death has been responsible for at least half the events in history !

The money Charles was receiving from Louis enabled him to keep going without often assembling Parliament, and for the last four years of his life it never met. The fabricated story of the Roman Catholic plot, moreover, acted against the Whigs, who had been its principal propagators, the consequence being that the King's Roman Catholic brother James, the Duke of York, instead of being excluded from the throne as the Whigs desired, became more popular and an important influence. Especially was this so during the last two years of the reign, a time which was clouded by the attempt of some of the more violent Whigs to murder the King in 1683 at a lonely spot on the London-to-Newmarket Road. The Rye House Plot, as it was called, was discovered, the leaders executed, and the Whigs were discredited.

Several additions were made to British possessions abroad during this reign. Catherine of Portugal, whom Charles married, brought with her Bombay as her marriage portion, the first British territorial settlement in India. William Penn[1] founded Pennsylvania, and then the Hudson Bay Company was formed, thus increasing Britain's ever growing hold on North America. A few outstanding men added lustre to this intolerant age, men who were really great and will be remembered long after the names of the intriguing and fanatical politicians of the time have been forgotten.

Sir Isaac Newton, the greatest of them all, has been mentioned in Chapter XI, but here we must refer to John Milton (1608–1674), who intended becoming an Anglican priest, but was too honest to swear belief in the Thirty-Nine Articles, and detested Episcopalian tyranny. So, instead, he devoted his life to literature, his best known production being

---

[1] Penn was the outstanding champion of Quakerism in his time, writing voluminously and ever preaching and arguing on its merits. In politics his best contribution was an *Essay towards the present and future peace of Europe* in which he puts forward the idea of a supreme court of arbitration to maintain peace and thus abolish war.

Paradise Lost, but the most eloquent, if not the greatest, of all his prose writings was his famous *Areopagitica.* It was published in 1644, deliberately unlicensed and unregistered, its theme being the scandal of press licensing and censorship. In his day savage punishment was inflicted on all who criticised either Church or State, and no book could be published without their permission. The number of printers in the country was limited to twenty, and all unlicensed books were publicly burned by the hangman. So Milton called for a repeal of the law which curbed the right to free expression. Though he was pardoned, yet the law remained in force until 1695, and it was only after that date that one could print and publish what he chose so long as it was not seditious or libellous.

Another rebel against the prevailing tyranny was John Bunyan (1628–1688). He was the son of a tinker, and ranks as the most popular religious writer in the English language. His most famous book, *The Pilgrim's Progress,* slipped silently into the world, to be read by only a few obscure people. Slowly its theme was appreciated, though today, with our higher ethical standard, some will regard it as quite unethical, because salvation is represented as being secured through the death of a divine victim and not by the way we live. Bunyan next produced *The Holy War,* which, like its forerunner, is one of the best allegories ever written. For twelve years this earnest brave man was confined in Bedford Gaol, in a cell not fit for an animal, because he would not subscribe to the Episcopalian form of worship, and fortunately he just escaped being hanged or banished.

Bunyan was typical of many thousands of innocent victims of Episcopalian tyranny during this dreadful period of religious intolerance. Another prominent religious reformer who had to suffer for his convictions was George Fox (1624–1690), the founder of the Society of Friends, or Quakers as they are more generally called. Scandalised at the debauchery and profligacy of the times, and the absence of righteousness in every walk of life, he left his relations "and broke off all fellowship with both young and old", at God's command, he tells us. So, from the "times of the first working of the Lord" in him, he lived in great perplexity and distress.

Evidently, from time to time, he went into a state of trance, like Peter of old, when he "saw heaven opened", and this had such an effect upon him that he left his home and wandered about the country, so as not to be tarnished by coming into too close a personal contact with anyone. Eventually he produced his new revelation, claiming, like Paul, the great apostle, that it had come to him direct from Christ in heaven. So he commenced its diffusion by going about as an itinerant preacher, and his sincerity was so obvious that he established a great influence over large numbers of people.

He did not approve of the teaching of any of the other different Christian sects, all being unscriptural, and he believed that the divine light came neither by the Scriptures nor through the Church. From now onwards his followers were called "Quakers", because "they bade the people tremble at the word of the Lord" as revealed to each individual. Many times was Fox imprisoned for blasphemy, during which periods his hand was not idle, as is shown by his voluminous letters and exhortations to his flock. He visited the colonies and America, taking with him his new revelation, but, on his return to England, he was again arrested and all Quaker meetings banned by law. Then he started on a missionary journey through Holland and Germany, to return home and live his remaining years in peace.

Fox was tall and strong, of graceful countenance, manly in his bearing, courteous and unaffected, civil in manner, tender, compassionate, sincere and pitiful, with little learning and no great intellect, but his moral character won for him friends and followers. He established a sect which more nearly corresponds in its beliefs to those held by the early Jesuians than any other bearing the Christian name. Moreover its adherents, whose talk and manners were quite unusual, lived more closely to the moral code than did most people in those days, when morality, honesty and common decency were so often absent. The courtiers and politicians scoffed at virtue and were quite unscrupulous, but the Quakers have always been noted for their opposition to slavery, for their virtue, and their deeds of charity and mercy. Nevertheless, they had to endure bitter persecution from those who considered themselves as orthodox, and also suffer from insults, social ostracism and many other hardships for the sake of their beliefs, in one year alone (1662) more than 4,000 being in prison.

The intellectual life of England in those days was represented by two outstanding men, Hobbes and Locke, both of whom worked for increased liberty and the advancement of knowledge. Thomas Hobbes

(1588–1679), the great political philosopher, assailed in his *Leviathan* the prevailing system of theological education for all who attended the universities. He attacked the fantastic claims made by the theologians for their religion, and advocated the abandonment of Church-controlled instruction in favour of education by the State, it to him being the pivot round which the national life should evolve, its unity and strength being of prime importance.

The other great reformer of those days was John Locke (1632–1704), the temperate humane exponent of Whig ideals. In the philosophical, scientific and political sphere he was a thorn in the side of tyranny and orthodoxy. This wise man reverenced facts, relied on reason, advocated philosophy and education as a guide to life, and was the intellectual leader of reform and progress. His *Essay on Human Understanding*, the *Essay Concerning Toleration* and *Two Treatises on Government*, a defence of the sovereignty of the people, are his most famous works, in which he advocated more humanity and greater kindness, deploring the constant severe floggings practised on both young and old.

In an age when the theatre, which had been suppressed by the Puritans, was reviving—and women for the first time were appearing on the stage in place of boys in women's costumes, and when the roofed-in Theatre Royal at Drury Lane was the only theatre in London—John Dryden (1631–1700) was accepted as the outstanding dramatist and poet of his age. He was the literary father and model of Pope (1688–1744), who was the greatest poet of the next generation.

This was also an era of diarists, Samuel Pepys (1633–1703) being the most outstanding, his *Diary* giving us an understanding of his times as no other book could do. His imprisonment in the Tower on the charge of being a traitor and a papist finally ended in acquittal and release. Then he returned to his post as Secretary to the Admiralty, and was elected President of the Royal Society. A Surrey squire, John Evelyn (1620–1706), the diarist and author, likewise gave a frank expression of his opinions about an age rich in great events, and this so stimulated the imagination of Daniel Defoe (1661–1731), the son of a London butcher, that he produced a series of interesting novels, the most famous being his widely read *Robinson Crusoe.*

In architecture, Inigo Jones (1572–1651) was the most distinguished exponent of his time. He acquired his style in Venice, and was patronised by royalty both at home and abroad, designing some of their stately palaces, including Whitehall in London. Then followed Christopher Wren (1631–1723), who was the greatest architect of his time, St. Paul's, and numerous other churches, being lasting monuments to his genius. It is unfortunate that it was not employed in the construction of better houses for the people, his ambitious designs for a planned and imposing London, with wide streets and open spaces, being turned down. Grinling Gibbons (1648–1721) decorated the interiors of a number of famous buildings, including St. Paul's, and besides being remarkable for his skill as a woodcarver he was an outstanding sculptor.

The foregoing pages record the prominent

leaders in philosophy, sociology, literature and the arts, but they were rare and quite exceptional men, the vast multitude being immersed in ignorance. Consequently this was an age of intolerance, when only those who thought alike were friends. It was a period of injustice, cruelty and oppression. Ignorance of hygiene made it one of filth, bad housing, deficient sanitation, and neglect of the poor. It was the time of the Great Plague of 1665, that ever recurring pestilence, due to these foul conditions, when the people were living in hovels and Wren was building his fifty magnificent churches out of public funds. From London's population of 500,000 the plague carried off 100,000 in six months.

Then exactly a year later came the Great Fire of London, now the hub of England's wealth and trade, and this destroyed in five days two thirds of the city (between the Tower and the Temple), made up of wooden houses, as were all towns in northern Europe in those days. It was after this great catastrophe that Wren produced his famous plan, to rebuild the city on a scale which would have made it the most majestic and stately capital in the world, but the people were too short-sighted, too poor, and perhaps too stupefied by all they had gone through to carry out the scheme. Houses built of brick now took the place of those constructed of lath and plaster, but the new city, which became the metropolis of the far-flung British Empire, never approached in magnificence to other cities abroad of much less importance.

Britain, for over three quarters of a century, had been ruled by three kings who claimed autocratic power derived from God, but, tyrannical as had been their rule, one form of government the people were determined never to have again. Never would the British return to the experiences they suffered under Cromwell, when a harsh military dictatorship, and a hateful puritanical way of life, had dominated the land. So bitterly was he hated, that some of his victims took their revenge after his death and dug up his body, which they hanged on a tree.

Consequently the people, now that the theatres were open again, and they had their pleasures and amusements, made the best of Charles II for twenty-five years, in spite of the long-drawn-out persecution of the Presbyterians, and when he died they foolishly allowed his brother James, Duke of York, to become their king. James II (1685–1688), an avowed Roman Catholic, who declared openly what Charles worked for secretly, was faced at the outset of his reign by a rival claimant in the person of the Duke of Monmouth, the illegitimate son of Charles II. His attempt to secure the throne was suppressed with the utmost cruelty, he being executed after his followers were defeated in 1685 at the Battle of Sedgmoor. This rebellion cast a beam of light on the depths to which the administration of the law had sunk in these days, justice being turned out of court and everything evil put in its place.

The Lord Chancellor of England at this time was George Jeffreys (1648–1689), a zealous Anglican, to whom every Presbyterian and Nonconformist was a lying knave. In this incarnate devil everything wicked flourished, and nothing good. His personal habits were bestial, drink and debauchery being his pleasure, but by cunning, servility and intrigue he rose to the highest legal position in the land, and became a peer of the realm. His insolence, intemperance and injustice were notorious, and, in his conduct of the trials of those who had been involved in the rebellion against the King, he brought English justice to its lowest depths.

During what came to be known as "the Bloody Assizes", Jeffreys was a monster of bloodthirsty cruelty, blasphemous rage and brutish savagery. Then he gave free rein to his ferocity, and his appetite for slaughter grew more intense as the proceedings advanced, the horrible glare in his eyes, the savage lines on his face, his fierce shouts of wrath terrifying and confusing innocent and guilty alike. No one pleading innocence had a chance to escape, and no evidence in defence carried any weight, as some 1,400 victims passed before him to be sentenced to death by revolting torture, or to banishment as slaves to the West Indies.

When his master James II fled, after his short inglorious reign of three years, Jeffreys knew that his tyrannical career was also closed. Realising that he would now receive no mercy, he shaved off his shaggy eyebrows and disguised himself as a common sailor, but, before he could make his escape from the country, he was recognised, and only saved from being torn to pieces by the timely arrival of some soldiers, who conducted the trembling wretch to the Tower. There he lay for some months until he died, soothing his tortured mind by copious draughts of brandy.

Again religion played a large part in this reign,

as James, an avowed Roman Catholic, claimed absolute power and was determined to bring Britain back
to the old faith. Realising how Cromwell had
obtained his power by having a large army, he decided
on a military despotism. He maintained a large
army, and appointed Roman Catholics to the high
offices in the State, Universities, Church, Army and
Navy. By his Declaration of Indulgence, giving
religious freedom, he planned to pave the way for
Roman Catholic domination, but the Episcopalians
and the Dissenters combined against him because, as a
publication of the time stated, "You are therefore to
be hugged now, only that you may the better be
squeezed at another time."

James ordered his Declaration to be read in the
churches, and when seven bishops petitioned the
King to withdraw it they were arrested and prosecuted
for seditious libel, to be later acquitted and released.
When the bishops were awaiting their trial Mary of
Modena, James's Roman Catholic wife, gave birth to
a son who, the people realised, would in all proba-
bility continue his father's policy. This made both
the Whigs and Tories combine to take decisive action,
and the same day as the bishops were acquitted an
invitation was sent to William of Orange—a man of
liberal and enlightened outlook, the champion of
European Protestantism, and the husband of Mary,
the Protestant daughter of James II by his first wife,
who was a Protestant—to come to Britain with an
army to help the people to defend their liberties.

When William landed at Torbay in 1688, thanks
to a favourable wind which kept the loyal Royal
Navy at the Nore, he found the country in revolt

against the King, who escaped to France. It was a bloodless revolution, but financially very expensive, as William was paid £600,000 for his travelling expenses from Holland, though only a small Dutch fleet accompanied him. William and Mary ascended the throne of Britain as joint rulers, both having previously accepted the Declaration of Rights, which declared that a British sovereign must not be a Roman Catholic. Further, it limited the royal prerogative and freed Parliament from royal interference, making the office of Sovereign a contract between the King and his people, and not one to be held by divine right.

So we have now reached a new era in British history, one which had come about by mental development. The people had grown up sufficiently to feel able to face their future by relying on Parliament making the right decisions, the days of paternal control being over and those of manhood begun.

After this speedy transformation was completed, Louis XIV realised that he had lost his chance of delivering a blow at Protestantism. This new development was not what he had expected, but behind the change we see his figure, and the fear he caused to both Anglicans and Nonconformists alike. Anticipating a bloody revolution, and a long civil war, Louis had done nothing to prevent his most bitter enemy from becoming King of Great Britain and Ireland. But now it was too late because his army was fully engaged in the Rhineland, and William had received a royal welcome in the south of England, while up in the north the Scottish Presbyterians were equally joyful. Nowhere else was the new regime more heartily acclaimed than in Scotland, as it meant religious toleration to the scarred and bleeding lowlands, groaning in agony from twenty-eight years of bitter persecution.

So the people in these northern parts, now liberated from Episcopalian terrorism, burst forth into song, every town, village, hamlet and glen echoing with the strains of the metrical version of the 124th Psalm, the Presbyterian Te Deum, set to stirring music:—

> Now Israel may say, and that truly,
> If that the Lord had not our cause maintained,
> If that the Lord had not our right sustained,
> When cruel men against us furiously
> Rose up in wrath to make of us their prey.
>
> Then certainly they had devoured us all,
> And swallowed quick for aught that we could deem.
> Such was their rage, as we might well esteem.
> And, as fierce floods before them all things drown,
> So had they brought our soul to death quite down.
>
> The raging streams with their proud swelling waves,
> Had then our soul o'erwhelmed in the deep,
> But blessed be God, who doth us safely keep,
> And hath not given us for a living prey,
> Unto their teeth and bloody cruelty.
>
> Even as a bird out of the fowler's snare
> Escapes away, so is our soul set free.
> Broke are their nets, and thus escaped we.
> Therefore our help is in the Lord's great name,
> Who heaven and earth by his great power did frame.

The joyful singing of this psalm of praise and thanksgiving in the year 1688 ushers in the time when active religious persecution ceased in Britain, and it is fitting that this famous paean of thanksgiving be given in full to mark this epoch-making event. Though general organised torture, imprisonment and death ceased in 1688, a youth of eighteen was hanged in Edinburgh in 1697 for disbelieving that the Bible was divinely inspired, and imprisonment for publicly expressing unbelief continued until the middle of the 19th century. Though bodily persecution ceased from the beginning of the 18th century yet intolerance of, and interference with, religious convictions still remained, as nearly a hundred years were to pass before the Roman Catholics received permission in 1779 to worship in public, cruel restrictions lasting in Ireland until 1829. The Nonconformists in England had, however, to wait for nearly 150 years before they received the same consideration as the Episcopalians, as not until 1828 were they allowed to sit in Parliament, and not until 1871 were the universities of Oxford and Cambridge opened to receive them.

The coming of the stern, dour, unsociable William also brought to an end in Britain the claim that the King ruled by divine approval, and could do no wrong. Thus was severed the last link of a long chain of superstitious beliefs which commenced with the ancient idea that the gods ruled each country through the priest-king, who did their bidding, as expressed through the nation's oracle, or medium, from the Holy of Holies of the chief temple of the land. The course of history has been changed over and over again by this belief, its effect on every nation, in many different subtle ways, being noticeable to those who know where to look.

Historians, during the Christian era, have passed

by unnoticed this potent influence, because it is a subject about which they were quite ignorant, owing to the ban laid by the Christian Church on the study and investigation of psychic phenomena. To maintain its power over the people the Church associated mediumship with the devil, terming mediums wizards and witches. Consequently, because mediums were regarded as "servants of the devil", a highly important biological and psychological study was neglected during the Christian era, to produce, on the one hand, much superstitious nonsense, and, on the other, the age of materialism in which we now live.

The British people, through the landed aristocracy, which then mostly comprised Parliament, had at long last, after centuries of conflict between their Parliament and the Crown, secured control of their own affairs and their destiny. First of all they removed the divinely guided Pope, and now they removed the divinely guided King. Only the divinely guided archbishops and bishops, who still claim to be controlled by the Holy Ghost, remain, and continue to legislate in the House of Lords, quite uncontrolled by the will of the people.[1] Some day they also will go, and Britain will then be free from all these false claimants, whose legislation in the past has been for their own selfish interests and not for the good of the people.

William III (1689–1702) had little sympathy with the Church of England and Episcopalian domination, but he could not get Parliament, dominated by

---

[1] In the Prayer Book this divine control of the bishops is emphasised, and further confirmed in their publication entitled *Doctrine of the Church of England*, issued in 1938 after sixteen years of deliberation.

Episcopalians, to do more than allow the dissenters freedom of worship. It would not repeal the Corporation and Test Acts, which excluded all but Episcopalians from the universities, Parliament, state and municipal offices, and the holding of commissions in the army and navy. Nevertheless a step was taken towards democratic government, because he was the first to choose his ministers from the party having the greatest number in Parliament. Consequently, when the Tories outnumbered the Whigs, his ministers were Tories, and likewise with the Whigs. Religion, as we have already discovered, brought about the present-day party system, as the Tories were mostly Episcopalians, and the Whigs supported the Nonconformists. Ministers of the Crown now took up office, and retired from office, according to the support they received in Parliament. So impeachment, and the execution of ministers who were no longer wanted, came to an end.

The political freedom of the Press was established in 1695, and a political literary campaign developed which was led by rival journalists, the most outstanding being Addison, Steele and Swift. Then also came into being the National Debt, when in 1693 the government raised the first loan on the security of the nation, the King no longer borrowing money for national expenditure. A year later the subscribers were formed into a corporation which was given the name of "The Governor and Company of the Bank of England", to become the national bank, this having become a necessity, as war was now so expensive that it could only be paid for by borrowing.

While on the subject of money, it is fitting that
mention should be made of the poverty then prevailing throughout the country, nearly a fifth of the
nation being in receipt of occasional poor relief.
Everyone who was not a landlord was liable to be
expelled from any parish but his own. His native
parish only was considered to be responsible for his
maintenance if in financial distress, and no parish
wished to be burdened with the native of another
parish. The fear of increasing the rates, by maintaining those for whom it was not legally responsible,
caused the authorities of each parish to inflict much
misery and suffering on many respectable people who
had settled away from the place of their birth. Even
those not in immediate receipt of poor relief were
liable to be harried out of their homes if they were
living away from their native parish. Not only did
these strangers feel unsettled, but this stupid law
prevented labour from going where it was in greatest
demand.

Another hardship and injustice in those days came
about from the Game Laws, which made illegal the
killing of game except by the privileged few. Game
was preserved only for the large landowners, and
all small freeholders were precluded from killing it
even on their own land. Later we shall read of the
grave social consequences which followed from the
excessive eagerness of the country gentlemen to
preserve the partridges, pheasants, hares and rabbits
dwelling on their land.

Privileges, once claimed by the King for himself
and his courtiers, had now been taken over by the
landed gentry. Parliament was now the powerful

force in the land, and they controlled the elections, each candidate being the man of their choice who was elected to Parliament on the votes of the landlord's tenants, who voted as he directed. We will remember that the squires arose from the dissolution of the monasteries, an event which we are now beginning to see had considerable consequences on the political and social life of England, now a country with a population of 6,500,000, the great majority of which had little to brighten their lives.

Britain was still a land without hedges, and on its soil men, women and children worked thirteen hours a day to cultivate in a primitive way the patches of ground from which they derived their livelihood. There were no village schools, much disease and early death, but nevertheless the country was approaching changing times, though two hundred years were to pass before the people received their rights and privileges. Slowly but steadily Britain moved towards an agricultural and industrial revolution which, when completed, would leave little trace of the way of life that had so far lasted from the beginning of civilisation.

The Scottish Highlanders, who were mostly Episcopalians or Roman Catholics, continued to support the exiled James II, and their army, under Graham of Claverhouse (Viscount Dundee), was victorious at Killiecrankie in 1689, but collapsed as an organised body after the battle because here their leader was killed, his savage followers stripping his body and leaving it lying naked on the field. England was then at war with France, but William, the following year, with the support of the Protestants in northern Ireland, some of whom were besieged in

Londonderry for 105 days, defeated James II and his French and Roman Catholic Irish supporters at the Battle of the Boyne. This decisive conflict, which settled the fate of Ireland for the next 242 years, also made England safe against a French invasion from the west.

A year later (1691) Limerick capitulated, and the treaty signed there ended the war, when the Roman Catholics were given religious freedom, but this was withdrawn four years later and severe penal laws were passed against them. Jacobitism remained strong throughout William's reign, especially in the Highlands, and received powerful Episcopalian support, one of the most tragic episodes in the struggle being the massacre of Glencoe (1692), not so much on account of the death roll, which was small, but because of the treachery which preceded it. It left bitter memories, and these remain to this day.

William, though a brilliant statesman, was never a popular monarch. His manner was cold and repellent, and we shall see how nearly the Roman Catholic son of James II received the throne on the death of Anne, his successor. Neither William nor Anne had any use for the gay court life, hitherto the centre of politics and fashion since the time of King Alfred, and beloved by the aristocracy. Much of his reign was taken up in an effort to settle the division of the Spanish dominions on the death of Charles II of Spain. Unfortunately all his plans and agreements collapsed by Charles leaving his country and empire to Philip of Anjou, the grandson of Louis XIV. Then Britain, Holland and Austria, in alliance, prepared for war, but William, a life-long sufferer from asthma, died without an heir two months before its outbreak, his death coming from falling off his horse, which stumbled on a molehill.

He was succeeded by Anne (1702–1714), the dropsy-afflicted, dull-witted, pious Anglo-Catholic daughter of James II, and the wife of Prince George of Denmark. This was the age of the Sedan chair and the Coffee House, then the centre of news, of commercial information, gambling and social life, where everyone could express freely his opinions about everything. The principal event of her reign was the War of the Spanish Succession, the account of which has already been recorded. To Britain this conflict was for the maintenance of the balance of power, for purposes of trade, especially to keep open the markets for English cloth, and also for religion, it receiving the support of the Nonconformist Whigs, who were against Roman Catholic ascendency in Europe. It did not receive the support of the Tories, and, when it ended, they obtained Parliamentary power.

Then the Tories nearly succeeded in upsetting the Act of Settlement of 1701, the measure which had been introduced when it became evident that neither William III nor Anne would have children to succeed them. This legislation provided that on the death of Anne the crown would go to the nearest Protestant branch of the Stuart family, and only her unexpected death, and a violent quarrel between the Tory leaders, saved the country from the calamity of a Roman Catholic sovereign again being enthroned. When Anne died in 1714 the Whigs outmanœuvred the Tories and proclaimed George, the son of the

Electress of Hanover, and the Protestant great-grandson of James I, as King.

Little do we realise the bitterness of political feeling in these days, when loyalty to the Stuarts was again reviving. Around Viscount Bolingbroke the Jacobites rallied, and this brilliant man, one of Britain's greatest orators, was finally impeached for treason and exiled. Politics have always been a dirty and disreputable occupation, and the time we are now considering was no exception, because everyone was out for his own advancement, and success meant titles, office, wealth and power, to secure which few hesitated to adopt the most corrupt methods. Treason was of common occurrence, and many names amongst the highest in British political life were tarnished by acts of the grossest treachery. Bolingbroke, who held high office, was a good example of the times, as he showed no consistent policy, and no higher motive than personal ambition, it being only his lack of nerve which prevented him from carrying through his plan to restore the Stuarts to the throne.

Seven years before the death of Anne the Parliaments of Scotland and England, composed mostly of landed gentry, were united in 1707 after much Scottish controversy, the endless difficulties which were raised only being settled after lavish bribes had been paid. The Presbyterian Church of Scotland was now recognised and firmly established, Scottish law remained, and the two countries agreed on equal trading rights at home and in the colonies, the Scotch taking their share of the National Debt. Scotland, moreover, agreed to the Hanoverian Succession, and this brought to an end the ill-fated House of Stuart, whose kings, like the Bourbons, would never move with the times.

The reign of the House of Hanover opens up a new period in British history, and one which will be considered in the next chapter. Meantime we must return to Europe.

(4) Spain Falls from Her High Position.

The story of Spain, from the time of the Moslem invasion in 711, has already been told, and here we shall briefly review the position as we find it in the 17th century. During the first part of the century there flourished in Spain famous artists and distinguished writers, the most celebrated being Cervantes (1547–1616), the author of *Don Quixote*, one of the most widely read novels in the world, over which the language of eulogy has been exhausted during the past three hundred years.

Other celebrities have been mentioned in Chapter XI, but one other distinguished Spaniard of this era was Calderon de la Barca (1600–1681), who was the most eminent representative of his country's national drama. After some fifty years most of this intellectual life had passed away, and Spain had sunk into a state of political and intellectual slumber. She seemed to suffer from all the curses which come from ignorance, her finances were precarious, and her financial structure the worst in Europe. Taxation was stupidly devised, because it ruined industry and brought little gain to the national exchequer.

The Roman Catholic Church dominated the entire country, and had financial interests in most of its enterprises. To this unscrupulous organisation Spain was a land from which it sucked into its own coffers the best of everything. The nobles, with their vested interests and privileges, misruled their districts and estates, keeping the peasants in a state of serfdom. Spain was just typical of what all Europe was like during the age of Christian civilisation, except that elsewhere, here and there, spots of intellectual light brightened as Christian influence weakened, but not so in Spain, because the Church always kept a firm grip over the people.

With the Roman Catholic Church dominating everything, there was reaction everywhere, and the Holy Inquisition established an intellectual tyranny which was the worst in Europe. Its victims, who were accused of heresy, numbered in Spain alone over 341,000 since it first commenced its devilish work. When Europe was making scientific progress, science in Spain was non-existent. When Europe was beginning to develop wealth on sound economic lines, the Spanish were thinking as they thought in the Middle Ages. Free thought, tolerance and progress were words unknown in Spain, and in such conditions literature and learning withered away. Politically, socially, religiously and scientifically, Spain was still in the Dark Ages, and the miserable streets of her towns and villages swarmed with priests and beggars, the latter openly displaying the horrible sores and diseases from which they suffered.

Her vast American possessions, her domination over much of Italy, and her hold over the Netherlands did nothing to improve the lot of her people. She had her military and diplomatic triumphs, but the

upkeep of her armies for a long period was a great
drain on her resources. Her rulers dreamed of
possessions and conquests, but neglected their subjects, until the entire imperial fabric grew weak and
rotten. The people eventually always get the government they deserve, and to the Spanish character must
ultimately be attributed the low state to which Spain
sank as the 17th century drew on.

Spain never recovered from the loss to her intellectual and commercial life by the expulsion of the
Moors, the last of them being expelled in 1609,
because they were the backbone of the agricultural
and industrial life of the nation. They had introduced
into Spain the cultivation of sugar, cotton, rice and
silk, and had established paper-making mills, besides
a system of irrigation which had greatly improved the
fertility of the soil, the province of Valencia having
become a model of agriculture to the rest of Europe.
Both in manufacture and in commerce the Moors
were superior to the Spaniards, and, in consequence,
Spain enjoyed a flourishing export trade. All these
advantages were sacrificed by the Christians, because
they felt that they could not have as fellow countrymen those who professed a different faith. The
year 1609 therefore marks the height of Spanish
greatness, and, from now onwards, Spain sinks ever
lower under the weight of ignorance brought about
by a slavish attachment to Christian mythology.

Much of what interests us in Spanish history
dovetails in with what took place elsewhere in Europe,
and has already been noticed. Philip II (1556–1598),
the husband of Mary Tudor, and the King who
attacked England with the so-called "Invincible

Armada" during the reign of Queen Elizabeth, was followed by Philip III (1598–1621), who completed his father's work of expelling the Moors, because he felt that he could not conscientiously reign over any subjects who were damned, and whose destination hereafter was hell. The reign of Philip IV (1621–1665) was one long series of misfortunes, as during it Spain lost Holland, the Spanish fleet was destroyed by the British during the Thirty Years' War, Catalonia revolted, and revolution also broke out in the Spanish Netherlands (1633). Two years later France and Spain were at war, and not until 1643 did the Spaniards succeed in forcing the French invader to withdraw from Aragon. In 1647 Naples rebelled against Spanish rule, a revolt which was not quelled until the following year. In 1658 Spain was defeated by Portugal, and again this happened five years later, after which disaster the King died, to be followed by his infant son.

Charles II (1665–1700), at the age of four, then succeeded to a throne whose two former occupants had preferred the more secular pleasures of hunting and amusement to government. His mother Maria Anna acted as regent, but, as by now royal authority had much declined, Spain was really governed until the King came of age by a junta consisting of the chief ministers of state. Meanwhile Spain and Portugal had made peace, Portuguese independence being recognised (1668), and three years later Spain and Holland entered into an alliance, to be followed by one with Austria so as to curb the growing power of France. When Charles died he left all his possessions to Philip of Anjou, a settlement which led to the Spanish Succession War about which we have already read.

When the 17th century closed, Spain had been stripped of much of her influence in Europe. Holland had secured her independence, Portugal was once again a separate kingdom, France had occupied a great part of the southern Netherlands, and had established herself in Italy as a counterpoise to that of Spain. The weakness of the extremities, to which these facts bear conclusive testimony, was the result of still greater weakness at the centre, because the country's population had fallen from 30,000,000 when under Moslem rule, to less than 6,000,000 during the reign of Charles II.

This decrease in numbers was doubtless due to the religious bigotry which had condemned many thousands of Jews and millions of Moors to torture, death or exile. Thus the most virile portion of the population had been exterminated or banished, and much of the once prosperous fertile lands fell into the hands of the Christian Church, one fourth being taken over by the monasteries, which, clinging to obsolete methods of cultivation, received not more than one per cent. on the capital expended. Moreover, the rest of the land was in the hands of a few wealthy nobles who lived in Madrid and quite neglected its cultivation, the consequence being that the peasants produced just enough to keep themselves alive and no more, as they knew that if a surplus remained over it would be taken from them.

Spain is a country which has suffered from the curse of ignorance from the time it adopted the Christian faith. This being so, we find here focused everything that is evil and stupid, its people in consequence suffering the hardships and misery which always comes from ignorance. Here, however, we must leave this tragic land, and consider one which has so far not come into the limelight, one whose influence and importance was just becoming evident.

(5) RUSSIA BECOMES A GREAT NATION.

To understand the reason for the rise in the power and importance of Russia, it is necessary to consider at the same time those countries lying round her frontiers. The climate in these northern regions, and the less fertile soil, has kept the nations placed there from playing as important a part in European history as they might have done, when consideration is given to the strength of character and intelligence of their inhabitants. Though they did not greatly influence the rest of Europe, they have a history of their own which is well worth remembering, and here a short account will be given of what took place around the time we are now considering.

But for the Reformation, and the religious differences it caused, Denmark, Sweden and Norway might have dominated the Baltic and its adjoining lands, but Christian II (1513–1523) shattered their union by trying to force Sweden to retain orthodox Catholicism. Northern Sweden broke away, and he remained king of only Denmark and Norway, the effect of this being that for the next two centuries Denmark and Sweden were intermittently at war. Gustavus Vasa, a Swedish nobleman, valiantly resisted Christian's religious policy, and the Swedes in 1523 offered him their throne. Under him, and his descendants, Sweden played a part in European affairs out of all proportion to her size and wealth, because the Swedes were sturdy fighters and at times had outstanding leaders.

In 1587 Sigismund Vasa was elected to the throne of Poland, but, being an orthodox Catholic, there arose great antagonism between him and the Swedish branch of his family, to end thirty-six years later in Gustavus Adolphus entering the Thirty Years War to break the Roman Catholic power in Poland as well as in Germany. This in turn led to Sweden, when the Peace of Westphalia followed, obtaining the bishoprics of Bremen and Verden, valuable possessions which enabled her to control the mouths of the Weser and Elbe. As she also held the lower reaches of the Oder her position in the southern Baltic was now strong.

Brandenburg, from the same peace treaty, secured Eastern Pomerania, beyond which were the lands the Teutonic Knights had Christianised by the sword in 1228, and taken for themselves after destroying many of the Slavonic inhabitants. Brandenburg became the nucleus of the kingdom of Prussia, a nation which eventually reached to the Rhine in the west, to Denmark in the north, and to East Prussia on the east, thus bordering the entire southern coast of the Baltic Sea.

In the 17th century we see only the beginning of this great expansion, as then Poland split the German lands by coming down to the Baltic, with Danzig as her port at the mouth of the Vistula, thus dividing East Prussia from Brandenburg. The lands lying farther north, on the eastern side of the Baltic, now called Lithuania, Latvia, Estonia and Finland, were the prey of both Sweden and Russia, but in 1617 Gustavus Adolphus, after much hard fighting, secured them for Sweden. Thus was Russia, then called Moscovy, shut out from the Baltic and from all ocean trade.

The important Jagellon dynasty of Poland, to whom her greatness was due, died out in 1572, and from this date onwards her kings were elected. Bitter rivalry for the throne followed in a land seething with unrest, as her nobles and squires, who numbered 80,000 and were mostly independent rulers, were for ever at war with one another. Poland is one of the worst examples of the art of government in European history, and, in her attempt to be democratic, she became chaotic with her peasantry in serfdom. John Sobieski (1674–1696) was the last of her great kings, and became famous for his march to relieve Vienna when besieged by the Turks in 1683. He it was who was principally responsible for their defeat, but this, and his other successful military adventures, did no good to Poland, because, as he himself said, "the only result of so many victories was irreparable ruin and the damnation of Poland".

So we now come to Russia, better able from what has been said to appreciate her rise to greatness. Poland became weak because of anarchy, whereas Russia became united by the hammer-blows of two powerful men. The inhabitants of both countries are of the Slavonic race, a brave proud people who have always gallantly maintained the meaning of the word they gave to their ethnical stock, because Slav is the Russian for glorious. Poland in religion was

Roman Catholic, while circumstance had decreed that Russia would be Orthodox, or Eastern, Christian, and, moreover, their development has been vastly different. Perhaps this was because of the infusion of Tartar blood into the Russians, which Poland never had, as she largely escaped the Tartar invasion, but besides this Russia was made by two ruthless men who stood at nothing to have their wills obeyed.

Ivan the Terrible (1533-1584) was the founder of modern Russia, and he was the first Grand Duke to call himself Tzar, or Caesar, because of his marriage with a Byzantine princess. He was cruel and barbarous to a degree, and delighted in seeing men, women and children being tortured and massacred, his atrocities at Novgorod and Pskov being notorious. Moreover, he was a deeply religious man and a devout Christian. His blows fell particularly on the nobles, against whom he was pitilessly severe, but the middle and lower classes had not such terrible experiences, as he showed special mercy towards them. He increased the country's trade and favoured the advance of knowledge. Still, he left a name that fittingly described his life, because he quite neglected that side of learning which pertains to the development of character, and the practice of the virtues, as expounded by the great philosophers of the past. To historians his greatness lay, not in himself, but because of his victory at Krazan (1552) which drove the Tartars beyond the Caspian Sea.

After his death many troubles came to Russia, including plague, famine, invasion, foreign and civil war. In 1612 the Poles occupied Smolensk and Moscow, the Swedes capturing Novgorod, but the following year the Russians arose and drove the Poles out of Moscow. Then they elevated Michael Romanoff, the son of the Patriarch, to the imperial throne, thus bringing to an end the dynasty founded by Ivan. From now onwards the throne was occupied by a descendant of Michael—or the wife of a descendant—until the revolution of 1917, the people regarding its occupants with such veneration that the Tzars were considered to be more like gods than men.

The Poles to the Russians were what the Roman Catholics were to the Protestants, and they have been fighting each other since the 15th century, each trying to subdue the other and secure increased territory. Between the Orthodox Russians and the Catholic Poles there was bitter hatred, as each considered that the other was not a true Christian because they each defined the Trinity differently, as was explained in an earlier chapter. The Pole to the Russian was a dangerous heretic, a hateful political enemy, and a contemptible creature who could not maintain law and order in his own country. Likewise to the Pole the Russian was a heretic, besides being a cruel drunken barbarian. So it is not astonishing that the war against Poland continued, to last for five years, until the Poles were driven out of Kiev and those parts inhabited by Orthodox Christians.

Peter I (1689–1725), called the Great, reigned for thirty-six years. By the standard of greatness set up by Pythagoras and Socrates he does not deserve this title, but our ancestors gave little thought to character and much to spectacular achievements when honouring outstanding men. They were not sufficiently developed mentally to realise that the conquering of

our lusts and passions is much more important than
territorial conquests and the booty which follows.
Peter was a man of great physical strength and ferocity
of temper, much given to buffoonery, quite lacking
in dignity, dirty in his habits, a profligate and hopeless
drunkard. Cruel and brutal though he was, yet he
was intelligent, progressive, versatile and displayed
amazing energy.

Peter was capable of the most diabolical cruelty,
and because his son did not approve of his advanced
methods he tortured him abominably, and then
murdered him. Moreover, he was a fierce tyrant,
and yet he was deeply interested in the prosperity and
progress of his country. He tortured his opponents
by the thousand, and at the same time he devoted
himself to the introduction of culture into Russia.
Trade and industry were his special interests, and the
man of business received his favour in preference to
the one of noble birth. He, however, attempted no
social reform, or any kind of national or local representative government. This latter was obviously
impossible, because Russia was a land sodden with
ignorance, drunkenness and vice in every form, and
her deeply religious people, wedded to their Church
and completely under the rule of its priests, present
another example of how religion has no effect on
conduct.

Husbands beat their wives, as did the masters
their slaves and serfs, and everyone wallowed in
bestial drunkenness. The poor received no alleviation in their distress, and the great multitude of
wretched serfs were ground down so that the landowners might get the uttermost from their labour.

There was no justice and no general education, but, if the lot of the down-trodden was hard, Peter saw to it that beyond their own domains the upper classes had no special privileges. He stamped out corruption, compelled servile obedience, and abolished old and venerated customs, not hesitating on one occasion to put to death, with unbridled cruelty, a thousand of his bodyguard who resisted the adoption of new methods of service.

His reign was certainly a great epoch in Russian history, as he forged the people into a powerful nation. To make Russia like the rest of Europe was his ceaseless aim, and he had to meet the constant opposition of the priests, who encouraged every form of gross superstition, and influenced the people against any change for the better. European male dress was introduced in place of the long skirts worn by the men, who also had long beards because they thought that God had a beard, and that every Russian man was made in his likeness. Peter cared nothing for tradition and, in consequence, both beards and gowns were abolished. Then he turned his attention to the unnatural lives lived by the women, and did his utmost to bring them out of their strict Eastern seclusion, just as Mustapha Kemal did in Turkey in our own time.

He reformed the currency, and brought the Russian calendar into line with the rest of Europe by making the year begin on the first of January, introducing to Russia the first hospital, newspaper and museum. The teaching of science and mathematics to a favoured few received his special attention for military reasons, and he thoroughly reformed the whole machinery of government. His reforms followed after a visit to Holland, France and Britain, where he went to learn how to build a powerful navy; a momentous journey, as it marks the beginning of Russia becoming a powerful factor in European affairs. There he learned the art of ship-building, to such effect that some years after his return home he was able to sail down the River Don, with his new fleet of warships, and, in 1696, capture the strong Turkish fortress of Azov.

He now had his navy, but ships without ports and access to the sea are of little use. So he had to find a way out into the open, but Turkey controlled the shores of the Black Sea, and Poland and Sweden those of the Baltic. His only sea was the Arctic Ocean, which he could reach through Archangel, but this was frozen during the winter. Because of this confinement, Russia, in 1699, joined Denmark and Poland, still smarting from the unjustifiable attack on their territories by Charles X of Sweden forty years earlier, and together they attacked Sweden, but Peter found that he was up against a formidable opponent in Charles XII (1697–1718), a young and resolute warrior.

Charles was as great a soldier as Gustavus Adolphus, but he lacked his wisdom and caution. First of all Charles turned on Denmark, and here a great victory enabled him to reach the walls of Copenhagen, when the Danes made peace, paid an indemnity, and withdrew from the war. Next he attacked Russia and defeated a force five times the size of his own at Narva, close to the Gulf of Finland. Then Poland became the next victim, and, after a series of brilliant victories, ending in the capture of Warsaw and the over-running of Saxony, he dethroned Augustus II, their ruler, and set his own nominee on the throne. Meantime, while all this was happening, Peter of Russia was most of the time hopelessly drunk, but this did not prevent his reorganised army from occupying Sweden's Baltic provinces, and so Charles next marched straight for Moscow, that magnet which attracts all invaders to their doom.

Like both Napoleon and Hitler, he found the task of destroying Russian resistance was beyond his powers, as its defence strengthened as his line lengthened. So he turned south, but the Russian winter was now upon him, and this proved to be his most formidable enemy. Victories could not overcome the weather, or the barrier made by the snow, and besides this the piercing of the fierce cold so reduced his army by illness, death and desertion that it melted away. Then at Poltava, in 1709, the Russians attacked his weakened force, defeated it and made it surrender. Charles, this military meteor, escaped and found his way home to Sweden by way of Turkey, to die nine years later fighting an obscure battle in Norway. Sweden's power was now broken, as she had no further men available for the army, and had to stand by helplessly and see her possessions falling from her.

Russia took all the Swedish provinces around the Gulf of Finland, and there, on the River Neva, at the head of the gulf, Peter founded the city of St. Petersburg, later to be called Petrograd, and to be changed to Leningrad when the people obtained the power in 1917, as for them the name of Peter I had no happy memories. Here he established his navy, and it became the chief seaport of Russia. Prussia obtained western Pomerania, to become from now onwards the most powerful Baltic state and Russia's greatest enemy. Peter I was followed by his widow Catherine I (1725–1727), then by his grandson Peter II (1727–1730), after whom came his niece Anne (1730–1740), and then, after a short interval, his daughter Elizabeth (1741–1762), each monarch in turn being guided by capable and responsible statesmen, who brought Russia out of her age-old isolation to a place in the diplomatic system of Europe. This was her status when another of her outstanding rulers came to the throne.

She was Catherine II (1762–1796), a handsome, strong-minded, ambitious woman, a German princess by birth, and French by education. She was the unhappy wife of the semi-imbecile Peter III, the son of Anne. Her husband's reign was a tragedy for Europe, as, because of his admiration for Frederick II of Prussia, he allied himself with Germany, and so saved that predatory monarch when on the point of collapse. Thus Peter enabled Prussian influence to become firmly rooted, and, though his reign lasted only four months, these were fateful enough. Peter was so coarse in his habits, so unfaithful to his wife, and such a drunkard, that Catherine, who was much beloved because of her interest in, and sympathy with, everything Russian, put herself at the head of 20,000 men when the miserable emperor abdicated without a struggle, to be assassinated later without his wife's knowledge.

The Russians then put aside the legitimate successor

and acclaimed Catherine as their Empress, her long reign being one of conquest and expansion. In 1767 Turkey declared war, to be defeated and lose the Crimea. Plague then swept away many of the inhabitants of Moscow, and this was followed by an uprising of Cossacks and Mongols on the River Don, which ended by the Cossack republic being abolished. Then followed the important work of codifying the nation's laws, but the serfs did not benefit, in fact a ukase forbade them to bring any complaints against their masters, who had the power to punish them by sending them to Siberia. In those days serfs were bought and sold in the public market, but Catherine deprived the monasteries of owning either land or serfs, and, at the same time, made the Church entirely dependent on the State.

Again Turkey declared war in 1783, and this time her defeat in several bloody battles enabled Russia to occupy all the land bordering the Black Sea as far west as Odessa, thus securing to Russia the entire northern coast. Already (1772) Russia had occupied two thirds of Polish territory, and then followed twenty-two years later, the capture of Warsaw and the massacre of its inhabitants, when Russia deposed King Stanislas, who was set on certain urgent reforms. Poland, as we shall discover in the next chapter, was divided between Russia, Austria and Prussia, a foul deed which was the last of Catherine's conquests, as she died of apoplexy two years later.

Only three times in her history has Russia departed from her traditional policy of isolationism from the rest of the world. Peter the Great lifted the curtain between the East and the West for a time, and so also did the German-born Catherine. Then again it was lifted for the last time under the reign of Alexander II in the latter half of the 19th century. Catherine, because of her French education, brought French culture and the *philosophe* movement to the Russian Court. Then it was that in France the discoveries of science were giving the intelligensia an entirely new outlook on the world, and Bernard Fontenelle, by his popular writings on the bewildering discoveries of his time, acted as an important link between the scientific revolution and the new philosophy. This, for a time, enlightened the Russian Court, its influence dissipating when the iron curtain came down again when Catherine passed away.

The magnificence of her court, the great extent of her empire, her foreign conquests, and the imposing position she held amongst the sovereigns of the world, only bring into prominence the moral corruption, the semi-barbaric nature, the cruelty and systematic corruption, which characterised her entourage and policy. She was certainly a woman of strong character and great ability, but in vice, immorality and violence she maintained the tradition established by her famous predecessors, her munificence towards her lovers costing the State some £20,000,000. Alone she ruled her vast domains for thirty-four years, and would permit no disobedience, to become known after her death as Catherine the Great. Here, however, we must leave Russia for a time and learn how it was that Prussia, her neighbour, grew into a great and powerful state.

CHAPTER XIV.

CHRISTIAN CIVILISATION.
(1611–1802.)

Introduction. (1) Prussia Becomes a Great Power. (2) Injustice in France Prepares the Way for Revolution. (3) The Old Order in France is Overthrown. (4) Britain is Ruled by her first Prime Minister. (5) The British Empire Grows in Size and Power. (6) Britain Experiences her Greatest Humiliation. (7) The First Comprehensive Social Welfare Scheme.

THE construction of the human body came about by combination. First the single cell, the Amoeba, floated about alone in the ocean, to increase in number by dividing itself. Then came the time when two cells remained together, to become a body which propagated itself by throwing off a cell capable of producing new cells. This combination of cells went on until what we call a worm came into being, and by this process of enlargement and propagation the oceans, and then the land, were populated by numerous different creatures with bodies each of which numbered millions of separate cells. Socially, when we come to the beings grouped under the comprehensive name of Man, the same method is noticeable, as the species mated and lived together first as families, then as relations, and then as tribes. Politically the same tendency continued, because the tribes became nations and the nations empires.

Certain definite benefits followed from this unification of individuals into groups. There was greater protection and development, besides an increase in the division of labour, so that concentration was possible on definite objects. Consequently, as this went on, progress was made in acquiring the different arts. Primitive man when alone had to find his food and make his clothes, erect his shelter and protect himself against his enemies; in fact, do everything. Now today this is all divided up, each one doing his or her bit, which division of labour has led to our having all the comforts and conveniences of modern society.

Primitive man had to fight his enemies alone, but now some do the fighting, some produce the weapons, some the food, and so on. Modern war, owing to machinery being so largely employed, is also a much more all-embracing affair than it used to be when wars and fighting went on without greatly affecting the balance of the entire community. Now a war upsets the lives of everyone. We are all combatants as the result of air warfare, and we know, by means of the radio, hour by hour, what is happening.

While invention has intensified our pleasures and comforts in peace-time, it has likewise increased our danger and reduced our comforts in war. The greater contrast between war and peace now, from what it was in the old days, may in time make the people realise that it is not an affair quite apart, for some adventurers to enjoy, but something which comes so near home to everyone that the unwelcome visitor should never be permitted to approach. This could be accomplished if all the people were strong minded enough to combine against it. The change from war to peace, from the old discredited method which nations still have of dealing with nations, to a new and peaceful form of procedure, could come overnight if all desired and willed it. War, poverty, over-population, ill-health and distress could be finally abolished within our life-time if the minds of the people everywhere advanced sufficiently to make this possible. It is all a question of mental development.

The mind in man must make the conditions favouring peace and happiness, it must override the difficulties in this respect as it has done those of other seemingly insoluble problems. It has produced shelter against the weather, ships that are safe, airplanes which defy gravity; it has discovered how to force water above its own level, how to cure sickness and so on, and it must now produce the conditions which make war, and all the other evils from which we suffer, unnecessary. All must unite to make this change possible, and it is just because the human race is so ignorant, or rather because we are at such different stages of ignorance, that we go blundering along in and out of war, in and out of prosperity, with poverty and misery, hardship and suffering, always our companions, when, by rational and intelligent foresight and planning, there could be plenty and comfort for all.

The human mind is king of nature, but it is only slowly learning to use its authority. To primitive minds nature is supreme, and to it they bow low in meek subjection. Mind can be king only if it develops to a point where it can exercise its authority and control nature, thus transforming an enemy into a friend. Nature is a good servant, but a bad master. Mind, even in its present partially developed state, is constantly interfering with, and interrupting, what nature, if left alone, would do, thus producing different effects from those nature intends.

Nature's laws work within strict limits, whereas mind can roam at will. Rain never thinks that there is no further need of water in a certain place, and that elsewhere there is a drought, but mind can arrange to store or carry water where it is most required. We dam up the river and irrigate the fields, instead of permitting the river to run along its course. By ice nature breaks open rocks, whereas we take from the earth certain ingredients, produce explosives, and blast the rocks to our own design.

Mind has decided to make its home, for a time at least, in matter, and both matter and force, which seem to be inseparable, can be either its friend or enemy according to the use it makes of them. Much of modern history is just a record of mankind using matter and force more and more for both purposes, for erecting houses and producing our comforts, on the one hand, and, on the other, manufacturing cannon, bombs, shot and shell for our misery and destruction.

Mind produces the tools for both production and destruction, implements to extract from nature that which makes for our happiness and misery. So we must go to the source to find a remedy for all our troubles. As we think, so we do, right thinking producing comfort and happiness, wrong thinking creating misery and unhappiness. Only by our learning to think aright can righteousness take the place of wickedness; only by individuals, and every nation of individuals, thinking the right, and not the wrong, way can war cease, and lasting happiness come to mankind.

Germany, more than any other nation in modern times, has thought the wrong way, and consequently has propagated evil, ignored the ethical code and the lessons history and experience have to teach us. Germany stands out as does no other nation, in her glorification of war, cruelty and hatred. Other nations have fought, been cruel and hated, but Germany has glorified and sung praise to these abominations. From the beginning of the 18th century Prussia has been the nucleus of German thought and action, making her influence more and more felt until she dominated the German race.

Our historical review has now reached the time when the Prussian influence began to be felt · in European affairs, a power which grew and developed until eventually all the other Germanic tribes were under her domination. This German combination then attempted, on two occasions, to become the complete master of Europe, but much was to happen before that time arrived.

(1) Prussia Becomes a Great Power.

The origin of what is now Prussia was a Germanic frontier outpost against the Slavs, a "Mark" as it was called. Around this centre of German influence, territory was acquired until a small state under a ruler came into being. In 1319 this region became the flourishing little state of Brandenburg, after a series of able rulers had governed it wisely and well. Then followed a century of confusion and bad government until 1415, when the emperor, Sigismund, made his friend Frederick of Hohenzollern the Elector of Brandenburg. Some sixty years later (1473) it was decided that Brandenburg must not be divided, but descend to the eldest son of the Hohenzollern family.

In Prussia, which in those days had no connection with Brandenburg, the Teutonic Knights had been plundering, slaughtering and converting the inhabitants to Christianity, seizing their land and settling down. Then, at the Battle of Tannenberg (1410), they were defeated by the Poles, and West Prussia was annexed to Poland, while East Prussia, or Prussia as it came to be called, had to recognise the King of Poland as its overlord. Feeling helpless, they asked Albert of Hohenzollern, a near relative of the rulers of Brandenburg, to be their chief, or Grand Master, a position which he accepted in 1511, to declare himself a Protestant at the Reformation.

When, in 1611, his family became extinct, Prussia was taken over by the Elector of Brandenburg, but Poland still retained what was once West Prussia, the land on the west bank of the Vistula, with the port of Danzig on the Baltic at its mouth. This piece of land came to be known in our own time as the Polish Corridor, which the Germans made the excuse for the war with Poland in 1939. By marriage, other possessions gathered round Brandenburg, including lands on the Rhine, but they were scattered and formed no unified state. Frederick William

Hohenzollern succeeded to these domains, and, as he is considered the founder of modern Prussia, became known as the Great Elector (1640–1688).

After the Thirty Years' War, at the Peace of Westphalia, Magdeburg and eastern Pomerania, on the southern shore of the Baltic, were added to his possessions. He gave the lands under him unified government, and was unflagging in promoting their commercial prosperity, building canals and fostering industry by means of a protective tariff. As already mentioned, his sheltering in Berlin of the French Huguenots, expelled by Louis XIV, marked the beginning of that city's greatness, they contributing much to the wealth of the entire state. He fought against Poland in alliance with Sweden and gained a great victory at Warsaw, after which the King of Poland relinquished his overlordship of West Prussia and recognised him as its ruler, but his greatest victory came later when at war against the Swedes in 1675.

The Great Elector was succeeded by his son Frederick, a man quite unlike his father, and one who was fonder of pomp and ceremony than of administration. For his services to the Emperor Leopold I he was given the title of King Frederick I of Prussia (1688–1713), the reason why Brandenburg was passed over being because it was within the Holy Roman Empire, whereas Prussia was not, and the Emperor wished no king within his realm. This accounts for Prussia instead of Brandenburg ultimately giving its name to all the territories of the future Hohenzollern kings.

Frederick William I (1713–1740) succeeded his

father. He inherited many of the qualities of his grandfather, the Great Elector, but these were exaggerated and brutalised. Pomp and ceremony he despised, and in place of lavishness he set about rigidly economising, though this did not detract from efficient administration. He reigned as a despot, permitting no liberty of opinion, or any form of representative government. He claimed all that the Stuarts had claimed, and these demands were accepted by his people, whereas the British, a century earlier, had rebelled against them, a fact which illustrates the difference between the British and German mentality towards representative government. It is strange that a nation like the Germans, so thorough and painstaking in everyday affairs, is so childlike in affairs of state.

Frederick William was typically Prussian in his narrow outlook, and considered everything from only the Brandenburg point of view, as if this petty state were the centre of the universe. He was coarse, brutal, savage, unlearned and very pious, living for three things only: the Bible and his religion, the efficient collection of taxes, and the building up of a well-equipped and highly organised army. He maintained peace throughout his reign, and handed down for his son's use a prosperous state, well-organised taxation, and an army of 83,000 men, half the size of the French army but much more efficient.

Quite the most notable, and one of the most wicked, of all the Hohenzollerns was Frederick II (1740-1786). When a young man he was both polished and cultured, a cosmopolitan, a patron of the arts, and quite unorthodox, the exact opposite of his father Frederick William, whom he succeeded. He so hated the life at his father's court that he tried to escape, but was caught and condemned to death. He was, however, pardoned, but his father tortured and executed all his accomplices without justice or mercy, and some without trial. Then this God-fearing parent forced his son to accept the Protestant form of Christianity, and marry a woman he disliked, both of which impositions seemed to alter entirely his outlook on life, because, when he became king, all his early idealism and humanity had vanished. He became a typical Prussian, the Prussians then being classed by Goethe as no better than barbarians. Henceforward he relied only on force and ruthlessness to attain his ends.

To understand what now follows we must go back some years. Charles VI (1711–1740), the Hapsburg Holy Roman Emperor, had only one child, a daughter Maria Theresa. His aim was to secure for her at his death all the Hapsburg territories, and the imperial title for her husband Francis of Lorraine. To make her position secure he obtained from his various domains, and the leading European powers, including Prussia, a signed document, known as the Pragmatic Sanction, which recognised her rights to his possessions. His foresight was unfortunately in vain, because, when he died in 1740, the avaricious Frederick II took the opportunity to steal from Austria the rich province of Silesia, whose lands embraced the upper reaches of the River Oder. Its prosperous linen industry, rich deposits of iron, and good waterways, made this land a golden prize for the criminally minded royal burglar, and the efficient army left to him by his father was not long in accomplishing its allotted task. Silesia was quickly overrun by the Prussians, and the Battle of Mollwitz (1741) decided its fate.

Thus this Hohenzollern robber obtained for himself and his descendants vast estates which made this royal house one of the richest in Europe, but the victory of Mollwitz did more than that, it achieved something which closely affected every one of us during the last thirty years (1914–1944). It made the Prussians, and then the Germans, believe that war could be made to pay. To this forerunner of Hitler a promise meant nothing if by breaking it the Germanic cause was furthered, and from this time onwards the Germans took the way of the common thief, to whom loot is everything and honour and righteousness nothing.

For the next twenty-one years, with an interval of seven years of peace, bloody and destructive war again cursed Europe. France, unable to lose an opportunity to secure the Netherlands and Luxemburg, broke the promise she gave to recognise Maria Theresa, and joined with Prussia. British and Hanoverian troops, under the command of George II of Britain, supported Austria, to keep France from having the Netherlands, defeating the French at Dettingen in 1743, which, it is interesting to remember, was the last occasion a British monarch led his troops into battle. Two years later, under the Duke of Cumberland, Britain was defeated by the French at Fontenoy, when France occupied the Netherlands.

This conflict, known as the Austrian Succession

War, centred round the pathetic figure of Maria Theresa (1740–1780) who, on her accession, found herself at war with Prussia, while Charles, the Elector of Bavaria, claimed, with the support of France, the imperial title. When Bavarian and French troops entered Bohemia, she appealed to Hungary for help, a request which the Hungarians could not resist from one so beautiful when she appeared before them with her child in her arms. A large force, composed of wild adventurers, quickly assembled and drove out the invaders, but, when the war ended in 1748, the Peace of Aix la Chapelle gave Silesia to Frederick II, neither Britain nor France gaining anything.

Then followed a complete volte-face. France and Austria, who had been deadly enemies for two hundred and fifty years, became friends, and in consequence Britain dropped her friendship with Austria, and allied herself with Prussia, who, without any justification, started a new war in 1756 by attacking Saxony and seizing its capital and treasures. The skilful diplomacy of the Austrian minister Kaunitz, and the influence of Madame de Pompadour, the mistress of Louis XV, brought about this French-Austrian alliance which was to drag France into another war with Prussia. The recent peace treaty was soon scrapped, and Frederick II faced alone the combined forces of Austria and France intent on his destruction. Black indeed as was his prospect, worse was to come, because Maria Theresa succeeded in winning the support of the hard-drinking, licentious Elizabeth, the Tzarina of Russia.

Frederick now found himself pitted against three formidable powers, and could only look to Britain for help, which at first lay chiefly on the sea and in money. For seven years Prussia was devastated by this conflict, known as the Seven Years' War (1756–1763), and experienced a time just as terrible as that through which she passed during the Thirty Years' War. Thus millions of innocent people suffered because of the greed and ambition of one man, Frederick, whom they later called the Great. By attacking Saxony, he brought all this misery upon them.

The Prussian armies at first were successful, but later were defeated by Russia at Kunersdorf (1759), when Berlin was captured, and Frederick contemplated suicide, as did Napoleon, and other similar scoundrels, when faced with defeat. In their hour of danger these so-called great men had not character enough to face boldly their fate, but considered a quick and easy way out. This shows that planning for others to fight for what one wants is not a sign of greatness but only of complete selfishness and greed, of thought for oneself alone, and entire neglect of the misery this scheming brings about.

Frederick, like Hitler and his gang, and all the other conquerors of the past, calmly sat down to work out beforehand wholesale criminal robbery with violence, a crime which in civil life brings the culprits to the gallows. They were so criminally minded that they resorted to crime instead of honest methods of accumulating wealth. The fact that we, and our ancestors, have in the past looked on such moral perverts as great, shows how our ethical outlook has been twisted and dazzled by their successes, as, if a country was devastated, captured, and some of its

inhabitants killed, maimed or ruined, the exalted
thief who did the deed was regarded as a brilliant
soldier, and a great and outstanding man.

Why not lavish praise instead on the great inventors and industrialists who have brought to us our
comforts and our pleasures? Why not talk of Edison
the Great, Ford the Great, Nuffield the Great, Marconi the Great, James Watt the Great, George
Stephenson the Great, and hundreds of others whose
capacity to build up great enterprises was far and
away beyond that of professional soldiers, whatever
title they bore—emperor, king, duke, marshal or
general—who used their power and position for
criminal purposes instead of for the good of
humanity? True, they changed national boundaries,
but, if there never was another such man, all mankind
would gain immensely.

To build up a great business requires ingenuity,
courage, fortitude, foresight, perseverance, industry,
skill, honesty, and even greater qualities than are
required to win a battle. The truly great men would
never descend to the degradation, criminality and
cruelty necessary to fight an aggressive war, but
history gives to their deeds and thoughts little attention, most of the outstanding industrial benefactors
and inventors being only vaguely known to most
people. In any case war is the greatest of all gambles,
because so many unforeseen events occur which
neither genius nor planning can prevent, and if
Frederick had not been lucky he would have been a
complete failure.

For a time it seemed as if Prussia would be
obliterated, but, after the defeat of the French at

Rosbach in 1757, he managed to extricate himself from his perilous position. Again, in the same year, he decisively defeated the Austrians at Leuthen by employing a new method of attack which revolutionised the practice of war. Britain then sent a large army to his aid, "to win Canada on the plains of Germany", as the Earl of Chatham, the British Prime Minister, declared, and by its great victory at Minden (1759) saved Hanover from being overrun by the French.

So as to secure Canada and India, Britain fought France and helped to save Prussia, a policy which produced modern Germany, a nation which has brought more ruin and desolation on the world than any other. On the other hand, France, in order to secure the Netherlands, poured out her men and treasure in a long exhaustive war which prevented her from reinforcing her troops abroad. Her navy was neglected, an error which was not repaired until both Canada and India had passed into British possession. Politically, France made as great a mistake as did Britain when she lost the American colonies, and few other mistakes have had such far-reaching consequences. Thus the destiny of two great continents was decided on the plains of Germany, and the Protestant faith became predominant in North America in place of Roman Catholicism.

Prussia was therefore a contributing cause to Britain securing India and Canada, just as Britain was a cause which helped Prussia to secure her dominance in Germany, and Frederick acknowledged with gratitude Britain's help in his time of danger. The complete putrefaction of French political life was also another reason for his success, just as it was to his successor Hitler in 1940. Still, in spite of the changed outlook, Frederick was by no means out of the wood, because Britain in 1761, after an expenditure of £82,000,000, withdrew from further participation in the war. Then the death of the Tzarina Elizabeth saved him once again, as she was followed by Peter III, who had a great admiration for Frederick's military qualities. An alliance between Russia and Prussia changed the entire aspect of the war, but Peter was murdered four months later, and Catherine, his German wife, reigned in his place as Catherine II, as told in the previous chapter. She annulled the alliance, though it was now too late to secure Frederick's defeat, and the Peace of Paris (1763) concluded the Seven Years' War.

Prussia was left in possession of Silesia, but not of Saxony. Her position was tragic, as not only was there everywhere devastation and destitution, both the nobles and the peasants being reduced to living in poverty and wearing rags, but her population had fallen by 500,000 to 4,500,000. Lord Malmesbury, the British Ambassador, reported in 1772 that not a chaste woman existed in Berlin, both sexes being completely corrupt. Women of rank were common prostitutes. Anarchy and lawlessness abounded, the administration of justice ceased, and everything was as chaotic as it had been after the Thirty Years' War. Britain, on the other hand, had secured Canada, India, Senegal, Florida, St. Vincent, Tobago, Dominica, and other islands for the cost of only 1600 British lives, her superior sea power, moreover, having enabled her to make this vast addition to her empire at a cost in money which was easily borne because of her rapidly expanding maritime trade.

Never again did Frederick engage in another serious conflict, as he came to realise that war is mostly a gamble, and that the best prepared plans do not always work out according to calculation. Instead he devoted himself to repairing the damage his greed had brought about. At his court there was little lustre, and no one worked harder than he did to bring prosperity back to Prussia. He is called an enlightened despot, and in the 18th century such rulers reigned in Russia, Sweden, Denmark and Austria, though he ranks beyond them all for the energy he displayed in raising his country from the depths of desolation to prosperity. He abolished torture, and gave complete religious toleration, being influenced by Voltaire and the other notable liberators of France, for whom he had a great admiration.

Poland meantime lay a helpless wreck, her people divided into numerous factions, her constitution and administration was in hopeless confusion, and her peasantry were in abject sordid serfdom. Here was the opportunity for some more grabbing, and Frederick, anxious to avoid another war, proposed (1772) that Austria, Russia and Prussia should each annex a slice of this distracted land. Maria Theresa, who had a higher ethical standard, and remembered how much she had resented Silesia being taken from her, refused at first to partake in such a deed, but, in the end, agreed when she found that if she did not take her portion the other two would divide between them what they wanted.

Russia obtained the largest share, but Prussia got

Western Prussia, and thus joined up with Brandenburg. From that date internal conditions in what remained of Poland improved under her king Stanislas II, who curbed the power of the aristocracy and restored law and order. Progress continued, much to the annoyance of her neighbours, especially Russia, who did not wish a strong power on her frontier. So a plot was hatched by Prussia, Russia and Austria to divide the entire country between them. Flimsy excuses were made for this further act of brigandage, when, in 1793, the three armies marched in and defeated the Poles, only to start to quarrel amongst themselves as to how the booty was to be divided.

In the end Russia took all the land east of Warsaw, Prussia received what lay north and west of the capital, and Austria everything to the south. Then they made a thieves' bargain never to allow Poland to rise again, and so it came about that this old nation was cut up like a dead corpse, but later on she did appear on the map, as we shall discover.

These brigands were so busily engaged in demolishing their victim, to prevent its newly elected King Stanislas from carrying out the much needed reforms he had promised to undertake, that they had not time to spare to attend to matters in the west. Here France, fired with revolutionary ideals, had become a rejuvenated power, and when at last they paused to look round they beheld to their dismay a new France firmly established, and determined that the fate which had befallen Poland would not come to her, a fact which, from now onwards, was to change the political map of Europe.

Meantime Maria Theresa, a woman with many fine

qualities, had died in 1780, leaving to her son Joseph all the Hapsburg possessions, he already having succeeded to the imperial title after the death of his father in 1765. Joseph II (1765–1790), though he regarded Frederick II as his enemy, set about to adopt the methods initiated by him to rebuild Prussia after the disastrous wars for which he had been responsible. Joseph was one of the enlightened dictators of his age, and, under the complete authority of the Crown, he attempted to build up a unified Austrian Empire, honestly governed without class or race privilege, one in which there was to be religious freedom and German the only language. He took Prussia as his model, but he found the Austrian dominions, with their various religions, races, ideals and antagonisms, to be quite a different proposition.

He was the ruler of (1) Austria, which was the original Hapsburg possession, whose people were German and mostly Roman Catholics; (2) Bohemia and Moravia, which was Czech and partly Protestant; (3) Hungary and Transylvania, whose Roman Catholic population consisted largely of Magyars, with a strong national sentiment; (4) the northern Italian territories, whose people were Roman Catholics but quite apart in language, character and outlook; and finally of (5) Roman Catholic Belgium, acquired from Spain under the Treaty of Utrecht, a land which was more French than Austrian, with her inhabitants of different race, language and ideals. Besides these there were other minor territories, but the foregoing gives an idea of the ramshackle empire over which Joseph ruled from his palace in Vienna.

This outstanding man made a noble effort at unification, but failed. When he proclaimed religious toleration everywhere in his realm the Roman Catholics, where they predominated, and the Protestants in Bohemia, were up in arms. When he announced the end of Church censorship of books, the freedom of the press, and education for the people, the clergy raised their flocks in active opposition. He abolished serfdom and capital punishment, instituted public libraries, an observatory, a medical college, a university and schools for the middle classes, besides abolishing monopolies and fostering trade, industry and the arts. Pope Pius VI, a weak and stupid old man, was so alarmed at the prospect of the people being educated that he took the unprecedented course of making a special visit to Vienna, to persuade the Emperor to drop his reforms, but without success.

When Joseph died, his aims were not accomplished, and his brother Leopold II (1790–1792), who followed him, tried to conciliate all the passions which Joseph's plans had aroused, but before he succeeded in doing so Europe was again in the melting-pot by the upheaval caused by the French Revolution, about which there is now a very interesting story to tell.

(2) Injustice in France Prepares the Way for Revolution.

Now we must go back again to the beginning of the 18th century, when, by a series of deaths, a child, the Duke of Burgundy, became the successor of Louis XIV in 1715, to be known as Louis XV (1715–

1774). The Duke of Orleans became regent during the King's minority, at a time when France was suffering from the reaction caused by the mistakes of Louis XIV ; her finances were in chaos, and her prisons were full to overflowing with many who knew not the reason for their confinement. The debt was immense, and the taxation, which exempted both clergy and nobles, so crushing that the experiment was made, on the suggestion of a Scotsman, John Law, to redeem the debt by issuing paper money on the security of the French North-American possessions. The scheme failed, and Law was disgraced. The Regent died in 1723, and Louis appointed his former tutor, the wise, patient, imperturbable Cardinal Fleury as his Chief Minister. So long as he lived France was on friendly terms with Britain and at peace.

Now we come to another of these succession wars, which are quite enough in themselves to make clear that it is wrong to have all the affairs of state resting on one man. Europe has wasted its blood and treasure over the question as to which family was to rule. England, France, Spain and Austria have been involved, and now comes the war over the Polish succession. France, Spain and Sardinia supported the claim to the Polish throne of the benevolent and enlightened Stanislas I, the former king, who had been exiled, while, on the other hand, Austria and Russia favoured the degenerate Augustus of Saxony. A Russian army arrived in the neighbourhood of Warsaw in 1734, and Augustus was made king against the wishes of the people, who had elected Stanislas by a large majority. Stanislas fled to Danzig, which capitulated after a siege of five months, and then he escaped to Prussia. Under Augustus the condition of Poland went from bad to worse, his influence on everything being evil, until finally, under his successors, the country ceased to exist.

The reign of Louis XV was one of the worst in the history of France. For the most part he lived a life of vice and immorality, and showed neither patriotism nor skill in diplomacy. He neither trusted, nor was trusted by, his ministers, and carried out intrigues without their knowledge, being influenced by his mistresses, Madame de Pompadour, in the early part of his reign, and then by Madame du Barri in the latter part. We have already read how Pompadour's influence caused France to drop her friendship with Prussia, and become involved in a war against Prussia in alliance with Austria. Her influence upon national policy was against the true interests of France, and the decline in French prestige, which went on throughout this reign, can be traced in part to her evil counsels.

By skilfully engineering quarrels amongst the Indian princes, and training Indian soldiers in European methods of war, Dupleix, and other unscrupulous diplomatists, had, with little fighting, obtained for France a dominating position in India. In Canada, and the south of North America, New Orleans and the lower Mississippi valley, France had large well-governed possessions, and everything then pointed to these being increased to the disadvantage of Britain. This state of affairs was of short duration, because France, by her wars in Europe, overstrained her resources, and was unable to protect her interests abroad or maintain large armies at home. To Britain, these European wars were no more than incidents, into which she could enter and withdraw at will, to shelter behind her ocean rampart. So Britain fought France in Europe, to prevent her from sending large forces overseas, and in this way took India and Canada for herself.

The Seven Years' War, and British naval supremacy, gave Britain these two vast possessions, and when the French realised that they had gained nothing in Europe but humiliation, disaster and bankruptcy, besides losing much abroad, Louis XV forfeited the loyalty of his people. This distrust, together with the disasters which had come to France from the autocratic rule of Louis XIV, weakened the people's confidence in the throne, and laid the foundation for the revolution. The spread of literature, moreover, enabled outstanding men, with the interests of humanity in mind, to denounce the rottenness of existing conditions, and, when they could not write what they thought in France they did so elsewhere, nothing being done to prevent the educated French from reading their advanced thoughts.

France had everything to make her a happy, rich and prosperous state, but she lacked the greatest of all assets: knowledge of how this can be achieved. A black cloud of ignorance shadowed the minds of the people, the upper classes being selfish and thinking only of themselves, while the lower classes were forced to do the bidding of their masters. Privilege abounded everywhere, at Court, in the Church, the Army and the Navy, and justice throughout the land was polluted, while finance and taxation were not based upon just or scientific principles. Agriculture was medieval, famines frequent, and poverty everywhere. Embittered by destitution, bread riots were chronic, as nothing was ever done to improve the fertility of the soil, the age-old theological method of prayer for daily needs failing to achieve any other results than to burden the poor with the upkeep of a great and wealthy Church organisation.

Though the States-General never met, Parlement (as the French spell it) did, but this body, which assembled in Paris, was not like the elected British Parliament, it being more a Court of Justice which was convened to protect the laws of France from illegal interference. This assembly now showed some independence of expression, particularly in its support for Jansenism, a religious body which the Roman Catholic Church had done its utmost to obliterate. We have already read of its beliefs and sufferings during the reign of Louis XIV, but, though reduced in numbers, the remnant was still bitterly persecuted. Repeatedly Parlement supported its cause, and attacked the government for allowing the Church to carry on such pitiless cruelty. More and more the people rallied round Parlement, and looked to it to protect their liberties.

The Jesuits were also the subject of attack by Parlement, because they represented everything reactionary in the Crown, which they loyally supported. They were unpopular with the people, who realised their evil influence, and how they had instigated the worst forms of religious oppression. Parlement enquired into the methods and organisation of the

Society, and declared that the members were not loyal citizens of France, because they would as readily take instructions from a foreigner, belonging to the order, as from a Frenchman. Its international character was resented by patriotic people, and the King was forced by popular opinion to suppress the Society in 1764. This ban lasted for only a short time, as the Jesuits were much too useful to the Church, and what the Church decided in those days came to pass. So the Jesuit order was again allowed to function. Similar attacks occurred in other countries against the Jesuits, all of which can be directly traced to the growing influence of the intellectuals, who, by their writings, were exposing the falsity and hollowness of the beliefs and claims of the Christian Church.

Then Parlement turned its attention to the question of taxation, and took exception to some of the methods and forms adopted. Instead of the King yielding, he arrested and exiled its members, decreeing that Parlement be for ever abolished, and that in future the place of the High Court of Justice be taken by new courts chosen by the Crown.

To prevent a recurrence of criticism it was decreed that the new courts would be deprived of wide powers, and thus be unable to interfere in public affairs. Never did Louis XV try to understand his people's wishes, and he would neither govern nor allow others to govern, he being both slothful and self-indulgent, so much so that he left behind him a long trail of evil. Had he been sufficiently wise and industrious to adjust conditions to the advancing intelligence of the people, the Revolution would have been unnecessary, but he thought little of the good of France, and only of himself and his own selfish pleasures.

Nations rise and fall. Some progress for a time only to return to primitive conditions. History, which covers only a few thousand years, certainly records progress, not continuous progress, but progress in the form of a spiral. Periods of recession follow those of advancement, the Dark Age of Christendom, when the Church took the place of the school and the priest that of the schoolmaster, following the Golden Age of Greece and the Silver Age of Rome. Now we are at the entrance to a new age, the dark age of Christian civilisation is closing, and the dawn of a new era is heralded by the growing demand for education to take the place of superstition.

In the long course of evolution, the time mankind has lived together as separate nations is like as a second is to a day. Some nations made greater mental progress than did others, only eventually to suffer decline—Greece, for example, during the Christian era, being unrecognisable as the land which gave birth to the great intellects of her golden age. Up to now all Christendom had suffered from the same mental blight which Christianity had cast on Europe, but, as the chains of ignorance slackened, the minds of the people stirred to ever greater effect. Within the compass of history man's evolution has seemed deadly slow, but now we are coming to the time when the use of paper and printing is beginning to make a very definite impression on his mind.

When thoughts were confined to the family or one's friends, all of whom were equally ignorant, no mental progress was possible, but now books were being written and read, and one new thought led to another, thus proclaiming the time when many would be found who would be eager to learn. The more the people read the more they realised how little they knew, and then it was that they took thought for their social conditions, as only sodden minds will live in filth like animals. Likewise the desire to know more quickened the wish for greater freedom of expression, to right wrongs, to improve conditions, and to have greater liberty, less toil and fewer hardships.

Conditions everywhere were bad, and France was no exception. The condition of European and British towns would have shocked a Greek or Roman of two thousand years earlier. Sanitation was lacking, the houses of all but the rich and well-to-do being filthy hovels. The poor and the sick received little or no care and attention, and the great majority lived and died in serfdom, tied to their crofts. The condition of the peasants in France was bad enough, but it was much worse throughout Europe, especially in Spain, southern Germany, Russia and Poland.

What the French most resented was their total inability to express themselves for the purpose of obtaining redress of their many grievances, one being that they could not prevent game, great and small, from spoiling their crops, because that would interfere with their overlord's shooting rights. The King was an absolute monarch, the States-General never met, taxation was unbearable, and pressed hardest upon the poor, while the Church and the priests were exempt, and the nobles, who had certain judicial rights over their tenants and employees, paid far less than their share.

The Church was the instrument used to promote this autocratic and unjust state of affairs, and both it and the King worked together for their own ends. Both the Church and the Court were corrupt, tyrannical and unjust, and the injustice in taxation was specially felt in the country districts, as the townspeople were to some extent exempt. In the country the peasantry were the chief sufferers, and in some districts they paid in taxation more than half of what they earned. There was no incentive to have attractive, clean, tidy homes, as, whenever anything was done to improve their property and conditions, the tax-gatherer had the right to increase arbitrarily the sum he demanded. Consequently French villages were left in a state of squalor, to impress the tax-gatherer with their inhabitants' poverty.

Eager as was the peasant to have his home freed from oppressive taxation and restriction, yet he saw in every government official and overlord an enemy, and heartily desired to experience a new system of administration. When the revolution came it received more support from these down-trodden people than from any other class, though many of the townspeople and trading classes equally desired a change of regime, in the hope of it bringing to them the prosperity Britain was then enjoying under her system of parliamentary government.

There is but one justification for government and law, and that is justice. If men and women do not obtain that for which they labour, if they have not the freedom and liberty to think and say what they believe, while not defaming anyone, then government and law are being used for wrong, instead of for right, purposes.

Liberty is the breath of progress and is what the blood is to the body, as without liberty the people mentally wither away. They become no better than animals, driven as their masters direct. Such were the Germans and Italians in our own times, and such were the French until Voltaire, and others, by their writings, quickened the dawning intelligence of their time to a point which made them demand the rights so long denied to them.

The people of France, as the century drew on, became more and more revolutionary in their ideas, and both the Throne and the Church slowly awakened to the fact that there was danger ahead. Less authority, and more humanity, was the cry of the intellectuals, and it was taken up by those who could read, to spread down to the lower grades of society. No churchman came forward to defend the poor and down-trodden, no Christian was found to write in favour of humanity and attack the injustice, cruelty and poverty of those times.

Those who wished to raise humanity did not believe in the claims of Christianity, and despised its creeds, dogmas and doctrines, but they believed intensely in the welfare of the human race, and passionately desired to see it educated and rise above its then sordid conditions. As always happened during the age of Christian civilisation, whenever anything occurred to benefit humanity, the humanitarians, who were responsible for the new ideas, were denounced by the Christians as men spreading dangerous opinions, because poverty and servitude were part of God's plan for humanity, it being recorded in their sacred writings that "ye have the poor always with you". (*Matthew* xxvi, 11.) That being God's will, some must do the drudgery so that the favoured ones could live in luxury.

In spite of being abused by the Christians, these eminent humanists of the 18th century persisted in proclaiming as wicked all persecution, torture, banishment and unjust imprisonment, a number of great and noble men risking their lives and comfort to help humanity to free itself from political and ecclesiastical bondage, but only the most outstanding can here be mentioned. Now we have come to the age of the really great men, those who inspire us to greater effort, and widen the mental horizon, in such marked contrast to the ignorant, selfish, cruel, debased creatures to whom so much of this book has been devoted up to now.

The most outstanding man of this age of great men was undoubtedly Voltaire (1694–1778), who was born into an orthodox Catholic middle-class home, when the King controlled the bodies and the priests the minds of the people of France. This time of tyranny, injustice, corruption, ignorance and vice was an era when the King and the nobles lived in comfort and luxury, and the great mass of the people like beasts.

Voltaire was born when Christian civilisation had been in existence for thirteen hundred years, when the King and the priests relied on torture, the rack, the thumb-screw and the contracting boot, prison, banishment and the stake, to prevent all freedom and expression of thought. He was born when the royal palace was a house of prostitution, the priests were libertines, the judges unjust, cruel and venal, and the nobles heartless, arrogant and proud. He was born at the time when creeds were more sacred than virtues, images and relics more precious than liberty or justice, and when faith was more blessed than reason and understanding. He was born when justice was unknown, when every witness in a court of law had before him the mental image of the thumb-screw if he did not testify as those in authority desired, and when most intellectuals and authors were in prison, exiled or ruined by crushing fines.

Voltaire was the greatest man of the 18th century. In looks he was little better than a skeleton, small and very thin, with a long nose and bright preternatural brilliant eyes. Yet this sober, good-living man, who was more brain than body, was decidedly vain, and when roused could be bitter in his reproaches. At a time when to attack the King for his crimes was treason Voltaire attacked; when to criticise the priests was blasphemy, he criticised. In his day the King said that God had made him king, and the people his subjects who must do his bidding. His place, said the King, was the palace, and the people lived where God had placed them. It was the divine will that he clothed himself in silks and that the masses wore rags.

The priests followed this up by teaching that God had made the common people ignorant and vile, and the King wise and holy. It was God's will that they obey the priests, because, if they did not, he would curse them, which meant misery on earth and everlasting torment in hell, he having mercy and forgiveness only for those who obeyed the priests, his representatives on earth. Consequently they must always accept and never doubt, as to do so was to rebel against God, and this meant that they must not think for themselves, as that was equally sinful. Everyone must believe only what the Church, acting on behalf of God, declared through the mouths of its priests was true and proper, all else being sinful and pertaining to the devil.

Fortunately for us, some men dared to be treasonable, and some accepted the hatred and contempt of their fellow men, who denounced them as heretics, blasphemers, atheists and infidels. Voltaire was the greatest of these outcasts, the leader of all who loved liberty and hated injustice, one of those who knew the value of knowledge and realised the degradation brought about by ignorance. A great man adds to the sum of human knowledge, he extends the mental horizon, and releases the mind from bondage and fear. He cares nothing for popularity, only for truth, which, when found, he does not keep to himself, but passes on so that all may benefit by his discoveries.

The great men are not the master plunderers, but those who have freed the bodies and minds of men, and then brought happiness and joy to all released from physical and mental bondage. Poets, whose words ring out in song and rhyme, inventors who add to our happiness and comfort, musicians who make the atmosphere vibrate with melody, discoverers who go farther than the rest into the unknown and bring back increased knowledge, artists who bring nature's beauties in our homes—all indeed who have added to the happiness and well-being of the human race—are the great men and women of this world. These we thank, while we pass by in contempt those men, made heroes by the ignorant mob, who have left behind them a trail of misery and destruction.

In the time of Voltaire the Church did a highly lucrative trade in selling relics and bones of dead saints, to cure those afflicted, because the Bible taught that all disease, insanity, and every ailment, came from devils which everywhere abounded. On their churches the faithful carved hideous gargoyles, and put figures of crowing cocks on their spires, to frighten away the evil spirits ever anxious to enter the bodies of the saved, the swinging censers filled with incense performing the same function inside these edifices. There was a different saint to be prayed to for every affliction, and it was thought that all having psychic gifts were wizards or witches under demon control. Except by a few there was no belief in an ordered universe, the vast majority believing in one governed by the will of God, who was for ever being thwarted by spiteful devils ever ready to interfere with his designs.

At the age of ten Voltaire was sent to a Jesuit school, where he was taught theology, which embraced all the prevailing superstitions. Instead of knowledge he was taught two dead languages, Latin and Greek, but no ethics, philosophy, economics, mathematics, history, geography or any science, and when his theological education was completed he entered a lawyer's office as well qualified for the affairs of life as anyone else in those days.

Fortunately he did not consider, as do most people, that education finished when school-days ended, and he began to read the thoughts expressed by the Greek and Roman philosophers, dramatists and historians. Imbued with this learning he began to write poetic verse and tragedies to such good effect that he became well known for his plays, but, being too candid with his pen, he was exiled. On his return he was again arrested and imprisoned in the Bastille, where he remained for a year. He went in as François Marie Arouet, but in prison, because his family had disowned him, he changed his name to Voltaire, by which he was ever afterwards known. Then he was exiled to England, where he met the best in English intellectual life, and, when he returned home, he began to study Church history and the origin of the Christian faith, to be again exiled.

From now onwards he devoted his life to humanise the Christians of his time, and free them from the bondage of the Church. He attacked its injustice, its cruelties, its tortures, its absurdities, its divine claims, and tried to reform the laws of France, enlighten the judges, civilise the people and banish the lust for war. He became the champion of the down-trodden and oppressed, advocated education, toleration, justice and kindess to all, including children and animals.

He made every priest his enemy, and every good man and woman his friend. For twenty-seven years, from his exiled home at the base of the Alps, he pointed a finger of scorn and ridicule at the ignorance of his age, and for sixty years filled Europe with his thoughts, essays, epigrams, epics, comedies, tragedies, histories, poems and novels representing every phase of life. He had great wit and humour, and on one occasion remarked that he did not believe God would damn even a priest for ever. Against oppression, injustice and slavery he waged ceaseless war, his exposure of the case of Jean Calas being an example of how he not only wrote but worked for justice.

The minority of Protestants who lived in France

were now mild and mostly unobtrusive people, because they had not the power, as the Episcopalians had in Britain, to be ferocious. One of these was a small tradesman, of good reputation, named Jean Calas, living in Toulouse, whose son committed suicide in 1761 because, being a Protestant, he could not become a lawyer. The Roman Catholics said that his family had murdered him to prevent him becoming an orthodox Christian. There was no evidence against the Calas family, but they were all imprisoned, and the father was tortured to force a confession.

He was made to lie down, when ropes were bound to his arms and legs, and each time they were tightened he had the cross shoved in front of his face and was told to confess his guilt. Gradually his arms and legs were dislocated, but, as he still lived, thirty pints of water were forced down his throat. His agony was excruciating, but, as he continued to declare his innocence, these Christian fiends strangled him, and then burned his body at the stake, after which the family property was confiscated and his widow turned adrift homeless.

As was always the case, people gathered around to witness the burning of a heretic, and in Toulouse, whose cathedral was believed to shelter the bones of seven of the apostles and part of the dress of the Virgin Mary, this event was looked upon as a festival by the inhabitants. To Voltaire it was far otherwise, as to him this wickedness of the Church was an outrage against an innocent helpless family, who, because they were Protestants, had no redress. Immediately he took one of the sons under his roof, supplied the family with money, and wrote an account of the case. He corresponded with royal courts abroad about it, and for years kept Europe echoing with the groans of the victim. Finally he was successful, as the French court of law declared Calas to be innocent and annulled the judgment.

Many other similar cases he exposed, and many of the dependants of the victims he helped with shelter, money and advice, but he could not cope with all the cruelty and injustice in a land ruled by fiends. Nevertheless he, the exiled outcast, the champion of kindness, justice and tolerance, in a land which knew not the meaning of these words, gradually made the name of Infidel stand for what was fair and right, just as he made evident that the name Christian stood for what was evil. When little thought was given to the rights of man he proclaimed the meaning of the brotherhood of man, and yet, up to our own times, because he was not a Christian, both Protestants and Roman Catholics have vied with each other in denouncing and maligning this great advocate of human liberty.

His life and work contradicts the Christian claim that the greater humanity which has come about in our times is due to Christianity, and also the falsehood that the non-Christian humanitarians were influenced by that religion. Voltaire lived and died an enemy of Christianity, repelled by the cruelty and squalor of his age, but he lived long enough to experience the gratitude of his fellow men. The King, the priests, and many of the nobles, hated this champion of liberty, but the people became his friends, as by now they had come to loathe the monarchy, priesthood and aristocracy. After an exile of twenty-seven years he returned to Paris as the recognised intellectual king of

Europe. The journey thither was like a victorious march, and he was met at Paris by representatives of the Academy and the Immortals, his triumph culminating at the theatre, where his tragedy "Irene" was performed, when he was crowned with laurel and bedecked with flowers.

At the close of his life he was recognised as the greatest man of his age, the idol of France, but, when he died peacefully at the age of eighty-four in 1778, the Church took its revenge by spreading the story that his last moments were filled with mental agony and remorse, a falsehood which the clergy have spread from that day to this. No other name so incites their malignity, as he it was who drew the teeth of what he called The Triumphant Beast, and so reduced its power for evil. From Constantine to Voltaire represents a period covering over fourteen centuries of crime, injustice, torture and suppression of liberty. As Constantine was responsible for the establishment of the Christian Church, which banished education and all freedom of thought, so Voltaire has the honour of again bringing liberty back to the continent which first gave it birth in ancient Greece, though a century was to pass before the people, whose eyes had been blinded by the darkness of their prison, learned to see again.

This is the remarkable position attained by the first outstanding humanitarian of the Christian era, and the most famous literary man of his age, to be fittingly recognised in 1791 when his body was removed from its grave to be placed in the Pantheon. Over the hundred miles it covered to Paris, the funeral procession passed through villages and towns hung with flags and bedecked with arches, every one anxious to do honour to the liberator of France. On the remains of the Bastille, which he had done so much to destroy, his body rested in triumph for a night, to be taken the next day to its last resting-place, which became a shrine to all who loved righteousness and hated evil.

Another intellectual who exerted by his writings a great influence on the times was Jean Jacques Rousseau (1712–1778). He rejected Christianity as an evil superstition, but passionately believed in God. He was a master novelist, and also wrote many books on the political conditions of his time. The one which exerted an immense influence was *Social Contract*, to become known as the Bible of the Revolution. This book set France aflame intellectually. Herein he makes clear his opinion that liberty and freedom are the heritage of mankind, that all government should come from the will of the people, and that those who govern should only do so according to the desires of those they serve. He fired the minds of his contemporaries with the idea that their destiny was in their own hands, that the practice of the virtues would bring happiness and contentment, and that liberty and justice could be secured if they so willed it.

Consequently the people have the right to elect the kind of government they desire, keep it in office, and put it out of office at their pleasure, all of which is very sound and reasonable in an educated community, but before this is possible the people, who set out to govern themselves, must at least be able to read and write, and this the French masses could not do. Rousseau realised this, and he advocated education from early childhood, but his ideas in other respects were far from consistent, as elsewhere he supported despotic rule. His sentimentality detracted from his arguments, and his belief that man in his primitive state was virtuous and happy until kings, priests and lawyers came on the scene, can only be explained by the ignorance of the times.

Likewise his excuse for all breaches of the moral code, that it is a return to nature, certainly does not make for righteousness, which stands for something idealised by the mind and unrelated to the unthinking cruelty of nature. It is just because we are mental beings, rational thinking creatures, that we can differentiate between right and wrong, good and bad, kindness and cruelty, and so on. If we were not something apart from the material universe, with its never-changing laws, we would not have words for the virtues and the vices, and it is just because we can become rational in our thinking that we have possibilities ahead of us far beyond anything we can imagine at our present stage of development.

Another of those 18th-century thinkers was Montesquieu (1689–1755), who tried to find a juster system of government, and, in *The Spirit of the Laws*, he shows what history has to teach, and how the claim to divine majesty pertained to an age that had passed. He was much impressed by the British parliamentary system, and advocated the adoption of a form of aristocratic government, similar to the one then in vogue across the Channel. His ideas on the separation of government into legislative, executive and judicial departments greatly influenced the framers of the constitutions of both the United States of America and of France during her Revolution.

Denis Diderot (1713–1784) was one of a group of outstanding men known as the Encyclopaedists, who set to work with other advanced thinkers to bring together human knowledge within the covers of a series of books. Then also lived the benevolent Paul Holbach, who used his brilliant gifts to overthrow the existing wickedness and superstition and put in their place the love of man for man. Claude Helvetius, the famous physician, was another of the noble humanists of that age, and so also was the humane and charitable D'Alembert, the great mathematician and philosopher, who used his wide learning to educate the people out of the Christian way of life into one that was grander and nobler, by putting knowledge before theology.

They, and others like them, formed a galaxy of enterprise and talent, and one and all in no uncertain way expressed their hatred of everything cruel and unjust, of trade in slaves, of inequality of taxation, of war, of the prevailing poverty and squalor, and of Christianity. They envisaged the social conditions we now enjoy, and put the love of their fellow men before the superstition of their times. Another band of thinkers, the Economists, set to work to study the laws relating to the production and distribution of wealth, some going the length of advocating a system on the lines which Russia adopted within our own times.

Meanwhile Louis XV went out hunting, his pleasures coming before his duties, and the rest of the Court followed his example, refusing to face the fact that for the first time during the Christian era men were seriously thinking and planning economic problems, and a better and juster form of government. To him it all seemed so ineffective, but, while he lived in the clouds, powerful mental forces were at work which were carrying the people forward either to evolution or revolution. Evolution it might have been had circumstances not upset the old established order. What these occurrences were, and how the effects of past causes changed the face of France, we are now about to read.

(3) THE OLD ORDER IN FRANCE IS OVERTHROWN.

The latter part of the 18th century was just about as uncomfortable a time as possible for a monarch, with absolute traditions behind him, to ascend the throne of France. Great wisdom and understanding were necessary to steer the ship of state safely through all the quicksands which had been slowly gathering round the throne over the past hundred years.

Louis XVI (1774–1793), who followed his grandfather Louis XV, was certainly well-meaning, virtuous, pious and amiable, but far from being a strong character. If this handsome man had been made in a stronger mould he would not have dismissed Turgot from the office of Controller-General, the very man for these difficult times. Unfortunately for France, the King had married a foolish woman, the daughter of Maria Theresa of Austria, and sister of the progressive Emperor Joseph II, and relied on her advice against his own better judgment. Marie Antoinette was endowed with good looks and great strength of character, besides being more intelligent than her husband, but she never grasped the problems of the time. When the people's minds were stirring ever more quickly, her thoughts were back in the time of Louis XIV, until she came to be looked upon as the leader of all the reactionaries in the land.

Sound financial methods have never been a strong point with the French people, whose facile temperament in money matters demanded a strong man to obtain the nation's revenue and spend it wisely. Turgot was a wise and skilful financier, who sympathised with the liberal ideas of the age. He put forward new schemes embracing juster and sounder methods of taxation, and the improvement of the government, but the Court, led by the Queen, intrigued against him until Louis submitted to their demands and dismissed him from office. Had the King been strong enough to support his minister, as Louis XIII had supported Richelieu, the necessary reforms would have been carried out, France would have been spared the trials of the Revolution and Europe the ravages of Napoleon. On such small matters hang the fate of nations, involving the happiness of millions of innocent people.

The post of Director of Finance was now given to Necker, a Geneva banker who was unpopular at Court because he was a Protestant and a Republican, but he was a sound financier, though lacking his predecessor's desire for reform. By economy and skilful borrowing, the country's financial position improved, but war again threw it into the melting-pot. His proposals to tax Church property, and increase the taxation of the lightly taxed and privileged upper classes, brought about his fall from office by the same clique which had brought about Turgot's·

downfall. The country's finances consequently became hopelessly involved, the deficit being met by borrowing at high rates of interest. The King issued edicts demanding more money from everyone, only to find them met by open opposition, Parlement giving its support to this outcry by the people, who demanded that the States-General, which had not met since 1614, must assemble and look into the state of the nation's finances.

Louis acceded to the growing demand, as he was not unsympathetic towards his subjects' desire for a greater share in national affairs, and in 1789 the States-General met, 1200 representatives of the people, consisting of priests, nobility and commons, gathering together at Versailles without an idea as to how they were to carry through their work. Was a majority sufficient to ensure a measure becoming law, or were they to divide into three departments, priests, nobles and commons, each having their own meeting-place, and each its own separate divisions for voting purposes? Nothing could be done until this question was decided. After much wrangling, the commons, who took the name of Third Estate, decided to form themselves into the National Assembly and produce a new constitution, the nobles and priests being told that if they did not co-operate they would be ignored.

The King now made the mistake of interfering with this decision. He promised to agree to many of the reforms demanded, but insisted on the three-chamber method of government. Under the lead of Mirabeau (1749–1791), a powerful orator, a nobleman by birth, and one of the greatest statesmen France has ever produced, the Third Estate refused to accept the King's demand, as to do so was to give the upper houses the power to veto all the legislation of the lower house.   The King gave way, and at his request the priests and nobles did likewise, because everyone was anxious for a settlement of the dispute, the country requiring money to carry on national affairs, and this only the Third Estate could produce. France now had all her representatives gathered together under one roof, whose majority vote carried a measure. A constitution was drawn up, and all might now have gone well if the King had been strong enough to resist the evil influence of his Court.

Necker, who had been recalled to office in the year prior to the meeting of the States-General, and had shown little administrative ability, was again dismissed, greatly to the annoyance of the citizens of Paris, with whom he was a popular hero. Mob orators harangued the crowd which proceeded to attack the Bastille, then regarded as the bastion of injustice, though for long it had been little more than a bogey fortress like the Tower of London in our time. With little opposition it surrendered, and, after the garrison had been killed or captured, the small number of prisoners were released, an event which chilled the hearts of all the tyrants in Europe, and gave hope to the down-trodden masses everywhere of a brighter era about to dawn.

The fall of the Bastille (1789) so thoroughly frightened Louis, and his courtiers, that Necker was restored to office, the King being also forced to dismiss his reactionary ministers, and then publicly to accept the new tricolour flag, the emblem of the new-found liberty. Besides this he was made to give thanks in public for the downfall of the famous prison, the symbol of tyranny. Having once bowed to the people's will, he was compelled to do so again, by being obliged to leave his palace at Versailles and take up residence in the Tuileries, the leaders of the National Assembly wishing to keep him under closer supervision.

On the advice of the Marquis de la Fayette (1757–1834), the chief of the newly formed National Guard, the King quietly made the change of residence, as the mob was now threatening the safety of the royal family, whose private apartments at Versailles had already been entered by a hostile crowd. La Fayette, who has the distinction of being the designer of the tricolour, the new national flag, was a much esteemed humanitarian and enemy of the Church. He played a noble and important part in the Revolution, and was always just and moderate in his deeds. Both he, and the other reformers, not only sympathised with the suffering of the people and wished them speedy relief, but they realised that the abolition of autocratic and aristocratic rule was only the beginning of the much needed reform, as economically France was in a pitiable plight.

Much of the country's financial trouble came from the war with Britain, when France took the opportunity to pay off old scores during the American War of Independence, she siding with North America when the colonists declared their independence, and giving them all the help possible. Nevertheless this policy of revenge pursued by the French king brought about the downfall of the French monarchy.

Britain's humiliating defeat at the hands of her own kith and kin was a great triumph for France, whose help had made their victory possible, but it was more than a military success, because the victory of liberty over tyranny acted as an inspiration to the French to make a further effort to overthrow the evils of the past, and establish liberty and justice at home. The French people, though not suffering more than those inhabiting the rest of Europe, were more conscious of their sufferings, and when the United States emerged victorious from the war they realised what was possible if only the people were determined.

Though France gained nothing material from the war—in fact her fleet was destroyed when attempting to capture from Britain Jamaica and Barbadoes in the West Indies—yet it brought her absolute monarchy to an end, and marked the beginning of a new era in which, short as it was, the people had a greater say in the management of their own affairs. A new democratic Republic had arisen across the Atlantic, and, as that was possible there, why not a democratic republic in France? The new spirit of revolt in France against the old order, which flared up after the American war for independence, can consequently be traced directly to what had occurred across the Atlantic.

The American colonists gained their independence in 1782, and seven years later (1789) we see the repercussion in France, her king for all practical purposes being a prisoner in the Tuileries. This being so, the National Assembly, which now called itself the Constituent Assembly, felt itself free to frame a new constitution for France, one which was to replace the old regime of absolute monarchy and a privileged artistocracy. As a prelude it produced the historic Declaration of the Rights of Man, in which the influence of Rousseau's writings is noticeable, this famous declaration affirming that:—

All men are born, and continue free and equal in rights, all social distinctions being purely conventional.

Society is an association of men to preserve the natural rights of men.

Sovereignty resides in the nation, and all authority, vested in an individual or a body of men, comes expressly from the nation.

Liberty is the power of doing what we will, so long as it does not injure another. The only limits of each man's natural right are such as secure the same rights to others, which limits are determined only by the law.

The law can forbid only such actions as are mischievous to society; "Quod lex non vetat permittit".

Law is the expression of the general will, and all citizens have a right to take part, through their representative, in the making of the laws. Law must be equal for all, and all citizens have equal rights (according to their fitness) to fulfil all offices in the state.

Accusation, arrest and detention can only be in accordance with the law, which all are bound to obey.

The law must be reasonable, and must not have any retroactive force.

Every one is to be deemed innocent until he has been convicted, and persons under arrest on suspicion must therefore be treated gently.

All men are free to hold what religious views they will, provided they are not subversive of public order.

Freedom of speech, of writing and printing (save in cases reserved by the law), is one of the most precious of the rights of man.

A public force is needed to guarantee the rights of man; such a force to be for the benefit of all and not for one class only.

To support such a force a common contribution is necessary; to be equally laid on all citizens according to their means.

All citizens have a right to show (personally or by representatives) that such public contribution is necessary, to consent thereto, to arrange its application, its incidence, its manner of ingathering, and its duration.

Society has a right to demand from every public servant an account of his administration.

A society, the rights of which are not assured, the power of which is not definitely distributed, has no constitution.

Property being an inviolable and sacred right, no one can be deprived of it, save when public necessity, legally established, evidently demands it, and then only with the condition of a just and previously determined indemnity.

The committee which framed these just and humane democratic expressions of opinion was not composed of men who accepted the Christian religion, in fact they were bitterly opposed to the superstition, and it is because the civilised world ultimately adopted their definition of the rights of man that some countries had the freedom and liberty enjoyed before the blight of Mussolini and Hitler cursed this earth. This famous declaration paved the way for the era of democratic civilisation, which can come to every country having reached the stage when its people are sufficiently educated to adopt adult suffrage. So, in spite of what the black clerical army, the B.B.C., and some of our newspapers, have to say on the subject, it was certainly not through Christianity, but very much in spite of Christianity, that we have the freedom and liberty we now enjoy.

How different the course of history would have been had Europe been ready to grasp this opportunity to dethrone tyranny everywhere, and establish

enlightened government, but the people were too
ignorant, and so both the Throne and the Church
continued to reign supreme. To both monarchs
and priests the revolution was anti-Christ, and
Britain showed no desire to stand with France for
freedom against tyranny. This united opposition
consequently weakened the influence of the great
majority of moderate Frenchmen, and strengthened
the extremists, who eventually led their country from
one folly to another. With the feeling in France
that all Europe was against her, she prepared to
defend herself against her enemies, but if they, her
enemies, had been sufficiently far-sighted to have
foreseen what was in store for them from an arisen
France, how differently events would have shaped
themselves.

After the French reformers had defined the rights
of man, under the frowns and abuse of the ruling
powers of Europe, they then set to work to frame
their new constitution, and its essential lines were
taken from the one adopted in England. In general
Louis accepted it, but objected in vain to the clauses
reducing the power of the Church, a reactionary
attitude, as to everyone who then worked for reform
in France this long-established tyrannical institution
required to have its power severely curtailed, though
no attempt was made to interfere with its legitimate
activities. Its lands and wealth, obtained by fear and
fraud, were consequently confiscated, the tithe was
abolished, the religious orders suppressed, all monks
and nuns released from their vows, and the clergy
became the salaried servants of the State, their respective offices being filled under government direction.

The King was forced to accept these drastic changes, but the Pope issued a Bull of Condemnation and excommunicated all responsible, a punishment once looked upon as something dreadful but now regarded with little concern by those affected. Otherwise there was no attempt to interfere with wealth, and the revolutionists were determined to do nothing to discourage individual effort. They were neither Socialists nor Communists; all they attacked was privilege, not property, and, in consequence, the peasant was freed from his serfdom, the iniquitous game laws were abolished, and the landlords were forced to give up their long-established privileged rights over the land.

Now that the people had liberty of expression, all their long-pent-up feelings against the monarchy, the priesthood, and the nobility, burst forth in a torrent against the unhappy Louis XVI, who became the victim of all his predecessors' crimes. The newspapers and politicians did not trust him, and accused him of working secretly against the new order, as across the border were large numbers of aristocratic émigrés, whose subversive activities with foreign powers did as much as anything to stimulate the excesses of the revolution. These embittered exiles did all in their power to foment war and encourage domestic strife, and, because it was believed that the King was in sympathy and in communication with them, he was not trusted, to forfeit eventually his life for his treachery.

More and more he felt his position less secure, so much so that in June 1791 he abrogated his constitutional edicts, and then fled with his family, only to be caught close to the frontier and brought back to Paris. Some now wanted the King deposed and a Republic established, but it was decided to complete the new constitution, giving the King limited powers, and then offer him the choice of accepting or refusing it. If he refused he would then be forced to abdicate.

The new constitution, completed in 1791, gave the King power to appoint his own ministers and control the army and navy, but no power to veto legislation permanently, all legislative power being placed in the keeping of 750 qualified elected members sitting as one body in one chamber. This new constitution was accepted by the King, and, though he was not always loyal to it, affairs would probably have worked out happily enough for the good of all concerned had not the German princes taken active warlike measures, to be followed by Austria, Prussia and Piedmont mobilising their armies. The other monarchs of Europe likewise threatened, and France, faced with a ring of enemies, called her troops to arms.

France had no wish to experience the treatment Poland was then receiving, the rump of that unhappy country being in process of being swallowed up by Russia, Austria and Prussia. Consequently the Girondists, the majority party in power, took up a strong defiant attitude, and complained against the French émigré nobles across the frontier plotting the downfall of the new order. Francis II of Austria impudently replied that Louis XVI was to be replaced in his former autocratic position, and that the clergy and nobles were to have their old positions and privileges returned to them. To this demand France replied by declaring war on Austria in 1792, and so began the long series of conflicts which were not to end until Napoleon was defeated at Waterloo.

Wiser and cooler heads could have settled these matters peacefully, but the French were intoxicated with their recent liberation, and rushed into war with confidence and enthusiasm. This folly occurred at a time when affairs in France had reached a climax, as Louis was now accused of siding with the enemy and the Church against France in the hope of having his power re-established. Danton (1759–1794), one of the most conspicuous figures of the Revolution, supported the Jacobins, the most rabid of all the revolutionary parties, who led an attack on the Tuileries, which was occupied but not before the King, the Queen and the royal family had fled, to find refuge in the Assembly Hall. The Jacobins next invaded their place of refuge and demanded that the King be deposed, which was agreed, the assembly later deciding on manhood suffrage and that a new election be held to determine the future constitution of France.

France was now without a head, as the King had been deposed just prior to the forthcoming election, and the Assembly, pending its outcome, was in a state of suspended animation. Because of this unfortunate situation an extremist clique took over the government of the country, and issued decrees which all had to obey. Paris, like all the other cities and towns throughout France, was then ruled by an all-powerful municipal council, known as the Commune, composed of men who held extreme views, and through them the extremists in power exercised their authority.

The chief of these was Marat (1743-1793) whose honesty cannot be doubted, but whose mind, by illness, poverty and suffering, could not be other than unbalanced. Numerous people in Paris and elsewhere kept their sanity, and deplored the lack of moderation in the legislation, especially the hasty action of deposing the King before a new head had been found. Many also wished to see the King return to rule as a constitutional monarch, but they were unable to make their voices heard.

Such, then, was the position during the time when rumour ran wild of conspiracies against the newly elected Assembly, helpless for want of a strong leader, and when suspicion also abounded towards many suspected of plotting to reinstate the King. Paris was searched for arms and so-called traitors, while the prisons filled to overflowing. Tribunals were established, charged with the duty of discovering all friendly to the monarchy, while day by day the Commune passed from one folly and excess to another, its members during the space of five days losing all sense and reason. Massacres took place in the streets, and people were arrested here, there and everywhere until finally some 1500 had been butchered, but it is well to remember that this number did not greatly exceed those hanged in England for petty offences during the same period.

All this insanity was manifesting itself in Paris while the country was still at war with Austria, now strengthened by the help received from Prussia. A joint Austrian-Prussian army had crossed the frontier under the Duke of Brunswick, and town after town fell to its onslaught, until at last it was checked by the French at Valmy in 1792, some forty miles east of Rheims. Then it fell back across the Rhine, pursued by the French, who occupied the Netherlands, and opened the River Scheldt to traffic, much to the indignation of Britain, who had encouraged its closure because of its competition with London.

This French victory, we might well think, was just one of the many episodes in history which led to nothing very decisive, but it was much more than that. It was a great event in history, because it gave the French renewed confidence in their fighting abilities, an assurance which was to end in making them temporary masters of most of Europe. Flushed with their success, they declared war on Britain and Holland, and defied the monarchs of Europe by the declaration that France shall be an armed camp, every Frenchman a soldier, to conquer or die to bring the principles of the Revolution to the down-trodden masses of Europe. This was the beginning of Conscription. Thus began a conflict which was to last for twenty-three years, with only one short interval, until 1815.

Meantime the criminal genius, who was to be responsible for this wide-spread conflagration, was a young artillery officer, Napoleon Bonaparte, a Corsican who had distinguished himself at Toulon. He was at the moment in Italy studying all phases of warfare, and ready to take the first opportunity to put his knowledge into practice. The story of this adventurer, this master criminal, this destroyer of the property, prosperity and happiness of millions, will begin three years later, but until then something must be told of the years which intervened.

They include the year known as the Reign of

Terror, when injustice, brutality and everything evil came to the surface. Then it was that the lust for retribution, the passion to avenge all that the poor had suffered at the hands of the rich and privileged for centuries past, gave the extremists, who had seized power, an opportunity they had never expected, but which, when it came, they used to the full.

When, however, we remember the past history of France, we cannot be surprised that when the ignorant, half-famished mob obtained power, extreme folly and violence naturally followed. How could it have been otherwise when theology had taken the place of knowledge, and supernatural religion the place of education over the past thirteen hundred years? France, when a province of the Roman Empire, was a highly cultured state with fine buildings, public baths and schools everywhere, but, since the 5th century, when it became a Christian country during the reign of Clovis, there had been no education, little justice, no baths and little progress, because ignorance, filth, squalor and poverty then replaced Pagan culture and education.

So, in the 18th century, the people, who had been like captives in a dark prison, when they first experienced the light of freedom, were dazzled by its brilliance and knew not the road to take. After sweeping away their tyrannical masters they had neither the knowledge, nor the tradition, to guide them on the dangerous and difficult path of self-government, the consequence being complete chaos because passion and hate took the place of reasoned thought. Consequently we read of terrible depravity, when the poor of Paris, and other towns, gave vent to their hatred of all that had gone before, by gloating over the beheading of "les aristocrates", many of whom did not deserve their wrath, some being executed only because they were opposed to the extreme measures pursued by the Jacobins, the clique in power.

The Reign of Terror opened with the decapitation of Louis XVI in 1793, after he had been found guilty of treason. Prior to this a Republic had been proclaimed which came under the control of the Jacobins, though they represented only a minority of the people; in fact the French as a whole were so ignorant of anything to do with politics that only six per cent. of the total electorate took the trouble to vote at the election of members to the Assembly.

On the other hand, the extremists, who did not represent one per cent. of the population, knew exactly what they wanted, and were determined to have it, while the more balanced-minded, humane, law-abiding Girondists, who were in the majority, and believed in parliamentary procedure, allowed themselves to be pushed aside. Though the latter expressed themselves in glowing speeches, full of fine phrases on the subject of liberty, equality and fraternity, they knew not how to act, and stood by helpless, shocked and stupefied while all the horrors of the next thirteen months (June 1793–July 1794) took place.

One strong man could have restored the power to the Assembly, but none arose to put down the extremists. Insurrection broke out in various parts of the country, and all Europe developed an enmity towards the young Republic. Only by adopting dictatorial methods, and abolishing all liberty, was it possible for the Jacobins to retain their illegal power, and so brute force, imprisonment and fear were used to preserve order. Terror took the place of justice, all opposition was cowed, and the charter of the rights of man was consumed in the heat of passion.

This terror centred in the Committee of Public Safety, a body of twelve men, of which Danton, fiercely republican, but always a statesman and a patriot, and Robespierre, merciless, cruel and calculating, were the controlling influence. It over-ruled all other authorities, and relied on the support of the Revolutionary Tribunal in Paris, before which everyone accused of offences against the State had to appear. High treason consisted of hostility towards the Jacobins, and all found guilty were murdered at the guillotine. The Queen thus met her end, and, in company with her, many less deserving of this fate, because the moderate republicans were classed along with the most ardent royalists. The leaders of the Girondists were first imprisoned, to be later executed, and if the criminal gang had not quarrelled amongst themselves who can say how or when this butchery would have ended?

These extremists now broke up into moderate and immoderate groups, the former led by Danton, and the latter by Hébert and Chaumette, who, when in power, inaugurated a new era dating from the formation of the Republic (22nd September, 1792), to last until Napoleon made friends with the Pope. New names were given to the months, the week was extended to ten days, and the decimal system of calculation and measurement introduced. Robespierre, and his followers, took a middle course, and were against the extreme views of Hébert, but equally opposed to Danton's moderation. Robespierre's oratory and singleness of purpose, his legal training, his elegance of dress, and his determination to stamp out all opposition to his narrow political creed, made him the outstanding figure of the Reign of Terror, all his opponents falling to the guillotine before he also, the last of the terrorists, met the same fate.

These zealots did not represent the people, only their own wild ideas. Arrayed in gorgeous uniforms and plumed hats, they sat around a table in the luxurious salon where, some years earlier, good earnest men, intent on the up-liftment of mankind, had debated on the rights of man. Now all that mattered to the successors of these earlier humanists was power and authority, no liberty or justice being granted to anyone who expressed opinions different from their own.

They could not even agree between themselves, and whoever amongst them obtained power guillotined all who opposed him. Robespierre (1793–1794) was the last to secure domination, and dispatched his rivals without discrimination. This tyrant was an ardent Theist, but to believe in God does not make bad men good, because every scoundrel, so far referred to in this history, believed in one or more gods. Robespierre was just as great a despot as any of his predecessors in office, and to retain his position he resorted to the same extreme methods as they adopted. He abolished the god of Reason, and put a deity of his own imagination in its place, but, as we have already discovered, supernatural religion, whatever its name, has no relation to justice, mercy, truth, honesty, kindness or any of the other virtues, all of which are the outcome of mental development and practical experience.

So the Terror continued, and Robespierre struck down enemies, and supposed enemies, in ever-increasing numbers. To do otherwise meant his own downfall. Consequently the blood-bath continued until his excesses united all his rivals against him. In 1794, after some months of this despotic rule, he was seized by his united enemies, to meet the same end as he had prescribed for so many others, the guillotine, without a trial. His death ended the Reign of Terror, and brought about the return of the Girondists to power, as the people were disgusted with all the slaughter, and quite determined to end this fierce oppression.

Victories beyond the French frontier, moreover, made repressive measures now unnecessary, because the country was in no danger from foreign foes; in fact her armies were carrying the slogan, "Liberty, Equality and Fraternity" into other lands. All the fine ideas of the early revolutionists, relating to peace and the abolition of war, were now forgotten, as were also their opinions on justice, kindness and mercy. The seed they had sown had fallen on stony ground, as those they had tried to raise were not yet ready to nourish their high ideals, the masses lacking knowledge, wisdom and ethical instruction, through which alone can develop a better and happier order of society.

The French were still suffering from the effects of the age-old policy of both Church and State to keep the people ignorant, so as to prevent them from thinking for themselves. This policy of maintaining ignorance has been followed in our time by the inculcation of false ideas by dictators, who had seized power and wished the young to think as best benefited their instructors, but now we know all too well that both methods lead to wickedness, and only the honest teaching of facts, material and moral, can produce prosperity, righteousness and lasting happiness.

In the year 1795 another new constitution was produced, and, now that the infant son of Louis XVI had died in prison, and the next heirs to the throne were fighting against France in the armies of her enemies, it was anticipated that all patriotic Frenchmen would rally round the Republic. An upper and lower house on the British model was planned, with a Cabinet of five, called the Directory, but the proposal that the first members of the two houses should consist of two thirds of the discredited Assembly, now to be abolished because of its weakness during the year of terror, led to an insurrection. It was feared that if the Girondists returned to power their now recognised feebleness would again open the door to the extremists.

On this occasion the mob did not have matters their own way, as it so happened that Napoleon Bonaparte was then living in poverty in Paris. Here he met the leading politicians, including Barras, a man of action, who had been responsible for the downfall of Robespierre, a bold deed which he had followed up by taking control of the Directory. To meet the new crisis Barras put this young man in charge of the army for the protection of the Directory and the Assembly, and Napoleon, who had no scruples about killing, poured volleys of grape-shot into the mob, thus quickly securing its dispersal and the return of law and order.

This episode is the historian's first introduction to Napoleon Bonaparte, a man who was soon to be both beloved and hated throughout Europe. Henceforth his promotion was rapid, as the French had now turned their thoughts from home affairs to conquest, thus giving him the opportunities he was quick to take. Social reform, and enthusiasm for the rights of man, were now replaced by the passion for plunder and military glory, victories in battle having more glamour for the ignorant mob than thoughts for the welfare of humanity.

Soldiers, and not reformers, caught the imagination of the populace, and soon Napoleon was to become the idol of the army and the entire nation, to which cause can be traced his rapid rise to fame. Already, after three years of war, France by 1795 had won territory from Prussia on the left bank of the Rhine. Only Britain and Austria, of all her former enemies, remained in the conflict, but the time had now come for a direct attack on Austria through the Danube valley, while her possessions in Italy were simultaneously invaded by an army under the command of Napoleon.

Here in Italy, this genius for war first showed his ability in the field of battle, as, by his capture of the bridge over the Adda at Lodi, he quickly occupied Milan, then besieged Mantua, and finally completely crushed the Austrians at Rivoli in 1797. Now that he was master of northern Italy he marched into Austria, to make terms with the Emperor. Austria renounced her hold over Belgium, which was already occupied by French troops, and agreed to recognise a free Italian state, comprising most of northern Italy, while France, on her part, passed Venice over to Austria, greatly to its inhabitants' anger, because for many years they had maintained their independence.

From now onwards, for the next eighteen years, the history of France is the history of Napoleon, a subject which is too large to continue here, and must be taken up again in the next chapter. His appearance on the stage of history marks the end of the French Revolution, a period which comprised important events, the effects of which will become more and more noticeable as we proceed.

Europe had now experienced the first attempt of a great nation to manage its own affairs by representatives elected by popular vote, but, as the French were quite inexperienced in parliamentary government, they made many and terrible mistakes. Take a child out of the nursery, and place it alone in everyday life before it has passed through the schoolroom, and it becomes the victim of every scoundrel. All the elevated writings of the intellectuals could not make illiterate people intelligent, and able to proceed wisely when faced with the events which came about so rapidly in France. The French were little better than children, whose ancestors had never been out of leading-strings, they never having thought for themselves, and only what the Church and State had told them to think. Consequently they made mistakes, but the guilt for the carnage during the Reign of Terror rests on those ferocious zealots who seized power, and, by terror, beat down all opposition to their fanatical ideas.

Thousands of innocent victims died during the birth of freedom, as we shall discover as we proceed, but, compared with the millions of innocents who perished at the hands of the Nazis, in their attempt to obliterate all that the reformers won in their struggle for freedom, the cruelty which accompanied the French revolution fades before what Europe has experienced in our own times. What to the 19th century stood out as a mountain of crime is now dwarfed by this new black towering meridian of wickedness which has arisen before it, and dimmed it to our eyes.

(4) BRITAIN IS RULED BY HER FIRST PRIME MINISTER.

Now we must return to the early part of the 18th century and pick up the story of events in Britain. We left her in the previous chapter when Queen Anne had died, and George, the Elector of Hanover, had accepted the British throne. He was the great-grandson of James I, whose daughter Elizabeth had married Frederick, the Elector of the Palatinate, the chief supporter of the Calvinist cause in Germany during the Thirty Years' War.

In those days Protestant royal blood was scarce, as, if it had not been so, such an unsuitable choice would surely never have been made. Because of short supply, this dull, unintelligent German, who was quite unfitted for the position, was picked out and brought over to Britain, attended by his family and mistresses, besides numerous retainers who filled their pockets with English gold. Not only so, but Britain paid George a bonus of £250,000 for consenting to accept the British throne, besides a huge yearly salary, the bonus being used by him to purchase the Duchy of Bremen, which he added to his Hanoverian possessions, and so enormously increased his already large private annual income.

George I (1714–1727) commenced a new dynasty, the House of Hanover. Most of its kings were licentious and weak, and the first two did not understand their people, both George I and George II knowing little of the English language. Consequently Parliament secured a position unequalled in any other country, because, when it has the support of the people, the King becomes a mere figurehead who performs the ceremonial which surrounds the throne. As George I could only reign but not rule, a selected body of men, drawn from those who were in charge of the chief state departments, and representative of the party with a majority in the House of Commons, met together as a Cabinet, thus to inaugurate a new era in British politics.

The present British system of Cabinet government came slowly into being, as did the office of Prime Minister, and it was during the twenty-one years when Sir Robert Walpole (1721–1742) was the Chief Minister that Cabinet rule became the established custom. As the King could not understand English one of the ministers presided, to become known in later years as the Prime Minister and leader of the majority in Parliament. Walpole was the first Prime Minister, though the title was not used until the reign of George III. He became the recognised leader of the country, its real ruler, but subject to the will of the people through Parliament. The Prime Minister did not then, as now, represent the majority of the people, because Parliament did not do so, both the Whigs and Tories being dependant on the landowners for their seats, and only gradually, over the next two centuries, was the suffrage extended to include all qualified adult males and females.

Britain, during the early years of the reign, was suffering financially as the result of the losses incurred by the collapse of the South Sea Company, formed in 1711 to trade with Spanish America, and, in the hour of crisis, when the horizon looked black, Parliament turned to Walpole to lift the country out of the morass. In private life he was a Norfolk squire, gay-living and, like most people in those days, coarse in his manners, but in public life he proved himself to be a humane, wise and prudent statesman endowed with great financial ability. He led the Whigs, who, after Anne's death, enjoyed fifty years' supremacy, because the Tories, tinged as many of them were with Jacobite sympathies, never could get the confidence of the electors. Walpole became First Lord of the Treasury and then Chief Minister in 1721, and succeeded in placing the national finances on a sound basis. Moreover, he pursued a peaceful policy abroad, and strove by negotiation to settle all differences, making an alliance with France and peace treaties with Spain and Austria.

During this period the country was cursed by terrible drunkenness, as the result of cheap gin, which took such a hold of the people that the death rate rose sharply. "Drunk for a penny, dead drunk for twopence", was the advertisement outside the gin shops, and abject poverty and misery spread amongst the poor at a time when fifty new churches, but no schools, had just been built in London at the expense of the tax-payer. Crime, filth, overcrowding and unchecked violence were common in every town, especially around the docks of ports like London, now the most democratically governed city, and by far the greatest trading centre in the kingdom.

A more pleasing side of the social picture is to be found in the opening of hospitals, when, between 1720 and 1745, Westminster, St. George's, Guy's, London and Middlesex Hospitals opened their doors to welcome those who needed medical attention. Some years earlier (1693) St. Thomas's was rebuilt and so also was St. Bartholomew's in 1739. Between 1700 and 1825 new hospitals and dispensaries in Britain numbered 154, all of which were the outcome of secular effort, the consequence being that from now onwards, in spite of the ravages of smallpox, the death rate was reduced by improved medical attention and better food.

This individual philanthropy is exemplified in the work done by three outstanding men: Jonas Hanway, a London merchant and the first to use an umbrella, who founded the Marine Society and the Magdalen Hospital. He also got an Act passed for the better treatment of parish infants, though he was unsuccessful in his endeavour to alleviate the lot of the boy chimney sweeps, who, stripped naked, climbed up chimneys for fifteen hours a day with bleeding elbows and knees, as many as twenty-five a day being cleaned by one boy. Thomas Coram, a merchant seaman, harrowed by the destitute and miserable condition of London East-End children, founded the Foundling Hospital, and lastly, General Oglethorpe, who founded the State of Georgia, got Parliament to stop the scandals connected with debtors' prisons, and the torturing of the inmates by the gaolers in an effort to extort money from those who had little or none to give.

When George II (1727–1760) succeeded his father, the mental development of the people was beginning to scatter the clouds of ignorance which had so far obscured the sunshine of wisdom and knowledge. Walpole, by his more humane policy, was the herald of the future statesmen who were to represent a more developed people. The King disliked him, but the Queen realised his value as a statesman, and appreciated his loyalty to the Hanoverian succession. To Walpole, more than any other man of his time, is due the permanence of this royal house. His policy brought peace and prosperity to the country, and a great reduction in the National Debt, his influence being always on the side of peace and against war. So he refused to have Britain involved in the Polish succession War of 1733, and was proud to be able to say that of the 50,000 men killed in this senseless conflict not one was British. Besides this he refused to allow the Church to persecute the Nonconformists, but he could not dispel the hatred of the Anglicans towards all dissenters, who were boycotted socially and professionally now that they could not be tortured and liquidated.

Under his wise guidance British trade, mostly in woven cloth, flourished, and rivers were deepened to enable them to carry the greater inland traffic. Wealth increased, and exports were encouraged by a reduction in the duties on imported material used in their manufacture. Nothing, however, was done to improve the roads, which were left to the attention of each isolated parish, a foolish system because there was no supervision and the parishioners were indifferent as they made little use of them. Walpole, however, stimulated colonial trade, and withdrew irritating restrictions hampering commerce between the colonies and foreign countries, his legislation being always on the side of moderation, and he never forced a measure which aroused vigorous opposition. Nothing, however, was done to alleviate the lot of the poor, whose children had to work to support themselves from five years upwards.

The age of humanitarianism was just at its dawn, but trade was uniting a country hitherto hopelessly divided by religion. The business man's Ledger was making men friends, whereas the Bible had caused sects and dissensions. In these days of transition, from the feuds and ideas of the Stuart era, to one with an outlook more tempered by scientific thought, a man as unique as Walpole was bound to have enemies, some of his own party despising his peace-loving policy, Swift and Bolingbroke especially being his bitter opponents.

Despite his policy to preserve peace, Parliament forced a war on Spain in 1739. This came about because of certain differences between Spanish officials and British slave dealers over Britain's contract to supply the Spanish colonies with 4,800 slaves a year. As these quarrels continued Philip V of Spain broke the contract, and a war fever developed in Britain, led by William Pitt, the elder, a fact which forced Walpole to declare war, though he stated that all the differences between the two countries could be settled peacefully. One successful British naval action, and some Spanish treasure seized, was all that occurred.

Then followed the war over the Austrian succession in 1740, and Walpole, soon after Britain participated in the conflict, was driven from office, as he wished his country to remain neutral. He became the Earl of Orford, a much more satisfactory way of terminating a life of service to one's country than had been experienced by his predecessors, who, after outstaying their welcome, had been impeached, imprisoned or executed.

Another change then took place which should be remembered, as in 1752 the Gregorian was substituted for the Julian Calendar, and henceforward the legal year commenced on the 1st of January instead of the end of March as heretofore. All the same, the beginning of April still marks the end of the old and the beginning of the new national financial year, after which the Budget is presented. In Scotland the new way of commencing the year had been in vogue since 1600, and England just followed in the steps of other Christian countries which at different times adopted January as the first month of the year.

After Henry Pelham's ministry (1743–1754), and one formed by the Duke of Newcastle, William Pitt (1757–1761), in conjunction with the Duke of Newcastle, formed a strong government. Pitt was the outstanding statesman of his day, incorruptible, original, far-seeing, enthusiastic, inspiring and eloquent, with great executive capacity, and to him more than anyone is due the fact that France lost her control of India and Canada. He was later created the Earl of Chatham, and, to avoid confusion with his younger son, also named William Pitt (1759–1806), who was Prime Minister from 1783 until 1801 and again from

1804 to 1806, Pitt, the elder, will be referred to as Chatham, and his son Pitt, the younger, as Pitt.

From the time James II fled from the country, some openly, and many secretly, had expressed the desire to have a Stuart again on the throne. The Jacobites, as they were called, hated a foreigner occupying the British throne, and awaited their chance to restore the old regime. The first attempt was made in 1708, when Louis XIV sent a squadron of twenty-six ships, with troops on board, to land in Scotland. Prince James, known as the Old Pretender, the son of James II, accompanied the expedition, which was to seize Edinburgh and proclaim him king, but the French were driven off and the attempt ended in failure.

Again in 1715 the Jacobites made a fresh effort, this time without the help of France, as Louis XIV, their principal supporter, had just died. The Earl of Mar raised the standard of rebellion in Scotland, and, along with the clansmen who rallied to his call, he occupied Perth. Some of his forces united with Jacobites in the north of England and moved south, only to be defeated at Preston, while the remainder fought an indecisive action at Sheriffmuir, near Stirling, against the government troops led by the Duke of Argyll. When the Pretender landed at Peterhead he realised that he had no hope of success, and to prevent capture both he and Mar fled to France.

This rebellion brought about the opening up of the Highlands by General Wade, because he constructed good main roads for the movement of his troops. These proved useful to the authorities three years later when some of the Highland clans were joined by Spaniards, who landed on the Argyllshire coast to support the Stuart claim to the throne. At Glenshiel the Spanish surrendered and the Highlanders were dispersed.

Much the most serious attempt to restore the Stuarts to the British throne occurred in 1745, when Britain was engaged in the war over the Austrian succession. The son of the Old Pretender, Prince Charles Edward, inspired many a waverer by his good looks and charm to rally to his side, and Louis XV prepared a large French expedition to land in England to support the Prince in his fight for the throne. A storm, however, sank the ships, the enterprise was abandoned, and when Charles Edward landed in Scotland he found no preparations to receive him. Three thousand Highlanders gathered to his standard, and, with them, he moved on Edinburgh, which was occupied without difficulty.

At Prestonpans nearby he defeated the government forces under Sir John Cope, and then marched on London. By the time he reached Derby the government had gathered such large forces together, under General Wade and the Duke of Cumberland, the son of the King, that the young Pretender decided to return to Scotland. After gaining a minor success at Falkirk he retreated northwards to Inverness, to be brought to battle at Culloden Moor (1746), about five miles from the town. Here his exhausted followers were completely defeated, and Cumberland, known as "The Butcher" because of his ruthlessness, pursued the defeated clansmen, slaying all he could find. Thus came to an end the ill-fated House of Stuart, four centuries having elapsed since it came into being.

Charles Edward escaped, hid in Skye, was sheltered

by Flora Macdonald, and finally found his way to France, where he died a hopeless drunkard, leaving behind him many romantic stories and sentimental songs. He brought romance to a dull period of British history, and the songs which were sung of him, and his deeds, have their echoes to this day in many a Highland glen. This is the lighter side, but those who supported him suffered severely; many were killed and wounded, eighty survivors were executed, some lost their land, the wearing of the kilt and the carrying of weapons was forbidden, and measures were taken to destroy the loyalty of the clansmen to their chiefs, from whom was taken the hereditary right to administer justice.

Throughout the 18th century Britain and France were always in opposite camps, fighting each other, and, by keeping France occupied in Europe, Britain added to her possessions in North America and India. We have already read about the Austrian Succession War, and of Britain fighting France in the Netherlands. At sea the British defeated the French off Cape Finisterre and Belle Isle, and they were consequently able to interfere with French communications to their colonies, but peace was made in 1748, when France agreed to expel Prince Charles Edward and recognise the Hanoverian succession in England, her hope of a Roman Catholic again becoming king having by now vanished.

Eight years later France and Austria became friends, and Britain supported Prussia against them. Britain, by the Treaty of Westminster (1756), agreed to recognise Prussia's conquest of Silesia in exchange for Prussia recognising the independence of Hanover, an thus the stage was set for the Seven Years' War about which we have already read. While all this was going on, the British in North America were striving hard to prevent the French from excluding them from the interior by a ring of forts which they were building. George Washington and General Braddock both failed in their attempts to capture Fort Duquesne, whereas the French, under the Marquis de Montcalm, captured some of the British fortified positions.

In India the position for the British was equally unsatisfactory, as Calcutta had been captured by one of the native rulers, but here something must be said to explain why, and how, it was that the British ever got so far from home and what they were doing there.

(5) The British Empire Grows in Size and Power.

In Chapter IX we read the story of India under Moslem rule until she came under British control. Now we must learn how this came about. From the time of Alexander to Vasco da Gama, Europe had experienced little direct intercourse with the East. An occasional traveller had brought back wonderful stories of strange races and powerful kingdoms displaying great wealth, and we remember the experiences related by Marco Polo. Until the compass conquered the vast expanse of ocean the approach to India, and farther east, was by land over wide deserts and hostile countries. To the European of the 15th century India was practically an unknown land.

We have read how Columbus attempted to reach India in 1492 by sailing west, and how Vasco da Gama started from Lisbon five years later and reached Calicut, in south-west India, by way of the Cape of Good Hope after a voyage of eleven months. Here he found various independent Afghan and Moslem kingdoms, but that was before Akbar I, a contemporary of Queen Elizabeth, had conquered the greater part of India, a story already recorded under Moslem Civilisation.

A second Portuguese expedition, consisting of thirteen ships and 1200 soldiers, sailed for India in 1500 carrying the following instructions from their King Emmanuel: "To begin by preaching the Gospel and, if that failed, to proceed to the sharp determination of the sword." That was how Christianity spread from Rome throughout the world, and Emmanuel did no more than follow the instructions of Saint Augustine, the greatest figure in the Christian Church, who proclaimed that all who did not accept the Christian faith were to be slain. All who were not Christians were considered to be damned heathen, who were destined to eternal torture in hell. Consequently Christians just anticipated what their god intended to do, and we need not be surprised at the trail of misery they left behind them wherever they went.

Thus was Christian civilisation carried to the people of India, but the Christians were ignorant of the fact that India is the cradle of many of the world's religions, in which was nurtured everything comprised in Christianity. Besides this, Indian philosophers produced an ethical code of conduct far in advance of anything the Western world could understand during the Christian era, when evil predominated and righteousness was smothered by the lust for power and wealth. The European conquest of the East revealed this passion for possession at its worst, no justice or mercy being ever exhibited towards the simple, helpless natives, who were enslaved, tortured and massacred, nothing ever being allowed to thwart the European in his aim for world domination.

During the entire 16th century Portugal enjoyed a monopoly of the trade in the orient, and occupied so important a position in India that she was there represented by a viceroy. Her trade extended from the Red Sea to Japan, but she never commanded the necessary resources for the maintenance and defence of the various lands and islands on which her seamen and traders landed. Moreover, they were so bigoted and superstitious that all who were not believers in Christ were considered to be their enemies. It is impossible for anyone who has not read the contemporary narratives of their discoveries, and conquests, to grasp the cruelties inflicted on the inhabitants of those eastern lands by these missionary traders while on their travels. It is a record which has left an indelible stain on Christian civilisation.

The cruelties of Vasco da Gama, and other viceroys, drove the natives, who were anxious to be friendly, to desperation, and encouraged the princes of western India (1567) to form a league against the Portuguese. More and more troops had to be sent to protect their possessions, until at last the resources of Portugal could not continue to support the strain. Meanwhile the British and Dutch appeared in these eastern seas, and before their persistent competition Portuguese trade and domination withered away.

The Dutch were the first Europeans to break through the Portuguese monopoly. At first, like the

British, they tried to get to India by the northern coasts of Europe and Asia, William Barents leading three expeditions. That failing, they next rounded the Cape of Good Hope in 1596 and reached Sumatra and Java. From the trade which followed came the Dutch East India Company, with its factories in India, Ceylon, Java, Sumatra, the Moluccas, and on the Red Sea and Persian Gulf, the city of Batavia in Java becoming the seat of their eastern government. They reached down to the coast of Australia, established a colony at the Cape of Good Hope, and in America founded the city of New Amsterdam, now New York.

During the 17th century Dutch maritime power was the first in the world, and at one time they seemed to have the East at their feet. The rapid downfall of this supremacy came about by their short-sighted commercial policy, deliberately based upon a monopoly of the trade in spices, and one which was destitute of the true colonising spirit. Moreover, they practised such cruelty towards the natives, and their European rivals, that they failed to secure any respect from the inhabitants of those lands they had occupied. In 1758 they were attacked by the British on both land and sea, to such effect that within fifty years Britain had taken from Holland every one of her colonies, though Java and Sumatra were later restored to her. Nowhere in India did Holland retain a foothold, but how this great continent fell into British hands will now be told.

The British attempted to reach India by the north of America, John Cabot in 1496 fitting out an expedition which failed to discover the North-west Passage. He discovered Newfoundland, and then sailed along the coast of America from Labrador to Virginia. Various other unsuccessful attempts were made until 1599, when English merchants decided to form the East India Company, to trade with India by way of South Africa, because the Dutch had raised the price of pepper from 3*s.* to 8*s.* a pound, this spice being in great demand to season the high meat, game and venison before the days of condiments and sauces.

Within ten years, English ships of 1100 tons were spanning the 10,000 miles, a voyage which took a year to complete, the crews being spared suffering and death from scurvy by being given oranges to eat and lemon water to drink. Then in Cromwell's time another company was formed, to be followed by still another in 1698, and these trading activities extended as far as China, tea and china-ware being thus introduced into Europe. Everywhere the English were opposed by the Dutch, but, in spite of conflicts, they gradually extended their roots into the East, especially India, which was in a state of disunity owing to the death of the Great Mogul Aurangzeb in 1707.

During the 18th century the only serious rivals to Britain in India were the French, who secured Madras (1746) from the British, only to have to return it two years later. The centre of rivalry between the French and the British was in the district known as the Carnatic, of which Madras occupies the centre.

Here two Nawabs, or native rulers, were fighting for the throne, one Mahomet Ali, who received British support, and the other Chunda Sahib, who was supported by the French. Mahomet, at one stage of the struggle, was besieged in Trichinopoly by French native troops under the command of Dupleix, the governor of Pondicherry, the first man to train native soldiers (sepoys) for war under the command of European officers. If the French had succeeded in capturing Mahomet, British influence in India would have received a crippling blow, but the situation was saved by Robert Clive.

From now onwards, for the next twenty years, the history of India centres round the name of Robert Clive (1725-1774), the son of an impoverished English squire. He was only twenty-seven years old, an employee of the East India Company, at the time when Mahomet (1751), was being attacked by the French, and to relieve the situation Clive planned an attack on Arcot, the capital of the district, so as to ease the pressure on Trichinopoly. With only 200 European and 300 natives he captured Arcot, and defended it against a force of 10,000 sepoys under the command of the French. Eventually the besieging army retired, and this marked the turning point in the war in favour of Britain, because Mahomet, the friend of the British, became the Nawab of the Carnatic.

Clive, who was described by Chatham as "a heaven-born general", now became a colonel and the governor of Fort St. David, whence he marched the following year against the Fort of Calcutta, formerly in British possession, but then in the hands of Surajah Dowlah, the Nawab of Bengal, who was hostile to the British. This he captured, releasing the twenty-three captives, all who remained of the 146 who had been imprisoned in what came to be known as "The Black Hole of Calcutta". After a period of negotiation with the Nawab, and of plotting with Mir Jaffir, a treacherous officer in the ranks of the Nawab's army, Clive attacked the Nawab at Plassey in 1757, just north of Calcutta, where he defeated a force twenty times as large as his own, and thus secured a decisive victory which cost him less than a hundred casualties.

Battles determine history and the fate of mankind; force and not reason having so far controlled our destiny. Some battles are more decisive than others, but the Battle of Plassey was one of the great decisive battles of history, as here the Nawab of Bengal was finally defeated, a large province and valuable plunder worth £1,500,000 falling into British control. Clive became Governor of Bengal, but this did not end his military operations. Though he was much occupied with the civil administration of his conquered territory, he found time to follow up his military success and pursue the French as far as Benares and Madras. Meanwhile he never ceased to improve the organisation and drill of his sepoy army, enlisting into it many stalwart men from Upper India, until eventually he had a formidable force at his disposal.

After four years of incessant labour his health gave way and he returned to England, leaving behind him his protégé, young Warren Hastings, who was destined to be his great successor. Clive by now had amassed a large fortune, though it could easily have been very much greater but for his generosity to all his friends and helpers. He was not greedy for his own enrichment, and always generous to his colleagues and the troops he led to victory. Nevertheless, like all conquerors, he was a robber, and had no justification for plundering the wealth of the Nawab of Bengal and stealing his domains. On the other hand, he brought peace to a distracted land which was just waiting to be exploited by the first nation with the necessary dash, resources and determination. Besides peace he brought prosperity, security and greater liberty to the natives, who for centuries had been the prey of oppression.

The French strove hard to secure their position in the Carnatic, besieging Madras, but the arrival of reinforcements from Britain turned the balance so much in favour of the British that General Eyre Coote decisively defeated the French at Wandiwash in 1760, after which Pondicherry and other French settlements fell into their hands. Five years later Clive returned to Calcutta, and commenced the work of making Bengal the base from which the mighty fabric of British India could afterwards steadily and proportionately grow. Meantime the East India Company became the real sovereign ruler over 30,000,000 people, occupying a vast territory, and yielding an annual revenue of £4,000,000, part of which was used for the improved government of the country.

He became Lord Clive, but his closing years were clouded by Parliament showing resentment at the use he had made of his high office for his own enrichment, though it also expressed the opinion "that Robert, Lord Clive, did at the same time render great and meritorious services to his country". The criticism he received so preyed upon him that he died by his own hand in his fiftieth year.

The early British occupation of India is just the same old story of conquest, pillage, intrigue, breaking faith, and all that is sordid in human nature. Bribery and corruption, in dealing with the native princes, was the accepted policy of those days, and this was continued by Warren Hastings (1732-1818), who became the governor of the East India Company, now attracting the attention of Parliament because of its corrupt methods and misrule. He arrived in India (1772) just after a terrible famine had swept away a third of the population of Bengal, and during his term of office he was engaged in fighting, bribing and scheming.

He it was who organised and extended British dominion over this vast continent, being responsible for establishing its system of civil administration. After thirteen years of office he was succeeded by Lord Cornwallis (1738-1805), who, ten years earlier, had surrendered the British Army to the American colonists. With him fell the British cause in what became the United States, but his prestige in no way suffered, and, during his seven-year term as Governor-General of India, he successfully built the superstructure on the foundations laid by Hastings.

From now onwards the policy of succeeding governor-generals aimed at ensuring that the British were the predominant power in India, and that the native princes, whose states cover nearly two fifths of the land, only retained the insignia of sovereignty by surrendering the substance of independence. The subsequent political history of India has been the gradual development of this idea, its culmination being reached when Queen Victoria was proclaimed Empress of India in 1877. On the conflicts the British had with the native princes, on how they finally drove out the French, on the twenty-one-year feud between Hastings and Parliament, and the long struggle between the East India Company and the Crown for the supreme control of Indian affairs, there is not space here to enlarge, but when Hastings returned home for the last time, he found in Edmund Burke, Sheridan and Fox severe critics of his actions in India, a conflict which ended in him being impeached in 1788.

For seven years he was on his defence on the charge of "high crimes and misdemeanours", to be finally declared innocent of all the accusations laid against him. Against his private character not even calumny has breathed a reproach, but, in his public life, it was his misfortune to be the scapegoat upon whose head Parliament laid the accumulated sins, real or imaginary, of the East India Company. He did much for the good of India, for its trade and welfare, and no one devoted himself more heartily to the promotion of every scheme, great and small, that could advance the prosperity of the land to which he gave his life. Clive's sword conquered India, but it was Hastings who planned its administration, and saved it in its darkest hour.

The dissolution of the Indian Mogul Empire, and the confusion which followed, gave Britain her opportunity to tighten and expand her grip on this great continent which had come within her control so quickly, so easily and so unexpectedly. Britain's conquest brought peace, prosperity and freedom from oppression, her small army of about 225,000 troops, and some 5000 British officials, having preserved this vast territory from outside attack and inside disorder, while the population, since her occupation, has grown from 120,000,000 to over 350,000,000. The country's trade, moreover, has so expanded that India is now the eighth largest industrial country in the world.

This alone is a great achievement, but, though much has been impossible because of religious prejudices, much more besides the foregoing has been accomplished, 40,000,000 acres, for instance, which were desert having been reclaimed for cultivation by means of elaborate irrigation systems. One common language, English, now binds together races which hitherto could not understand each other, this diversity of language having made intellectual progress so difficult. Ninety per cent. of the population is still illiterate, but her numerous languages and creeds have so far been responsible for the absence of education, other reasons being the custom of child marriages, and the impossibility of having women teachers because of caste, the result of social and religious prejudices.

By their contact with Britain the native leaders have absorbed her science and culture. This was freely imparted to them, with the intention that they in turn would be the means of enlightening their own people in the way of a more advanced form of existence, and the art of government freed from the corruption so prevalent amongst Easterners. So successful has this policy been that India today possesses some 2,000,000 educated and intelligent native administrators, officials, judges, lawyers, teachers, scientists and politicians who have so acquired British ideals that they now feel themselves competent to manage their own country without outside interference.

This, then, is the fruit of the Indian Charter of 1833, the essence of which was that "the interests of the native subjects are to be preferred to those of Europeans wherever the two came into conflict", and "that no native of India, or natural born subjects of

His Majesty, shall be disabled from holding any place, office or employment by reason of his religion, place of birth, descent or colour". How important for orderly and disinterested government these principles are will be better realised when we remember that religion, which determines caste, is the curse of India seething with hostile creeds.

No country on earth better demonstrates the theme of this book—the curse of ignorance. Here we have a vast mixed population of illiterate, ignorant people, who, through lack of knowledge and stupid prejudices, are often miserable when they could be happy. There is probably no other country on earth in which there is more suffering and misery, the deadening hand of orthodox religion being everywhere noticeable. Hinduism, with its numerous castes and taboos, has the same paralysing effect on progress as had Christianity during the Middle Ages, and consequently life in India is still medieval in many parts.

Because of religion, the Moslems and Hindus hate each other, and will not work together for the common good. Because of religion, the Hindu caste system brands 60,000,000 men and women as untouchable. These cannot use the public well, their children cannot go to school, they cannot wash at the public washhouse, they cannot sit with others in public places, and, if they cast their shadow on a Hindu of a higher order, he has immediately to wash his entire body to cleanse himself of the pollution.

Religion keeps women in purdah and their faces veiled. Religion considers nursing a dishonourable and degrading profession. Religion allows children to play in the temples amongst phallic obscenities.

Religion encourages child marriages and makes child-birth a nightmare of filth, suffering and danger. Religion teaches that Karma is the explanation for suffering. When even the tiniest child suffers, it is because of sins in a previous life. Consequently it is wrong to try to alleviate suffering and cure disease.

Because the Hindus are so impractical, they have produced a religion contrary to all sense and reason. The fakir who sits motionless gazing at the sun until he is blind, is looked upon with greater reverence than the doctor, the teacher and the social reformer who wish to improve hygienic conditions, remove filth, stamp out plague and disease, develop the mind and raise the standard of life.

Britain's successful occupation of India was largely due to her command of the sea. Chatham based his foreign policy on blockading the French coast and keeping France from sending troops and supplies to India or Canada. During the Seven Years' War, when France and Britain were enemies, he made full use of British sea power to this end. Britain's share of the fighting in Europe was a side issue to this main plan for securing from France both Canada and India, besides other of her colonies, and Britain continued to subsidise Frederick II of Prussia to keep him fighting France, so that France could not spare the troops to protect her overseas possessions. At sea (1759) the British defeated France at Lagos and Quiberon Bay, after which they had command of the ocean routes, and the French were cut off.

At the time Clive was conquering India, in the year after his great victory at Plassey which gave him control of Bengal, Chatham set out to conquer Canada.

Under the able command of Generals Amherst and James Wolfe, the British (1758) attacked the French, who were skilfully led by the Marquis de Montcalm. Louisburg, a fort at the mouth of the St. Lawrence river, was captured, and this was followed by the surrender of Fort Duquesne, the key to the west, as it commanded the Ohio river, and whoever controlled that waterway could expand westwards to the Pacific. The following year Quebec, situated on a steep promontory in the centre of the French settlement, was attacked and captured by Wolfe. Two attacks were made, one by land and the other by river, which latter was under the command of Wolfe. Amherst failed to get through, but Wolfe reached Quebec by water, and found it so strongly fortified that no direct attack was possible.

After a siege of over two months Wolfe decided on a surprise attack, during the night, by a steep path leading from the river. To keep the garrison ready for a frontal attack his fleet meantime bombarded Quebec, and this enabled him and his men to reach the Heights of Abraham well prepared to fight the enemy on equal terms. Within twenty minutes the French were defeated, and Quebec surrendered, but both Wolfe and Montcalm were mortally wounded. When Montreal surrendered (1760) French resistance was at an end, and Canada consequently became a British colony.

The Seven Years' War in Europe, from which Britain by the use of sea power gained other territories from France, came to an end in 1763, a date which marks the time when this island kingdom was approaching the height of her power. Securely settled in Bengal, only time was now required before nearly all India would come completely under her control. In North America she had no serious rival, and elsewhere she was picking up new colonies all over the world. At this stage of the construction of the British Empire it is interesting to review the British gains throughout the 17th and 18th centuries, and to remember that then was revived the name of Great Britain, which had first been used abroad to distinguish her from Brittany in France.

The first British colony was Newfoundland, which was occupied in 1583, though the Channel Islands came with William the Conqueror. From the 16th century onwards the story is one of continual growth, either by conquest or peaceful settlement. In 1600 St. Helena was captured, and seven years later the first permanent settlement by the English was made in Virginia by Captain John Smith, who founded Jamestown in 1607, to be followed by one at Plymouth in New England (1620), where landed the hundred pilgrims from the *Mayflower*.

This expansion went on until there were thirteen separate colonies on the Atlantic seaboard of America, each one politically quite independent of the others, and kept apart by religious and other differences. Their inhabitants were mostly of English descent, and they thrived on the natural wealth with which their land was endowed. They brought with them the customs and ways of life to which they had been accustomed, and also the same intolerance from which they had suffered in the land of their birth. Eight of the colonies had a governor appointed by the King, an elected assembly, responsible for local affairs, but dependent on the home government so far as tariffs and external trade were concerned, which latter was controlled for the benefit of Britain.

Colonists arrived in the Bermudas as early as 1612, and in Barbadoes in 1625. Several of the Leeward Islands were occupied in 1632, Jamaica was taken from Spain in 1655, and the Gold Coast was occupied in 1661. The first settlements in the North-west Territories of Canada occurred in 1670, and Gibraltar was captured by Sir George Rooke in 1704. In 1713 Prince Edward Island, Nova Scotia, the Hudson Bay Territories, New Brunswick and Minorca were ceded to Britain by France in the Treaty of Utrecht, following her defeat in the war of the Spanish succession. Britain also obtained the contract held by France for supplying the ever increasing number of slaves now being sent to Spanish America. In 1760, Canada, and all the other French settlements in North America, were conquered and came under British rule.

After her defeat in the Seven Years' War, at the Peace of Paris (1763), France ceded to Britain, Dominica, St. Vincent, Granada in the Windward Islands, and Tobago. Then came the occupation of the Falkland Islands (1765), British Honduras (1786), Sierra Leone (1787), New South Wales (1788), the capture of Ceylon in 1795, and Trinidad in 1797, which brings us up to the end of the 18th century. More was to follow in the years to come, but that is a story which will be told in the following chapters, as a black page in British history must first be read before this came about, and to it we shall now devote our attention.

(6) Britain Experiences Her Greatest Humiliation.

Neithe: of the first two Georges took much part in the administration of the country, leaving Parliament a free hand to do as it pleased, but, when George II died in 1760, his grandson George III (1760–1820) decided that the time had come to break the long rule of the Whigs and restore the authority of the Crown. The Tories, who had displayed Jacobite leanings in the past, were now loyal to the Hanoverian dynasty, they realising that the Stuart cause was hopelessly lost. George III was a man of third-rate intelligence, but imbued with the belief that a king must rule as well as reign. So he set about having ministers of his own choice, and the man he chose to do his bidding was quite inexperienced and lacked the genius of his predecessors.

The Earl of Bute, the new Secretary of State, disagreed with Chatham over Britain's continued participation in the Seven Years' War, Chatham objecting to leave Frederick II, who was in desperate straits. The King supported Bute, Chatham resigned, and Lord Bute became Prime Minister, he being the first to receive this title. Chatham, the proud, despotic empire builder, had no use for the inexperienced Lord Bute, his disgust for him reaching its peak when Bute made the Treaty of Paris. Britain was now the world's supreme power, but Bute feared attack from those she had stripped of their possessions, and, as a sop, the Treaty of Paris was signed in 1763, which gave back to France and Spain a few of their minor losses, but the major ones Britain retained. Bute was so despised because of this faint-heartedness, that a body-guard of prize-fighters had to protect him in the streets until he resigned within a year.

The new Prime Minister was George Grenville, an able honest man, and he was followed by the liberal-minded Marquis of Rockingham. These two administrations occupied the years 1763–1766, and then came the Grafton-Chatham ministry from 1766 to 1770, to be followed by Lord North's, which lasted until 1782. This Tory peer was just the King's tool, and nothing more. From now onwards George pulled all the political strings, and kept the Whigs out of power and office. Around North's administration the tragic tale unfolds, of how the thirteen American colonies separated from the mother country to form the United States of America.

The quarrel started by Britain trying to get the colonies to pay their share of the Seven Years' War, in which Britain participated in Europe to prevent the French in Canada from extending their domination southwards. The Whigs, who were mostly in favour of conciliating the colonists, had little opportunity to carry their policy into effect. Had they done so they might have smoothed the differences that had arisen between them and the homeland, but the Rockingham ministry was in power for only one year.

The Tories, represented by Lord North's ministry, and lorded over by George III, must be held responsible for the calamity of the American War of Independence, the King being the chief culprit, as the position which he assumed was as contrary to the principles of parliamentary government as had been the encroachments of Charles I. On the accession of George III the Whigs were disunited, and he played one off against the other, making changes in the administration at will, so much so that the King, and not Parliament, ruled the country for the next twelve years.

Some enlightened politicians protested against this reactionary procedure, one of the most outstanding being John Wilkes (1727–1797), who was the champion of the right of free representation by the parliamentary constituencies. He was imprisoned for his criticism of the King and his ministers, but gained release on the plea of privilege. He secured the right of a constituency to the member of its choice, a representative who could not be declared disqualified by the government, but he pleaded in vain for a just and equal representation of the people.

Another of his victories was the recognition of the right of printers to publish parliamentary debates. He bore an unsavoury reputation, because of his loose sexual morality, but his work for liberty, justice and democratic government impelled Gladstone to say that "Wilkes must be enrolled among the greatest champions of English freedom". After being Lord Mayor of London he became member for Middlesex, which seat he retained for many years, during which time he proved himself to be one of the outstanding pioneers of government of the people by the people.

One of the greatest men in the history of political literature, Edmund Burke (1729–1797), who stood for complete American liberty, was likewise an outstanding critic of the policy of the King and his subservient

Tory ministers. Though he never attained the position of supreme responsibility, few, if any, before him came so close to the details of practical politics, with which he combined a broad conception of political philosophy. The variety of his literary and rhetorical gifts is striking, but his judgment on the French Revolution is open to deep criticism, as he failed to realise the rotten core which had to be cut out of French political life. Evolution is generally the best way to attain progress, but sometimes this can only come by revolution, an idea with which Burke would never compromise.

A deep longing for greater freedom and liberty, which sprang from a quickening of the minds of the people, prevailed in Britain, as well as in France, in the years preceding the Revolution. Fortunately the more flexible system of government in Britain made its realisation possible, without the upheaval which occurred across the Channel, but unfortunately the reactionary George III took command at a critical time, when the colonies in North America likewise desired greater liberty of action, an urge which was quickened by the fact that the fear of France had now been removed.

Hitherto the French hold on America had made the colonists look to the home country for protection, as prior to France's removal she had controlled the North American hinterland from Labrador to the Gulf of Mexico, except those tracts in the south-west claimed by Spain. France, following her defeats in Europe and Canada, had by now (1760) retired completely from North America, though Spain retained her claims west of the Mississippi and around New Orleans. The rest of the vast continent, including Canada, which had just been won from France, belonged to Britain.

This immense area covering over 7,000,000 square miles, nearly 3,000 miles wide, and about the same from north to south, was the greatest prize and opportunity which ever fell to any country. Sparsely populated, the colonists numbering only some 2,000,000, rich in virgin soil, minerals and everything mankind needs or desires, it had come into the possession of a small island people who, had they been wise, would have made sure that nothing would occur to prevent them keeping it secure, and developing it according to the wishes of its inhabitants. How half of this continent was lost to Britain is the story now about to be unfolded, a tragic tale of stupidity and folly which reveals how heavily the curse of ignorance enveloped Britain in the 18th century.

For nearly one hundred and fifty years, colonists, tempted by the gift of free land, had been leaving the shores of Britain and Europe to make their homes in this far-distant land, glad to be free of the tyranny, injustice and warfare which afflicted the continent of Europe. It was a dangerous enterprise in those days to cross the 3000 miles of storm-swept ocean in ships of only some hundred tons, but increasing numbers took the risk, well knowing that never again would they see their home land. They thrived and multiplied in their various settlements, and, as time passed, England became to most of them a far-off land about which only the older people knew anything.

Consequently a national feeling developed amongst the American colonists, as very naturally they wished to manage their own affairs, and this was just what Britain did not want them to do. Such an idea was monstrous in the 18th century, when government without a monarch and an aristocracy was considered impossible, but it required a terrible war before the seemingly impossible was proved to be quite possible.

The expulsion of the French from North America, after years of hard fighting, was the prelude to the American revolution, because this conflict with the French had trained both officers and men in war. Moreover, it had given the colonists a feeling of independence and self-reliance, besides uniting the thirteen separate colonies. Much to their resentment, Britain now declared all territory west of their present boundaries to be Crown Land, a decision which was contrary to the original charters.

This was the seed which ultimately developed into open revolt, because the colonists felt that America belonged to them as they had played a large part in driving out the French. Moreover, they expressed great contempt for the British fighting qualities, and the inferior type of officers sent from the homeland, men with little ability, who held their positions only because of social qualifications. Such was the delicate position George III and his ministers were called upon to handle, one which required much tact and understanding to be successfully negotiated.

Three thousand miles was a great distance in those days, and for over a hundred years the British in America had been separated from the motherland. Naturally they felt more American than British, but still the home government treated them as Britishers, and expected them to carry out its bidding, just as if

America was an addition to the British Isles, like some new counties which had come into being. The Americans still remained British both in their ties and outlook, with British sympathies and prejudices, but for all that they now felt that they had grown up and were quite capable of managing their own affairs, while remaining loyal to the British Throne. There was no desire whatever to break this vital link, and George III, when he became king, had no more loyal subjects than the people comprising the American colonies.

The Americans rightly said that if the British would only pay taxes sanctioned by the British Parliament, they likewise would only pay taxes authorised by their representative assemblies. American affairs, they claimed, were their concern, and, as they did not interfere with home affairs, the King and Parliament had no right to meddle with what did not concern them. If Britain required money from America, she would get it by applying to the representative assemblies through the governors. Even as late as 1774, a year before the rebellion, the American Congress agreed that it was right and proper for the British Parliament to make such regulations as would best benefit external trade, but it maintained that only the colonial assemblies could levy internal taxation and make local laws, Britain having no right to raise revenue from the American colonies without their consent.

This resolution was reached after years of irritating British enactments, which can best be followed if summarised in their correct order.

1763.—All American judges to hold office during the King's pleasure, their salaries being independent of the colonial assemblies. A regular British army in

America of twenty regiments to be paid by America. Lord Bute was driven out of office by the uproar created by Wilkes, who saw in this a plan to subdue the Americans by force. The exportation of European products to America was forbidden, except in British or colonial-owned vessels, manned by British seamen.

1765.—The Stamp Act was passed to raise revenue in America from stamps on official and legal documents, coupled with a command to the American Assemblies to furnish the royal troops in America with fuel, candles, vinegar, bedding, cooking utensils, and secure the billeting of soldiers in inns, barns and vacant houses.

This meant that the colonies were to be taxed without their consent, and the revenue was to be employed to support a standing army which was to be used to maintain Britain's right to tax the Americans as she thought fit. Objection to this was taken in America, but no forcible resistance occurred, though arrangements were made for the formation of an all-American Congress, to be composed of representatives of all the colonies. When this met a petition was sent to the King and Parliament, asking recognition of their powers of legislation "agreeably to the principles of the English constitution", acknowledging allegiance to the Crown, and claiming "all the inherent rights and privileges of natural born subjects within the kingdom of Great Britain", including the right of petition, trial by jury, taxation by representatives, and of granting supplies to the Crown.

In the same year the Navigation Laws were enforced, which limited to Britain alone the destination of certain American produce, and from time to time new articles were added, such as sugar, tobacco and indigo.

1766.—The Rockingham ministry repealed the Stamp Act, resolving that taxation without representation was a violation of the British constitution, but that Parliament reserved the power over all other legislation.

1767.—The Grafton-Chatham ministry passed a measure to tax imports into the colonies. The effect of this was that the colonies ceased to import all dutiable articles.

1768.—The Governor of Massachusetts prorogued his Assembly, because it issued a circular letter to the other Assemblies, which urged a petition to the King that he act as umpire between them and the British Parliament in their attempt to redress their grievances. Protests followed this action by the Governor, when those who had protested were censured by the British Parliament, which demanded that they be sent to England for trial on the charge of treason.

1770–1773.—When the Assemblies met they would pass no other resolution except one, which denounced the acts of the British ministry, and because of this they were prorogued by the governors. Tryon, the governor of North Carolina, one of the worst of the Crown officials, crushed a rising by the people, who were denied justice and defrauded of legislative power, and used his victory so savagely that he forced an increasing stream of settlers over the mountains into Tennessee.

1772.—Owing to the boycott of all dutiable imports the revenue for this year was £80, a sum which cost

£300,000 to collect. This revenue was produced from tea imports only, because in 1770 the import tax on all other imports had been removed.

1773.—At Boston some fifty persons, disguised as Indians, went on board the vessels in harbour, and threw the tea which was in their holds into the sea, in the presence of a large crowd of spectators.

1774.—The British ministry decreed that Boston was to be closed as a port until an indemnity had been paid for the tea destroyed, this closure to continue until the town returned to loyalty to the Crown. Then Parliament passed a measure extending the boundaries of Canada over the whole territory lying north of the Ohio, and east of the Mississippi.

This Quebec Act, as it was called, was to prevent the northern colonies from expanding westwards, but it also meant to the Puritans the establishment of the Episcopalian Church in their midst. For many years they had dreaded this calamity, because of the way some of them, and their ancestors, had suffered from the persecution of the Church of England before they had emigrated. In this year also met the First Continental Congress, the first really national body in American history, which adopted an address to the King, to the people of Great Britain and the colonies, declaring the rights of the American colonists, and summing up the various violations of these rights, for which Parliament had been responsible. Another resolution stated that force would be used if necessary to secure to Americans their rights and liberties.

All the American pleading, arguments and threats made no impression on the British government, which now began to act in earnest, instructions begin dispatched to Canada that troops were to be mobilised and moved against the American colonies, General Gage, the British commander in America, being instructed to arrest all the colonial leaders. This was followed by the two British Houses of Parliament presenting a joint address to the King offering all the resources of the Empire to suppress any rebellion in America, and the King replied that he would act as Parliament desired.

For nine years the Americans had been restraining themselves, and practising patience. Though their feelings became ever more difficult to control, increasingly scrupulous care was taken to keep within the law, but popular excitement was now steadily rising. Finally, when British troops fired on some Americans guarding a stock of powder, the dam burst, and the flood of feeling, which had been repressed all these years, carried all before it. Men left their ploughs in the furrows, and rode off to Boston in such numbers that before many weeks had passed the town was occupied by a mass of undisciplined and half-armed soldiers. British officials, who had been responsible for so much of the trouble, and on whose bad advice to the government at home the calamity was largely due, now fled to England, or the nearest military depot, but some joined up with the Americans.

It is sad to think that as late as the 18th century the British army was employed in the disgraceful task of subjecting to death and mutilation people of British stock, whose women and children saw their homes devastated and were themselves cruelly insulted. Its evil record of cruelty and destruction during some of its many wars in Europe, and its crimes against the

Irish and Scottish people, were now continued in America, and no good can come from misrepresenting the past, which should be remembered with regret. It is true that the British soldier was then no worse than the soldiers of other lands, as everything to do with war and destruction is degrading, but to tell a wide audience, mostly composed of ill-informed listeners, that "the British army has always fought for liberty and justice" is false. The B.B.C., which allowed a prominent cabinet minister to make this remark (23-3-44), when fulsomely expanding on the perennial zeal of the British for righteous causes, consequently lowered itself to the German level and made itself ridiculous to all who are acquainted with history.

On 19th April, 1775, the United States of America was proclaimed as now in being, but George III still remained her king, and her flag retained the crosses of St. George and St. Andrew. The struggle for liberty was long and bitter, lasting for six years. George Washington (1732–1799) became Commander-in-Chief of the American forces on the same day as the Battle of Bunker Hill (1775), when the British defeated the Americans, but at terrible loss to themselves, half the British forces being wiped out. Nevertheless there was as yet no idea of this being a struggle for independence, the fight being only for self-government. Another petition was now sent to the King proclaiming a state of open rebellion in the colonies, and to this he refused to reply. Some of the people in Britain were in sympathy with the Americans, and a number of British officers resigned their commissions rather than fight against their fellow countrymen in their struggle for liberty. Parliament, however, by more than two to one, still supported their previous decisions to force the rebels into submission, but it had to go to Germany to obtain the 25,000 men now required for the army.

In 1776 independence was declared and the British flag was replaced by the Stars and Stripes, Congress and the people being greatly influenced by Thomas Paine's pamphlet *Common Sense*, advocating complete independence. This was read everywhere, and the open movement for independence dates from its publication. France now supplied the young nation with arms and money, and the conflict commenced in earnest. A committee consisting of Thomas Jefferson, John Adams, Benjamin Franklin, Roger Sherman and Robert R. Livingston then drew up the Declaration of Independence, disowning all political connection with Great Britain, and this was adopted by Congress.

An invasion of Canada met with partial success, Montreal being captured, but the Americans were defeated at the Battle of Long Island (1776), and Washington had to retreat because his position was becoming increasingly precarious. Undismayed by adversity, he now planned and carried out a movement which was to be the turning point of the war, the capture of Trenton, whose garrison surrendered. Next he captured Princetown (1777), and shortly afterwards was joined by the young Marquis de la Fayette, and other foreign officers, who brought with them a shipload of supplies from France. Meanwhile, Benjamin Franklin (1706–1790), one of the great personalities of the revolution (a man of exceptional inventive genius, and one of the most eminent journalists, diplomatists, statesmen, scientists and philosophers of his time), went to France, and succeeded in making her an ally of the United States.

General Burgoyne, moving south from Quebec with reinforcements, failed to meet Howe, the British commander, as arranged, and was defeated, being forced to surrender at Saratoga. A difficult position was made worse when Spain, hoping to regain Gibraltar, now entered the conflict, and then Britain declared war on Holland because of her help to the colonists. Britain now discovered that she could not keep supplies from reaching her enemies, because her fleet was scattered and inferior to the French navy, though it managed to defeat a Spanish squadron (1780) off Cape St. Vincent, a victory which gave her little comfort, as by now she had no friends, and wherever she looked there were enemies eager for her defeat and humiliation.

Besides this the colonists bitterly resented the use she made of the Indians to fight against white people, but, most of all, their feelings were outraged by the way the British army, composed largely of Hessians and Hanoverians, pillaged and insulted both friend and foe alike. Truly ignorance produces folly, and the blank stupidity displayed by the British king and Parliament certainly led Britain in those days far down the path which leads to destruction.

Two years earlier, the British, having failed in the north, commenced a campaign in the south, capturing Charleston. Cornwallis was now in command, and, after victories at Camden and Guildford Court House, he advanced into Virginia, to encamp finally on the narrow peninsula of Yorktown (1781), to await reinforcements. Meantime the French had defeated the British fleet, and were in command of the approaches, the consequence being that Cornwallis was cut off from receiving supplies by sea, a situation which led to his destruction. Washington, quick to see his chance, marched against him, penned him in, and forced him, and his army of 8000 men, to surrender after a siege of three weeks. The Battle of Yorktown thus became one of the world's great decisive battles, as from it arose a new independent nation, the United States of America.

This British military disaster brought the war to an end in America, and all Europe now considered Britain to be down and out, her empire on the verge of disintegration, and her role in world affairs at an end. Washington became the first President of the United States, now for the first time a free and independent state, and one of its first acts was the confiscation of all the huge tracts of land which had been in the possession of British private owners.

The naval struggle between Britain and her European enemies still continued, the Spanish investing Gibraltar for three years, when it was eventually relieved, but they succeeded in capturing Minorca, and the French seized several islands in the West Indies. Only after the British had defeated the French fleet off Saints Islands were peace discussions opened, to end in the Peace of Versailles (1783), when Britain ceded Tobago and Senegal to France, and Minorca and Florida to Spain, all other captures being returned to their previous owners.

Such, then, was Britain's punishment for her stupid reactionary policy, and France certainly could feel that she had, to some extent, paid Britain back for turning her out of India and Canada, the Americans winning the war only because of the help she gave them in men and weapons. Justice was certainly on the side of the Americans, because they only claimed what the British themselves for centuries had fought for—the right to determine their own taxation.

No taxation without representation had by now become the established principle of a free people, and why the British at home lacked the sense to realise that the colonists loved their liberty just as much as they did is difficult to understand. Most of the colonists had left their island home for the sake of freedom and liberty to live and think as they thought right. Why then was it to be expected that they would now submit to an autocratic King, a tame Prime Minister who did his bidding, and a subservient Parliament which was not of their own choice?

We cannot get back to the mentality of those days, because the people of democratic lands now look on such matters in quite a different light. Our minds have developed on the question of the people's rights and liberties, whereas in those days the dawn was just approaching. Then, in Britain, it was a period of bribery and corruption, when politicians were bought by money, positions and titles. Both Lord Sandwich, responsible for the Navy, and Lord George Germaine, in charge of the Army, were corrupt unprincipled men, and their incompetence was reflected in both services. Time-servers, place-seekers, those who were against progress and reform, and bent on maintaining the existing sordid social order, received decorations and titles which their direct descendants carry to the present day, while the advanced thinkers and pioneers, the really great and good men, were treated with disdain or as outcasts.

To them no honours were ever offered, as those who had the power to bestow such gifts were quite uninterested in reform or progress, and consequently retained their bribes for their own reactionary supporters. Thus the truly great of those days were generally men who lacked these relics of a bygone age, honours which still so appeal to many, but which were rightly discarded by those countries that freed themselves from monarchy, and the ancient traditions surrounding the throne.

(7) THE FIRST COMPREHENSIVE SOCIAL WELFARE SCHEME.

At the close of the 18th century the common people everywhere were living in a state of moral depravity and intellectual darkness, and nowhere was this state of affairs more pronounced than in Great Britain. It is difficult to find words to describe the appalling conditions in which the poor lived, and how little was done for their social and moral upliftment. The utter indifference of the rich to the surrounding misery is impossible for us to imagine, and they seemed to lack entirely the qualities of compassion and mercy.

Nothing could better illustrate this mentality than to record the treatment of that age towards one of the greatest benefactors of mankind, a man who devoted his life to raising the people and freeing them from all religious and political tyranny. He was the pioneer of social welfare, of free education for every child, and the originator of our present social system, though his ideas were not put into practice for about a hundred years. He is known by name to few, and yet he was one of the greatest men of his age, a master mind which helped to shape the destiny of the world.

This great champion of liberty and justice was Thomas Paine (1736–1809), whose influence for righteousness and truth was so pronounced that this last section of this chapter will be devoted to his life and work. He was the son of a Quaker, a Norfolk stay-maker, being first an exciseman, then a schoolmaster, shopkeeper, artisan, and finally a journalist. For the good of mankind he accepted poverty and calumny so that he might speak his honest thoughts, and thus help the people to live freer and happier lives. Paine did for Britain and America what Voltaire did for France, and to him we are indebted for much of the liberty we now enjoy.

Born in poverty, in a country where liberty was preached but not practised, where the privileges of class were more important than truth and honesty, and where the rights of the ordinary individual were ignored by both the clergy and the aristocracy, Paine lit the lamp of reason which illuminated the darkness of his age. He saw oppression on every hand, injustice everywhere, hypocrisy at the altar, bribery and corruption in Parliament and in the Law Courts, and imbecility on the throne. With outstanding courage he espoused the cause of right against wrong, of the weak against the strong, of the poor against the rich. For such a man there was no place in Christian England and no living to be made. So he went to America in

1774, to help the colonists in their struggle against George III and his subservient, incompetent, corrupt ministers, his pamphlet *Common Sense*, published two years later, about which we have already read, being his first contribution to the cause of justice and freedom.

Then, when serving in the ranks of the American army, sharing its defeats and dangers, at the time when the situation seemed to be desperate, he produced his second pamphlet *The Crisis*, which acted as a beacon in the fog of war, cheering the downhearted, and pointing the way to victory. No other two pamphlets ever accomplished such terrific results; no other publications, before or since, ever created a nation. Nothing from the pen of one man had ever laid the foundation, not only of a nation, but of the greatest and wealthiest unified community of all time. That was Paine's greatest contribution to mankind, but he did more than that.

At the end of the war, when independence was won, no one stood higher in the estimation of the American people than Thomas Paine, the best and greatest being his friends and admirers. Still, he felt that he had further work to do, and that he must now bring light to darkest England. So he returned home (1787) to a land where 223 offences were punishable by death, where criminals abounded, the prisons were dens of abomination and filled to overflowing, the scaffolds were crowded, national and local government was corrupt and unrepresentative, and tyranny, injustice, intolerance and cruelty reigned everywhere.

In this atmosphere he wrote *Rights of Man*, a work which everyone should read. It is concise, compact, logical, accurate, natural and convincing; it is the

Magna Charta of Democratic civilisation, and it laid the foundation of the liberty we now enjoy. Evil is exposed, and unrighteousness uncovered in brief pithy sentences, some of which bring home his meaning by apt comparison, such as "He pities the plumage but forgets the dying bird," this being a reply to Burke, who was lavishing so much sentiment on the royal family and aristocracy of France during the Revolution, while quite forgetting all that the people had suffered in the past.

The British revolution of 1688 had placed the landed aristocracy firmly in political power. Mostly Tory in politics, the squires had great influence in the parliamentary elections; Episcopalian in religion, they had the appointment of the village priest, and, as Justices of the Peace, they administered the local laws. Besides this they regarded all non-Anglicans as a class apart, as outcasts and untouchable. Since the Revolution the wealth and power of the squires had steadily increased, and they received a terrible shock from the French Revolution, which overthrew the autocratic orthodox oligarchy that had so mis-ruled France.

Consequently, when *Rights of Man* was first published in 1791, a writ was issued the following year for the arrest of Thomas Paine, its author. This was the beginning of the great repression of British Liberal opinion, because it was feared that what had happened across the Channel would likewise take place in Britain. In those days the leaders of the nation could not imagine England without a dominant aristocracy, buttressed by the State Church. Neither could they imagine a country with all its people free and educated, it being considered necessary for the good and safety of the realm that the masses be kept illiterate and in servitude.

Education, in the opinion of both politicians and priests, was the prelude to anarchy, as the State in those days did not rest on reason but on tradition. Into this fabric of custom *Rights of Man* burst as a bomb, because Paine wrote in favour of republican government, and denounced an hereditary monarch who ruled through the ministers he alone appointed. He did not envisage what time and circumstance brought about, a constitutional monarch who represented his widely scattered people but was prepared to leave to their representatives the management of the affairs of state. With the reactionary George III on the throne, we can well understand how the reformers of the time saw salvation only by means of a republic, especially so as only a few years previously the ministers appointed by the King to do his bidding had, by their crass stupidity, thrown away the greatest and richest part of the Empire.

Within a few months of publication, *Rights of Man* had run into many impressions, because, in spite of the ban placed upon it, the people felt that here at last was a book by an author whose every page glowed with sympathy for their condition. It became the Magna Charta of the poor, because it was the first book to make out a case for the working class from their own point of view. This the author did by setting forth for the first time a sound and reasoned programme of social reform, which gave the illiterate unfranchised masses a goal to strive for, and a programme to work upon.

Paine was 80 years before his time in advocating general education, 120 years in advance in advocating old age pensions, 130 years ahead in his scheme for a League of Nations to prevent war, and 150 years ahead in his ideas on general social welfare, but we have not yet caught up with his programme of the unemployed being given work which will be of service to the nation. He envisaged an era of happiness and prosperity when his programme of reform was put into practice, his words being:

When it can be said by any country in the world, my poor are happy, neither ignorance nor distress is to be found among them, my jails are empty of prisoners, my streets of beggars, the aged are not in want, the taxes are not oppressive, the rational world is my friend because I am the friend of happiness. When these things can be said, then may that country boast its constitution and government.

Paine was the first true democrat in Britain, and declared that "By engrafting representation upon democracy we arrive at a system of government capable of embracing and confederating all the various interests and every extent of territory and population." Only when all are everywhere educated, and then given the vote, would there be "universal security as a means to universal commerce", when riots and revolutions will cease. Thus only by democratic government would come human freedom and liberty without licence, when toleration would triumph over orthodox religion and political bigotry. He had no use for uniformity, believing that differences of opinion were both beneficial and creative.

After drawing attention to the wretched state in

which the majority of the inhabitants of civilised countries lived, due in large part to war, and to governments confining their attention only to maintaining law and order and the safety of each country's frontiers, he advocated a government by the people which would plan for the welfare of the people. The following eight points comprised the first essential legislation for this purpose.

(1) Provision for 250,000 destitute families at the rate of £4 per head per annum for each child under fourteen years of age.

(2) Education of the country's 1,030,000 illiterate children.

(3) Annuity of £6 per annum each for all poor persons, decayed tradesmen, and others from 50 to 60 years of age.

(4) Annuity of £10 a year for life to each poor person from the age of 60 upwards.

(5) Gift of £1 for each child born, limit being 50,000 births.

(6) Gift of £1 on marriage, limit being 20,000 marriages.

(7) Funeral expenses under exceptional conditions.

(8) Employment at all times for the casual poor of London.

After giving in detail how the necessary money would be raised, and the procedure necessary for its distribution, Paine concludes:

By the operation of this plan the poor laws, those instruments of civil torture, will be superseded, and the wasteful experience of litigation prevented. The hearts of the humane will not be shocked by ragged and hungry children, and persons of seventy and eighty years of age, begging for bread. The dying poor will not be dragged from place to place to breathe their last, as a reprisal of parish upon parish.[1] Widows will have a maintenance for their children, and not be carted away on the death of their husbands like culprits and criminals, and children will no longer be considered as increasing the distress of their parents.

The haunts of the wretched will be known, because it will be to their advantage, and the number of petty crimes, the offspring of distress and poverty, will be lessened. The poor, as well as the rich, will then be interested in the support of government, and the cause and apprehension of riots and tumults will cease. The plan is easy in practice. It does not embarrass trade by a sudden interruption in the order of taxes, but effects the relief by changing the application of them, and the money necessary for the purpose can be drawn from the excise collections which are made eight times a year in every market town in England.

Only £4,000,000 a year was necessary to put this plan into operation, but nothing came of it. It was beyond the range of Christian charity and Christian ideals, though the national revenue was nearly £16,000,000, at a time when there was no income tax, and the interest on the National Debt was only £9,150,138 a year. Nevertheless, as Paine remarks, "Britain, which cannot educate her children, nor make life even tolerable for her poor, spends £1,000,000 a year to support men from Holland and Hanover, men who understand neither her laws nor her language, and are quite uninterested in her destiny, their capacity moreover hardly fitting them for the office of parish constable." This was taken to refer to the House of Orange and the House of Hanover.

Because Paine wrote in this way about the reigning

---

[1] In these days each parish tried to avoid having to pay for the expense of burying the poor, and so the dying were moved from parish to parish until they expired.

House of Hanover, which had just lost for Britain her most valuable colony in North America, he was prosecuted for treason. His effigy, with a rope round its neck, was flogged through the streets of the principal towns of the land, every possible indignity being heaped upon it. All who published or sold *Rights of Man* were imprisoned or banished, one after another going to prison during the next thirty-five years for the crime of reprinting it or offering it for sale; Thomas Muir, a Scottish advocate, being banished (1793) for fourteen years because he passed the book on to his friends.

These prosecutions, and this persecution, were maintained to enable the authorities to retain the ban they had placed on the book. They wished to prevent the people from realising how much the government could do for their welfare, if intelligent planning took the place of the antiquated method of leaving everything for God to provide.

For thousands of years the people had relied on God, or the gods, to order their lives through the dictates of the priests, and in consequence they had lived in misery and poverty. Now the inhabitants of Europe were beginning to realise that nothing would ever come of this insane way of living, and that they must rely on themselves for increased comforts and greater happiness. The Church-controlled aristocratic government, in order to maintain past tradition and their own position and prestige, fought this rising tide of revolt, but their repressive measures did not have the effect desired, because rioting and unrest continued for the next sixty years, when at long last the people began to obtain their rights as advocated by Paine.

Before the date of his trial Paine was elected in 1792 by the Department of Calais to the French Assembly, and he succeeded in slipping away to France. Instead of being tried, and probably hanged, he was now outlawed. After taking his place in the Assembly he was appointed to the committee to draft a new constitution for France, and, if the French had followed his advice, there would have been no Reign of Terror. He was, however, too wise and cautious to please the extreme politicians, who had many old grievances to pay off. Paine wanted these forgotten, and, in his speech against the decision to kill the King, he uttered these wise words, "We will kill the King but not the man. We will destroy the monarchy but not the monarch."

Filled with unbounded love for mankind, his philanthropy boundless, he voted for the destruction of the monarchy, the instrument of tyranny, but against the death of the King. He desired a new order in France, giving privileges to none and justice to all, but had no wish to see this preceded by murder. To vote against the death of Louis XVI was a brave act, as he became at once a suspect. He was arrested in 1793, imprisoned and sentenced to death. George Washington was appealed to, but took no notice of the man who had saved him in his hour of peril. Others, however, made the effort, and he was released the following year.

Now it was that this man of untiring energy, whose one object in life was to free mankind from the bondage of State and Church, turned his attention to the prevailing curse of religious intolerance. When in prison he completed his book *The Age of Reason*, one which every intelligent individual can read with profit and delight. It set out his belief in God and the after life, but argued that the universe had not been made in six days, a flood had not covered the earth because of man's wickedness, that there were many mistakes and contradictions in the Bible, that Jesus was not God, and that Christian doctrines had not been revealed from heaven but were the work of ignorant men.

He believed in natural religion, and not in supernatural religion sponsored by priests. His arguments have never been answered, and never will be, because he kept strictly to facts, reason and experience, which in those days was a dangerous thing to do. Not only did he have to suffer for the sake of truth, but 150 people in Britain, who thought like him, were imprisoned for selling this book.

In those days of ignorance such matters as facts and reason in religion received no consideration from the vast majority, the people preferring their mental chains to liberty, and Paine became the object of bitter hatred and loathing. From the time he published *The Age of Reason* he has been cursed and maligned by most of the clergy in Christendom, the ignorant multitude following their lead, all his past services to the people being forgotten. When he returned to America in 1802 he found that his former friends had deserted him, and that it was unsafe to appear in the streets for fear of being mobbed. The pulpit became the factory for everything vile and false which the priestly mind could imagine.

Under the flag of freedom he had helped to hoist, his life was in danger, and, amongst the people he had worked so hard to set free, he was shunned, loathed and slandered, being treated as if he had some foul disease. All that he had done to secure their independence seemed to have been blotted from their memory.

In America, this land of the so-called free, where intolerance, bigotry and ignorance were as rampant as in Britain, this great champion of liberty was treated as a despised outcast, because he had declared himself not to be a Christian. The all-powerful Protestant Church sacrificed him on its altar of lies, and tore his character to shreds with the sharp-edged knife of hatred. He was a man of unblemished reputation, but he stood for liberty of thought, which, during the era of Christian civilisation, was the greatest of all crimes.

Paine gave his life to secure justice for all, introducing a measure in the Assembly of Pennsylvania to abolish slavery, but without success. He was the first man to write an article for a magazine (1775) advocating the abolition of slavery, and upholding the rights of the negro, every line of which was filled with pity, tenderness, justice and humane feeling, the effect being that the American Anti-slavery Society was formed. Next he wrote against duelling, which, he argued, did not settle the rights of a dispute, and then followed this up with an article against the prevailing cruelty to animals. Lastly, the same magazine printed his article on the rights of women, who were then considered as chattels at law, he being the first to propose that they should have the same rights as men.

His article against slavery aroused violent opposition, and the Bible was quoted in almost every Church to prove that it was a divinely decreed form of labour. Excuse can be made for slavery in Pagan times, when money did not freely circulate, but no excuse can be found for Christian slavery in the 18th century, except for the reason that the Bible, which nearly everyone in those days believed was dictated by God, supports it, an argument which carried no weight with a non-Christian like Paine.

Paine advocated the Religion of Humanity, declaring that his creed was "The world is my country and to do good is my religion." The Trinity he worshipped was Truth, Liberty and Justice, and yet, because this ardent worker for the upliftment of the human race was honest enough to say that he could not believe in Christian dogma, he became an outcast, and his name has been besmirched by the lie that he was "a dirty little atheist", he being neither dirty, little, nor an atheist. Though he loved his fellow men more than his own comfort, he was maligned, and for being one hundred years before his time his name was tarnished by every abominable lie, all of which still go around even in our own times. He despised senseless pomp, scorned titles and titled stupidity, the wearing of stars, sashes and ribbons, knowing only too well that fine feathers do not make fine birds, and yet he was greater than most monarchs because his sane and lofty ideals made multitudes better, freer and more intelligent in the century which followed.

Adolf Hitler wrote a book in prison which bound much of Europe in mental chains, and caused untold world-wide destruction and misery. Thomas Paine wrote a book in prison which liberated humanity from the shackles of Protestant bigotry and intolerance. Paine hated war, slavery, injustice, tyranny, intolerance and every form of cruelty—in fact, everything evil—

and loved all that was good and kind. He did much to lay the foundation of democracy in Britain, and bring about our age of liberty and tolerance. This being so, the treatment he received, in his day and generation, tells more powerfully than any other record could do of the social and mental conditions at the beginning of the 19th Christian century.

His life and work are a political and religious history of the times, and throw a much more illuminating light on what is called "our Christian heritage" than a bare mention of all the stupidities, cruelties and injustices prevalent in Britain, Europe and America not much more than one hundred years ago.

CHAPTER XV.

CHRISTIAN CIVILISATION.
(1780–1858.)

Introduction. (1) *Science and Invention Increase Wealth, Trade and Industry.* (2) *Pioneers of Modern Literature, Music and Art.* (3) *The Rise and Fall of Napoleon Bonaparte.* (4) *Tyranny and Injustice Cause Revolution in Europe.* (5) *Independent Republics Arise in America.* (6) *The United States Grows Rich on Slave Labour.* (7) *Sordid Social Conditions in Britain Cause Unrest.* (8) *Social Reform in Britain while her Empire Expands.*

EUROPE, at the close of the 18th century, could certainly not be called civilised, as we now understand the word. The roads between the towns were infested by highwaymen, and the dark filthy city streets by gangs of thugs ready to strike down any unprotected person. In Britain, Dick Turpin, and men like him, made travelling dangerous, and a journey from St. Paul's to Westminster at night was a hazardous undertaking. Street brawls were common, blows were readily given and returned, drunkenness was accepted as something quite natural, tempers were hasty, and there was little self-control. Baths were unknown, and the poor were filthy and verminous. Sport included bear-baiting and cock-fighting, both cruel and debasing forms of amusement.

Children, in rags, swarmed the filthy smelly city streets, receiving neither education, care nor attention from their elders, whose moral standards were of the lowest order. Socially, Britain was more backward, and the condition of the poor more deplorable, at the end of the 18th century than France was before the Revolution. Under such sordid conditions both corruption and apathy flourished in Church and State, so much so that Walpole and Pitt condemned their fellow politicians for their entire lack of ethics and social conscience.

A much more severe shock was administered to the Church when three of its own priests commenced a reform movement within its sacred walls. They were John Wesley (1703–1791), his brother Charles Wesley (1708–1788) and George Whitefield (1714–1770), and while Charles produced his 4100 hymns the other two preached in the open with great earnestness and eloquence, especially amongst the poor, who were quite neglected by the state religious organisation.

Against them, and their followers, the Church closed its door, refusing them membership or participation in the sacrament. Samuel Taylor Coleridge (1772–1834), one of the most remarkable of English poets and thinkers, well expressed the hypocrisy and selfishness of those days in his *Aids to Reflection*, in which he wrote, "He who begins by loving Christianity better than truth will proceed by loving his own sect and church better than Christianity, and end in loving himself better than all."

It is always interesting to note the large issues which come from small causes, because if John Wesley (who had given up his curacy in England and gone to Georgia in America as a missionary of the Society for the Propagation of the Gospel) had remained there, his movement might never have been born, and the Church of England not split in two as was the Catholic Church at the Reformation. Instead of continuing his missionary work, he had to leave hurriedly from Georgia, in time to escape the consequences of a suit filed by the husband of a lady to whom he had been paying too intimate attention. Likewise when in Georgia, during a period of great mental agitation, his emotions influenced him to believe that salvation came only by faith, and, on his return home, he set about to put new life into the traditional religion of England.

Wesley, who was neither a deep thinker nor learned, founded Methodism, and in its organisation he displayed not only extraordinary energy and capacity for work but also remarkable administrative powers. His movement in the Church of England corresponded to the Jansenist movement in the Roman Catholic Church, because it was a protest against the lethargy and corruption which had eaten into the Episcopalian organisation. The effect it had was so great that it disrupted the established Church, and produced a rival organisation which held just the same cardinal beliefs as the one from which it came.

Wesley and Whitefield sincerely thought that by preaching the Christian scheme of salvation they would raise the people, and in those days that was the common belief. We now know, and events since then have proved it to be true, that only by education and ethical instruction can character be developed, poverty abolished, and the standard of living raised. Organised orthodox religion, relying only on the belief in a creed and the performance of ceremonies, never has done, and never can do, more than soothe the individual's fear of death, because its foundation is belief in the sacrifice of an innocent victim who had relieved all believers of the consequences of their misdeeds. This unethical doctrine had tragic consequences, as the history of Christian civilisation reveals, and neither Wesley nor Whitefield contributed anything to the improvement of the lot of the people.

The threat of hell for unbelievers, and heaven for the baptised and saved, remained their only remedy for all the world's troubles, they producing a mass hysteria amongst their hearers, but, as they could not agree on the correct definition of the Christian scheme of salvation, they quarrelled and parted company. Wesley certainly awakened the state Church from its apathy, and frightened its priests by the disruption he caused, but neither he nor Whitefield succeeded, as they hoped, in raising the mental and moral level of the people, and consequently the sordid social conditions continued everywhere as before.

Let us, however, get away for a little from the abysmal ignorance of the times, and turn to a phase of life which was showing signs of quickening intelligence. Now we have arrived at the time when something at long last was being done to improve the lot of the people, to make life easier and happier, and this great work was carried out, not by the politicians or the priests, but by the inventors, constructors and engineers, by those who studied nature and set about making natural forces work for the improvement of the entire human race. So far priests, politicians and soldiers have made history, but now we come to the deeds of the really noble men, to those who by rational thought and intelligent industry have made life more pleasant, happier and fuller for everyone, to those whose names should be enshrined and remembered with gratitude, as they rank amongst the great benefactors of humanity.

(1) SCIENCE AND INVENTION INCREASE WEALTH, TRADE AND INDUSTRY.

We remember how knowledge came to Europe from the Moslems, and by the discovery of the Greek classics in the 15th century. The Moslems by the 10th century had acquired an advanced understanding of science, but, at that time, and during the seven centuries which followed, Europe destroyed its thinkers, and so it came about that the knowledge the Moslems had acquired was only very slowly absorbed by the Christians. The Renaissance was followed by two hundred years of religious wars and persecutions, and only in the 18th century did the leaven begin to rise, to stimulate some minds to think as Christians had never thought before. Now we are beginning to see the first fruits of intelligent thought, but, if this had not been suppressed over the previous fifteen centuries by war, persecution and superstition, where might we not have been today? Certainly many centuries in advance of what we are.

For all our past and present troubles, for all the ruination and destruction of war, for all that prevents us from enjoying life to the full in peace and happiness, with ill-health and disease a nightmare of the past, the curse of ignorance is to blame. There is no darkness like ignorance, and only by flooding the world with intellectual light will mankind be able to gather from life all that it has to offer to those who acquire knowledge, and apply it with wisdom and reasoned thought to their everyday life.

Throughout the 18th century, while soldiers were plundering and destroying, and the Church lay steeped in its wicked superstitions, some were thinking and scheming to improve methods of production and distribution. Except London, with 500,000 inhabitants, towns in England were few and small, four fifths of the population earning its livelihood in the country by means of agriculture, or by spinning and weaving wool in their own homes. Other industries existed on a small scale, but, with the coming of the Huguenots from France, after the revocation by Louis XIV of the Edict of Nantes, Britain, like Prussia, benefited from her hospitality. Many of these exiles were skilled craftsmen besides being expert silk weavers, and, as the century drew on, British capital more and more found its way into financing industrial undertakings, to produce finally what is now called the industrial revolution, when machines replaced much manual labour.

This financing of industry would have been impossible without an organised banking system, and because one grew round the Bank of England, by the formation of private banks throughout the country, it became possible to provide the necessary capital for the new undertakings then springing up. The first bankers in ancient Babylon, Egypt, Greece and Rome were pawnbrokers, who advanced money on the security of household articles, but, when this came to be done on a much larger scale, they became known as bankers, those who lent money on all types of security, besides receiving it at a lower rate of interest than that at which they lent it.

Consequently great and wealthy banking establishments arose which, in power and influence, exceeded that of the feudal barons, and for many years the Holy Roman Empire was financed by the banks of Augsburg, Florence, Lyons, Venice and Rome. Banking encouraged thrift, and made possible the use of the people's savings to produce still more wealth, which, when thus employed, is called capital.

The sound system of banking established in the reign of William III, and copied from the Dutch, was consequently a vital contributing cause of Britain's rise to industrial prosperity from the 18th century onwards. In France the banking system was defective, but in Britain it was so strong that it carried the country successfully through the new industrial age, and was also able to finance the long-drawn-out expensive Napoleonic war. Large undertakings were now possible, because Britain was blessed with a moist climate, eminently suitable for the manufacture of cotton goods, and amply endowed with both iron and coal in close proximity. Wealth increased rapidly, the population between 1760 and 1821 doubled to 12,000,000, and comforts unimagined heretofore became the necessities of the people.

Nevertheless, in many cases, the changes brought about by the mechanical age did not increase the common people's happiness. The machine turned the old way of life upside down. The craftsman of every trade, to be found in every large village, gradually disappeared, and this meant that a hitherto tough, healthy, primitive, but contented, people, who had lived a free open-air life, brewed their own beer and grown their own food, had in many cases to readjust their lives to the changed conditions.

England in those days was a land of extreme contrasts, the upper classes enjoying life in a way probably never before experienced. Thousands (in 1785 some 40,000 English people, many with their own coaches) toured the Continent, and each one to the obsequious landlords was "My lord" or "My lady". No one spent money more lavishly than the notorious Frederick Hervey, who was Earl of Bristol and also received a huge income as Bishop of Londonderry. He left, as a memorial to his extravagance, the numerous Hotels Bristol named after him throughout Europe.

While the rich were living luxuriously, life for the poor was indeed sordid. Squalid towns grew up to house those who heretofore had worked their own looms in their own village homes, but now had to congregate together to be near the mills which sheltered the new looms, run first by water-wheels and then by steam engines. These latter increased the demand for coal, the production of which in Britain advanced to 10,000,000 tons a year against 200,000 tons in the 16th century. At the same time, the miners became a class apart, to become segregated from the rest of the community, no one, their employers least of all, caring in the least that their working and housing conditions were the worst in the land.

Prior to the 19th century merchandise was carried from one part of the country to another by means of pack-horses, a method which showed no advance over the customary form of transport in use by primitive man. The roads were mere tracks, with such ruts that wheeled vehicles could only pass over them with difficulty, and many were impassable during winter. Only on certain main roads could wheels be used with ease, but, as they were very rough, a journey by stage coach was most uncomfortable. When the Turnpike Act was passed in 1767 it was possible for companies to take over old roads, build new roads, keep all roads in repair, and erect toll-houses to collect money to meet the cost, but it was not until 1815, when John Macadam, a Scottish engineer, produced an endurable road surface, that traffic increased in both speed and comfort.

Important consequences followed, as improved communication made possible both the agricultural and industrial revolution. The beauty spots of the country, hitherto unknown to most people, were now for the first time appreciated, and some became attracted by the seaside to indulge in the novelty of sea bathing. Roads opened up the seaports to the midlands and substituted the wagon for the pack-horse, and both exports and imports increased in consequence. Moreover, they made the self-sufficing village no longer necessary, and it became dependent on the nearest town for many of its needs.

As this silent revolution was going on an illiterate engineering genius, James Brindley (1716–1772), further improved transport by constructing (1761) a canal six miles long between Worsley and Manchester, and this formed the first of a chain of canals which gradually covered the entire country, he being responsible for the construction of 360 miles of these water-ways. Thomas Telford (1757–1834) was another great canal builder, being employed in the construction of the chief canals in Great Britain, the Caledonian (1804) being his first great achievement. He built 920 miles of roads in the Scottish Highlands, the Menai Suspension Bridge, and greatly improved the Great North Road. He constructed harbours, docks, great bridges, and drained 48,000 acres of land in the English Fen district; truly a life devoted to the increase of wealth for the benefit of humanity.

Another great engineer of those times was John Rennie (1761–1821), who built mills, warehouses and many bridges, Southwark Bridge, Waterloo Bridge and London Bridge being amongst his achievements. He constructed canals, docks, harbours, government dockyards and drained a vast tract of land bordering the rivers Trent and Ouse.

Quickening intelligence was also noticeable in agriculture, farmers seeking ways of producing more from the land, they being now encouraged to do so by Parliament passing legislation authorising the enclosure of land which had hitherto been mostly open to general village use. When the 18th century began about three-fifths of the country's arable land was open fields, each village having its pasture so arranged that one-third of this open land was always left fallow each year, the remaining two-thirds being divided into strips amongst the villagers who also had grazing rights on the rough uncultivated land. Each year the peasant often received a different strip, and this meant that he had no inducement to improve his holding, as he might not have it again.

By enclosing the land with fences and hedges,

improving the drainage, manuring scientifically, and letting out the same pasture to the same farmer each year, a revolution took place in farming methods, though it caused a great upheaval in the lives of the village communities. More land came under the plough, and less land lay fallow, because the farmer discovered that he need not always leave some of his fields idle to recuperate, he being able to achieve the same results by a rotation of crops.

By a four-crop rotation, wheat one year, turnips the next, barley the next and clover the next, then back again to the same rotation, the land was able to produce just as well as when it remained fallow every third year. Now, for the first time since agriculture began, it became unnecessary to kill off cattle at the end of summer, as the farmer grew root and other crops on some part of his land to feed them during the winter. Thus began the scientific breeding of stock, and it made possible the supply of fresh meat all the year round, scurvy and other skin diseases consequently coming to an end.

Early in the 18th century Viscount Townsend introduced this method of crop rotation, and then Jethro Tull invented the drill (1701), which made rapid sowing possible. Within a hundred years 2,000,000 acres were added to the agricultural land of England and Wales. As the century drew to a close the Duke of Bedford, Robert Bakewell and Coke of Holkham, after many experiments, greatly improved the breed of cattle and sheep, this having the effect of doubling the average weight of cattle and increasing the number of sheep threefold. Bread was now made from refined wheat, and beer and meat were sufficient to meet the requirements of a population that nearly doubled itself over the century, but the small village farmer had to suffer.

He lost his strip of land, which now became enclosed in what is today called a farm, but, as industry in the towns was requiring more and more labour, many peasants drifted there, where much less healthy and congenial work was to be found in the newly built badly ventilated factories. Here they started a new way of life at low wages, with no political influence, taking the first job they could get to keep them and their families from starvation, the rise in the population making the supply of labour much in excess of the demand.

Consequently the towns grew in size at the expense of the villages, a development which has raised much controversy, as we are now beginning to realise that to put industry first and agriculture last is a very short-sighted policy, and one that brings disaster in its train if not checked before the countryside is completely denuded of workers. A much more balanced economic plan must follow as the result of our past experience, because it is just as important for the welfare of the country to have a prosperous agriculture as it is to have a prosperous industry.

William Lee invented the stocking frame (1589), the machine which mechanically produces the loop stitch in hosiery. This great boon which he conferred on mankind came into extensive use, and was not improved upon until 1758. In 1733 John Kay invented the "Flying Shuttle", which doubled the weaving output, but, as the primitive spinning wheel could not now supply sufficient yarn, James

Hargreaves devised the "Spinning Jenny" in 1764, thus making it possible to produce eight times the quantity. Richard Arkwright (1732–1792), the founder of the British cotton industry, then created a new type of spinning machine, to be followed by the invention by Samuel Crompton (1753–1827) of what is called the "Spinning Mule", which incorporated both Hargreaves's and Arkwright's ideas. Then in 1785 Edmund Cartwright (1743–1823) invented the power loom for weaving, and so the textile industry was revolutionised by these new ideas which, with less labour, greatly increased production.

Thomas Saint, an Englishman, was the first to think of the idea of sewing by machinery (1790), but it was left to a poor tailor in France, Barthélemy Thimmonier, to produce the first practical sewing machine in 1830. Eighty of these machines were at work in a factory in Paris (1841) when a furious mob, fearing that the machine would deprive them of their livelihood, which came from sewing by hand, wrecked the establishment and nearly murdered the inventor. This state of affairs existed wherever new machines were introduced and factories built. Arkwright, Hargreaves, and all the other inventors, had their machines smashed, and the factories attacked, by those who lived by weaving at home and now feared loss of employment, they not realising that the cheaper one can produce the greater becomes the demand.

Other great men were likewise at work in other branches of industry, striving to find improved methods of production. Josiah Wedgwood, a master potter, ever zealous to create more beautiful designs, discovered new and better methods of producing artistic pottery, to such effect that the china of England surpassed in beauty and utility that produced abroad. Even China, whence it derived its name, was unable to produce the masterpieces made in England.

The first man to build an iron bridge, one over the Severn, was Abraham Darby, who, by using coke instead of charcoal to smelt iron ore, invented the blast furnace, which greatly increased Britain's iron production. This was followed by Henry Cort's "puddling" process for eliminating impurities from the finished product, the cost of fuel consumed being greatly reduced by Neilson's invention of the "hot blast".

Improving the means of production was not enough, because a new method of obtaining power was now required. The power developed by compressed steam had long been known—Heron, the Greek, in 130 B.C., being the first to turn it to practical use—but, as no one in his day followed up his ideas, his inventions were forgotten. From his time to the 17th century there is no practical progress to record, and then Giovanni Branca (1629) designed an engine shaped like a water-wheel, which was driven by the impact of a jet of steam directed on protruding vanes. Edward Somerset, the second Marquis of Worcester, however, deserves the credit for making the first useful steam engine, but it never became a commercial success.

Thomas Savery in 1698 produced the first steam engine to come into general use, it being employed to pump water out of mines and for other purposes. To Newcomen, however, is due the honour of inventing (1705) the steam engine, as we now know it, in the form of a cylinder, in which is placed a piston forced backwards and forwards by expanding steam supplied by a separate boiler. By 1725 this engine was in common use at coal mines until James Watt so improved upon it that it became obsolete. Then James Nasmyth (1808–1890) made use of this idea to invent a steam hammer, which is so strong and yet so gentle that it can forge a propeller shaft into shape or just crack an egg.

In 1763 James Watt (1736–1819), a delicate, morose, mechanical genius, when an instrument maker in Glasgow, and engaged in repairing one of Newcomen's models, was struck by the waste of steam. So he set to work to produce a really serviceable steam-powered engine, thus becoming the inventor of the modern condensing steam engine, an invention which has conferred untold blessings on mankind. His ideas were so successful, when put into practice, that he became the pioneer in the manufacture of steam engines. These superseded all that had gone before, and for years he had no rival. One other name, however, deserves special mention, that of Jonathan Hornblower, who, in 1781, invented and constructed a compound engine of two cylinders. This was found to have so many advantages that the system is now used in all large engines for the sake of economical running.

Woolf in 1814 made further improvements in the compound engine by using high-pressure steam, but to Richard Trevithick (1771–1833) is due the credit of inventing the first locomotive, known as "Puffing Billy", which, in 1801, carried the first load of passengers ever conveyed by steam. He improved upon this (1804), and produced one to run on rails. His ideas were successfully developed by George Stephenson (1781–1848), whose locomotive "The Rocket" in 1829 definitely proved its superiority in power and speed over horse traction on railways. Under his direction, and that of his son Robert, the locomotive took the form which it has maintained in all essentials up to the present time.

Robert Stephenson (1803–1859) now turned his father's invention to practical account by building our first railways and great bridges. His most remarkable achievements were his viaducts built on the tubular system, and amongst his most notable bridges are the Royal Border Bridge at Berwick-on-Tweed, the High Level Bridge at Newcastle-on-Tyne, the Britannia tubular bridge over the Menai Straits, the Conway tubular bridge, and the Victoria tubular bridge over the St. Lawrence in Canada. Such a man stands out far above all the so-called great monarchs and soldiers, who carried destruction in their train and left the world poorer for having lived.

Then also lived another outstanding master builder, Isambard Brunel (1806–1859), one of the most distinguished engineers of the age, who built the track, bridges and great viaducts of the Great Western Railway. Then he became a shipbuilder, constructing the *Great Western*, so as to extend the terminus of the system to New York. This was followed by the *Great Britain*, the first large ship built of iron and the first big vessel to be driven by a screw propeller, and then came the famous gigantic *Great Eastern*. With great devotion this noble-minded genius dedicated his life to the good of humanity, and when he died he left the world richer and better than he found it.

While inventors were thinking out means of more rapid and powerful traction, others had been wondering how to apply the use of steam to ships at sea. A Spaniard, Blasco de Garay, produced (1543) a small boat which he moved by steam power in Barcelona harbour, but nothing more was ever heard of it. An American, John Fitch (1743–1798), holds the honoured position of being the first man to build a boat propelled by a steam engine to carry passengers (1790), but, as it was a financial failure, the enterprise was abandoned. Consequently he never received the credit he was due as the pioneer in steam navigation.

William Symmington was the man who built the first practical steam-boat in 1802, the *Charlotte Dundas*, fitted with a Watt double-acting condensing engine, connected by a shaft to a paddle-wheel at the stern, and this ship plied successfully on the Forth and Clyde Canal. Henry Bell (1767–1830) improved on this, and ten years later (1812) constructed the *Comet*, with side paddle-wheels. This vessel was employed as a passenger steamer on the Clyde, though five years earlier (1807) Robert Fulton, an American, had fitted a ship with a Watt engine and successfully propelled it on the Hudson river.

These four men were therefore the pioneers of all ocean-going steamers, which, from now onwards, became a commercial possibility, the *Great Western*, in 1838, being the first to cross the Atlantic in fifteen days on steam power alone. Soon, on the seven seas, smoke was to be seen rising from the decks of ships in place of sails, the only method of propulsion hitherto known apart from the use of oars.

As the means of production developed, and the methods of transportation advanced, so safety at sea increased by the use of improved instruments. John Hadley invented the sextant in 1731, and John Harrison an accurate mariner's chronometer in 1761. As trade expanded and wealth accumulated, some had sufficient time to study the causes which produced disease, the consequence being that health improved and the people were better nourished. Besides this our means of livelihood was no longer confined to livestock and agriculture, but also came from producing and exporting finished goods in exchange for foodstuffs and raw material from abroad, a more varied form of life, dress and diet being the result. With fewer deaths the population in Britain increased, the populous districts moving from the south to the north and the midlands, where industrial towns, near to coal and iron ore deposits, expanded rapidly in size.

Britain consequently became the principal manufacturer in Europe, and her goods found their way in increasing quantities all over the world, especially to America and India. She obtained this position because of her inventors, who were in advance of any other country, but besides this she had command of the sea, and enforced the Navigation Acts which made her the world's clearing centre and her ships the principal carriers. For long she had no rivals, and only slowly did Europe obtain her share of world commerce.

Because of the number of lives lost by wrecks on the Eddystone Rock, Winstanley, in 1698, erected there a lighthouse. Before he could start work on this he had to fight the opposition of Trinity House, which was founded by Henry VIII for the purpose of accommodating the Trinity House brethren, whose duty it was to pray for the souls of all who were lost at sea. In return for this effort they were given the salvage of all the wrecks around our coasts. The more wrecks there were the more they earned, and for this reason they objected to anything being done to reduce the number. Winstanley, however, eventually obtained permission to build the first British lighthouse. It was built of wood, and destroyed in 1703 in a storm, the brave constructor perishing with it. John Smeaton (1724–1792), the first engineer to construct a modern lighthouse, built a new Eddystone tower in 1759, and this was replaced in 1882 by the present edifice.

The famous pioneer chemist Robert Boyle (1627-1691) was followed by Lavoisier (1743-1794), a great humanitarian, and one of the founders of modern chemistry which has so changed our way of life. Then also lived Joseph Priestley (1733-1804) who investigated gasses and discovered oxygen. John Dalton (1766–1844), the celebrated physicist, propounded the atomic theory to explain the structure of matter, and Sir Humphry Davy (1778–1829), the eminent natural philosopher, and inventor of the miner's safety lamp, made many electro-chemical discoveries from which much was learned of the properties of light and heat. Murdock (1754–1839) discovered how to extract gas from coal about the same time as Volta (1745-1827), the famous Italian physicist, and Galvani (1737–1798), the eminent Italian physiologist, were laying the foundation of all we know today about the power and use of electricity. Humboldt (1769–1859) was the greatest naturalist of his time, travelling extensively to ascertain with certainty the geographical distribution of plants. His wide knowledge of all the sciences led him to declare that "The Universe is governed by law".

The extent and majesty of the starry heavens on a clear dark night have always aroused in the mind of man the feeling of wonder and awe. Man, a speck in infinity, contemplating the visible universe, discloses the superiority of mind over matter. Consequently the meditation and study of the limitless dome above us has been the attraction of wondering minds from early times, but, without the necessary instrument, the vastness of space was never grasped. The illustrious astronomer, William Herschel (1738–1822), who discovered the planet Uranus, did much to extend the power of the telescope, and his son John Herschel (1792–1871) further advanced his father's survey of the heavens.

Another outstanding astronomer was the Marquis de la Place (1749–1827), who was one of the greatest mathematicians of any age, and the author of the nebular hypothesis. In a series of brilliant treatises, published by the French Academy between 1784 and 1786, he laid bare the general working of the celestial machine, for which he deservedly earned the title "the Newton of France", his discoveries, moreover, leading him towards atheism because he could find no place for God in the universe.

In quite another sphere of science the celebrated naturalist Lamarck (1744–1829) stands out as the forerunner of Darwin, whom he anticipated in some of his theories on the evolution of the species. By men such as these science was raised to the place it now occupies, and to them we must be grateful for enlarging our mental horizon, thus enabling us to determine better our place in the universe.

Now we have arrived at the opening of a new age, the Scientific Age, which relied on experiment, observation and experience in its pursuit of knowledge. During the past two centuries science had been slowly emerging from its obscurity, and ever more loudly proclaiming its momentous discovery that the universe is governed by law and not by the dictates of the gods. Untold good followed from this discovery, because from it emerged our present-day knowledge of all that is comprised under natural law, and all the blessings that this has conferred upon humanity.

Unfortunately, some assumed that because science had banished the gods into the mists of obscurity, and relegated mythology to the childhood of mankind, the natural urge which had produced every religion had come only from childish imagination. No greater mistake could be made. Childlike imagination was certainly responsible for many foolish and fantastic ideas, which, during different periods and in diverse places, produced the numerous world religions, but science has never disproved the belief that we are basically etheric beings, and that we continue to live after death. Upon this foundation stone every supernatural religion was born, developed and flourished, to produce half the events of history.

Science, instead of disproving the after life, has discovered how possible is the seemingly impossible, it having found a place for it within the multitude of vibrations which make up the universe. Besides this it has thrown such a flood of light upon the human body, that we now realise that we are not just a mass of flesh and bones, but a marvellous trinity of physical and etheric substance which is dominated by a mind quite unrelated to physical matter. Death, the only certain thing in life, is no more than a separation of the flesh from the other two substances, and this makes possible the functioning, after death, of the mind and the duplicate etheric body within a range of vibrations which are different from those we experience when enveloped in the physical body.

Our mind being ourselves, we consequently continue to think and act hereafter as we do on earth, our etheric body, and our mind which produces our individuality, our character and our memory, being the only earthly possessions which we carry with us to our new abode. Our new surroundings are in vibrational harmony with our etheric body, and consequently everything there seems real and solid, just as it does on earth, and there we appear to each other just as we do to one another here, we being the same men and women there as we are here, but old age and deformities appertain to the flesh and not to the etheric body.

What a marvellous creation is man; how very different from what he seems to be; but that is nature's way, to make everything appear different from what it really is. How difficult it is to grasp and truly envisage this wonderful creature, each one with his or her individual thoughts and outlook. No one can think the same as someone else, and to adopt the mental outlook of another is impossible. Each one is a highly developed individual unit, and to force uniformity of thought on everyone, as did our ancestors, is not only the height of folly but mentally impossible.

Each one of us, each individual unit, has some great inscrutable purpose ahead, which it is the duty of psychic science and natural religion to discover. "Man know thyself" was the urge which produced the Socratic outlook on life, and this is a study which will some day raise mankind above his present aggressive, intolerant, narrow outlook, to a plane of thought which will transform life and ideals beyond present-day imagination. Its effect on our conduct, one towards another, should consequently be so beneficial that peace, harmony and happiness will take the place of the dispeace which has so far marred life in the past.

So, although this chapter introduces us into the Scientific Age, which has swept away so many religious misconceptions, and will finally sweep supernatural religion into oblivion, science has not destroyed, and never can liquidate, natural religion, and raise up a materialistic philosophy devoid of everything except physical matter and force. It can never override facts and truth, though mistaken conclusions have been drawn from pronouncements made by those who have never studied psychic phenomena. Similar mistaken conclusions were made by our ancestors when they transformed the men and women of the other world into gods and goddesses, and allotted to them omnipotent power over the earth and the universe.

We certainly live within the grip of a vast unthinking machine, but, when we know the levers, and learn how to pull them, we can make it work for us and not against us. Here on earth it can destroy our physical bodies, which are akin to it, and are subject to its laws, but it cannot harm our psychic structure which houses our invulnerable mind, both of which are beyond its reach, because they belong to another order of existence. Slowly mind is finding its true place in the universe, and, as its development continues, man becomes the master of his destiny, and ceases to be the slave of fate.

(2) PIONEERS OF MODERN LITERATURE, MUSIC AND ART.

The triumph of art is the true presentation of nature, the artist employing method for the symmetrical formation of things that are beautiful. In all works of imagination, painting, sculpture and literature we behold the mental image materialised, and this is no less true regarding things in everyday use.

As mind developed, and as wealth increased, so did the desire to be surrounded by elegant furniture. Looking-glasses, or mirrors, were produced in Venice in 1690, and in a few years these were being made in Paris and London. Carved and gilt furniture was first made in Italy, and there furniture-makers copied the elegant designs of the Greco-Roman period, laid bare by the uncovering of Pompeii. Riesener, Roentgen and Gonthière in France, and Chippendale, Lock, Sheraton, Hepplewhite, James and Robert Adam in England produced the furniture of the 18th century, when the homes of the rich were not only well and comfortably furnished for the first time during the Christian era, but were also filled with many beautiful pictures and objects of art.

Besides having good furniture, the rich and well-to-do now decorated their walls with the pictures produced by the great artists of the time. They had several from whom to choose, such as William Hogarth (1697–1764), who was the outstanding pictorial satirist, and whose engravings vividly display the grossness of the times. Thomas Gainsborough (1727–1788) is famous for the elegance of his portraits, and the simple beauty of his landscapes. Sir Joshua Reynolds (1723–1792), the first President of the Royal Academy, is noted for the richness and splendour of colour of his portraits, his studio being thronged with women who wished their portraits to be etherialised, and with men who wished to appear as philosophers or heroes. Joseph Turner (1775–1851) is one of the greatest of English painters, John Constable (1776–1837) is famous for his landscapes, Landseer (1802–1873) is celebrated for his pictures of animals, and Francisco Goya y Lucientes (1746–1828) was certainly the outstanding portrait-painter in Spain of his time.

The more thoughtful now commenced to collect books, as, besides furnishing their houses, they were also furnishing their minds with new ideas. So libraries were set apart in the larger houses to protect these new treasures, and now that we have come to the age of modern literature a few words about its pioneers will not be out of place.

Samuel Johnson (1709–1784) was one of the great literary giants of this period, when intellectual light was beginning to glow in Christendom. He was not only one of the most eminent of English writers and thinkers of the 18th century, but he produced the first English dictionary, which was a novelty for those times. In 1755, after eight years of labour, and with the help of several poorly paid assistants, he published a *Dictionary of the English Language*, for which he received from the booksellers who employed him in this task the sum of 1500 guineas, out of which he had to pay his assistants. Johnson was kind and generous, but gloomy and irritable, the latter failing being perhaps due to the fact that he suffered all his life from scrofula. His voluble opinions about everything received more attention than they deserved, through the dog-like devotion of his biographer Boswell, who, in this way, made himself almost as famous as his hero.

In an age when little was known about history by people in general, Edward Gibbon (1737–1794), one of the most celebrated historians of any age or country, produced his famous book *The Decline and Fall of the Roman Empire*. During an inconspicuous period in Parliament, as he was shy and a poor speaker, he devoted his very retentive memory to history, and then gave to the world this masterly, rich and vivid description of the history of Rome, which, because of the many centuries he covered, embraced the history of the Western world.

Precise and brilliant as it is, he wrote in the somewhat ponderous style of his time, and, sometimes lacking lucidity, his story ceases to flow as a natural winding stream. Much to his disappointment, it excited no controversy on its appearance, and was seldom mentioned, but how few realise the long hours given by the historian to research, and the care necessary over every detail. Besides this labour, much patience and careful planning are required to reduce a wide range of historical episodes into a compact, interesting and easily absorbed form for all to read.

If Gibbon was the most notable historian of his age, then Adam Smith (1723–1790) can well be described as the most outstanding political economist of all times, his most important work, *Inquiry into the Nature and Causes of the Wealth of Nations*, appearing in 1776. Herein this wise, rational, Fifeshire man, who was Professor of Logic and Moral Philosophy at Glasgow University, proved conclusively that if man only understood the laws of nature and used them for his comfort and happiness, then poverty, misery and famine would be no more. This great humanitarian infidel, this outstanding apostle of reason, the man who made Glasgow University famous throughout Europe, was the first to demonstrate and expound the economic law, and develop into a practical science the method to be employed in the efficient production and distribution of wealth.

He stood at the cross-roads pointing the way to human happiness. If he had lived a century or so earlier he might possibly have been tortured and put to death, but the Christian theologians could only now bitterly denounce him as a heretic and blasphemer.

Since the time of primitive man up to now, the vast human throng had plodded wearily along the theological road, stopping repeatedly to seek divine help to alleviate the distress which comes from ignorance. Now, in the 18th century, Adam Smith directed them on to the road of reason, and told them that only by observation, experiment and experience could all the troubles that afflict mankind be solved. He was one of those notable human signposts which arise from time to time, one of the really great men who by his thoughts and deeds made possible the greater comfort, prosperity and happiness of those who lived after him.

Another outstanding man of this age, likewise bitterly attacked by the theologians, was David Hume (1711–1776), one of the most subtle metaphysicians, who also ranks amongst the most eminent of British historians and political economists. A fellow country-man and a contemporary of Adam Smith, he, with other notable Scotsmen of this time (such as Smollett, Pringle, Hunter, Smellie, Robertson and Dugald Stewart), stands out as one of an illustrious band of heretical humanists who had a powerful influence on civilisation. Smellie founded the *Encyclopaedia Britannica* in 1771, and was its first editor. Edinburgh, which hitherto had looked to France for its culture, now became famous for its intellectual wealth, a veritable modern Athens. Scotland, during her golden era, contributed as much as any country to the ushering in of the age of reason, and thus brought about the dis-credit of the Church, which for so long had held down the people by its deadly paralysing grip.

Sir Walter Scott (1771–1832) first made his name as a poet, but his prose romances give the fullest measure of his genius. He made his great literary reputation by his first book *Waverley*, and then followed many others which were equally enthralling to the readers of his day. Another famous Scotsman was Robert Burns (1759–1796), the Ayrshire, free-thinking peasant poet, the humanitarian democrat who delighted his contemporaries, just as he has those who followed them, with his songs and verse packed with humour, satire and pathos. Pope (1688–1744), Shelley (1792–1822), Keats (1795–1821) and Wordsworth (1771–1850) are the outstanding names of English poetic expression. Goldsmith (1728–1774) is one of the most pleasing of English writers, while the genius of Byron (1788–1824) as a poet was more lyrical than dramatic. David Garrick (1716–1779) was the leading tragic actor of his time, Sarah Siddons (1755–1831) being the greatest tragic actress of the next generation.

Thomas Malthus (1766–1834) was the scientific expounder of the principle of population, a subject which will require much more serious consideration than it has yet received if war in the future is to be prevented. His work, *An Essay on the Principle of Population*, was the first serious attempt to solve the vast problem of over-population and the scientific dispersal of mankind. Auguste Comte (1798–1857) was the most outstanding and important of that interesting group of thinkers whom the overthrow of the old institutions in France turned to the study of social problems. He was the founder of the "Positive" school of philosophy which aimed at the development of new principles to co-ordinate social relations, and guide society to a higher standard of conduct.

Without doubt the greatest philosopher of the 18th century was Immanuel Kant (1724–1804), who combined in quite an unusual degree the knowledge of physical science with speculative acuteness to philosophy. No other thinker of those times shows such a fundamental conception of physical science, or held the balance between empirical and speculative ideas with such firmness. Arthur Schopenhauer (1788–1860), born in Danzig, expressed in his book *Die Welt als Wille und Vorstellung* his ideas of man's nature and destiny, and Georg Hegel (1770–1831) published his *Grundlinien der Philosophie des Rechts* in 1821. Herein he combined a system of moral and political philosophy, a sociology dominated by the idea of the state, turning fiercely against all the aspirations of reformers who were possessed with democratic ideas. Fichte (1797–1879), on the other hand, advocated a moral theism, and supported the Spiritualists in his ethical, individualistic outlook on life, based on the discoveries of psychic science.

Fichte, like Immanuel Kant, and William Blake (1757–1827) the English painter, engraver and poet, was influenced by the life and work of Emanuel Swedenborg (1688–1772), a Swedish nobleman and son of a bishop. Swedenborg, a man endowed with unusual intellectual power, and by profession a mining engineer, was, like his father before him, a medium, and in trance was controlled by men and women of the other world. He was both clairvoyant and clairaudient, and in his presence could be heard what is today called the direct voice, a voice heard though the speaker is unseen.

The revelation which he thus believed he received from the Lord brought a new religion into being— Swedenborgianism—a mixture of Christianity and Spiritualism, because he could not get away from his early orthodox training and, like the early Jesuians, believed in divine spirits, angels and devils. The expressions he uses in his writings resemble those of Saint Paul when writing about his own psychic experiences. Fortunately for Swedenborg, the burning of wizards and witches was in his day coming to an end, and he ranks as the first outstanding medium to be allowed to live during the Christian era.

Resurgent Europe of the 18th and 19th centuries produced many men great in literature, but none more illustrious than Johann von Goethe (1749–1832), who, during his long life, which saw many changes, did so much to raise the intellectual level of Europe. This great individualist and humanist, who was neither a Christian, a patriot, nor a hero to his generation, radiated from the small town of Weimar his lyric poems and lucid prose, which were rich in science, ideas and suggestions. For many years he was the intellectual giant of Germany, his mind touching and brightening all aspects of thought. An edition of his works in thirteen volumes was published in 1808, and contained the first part of *Faust* in its complete form, an effort which stands at the head of all his other achievements, and deserves a very high place among the best works of every age.

During a time when German patriotism was at its lowest depth, when there was no cohesion or unity, and the land was being devastated and humiliated by the armies of Napoleon, Germany reached the height of her literary and scientific greatness. Later on, as power politics took the place of mental development, her notable earlier achievements declined, never to return. Besides Goethe, we must mention his friend Johann Schiller (1759–1805), the benevolent German poet and dramatist, who helped to kindle in the minds of the people a longing for a free and worthy life. Both these men did more to bring refinement, peace and happiness to Germany than did any others, but unfortunately the generations that followed, by worshipping that which is evil instead of righteousness, brought upon themselves misery, heaped down by world hatred.

A fearless and independent writer, to whom the Germans owe a deep debt of gratitude, was Gotthold Lessing (1729–1781), and in Johann von Herder (1744–1803) they had one of the most prolific and influential of literary men. Johann Paul Richter (1763–1825) was the greatest German humorist, the publication of seven popular books securing for him a leading place in German literature, and Heinrich Heine (1799–1856) made his reputation from his poems and songs, they having the good fortune to be wedded to the music of Schumann and Mendelssohn.

In Britain, Jane Austin (1775–1817) was one of the most distinguished of early novelists, who finely expressed the feminine viewpoint of her day, and her contemporary Charles Lamb (1775–1834) was both an original and delightful essayist and critic, his writings being characterised by great felicity of expression. A generation later Thomas Carlyle (1795–1881), the harsh, pessimistic genius, by his power of graphic description, his balance and biting humour, brought vividly to the readers of his two great books, *The French Revolution* and *Frederick the Great*, a picture of these times, and from the first their success was assured. Charles Dickens (1812–1870) is considered to be one of England's greatest novelists, some of his books showing up vividly the terrible social conditions of the times, and the need of drastic improvements in the lives of the poor. *Oliver Twist, David*

Copperfield, Pickwick Papers and *Nicholas Nickleby* are amongst the best known of the many works of this prolific writer.

William Thackeray (1811–1863) was another of England's greatest novelists and authors, *Vanity Fair* probably being his best-known and most popular work. Lord Macaulay (1800–1859) made his fame by his *History of England*, published in 1848, a work which was a success beyond all expectations, its sale in Britain and the United States being enormous. In France, his contemporary Victor Hugo (1802–1885), the dramatist, poet and romance writer, produced works which show that he was one of the greatest of poets, unsurpassed in sublimity, in spontaneity of utterance and variety of power.

The greatest name in the post-revolutionary literature of France was Honoré de Balzac (1799–1850). He holds a more distinct and supreme place in French fiction than does any English author in the same field, his *Comédie Humaine* being his greatest enterprise. Here, however, we must leave these literary luminaries, because we can only confine ourselves to the pioneers of literature in its various branches.

This was also the age of the great musicians, Purcell (1658–1695), Handel (1685–1759), Mozart (1756–1791), Beethoven (1770–1827), Weber (1786–1826), Haydn (1732–1809), Schubert (1797–1828), Mendelssohn (1809–1847), Schumann (1810–1856), Franck (1822–1890), Chopin (1809–1849), Liszt (1811–1866), Joachim (1831–1907), Brahms (1833–1897) and Wagner (1813–1883), whose compositions have elevated, delighted and enraptured millions.

At this point we must leave the sublime, those

who helped to lift the black curtain of ignorance which hangs between humanity and reality, and return to that sordid side of life which makes up so much of history. How little we read of all the good and kind things done in the past, the things which are evil for ever forcing themselves before us. We think less of the peaceful, pleasant, quiet summer days, and remember the tempests and storms, we recollect the events in life that upset us, and do not dwell so much on the times when we were tranquil and happy. So it is with history, because it is the gaps in the harmony of life which are generally recorded, and not the days of peace and prosperity.

Now there breaks upon us the greatest of all the hurricanes which had so far ever swept over Europe, when a monster of selfishness, a pitiless creature, led his armies of dupes and plunderers over its fertile lands into the towns and cities, creating devastation and misery wherever they went. So far we have not kept within the dates mentioned at the beginning of this chapter, as the age of invention and literature commenced early in the 18th century, but now we return and take up our tale where we left it off in the previous chapter.

(3) The Rise and Fall of Napoleon Bonaparte.

After his ghastly failure in dealing with the American colonies, the pious and foolish George III decided that he would now only reign and allow others better qualified to rule Britain and her empire. His puppet, the devout reactionary Lord North, the darling and champion of the Church, resigned in 1782 along with the rest of the bribed subservient Tory ministers. These political lackeys, titled, and paid by the King out of the country's revenue to do his bidding, gave place to the Whigs under the leadership of Lord Rockingham, who had as his Secretary of State Charles James Fox, a singularly kind, generous and progressive statesman, his failing being gambling.

Rockingham formed a more respectable administration, but he died the same year as he took up office. Fox resigned, and the next two Whig ministries, the first under Lord Shelburne, and the next under the Duke of Portland, passed in quick succession. These short administrations were two years of confusion, when the Whigs were split by Fox and his followers, and then William Pitt, the younger, son of Lord Chatham, formed his first administration at the age of twenty-four. Though he was under constant attack from the opposition, led by Fox and North, his ministry lasted for more than seventeen years, and about this famous man something must now be said.

William Pitt (1783-1801) derived his power from his great command of language, and as an orator he surpassed Burke, Windham, Sheridan and Fox. His grasp of detail was remarkable, his honesty and rectitude, in an age of corruption, were beyond reproach, and his private life added much to the dignity of his public character. Though he handled millions honestly for the State, he was so engrossed in national affairs that he became deeply involved in debt. He seemed quite uninterested in his own private affairs, his entire life being dedicated to his country and the House of Commons.

Though he bestowed titles right and left, and could

have had for himself what he pleased, he spurned them all, and lived and died William Pitt. He inherited no money and refused all sinecure offices carrying large emoluments. These he gave to his friends, and died at the age of forty-seven a poor man, his life being cut short by the constant burden and load of care he was called upon to carry for so long. He led the country in the early stages of the long-drawn-out war which ended at Waterloo, but died in the belief that all he had worked for had been in vain.

By skilful diplomacy Pitt re-established Britain's prestige in Europe, after it had been so heavily damaged as the result of the American war. He regained Prussia's friendship, which had been lost when Britain deserted her in the Seven Years' War, and then he made a commercial treaty with France. He tried, with the help of Fox and Wilberforce, to abolish the slave trade, but without success, and he likewise failed to improve parliamentary representation. His policy, to begin with, was progressive, his aim being to restore the country's finances and commercial prosperity, so badly shattered by the American war. Greatly influenced by Adam Smith's arguments in favour of free trade, he reduced the import duties on articles in common use, and thus incidentally lessened smuggling.

The French Revolution broke out in 1789, but, as friendly relations existed between the revolutionary government and Britain, everything seemed to be set fair for more peaceful and happier times, so much so that Pitt declared in 1792, "There never was a time in the history of this country when, from the situation of Europe, we might more reasonably expect fifteen years' peace than at the present moment." Yet, as events turned out, within a year of this bold prophecy Britain was at war with France, to continue in this state until 1815, with only one short interval of peace, during which time her National Debt increased to £830,000,000.

Most of Great Britain's 9,000,000 inhabitants were at first sympathetically neutral towards the French Revolution, and did not regret the fall of the Bastille, which symbolised the end of tyrannical monarchs, but feelings changed when the massacres began, so much so that Pitt became violently reactionary, fearing that the infection would spread to Britain. Meetings of more than fifty people were forbidden, the Habeas Corpus Act was suspended, and to speak or write of reform became treason. It says much for the stolidness of the British character that a revolution did not also occur in Britain, as conditions amongst the poor were so deplorable that anything might have happened.

Looking back on these fateful years we see how affairs might have worked out so very differently had a wiser and more enlightened policy been adopted from the first towards France, and thus Europe would have been saved the ensuing twenty-three years of carnage, waste and destruction. Unfortunately Britain, because of ignorance, was not ready for the drastic changes brought about by the French Revolution, and because of this she missed her opportunity to carry through many urgently needed reforms which were not accomplished for another hundred years. Moreover, if Britain from the first had been the friend and active collaborator with the majority, and the best, of revolutionary France, when they appealed to her for help, and had she backed them in their determination to destroy tyranny, and establish liberty and justice, how different history would have been from that time onwards !

That was the policy advocated by Fox and his followers in Parliament, but they were not strong enough to force the government to adopt their far-sighted programme. Instead of being appreciated they were denounced as Jacobins and anti-Christ, the enemies of Religion, the Throne and the Church. Ignorance, which causes fear, was the reason of this stupidity, but, if Britain had been behind the moderates in France, they would probably have been quite able to keep down the minority of extremists. Unfortunately she was not, and, as events developed, Britain found herself on the side of all the reactionaries in Europe, besides being the advocate both at home and abroad of everything the best minds everywhere condemned as evil. A Reign of Terror ruled in Britain, and, in the name of law and order, cruelties and outrages were inflicted on the people which were just as terrible in their own way as the atrocities perpetrated in France.

So much concern in those days was given by the middle and upper classes in Britain to the royal family, the nobles and the gentry of France, who had brought all the trouble on their own heads, but how little was expended on the millions of working-class British subjects who needed and deserved their sympathy and help. Many of these unfortunates lay suffering in sordid foul prisons, or were exiled to the colonies, or hung from the gallows to be seen everywhere, because they had contravened one of their country's numerous barbaric laws. Rarely a thought was given to them, or to the poor and afflicted who formed such a high proportion of the population, but this tragic story will be told in its right place.

It was fortunate that George III gave up the attempt to rule his kingdom, because his meagre intellect became more and more clouded as the years passed, to end in him becoming quite insane. Never again did the British people allow their monarch to have autocratic power, as, after the loss of the American colonies, they developed the democratic art which has served them so well. Out of an aristocratic Parliament, whose ministers were chosen by the King, Britain evolved her present parliamentary system of government of the people, for the people, and by the people, but in France things were far different, because when the Revolution began there was no foundation on which to build up a democratic regime.

Moreover, her aristocracy was hated, whereas the local affairs of England and Scotland were largely controlled by the country gentry, each one having great influence in his own district. The gentry of Britain, moreover, mixed more with the people, and many were much respected. There was no place for the Guillotine in a land where all classes met on the village green to see cricket played by squires, gentlemen and villagers, the best man amongst them being captain.

For these reasons the Revolution did not spread to Britain, though Pitt was in terror that it would do so. Consequently he took drastic action, and banished or imprisoned all who circulated *Rights of Man*, which advocated education, adult suffrage and the abolition of hereditary monarchy. Many, including Fox and

Sir Charles Grey (later Earl Grey), thought that Pitt had introduced panic legislation, and opposed it, advocating reform in place of repressive laws.

Pitt, however, saw danger on every side, as is evident from the remark he made to his niece, the beautiful gifted Lady Hester Stanhope, that "Tom Paine is quite in the right, but what am I to do? As things are, if I were to encourage Paine's opinions we shall have a bloody revolution." Surely to teach the people how to read and write, to improve their social conditions, and extend the suffrage beyond the land-owning and trading classes, would not have brought about a revolution; in fact riots and demonstrations for reform were frequent for the next seventy-four years until this came about. So Paine and others were imprisoned or banished, but that part of the story has already been told.

When the French won their victory at Valmy in 1792, thus obtaining renewed confidence in their fighting abilities, and then invaded the Netherlands, Britain took fright, as these parts have always been considered danger areas. Moreover, the French were encouraging revolution in Britain and, contrary to the treaty of 1648, they had opened the Scheldt to shipping, thus making Antwerp a rival port to London.

The French declared war on Britain in 1793, Pitt being regarded as their most formidable enemy, and Britain found herself in a coalition with Austria, Prussia, Holland and Spain against France, all the sovereigns of Europe now greatly fearing for the safety of their thrones, each and all, by every possible means, striving for the return of the French monarchy. An ill-equipped British expedition to the

West Indies, which was sent there to seize the French possessions, ended successfully, but only after 40,000 British lives had been lost. Off Brest (1794) Lord Howe defeated the French fleet, but on land matters did not go so well, France not only driving out the invading allies, but overrunning some of their territories. In 1795 Prussia, Holland and Spain made peace with France, and Napoleon, as recorded in the previous chapter, forced Austria (1797) to make peace after her defeat in Italy.

So Britain now stood alone in a war with France, the conflict being continued by Britain more for the purpose of re-establishing the old order of hereditary monarchy than for any other reason. This reactionary policy, however, imposed such a drain on her finances that Pitt found it necessary to introduce a new form of taxation. As a war-time measure a tax was imposed on income in 1798, and so began the Income Tax, to increase in its scope and incidence as each new war enlarged the National Debt, which now amounts to a gigantic sum, the result of 250 years of war.

We have now arrived at the point where we left off in the previous chapter, and from this time onwards the history of Europe centres round the young military genius Napoleon Bonaparte, a man of almost super-human energy and magnetic power. Just as no one foresaw the calamity which the election of Hitler to the office of German Chancellor in 1933 would bring to the world, so no one then realised the trouble this merciless creature would cause to his generation. How Napoleon managed to get the grip of affairs into his own hands, how he started off as a military missionary to convert Europe to the blessings of Liberty, Equality and Fraternity, how his ambitions, and genius for war, made him master of much of Europe, and how he finally fell, to die a prisoner, is the tale now to be told. So we return to France and renew the acquaintance already made with this man whose shadow was beginning to fall on Europe.

Napoleon Bonaparte (1769–1821) was another of those men endowed with an ill-balanced mind who, because of the greatness of his conquests, was styled the Great. To our half-civilised great-grandparents he was more a hero than a scoundrel, but their lack of moral development was the reason why success and not righteousness was their measure of greatness. As an individual Napoleon exhibited everything in human nature which every good man and woman despises: vanity, deception, greed, selfishness, debauchery, egotism, passion for domination, pitiless cruelty, bad temper, and unbridled ambition to achieve his aim regardless of the misery, suffering, destruction and ruination it might cost. Nothing he relished more than to witness the humiliation of a defeated enemy. His manners, which could be dignified and courteous, were often brutal and harsh. He was quite devoid of any moral sense, and before every campaign he promised his troops all the loot and women they wanted.

Born in Corsica, the second child of a lawyer of noble Italian origin, and a full-blooded Corsican mother who had thirteen children, eight of whom lived, Napoleon was educated in the art of war, first at the military school at Brienne and then at Paris, to pass into the artillery of the French army in 1785. He was industrious and showed a great aptitude for history and mathematics, being much helped by having an exceptionally good memory. Otherwise he displayed no special intelligence. Then came the Revolution, and he became an ardent Jacobin.

Because of his acquaintance with Robespierre's brother he was given the command of the artillery outside Toulon, then occupied by a British and Spanish fleet, and there, in the fight which drove out the enemy, he proved himself to be a capable officer. Later on he was sent to Italy, where France and Austria were at war, and here, on one occasion, he exhibited his cynical insensibility to suffering by ordering a quite unnecessary attack of outposts in order to treat a female friend to the sight of active war, men on both sides being killed and wounded.

Then came the uprising in Paris (1792), when Napoleon, who was in command of the troops, subdued it by firing grape-shot at the mob. Next he obtained command of the forces in Paris and the army of the interior, an appointment which enabled him to marry Josephine de Beauharnais, the widow of an officer guillotined during the Terror, a woman lacking both character and intelligence but of a real sweetness of disposition. The prominent position she occupied in Parisian society proved of priceless value to the lonely Corsican soldier, and she gave him a social position he would not otherwise have had. On the day of his marriage he was appointed to the command of the French army in Italy, and now began, in the year 1796, his dazzling career, his victories being achieved by him massing his artillery on a

section of his enemy's front and then driving through
the battered mass. This was successful until he met
Wellington, who fought him only two lines deep, and
thus saved his troops from being massacred, while
they still retained the power to destroy the French
when they attacked.

During the next two years, as told in the previous
chapter, Napoleon achieved a remarkable series of
successful victories in Italy, which country, including
the Papal States, he thoroughly plundered like any
common thief, while the Directory in Paris, acting on
his instructions, liquidated all the royalists and leaders
of moderate liberal opinion. Success now generated
dreams of victories and conquests, in his warped
imagination, of much greater magnitude than Europe
could supply. So he turned his thoughts farther east,
envisaging the creation of an eastern empire, and the
securing of booty more valuable than could be found
in Europe. India, with its vast wealth, was now his
goal, but, as a stepping-stone, Egypt must first be
captured from the Turks.[1] Ignoring the fact that the
British were stronger at sea than the French, he
persuaded the Directory, now mesmerised by the
young hero, to give him an army to invade Egypt.
Evading the British fleet, he first captured Malta and
then Alexandria, the Battle of the Pyramids, in which
the Turks were defeated, making him the master of
Egypt.

By now Horatio Nelson (1758–1805), a devout

---

[1] The Turks who ruled Egypt in the time of Napoleon were known
as the Mamelukes, a name which was originally given to the bodyguard
of the sultans who succeeded Saladin. They became so powerful that
they overthrew the Sultan in the 13th century and ruled Egypt under
their own sultans.

reactionary, but as great a genius at sea warfare as was Napoleon on land, had sailed from the Atlantic as fast as wind would carry his ships to Aboukir Bay, where he found the French fleet at anchor with many of its men ashore. Evening was approaching, but, in spite of bad light, Nelson engaged at once, and by midnight (1798) the Battle of the Nile was over, the French fleet being destroyed, thus leaving Napoleon high and dry on the desert sands without contact with his home base. It took two months before the news of this great victory reached Britain, during which time Napoleon realised ever more clearly how desperate was his position, to be made worse by plague attacking his army at a time when the Turks were again mustering for a fight. However, he marched on victoriously to Jaffa, where he murdered all his prisoners and poisoned those of his own men who were too weak to fight.

When the news arrived that their hero had captured the Holy Land, and made his headquarters at Nazareth, every Christian in France became delirious with pride and joy. Then later it was told how he had gathered his officers together, conducted religious services, read to them the Gospel story and reminded them how Jesus, now the Christ in heaven, had lived in this very place and then died for their salvation. He became a veritable modern crusader, the saintly warrior appointed by God to liberate Palestine from the infidel Turk, but their rejoicings were premature, as he was unable to capture Acre, and had to abandon his conquests, returning to Egypt, where he again defeated the Turks at Aboukir.

Here he received news of French military disasters

in Italy, all that he had won there being now lost, and, as he came to realise that victories in Egypt brought him nowhere so long as he did not command the sea, he put his army in charge of his Chief of Staff and sailed (1799) for France, being nearly captured by the British off Sicily. Meantime the British admiral Jervis had defeated the Spanish fleet at the Battle of Cape St. Vincent (1797), Spain the previous year having allied herself with France. Moreover, Admiral Duncan, the same year, had won the Battle of Camperdown against the Dutch fleet, Holland now being under French control and made to fight for France. These successes prevented the Dutch and Spanish fleets from uniting, to the great relief of the people in Britain, who were expecting a French invasion at the time when serious disturbances were occurring in the British navy, its sailors, who had genuine grievances, having mutinied at both Spithead and the Nore. The leaders were hanged, and then the worst of the hardships were alleviated.

The living conditions then prevailing in the British navy were a scandal to any civilised country, the lot of the British seaman differing little from that of a galley slave. The men lived under deck in a state of neglect and hardship difficult to describe, and their food was of the poorest quality. The Press Gang collected the scum of England, and sent them to these floating prisons, leave ashore being always difficult to obtain, as, once free from their bondage, few would return. Such were the seamen and the conditions at the time when Britain was proudly securing her position as mistress of the seas, but, when we consider the condition in which the poor lived in those days, we need not be surprised that affairs at sea were much the same as those on land.

Neither need we be surprised, when we remember that reaction then ruled supreme in Britain, and that Nelson, after the Battle of the Nile, carried forward this policy with diabolical thoroughness. Then reigned in the kingdom of Naples the reactionary Bourbon, King Ferdinand, who gave Nelson a tremendous welcome for so thoroughly defeating the revolutionary French. Nelson now made his base at Palermo in Sicily, and, when there, the French invaded Naples to cause the King, the royal family and court, accompanied by Sir William Hamilton, the British representative, and his wife Emma, to hurry to Palermo for safety.

Nelson in those days was consumed by two great emotions: his love for Emma, who was now his mistress, and his hatred of the French. Consequently, when the French withdrew from Naples, he was determined to undo the good work they had left behind, as there they had set up a new government composed of all that was best in that despotically governed state. Though this new order was long overdue, and its new enlightened rulers had restored liberty and justice to a people who for centuries had groaned under tyrannical misrule, Nelson, with the help of the Church, and all the reactionary forces he could command, overthrew the new republic and reinstated the reactionary King Ferdinand.

The Liberals fought courageously for their new-found liberty, and only surrendered eventually when the King promised pardon to all who would capitulate. This amnesty Nelson declared null and void, as to him a promise to a rebel or a traitor was never binding. Then, with his consent, began the massacre when outrages were perpetrated by the royalists, who produced as bloody a reign of terror against the Liberals of the Republic of Naples as the Jacobins had pursued towards the aristocrats of France. The British public, which was aghast at the beheading of the pitiless despot Marie Antoinette, passed by without a murmur the murder of Eleanora Pimentel, a cultured intelligent woman, who, by her writings, had advocated toleration, justice, education, parliamentary representation and the rights of man.

She was publicly hanged, along with many of her friends and colleagues, but in those days it meant much that Marie Antoinette was a Christian queen by divine right, and Eleanora Pimentel, like most of the reformers, was an infidel. Here we are only at the beginning of a tragic story of cruelty and injustice towards the people of Naples, and it will be continued in the next section. Meantime, while this ghastly massacre was proceeding, the pious Nelson, and his mistress, held each day a religious service to thank God for this victory of tyranny over liberty, besides acknowledging their thanks for the British navy and the fact that Britannia ruled the waves.

Napoleon's Egyptian campaign was certainly one of the rashest military ventures in history, and it ended in complete failure, because what was left of the French army surrendered to the British two years later. When Napoleon returned home it was still a force in being, and the French were never told that their great army was hopelessly trapped. Instead of appreciating the true position, they gloried in the wonderful victories told them by their hero, and were so impressed with his marvellous military power that he was able to carry off successfully a daring conspiracy which replaced the existing Directory by three Consuls, of whom he was made the chief.

All France in those days was in confusion, and everyone was tired of the prevailing chaos, the desire for ordered government being intense. On Napoleon the eyes of all Frenchmen were turned as the only hope of political salvation ; in fact the situation in France in 1799 was in some ways similar to the position in Germany in the years before 1933, when the Germans almost unanimously chose Hitler as the one to restore authority and lead the country to peace and prosperity. Another of the many similarities between the careers of Napoleon and Hitler, which are obvious to all who study the events of the momentous years when these two men dominated Europe, was the false explanations put forward by Napoleon for the abolition of the National Assembly, charges of conspiracy being made the excuse, while everyone who showed hostility was arrested and put out of the way.

When this crime was successfully accomplished the road was clear for a new constitution produced by Sieyès, a remarkably shrewd politician who was one of the three Consuls. This gave Napoleon, as First Consul, almost absolute power for the next ten years, and brought to an end all the aspirations for a new democratic order. So we arrive at the final scene of the tragedy, known as the French Revolution, an outstanding historical event which lasted for eleven years, the end being an orgy of murder and violence when the stage was set for a new drama that was to prove equally tragic.

With the brilliant, shrewd and unscrupulous ex-priest Talleyrand at the Foreign Office, pursuing the same tortuous policy as did his counterpart Ribbentrop in our time, and with Fouché, the Himmler of these days, as Chief of Police, all royalists, including a completely innocent Bourbon prince, and men of moderate and liberal opinion were run to earth and murdered, there being now no place for more than one political opinion in all France.

The Revolution can now be considered as over, and the public services, for so long in disorder, again began to function, but no one then realised the terrible price the country would have to pay for giving one man complete power, and elevating him to the status of a god.

France, like Germany and Italy in our own time, put herself body and soul at the mercy of this crazy adventurer, with similar disastrous results. Three times he received the overwhelming votes of the French people: in 1800 as First Consul, in 1802 as Consul for life, and in 1804 as Emperor. The people welcomed manacles to prevent their hands from shaking, and, from fear of being lost, they preferred being confined in a mental prison. Still, can we wonder at this complete surrender of their newly won liberties? They were not much better mentally than children, quite uneducated, and few could even read or write. They felt like people lost who at last had found a guide whom they could trust, one who at least could win battles, protect their frontiers and secure valuable loot. They had no ethical standard, religious dogma having been their only mental food from childhood to old age.

All the revolutionaries had promised so much, but the people could not rise to the level necessary to achieve what the humanists had envisaged. The failure of the Revolution did not lie with the great men of a generation earlier, but with the people, who, poor creatures, could do nothing to help themselves, as they were both ignorant and debased. Consequently, as they could not by themselves reach the Promised Land, it is not surprising that when a brilliant soldier, a daring adventurer, a man who could lead, and act, and knew exactly how to bring order out of disorder, came before them and asked for their confidence, they gave it to him in full measure.

Before their eyes he dangled imaginary fruits of conquest, and made them believe that by following him all the treasures of earth would some day be theirs to enjoy. So we need not wonder that they forsook the ideals of the earlier humanists on the subject of the rights of man, and took what they thought was the easy and quick road to happiness, rather than attain their salvation by intelligent industry along the hard but sound economic road which only leads to lasting prosperity and contentment.

Napoleon's policy, based as it was on ignorance, inevitably led to disaster. After fifteen years of military glory came crushing defeats, when France, after dominating all western Europe, had to return to her former frontiers stripped of many of her valuable foreign possessions. Following her "crowded hour of glorious life", she was bankrupt, weak, helpless and despised, her manpower so decimated that years passed before she recovered her vitality.

Napoleon as First Consul (1800–1804) soon made

it clear to all the world that he had never been sincere in all his previous declarations that the old bad order must be swept away, to be replaced by liberty, equality and fraternity. No man ever had a greater chance to establish a new order of righteousness, peace and good-will amongst men, and no one failed more miserably. Instead of peace he brought the sword, instead of kindness, cruelty, and instead of prosperity and happi-ness he involved Europe in war and misery. The course he took from now onwards, with France as pliable as a child in his hands, proves him to be a man of no vision and without a redeeming noble quality, he being intent only on his own self-aggrandizement at the expense of those who had put their trust in him.

Bad men, or men with no pronounced sense of right and wrong, have often reached the top in time of national difficulties, when an ignorant community had no leader in whom it could trust, because they only stooped to the acts of intrigue and dishonesty necessary for the attainment of their ambitions. Only by increased intelligence, greater knowledge, and the critical faculty becoming more fully developed, will the tragedies which history records, of evil men obtaining power, cease.

So long as people are carried away by pomp, ceremony and hero-worship, their judgment is dulled and their reasoning power unbalanced. So it was with the French when Napoleon by his victories in Italy became the national hero. These conquests threw his countrymen into paroxysms of enthusiasm, so much so that sane and rational thinking vanished, and, when the opportunities offered, he took them one by one until he became the complete dictator of

France. This childlike simplicity of the human race leaves wide open the door for the clever unscrupulous adventurer, and, until it grows from childhood to manhood, every community everywhere can be imposed upon by priest, politician or soldier as the circumstances occur to give one or other the opportunity.

In 1800 we find Napoleon once more in Italy, where, at Marengo, north of Genoa, he succeeded, after nearly coming to disaster, in regaining his former conquests by again defeating the Austrians, and this event was followed by the great victory of Hohenlinden in Bavaria, which was achieved by his general Moreau. Now came a breathing space, the Treaty of Luneville (1801) bringing peace with Austria, and marking the beginning of the end of the Holy Roman Empire. The same year the British, under Sir Ralph Abercromby, defeated the French at Alexandria in Egypt, and Sir Hyde Parker, thanks to Nelson disobeying an order to withdraw, vanquished the Danish fleet at the Battle of Copenhagen in 1801.

These victories, together with the assassination of the tyrannical Paul I of Russia, brought the Northern League to an end, Russia, Sweden, Prussia and Denmark having united against Britain because her navy was searching their vessels for contraband. Equally important to Britain was the fact that these successes at sea frustrated Napoleon's attempt to exclude all British goods from Europe, his Continental blockade being the principal weapon on which he relied to defeat the otherwise impregnable island.

While all these stirring events had been happening at sea, Britain was going through a religious turmoil,

Ireland being in rebellion because of the severe restrictions imposed on the Roman Catholics, who were battened down like dangerous animals. Ireland was now in open rebellion, and terrible atrocities were committed by both sides. So the majority in that misgoverned land stood ready, with open arms, to welcome a French army whose ships were fortunately scattered by a severe storm in 1796 before reaching their destination. England took fright, and Pitt now proposed to remove some of their disabilities, his plan being that Ireland, instead of having a corrupt and inefficient Protestant parliament in Dublin, should now merge her Parliament with the one in London, all Irishmen, both Protestants and Roman Catholics, being eligible.

To this plan both sides in Ireland consented, but George III refused to agree to Roman Catholics being Members of Parliament, a reform which would then have reconciled the Irish to the idea of union and participation in the wider problems of the United Kingdom and the Empire. Instead, he made the excuse that to allow Roman Catholics to sit in Parliament was contrary to his Coronation Oath, and, in consequence, only Protestant Irishmen came over to Westminster. Because of the King's obstinacy Pitt resigned in 1801, quite disgusted with this narrow interpretation of his sovereign's obligation. So it came about that ignorance of natural religion, and the belief in supernatural religion, brought injustice to Ireland, and the tragic repercussions have reverberated one after the other right on to the present time.

Once again the opportunity was missed to appease Ireland, bitter hatred towards Britain following this latest failure to bring about peace and unity. The history of Britain's relations with Ireland is one of missed opportunities, and the man who was responsible for the loss of the American colonies, George III, was now to blame for beginning the century-long conflict between Britain and Ireland over the question of Irish government, one which unfortunately ended in the complete separation of all central, southern and western Ireland from Britain in our own times.

Henry Addington (1801–1804), a politician who commanded little respect, replaced Pitt as Prime Minister, and the following year signed the Treaty of Amiens (1802), which brought the war between France and Britain to an end. Napoleon now became Consul for life, a position he could attribute to the prestige he gained from his fortunate victory at Marengo, the influence of which was to carry him forward until he realised his ambition of becoming Emperor of France.

The treaties of Luneville and Amiens had extended the boundaries of France to the Rhine, and deprived Austria of much territory in Italy. So Napoleon had now his chance to consolidate and enrich the land over which he had been placed. No enemy was on his border, but this modern Caesar was soon to make one, as his ambitions far outdistanced that of improving the happiness of his people. He could have made a new France which would have been a torch of inspiration to all Europe and the world, because the material was there awaiting some skilled hand to use it wisely for the advancement of the common good. Instead of so doing he decided to conquer and unify Europe, so as to realise his dream of a great European empire, of which he was to be the first emperor.

The preliminary step to empire lay in a settled and prosperous France, as his ambitions could not be realised without men and money. So he founded the Bank of France (1800), reorganised the banking system, introduced an equitable method of taxation, improved the roads, enlarged the canals and encouraged trade, all of which reforms had already been prepared by others years before, the turmoil of the Revolution making their earlier materialisation impossible. With France now set upon the high road to recovery from all her past troubles, Napoleon next made a Concordat with Pope Pius VII, whose domains in Italy had just been returned to him by the French, and negotiations commenced for the purpose of re-establishing and re-endowing the Church of France.

The Revolution had not only swept away the monarchy, but it had also deprived the Church of its rights and privileges, besides all its ill-gotten lands and wealth, it being now entirely dependent on the civil power. By means of the Concordat the Pope anticipated the return of all its ancient privileges, but Napoleon, as First Consul, retained the prerogative to appoint all Church dignitaries, and France's broad acres, which had once been Church possessions, were never again to be known as Spiritual land.

Whenever the agreement was signed, Napoleon shattered all the expectations of the Vatican by issuing what were called "Organic Articles", which became immediately binding on the Church. These decreed that no papal Bulls were to be received in France, no synod of the Church was to be held in France without government permission, no bishop was to leave his diocese upon the summons of the Pope, that all had a right to worship as they pleased, and that religious persecution must cease from now onwards.

So the Church authorities were thus prevented from exercising their inveterate custom of torturing and slaying unbelievers, the priest being compelled to confine himself to preaching and the performance of his ritual and ceremony. One exception only was made to these priestly duties, as he was expected to exert his influence for the purpose of inducing the young men of his flock to join the army, besides instilling into the minds of the faithful the necessity for implicit obedience to the man who now ruled the nation.

Probably the most enduring work of this period is the *Code Napoleon*, which codified, unified, humanised and simplified the laws of France, a dream long held by French legislators, and one of the first planks in the revolutionary platform. During the Revolution's tempestuous career it could do no more than start this great undertaking, which Napoleon instructed members of the Council of State to carry through to a finish. In clear and simple words these legislators produced a short and concise legal foundation for a modern civilised society, established on social equality, religious toleration, private property and family life.

Freed from revolutionary extravagance on the one hand, and despotic injustice on the other, it contains all for which the 18th-century humanists worked, privilege, persecution and injustice being absent from its pages, the same justice being meted out to everyone. Religion is ignored, marriage and divorce becoming a secular affair and quite apart from the priest. Liberty, combined with order and the family life, with the husband as the recognised head, comprises its leading feature. Women, however, received no equal position with men, their land and money became their husbands' property, and it was not until the Married Women's Property Acts of 1870 and 1874 that they, for the first time during the Christian era, obtained their legal rights and were able to own and dispose of possessions apart from their husbands. This reform, however, applied only to Britain, to be accepted by other countries in later years.

The *Code Napoleon* contained other blemishes, especially in its savage punishments for crime, such as branding and confiscation of property, and, although everyone was entitled to open trial by jury, a heritage of the Revolution, the weak and innocent were not so carefully cared for as we would now think proper. Still the fact remains that this code marked a decided advance in justice, privilege being abolished, and all men and women were treated as human beings, with equal justice, for the first time since the beginning of Christian civilisation.

Abroad Napoleon established Christian missions, each missionary being his agent, who, under the garb of religion, strove to advance the political and commercial policy of France. At home he entirely neglected elementary education, as he showed no wish for the people generally to have knowledge, only those who could serve to gratify his ambitions receiving instruction. The army needed technicians and men versed in the knowledge required for his ambitious schemes, and these he encouraged by establishing the University of Paris and seventeen subordinate

academies in the provinces, where youths experienced
Spartan discipline and were trained to glorify war and
all the evil it represents. What a change from the
all-embracing scheme for the rational education of
every child, which was the aim of those who carried
through the Revolution !

As Emperor, Napoleon did not freely reintroduce
the bestowing of titles, but instituted instead the Legion
of Honour, his most popular deed. This enabled
those favoured with the distinction to wear a piece of
ribbon, and have the feeling of a certain claim to
superiority, a failing above which few can rise.

With the stage now set, and everything ready, he
commenced to put his schemes in motion, but in so
doing he showed himself to be a gambler without
vision or wisdom. He again quarrelled with Britain,
though he lacked greater sea power, having apparently
learned nothing from his ignominious experience in
Egypt. In 1803 his army occupied Switzerland, thus
upsetting the Treaty of Luneville, and Pitt, who again
became Prime Minister, foreseeing that this was just
the first bite of a hungry man eager to devour all
Europe, declared war on France. Spain was forced
into an alliance with France, but otherwise nothing
of importance happened immediately.

Napoleon, however, was not idle, and much
to the disgust of all democratically minded Europeans
he was active in consolidating his power by washing
out all traces of the new order for which he had
hitherto stood. Nevertheless he remained the hero of
the French, who had abandoned some of their former
high principles relating to the rights of man, so much
so that they now created him emperor in 1804 by an

overwhelming majority of votes. Consequently the next act in the drama proceeded in more glamorous surroundings, greatly to the astonishment, stupefaction and terror of the rest of Europe.

Napoleon I, Emperor (1804–1814), was crowned at Notre Dame in Paris, not by Pope Pius VII, who had come all the way from Rome to perform the ceremony, but by his own hands, the Emperor seizing the crown from the grasp of the Holy Father and crowning himself. He would be indebted to no one for his position, having perhaps in mind the strange experience to which Charlemagne was subjected by the Pope of his day. Next year he was crowned at Milan, as King of Italy, with the iron crown of Lombardy.

Meanwhile he distributed other crowns amongst his brothers, all very plain ordinary people, who thus obtained some of the pickings from the successful brother's table. Louis was made King of Holland, Jerome King of Westphalia, Joseph King of Naples, to become later King of Spain, and Eliza's husband was given the principality of Lucca on the frontier of France, the Grand Duchy of Berg being reserved for Murat, who had married Caroline. During all this period of prize-giving, wise Madame Bonaparte, this mother of monarchs, remained quietly at home saving the money her prosperous son was sending to her, ever fearing that the grandiose bubble would some day burst.

While much of this ceremonial was proceeding an army of 100,000 men and 2,000 barges assembled at Boulogne, awaiting the first opportunity to cross the Channel and conquer Britain, a medal having already been struck and a column erected at Boulogne to commemorate the great victory. The barges were ready, all that was wanting being a fleet to protect them, but unfortunately for the Emperor the British admiral Calder had so crippled the French fleet, under the direction of Admiral Villeneuve, in the Bay of Biscay that it could do nothing to help him. So Napoleon's cry "Why will Villeneuve not come?" went unheeded, and when he realised that an invasion of England was impossible he withdrew his army, to win a series of victories which made him master of Central Europe.

Napoleon's aggression in southern Germany had already decided Austria and Russia to join Britain in a coalition against this new enemy of liberty. So the Emperor moved his army from Boulogne across Europe, and decisively defeated the Austrians at Ulm and then again at Austerlitz (1805), following this up with the formation of the Confederation of the Rhine. Prussia, in haste, and not fully prepared, now joined in the conflict on the side of the allies, only to be defeated at Jena in the following year (1806), after which she completely collapsed, when the French, meeting little resistance, marched into Berlin. Austerlitz killed Pitt, and Fox became Secretary of State, to die six months later, but within that time he secured the passage of a Bill for the suppression of Britain's part in the capture and selling of slaves.

These French victories were indeed terrible blows for Britain, though they were softened by Nelson's great victory at Trafalgar in October 1805, when he destroyed the combined fleets of France and Spain under Admiral Villeneuve. Nelson did not live to see this victory, as he was killed by a musket ball an hour after·the battle started, but this great achievement made Britain definitely mistress of the seas, with the French and Spanish colonies at her mercy, an important development which was withheld from the French people, who remained in ignorance of this great sea battle.   For Britain it was a sad victory, as when the news reached England, two weeks later, Nelson's grateful admirers, amid their rejoicings, too clearly realised that never again would they welcome home their hero who had done so much to protect their island from invasion, a danger which his genius and daring had now fortunately removed.

Italy, Austria, Prussia, the German states and the Netherlands were now completely in the power of Napoleon, who became President of the Confederation of the Rhine, comprising all the states of western Germany.   The defeat of Austria brought to an end the Holy Roman Empire, the cause, since its formation, of so much wickedness and bloodshed, and the Emperor Francis confined his title to embrace only Austria, but the Prussian collapse at Jena had just the opposite effect.   Out of that defeat arose the Germany of our time.   As the star of Germanic Austria declined, so did that of Germanic Prussia arise, until she had absorbed all the German people of Central Europe into one great aggressive community, intent on the domination of Europe as a preliminary to world conquest.

The defeat at Jena, and the harsh humiliation which followed, raised up a group of energetic, thoughtful, calculating men such as Scharnhorst, Hardenberg, Stein and Clausewitz, who were determined to make Prussia again great, powerful and respected. To Clausewitz, the greatest of all military theoretical writers, war was "the continuation of policy", and his opinions have always been deeply revered and respected by the German military caste, so much so that what he wrote became the foundation on which Germany built up her great armed power. History teems with great effects following sometimes from insignificant causes, but surely, amongst the many tragic events of history, few stand out more boldly than those which grew out of the bloody field of Jena.

Spain and Turkey were safe from devastation and humiliation because they were France's allies, but Russia still remained outside the conquered lands, and before the end of 1806 Napoleon was in Warsaw, making preparations to strike her down. At Pultusk and Eylau he had a bad mauling, but at Friedland (1807) he decisively defeated a combined force of Russians and Prussians.

Instead of advancing into Russia, he induced the young and genial Tsar Alexander I (1801–1825) to meet him on a raft on the River Niemen at Tilsit, the purpose being to form an alliance, called the Peace of Tilsit, which decided on the division between them of Prussia, Poland, Turkey, India and most of Asia. Britain alone appeared invulnerable, but the denial of European ports to her ships seemed the best way to bring about her ruin. So that was also agreed, and, as a further reward for Russia's help, she was to be given Finland, which was to be taken from Sweden. All this being satisfactorily settled, the end of the year 1807 saw Napoleon practically the master of all

Europe, his troops, with the help of Spain, having just conquered Portugal, entered Lisbon, and sent the royal family hurrying off to Brazil.

Britain stood alone against this mighty combination, even more formidable than the one which confronted her when France collapsed in 1940. Her industries were being ruined by the almost cessation of European trade, unemployment was acute, food was very dear, and poverty and starvation were terrible, but she still had command of the sea and did not falter. Napoleon tried to rectify France's naval weakness by forcing Denmark to declare war on Britain, so that he might have the use of the Danish fleet of twenty warships, but this manœuvre was foiled by Britain seizing them in Copenhagen harbour.

On the high pinnacle from which he now surveyed Europe his loving Josephine did not seem to him to be sufficiently exalted to share his throne, and, moreover, she had given him no heir to continue the dynasty he had founded. So for a time his thoughts turned to marrying a Russian princess, but as nothing came of this the young ladies of the royal courts of Europe passed one by one beneath his gaze, during which time his temper became daily worse, his attitude towards everyone becoming increasingly intolerable. His judgment became warped, so much so that he quarrelled with Spain, his ally, a fatal blunder which was to mark the beginning of his downfall. So far his victories had been against governments, and their paid mercenary troops, who had no real interest as to which way the fight went so long as they were paid, but from now onwards a change occurred, as the people in the occupied countries commenced to take part in the struggle, fearful that this new tyranny would in the end strangle all liberty and justice, and bring them to utter destruction.

Quite indifferent to any outlook except his own, and unmindful of the advice given to him by the sagacious Talleyrand, the Emperor now decided (1808) to depose the Bourbon King Charles IV of Spain, and put his own brother Joseph in his place, Murat, his general, being given the kingdom of Naples, which Joseph had vacated. Spain and Portugal were to be united, but the Spanish, incensed by this high-handed action, arose in their fury at such interference with their independence, and, though ill-equipped, commenced a long guerilla war which thoroughly exhausted the French. Anxious to get a foothold in Europe to bring their enemy to defeat, the British quickly seized the opportunity to support Spain in the conflict, and sent Sir Arthur Wellesley, later to become the Duke of Wellington, to Portugal with an army composed of privates "drawn from the scum of the earth", as he described them.

In the first two battles, Rolica and Vimiero (1808), Wellesley defeated the French, and this brought the Emperor on the scene. Napoleon occupied Madrid, and abolished the Inquisition and feudalism, besides reducing the power of the priests. Then in 1809 he marched successfully against a British army, to be driven back at Corunna, thus enabling the British, who were encompassed, to withdraw their troops in safety by sea, though unfortunately their gallant leader Sir John Moore was killed during the conflict. The French then captured Saragossa, during which

action the Spanish showed heroic bravery and determination.   In Austria the French were also victorious
at Abensberg, Eckmühl and Landshut, but they lost at
Aspern, only to win again at Wagram, a hard-fought
battle in which the Austrians displayed increased
resistance and improved leadership.   Vienna was now
captured, but all this time, while Napoleon was busy
occupying the capitals of Europe, the French possessions abroad were falling one by one into British
hands.

The frontiers of Europe were now altering rapidly,
as Napoleon annexed first this country and then that
to France, and Russia took what she wanted.   In a
determined effort to get to closer grips with the
enemy, Britain, in 1809, landed 40,000 men on
Walcheren Island at the mouth of the Scheldt, her
aim being to capture Antwerp, through which she
could pour troops on to the Continent.   Though
this venture failed, and the invading force perished,
largely through incompetent leadership, besides lack
of hospital equipment and supplies, the British
strategy was sound, as Antwerp leads directly to the
heart of Europe.

On the banks of the Scheldt England made her
base for the Hundred Years' War, and from Antwerp
the Spanish planned to invade England if their great
Armada had sunk the British fleet in 1588.   Britain
always feared that France would permanently occupy
Antwerp, and this was one reason why she and
France fought so many battles in the 17th and 18th
centuries.   So Antwerp has played a great part in
European history, it being the prize sought for by
those who were Britain's enemies, just as it was the

door used by Britain to enter Central Europe in the closing stages of the Second World War.

During the Napoleonic War Lisbon was the door used by Britain to enter Europe. This natural land-locked harbour is at the tip of a peninsula, across which Wellington constructed the famous bulwark of Torres Vedras in 1810, behind which he built up his army and his supplies. Attempts by the enemy to break these fortifications failed, and, while Europe was writhing under the thraldom, Britain prepared for the day of liberation. Meantime Prussia reorganised her constitution, abolished serfdom and privileges, and established popular education, while Alexander of Russia drifted farther and farther away from his ally. This separation was intensified by Napoleon divorcing Josephine and marrying Marie Louise of Austria, the amiable simple-minded niece of the decapitated Marie Antoinette, who gave him a son (1811) known as the King of Rome, a child who was fated to live a life which was short, sad and tragic.

The Emperor next angered Alexander by annexing North Germany from Holland to the Weser, and now (1811) the tide began to turn in favour of the British. First of all they drove the French out of Portugal, and then won the Battle of Salamanca in the following year. Alexander withdrew from the boycott of British trade, a policy which was hurting Russia in common with every other country in Europe, and Napoleon made this the excuse to declare war and invade Russian Poland. In 1812 600,000 men, including conscripted Austrians and Prussians, crossed the frontier and fought their way through Poland and on to Moscow, which they reached in September, the

Russians retreating but always keeping their armies intact, adopting just the same tactics as they used against the Germans in 1941.

Defeating the Russians at Borodino, seventy miles west of Moscow, where they made their first stand, Napoleon entered the capital to find his position decidedly uncomfortable. Already he had lost 150,000 men in his advance, and now his communications were being constantly raided. Though his troops were continually being reduced by disease he remained on, uncertain what to do, leaving it too late to retreat safely. Then his stay in Moscow was cut short by the Russians setting fire to their capital and smoking him out. On 18th October, 1812, he and his troops had no other alternative than to set their course for home, and traverse the bleak road they had devastated on their advance. First they struggled on through mud, then through snow, and still more snow, and then through biting blizzards, until at last their morale snapped, and the Grand Army broke into bands of marauders to be shot down by Russian soldiers and the irate peasants ever in their rear and on their flanks.

This famous event, once looked upon as the greatest military tragedy of history, is now eclipsed in our own time by the experience of the Germans and their allies in attempting to do what Napoleon failed to do. How like is all that we have been reading to what we have lived through these last few years. The most important resemblance is in the fact that Russia, after holding back while all Western Europe was over-run by a well-prepared aggressor, during which time Britain stood alone unbeaten, then entered the fray to play a similar decisive part which helped to ensure the final defeat of the enemy.

Only about one tenth of the French army survived the Russian ordeal and reached France. What remained of the Prussians had already surrendered, and the Austrian remnant, tattered, hungry and sick, returned home by straggling south, spreading the news everywhere of the disaster.

This staggering defeat of France gave increased courage to Austria and Prussia, who once again began to show resistance, but Napoleon made a desperate effort to avoid defeat. With all speed he rushed to Paris to mobilise a fresh army, a difficult task as the war in Spain had already drained 250,000 men from his reserves, and now he was faced with resurgent Austria and Prussia, besides Sweden and Holland, as his enemies. In spite of this now powerful alliance against him, which was the work of the brilliant diplomacy of Castlereagh, the British Foreign Secretary, Napoleon secured sufficient men to win the Battle of Dresden in 1813, but at Leipzig, a few months later, his army was encircled and crushed during the bloody slaughter which followed.

Definitely his star had now set, and, like a wild animal, he was driven back on Paris, bellowing all the way that he would not abandon one of his conquests. Nevertheless the forces arrayed against him moved in deadly earnest, the Swedes, Austrians, Russians and Germans coming in from the east, while the British, who had won five battles in Spain,[1] the last being Vittoria, moved across the Pyrenees

---

[1] Talavera (1809), Busaco (1810), Fuentes d'Onoro (1811), Salamanca (1812), and Vittoria (1813).

accompanied by their Spanish allies.   Like a cornered
rat Napoleon fought well and furiously in the valleys
of the Seine and Marne against the troops led by
Schwarzenberg and Blücher, but gradually they pushed
him aside and entered Paris.

The Emperor abdicated a few days later, and was
banished to Elba, but he was allowed to retain his
title and consider himself the sovereign of the island.
If he had been a poor man in England in those days,
and had stolen some meat for his starving family,
he would have been scourged and then hanged.   Though
he had driven 2,000,000 to their death, and devastated
a continent, our ignorant ancestors, who ruled Britain
and Europe, saw in that no reason for punishment;
in fact all they wanted was to get him out of the way
so that the bad old order could be restored.   This
was done right thoroughly, as the Bourbon dynasty
returned, Louis XVIII, the brother of Louis XVI,
becoming King of France, Louis XVII, the titular
King of France and son of the executed Louis XVI,
having died in prison in 1795.

The revolutionary idealists thought that by removing the tyrannical crown, peace, justice and happiness
would follow, but they failed to realise that the people,
who had never been taught the way of righteous
living, were incapable of self-government.   It requires
over fifty years to educate the entire population from a
state of illiteracy, and the well-meaning attempt by the
revolutionaries to make a start was killed at birth.
Now that Napoleon was out of the way a new opportunity arose to establish enlightened government in
Christian Europe, but it was not to be, as we shall see.

Europe was in chaos.   So the European monarchs

and their representatives met in Vienna to clear up the mess and settle the new frontiers, the old ones having been so badly knocked about. To this conference came Alexander of Russia, the most enlightened monarch of his time, as well as the representatives of the Roman Catholic reactionary Hapsburgs, the revengeful Hohenzollerns, and those of aristocratic Britain. The brilliant ex-priest Talleyrand (1754–1838), who had been created Prince of the Empire by Napoleon, was also there to see that the return of the Bourbons to the throne of France was assured.

The rights of the people consequently received little thought, the chief concern of these envoys being the firm establishment of their own despotic thrones. Nevertheless, amidst the scramble for power and territory, in the intervals between their secret intrigues and open disputes, they thoroughly enjoyed themselves with their lady friends at sumptuous banquets and glittering balls, but in their midst stalked the ever-present spectre of ignorance which presided over all their deliberations.

While all this was going on Napoleon slipped through the protecting British warships and landed at Cannes in 1815, to be welcomed enthusiastically by the men he had led on his plunder marches. Thus began "the Hundred Days", during which the master criminal was again loose, much to the consternation of the new King Louis XVIII, and all the royalist émigrés, who had just returned to France from their places of refuge in foreign lands. So the French had to make their choice between a representative of the old tyranny, which they hated and never wished to experience again, and the man who had bled them white to satisfy his ambitions.

They mostly chose the latter, driven to do so by the policy of Louis XVIII, which convinced the people that the Church would recover its old power and that all the land it had lost during the Revolution would be returned to it, thus depriving innumerable small farmers of both the land and houses which they now considered to be their own. Napoleon had never tampered with the new order's land settlement, whereas Louis proposed to do so, and that was the deciding factor which gave Napoleon one more chance to save his throne.

It was a perplexing position for every patriotic Frenchman, but Napoleon quickly settled opinion in the minds of all who wavered. His march on Paris, gathering soldiers and admirers all the way, was a triumphal procession, and before he entered the capital Louis had fled, leaving the Emperor again the master of France. Many French people would have liked a republic, but the monarchs of Europe were determined against this form of government, and, as Napoleon promised to reign as a constitutional sovereign, his countrymen took him at his word and accepted him.

The rest of Europe naturally felt that they could not leave such a man loose in Europe, and, knowing this, he prepared for the inevitable clash, gathering together an army with all possible speed. Eighty-seven days after his entry into Paris he struck swiftly at Brussels, hoping to divide the British from the Prussians, and that by capturing the Netherlands, with its rich cities and great natural river ports, he would restore his prestige in France. To incorporate within the borders of France this wide delta, laid down by the rivers Rhine, Meuse and Scheldt, had for long been the French desire, and its loss had been their greatest blow.

Nothing could better unite a distracted France than an attempt to recapture this great prize, and consequently Napoleon struck swiftly at his goal, first of all defeating the Prussian general Blücher at Ligny, while Marshal Ney was fighting the British at Quatre Bras, but in neither battle was anything decisive reached. Two days later at Waterloo (1815) the French were completely defeated by "the worst equipped army with the worst staff", according to Wellington, its commander, who also added "and it was a damned near thing". This force comprised 23,900 British, 17,000 Belgian and Dutch, 11,000 Hanoverians and 9000 from other German states, decisive victory being secured when the Prussians came in on the enemy's right flank as the day drew to a close. The French retreated in disorder, pursued by the allies, who occupied Paris.

Before they reached the capital Napoleon had abdicated and fled in an attempt to reach America. He got as far as Rochefort, where he took refuge on a British frigate, the *Bellerophon*, hoping that he would not be treated as a prisoner. Thence he was taken to Plymouth, whence he was packed off to St. Helena. There he remained until his death from cancer in 1821, quarrelling with everyone, and writing his memoirs with the object of showing that he was in reality a very fine and clever fellow, whose deeds had been quite misunderstood. Much has been written about this extraordinary individual, but no one compressed more into so few words than did Robert G. Ingersoll, when recording his thoughts after gazing down from the encircling marble balustrade upon Napoleon's sepulchre in Paris.　They are indeed a fitting epitaph:

A little while ago I stood by the grave of the old Napoleon, a magnificent tomb of gilt and gold, fit almost for a deity dead, and gazed upon the sarcophagus of rare and priceless marble, where rest at last the ashes of that restless man.　I leaned over the balustrade and thought about the career of the greatest soldier of the modern world.

I saw him walking upon the banks of the Seine, contemplating suicide.　I saw him at Toulon, I saw him putting down the mob in the streets of Paris, I saw him at the head of the army of Italy, I saw him crossing the bridge of Lodi with the tricolor in his hand, I saw him in Egypt under the shadows of the pyramids, I saw him conquer the Alps and mingle the eagles of France with the eagles of the crags.　I saw him at Marengo, at Ulm and at Austerlitz.

I saw him in Russia, where the infantry of the snow and the cavalry of the wild blast scattered his legions like winter's withered leaves.　I saw him at Leipzig in defeat and disaster, driven by a million bayonets back upon Paris, clutched like a wild beast, and banished to Elba.　I saw him escape and retake an empire by the force of his genius.　I saw him upon the frightful field of Waterloo, where chance and fate combined to wreck the fortunes of their former king.　And I saw him at St. Helena, with his hands crossed behind him, gazing out upon the sad and solemn sea.

I thought of the orphans and widows he had made, of the tears that had been shed for his glory, and of the only woman who ever loved him pushed from his heart by the cold hand of ambition.　And I said, "I would rather have been a French peasant and worn wooden shoes.　I would rather have lived in a hut with a vine growing over the door, and the grapes growing purple in the amorous kisses of the autumn sun.　I would rather have been that poor peasant, with my loving wife by my side, knitting as the day died out of the sky, with my children upon my knees and their arms about me, I would rather have been that man, and gone down to the tongueless silence of the dreamless dust, than to have been that imperial impersonation of force and murder known as Napoleon the Great.

(4) TYRANNY AND INJUSTICE CAUSE REVOLUTION IN EUROPE.

When Napoleon was finally secured and put out of harm's way, Louis XVIII (1814-1824), a wise and witty old man, returned to Paris, and the Congress of Vienna resumed its sittings, to draw up the Second Treaty of Paris, the first treaty signed in 1814 having been abrogated by the unexpected return of the deposed Emperor. Under the new agreement France had to give up all her conquests, pay an indemnity, and return to the frontiers of 1790, her twenty-five years of expansion having cost her dearly, and in the end gained her nothing.

The Congress then set to work to define the boundaries of the different states of Europe which had been so badly knocked out of shape, to end in the Continent being divided up like this if we start with Switzerland as the centre. Germany became a loose confederation of thirty-nine sovereign states under the presidency of Austria, her neighbour Prussia being increased by being given part of Saxony and the districts of Danzig, Posen and Thorn. Russia got Poland, while Austria secured Hungary, Galicia, Lombardy, Venetia and Dalmatia. The Ottoman Empire in Europe embraced Bosnia, Serbia, Rumania, Bulgaria and Greece. Italy was divided into the Kingdom of the Two Sicilies from Naples southwards, the Papal States, including Rome, forming a wide band across the centre, north of which were the states of Tuscany, Moderna and Parma. Due south of Switzerland was Piedmont, which, with Sardinia, comprised the Kingdom of Sardinia. Luxemburg, Belgium and Holland became the Kingdom of the Netherlands. Norway and Sweden were united, and Spain, Portugal and Denmark were left unchanged.

Britain was given her choice of renouncing or retaining all the French and Dutch colonial possessions she had captured, and, after returning Java to Holland, her possessions abroad were increased by Malta, Ceylon, Trinidad, British Guiana, St. Lucia, Cape of Good Hope, Seychelles, Mauritius, Ascension, Tristan d'Acunha, the Ionian Islands and Heligoland.

After the world was rearranged, the first wish of everyone was that such a catastrophe should never happen again. So in 1815, on the suggestion of Russia, the first attempt was made to form a league of nations to preserve peace. This combination, which included Russia, Prussia, Austria, France and Spain, called itself the Holy Alliance, the charter opening with the words "In the name of the Most Holy and Indivisible Trinity". Christ, it declared, was the King over all Christendom, and he had appointed all monarchs to act for him, which they intended to do "in accordance with the principles of the Christian religion".[1]

---

[1] "The Lord hath set a King over you" (*Samuel* xii, 13), and other similar texts were taken by both Church and Monarch to mean that kings ruled by divine right, and had been endowed with absolute power over their subjects. Sir Robert Filmer, in his work *Patriarcha*, published in 1680, traces this divine authority from Adam, through Noah, Abraham, Isaac and Jacob on to the rulers of Israel, after whom it was conferred on all Christian kings, who in consequence could do no wrong.

This meant absolute monarchy, persecution, tyranny, ignorance and the obliteration of all hope of education and freedom. The Popes had worked on the same Christian principles for centuries, and had thus accumulated vast possessions and maintained autocratic power. So Pius VII, who had abolished torture and many feudal survivals at the Vatican on the instigation of the French, was not invited to enter the holy circle, because the signatories now wanted to keep the magic formula to themselves. The British monarch, with Parliament over him, did not identify himself with the Holy Alliance, but all the other minor sovereigns of Europe joined in except the former King of Poland, because Russia, during a moment of carnal weakness, had deposed him and taken his country.

This alliance, based on Christian principles, achieved its object, and in every country the tyranny which it established received the support of the Christian Church. With this wonderful opportunity to return to the methods it had always adopted before the French Revolution, all freedom of thought was speedily stamped out. Torture and the Inquisition, which the French had abolished, were reintroduced, the Index of Prohibited Books, which had been suppressed, was republished to destroy again all the seeds of progressive and intellectual thought which developed in the finest minds in Europe.

So the Church continued her policy, relentlessly pursued since the 4th century, of confining all knowledge within the borders of the Bible, her creeds, doctrines and dogmas, while Christian monarchs, whose prestige had suffered from the French

Revolution, were again placed within the sacred circle, their divine rights being re-emphasised to check the increased yearning of the people for greater political freedom and more control in the affairs of their country.

Behind the troops, who kept down those who writhed under despotic rule, and at the back of the police, who suppressed all expression of opinion, stood the priest who controlled the press and guided public thinking along the narrow path of Christian orthodoxy. With its influence everywhere, its enormous wealth and power, its multitude of ignorant adherents, and its freedom from taxation, the Church once again controlled the universities, besides the policy and the life of Christian Europe until the time came when evolving mind again revolted, to bring about another revolution as the century drew on.

The Christian despots had not only the Church as their ally, but also a depraved philosopher, possessed of a powerful intellect and great volubility. He was Georg Hegel (1770–1831), who, as Professor of Philosophy at Berlin University, influenced and moulded the minds of the German ruling class with his teaching that "the State was God walking upon earth", which meant that the State was superior to the individual. According to him God was present in the governing princes, to whom the people must always bow down in reverence.

He believed that democracy and liberalism were contrary to the will of God, the State being supreme and the people but cogs in a great soulless wheel, for ever turning for the purpose of lifting this material structure to an ever higher level of power and greatness. To Hegel the wellbeing and happiness of the individual did not count, if it conflicted with the interests of the State. Consequently force was superior to righteousness, might more important than right, and, as states are founded on force, war is justified for the wellbeing of the State which does not recognise the ethical code.

Into this depraved scheme, Hegel, a devout Christian, wove the beliefs of his religion, in which he found all the necessary support for his debased doctrines. The State being God on earth, it followed that the individual must be sacrificed for the State as the Son of God was sacrificed for the world. As the State was a divinely appointed institution, so the will of God was expressed by the monarch who was endowed with divine rights, which privileges also had been conferred on the nobility as the divinely appointed ruling class. Hegel thus reaffirmed the Christian political ideology which had so degraded mankind during the past fourteen hundred years, and he passed on to National Socialism the ideas which have in our own time brought misery, suffering and destruction, not only to Germany, but to Europe and the entire world.

At the same time as the Christian Hegel was teaching his reactionary doctrines to well-filled class-rooms of aristocratic Germans, who treated everyone beneath them as menials and their peasants as serfs, the benevolent philosopher Jeremy Bentham (1748–1832), his contemporary in England, who rejected the Christian faith, was propounding quite the opposite opinion. This was that the duty of the State was to procure the greatest happiness of the greatest number of its citizens. To the devout Hegel the wellbeing of the individual meant nothing, but to the non-Christian Bentham it was everything, everyone being entitled to equal justice, equal rights and the same privileges.

What a contrast there was in those days between the opinions and deeds of those smeared by the Christian revelation, and those of the heretical humanists who had worked themselves out of its evil embrace into the humanitarianism all good men and women in our day support. Today we witness the philosophy and philanthropy advocated by the noble non-Christians of the 17th and 18th centuries accepted by the good, and the Christian ideology, which had kept all Christendom in subjection for fourteen hundred years, advocated by those evil men against whom we fought in the Second World War.

Today we try to follow in the steps of these infidel reformers, whereas in their day they were denounced by all Christians as servants of the devil, their attempts to raise mankind to a higher level of thought, and an improved way of life, being considered as contrary to the will of God. Today we see the results which have followed from Germany and Italy pursuing the Christian tradition, devastation, misery and suffering covering most of Europe and much of the civilised world, the worst in humanity having come to the surface, and a long trail of hatred laid which will take generations to overcome.

Instead of the monarchs of Europe profiting from the good which came from the minds of the men who set in motion the French Revolution, they again put their faith in the supernatural gods, a belief which has been the curse of the human race. Consequently they learned nothing from experience, becoming ever more determined that the people would remain servile and ignorant, and obey the commands of their rulers whom the powers in heaven had set over them.

The excesses of the Revolution in France, and the deeds of Napoleon, who arose from its ashes, unfortunately gave absolute monarchy the opportunity it desired, so much so that despotic power, under clerical direction, returned to the hereditary rulers of Europe. Never again, they definitely decided, would the people have the power to govern and determine policy, their duty being to obey as simple obsequious subjects what their masters considered was right.

Consequently all free institutions, all intellectual aspirations, and every form of liberty were everywhere suppressed. This was particularly the case in Austria, about which benighted land more will be said some pages farther on. In that priest-ridden country the Hitler mentality was cultivated, the Nazis in our time only continuing the pernicious system in which Hitler and his forbears were nurtured. When we therefore consider his upbringing, and the tradition on which he was reared, we need not be surprised at the depravity of the Hitler ideology, which found a fertile soil in the Germanic mind likewise poisoned by the same befouled heredity.

What happened in Austria happened all over Europe to a greater or lesser degree, and her divinely guided monarchs never lost a chance to suppress every reform movement in other states besides their own, especial attention being given to the stamping out of any attempt made for the people to have a voice in the election of their own government. In Britain thousands were either imprisoned or exiled to Botany Bay, in the early years of the 19th century, the only crime of some of these being that they voiced the opinion that the corrupt and unjust parliamentary system of representation should be reformed, and that something should be done to improve the living conditions of the labouring classes.

Christians are very proud of Christian civilisation, and we are for ever hearing from them how much better the world would be if Christian principles, Christian culture and the Christian way of life took the place of the humanitarianism which has developed over the past hundred years since Christian doctrines, and the Bible, have ceased to guide the great majority in Christendom. Only within living memory have we emerged from the thraldom to which these devout people would like to see us return, because the laws of Christendom up to last century were little better, and in some respects worse, than those codified by Hammurabi some four thousand years earlier.

Then, in those far-off days, women received similar legal rights as did men, and engaged freely in commerce and the learned professions, the poor, widows and orphans being specially protected by the laws of the land. Many Egyptian laws, of an even earlier date, were likewise wiser and juster than those prevailing in Europe in the 19th century. Those termed the heathen, who lived in ignorance of the gospel of Christ, and wandered in spiritual darkness, deprived of the light of heaven, nevertheless produced a juster, wiser code of laws than came from those who had been favoured by what is claimed to be the only revelation from God to man. As Farrer, that thought-ful classical authority, says in his book *Paganism and Christianity*:

There is indeed no fact more patent in history than that, with the triumph of Christianity under Constantine, the older and finer spirit of charity died out of the world, and gave place to an intolerance and bigotry which were its extreme antithesis, and which only in recent years have come to be mitigated.

In the first part of the 19th century it was legal to inflict torture on suspects. One hundred years ago Germany and Austria were practising the age-old custom of breaking the live bodies of victims on the wheel or rack, burying people alive, impaling them on pointed stakes, and tearing off their flesh with red-hot pincers. Not until 1831 was torture abolished in Germany, it being abandoned by Russia in 1850, by Italy in 1859 and by Spain much later. In France, Britain and the Netherlands it had largely died out by the beginning of the century, but in some European countries torture is still practised by means of flogging with a whip of thongs to which pieces of metal or wire prongs are attached, which so cut into the flesh that the victim generally dies from the effects.

Imprisonment for correction is of comparatively recent date, no attempt before then ever having been made to reform prisoners, who were detained only for the purpose of retention before their punishment. In 1593 the first institution to reform women offenders was built in Amsterdam, but prison reform only seriously commenced at the beginning of the 19th century, before which time both innocent and guilty men, women and children were herded together in

filthy appalling conditions awaiting trial. Not until
1840 did Britain abandon the policy of transporting
her lawbreakers to her colonies, many of whom were
guilty of no greater a crime than the desire to reform
her barbarous laws, which Sir William Blackstone
(1723-1780), the eminent legal authority of his day,
declared were founded on the Bible, his words being:

> English law is presumed to be founded on the Bible, so much
> so that where it can be found to be contrary to the Law of God
> it is doubtful if it is valid.

Injustice in Britain in these days was so pronounced that Sir Samuel Romilly, the famous legal
reformer, truthfully exclaimed in 1817 that "The laws
of England are written in blood." This ever
courteous and benevolent man, and other reformers
in Britain and in Europe, consequently set about
to make Christians everywhere more humane, their
every endeavour being opposed by the authorities
in power, the House of Lords, true to its tradition of
opposing all legislation for the good of the people,
being particularly reactionary. It was not until
1870 that the practice of drawing and quartering the
victim was abolished in Britain, the prisoner before
1814 having his entrails cut out, while he was alive,
and burned in his presence, a relic of the time when
the mind was believed to be centred in the bowels,
which were burned for the purpose of its destruction.

It was because of this savage way of killing
criminals that a Frenchman, Dr. Guillotin, in 1789,
advocated the use of a more humane method—that of a
weighted axe which beheaded the victim instantaneously.
This method was adopted in France, but, unfortunately
for the doctor, the instrument received his name.

Those termed "Infidel" by Christians were becoming more and more horrified at the civilisation, the lack of education, the social conditions and the depravity of their times, and the only way they could suggest for the abolition of the existing abominations was by political reform. Thus it was hoped that the people, when they were able to control affairs, would have the say in the ordering of their lives, and the Church, and its God-appointed monarchs, none whatever. This outcry against existing conditions was confined to no one European country. Southern Italy, in these days, was well advanced politically, and ardently desired democratic government, but against all freedom and justice stood the divinely appointed sovereign and the Church, both determined that the people would have no political or religious liberty.

To exterminate this liberal movement, which swept through Europe between 1790 and 1870, terrible abominations were inflicted on those who desired to secure representative government. Within this period nearly 500,000 of the finest and best men and women in Russia, Germany, Spain, Portugal, Austria, Italy and France were executed, murdered, exiled or died in prison for peacefully, not in armed revolts, trying to improve Christian civilisation and raise the standard of life. Always the Church, and its priests, supported and encouraged the monarchs in their efforts to liquidate all forms of liberal and democratic thought. They supported every form of barbarism against these harmless good-living citizens, who only asked for constitutional monarchy, representative government, humane laws, education, freedom of thought, and improved social conditions.

Instead of being granted their just desires, the Inquisition, which Napoleon's generals had abolished in Spain, was re-established there and in Italy, to remain in being in Italy until Garibaldi drove it within the walls of the Vatican in 1870. Besides the Inquisition, which the popes claimed to have been founded by the inspiration of the Holy Spirit, the priests in Spain organised the Society of the Exterminating Angel, whose members expended their savagery on all having liberal ideas, the most abominable tortures being carried out in the prisons throughout the land, a state of affairs which continued up to the end of the 19th century. The victims in Russia throughout the 19th century are impossible to number, but, under the Tzars, every possible cruelty and horror occurred towards those who strove for better and more humane social conditions, 174,000 being confined in prison as late as the year 1910.

Within the Papal States, "whose very soil was contaminated by the abominations of the past", 15,000 unarmed men and women were massacred by various popes over thirty years because of their attempt to secure liberty and justice, the troops being led at times by cardinals. Others were left to rot to death in foul dungeons. A similar movement in Spain brought about the death and imprisonment of 150,000 unarmed men and women, while, at the same time in Portugal, 67,000 were murdered, imprisoned or sent to penal colonies, the number in southern Italy being 100,000.

Here once again we have an example of the way history has been distorted by Christian historians. We remember how much has been made of the

2000 Christian martyrs who suffered under Pagan persecution, but, as emphasised when considering this matter in Chapter VIII, nothing is said in our history books about the 25,000,000 who were slain by the Christian Church. So, likewise, in the period we are now considering, the same dishonest rrepresentation is noticeable, because we are for eve reading about the few thousands who perished during the Reign of Terror, but nothing of the 500,000 victims who were sacrificed for demanding political representation, education and improved living conditions. Everyone has heard of the Reign of Terror, but few about the European revolution and its terrible history, because it shows up so clearly the Christian way of life, and historians had to be careful not to offend their readers.

Every ideology, whatever name it bears, Christian, Nazi, Moslem, Buddhist, Communist, Spiritualist or Materialist, must stand or fall by its past record, and the effect it has had on its adherents. All good men and women outside of Germany were repelled by the deeds of those who had adopted the Nazi creed, and, as their evil works were committed within our own lifetime, they are known and remembered. The wicked deeds performed in the name of the Christian ideology, whose creeds and dogmas are even more repulsive than anything propounded by the Nazis, are less well known, because historians as a rule, who write for schools, have not dwelt on such matters. Consequently the vast majority, whose knowledge of history is confined to what they were taught at school, are sublimely ignorant of the true history of the Christian era, and do not realise the abominations which have taken place down the centuries, it being difficult to imagine conditions greatly different from what we experience from day to day.

All we hear about Christian civilisation today, apart from sermons delivered to the faithful, is through the B.B.C., the exclusive mouthpiece of the Christian Church. This organisation brings prominent ecclesiastics and churchmen to the microphone to tell listeners about the beneficence of this civilisation, which they affirm we fought the Second World War to save from destruction, but no one is allowed to broadcast the truth, or in any way to criticise this Nazi method of deluding the people. So the millions of B.B.C. listeners, whose knowledge of history is slight, have by now been well saturated with the idea that the Christian era was one of outstanding blessing to mankind. Because of this false propaganda most people now believe that only through Christianity was slavery abolished, and did hospitals, doctors, social services, schools, teachers, representative government, liberty, tolerance and the love of peace and justice come to a benighted world, which before its time was in a state of heathen wickedness.

These Christian propagandists have invented the name of "Christian democracy", to stand for a Christian form of society based on past achievements and future plans. No two words could be more unsuitably joined together, because each in the past has stood for ideas diametrically opposite, and yet the curse of ignorance weighs so heavily upon the multitude that the incongruity of this combination of words never strikes them. We might just as reasonably talk of Nazi or Fascist Democracy. With a church and a priest in every parish in Christendom, supported by the tenth of the produce of the land, and the monopoly of the B.B.C. so far as Britain is concerned, we need not be surprised that Christian propaganda has succeeded in completely falsifying history, and achieving its aim to represent Christianity as standing for everything that is good and kind, all the other religions and ideologies being subject to the weakness inherent in human nature.

Now that we are set out to build up a new structure of society, after the recent world-wide tempest which has shattered so much of what is called civilisation, it is more than ever necessary to have a correct knowledge of the past, and keep strictly to that which is true. The historical facts related in this book may therefore help to correct the false information which Christians are for ever spreading about the benefits their religion has conferred on the human race. Many there will be who will continue in the years to come to propagate and believe these falsehoods, but at least those who have read the pages of this book so far, and continue on to the end, will not be misled by Christian propagandists, and those who always put faith before knowledge, in their zeal to advance what they believe is the only revelation by God to mankind.

During the Christian era there has always been a church in every parish in Christendom; the towns had many, and every village had at least one. Likewise in every parish there was at least one priest. In every

community up to seventy years ago there was a church
but no school, a clergyman but no schoolmaster, the
people being kept in order by the fear of God, which
meant the fear of hell, but they were never taught
righteousness for the sake of righteousness and the
benefit it brings to everyone. Up to within the
past seventy years Christendom was in a deplorable
condition, mentally, socially, physically and ethically,
and only within the past half century have all the
people had their health well cared for and been
educated to read and write. This terrible state of
affairs was after eighteen hundred years from the
foundation of the Christian religion by Paul, no
expense, no effort, no opportunity having been spared
to force its ideology into the plastic minds of the
young. Christianity took the place of education; in
fact it was to the people of Christendom their only
form of mental nourishment.

Consequently this chapter is just a continuation of
the same old sordid story, the result of ignorance, as
told in the pages which preceded it. Only within
the present century, within the lifetime of most of us,
has real social progress been noticeable, the reason
being that religion in most countries now takes its
proper place, it having become, as it always should
have been, a personal matter for everyone, and not a
series of theological assertions, composed by priests,
who chained the mind by threatening all unbelievers
with the wrath of God and eternal damnation.

Hitherto the State had confined itself to keeping
internal order, protecting its frontiers, and conducting
wars, the condition of the people being left entirely
to the Church, which was responsible for their

social, mental and, what it calls, their spiritual development. This duty it carried out by confining their minds within the bounds of an ancient creed, and still more ancient formulas and dogmas which all had to believe. With that done nothing further was considered to be necessary, the people being taught that to be good citizens they must obey the king and priest whom God had appointed to rule over them, or be punished for their disobedience.

Whatsoever prolongs or encourages ignorance is evil, and that which stimulates knowledge is good, because only through knowledge, wisdom, and a high standard of ethical conduct, can the race rise to a higher level of thought and action. Judged by this standard, Christianity has been a curse and not a blessing to mankind. In fact it was the cause of most of the troubles of the past, and is the cause of many of the present time, as from its inception it has been the avowed enemy of education, the accumulation of knowledge, and of the people receiving proper medical attention. Prayers took the place of the healing methods adopted by the Pagans, and it was thought that everything worth knowing was contained within the teaching of the Church. Consequently, from the time it obtained power in the 4th century, education withered away, and the ideology it put in its place was both unethical and debasing. The effect of this is clearly noticeable in the events which make up the history of the Christian era.

The first half of the 19th century was a time of unrest and revolution, a black period of cruelty and political and religious intolerance. The attempt to restore the old order was greatly resented by all liberal-minded people, who, in spite of persecution, continued to clamour for education, and also the reform in the structure of their country's constitution, so that the people, by their votes, would have a say in their own government. Europe was growing out of the Theological Age, but the monarchs and the priests, who had hitherto ruled the people, did not wish to forgo their age-old authority. So they told their subjects that God would be angry with them if the divine monarch was deprived of the power he received from heaven. Everywhere, so far, in Christendom this had been the way the people had been governed and now, because of their mental development, the old order was beginning to weaken, but before it finally collapsed a stiff fight was inevitable.

From the time of the formation of the Holy Alliance the ferment amongst the people of Europe continued, and many looked across the Atlantic to see how the new Republic of the United States would fare in her experiment with a government which had no place for God, or the divine monarch and the inspired priest. This young community certainly acted as an inspiration to all reformers, but the spark which set alight the European revolution of 1848 occurred a year earlier in Germany. Then a convention was called to institute certain pressing reforms, but, before that happened, there is much to tell. So far, in the previous pages of this section, we have only covered the revolutionary movement in outline, but now a survey will be made of each country during the years preceding this important event.

Though the spark of revolution was lit in Germany all Europe was ready for a blaze, and consequently we shall not start there but at the powder magazine in Austria, and take each country in turn until we reach the time when Metternich, the most outstanding of all the reactionaries of the time, was driven from office a year after the revolution began. He, of all the statesmen of his day, radiated from Vienna the policy which produced the revolution, and to him the European monarchs looked with gratitude in their fight against reform. This being so, it is fitting that we start with Austria, if we are to understand matters aright.

This pious and retrograde land, the seat of the Holy Roman Empire, was ruled by her famous statesman Prince Metternich, who, for forty years (1809–1848) as First Minister, was the undisputed autocrat of the Austrian Empire's millions composed of diverse nationalities. Besides this he played the leading part in the tragic drama entitled The Holy Alliance. He was a man of noble birth, of engaging personality and determined will; and from the time of the Congress of Vienna (1815), where his forceful character was recognised, his work lay in the re-establishment of the bad old order which the French Revolution had failed to destroy.

His hatred of democracy guided his entire political career. To him there was no choice between autocracy and chaos, and, on the former system of government, he rebuilt Austria, which had suffered so severely from the hammer-blows dealt her by Napoleon. Consequently in that benighted land there was no liberty, no progress, and no reform, his idea of government being that the subject was completely subservient to the Monarch and the Church, whose priests, appointed by God, were the only teachers, and theology the only subject worthy of respect. From the highest official downwards to the humblest policeman and soldier, duty lay in complete obedience to the Holy Father at Rome and the laws of the State.

This being so, there was no education, and the people remained serfs, miserably poor and pitifully ignorant. There were no social services, and nothing was done for the upliftment, the comfort or the improved health of the people. There was no liberty, no freedom, no escape from the tyranny of the secret police, ever alert to hear and punish anyone expressing an enlightened opinion, and there was only repression for the subject nations yearning for their own form of government. There was no art, no literature, and only music flourished, the reason being because no heretical or political reformer could, by his compositions, contaminate the listener's mind.

Austria's compensation for losing Belgium, when the frontiers of Europe were being redrawn by the Congress of Vienna in 1815, was Venice, Lombardy, Illyria (now Yugoslavia) and a portion of eastern Bavaria, but only 4,000,000 of her Emperor's 28,000,000 subjects were Germans, the rest being Bohemians, Hungarians, Italians, Poles, Serbians, Croatians and Rumanians, all loosely held together by their recognition of the same crown. Nevertheless Austria was placed by the Congress over all the other German-speaking states for the purpose of military defence.

Northern Italy, divided as it was into different states, again came under Austrian domination, and their rulers, of Austrian birth or in close alliance with Vienna, returned to the thrones they had lost when Napoleon conquered their kingdoms. The Papal States were restored to the Pope, and the Bourbons came back to rule Naples and Sicily. The King of Sardinia, whose house at a later date was to give the sovereigns to a united Italy, received Piedmont and Savoy. With the Hapsburgs, Bourbons and the Pope again in control of most of Italy, we can now understand why it was that there was so much cruelty and suffering amongst the enlightened people of these parts, who desired liberty and reform in place of suppression and reaction.

The southern Netherlands, now called Belgium, were again the sport of the great powers, and became attached to Holland so as to provide a strong state against a French invasion of Germany. Like Palestine, in the days gone by, it was a highroad between East and West, a most unfortunate situation for any nation desiring to live in peace. The Dutch and the Belgians were of different nationality and language, the Roman Catholic Belgians particularly disliking the stern Dutch Protestant rule. In 1830 they revolted and the leading powers, in fear of Belgium becoming a republic, a hateful idea in those days, or being annexed to France, agreed to her being a separate nation under Leopold I of Saxe-Coburg, the wise, intelligent uncle of Queen Victoria.

Though Belgium lost Luxemburg and Limburg, and had to suffer from a Dutch invasion which was repelled by the French, she secured her independence, the neutrality, which was imposed upon her indefinitely, being agreed to by France, Britain, Austria, Prussia and Russia in the treaty of 1839, which became a "scrap of paper" in 1914 when Germany invaded the country at the beginning of the First World War.

Away up in the north changes were taking place in the frontiers of these hard bleak lands. Bernadotte, a former marshal in Napoleon's army, had been King of Sweden since 1818, this position having been given to him because of his great military talents, and there he reigned as Charles XIV (1818–1844) His predecessor had conquered Norway in 1814, over which kingdom Bernadotte was also king, this union lasting until 1905, when Norway became a separate kingdom, quite peacefully, without even a war to celebrate the event.

Across the Baltic Sea lay Finland, for long the prey of both Russia and Sweden. In 1808 the Swedes and Finns were defeated by Russia, and Finland passed over to her possession, to become the freest and best governed part of the Russian Empire, a state of affairs which lasted until 1914, when she declared her independence at the beginning of the First World War. Poland was not so fortunate, because, after a rebellion against Russian rule in 1830, she was decisively defeated, to lose every vestige of her former independence until she rose again as a republic in 1918.

Those countries situated in the northern extremities of Europe have contributed little to European history, and when we leave the north for the west we find the people of Spain likewise living lives apart from the central hub which has played such an important part in European policy, a state of affairs which came upon Spain after she fell from her prominent position in the 17th century. Here we find different ideas and another way of life, a proud, patriotic, indolent, negligent people whose way of life consisted of alternate siestas, riots and revolutions. Less than one third of the country was cultivated, ignorance abounded, and only in the large towns was interest taken in the liberating philosophy which was now sweeping over the rest of the Continent. The people were content to remain serfs, vagabonds, monks or smugglers, their only mental refreshment being that supplied to them by a corrupt Church and priesthood who took the best the land provided.

Even their most enlightened sovereign Charles III (1759–1788), who put an end for a time to bullfights, curtailed the power of the Church, modified the severities of the Inquisition, expelled the Jesuits, and did his utmost to stimulate the country's industries, was hated for his efforts, and when he died things slipped back to their old easy-going ways. Everything foreign, anything new, was despised by the majority of the Spaniards, who cared nothing for humanitarianism, progress, reform or learning, but only for their simple needs and their religion. Nevertheless this was the land which had given to the Roman Empire four of its greatest emperors, and some of its most notable philosophers and literary men, besides Quintilian, who founded and developed its splendid educational system. Hedged in by the Inquisition during the Christian era, few Spaniards added to the world's knowledge, and only during the period of Arab occupation did Spain send forth beams of culture and learning which eventually lit up the rest of Europe.

Spain, after being knocked about as the result of the Napoleonic wars, when Joseph Bonaparte was forced upon her for five years (1808–1813), again replaced the exiled Ferdinand VII (1814–1833), whom Napoleon had dethroned. He was a devout and wicked man, possessed of every vice, and quite wanting in the power to rule. Under Napoleon the power of the Church had been curtailed, and the Inquisition abolished, but, with the return of Ferdinand, its power and evil practices returned, the Inquisition being re-established. This meant the end of all liberty, mercy and justice, and the return of frenzied intolerance, but sufficient French republican influence remained to be the cause of a revolt in 1820. This aimed at securing a constitutional monarchy, representative government, education of the people, the freedom of the Press and the abolition of the wickedness and privileges of the Church and monasteries.

When Ferdinand was forced to yield to the demands of the reformers, the leading European powers, "guided by the principles of the Christian religion", and with the help of the French army under the control of a divinely guided monarch, crushed the revolt. Britain protested at this outrage, but to no effect, as the Holy Alliance, and 100,000 French troops, replaced the reactionary Ferdinand in his previous despotic position. All the reforms which he had been forced to concede were revoked, and then began the massacre of all the reformers, the French army remaining in Spain for five years to make sure that the King's authority would be nowhere disputed.

Spain's alliance with Napoleon had for her unfortunate consequences, as the break which this caused in the royal line convinced the South American colonists that the time had come to sever their connection with the homeland. Consequently the Spanish colonies, sufficiently distant to be more independent, declared themselves republics, which policy of separation from the mother country received the support of Great Britain. Thus Spain lost her vast South American possessions, because, by 1830, eight independent republics had come into being, severed as completely from Spain as was the United States from Great Britain, reactionary government in the homeland being the cause of both events.

A year after the Spanish revolution the Greeks in 1821 rebelled against their Turkish overlords, and fought gallantly for the national freedom which had been denied them for centuries. The birth-place of democracy and freedom had known no independent national life since the time of the Roman conquest (146 B.C.), the only form of independence being that maintained amongst the mountains, where brigands and guerillas lived precariously. These outlaws were only distantly related to the ancient Greeks, being now mostly of Slavonic or Albanian extraction, and they spoke a language somewhat resembling the old Greek but greatly intermixed with Turkish, Latin and Slavonic words and phrases. They had a hazy memory of their country's past greatness, and secret societies had prepared the way for a return to independence. When the day arrived, all lovers of the Greek classics gave her their sympathy, some, like Lord Byron, giving the movement active help and their lives. First of all Great Britain, and then Russia, supported the Greeks, the Turkish fleet being destroyed at the Battle of Navarino (1827), a victory which secured to the Greeks their independence, but many horrible things were done by both the Turks and the Greeks during the conflict.

From the time of the overthrow of Napoleon I, France had experienced the benevolent autocratic rule of Louis XVIII, but when this kindly old monarch died he was succeeded by his brother Charles X (1824–1830), a religious bigot and despot. Living as he did in the past, every trace of freedom went with the enactment of the Ordinances of St. Cloud. Revolution followed in 1830, led by a young journalist Louis Thiers (1797–1877), who, by his writings, roused the people to right their wrongs. Charles, remembering too well what had happened to his brother Louis XVI, when at the mercy of the Paris Commune, fled to England, and Louis Philippe (1830–1848), who was Duke of Orleans, a benevolent and well-meaning man, was proclaimed king in his stead, to give to his country eighteen years of prosperity and peace.

Constitutional government was established, industry was encouraged, railways were built, a telegraph system was organised, Algeria was colonised and developed, and the trading classes became prosperous. If France had been Britain, progress would have continued, wrongs righted in time, and national evolution would have taken its slow and tortuous course to higher and still higher levels of social well-being and culture. But the mercurial French do not think and act like the slower-moving, but more stolid and reliable, Britisher. Otherwise they never would have behaved as they did after their defeat in the Second World War. So, remembering their peculiar mentality, what happened now will surprise no one.

Some longed for the great and glorious days of Napoleon I to return. Thiers wrote a panegyric about him, and when what remained of his body was brought back in 1840, to be placed in its last resting-place in the Hôtel des Invalides in Paris, the finest possible tomb was erected to hold it. All the misery and destruction caused by the mind which had once inhabited this garment of flesh were now forgotten, and his past conquests and brilliance were compared with the existing peaceful conditions. Instead of peace causing content, past memories arose and produced dissatisfaction and longing for something spectacular.

That was one side, but there was another much more real, namely the shocking social conditions of the people who were employed in industry. Because of this terrible state of affairs three outstanding men, Fourier, Simon and Louis Blanc, advocated Socialism, and the putting into practice of the liberal ideas of the intellectuals of the Revolution. Conditions were sordid, the great majority having no electoral powers, but the position was just as bad, if not worse, in Britain, which slowly found ways to right the wrongs.

In France things work differently. So they had another revolution, and Louis Philippe, now old and tired, lost his nerve and fled to England, a Republic being declared in 1848. An attempt was now made to provide work for all, but the dislocation this caused produced riots and much bloodshed so it was abandoned as impracticable, 10,000 casualties being the price paid for the experiment.

Louis Napoleon, the son of Louis Bonaparte, who was the brother of Napoleon I, the eldest representative of the Napoleonic dynasty, now stood for election to the Assembly and was duly elected. Next he stood for the Presidency, and was elected by an overwhelming majority, the votes given to him swamping those cast for two leading reformers, his name being sufficient to open the magic door to power. Then he abolished constitutional government, and proposed that the President could hold office for a second time, to which suggestion the Assembly did not agree. Consequently he arrested all the leaders of the opposition and their leading supporters in the country, 100,000 being put to death, imprisoned or exiled, the clergy being particularly active in their support of these atrocities.

Then he introduced a new constitution, which made ten years the length of time the President could hold office, and when this was carried by an overwhelming vote of all the people, he proposed that he should reign not as President but as Emperor, to which the people agreed, the voting in favour being 97 per cent. of the votes cast. Thus he reached the throne in four years, and within a shorter time than his uncle took to rise from First Consul to the same position, his uncle's fame being the reason for the nephew's achievement. Once again the French had an emperor, their new ruler reigning as Napoleon III (1852–1870) until he abdicated after the disastrous defeat of the French in the Franco-Prussian War of 1870–1871, but that period in history comes into the chapter which follows.

The Austrian Empire, containing various different races and languages, was not unaffected by the stirring of the minds of the people of Europe during the first half of the 19th century, because the desire for freedom and independence came from all quarters. Belgium, as we have read, quickly secured her separation from Holland, but the Poles, Irish, Finns, Norwegians, Bohemians and Hungarians were all restless under foreign rule. Metternich's despotic rule over Austria kept the people for many years from exhibiting any form of self-expression, but eventually a revolt in Vienna (1848) forced him to resign. This was followed by the formation of a Constituent Assembly, which produced a constitution for each part of the Empire, and abolished the feudal laws from which the land still suffered.

Bohemia was likewise infected by the prevailing desire for greater liberty, and her people rose to demand that her Czech population should be given the same privileges as those enjoyed by the Germans, who formed an important part of her population. A Pan-Slav congress met in Prague at a later date, but, beyond considering the future of the different Slavonic people in Europe, nothing occurred. Hungary took the opportunity, which came from the prevailing desire for freedom, to demand many reforms, and finally declared herself independent of Austria in 1848, though still recognising the Emperor as her sovereign.

Louis Kossuth, a journalist and brilliant orator, inspired the movement, but the Serbs, Croatians and Rumanians, who comprised part of the Hungarian population, fearing the domination of the more numerous and detested Magyars, supported Austria. Russia sided with the minority Slav races, and a joint Austrian-Russian army defeated the Magyars at

Villagos, exacting from them such severe penalties that all Europe shuddered with horror. Kossuth escaped into exile, and the Magyar attempt to secure independence collapsed. How like this was to the conditions then prevailing in Ireland, when the Protestant minority, in fear of domination by the Roman Catholic Irish, was loyal to the British crown, and resisted all attempts in later years to create a united Ireland governed from Dublin.

The weak-minded Austrian Emperor Ferdinand (1835–1848) was not yet at the end of his troubles, as the Austrian Empire's Italian possessions took their tune from the others; in fact the entire assembly of non-German races comprising the Empire, made up of Poles, Rumanians, Serbians, Croats, Czechs, Italians and Magyars, were in a fever of unrest. They not only wanted their freedom and independence, but an end of tyranny, there being little justice, and the peasantry lacked all rights, being no better than serfs. Privilege abounded, the aristocracy and priesthood paying no taxes and not being subject to the common law, while the tax-gatherer bore heavily on the traders and small farmers. Poverty and ignorance induced tyranny and superstition, but the seeds laid by the French Revolution had not all died off, and in places growth was to be found.

Napoleon I, by his defeat of the Austrians in Italy, had given the Italians their first taste of freedom from foreign rule since Otto I first conquered Italy in 951. Their geographical situation and disunity made for domination by the German race, and their alliance with Germany in the Second World War was only in keeping with the subservience which circumstance had forced them to adopt towards their powerful northern neighbour over the previous thousand years.

The different states of Italy, since the fall of the Roman Empire, had never united, though they were composed of people of the same race, speaking the same language, and proud of the same history and great traditions. Now, however, the longing for unity and freedom increased, the thirty years following the formation of the Holy Alliance in 1815 having witnessed the growing desire for independence from Austrian rule, and the retention of the taxes coming from the rich and fertile Italian lands then passing into the Austrian exchequer. Italy thus became a pressing problem, because, under her ardent patriotic leaders, it seemed as if it would be no longer possible to keep what was becoming a united nation for ever divided and in bondage to a foreign rule.

Many thought that the Austrian Empire was about to collapse, but the loyalty of the army, and the bitter conflicts of the subject nationalities amongst themselves, besides the aid given by Russia along her borders, saved the situation. Then arose a remarkable man, Count Felix Schwarzenberg, the successor to Metternich, who, within four years (1848–1852), accomplished great things, only to die before his work was done. During this short period this haughty aristocrat, a man of great ability, procured (1) the abdication of the insane Emperor Ferdinand, and put his nephew the young Francis Joseph (1848–1916) in his place, (2) broke the Hungarian revolt with the help of the Russian army, as already recorded, (3) consolidated the administration of the Empire, and (4) restored

Austrian supremacy over the German-speaking people of Europe.

If he had lived it is possible that the German states would have been united as one nation under Austrian domination, instead of coming under Prussian mastery, as happened a generation later when Bismarck took in hand their unification. After Prague was bombarded the Bohemian revolt collapsed, but in Italy things were different and a veritable reign of terror followed, its object being to crush all liberal ideas, every petty Italian potentate, each one of Austrian birth, binding himself ever more closely to Vienna, in return for the promise that Austria would ruthlessly crush all attempts to form a free united democratic Italy.

That was the position in 1848, but we must go back some thirty years to better understand the position. The revolutionary movement had been gradually growing in strength all these years since Lombardy and Venetia had become powerful Austrian strongholds, a perpetual menace to any Italian province which attempted to take a lead to right the wrongs from which the Italians suffered. Under this tyranny many otherwise moderate Italians joined secret revolutionary societies, as it was felt that only through them could redress eventually be secured for their sufferings. Tyranny was thus met by conspiracy, Carbonari, and other revolutionary societies, quickly spreading throughout the land, to end in the smouldering fire breaking out in 1820 when the Spanish Liberalés proclaimed a new constitution on the lines laid down during the French Revolution.

Moved by this example, the army mutinied in

Naples, and the Bourbon Ferdinand, the King of Naples, fled to Austria, which country was now filling Lombardy with 80,000 armed men. Meantime Britain and France overawed the revolutionaries by patrolling the Bay of Naples with their warships, and a Congress of European powers met to authorise Austria to crush the uprising in all southern Italy. Along with the Austrian troops came back the despotic Ferdinand, to mete out his vengeance on his insurgent subjects. His abominations, however, did not prevent Piedmont in the north from overthrowing her king and proclaiming a democratic constitution, the liberal-minded Charles Albert, a distant cousin, being appointed regent until the legitimate heir Charles Felice returned from abroad. On his return Charles Albert resigned, and Charles Felice re-established the former autocratic government, forcing underground once more the revolutionary movement for justice and reform.

These two examples typify what was happening throughout the different kingdoms of Italy from 1820 onwards, every monarch of each state from the Pope downwards maintaining a reign of terror against all who demanded justice, reform, liberty and democratic government, to end in a fresh uprising in 1830 which was quelled by Austrian troops.

From that time until 1846 Italy remained uneasily tranquil but discontented, the infamous government of the Papal States and southern Italy continuing as before. The people everywhere were poor, miserable, ignorant and ravaged by disease, the discontent from north to south turning all Italy into a rumbling volcano ready at any time to overflow and sweep away for ever the despots from their thrones. Meanwhile the revolutionaries were preparing to strike again, and this time they were to be aided by powerful leaders, who did not rest until all Italy was a free democratically governed country.

The most outstanding revolutionary was Giuseppe Mazzini (1805–1872), who hated priests and distrusted kings, an enthusiast for the cause of Italian liberation, and a man who devoted his life to the realisation of one indivisible republic embracing all Italy. This notable visionary dreamed of a free Italy, under republican rule, linked with all other freedom-loving people everywhere, radiating the gospel of liberty over all the dark places of the earth, a chimera because he failed to realise that the theologically instructed Italians, who completely lacked knowledge, were quite unfitted to play such a role.

Enthusiasm, without a foundation of knowledge and wisdom, will never make a better world, and Mazzini, who founded the Association of Italian Youth in 1831, in a Marseilles garret, relied only on this emotion to raise the Italian people from their bondage. Bereft of all else, and with only an ignorant and down-trodden people to lead, and no worthwhile army to drive out the hated Austrians who dominated the north, he could do no more than keep alive the ideal of a united Italy. Thus he sowed the seed that fructified in later years, because meantime he could place little hope upon the poorly equipped and badly led force of Charles Albert, the King of Sardinia and Piedmont, who had succeeded his reactionary relative Charles Felice.

Only Charles Albert remained loyal to the aim of a

united Italy, all the other rulers of the Italian states being in favour of the bad old order which every right-minded Italian wished to have for ever abolished. The humane and democratic ideas, as expressed by the moderate French revolutionaries, which Napoleon had so grossly betrayed, were never again to be allowed if these reactionary rulers had their way. Only by keeping the people in subjection, they declared, could Europe be ruled by monarchs from thrones which would be safe and stable. Mazzini's policy to sweep them off their thrones can therefore be understood, but the great majority of Italians were not prepared to follow him in his extreme measures of conspiracy, and, if need be, assassination.

The publication of two books, one by Gioberti and the other by Balbo, deeply affected the more moderate Liberals by their discretion. Condemning, as they did, the violent methods adopted by Mazzini and his party, they yet put forward constructive plans for future action. As the years passed these more prudent reformers found their leader in Count Cavour, who became the champion of a united Italy under the sovereignty of the King of Piedmont, as will be told later. Meanwhile Mazzini, who was joined by the exile Garibaldi, was the only effective force resisting the tyranny and oppression of the age, which, under the direction of the infamous Pope Gregory XVI, was driving the people of Rome mad with rage and despair.

On the death of this tyrant in 1846 a temporary change occurred, because his successor, the treacherous Pius IX (1846–1878), known as Pio Nono, declared himself a Liberal under pressure from the laity now bent on reform. This greatly strengthened the moderate Liberal party to assert its demands openly, so much so that the idea of a united Italy under the sovereignty of the Holy Father made headway. Thus there existed at this time three parties, each one set on its own way as to how best to achieve a united Italy, the first led by Mazzini, who favoured a republic, the second which wished the Pope as sovereign, and the third which believed the country could be best united under the sovereignty of the House of Piedmont.

Before long only two alternatives remained, as, after first blessing the formation of a united democratic Italy, Pius IX turned round and cursed it, becoming violently reactionary and the tool of autocratic might, because his power rested on retrograde Austria. So Austrian tyranny over northern Italy remained, and, with the changed situation, the dream of a united Italy under papal rule vanished into thin air, a fortunate dénouement as it turned out in the end, because an Italy ruled over by the Pope would never have secured democratic government and the freedom so longed for by the people. This will be better understood by referring to Chapter XVI, p. 681 which gives the opinions of Pius IX on the way the people should be governed.

This period in Italian history is known as the Risorgimento, meaning the Resurrection, a memorable time when the flames of revolution were spreading through the rotten foundations on which were erected the despotic thrones of all the kingdoms of Italy and Sicily. Commencing in the south and blazing northwards, they engulfed Rome, Turin, Florence, Milan, Pisa, Leghorn and Venice, and, when it became known that the outraged mob was in control of Vienna, whence had stretched the long strong despotic arm, and that the tyrant Metternich had been overthrown (1848) and had fled to England, some of the hitherto timid Italian states took courage and proclaimed republics. Then it was that Schwarzenberg took command and put the young Francis Joseph on a somewhat shaky throne, an event which brings us up to the year 1848, when all Europe was seething with discontent and the desire for justice and reform.

To be free of fear, to be able to live without the constant dread of being overheard by the secret police, to have those elementary political and civil liberties which were enjoyed in Britain, and to receive an elementary education was the cry of the oppressed Italian people, who could be cast into prison without reason, and without defence, where they rotted away forgotten. A free Press, unrestricted travel, education and representative government, they demanded as their right as human beings, and because they could not get it they arose in rebellion.

The outraged people went over to Mazzini following the treachery of the Pope, and in 1848 the revolution began after the uprising in France had dethroned Louis Philippe. Sicily declared her independence and dethroned the despotic Ferdinand, Lombardy rose in insurrection, the Austrians were thrown out of Milan, where a republic was formed, and then Venice expelled her Austrian governor, also to form a republic. Impelled by the overwhelming enthusiasm of the populace of northern Italy, Charles Albert of Piedmont declared war on Austria, and this act caused the states of Piacenza, Parma, Modena, Lombardy and Venetia to decide on union with Piedmont, each citizen casting his vote.

In the first encounter with the enemy, Piedmont won at Goito, but at Custozza the Austrians were victorious, which news encouraged Ferdinand of Naples to crush the Sicilian rebellion, when Messina was bombarded, and such atrocities perpetrated that the admirals of the British and French fleets had to interfere to stop the massacre. In Rome Pius IX, now a declared supporter of Austria, witnessed the assassination of his minister Count Rossi and anarchy seizing the city, a state of affairs which impelled him to escape in disguise to Gaeta to be under the friendly protection of Ferdinand of Naples. From this refuge he excommunicated every one of his subjects in the Papal States, who, in the meantime, had deposed him from temporal power and declared a republic with Mazzini at its head.

All Italy north of Naples was now divided between the Republicans, led by Mazzini, the moderate Liberals, under the leadership of Gino Capponi, and the Democrats, whose leader was Urbano Rattazzi, but it became clear that Italian liberation and unification could come only from the House of Piedmont, because all the other petty monarchs were treacherous or hostile to the wishes of the people. Even the disaster at Custozza had not shaken this belief, and when again the Piedmontese army met the Austrians at Novara in 1849, to be decisively defeated, the hope of everyone continued to be placed on Piedmont for ultimate deliverance.

Charles Albert, a sick and disappointed man, now

abdicated, to die shortly afterwards at Oporto, and become a national hero, around whose memory all parties fighting for freedom joined as one. He was succeeded by the Duke of Savoy, who became Victor Emmanuel II (1849–1878), and, as the son of the unsuccessful liberator, he dedicated himself to bring to fruition the enterprise for which his father gave his throne and his life. The final act of this bloodstained drama centred in Rome, still held by the Republicans, against which city converged the troops of France, Naples, Spain and Austria intent on re-establishing the Pope over his former domains. In spite of spirited resistance led by Garibaldi, the city, after a siege of four weeks, capitulated, when he and his 4000 irregular troops, along with Mazzini, escaped; but a year elapsed before the Pope felt it was sufficiently safe to return. Then, for the next twenty years, tyranny, persecution, exile and bloodshed were the lot of his subjects.

The fall of Rome (1849) brought the Revolution to an end, Austrian troops occupying all northern Italy, while, from Naples southwards to Sicily, Ferdinand, urged on by the Pope, terrorised his people into silence with the help of Swiss mercenaries, his many loathsome dungeons becoming the graves of the most enlightened people then existing in Europe. Then it was (1851) that Gladstone visited Naples, to be so shocked by the many abominations taking place there that he renounced his reactionary Tory principles, to become the most outstanding of all Britain's Liberal statesmen.

Only Venice still held out, to suffer from siege, fire and bombardment, but famine and disease so reduced the population that eventually it also had to capitulate. Thus did the Holy Alliance, "in the name of the most Holy and Indivisible Trinity, and in accordance with the principles of the Christian religion", triumph in Italy as elsewhere in Europe. Everywhere liberty, justice and righteousness were suppressed and evil unashamed was crowned as King, nearly 500,000 victims, as detailed in the early part of this section, being imprisoned, exiled or slain in their attempt to secure justice, education, parliamentary representation and a fuller, freer, better way of life for the ordinary individual.

Only Piedmont remained free, to become the base for future operations designed to unite and liberate Italy, a story which will be told in the next chapter, as here we must consider another phase of this everlasting fight for freedom, and one which had a marked bearing on the future of Europe. Now we come to the time when the causes were becoming evident which produced such terrible effects in the first half of the 20th century. Here indeed we see the two roads clearly marked, the right one so nearly taken but, after much hesitation, the wrong one followed, to lead in our time to the tragedies, destruction, suffering and misery unequalled in any other period of history.

The revolutionary movement, which was sweeping through Europe like a tornado in the year 1848, did not pass by Prussia and the different German states, but what then happened will be better understood if we go back some years. The Congress of Vienna brought into being new petty kingdoms and grand duchies, while Prussia was enlarged, but no attempt was made to form a united Germany, though the people were prepared for new and far-reaching changes in this direction, and in the constitutions of the different states.

The jealousies of Austria and Prussia, and the hostility of the petty princes, prevented the popular policy from being carried out, and, instead of the desired union of all the states into one united nation taking place, a confederation of thirty-nine states emerged, each one being independent with regard to its internal affairs. A permanent Diet was, however, formed, presided over by an Austrian plenipotentiary, which sat at Frankfurt to settle all disputes between the various states, they agreeing never to make war on each other or to form alliances which would be injurious to the states collectively or individually.

The far-reaching effects of the French Revolution had, however, kindled in the minds of the people the desire for changes much more drastic than the Congress of Vienna proposed, as developing mind had reached the stage when the common demand was not only unity, but freedom, justice and progress. The time had come for the people to have a voice in their own government, the day of the autocratic monarch having gone, while the removal of the injustices of the past were long overdue. In those days the prestige of the despotic sovereign was at a low ebb, his only safety lying in the fact that all Europe was illiterate and ignorant, and to retain his power he must keep it so or perish.

So the monarchs of Europe appealed to the emotions of their subjects, proclaiming that what had gone on in the past was the will of God, who had decreed that the people must be subservient to their masters, and that the truly Christian State was the one in which the king commanded and the people obeyed, they basing this opinion on the verse "Obey them that have the rule over you, and submit yourselves." (*Hebrews* xiii, 17.) To do otherwise, they declared, was to flout revealed religion, and act directly contrary to the dictates of the Christian faith.

Up to now Christendom had been ruled by Biblical texts which the people believed had been written directly by God from heaven, and if intelligence had not increased we would still be in the Dark Ages. Fortunately Voltaire, and other French heretics, had exposed this false claim, and the people in Germany were timidly emerging from this form of Bible worship, the influence of the French during the Napoleonic occupation having introduced them to a wider outlook. Consequently from 1815 onwards there was constant unrest, to end in revolution in 1830 when Brunswick, Hanover, Saxony and Hesse-Kassel received constitutional government, while elsewhere greater freedom was given to the Press.

The coming of the reactionary Ernest Augustus, who succeeded William IV of Great Britain to the throne of Hanover, brought about the abolition there of the new constitution in 1837, but, with the accession of Frederick William IV (1840–1861) to the throne of Prussia, the hopes of German Liberals were reawakened, as he was known to be a thoughtful and cultured prince. His reign began well by him pardoning heretical and political prisoners, and restoring deposed professors to their former posts. Unfortunately the autocratic power which this vain and unstable monarch enjoyed altered his former outlook, and he became more and more reactionary under the belief that he reigned by divine authority. When therefore he announced that Prussia was in future to be governed as "a Christian State, based on the principles of the Christian religion", all hope of better times was shattered.

Within a few years his "Christian State" was a bastion of tyranny, when injustice was rampant, and arbitrary imprisonment was inflicted on all expressing enlightened opinions. Schoolmasters, judges and politicians followed one another in melancholy succession to confinement, no one being safe from the ever watchful secret police. Similar conditions now existed everywhere throughout Germany, and the hostility of the people towards their rulers was at fever heat. So much was this so that reactionary ministers everywhere were violently confronted by the outraged people, who were led by revolutionaries whose influence over them steadily increased.

In so many threatening forms did the rising temper of the Prussian people reveal itself that in 1847 the King summoned a representative Diet to meet in Berlin. With excessive moderation, and in all humbleness and servility, it expressed the popular feeling, to which Frederick William replied that he would never abate the rights which he as God's lawful prince enjoyed. His words were: "According to the law of God and the country, the Crown must reign according to its free decision and not according to the will of majorities." He thereupon dissolved the Diet, to arouse intense indignation and bitterness amongst his subjects, who now regarded the monarchy with loathing and contempt. This tyrannical action on the part of the King acted as the spark which set alight the European Revolution of 1848, the flames first catching hold in France, to bring about the downfall of Louis Philippe.

No longer was any trust put in princes, and at no time was monarchical government so discredited. In despair of any reform coming from this quarter, the cry arose that "the people must save themselves", and a convention was held at Mannheim in 1848, when four demands were formulated: (1) freedom of the Press, (2) trial by jury, (3) a national army, and (4) national representation, which four essentials were adopted as the Liberal party's programme. Within a few days the popular excitement became so intense that when word came that the reactionary Metternich had been deposed in Vienna every small German prince took fright, and appointed Liberal ministers in place of the old diehards.

In Berlin occurred scenes of great violence, which forced the King to announce that the Diet would be recalled and could meet periodically, when a constitution would be framed to meet the popular demand. No one believed him, and only after the troops and the people had been in conflict did he lay aside his divine pretensions and appoint new ministers with Liberal opinions. Peace was now restored, some progressive measures were enacted, and arrangements were made for the election of a national assembly.

The cleansing tide of liberal thought was sweeping over antiquated ideas and age-old traditions. Many questions of reform were agitating the minds of the German people, but there was a general conviction that the new day would not dawn until all the different states were united into one nation. Consequently the movement for a united Germany proceeded along with the reform movement, to end in a number of deputies, belonging to different legislative assemblies throughout the land, meeting at Heidelberg. From this gathering came an invitation to all who were, or had been, members of Diets, to meet at Frankfurt for the purpose of considering the most important problems then confronting the German people.

About 500 accepted the invitation, and these became a preliminary assembly which made preparations for the election of a national Parliament which would be composed of elected members, each of which would represent 50,000 inhabitants, every adult to have a vote. In spite of many difficulties being put in their way by the German kings and princes, the Parliament was elected and met· at Frankfurt If only its members had acted with courage and promptitude, their prestige would have been sufficient to enable them to overcome the numerous difficulties and obstructions ahead, but this was just what they did not do.

These representatives came from the best that Germany could provide, but they were without parliamentary experience, and, moreover, there was no clear-cut programme for them to accept or reject. Consequently everyone had a different opinion as to how to proceed, and, though there was much learned talk by professors, journalists and other leaders of public opinion, no legislative progress took place. Because of this feelings began to run high, and the ignorant electors, who expected immediate reforms, became impatient, but, as general agreement could not be reached as to how the united Germany was to be governed, we can understand why the question of pressing reforms was never considered.

Eventually it was agreed by a large majority to appoint the Archduke John of Austria as Imperial Vicar, he being authorised to carry on the government for the time being by means of a Cabinet appointed by himself. Unfortunately, after this was carried into effect, a discussion arose on certain fundamental laws which made clear the fact that the members could not agree on the wording of the new constitution, some being in favour of a republic and others of a constitutional monarchy. These two parties attacked each other with such vehemence and animosity that within a few weeks the people feared that the new Parliament was quite incapable of settling their first and most important problem.

Finally the Frankfurt Parliament succeeded in formulating the fundamental laws, after which the principal clauses in the constitution were discussed. Then the difficult question arose on the subject of Austria, the general wish being that her German-speaking inhabitants be included in the new German state, there being no desire to include the non-Germans and so make a quite unmanageable empire. Austria, on the other hand, would not consent to become a German state and renounce her empire, especially as she had just quelled the revolt in Vienna and had again tightened her stranglehold on her subject nations. Moreover, Count Schwarzenberg, the strong and ardent patriot, who had succeeded the reactionary Metternich, was convinced that Austria, and not Prussia, was the divinely appointed leader of the German people.

Bitter strife now broke out in the German Parliament, some favouring Austrian predominance, while others looked to Prussia to lead the German people to the unity, contentment and prosperity all desired. Ultimately the majority in favour of Prussia carried their proposal against the wishes of Austria and Bavaria. Frederick William IV of Prussia was now chosen as German Emperor, an office which was to be hereditary, but, fearing to offend Austria, he refused this tempting offer, and thus gave the death-blow to all the aspirations for a united Germany under one sovereign. This decision consequently meant that unity was not to be achieved by agreement, but twenty years later through Bismarck's policy of Blood and Iron.

Behind the King of Prussia's refusal there was another reason which in those days was all-important. In the middle of the 19th century the people generally were still uneducated, crude, rough and steeped in theological superstition, and Frederick William, like all monarchs before him, looked upon them as no better than ignorant children who must do as they were told. He believed that only the nobles could elect the sovereign, who received his crown from God through them, and consequently he rudely remarked to the deputation which offered him the imperial throne that to accept his authority from the people's Assembly would be like "picking his crown out of the gutter".

Lacking a crowned head, there was now not much hope of securing a united Germany. Consequently a violent agitation arose throughout the land for the democratic constitution produced by the Frankfurt Parliament being adopted by each individual state, so as to give the people a say in their own affairs. Armed mobs paraded the streets everywhere and terrorised their governments and rulers, when an event happened which entirely changed the position. Austria and Prussia withdrew their representatives from the Frankfurt Parliament, and this was followed by the resignation of most of its members. This unfortunate end to a noble effort gave the rulers their opportunity, and they once more took control, their armed forces bringing back law and order to a distracted land.

Looking back, we can clearly realise how foolish was Frederick William to pass by the golden opportunity which was within his grasp—to unite all Germany under an imperial throne. If he had taken this occasion to consolidate the numerous German states, the history of the next hundred years might have been entirely different, because Germany was then ripe for a democratic constitution. At a later date he realised his mistake, when he proposed a similar scheme, which was termed "The Union", but Austria, by that time, had quelled her internal disturbances and was again in the position to take up the role of leader of the German states. Her influence disrupted the Union, and then she invited the different states (1850) to send representatives to Frankfurt to consider the re-establishment of the national Parliament.

Germany was now divided into two camps, namely those states which remained in the Union, under the lead of Prussia, and those who joined Austria in the revived Frankfurt Parliament, a state of affairs which nearly led to civil war over a dispute relating to Hesse-Kassel. In this small state her ruler, termed the Elector, had abolished the democratic constitution, an action which brought about a state of anarchy. Austria supported the Elector, and Prussia the rebels who were fighting for their constitution, the troops of the former occupying Hesse and those of the latter Kassel, but Prussia shirked a fight and yielded to everything Count Schwarzenberg, the Austrian dictator, demanded, including the dissolution of the Union.

Austria had now the supreme power in Germany, but everything she did from this time onwards was opposed by Prussia, who was becoming more powerful each year as her trade and wealth increased, and in this unfriendly atmosphere the Frankfurt Parliament continued its deliberations. War against Denmark over her claim to the provinces of Schleswig-Holstein, however, again brought Prussia and Austria together. When peace came in 1852 they agreed on the conditions imposed on Denmark, requiring her to do equal justice to the German and Danish populations, and give each province a separate minister. Later a conference met in London which decided that these two provinces be indissolubly united to Denmark, to which both Austria and Prussia agreed.

This minor war with Denmark was but an interlude in the much greater conflict for liberty and justice demanded by the German people. The movement for democratic government, from which so much had been hoped, had so nearly reached its goal, only, in the final phase, to be flung back by Austria, now the dominating power, whose influence was all against progress and reform. Her imperial policy was despotic to a degree, her influence over Germany being equally reactionary, so much so that Frederick William was able to curb the Prussian Parliament sufficiently to reduce to a minimum the power of its representatives, and thus increase that of the King.

The Liberal Ministry elected in 1848 was dismissed, the freedom of the Press abolished, and anyone who uttered a complaint was rushed to prison. The smaller states followed with alacrity in the steps of Prussia, the Liberal ministries which had been established being abolished, and the new constitutions torn up. If the battle for freedom had been fairly fought the people would have triumphed, but the Frankfurt Parliament became a fiasco and revealed the unfortunate fact that the Germans were unripe for democratic government, they fearing their rulers so intensely that they would never act seriously against them. So the members of the Frankfurt Parliament disgraced their new institution by allowing it to be dominated by the monarchs and not by the people, the federal army, with its sanction, being used to quell all those who arose against the revival of the old tyranny it had been elected to abolish for evermore.

Martial law was everywhere proclaimed, and all officials who had shown liberal tendencies were dismissed, they being so penalised that thousands, unable to find employment at home, had to emigrate. The misery that followed from the persecution of all having democratic ideas is difficult to exaggerate. Germany was again under the old despotism which her people had tried so hard to remove, but, with the army under the Sovereign's control, and always loyal to the throne, their ability to right their wrongs was limited, whereas in Britain, with no standing army, the King had not the power to terrorise his subjects. Democracy has developed in Britain since the 17th century because she is an island, and did not require to keep a conscript army for the purpose of defence, a force which on the Continent was also used by the monarch to maintain his despotic authority.

After the different unsuccessful attempts of the German people to secure democratic government, it is strange that when they obtained it in 1919, following the First World War, they did not hold on to it as something too precious to lose. Only people quite lacking in the art of representative government, and completely subservient to autocratic rule, would have then changed their republic for a maniac like Hitler, who, immediately his dupes gave him complete power, tied them up again as firmly as did ever their most despotic rulers in the past. Truly the people get the government for which they are best fitted, and the Germans have clearly revealed to all the world that they completely lack the capacity of self-government, being politically no better than children who require an autocrat to tell them what to do.

Consequently, from 1850 onwards, Germany lost by emigration or imprisonment many of the most enlightened minds she possessed. Instead of men arising, as they did in Britain and America, to lead the people into the green pastures of intellectual freedom, justice, righteousness and representative government, her political leaders were men imbued with reactionary opinions. Liberty and freedom ceased to be cherished in Germany, and, from now onwards, her people adopted a political ideology founded upon the debased teaching of Georg Hegel, one which eventually led them into a morass, out of which it will take them generations to crawl.

(5) INDEPENDENT REPUBLICS ARISE IN AMERICA.

The history of Christian domination over the native populations of both North and South America is one of the most appalling records of crime, cruelty and injustice in the annals of mankind. Nevertheless we constantly hear from the lips of ignorance, the never-ending claim that Christianity brought light into heathen darkness, it being the first and only religion to recognise the dignity of man. Continually this old parrot-cry is to be heard on the radio and in the churches, besides continually appearing in books and the newspapers.

The ruin, degradation and misery which Christian civilisation brought upon the native population of both North and South America is impossible to express in words. When millions suffer, how inadequate words become, and nothing that can here be written will encompass the sum of human misery which the Christian occupation of America brought to mankind. In early life Columbus had been familiar with the slave trade, and he carried with him to the lands which he discovered the command of the Christian god:—

And ye shall take them as an inheritance for your children after you, to inherit them for a possession; they shall be your bondmen for ever. (*Leviticus* xxv, 46.)

Columbus considered that all the natives—or the heathen, as Christians prefer to call them—together with all their lands, were now the absolute property of the Spanish sovereign, who could order and dispose of them as he, and his agents, thought fit. Nevertheless Columbus only acted on what was the recognised method of those days, and what he did towards the natives was done by all the Europeans who descended upon the new-found world.

The Spanish government gave him and his followers the land which belonged to the natives, including all the inhabitants who were to be found living thereon, to do with them as they pleased. Besides getting their lands and their labour free the Spaniards commenced to Christianise the "damned heathen", but their cruelty towards them was so brutal that we are told by Las Casas, who did what he could to protect the natives, that they shunned their masters "as naturally as the bird shuns the hawk".

The natives, when captured, were passed on to Spanish masters with only one condition, that they be instructed in the Holy Christian faith, and it became the regular custom for King Ferdinand of Spain to reward his friends and well-wishers at home with grants of land in America, and all the natives they required. The popes and cardinals amassed great wealth from these new-found lands, but, besides the Church, thousands of Spaniards received payment for their services to king and country in this fashion, and, with their newly acquired wealth, they set to work by every possible kind of brutality to extract the utmost from their slaves.

Under these conditions the natives died off in

such rapidity that labour became scarce. Consequently negroes, on the advice of Las Casas, who was
anxious to preserve the natives from being exterminated, were then imported from Africa, and so began
the negro slave trade to America which continued until
the middle of the 19th century. Many parts of Mexico
were depopulated, a report addressed to Ferdinand
of Spain, dealing with the devastations of Cortes
and his Spanish soldiers, stating that "nothing is now
remaining but the sites" of the towns and villages. In
Peru an eye-witness of the times asserted that "one half,
or two thirds, of the natives and their cattle have been
destroyed". So far only the coastal regions had been
occupied, the conquerors not yet having penetrated
into the interior, but wherever they settled the same
desolation occurred, in fact the Christian settlement
of South America was even more devastating than a
plague, and it is estimated that 12,000,000 perished.

The Spanish government, now alarmed at the
depopulation of its colonies, made efforts to curb the
brutality of its citizens. Enslavement was forbidden,
but to no effect, as the reply came back from the
settlers that the land and its inhabitants had been given
to them by the King to do with as they pleased, and
that these privileges could not now be withdrawn. To
this the King agreed, and annulled the law against
slavery, thus making it legal, and this continued until
last century, though the Spanish government tried to
improve the lot of the natives whenever opportunity
offered. From afar it realised the appalling calamity
which had befallen these simple creatures in being
forced into a way of life entirely unnatural to them,
and for which they had not the stamina to endure.

The early English, French and Dutch colonists discovered and occupied most of North America, but there they could not find sufficient labour, the conditions in the north being quite different from those in the south. The Red Indians, as they were called, were comparatively small in number, and lived on the animals they could kill. Being nomads, they were not so easily captured, and, though many escaped the experiences of the inhabitants farther south, those who were captured were enslaved and often cruelly treated. The white man, however, did not have it all his own way, as, if he travelled any distance from his fortified encampment, he was set upon and slain by these roving tribes. Only slowly was it possible for the European to find security, by driving these nomadic warriors farther and farther into the interior and erecting defences against their depredations.

As native labour could not be secured in sufficient quantity, negroes were shipped over from Africa. A shipmaster named John Lok was the first (1557) to capture five negroes, whom he brought to London. From being trusted by the African natives, the British were now feared, but that did not prevent expeditions setting out to capture them for transportation to America. Sir John Hawkins, in 1562, was the pioneer in this traffic, his first catch being 300 negroes, whom he sold, we are told, at great profit in St. Domingo. This profitable transaction in human beings resounded throughout England as if a gold-mine had been discovered, and companies were formed for the development of this new-found wealth, Queen Elizabeth, and her nobles and clergy, being amongst those who took shares in the undertakings.

Hawkins's next raid yielded him 500 negroes, and on the voyage with them to the West Indies he was becalmed. He had decided to throw his human cargo overboard when wind came, or, as he put it in his diary, "Almighty God, who never suffers his elect to perish", brought him, his ship and her cargo safely to port without the loss of a man. Again he sold his catch at great profit, returned to England, and divided his ill-gotten gains amongst the shareholders. Thus was the slave trade established, to grow to enormous dimensions, because a large proportion of the slaves never reached their destinations. Very many succumbed from the terrible treatment they received and the revolting way they were packed together on board the slave galleys.

For three hundred years Spain governed the rich possessions she had so easily won, but, though thousands had emigrated from Europe, the native population of her territories at the beginning of the 19th century was less than it was when these lands were first discovered. Out of a total population of 16,000,000, 2,000,000 were Spanish, the remainder being natives, negroes and mixed breeds, and all were ruled by nine distinct governments under Viceroys or Captain-generals. Spanish rule was selfish and short-sighted, the aim being to squeeze all it could out of the land administered. Her colonial governors were sent to America for that purpose, the only qualification demanded being that these agents were Christians, and that they came of Christian ancestors.

This was necessary, as otherwise the unorthodox might have been inclined to consider the welfare of the colonies and natives first and the motherland last, but seldom did her well-trained agents depart from their instructions, or disappoint the hungry vampire at home, for ever sucking dry the life-blood of her vast American empire. No Spaniard in this empire, outside the official class sent out from Spain, had any share in the government of the land which was now his home. Many had now amassed great wealth and lived in luxury, but all were quite indifferent to political and social matters, as in those they had no say. None did better for themselves than the priests, who were powerful, numerous and rich, with great influence over the superstitious people, their systematic policy being to keep everyone ignorant from the richest down to the poorest.

Only books on Christian devotion were allowed to be printed or imported, and not even books on geometry, chemistry or botany were sanctioned. No schools of any kind existed, and no one was allowed to go abroad to be educated. By such means the priests kept the people servile, and frightened them into parting with a large share of the proceeds from their toil.

Documents discovered last century depict acts of extortion, perfidy, cruelty and oppression practised by the priests on the people which have rarely ever been paralleled. The natives were the principal victims of this tyranny, they being treated as only beasts of burden, to be ground down until they expired. Truly the discovery of America proved a fabulously rich gold-mine to the Church, and one which it worked thoroughly to its own immense enrichment, as did also the Spanish kings and ruling classes. They likewise enriched themselves handsomely from the labour of their subjects, who were obliged to trade only with Spain.

On the rich plains of South America cattle grew and multiplied, to become a source of great wealth. Precious metals and minerals were found in abundance, and these, with the crops gathered from the plantations, produced a large export trade. Spain, in 1809, took from her colonies £18,000,000 sterling and sent back only £15,000,000 in exchange, from which figures it will be seen how profitable these possessions had become.

The American War of Independence, and the French Revolution, were not without their effect on these prosperous Spanish colonists, who now began to wonder why all these millions should go into the treasury of a corrupt government at home. A revolt in Peru (1780) was the first warning of things to come, but it was suppressed, its leader being compelled to witness the death of his wife and children at the stake, after which he was torn to pieces by wild horses in the square of Lima, its capital. Nothing was done to remove the grievances from which the people suffered, and for thirty years discontent increased. How long this state of affairs would have continued had Napoleon not cast his covetous eyes on these rich domains who can say, but in 1808 an event happened which changed everything.

When Napoleon placed his brother Joseph on the throne of Spain, and made her a dependency of France, the colonists refused to transfer their allegiance to the new king, whom they unanimously rejected. Without a king, and now free for the first time from Spanish domination, they set up for themselves provisional governments. These later developed into independent republics, when Spain declared that she had no intention of instituting reforms or lightening the burdens of her colonies. Then followed a long and costly war which ended in her utter defeat in 1824, after fourteen years of bloody fighting.

The war commenced when seven of the northern provinces united in 1810, to become the Confederation of Venezuela, their first act being to dispatch home the Spanish governor and his staff. An earthquake now destroyed several towns, and killed 20,000 people, an event which the priests declared was a judgment from God for throwing off the Spanish yoke. So the stupid deluded people turned on their new government, whose leader, Miranda, was captured. They allowed him to perish in a dungeon, but he left behind him Simon Bolivar (1783–1830), who was to become the liberator of Spanish America. In the war of liberation his love of liberty was the animating impulse of his life, but his savagery caused many ruthless massacres and bloody deeds.

For the first ten years Spain continued her effort to reconquer her empire, the fight centring in the north against Venezuela, whose inhabitants had recovered from the effects of the earthquake to fight again for their liberty. No quarter was given on either side, and Bolivar declared that the "cursed race of Spaniards" must be destroyed. Those of his soldiers who collected the most Spanish heads were made officers, and there was no discrimination, as all heads were welcomed, quite irrespective of sex and age.

Thus again we see the same pitiless cruelty which follows after centuries of oppression, the Spaniards suffering in South America just as did the French aristocracy during the Reign of Terror when the down-trodden masses secured power.

Bolivar, reinforced by veterans disbanded after the overthrow of Napoleon, was able to press hard against the Royalists, and at Carabobo (1821), with the help of 6000 British, he decisively defeated his enemy and secured the liberation of Venezuela. The revolutionary movement, with British military and naval help, had by now spread to all the Spanish possessions, Mexico also gaining her independence in 1821, and Peru and Guatemala two years later. One by one the different provinces secured their freedom, the combined forces of Chili and Buenos Aires finally defeating the Spaniards at Maypu in 1818, though fighting continued until 1824. This year marked the end of the war for independence, only Cuba and Porto Rico remaining under Spanish rule. So it came about that Britain, by the help she gave to the Spanish colonies in their struggle for freedom, had her revenge on Spain for the help she gave to the American colonists in their war for independence.

Brazil, it will be remembered, was given by the dissolute Pope Alexander VI to Portugal in 1493. The Holy Father not only claimed the right to dispose of all the lands inhabited by the heathen as he pleased, but, in addition, he pardoned the sins of all Christians who died while engaged in their exploration. Consequently, when giving to Spain all the rest of North and South America, outside of Brazil, he absolved all Spanish wrongdoers who were then devoting their lives to enslaving and plundering the heathen. This perhaps explains why both the Spanish and Portuguese unleashed all the cruelty within them upon the helpless natives whose destination they thought was hell. Such was the curse which came upon the world when Christianity arose, because it divided the human race between the saved Christians and the damned heathen. This state of affairs never had such terrible results in earlier times, when the gods were worshipped because, under different names, they were accepted by all mankind.

So Portugal secured a large portion of the earth's surface, a hundred times as large as herself, and for three hundred years this small European state controlled this vast territory. The French and the Dutch tried to secure thereon a firm foothold, but in the end they were driven out. Gradually the interior was explored and developed, while on the coast large settlements sprang up as immigration increased. Coffee became Brazil's principal product, the surplus being sent to Europe, but her government was bad, insurrections occurred, one province fighting another, and she had her full share of the miseries which always come from ignorance.

Nevertheless commerce, though hindered by these conflicts, developed, until the time came when her inhabitants began to wonder why a country almost as large as Europe should remain dependent on an insignificant country like Portugal. The American War of Independence and the French Revolution exerted a considerable influence in their outlook, but not until Napoleon overthrew the royal house of Braganza in 1807 did a change occur. Then, as the bedraggled

French army, numbering only 1500, entered Lisbon, without encountering any resistance from a Portuguese army of 14,000, the royal family, and many officials and nobles, fled to Brazil, which now became a kingdom united to Portugal under the same crown.

The next step in this strange story was the demand of the Portuguese for their king to return home, and this he did in 1821, leaving his son and heir in Brazil to act as his regent. The Brazilians resented the King's departure, and the Prince Regent in 1822 was proclaimed Emperor of Brazil, thus bringing the union of the two states to an end. Constitutional government was set up, but, as the Emperor was not sufficiently liberal to satisfy his people, he resigned after a reign of nine years, during which time he became more and more unpopular.

He was succeeded by his five-year-old son Dom Pedro II (1831–1891), who reigned for fifty-eight years. Pedro II and his empress were held in the highest veneration and respect by their subjects, but two years before his death he was forced to abdicate. He was a model constitutional monarch, but preferred literature to legislation, and this impaired his position, which was already weakened by the desire for a republic. Slavery continued to be legal in Brazil until 1871, but only gradually did it die out, because in 1882 1,000,000 out of the former 2,500,000 slaves were still in bondage.

The vast wealth of Brazil, and her great size, are hardly yet realised, but both she, and the immense continent of which she forms a part, have already exercised an important role in human history. One third of the surface of the earth, which was unknown to all except its own inhabitants until four hundred years ago, is now yielding increasing wealth year by year for the greater wellbeing of mankind. In the centuries before Columbus, lay countless years of poverty and destitution, but to us today, looking back, he now appears as the herald of a new era in which, as the centuries pass, both North and South America are destined to play an ever greater part.

(6) The United States Grows Rich on Slave Labour.

After the War of Independence the United States enjoyed thirty years of peace, except for continual clashes with the native Indians, who generally got the worst of the encounters. The whites showed no mercy towards the natives, whose lands they took as they moved west, and the most appalling massacres and cruelties were inflicted on innocent men, women and children who had been deprived of the land on which they grew their grain. The story of the exploration of the unknown lands stretching westward towards the Pacific is one of cruelty and suffering, combined with great heroism, endurance and enterprise.

Under the lead of James Madison and Alexander Hamilton the different states produced a constitution in 1787 which was to be administered by two chambers, one in which the states were represented according to their population, and a Senate where they were equally represented. Over all was a President chosen for a term of four years. Each state was responsible for its own local government, such as police, schools and roads, the federal government having charge of the Post Office, coinage, army, navy and foreign policy.

George Washington (1789–1797) became the first President of the new republic, which position he held for eight years, greatly aided by the brilliant financial and administrative gifts of Alexander Hamilton, who became Secretary of the Treasury. Two years after Washington's retirement he died (1799) in his sixty-eighth year, to be greatly mourned, his memory being much esteemed. During his term of office the country passed from a state of chaos to one of settled constitutional government, and each year, with a steady flow of immigration adding to its population, it consolidated the new democratic way of life which increased intelligence, the world over, will some day put in place of the old despotism caused by ignorance.

Then followed as president three men who had taken a prominent part in the creation of the republic, John Adams (1797–1801), Thomas Jefferson (1801–1809)[1] and James Madison (1809–1817). They it was who guided the nation along the path of liberal democracy, freed from domination by either Church or King, both institutions to them being in every way hateful. Moreover, the tyranny from which the people had suffered under British rule left bitter feelings towards their kith and kin in Britain, but towards the French, who had helped them in their time of trial, cordial relations existed. As regards Napoleon, America was a passive spectator, and for six years gained greatly by supplying Europe with the

---

[1] The great work of liberation done by Jefferson, the author of the Declaration of Independence, that the people might enjoy "Life, Liberty and the Pursuit of Happiness", is remembered by a magnificent marble memorial in Washington, designed after the Roman Pantheon.

commodities Europeans required either to destroy each other or maintain existence. Then the position changed to her disadvantage, to bring about ruination and much distress.

When Britain decreed (1806) that the coasts of Europe be blockaded by her fleet, and that all vessels would be seized which tried to enter a European port, American opinion took great offence, only to be heightened by the British attitude towards the sailors on American ships. America held the view that anyone could change his nationality, but this Britain denied. To become safe from the British Press Gang, which boarded British merchant vessels and siezed the men to make them fight in her warships, many British seamen became American citizens and found employment in American ships. America claimed them as her citizens, while Britain held that they were still British, and boarded American vessels to carry them off. Six thousand men, who claimed American citizenship, were thus enslaved by the British government, according to the American estimate, and the time came when, to have her grievances put right, she set a ban on all ships sailing to Europe.

For four years this state of affairs lasted, cotton, tobacco, grain and timber accumulating at the American ports, thousands being thus rendered idle. Hatred towards Britain increased, and, when negotiations for a settlement failed, America declared war on Britain (1812), thinking that as her hands were full with affairs in Europe she could be forced into agreeing to America's demands. The same month in which war was declared, Napoleon started on his disastrous Russian adventure, and the British were driving the French out of Spain. Britain, moreover, had now 1000 warships against 20 owned by America, and 1,000,000 men in her army against the American army of 24,000.

Britain now repealed the blockade decrees, but maintained the right to search ships bound for Europe. As this would not satisfy America the war took its course, first by America invading Canada, with disastrous results, her army being forced to surrender in Fort Detroit. A second invasion had similar results, but at sea she was more successful, her ships attacking single British ships wherever they were found, five being thus destroyed. Britain was much depressed by these incidents, and not until the U.S.A. *Chesapeake* was destroyed by the *Shannon* off Boston in 1813 did she feel avenged and again secure.

So ships went on being destroyed, and men killed each other who had no personal quarrel one with another. Many were wounded and lived out the rest of their cheerless lives in suffering and want, all because some men in Washington and London could not agree on questions about which the victims had no say whatever. Then came the overthrow of Napoleon in 1814, which enabled Britain to send some regiments, comprising 3500 men, to America for the purpose of attacking Washington, defended by 7000 men, this being all that the Americans could muster. The hardy British veterans defeated their untrained foe without difficulty, entered Washington, destroyed the Capitol, the President's residence, the government offices, the navy yard, the arsenal, and the bridge over the Potomac River, after which they withdrew to the coast.

America was now tiring of the struggle, her large export trade had shrunk by nine tenths, her taxation was oppressive, and two thirds of her traders were bankrupt. The British proposed peace, to which America agreed (1814), but before this became known the British, 6000 strong, had attacked New Orleans without success, to lose 2000 men against an American loss of only 14 killed and wounded. As peace had been signed seven weeks earlier at Ghent in Belgium, all this slaughter availed nothing, in fact the war achieved nothing except destruction and misery.

The United States, when she threw off British rule, had a population of 3,000,000. In 1826 it numbered 12,000,000, and the thirteen states had increased to twenty-four. By now there were eight flourishing universities, and many states had made education compulsory, while literature poured out of the printing presses, first set up in 1639. Louisiana, a vast tract of more than 1,000,000 square miles, which Napoleon had stolen from Spain, was now in American possession, he having sold it to the United States to obtain more money to carry on his war in Europe. Florida had been ceded to America by Spain, and large tracts, with their native inhabitants, had been annexed to the Republic.

Her territory now extended from the Gulf of Mexico to the Canadian lakes, and from the Atlantic to the Rockies. Canals, joining the great lakes with the Hudson river, had been constructed and were now bringing grain from the interior to the coastal regions. Extensive factories were producing goods for home consumption and export, while the National Debt was being rapidly reduced. Millions of acres of rich land awaited cultivation. Everywhere there was expansion and abundance, besides a boundless faith in the future, a confidence which has been fully realised, though not without interruptions which could have been avoided by knowledge and wisdom.

Cotton, more than any other staple product, has brought great wealth to the Americans. This two-foot-high plant, studded with pods somewhat larger than a walnut, and each containing a soft white fibre in which the seeds of the plant are embedded, has revolutionised the life of mankind. The cotton plant was known to the Romans, and it was also grown in India from a remote period, but never appreciated, because linen made from flax was in much greater use. Its value was recognised only when the discovery was made that it grew luxuriantly in the southern states of North America, its popularity increasing after Arkwright invented his spinning machine in 1768 and Watt perfected the steam engine. Both these inventions greatly increased the use of cotton, but the supply was limited until the seeds which stuck to the cotton could be removed more rapidly.

Eli Whitney, when quite a youth, set his mind to solve the cotton planters' difficulties, and, by his invention of the cotton gin (1792), he produced a machine which removed the seeds hundreds of times more quickly than human hands could do. That made cotton production on a large scale possible, as it could now be sold cheaply enough for all to use. This young American, by his genius, opened up a new era for his country and the world, but how few even know his name—the glamour of conquerors, the destroyers of property and happiness, who drive men to their doom, appealing more to the multitude, who prefer to read about something exciting which becomes increasingly fascinating the more the ethical code is broken.

When the American colonies gained their independence slavery was the common custom, no state being an exception. The Puritans saw nothing wrong in holding a man in bondage, because their god had not only instructed the Hebrews, his chosen people, to enslave their captives, but had laid down cruel and pitiless laws to which all slaves were to be subject. The Indians were the first slaves, and then came the African captives. The land and climate of the southern states was more suitable for negro labour than that of the north, so much so that at the opening of the 19th century there were 500,000 slaves in the south and only 40,000 in the north. The cultivation of rice, tobacco and cotton was the work which the unintelligent African was best suited to perform, and the plantation owners were always willing to purchase from the slave dealers all the negroes they could catch.

Some masters treated them kindly, others harshly, but, as it was a cruel age, many of the unfortunate creatures, who had been dragged from their land and homes, suffered great misery. All this suffering passed unnoticed, as the Christians of those days seemed to have been quite devoid of pity or humanity. Otherwise we cannot explain how John Newton (1725–1807), the master of a slave galley, and author of *"How sweet the name of Jesus sounds in a believer's ear"*, and other well-known hymns, could have written that he "never knew sweeter or more frequent hours of divine communion than on his last two voyages as a slave dealer in Guiana".

One hundred years later the Reverend Samuel
Seabury, D.D., published in 1861 *American Slavery
Justified by the Law of Nature,* a book of 316 pages,
written to prove that slavery is morally and socially
right, and justified by *The Holy Bible,* the author concluding by invoking the benediction of Almighty
God on all true Christian believers. His opinions
were shared by the clergy of the Episcopalian, Metho-
dist and Presbyterian sects of the southern states, who
published about the same time their unanimous opinion
that slavery was justified by the Christian religion.

The invention of the cotton gin, and the purchase
of Louisiana, with its vast tract of the most fertile
land in the world for growing cotton, increased
enormously the demand for slaves, so much so that
importations from Africa could not meet the demand.
Kentucky and Virginia consequently turned their
attention to the breeding of slaves, exporting an average of 23,500 each year to the southern states over a
period of ten years (1840–1850), for which they
received an average price of £150 for each slave.
John C. Calhoun of South Carolina was the leader of
the slave owners in Congress, and they justified every
injustice and cruelty by a text taken from the Old
Testament.[1] Ham, according to this ancient literature, was to bè the servant (slave) of his brethren.
(*Genesis* ix, 22–27.) Consequently all the descendants

---

[1] When *Uncle Tom's Cabin* was published, it was denounced from all
the pulpits of the southern states, and from some of those in the northern
states. This book gave a vivid picture of the misery of the slaves in the
United States, and the author amplified it later by publishing *The Key to
Uncle Tom's Cabin,* a book of 500 pages, with documented statements of
resolutions passed at church meetings, official assemblies, and sermons
by Christian preachers, all of which accepted the institution of slavery as
an essential part of the Christian religion.

of Ham, believed to be the negroes, were the God-given property of the white man.

So fanatical did the southerners become that no one dared to express an opinion against slavery, as to do so meant that life would be made impossible, those who were suspected of hostility being tarred, feathered and turned out of the state in which they lived. Some were shot or hanged, and others were burned alive. The southern mobs were particularly brutal, and the slave owners found many willing hands to do their work of clamping down all criticism, the clergy passing resolutions and preaching sermons in support of this mob violence, and never did the law interfere to prevent or punish these atrocities.

This was the treatment accorded the white man who championed the rights of the slave, but what must it have been like to be a black man amongst these Christian fiends in the middle of last century? The slave was regarded as a thing, and not as a person. He had no civil rights; in fact the legal ruling of the time was that the white man was in no way bound by any law, civil or divine, towards the negro. The master could do with him and his wife just as he pleased, and his children could be taken from him as a calf is taken away from the mother cow. It was a grave offence to teach a slave to read, and debates took place as to whether it was more profitable to work a slave to death, or only moderately so that he would last longer, each master acting on the principle he thought best.

A slave was flogged or tortured for any petty offence, and, if he resisted, his master could legally slay him on the spot. A slave who would not stand to be flogged could be shot, and the master was blameless if the slave died under flogging or torture; in fact the law permitted him to flog the slave to death. Any means could be taken to kill a fugitive slave, and, if the master cut out the slave's tongue, or put out his eyes, the slave had to prove the deed, but, as no slave could witness against a white man, he had no remedy. Public whipping-houses became an institution, slaves were bought and sold like cattle, and the hunting of escaped slaves developed into a regular profession, dogs being specially trained for the purpose. All slaves suspected of the intention of escaping were branded or otherwise mutilated.

The attitude of these southern Americans towards slavery was quite logical, because they believed, like all other Christians, that the Bible, which everyone those days took in the raw, so to speak, was a direct revelation from God to mankind, and they adopted Jehovah's injunctions about slaves as readily as they believed that by the death of the Son of God they were saved for all eternity. How little we have advanced in our ethical standard when the book which contains so many fiendish injunctions is still termed "Holy" by Christians! It is to be found in all the churches and is referred to as "God's Holy Word", without evoking a protest from anyone in the congregations which assemble every Sunday throughout Christendom. Little wonder that Christian civilisation has such a terrible record, when Christendom received its ethical teaching from this ancient literature, much of which was compiled by the priests of an eastern tribe composed of people who were little better than barbarians.

Jehovah, so the Israelites thought, fought for

them just as Jupiter, the Romans thought, was their strength in the day of battle. How little Christian countries have got away from these barbarous times will be better realised when we remember that the savage instructions contained in the Bible form the basis of what the German youth have been taught in our own times. When we come to the next chapter we shall discover that the German warmongers, who were responsible for all the tragedies of our time, devoutly believed that war is a divine institution, and many based their arguments on appropriate texts in the Old Testament. In this way the German people were led to believe that they had replaced the Jews as God's chosen people, and that under divine guidance they would conquer the earth.

Few there be who realise the evil effect these cruel passages have had throughout Christendom during the Christian era, since the time it was decreed in the 4th century that the Bible was to be read in the churches, and taught as the only message from God to man, all other books being burned or banned. Pythagoras, Socrates, Plato, Aristotle, Seneca, Quintilian, Epicurus, Epictetus, Zeno and the other Greek and Roman philosophers would have been shocked to have been asked to regard the Bible as their ethical standard, but it was on this book that Christians everywhere relied for their moral teaching up to last century, and many still do even today.

They scatter it, and its terrible laws and stories, far and wide, and, by means of different societies, which are supported by Christian money, it has been translated into 761 languages and dialects, many millions of free copies having been distributed all over the world.

The British and Foreign Bible Society, as an instance, reported that for the year 1943 its income was £438,000, an increase of £59,000 over the previous year, which vast sum is used to promote the distribution and reading of a book which, in the name of God, advocates war, plundering, destruction, slavery, intolerance, lying, treachery, torture, ignorance, the slaying of mediums and much else that is evil. Though the history, science and chronology of the Bible are false, and its powerful influence during the Christian era has been reactionary and bad, Dr. Temple, when Archbishop of Canterbury, described it at an annual meeting of the above society as "a foundation for world unity—and a guide to God's purpose".

That opinion is to be expected from a theologian, but, when we hear a similar expression from the lips of a British Minister of Education, we may well wonder what hope there is for the future of society. R. A. Butler, who held this responsible position, when broadcasting in one of the B.B.C. religious services on 25th October, 1942, described the Bible "as the proper heritage of children", a startling remark which envisages a disastrous end to all our hopes of a better order of society emerging out of the furnace of the Second World War. Already we have discovered, in the preceding pages of *The Curse of Ignorance*, what terrible results Bible worship has had on the morals of Christendom in the centuries gone by, when all that is evil in the Bible was seized upon to justify wickedness, while that which is good was passed over and ignored.

Both the Old and the New Testaments form the basis of the Christian religion. We cannot have one without the other, because both hang together to make up the Christian scheme of salvation. "For as in Adam all die, even so in Christ shall all be made alive" (1 *Corinthians* xv, 22) is the foundation of Christianity. Both Adam and Christ are integral parts of the whole affair, and Christians, throughout the Christian era, have, in consequence, venerated and been guided by the Old as much as by the New Testament. This is true, but what is untrue is the Christian claim that their religion was the first to preach the brotherhood of man, and recognise his rights and dignity.

This humane idea only occurred to some Christians for the first time within the past hundred years, but it was propounded more than two thousand years earlier by the Greek philosophers. Not until the middle of the 19th century did Christians cease from imprisoning and persecuting those non-Christians who tried to teach the Christians to live righteous and decent lives. Up to last century all Christians believed that they only were the saved and the elect of God, his chosen people, and that all who were not Christians were the outcasts, the damned, anyone suggesting that the good of other faiths, or of no faith at all, could reach heaven being considered a heretic, and persecuted. Only by realising the mentality of the past can history be correctly understood, and, as the evil and intolerance which came from the belief in supernatural religion played a major part in the lives of our ancestors, this aspect of their outlook on life cannot be passed over.

Now we come once again to another ever recurring phase of human thought and action, namely the desire to steal something which is owned by a neighbour. What a long time it has taken the more intelligent members of the community to realise that it is wiser to trade and barter than to steal, and here we reach an interesting half-way development, when a nation first steals land by conquest and then pays the defeated victim a comparatively small sum as conscience money. Ethically this is wrong, as to knock down someone, take his goods, and go off leaving behind a shilling instead of a pound is just about as wicked as out-and-out theft. All the same, even this meagre payment represents an advance in ethical development, and points to the prospect that some day international robbery will be outlawed just as is the thief in every civilised land.

When the United States annexed Texas, which was a vast wilderness lying between the Mississippi and the Rio Grande rivers, Mexico was displeased, but not until 1846 did relations between the two countries become so bad as to cause war. This event was desired by the States because Mexico covered a vast territory, containing fabulous wealth, just waiting to be developed. To provoke Mexico into giving a cause for war, 4000 American soldiers were sent to the frontier, where, on the Mexican side, was stationed an army of 6000 men. There also was situated the city of Matamoras. So the Americans, on their side, built a fort whose guns had the city within easy range.

The Mexicans fell into the trap so cunningly laid for them, as, after some hesitation, they attacked, to suffer a severe defeat. Thus the war began, to come to an end in Mexico City (1847), outside of which the Americans won their last battle. Then Mexico was told what she would be paid for the land the United States intended to take, and she had to accept the sum of only $15,000,000 for an enormous territory of nearly 900,000 square miles, or four times the size of

France, stretching westwards from Texas to the Pacific, part of which was California, to become one of the richest of all her possessions.

In 1848, the year revolution spread throughout Europe, a revolution began in our outlook on the make-up of the human being, and his destiny, because in that year knowledge took the place of ignorance. In the little town of Hydesville in New York State lived John David Fox, his wife and two daughters, Margaret and Kate, aged fourteen and eleven. In this quiet little place, in March of that year, began rapping noises in the house into which they had just moved. No one could account for them; they terrified the children, and they disturbed the entire family.

After every effort had been made to discover a normal explanation, Kate challenged the unseen power to rap the number of times she clapped her hands. Every time she clapped, the correct number of raps followed, and the correct raps were given of the number of fingers or hands held up. So the unseen force could both hear and see. Mrs. Fox then asked how many children she had, and received the correct reply. Quickly it became apparent that there was an intelligence working behind the raps.

From this stage it was easy to get intelligent answers by means of a different number of raps for each letter of the alphabet, the communicator thus stating that he had been murdered in this house, and that his body was buried in the cellar. He gave his name, and the name of the previous tenant, called Bell, whom he accused as the man who had murdered him. Remains of a body were discovered in the cellar, and all else that was told was proved to be true, though quite unknown to anyone at the time except the murderer, who had vanished years earlier.

Out of this small seed grew a great tree, because this was the beginning of what is now called Spiritualism, whose adherents today number millions, with churches in every large town throughout Brazil, the United States, Canada, Britain, South Africa, Australia and New Zealand. Psychic phenomena have now been investigated and confirmed, not only by leading scientists, but by people of repute in every walk of life, and its literature is immense.

Communication between men, women and children out of the flesh and those in the flesh is not new, and did not begin for the first time in 1848; in fact ancient literature contains many references to the subject. What was new was the fact that the phenomena now came to be carefully studied and made a subject of scientific research. The people of old called the communicators gods, and built upon this basis all their stories of the gods coming to earth and fraternising with its inhabitants, tales which are now embraced in what we call mythology. Numerous instances of the gods being seen and spoken to are recorded in ancient literature, and, if the Bible had been correctly translated, the often recurring words "The Lord" would have come down to us as they were originally meant, namely "The Spirit".[1]

---

[1] In *Genesis* i, 2, we read of "the Spirit of God", which is a mistranslation of "the Spirit of the gods". This was none other than the etheric man or woman who took control of the medium when in trance, to receive different names in different religions. To the Hebrews he was "The Lord", to the Greeks "Hermes", to the Romans "Mercury", to the Persians "the Vohu Mano", to the Jesuians "the Divine Spirit" and to the Christians he became "the Holy Spirit", the origin of which was forgotten when the medium was banished from the Christian Church.

There is now no doubt that some people from earliest times have been so constituted that they were able to make contact with beings in another order of existence, in close proximity to our earth, and to such people we today give the name of mediums. From this contact every religion can trace its origin, its beliefs, eucharists, ceremonies and ritual. From this contact came all theology and all mysticism, the work of priestly minds whose speculations developed into the world's different religions. Before the advent of the priest the entire human race accepted things much as it found them, realising that the departed returned and communicated with those they had left on earth.

That is now called Ancestor Worship, which was the first religion, and it covered the entire earth,[1] but, when priestcraft came into being, those sensitive people now called mediums, who could detect the presence of the gods, were termed witches and destroyed. One important effect of the events which took place at Hydesville was the fact that they were the means of bringing to an end the belief in witchcraft, and putting in its place the recognition by the well-informed that those so-called witches were natural mediums, endowed with the faculty of sensing another order of existence outside our normal range of sight and hearing.

Future historians will, moreover, place the Hydesville rappings as an important cause in bringing to an end the Theological Age. They, together with the discovery that the universe is ruled by law, swept

---

[1] *The Psychic Stream* amplifies this subject and makes clear that if we were today as ignorant as our ancestors, we would still be worshipping the men and women controls of mediums as supernatural gods or devils.

away the idea of all-powerful supernatural gods ruling this earth, "which was their footstool and the heavens their throne". The discovery that the gods are men and women like ourselves, living in a world similar to this earth, and subject to natural law, banished the mystery encouraged by theology for thousands of years.

With the curse of ignorance some day removed by knowledge, the events at Hydesville, in the years to come, will receive as prominent a place in the opening chapters of the Scientific Age as any other discovery, and here their importance is fully recognised. We have recovered, from under the heap of theological refuse, vital facts which cannot but increasingly influence our outlook on life, and, as this is so, the Hydesville discovery becomes a great event in history.

In the distant past, when the priest displaced the medium, what was natural was turned into something unnatural and irrational, and mediums, who were intended by nature to reveal the other order of life, were destroyed because they were the means through which came the evidence of the falsity of the priestly speculations and inventions. The fight between the prophet (the old name for medium) and the priest runs through all religious history, away back for thousands of years, and, though the clergy cannot now destroy mediums in civilised countries, they continue to misrepresent them and prejudice those who are sufficiently ignorant to believe them.

So the Hydesville rappings stand out as a prominent event in history, because the etheric beings who communicated were accepted for the first time in Christendom as they really are—men, women and children, who had discarded their flesh garment, and now live in duplicate etheric bodies in close contact with this earth. Intelligence had developed sufficiently by 1848 to treat them as human beings who had died, and not as gods who controlled the ordering of the universe. This was an outstanding discovery, which every day since then has received cumulative confirmation, and, though many still disbelieve this to be true, the fact remains that their ranks are yearly becoming smaller.

With the origin of every religion now uncovered, both religious and philosophic beliefs have already been greatly influenced by the massive collection of evidence secured by the Spiritualists, who, like all who held opinions different from those accepted by the majority, were persecuted by the Christians and stoned when attending their services. Today their meetings are sometimes banned by the police, and honest mediums are heavily fined or imprisoned for no other reason than the fact that they are mediums, but, despite prevailing injustices, both religion and philosophy will continue to be influenced by this new knowledge, to the lasting benefit of generations yet unborn.

(7) Sordid Social Conditions in Britain Cause Unrest.

Throughout the greater part of the 19th century social conditions in Britain were deplorable, but here we shall confine ourselves to the first half of the century. The upper classes exhibited complete apathy towards the degradation in which so many lived, and, even up to within our own times, they regarded the poor as belonging to a different creation from themselves, and lacking in human feelings and emotions.

A small number of reformers, known as Radicals, the most vehement and outspoken being William Cobbett, voiced the grievances of the vast majority, and amongst these there was a decided leaning towards abolishing the monarchy and setting up a republic, an idea which found no favour amongst the well-to-do. Most of the aristocracy, the landed gentry and the prosperous business people were pompous and over-bearing, and received servile obeisance from all on a lower social level, the belief being general that titles, land and wealth made the favoured few superior to those who lived by daily toil.

Everyone in those days was too ignorant to realise that nobility, which comes from deeds, is not the gift of any monarch, and that the great are only those who have achieved much for the good of humanity. Then the rich and well-to-do lived in comfort and luxury, with their carriages and horses, while the poor lived in houses little better than hovels, and worked long hours for small wages, their condition being often not much better than slaves. The government made no effort to check the evils which followed the factory system, and the owners of mills and workshops took full advantage of the freedom they enjoyed.

The factory killed the cottage industry, which had employed men, women and children from the earliest ages of mankind. Many small rural households were broken up, single women especially being the victims, as the world in those days had little use for the un-married female, who too often against her wishes was forced into prostitution. The mill replaced the home as a workshop, and discipline and fixed hours of work took the place of the cottager's own way of doing things as and when he pleased.

In the long run this separation of labour from the home made home life more comfortable, the removal to the mill of the picking and cleaning of cotton making for greater tidiness and cleanliness, but during the change over many hardships and much unemployment had to be endured. Old ingrained habits and customs were changed. The workers in the factories became cogs in a giant soulless wheel, so much so that they themselves were looked upon more as machines than human beings, and their working conditions were both insanitary and unhealthy. The factories were badly lighted and ill ventilated, and the houses provided for the workers were squalid and poorly lit.

In those days every window was taxed according to its size, daylight and air having to be paid for by our ancestors, not only in Britain but also in Europe. Surely this form of taxation reveals their crass stupidity better than anything else. Small-roomed tenements, in which families would live in one or at most two rooms, with no amenities or sanitation, were the only living accommodation available for the artisan working in the towns. No baths or water and no light were provided, and only bare walls, small windows and a roof made up a house, the nearest pump and lavatory, for the use of everyone in the block, being out in the open some distance away. Their garments were coarse, the children were clothed in sacking, and lacked both shoes and stockings.

Children, boys and girls from five years of age upwards, had to work seventy, and even ninety, hours a week, and when they went to sleep at their work they were beaten. The death rate under these conditions was terrible; there was no supervision, no protection against deaths and accidents; in fact their living conditions would have caused consternation and horror to a Greek or Roman citizen in Pagan times. Children, moreover, were gathered from all over the country and apprenticed to millowners until the age of twenty-one, and this meant slavery, because they were no better off than the negroes. They lived behind locked doors, had no freedom or liberty and received neither pay nor holidays, only their food and clothes. Both boys and girls were employed by chimney-sweeps and forced to climb up chimneys naked to clear away the soot. Often they stuck and could get neither up nor down, only to hear their brutal masters cursing and swearing at them from below. Frequently they were burned by the heat, and at times taken out dead.[1]

Only in Britain was this method of cleaning chimneys practised, and even after long brushes were invented it continued until 1875, when an Act was passed for its abolition, an earlier Act of 1840 never having been made effective. In the coal mines children of from five to eight years of age worked in darkness for long hours attending to trap-doors, or, like animals, harnessed to trucks, which, on all fours, they pulled through the narrow passages. Women, moreover, were employed carrying coal on their backs up long stairs to the surface.

[1] Starved and neglected children were left to die in the gutter, a not uncommon sight to those who passed by.

Here surely was an opportunity for the Christian Church, which was then an organisation more powerful than any government, to step in and protect the dignity of man, but no, it did nothing. The unorthodox Radicals protested, but not the Anglican Church, which drew in royalties from the mines of Northumberland and Durham £400,000 annually, and the Bishop of Durham £40,000 a year from coal-pits in his own diocese. The long hours worked, and the unnatural conditions, brought disease and early death, but no recompense was made for mutilation or disability. When the mines and factories were sold, the workers were sold along with them as part of the gear and machinery.

In the first half of last century much labour and money was devoted to bring the knowledge of Christ to the heathen abroad, and world-wide Christian missions sprang into being supported by lavish subscriptions. Nothing, however, was done for the poor and wretched at home, the reason being that they were regarded as already saved by baptism, and in those days the conversion of non-Christians was considered to be more pleasing to God than the improving of living conditions in Britain. Only the unorthodox reformers, whose humanity exceeded their zeal for theology, gave a thought to improved social conditions, and they were hated by the orthodox for their "worldly ways".

The children of the poor were everywhere so neglected that Robert Raikes in 1780 commenced what were then called Sunday schools, their purpose being to teach the young to read and write on the only day they were not working. To this the Anglican clergy objected because Nonconformists were amongst the teachers. The same clerical opposition came about when Hannah More, in the early part of the 19th century, commenced to teach some children to read and write. So fierce was this resistance that she was prosecuted in an Ecclesiastical court, at the instance of some of the clergy, on account of one of her school enterprises.

The Church authorities did not wish the children to be educated, and this they made abundantly clear when the first Education Bill was introduced into Parliament in 1807. It passed through the House of Commons, but the bishops in the House of Lords raised so much opposition that it was thrown out, and so ended this first attempt by the State to educate its children. Then in England, only one in every seventeen could read and write, and, moreover, the education that was given in the private schools was deplorable, the teachers being quite untrained and unfitted for their positions. Consequently, although illiteracy in Europe was at the high figure of 85 per cent., "the English people are the lowest in the scale of knowledge", as was said at the time and never contradicted.

To the Church everything that really mattered was contained in its theological teaching, and what little the people knew and how they lived counted as nothing. Its leaders, consequently, not only opposed all legislation which the humanists proposed, but it was then, and still is, the largest ground landlord of slum property in the country. Even so recently as the end of the 19th century forty out of every hundred town-dwellers had only one room in which to live.

Not only was there white slavery in Britain, but negroes were captured in Africa and brought to work in Britain as slaves. It was quite a common sight, in places like London, Bristol, Liverpool and other ports, to see negroes going about with iron bands round their necks on which were inscribed the words, "This slave is the property of", and then followed the owner's name and address.

With labour conditions at home, during the first half of the 19th century, not far removed from slavery, we need not be surprised that slavery abroad was also accepted as part of God's plan, the Society for the Propagation of the Gospel considering it to be quite in accordance with Christian principles, and Christian ideals, to employ slaves from the year 1711 until 1830 on the two plantations it owned in Barbados. After the slaves in British colonies had become Christians the question arose as to whether it was in accordance with the Christian religion for Christians to own Christian slaves. This problem was submitted to the archbishops and bishops of the Church of England, who pronounced unanimously that it was quite within the beliefs of the faith for Christians to own Christian slaves, and then Parliament enacted legislation to this effect.

This being so, the owning of slaves must still be within the precepts of this religion, and, when we hear it said today that Christianity abolished slavery, let us remember this pronouncement by the Anglican bishops, and regard such a claim as quite untrue. The truth is that slavery came to an end when the people developed mentally beyond the Old Testament way of life, their attachment to which kept Christian civilisation, up to the 19th century, on much the same level as that maintained by the barbarous Hebrews.

When those interested in the slave trade realised that public opinion was rising against its continuation, petitions were made to Parliament for the purpose of impressing on members how grievous would be the loss to those financially involved if it were brought to an end. So the manufacturers of instruments of torture, and fetters of all description, combined to petition Parliament to refrain from passing legislation which would in any way interfere with their lawful and age-long industry, their petition being worded as follows:

To the Honourable the Commons of Great Britain in Parliament assembled, the humble petition of persons concerned in the manufacturing of neck-yokes, collars, chains, handcuffs, leg-bolts, drags, thumb-screws, iron coffins, cats, scourges and other necessary instruments of torture for the African Slave Trade humbly sheweth that your petitioners, justly alarmed at the present attempt to procure an abolition of the Slave Trade, humbly implore the protection of this Honourable House for a manufacture so essential to the true interests of this country.

Your petitioners apprehend that although torture be prohibited in this island, it is nevertheless absolutely necessary to the proper regulation of heathens and infidels; highly useful to the propagation of the Gospel of Christ, and very salutary to the persons on whom it is inflicted.

When we remember that this happened in the life-time of people whose children are living today, we realise how great is the change of outlook of civilised people living in the middle of the 20th century from that of those who lived one hundred years earlier. Seventy-five years of education, seventy-five years between the age of faith and the age of reason, and seventy-five years of mental development, have wrought a wondrous change amongst civilised people in their attitude towards their fellow men. Only those infected with the German mentality now remain to perpetuate the horrors which so many thought, when the 20th century opened, were of a bygone age.

Protestant Britain from the days of Queen Elizabeth was the world champion of the slave trade, and Parliament did everything possible to encourage this hideous traffic, one Act of 1749 declaring that "the slave trade is very advantageous to Britain". Besides constant legislation being enacted for the purpose of opening up new slave markets, Britain built forts along the African coast for the protection of this lucrative traffic, which further expanded when the British government gave free grants of land in the West Indies, on the condition that not less than four negroes be kept to every hundred acres.

The law officers of the Crown, namely the Attorney-general and the Solicitor-general, moreover, declared in 1729 that slavery was, and always had been, legal in the British Isles, and that slaves under British bondage anywhere need not be released when they became Christians. The newspapers of Britain in those days contained advertisements offering rewards for the return of runaway slaves, and anyone walking along the streets of London, and other cities, could see negroes being taken for sale at the slave market. Then every man in Britain of dark skin was in danger of being kidnapped and sold into bondage.

A fleet of 192 British ships was employed in the slave trade, and they had a total carrying capacity of

47,146 negroes, as great as the combined capacity of all the other slave ships belonging to the nations of Europe. So Britain carried half of this lucrative traffic in her own ships, and from London, Liverpool and Bristol slave galleys started on their regular voyages to the coast of Africa, being always speeded on their journey by prayers in the churches at the port of departure for a good catch and safe return. When they reached the African coast, they made for one of the many slave-catching centres, where armed men were stationed whose business it was to go into the interior, and in the dark set fire to a native village.

In the confusion which followed they seized as many natives as possible, put an iron collar round each neck, and then chained them together, these shackles being made in Birmingham, where also were manufactured the instruments of torture so freely used to break the spirits of the captives and produce the slave mentality. Then the poor creatures were dragged to the coast and put on board a galley, in which they were packed like cattle, but often only half those captured survived their horrible ordeal. From time to time the entire cargo of negroes was flung overboard to lighten the ship in a storm, or when the crew was short of water after being becalmed.

When our great-grandparents saw nothing wrong in the conditions of their times, we need not wonder that the law showed no mercy to the delinquent, however trifling his crime. Children were put to death for petty thefts; in fact, as already mentioned, there were 223 offences punishable by death, including one for appearing on the public highway with a blackened face. Old and young flocked to see the public hanging of criminals; there were always crowds to see some delinquent whipped through the streets by the local hangman, and there was always someone in the pillory to be made miserable by jeers. It was considered good sport in those days to throw rotten eggs at these helpless creatures, and to taunt some wretch who was being whipped through the streets tied to the back of a cart. Unwanted wives were taken to market, sometimes with halters round their necks, to be sold to the highest bidder. Advertisements announcing these wife sales appeared beforehand, the following, dated Carlisle 5th October, 1832, being a good example:

> Let it be known that on the above date James Thompson of the Valley Farm will sell his wife Mary by auction in the Market Square at twelve o'clock noon. The article will be offered without a warranty.

The last of these quite common occurrences took place in 1852, when a man led his wife into the market square at Aylesford, near Maidstone, with a halter round her neck, and sold her for half a crown. When that was tolerated we need not be surprised that there was no justice or mercy in the Law Courts, as, when people had money, they could escape the penalties of their misdeeds by bribery and intrigue, whereas if the people were poor they received no mercy. It was very dangerous for a poor man to go to law, because, if he were successful, the Court and lawyers often charged so much that he received next to nothing, but, if he lost, their charges ruined him, and he spent his life in a debtors' prison. Widows and orphans, on the death of their husbands or parents, if poor, were turned out of their homes, and, as there was no place for them to go, they had to beg on the streets. In those days there was little justice, mercy or kindness, and the lot of many of the poor was so miserable that it would have been much better if they had never been born.

A schoolmaster, Peter Annet, in the latter part of the 18th century, had the audacity to criticise some of the bloodthirsty passages in the Psalms. He said that it was not right to sing or read about dashing babies against the wall, exterminating unbelievers, devastating their habitations, hating our enemies, and the righteous washing their feet in the blood of the wicked, and much more in the same strain.

The people in those days thought that this was quite the correct thing to do, and Christians evidently still do so, because they lustily sing or read these bloodthirsty psalms in their churches. Annet, however, had to suffer in his attempt to make Christians humane, as he was brought before the King's Bench and sentenced to one month's imprisonment in Newgate, after which he had to stand twice in the pillory with a label round his neck on which was printed "For Blasphemy". Then, as if that was not enough, he was given a year's hard labour, and made to find sureties for his good behaviour during the rest of his life.

Both young and old of both sexes, hardened criminals and unfortunate debtors, were herded together in the prisons, where gaol fever always raged, and this was the lot of those awaiting trial, who, after being tried, were not always found guilty. The gaolers depended on what payment prisoners gave them, keeping in gaol those who could not pay the sums demanded, even after their term of imprisonment had expired. Sanitary conditions were unknown, the atmosphere was foul, and the only way to find rest was to lie down on a stone floor.

Two noble figures stand out at this period, a man and woman, who dedicated their lives to rectify these evils, John Howard (1726–1790) devoting his life to the improvement of prison conditions, the good work he commenced being carried on by Elizabeth Fry (1780–1845), a Quaker. Such was the intolerance of the time that Howard was precluded from taking the oath of loyalty on his appointment as High Sheriff of Bedford, because he was not a member of the Church of England, this powerful organisation doing nothing to remedy the evils Howard was devoting his life to eradicate.

These facts give some idea of the conditions in the towns, factories, coal mines and prisons in the first part of the 19th century, a state of squalid wretchedness that came from centuries of concentration on theology to the neglect of sociology, but the lot of the country labourer was just as hard. His position in some ways was even worse, as his wages, which were fixed by law in 1795 before the Napoleonic war, were now quite insufficient to maintain him and his family, because of the greatly increased cost of living which the war and the Corn Laws had brought about. Bread was so dear that to buy a loaf a day absorbed most of his pay, and he and his family had to live on oatmeal, potatoes and other vegetables, his children being clothed in sacking. Even this was only possible by his wages being supplemented, from time to time, from the Poor Law funds. To live, the labourer had to become a pauper. Naturally he became degraded and desperate, and poached to keep his family from starving, but man-traps were set up by the gamekeepers which crushed or broke the leg of anyone unfortunate enough to be caught, when seven years' transportation, from which few returned, was the legal punishment.

Not until 1825 were labourers, or factory workers, allowed to form a union to enable them to take combined action to improve their way of life, the Combination Acts of 1799–1800 making it illegal for workmen to form associations for mutual aid. These Acts were introduced by William Wilberforce, the champion of the negro slaves, and it is regrettable that one who did so much to free the slaves from bondage was so fearful of his own countrymen. With the one hand he helped to strike the shackles from the black men and with the other he forged the fetters for the white men. He instigated legislation to keep his own people in miserable servitude, but, though callously blind to the miseries at home, he enthusiastically supported Christian missions abroad.

He, as much as anyone, was responsible for the bondage under which the working class in Britain then laboured, and yet he more than anyone gave over his life to secure the freedom of others not of his own race. Wilberforce did not fear the negro, but he did not trust the British working man, who, it was thought in those days, might overthrow the aristocracy, if given the opportunity, as had happened in France. This state of affairs was the outcome of the policy adopted throughout the Christian era of keeping the people ignorant, and, when their hitherto stagnant minds began to stir, all who were responsible for perpetuating this injustice shivered in fear, and could only think of more and more repressive measures to curb the aspirations of the common man.

Consequently legislation was both brutal and unjust, and many examples of this could be given, but two will be enough. In the winter of 1830, the starving farm labourers south of the Thames revolted and caused a riot by their demand for a wage of half a crown a day. The revenge of the State was terrible, three of the rioters being hanged and 420 torn from their families and transported to Australia as convicts. Then again, in 1834, six Dorset labourers met for the purpose of forming a trade union. They were arrested and transported for seven years to Tasmania, to become known as the Tolpuddle martyrs. The action of these men was then perfectly legal, as nine years previously the House of Commons had passed an Act making trade unions lawful, but it did not withdraw an old Act making the taking of an oath of secrecy an offence. Because these men had taken this oath they were pounced upon by Lord Melbourne's government, who feared that if the workers combined it would be the end of all things. Protest meetings followed this outrageous punishment, but nothing was done, and only one victim ever returned to his native land.

Twelve hundred years of Christianity in Britain had done nothing for education or ethical development, the consequence being that we now find an upper class that was ignorant, pitiless, cruel and selfish.

The poor were little better than beasts, entirely
uneducated, coarse and brutal to a degree, while most
of the rich thought only of their own comforts, and
showed a callous indifference towards the poor.
The minds of our Christian great-grandparents were
so brutalised by their ignorance, and their religion,
that Edmund Burke stated that he could obtain the
assent of the House of Commons to any measure
imposing the punishment of death.   Both the upper
and middle classes strove to have the offences which
injured their interests made subject to the death
penalty, to such effect that during the reign of the
Georges 156 additional offences punishable by death
were added to the Statute Book, thus making in all
223 human actions subject to the death penalty.

If anyone chipped a piece off a bridge or building
he was hanged; if he appeared disguised he was
hanged; if he cut down a sapling he was hanged; if
he shot a rabbit he was hanged; if he stole anything
worth over five shillings he was hanged; if he stole a
handkerchief he was hanged; and if, starving, he stole
some food he was hanged.   As Judge Heath said at
this time, "there is no hope of regenerating a felon in
this life, so better hang him and get him out of the
way".   Consequently the gallows were everywhere,
and from them, for the sake of example, the corpses
of the slain were left hanging, bodies of children of
tender years swaying in the wind along with those of
hardened criminals.

Some were beheaded, and their heads exposed to
public view; many were transported for seven years,
and others for life; but this recital could be continued
for pages, because there was no limit to the cruelty

and savagery of our devout forbears. Soldiers and sailors were flogged to death in the presence of their fellows, the master flogged his workman, the schoolmaster his pupil, the husband his wife, and in those days of violent and uncontrolled tempers the floggings were ferocious.

Manners were as coarse and foul as were the people's minds. Profane swearing was the regular custom with everyone. They swore at one another, and at their inferiors. Husbands regularly swore at their wives. The clergy cursed their congregations, the judges swore on the bench, and society ladies used as foul language as their menfolk. The most commonplace remark could not be made without an oath. Every fashionable man was a gambler, and the clubs of St. James's Street were places of iniquity. Adultery was "a little affair", the man without a mistress received the jeers of his friends, and landowners considered that they had the right of intercourse with the girls on their estates. Filthy stories and obscene books circulated freely, and indecent songs and pictures were openly on sale in the shops and on the streets.

Drunkenness was as common as swearing, members in Parliament being often unable to express themselves, and it was not considered correct for a gentleman to rise from table after dinner in the evening as etiquette demanded that he fell under it drunk. A host was offended if his guest left his house sober, and one of the duties of the servants of the rich was to unbutton the collars of the men guests under the table, to prevent them from choking.

Education amongst the greater part of the community was non-existent during the first seventy years of the 19th century, only some 15,000 British children, when the population was 20,000,000, being taught to read and write. Instead of going to school, children went to work in the factories, on the fields, and many ran about the streets in rags, picking up what food they could, sleeping in the open or in some archway. Prisons took the place of schools, the gallows the place of the reformatory, and churches the place of free libraries.

Nearly everyone who had decent clothes went to church in those days, and was doped into feeling that the then prevailing social conditions were all part of God's plan, the poor being placed where God intended them to be, and so must be content with their lot in life. Sermons were preached from the texts "Take therefore no thought for the morrow" (*Matthew* vi, 34), "For ye have the poor always with you" (*Matthew* xxvi, 11), and "I have learned, in whatsoever state I am therewith to be content" (*Philippians* iv, 11). So both squire and farm labourer came out of church with the feeling that God is in his heaven, and all is right with the world. Yet the squires of those days, as Justices of the Peace, with their great authority and uncontrolled power, too often misused it, and contemporary Radicals bitterly criticised their tyranny, injustice and favouritism.

Ignorance of how best to produce and distribute wealth was, of course, one cause behind these terrible social conditions. So we should give thanks to the inventors, the discoverers, the engineers, the economists, the scientists, to those who have increased and imparted knowledge, and to all who brought about the industrial revolution. This great event quickened mental development to such effect that the people arose and demanded education, which, in turn, brought their sordid lives to an end and opened up for them a new era. Education is still in its infancy, a young and growing child with boundless possibilities. The more we know, and the more we discover, the greater becomes the stimulus for greater knowledge, and we should always remember that the popular urge which brought education to the people at the end of last century came from the discoveries made during the previous two centuries.

To the pioneers in every branch of knowledge can be directly traced the improved conditions in which most people find themselves in our own times, to which advance there seems no end, so long as new inventions are used for constructive and not destructive purposes. By rational thinking, and not by subservient faith, by trusting in ourselves and not placing all our troubles on God, by using our minds to overcome and exploit nature, we have advanced physically, mentally and morally. Man is his own saviour, and in himself only can he trust.

The Church, a hundred years ago, was a dope-house under the special protection of the squire, who represented the King, and the priest, who represented the will of God. Both these representatives of the law, human and divine, lived in comfortable spacious homes and had every reason to wish social conditions to remain as they were. Because of cheap labour the industrialists had become rich, and the high price of wheat and cereals had made the landlords and farmers prosperous at the expense of the labourers who were living in poverty at a starvation level.

Yet it was the working class, who had no rights or privileges, that provided the labour which produced all the comforts the rich enjoyed, and it was the common soldier, and the Press-Ganged sailors, who fought Britain's battles overseas underliving conditions which were degrading, and whose food was of the poorest quality. These conflicts had already added greatly to her possessions abroad, from which the rich were obtaining additional wealth and remunerative appointments. To suggest to the upper and middle classes that social conditions were bad and could be improved was treason, and, as they had the power, all who did so suffered for their audacity.

Such then was the condition of Britain in the first half of the 19th century, and conditions abroad were much the same. For the cause of evil always look for ignorance, and for the cause of good seek for the knowledge which brought it about. From the time primitive man left the jungle, knowledge and wisdom have been slowly increasing. Mind has been conquering matter, at times very slowly when theology reigned supreme, at other times more quickly, when theology was brushed aside. and man relied on himself and not on the gods. The more he discovered the more he depended on himself, on his own reasoning powers, and, in consequence, over the ages, intelligence has increased, and just as surely as it advanced did evil decrease.

Organised orthodox religion brings comfort to the simple, but not knowledge, and only now do we realise that it is much wiser to know how to avoid both sickness and trouble than to be ignorant. Priests are opposed to knowledge because their system of belief relies on the gods, and not on man himself. So it follows that when priests have ruled, learning made little or no progress. The intellectual age of the Greeks, Romans and Moslems was a time when the priests had lost their power, only to regain it and drag the people back into the abyss.

Then came the discovery of printing and paper, which in the end defeated these enemies of progress, because the greater dissemination of knowledge became possible. By making use of these two discoveries, Voltaire, Thomas Paine and others, by logical arguments, and the knowledge accumulated by the scientists since the Renaissance, exposed the evil of priestly rule. They proved all Christian claims to be false, and urged the people to think for themselves and cease being doped by pious platitudes about accepting their conditions as part of God's plan.

Most people could not read the books these reformers wrote, but some could, and they passed on to others what they had read. Thus doubts arose about the teaching to be heard in the churches, and when people doubt it means that they are thinking. To doubt has always been the greatest religious crime, as a doubting flock means that the priest has no longer sheep to shepherd. This was realised by the priest-hood thousands of years ago, and, in one form or another, the story of Adam and Eve is to be found in nearly all religions. Its moral is that to seek fruit from off the tree of knowledge is sinful. Up to the 19th century the priests had managed very successfully to get this accepted by the people, but paper and printing were now proving too much for even their subtle cunning.

Consequently more and more doubted the truth of the claims made by the Christian religion, just as more and more doubted the statements made by the politicians, who, by their Christian upbringing, accepted everything as part of God's plan, and tried to impress upon the people that everything was just as it should be. Nevertheless both priests and politicians became fearful about the future of society. For the first time during the Christian era the people were beginning to think and wonder, and, when the French Revolution came and went, leaving on record that the people could come into their own when they liked, the ground was cleared for the battle between those who could see no reason to change, and those of greater intelligence who realised that the poor were entitled to their rights as well as the rich.

As we have already read, two beacons lit the minds of 19th-century reformers, *The Age of Reason* and *Rights of Man*, both of which were the outcome of increased knowledge. The all-powerful Church, in the 16th, 17th and 18th centuries, fearful of losing its control, because the people were beginning to think about their religious beliefs, leapt on the unorthodox like a savage beast at bay. Then in the 18th and 19th centuries a further step forward was made when, all over Europe, some, more advanced than the rest, began to think about their social conditions, now that the deadly grip of the Church had been somewhat relaxed. Consequently the all-powerful ruling class, in fear of losing its privileges, turned furiously on the reformers in an attempt to repress their desire for the people having a greater say in their own affairs.

Hence the cruel oppression all over Europe after

the French Revolution, and all the additional laws which were passed in Britain imposing the death penalty. Fear, first of all, caused the Church to be brutal in its treatment of the thinkers, and now fear caused the State to be equally ferocious. Both Church and State throughout Europe, including Britain, wished no change in the religious and social outlook of the people, a desire which explains their opposition to all the reform movements about which we shall now be reading.

Ignorance breeds cruelty, and, as nearly everyone in those days was ignorant, they were likewise cruel. As we have become less ignorant we have become kinder, but a hundred years ago pity for suffering was only to be found amongst the most advanced intellects. Only by means of meetings of protest, and riots, did the people in the end secure their rights. In the midlands, machinery was destroyed and factories set on fire. A mob marched on London, but was dispersed. At St. Peter's Field, Manchester, in 1819, a large crowd, which had assembled to hear about the need for parliamentary reform, was broken up by a body of yeomanry and the speaker arrested, many people being killed and injured. This came to be known as the Peterloo Massacre, and the injustice of it all caused great indignation everywhere, but the result was not reform because prohibition of all similar meetings followed. For a time free speech in Britain came to an end.

The Government, fearing a revolution, passed what is called the Six Acts (1819), making it illegal (1) to have meetings of more than fifty people without a licence, (2) for men to possess or train in the use of arms, and (3) to publish literature defined as blasphemous and seditious. Henry Addington (1757–1844), Viscount Castlereagh (1769–1822) and George Canning (1770–1827), the outstanding politicians of the early 19th century, were responsible for these measures, to which some desperadoes replied by hatching a plot in 1820 to assassinate the leading ministers of the Crown. This was discovered, and its leader, and four others, were put to death.

During a short interval of more enlightened government, Britain's policy in foreign affairs was decidedly liberal, and, under the lead of George Canning, when Foreign Secretary in Lord Liverpool's administration (1812–1827), and, during Canning's own short term as Prime Minister (1827), help was given to the South American Spanish and Portuguese colonies and the Greeks to win their freedom, the former being saved by Britain from a French invasion. While Europe lay in bondage to tyrannical rulers, Britain thus secured the friendship of young and virile republics across the Atlantic, possessed of vast resources, to the great advantage of her trade. Then, after recognising their sovereignty, she turned her attention to help Greece in her struggle to throw off the Turkish yoke.

Austria and Prussia had no wish for a resurgent Greece bringing modern ideas to the Danube valley, but the statesmen of Britain, thinking of the glorious days of ancient Greece, did not hesitate to give the Slavonic-Albanian merchants, hill shepherds, pirates and brigands of that once-famous land, her support. So, when reports spread that captive Greeks were being sold in Cairo as slaves, and that the people of

Greece were in danger of extermination, Britain joined with France and Russia to liberate them from their long term of bondage under Turkish rule. The struggle which followed has already been told earlier in this chapter, its significance in history being the fact that it marked the beginning of the overthrow of imperialism in Europe, and the rise of the spirit of nationalism which spread through the Balkans to Italy, Poland, Finland, Bohemia, to end finally in Ireland.

George IV (1820–1830), who had been acting as Regent since 1811, when George III became permanently insane, became king in 1820, on the death of his father. Thus Britain was free of a monarch who, during his long reign of sixty years, was such a blight on progress and reform. No British sovereign, by crass stupidity, did more damage to the British Empire than did George III, and no Stuart king ever proved himself more unfitted to be at the head of a great nation than did this German prince. His son and successor, George IV, was a retrograde profligate dandy, licentious, dishonest, and his word could never be trusted, in fact not even an occasional gleam of brightness enlightens the dark picture of his unsavoury career, which was given over to folly pleasure and the squandering of money.

In those days, when Britain led the world in ocean trade, and possessed the greatest mercantile fleet in the world (2,500,000 tons), her social life had reached the depths of degradation. Wealth and display were confined to the favoured few, and arduous toil and abject poverty prevailed amongst the many, who lived in bleak squalid towns, lacking drainage, with filth festering in the streets and poisoning their lives. The machine had brought new problems which were not faced, the Napoleonic war and its aftermath being one reason, but the principal cause was the selfishness and indifference displayed by those who had the power and wealth.

They, being ignorant of the ethical law, sought their happiness by thinking only of themselves, whereas greater knowledge would have made them realise that real happiness comes from creating harmony. Outside this small circle of selfish rich lived the great majority, many of whom passed their lives in bondage, squalor and vice. Having no say in the affairs of the State, we need not be surprised that they expressed themselves by means of riots and indignation meetings, and these took place up and down the country.

So, when Castlereagh (now Marquis of Londonderry) committed suicide in 1822, the mob, which attended his funeral, cheered and jeered loudly as his body passed to the grave, he being the recognised leader of the aristocratic and reactionary party which owed its power to the excesses of the French Revolution. Few remembered that he had, as Foreign Minister, carried the country successfully through the final stages of the Napoleonic war, been Britain's representative at the Congress of Vienna, and brought about the Irish Act of Union. Likewise the mob made clear its disapproval of the policy pursued by Addington (Lord Sidmouth), the Six Acts, for which he was mainly responsible, having raised their hostility towards such forms of legislation. In these ways the ignorant but aspiring masses determined future policy, because in Britain all could criticise, grumble and demonstrate, the effect being that the selfish aristocratic and capitalistic classes were forced to make the reforms they so dreaded and disliked.

When the reactionary Addington resigned the office of Home Secretary in 1822, the more liberal-minded Sir Robert Peel took his place in Lord Liverpool's government, and abolished the death penalty for over a hundred petty crimes. His name, however, has been perpetuated for quite another reason. London streets were then so unsafe, and without protection, that he instituted a proficient police force, the "Bobby" taking his name from him. This wise constructive effort did more to lessen crime than all the penalties of the law, as prevention is always better than cure.

At this time the progressive William Huskisson became President of the Board of Trade, and secured the repeal of the Combination Act, which enabled the workers to form associations to bargain with their employers. This enlightened man was also responsible for the removal of many of the restrictions associated with the Navigation laws, which limited the cargoes and destinations of ships, and he helped to free trade by removing the high duties and restrictions under which it laboured. By a strange irony of fate he was killed in 1830 by Stephenson's engine "Rocket" at the opening of the Liverpool and Manchester Railway.

Huskisson's death coincided with the expiration of reform, its brief life having lasted only a few years. In 1827 Lord Liverpool retired, and his place as Prime Minister was taken for a few months by the feeble Lord Goderich, who was succeeded by the Duke of Wellington, a diehard Tory, with no

sympathy whatever for reform of any kind. He had
been drenched with different titles since his defeat of
Napoleon, honours having been showered upon him
in profusion, but he gave no thought to the class
from which the 50,000 men had come whose
nameless bodies rotted in the bloody battlefields of
Spain, Portugal and Belgium, and by whose exertions
he had reached his exalted position. For their class,
and those who had survived the Napoleonic war,
he was quite indifferent, his concern being only for
his own grade in society.

Through the influence of Peel, and from fear of
civil war in Ireland, he agreed, in spite of bitter
Protestant opposition, to the Roman Catholic Emancipation Act, a measure which enabled Roman
Catholics to become members of Parliament and hold
all offices except Regent, Lord Chancellor and Lord
Lieutenant of Ireland. This was a personal victory
for Daniel O'Connell, the powerful and eloquent
Irish Roman Catholic leader, whose fight for liberty
had finally triumphed after his long uphill struggle
against suppression.

Parliament in those days, as we have already read,
was quite unrepresentative of the people, and constituencies were very unevenly distributed. Cornwall
had forty-four members, and all Scotland only forty-
five. Old Sarum was the site of a town which existed
no longer, but two members from this nowhere sat
and voted in Parliament, a state of affairs which was
typical of thirty-five other similar. places. Some
landowners could give seats to their friends. Some
places had so few voters that a candidate could
easily buy all the necessary votes to secure election.

On the other hand, Birmingham, Manchester, Greenock and Paisley had no representation whatever. Seats in Parliament, like Church of England livings, were bought and sold, while graft, bribery and corruption were rampant everywhere; in fact the entire parliamentary system was thoroughly rotten and reform was long overdue. Hundreds of petitions demanding reform reached the government, but not until the retrograde George IV died in 1830 was anything done.

He was followed by William IV (1830–1837), the third son of George III, who was a more enlightened individual than his diehard Tory brother. Nevertheless he was an utterly fatuous being, irresolute, irresponsible and undignified, but it was in his reign that the first rays of a brighter day dawned for the British people. The factories were bringing together men of all shades of thought, hitherto separated from each other in villages and farms, but now able to express their grievances to hundreds of fellow sufferers. Some of these drowned their sorrows in drink, others became politically minded, while others again were sustained by Evangelical religion, which gave them the hope of greater happiness hereafter.

Combination consequently made the voices for reform louder and more numerous, but the retrograde politicians, living in the past, were too self-centred to realise that machinery had changed the old order and that a new one was impatiently waiting to take its place. Britain's rulers had just completed the lighting of the British coast by means of lighthouses and lightships to prevent shipwrecks, but they themselves were living in mental darkness and could not see that their policy was carrying the ship of state to disaster.

Nevertheless, in spite of Wellington's continued opposition, and the determined obstruction of both the peers and bishops in the House of Lords, the British reform movement gained ground after the despotic Charles X of France was deposed, and the more liberal-minded Louis Philippe took his place. So the reactionary Wellington was put out of office by the Whigs in 1830, and the long Tory ascendancy, which had been brought about by George III, came to an end, the progressive Earl Grey becoming Prime Minister.

For long an ardent parliamentary reformer, Grey, a wise and courageous man, at once introduced the Reform Bill (1831) for improved and increased parliamentary representation. This was passed in the House of Commons by a majority of one vote, only to be defeated in Committee. A general election followed, and this brought about a majority of a hundred votes in the Commons for a second Reform Bill, but this was thrown out by the House of Lords, the bishops voting twenty-one against and only two in favour. Because of their opposition they were mobbed when they appeared in the streets, and some of their palaces were set on fire. At a time when the opera was in its hey-day in London, riots broke out all over the country, but these did not prevent this unelected Chamber from mutilating the third Reform Bill.

Only in 1832, when Wellington and his reactionary Tory peers were threatened by the King that enough Whig peers would be created to pass the Bill, did the House of Lords capitulate and agree to pass the measure as received from the House of Commons.

The Church and Toryism had had their long fateful spell of despotism, but, though they knew that their power was on the decline, they fought bitterly to the last. Their defeat confounded them, while many Whigs were fearful of the future, but the Radicals, regarding the Bill as the first necessary instalment to a wider franchise, were joyful at their epoch-making victory which had immediate results.

From this time onwards the Church commenced to lose some of its reactionary power, one outstanding reform being the ending of the application of public money, at the expense of the taxpayer, to the maintaining and building of churches. Along with its allies, the Tories,[1] the Church and its priests were now decidedly unpopular with a large number of Englishmen, so much so that the unorthodox Radicals, and many Dissenters, had for long dubbed it "Old Corruption" the village priest being known as "the Black Dragon" because his influence was always on the side of tyranny and reaction.

The Reform Bill of 1832 eventually broke the power of that twin partnership, the squire and the priest, just as the Municipal Reform Bill of 1835, enfranchising all rate-payers, broke the power of the Church in municipal elections, the old rotten municipal corporations, with which the Church was so closely allied, having long outlived their usefulness. The Reform Bill, moreover, was the prelude to education, because until the people themselves had the say, the exclusiveness of the Church, fearful that increased

---

[1] The Tories, or Conservatives as they are now called, still claim to be the champions of Christianity, Winston Churchill, their leader, placing first in the party's programme, announced by him on 5th October, 1946, the policy "To uphold the Christian religion, and resist all attacks upon it".

knowledge would upset its dogmas and doctrines, made general education impossible. Likewise the Reform Bill broke the power of the squire, who, since the time of the Restoration, had intimidated the small electorate, mostly his larger tenants, to vote as he directed. Therefore the passing of the Reform Bill was a very important historic event, because it lifted from the people the tyranny of both squire and priest.

Whenever an increased number of the people (mainly the middle classes, farmers, tradesmen and professional workers) obtained a say in their own affairs, reforms became numerous, but another thirty-five years had to pass before the franchise was further extended to include the artisans and labourers who lived in houses little better than hovels. Only when they in turn obtained the vote was a start made to remedy their many grievances.

One important and ever-to-be-remembered fact emerges during this period of reform, and that is the opposition of the Christian clergy to every effort made to improve the lot of the people. The bishops in the House of Lords were particularly strong in their opposition to all reform measures and the abolition of the death penalty for thefts of 5s. and over, their antagonism to every form of education, apart from their own theological sectarian brand, being particularly violent. So objectionable became the attitude of the clergy to every measure to improve the lot of the down-trodden workers, who were earning less than 12s. for an eighty-hour week, that the Earl of Shaftesbury (1801-1885), who gave his entire political life to raise the standard of living for the poor, remarked:—

"I can scarcely remember an instance in which a clergyman has been found to maintain the cause of the labourers in the face of the pew-holders."

On another occasion Shaftesbury described the clergy as "timid, time-serving, and great worshippers of wealth and power", and he had every reason for this caustic remark. When the Prevention of Cruelty to Animals Bill came before the House of Lords in 1809 no bishop supported it. When a Bill was introduced in 1815 to prevent the use of British money in the Slave Trade, only three bishops were interested enough to attend to vote for or against it. The Prevention of Cruelty to Cattle Bill of 1824 did not interest them, and no bishop attended, but, as we have just read, when Wellington opposed the Reform Bill in 1831 all the bishops except two supported him.

Up to the end of the 18th century Christian Europe had practised slave-catching more extensively, and for the longest period known to history, but, with the extended franchise, the humanists were enabled to increase their opposition to Britain's participation in slavery in her colonies. Already progress had been made to this end, because sixty years earlier (1772) the Law Courts had decided that whenever a slave set foot on British soil he was free. This decision meant the freeing of some 15,000 negro slaves in Great Britain, and the credit for this is due to Granville Sharp, to whom more than any other individual the abolition of British slavery is due.

This happy event came about by him bringing into court a slave he had taken away from a brutal master in England, and, with the negro beside him, he demanded a decision as to the legality of his bondage.

When the court decided that it was now illegal to own slaves in England, thousands of these strangers in a strange land were set adrift to wander about the country, hungry and homeless, no one caring for them or giving them refuge. Finally 400 of them were despatched, along with fifty white prostitutes, to Sierra Leone, the idea being to establish a new colony, but all the women and half the negroes died, the remainder finding their way back to their own people.

The decision that it was now illegal to own slaves in Britain in no way ended the trade in slaves, from which she derived a very profitable revenue. Her slave traders continued to capture and transport slaves from Africa to the West Indies and North and South America, but this debased traffic was now beginning, under the lead of the despised Quakers, to revolt the conscience of the more intelligent amongst the people. The Christian Church still firmly opposed its abolition because it was in accordance with "God's Word", only two bishops supporting the abolition measure brought into the House of Lords in 1807. Abroad the same agitation for its cessation increased, and books were written against this degradation of man. The idea of a common brotherhood amongst men so roused the indignation of the clergy that the Pope excommunicated every Roman Catholic who took a stand for abolition, and ordered every book written in its favour to be burned.

In ancient Rome slaves could become schoolmasters, philosophers and engage in the arts and crafts. Under the emperors slavery was educative and often humane, but all authorities agree that

Christian slavery was more brutal and inhuman than anything experienced in Pagan times. Regimented gangs of slaves, crowded in barracks, took the place of the domestic slaves of Roman times. Herded together, they were treated like cattle, the utmost use being made of them so long as they were fit to work. In the British colonies and America the Christian Church did nothing to alleviate the condition of these victims of man's inhumanity to man, "no more than for the brute animal that shares his toil", said George Canning, Britain's Prime Minister in 1827, when referring to the attitude of the Protestant Church of his day.

After years of effort, Charles James Fox, Thomas Clarkson, Thomas Fowell Buxton, Lord Brougham and William Wilberforce, who had devoted their lives to abolish slavery, succeeded (1807) in passing a Bill to bring to an end the capturing and selling of slaves. The resistance to any change was particularly fierce, sermons being preached everywhere throughout the land against any departure from God's commands. Wilberforce, who was a man of great social charm, bitterly complained, just as did Shaftesbury, that in all his efforts to secure freedom for the slaves he had to encounter strong opposition from the clergy. To the non-churchmen, and the non-Christians, he gave praise for their help and encouragement during the dark days of obstruction, when every possible obstacle was put in his way to discourage him in achieving his aim.

Though he and his supporters ultimately won their fight against the powers of wickedness, the traffic continued, as the slave dealers secured immunity by sailing their galleys under the flag of the United

States, which was eager for all the slaves she could obtain. In the face of fierce opposition Clarkson and Wilberforce next worked for the emancipation of the slaves already in British possessions, but not until 1833, under the reformed Parliament, was a Bill passed which secured their release in 1840. Even this victory over evil was only possible by the additional Irish votes in favour of emancipation, because the Irish had no financial interest in the trade, and consequently lost nothing by the passage of the measure.

Mental development was responsible for this great achievement, as the minds of most Christians were rising above their former barbaric level. Up to now they had believed that God had delivered the heathen over to them to be their bondsmen for ever, to be handed down to their children as an inheritance. (*Leviticus* xxv, 46.) Only by mental evolution did the conduct improve of those who professed to live the Christian way of life. By that alone, and nothing more, though Christians claim today that it was Christianity which abolished the slave trade! What a hindrance to progress this queer assortment of Pagan and Hebrew beliefs has been to mankind, ideas which halted civilisation and progress for over a thousand years.

Drunkenness was the curse of Britain in those days, but only two bishops supported the various temperance measures introduced from 1839 to 1844. Lord Brougham was so angry with their indifference to anything for the good of the people that he remarked, "Only two out of six and twenty Right Reverend Prelates will sacrifice their dinner and their regard for their bellies . . . to attend and vote." All this is a terrible record, but we must remember that the bishops (who then claimed, as they still do, to be filled with, and guided by, the Holy Spirit) looked upon themselves as the guardians of Christian civilisation, an era which they believed was ordained by God. This being so, they considered that democratic civilisation, with its belief in the rights and dignity of man, in social welfare and in its parliamentary measures to raise people to a higher level of life and thought, was an invention of the devil.

If the bishops, and the Christian Church as a whole, did nothing to help forward a better civilisation, who then did so? Did individual Christians make themselves prominent in the movement for the betterment of the people? Certainly very few Christian clergymen did so; in fact they ranged themselves so heavily on the side of the reactionaries that the reformers branded them with names only associated with tyranny and injustice. Nearly everyone in those days was a Christian, and it would indeed be strange not to find some Christian layman infected by the arguments of the infidel reformers. Some were, but it is remarkable that in an age when Christianity was part of the everyday life of the people, everyone being born into it, the great majority of the reformers were professedly not Christians, a difficult stand to take in those days. This clearly points to the reform movement coming mainly from those who put the love of humanity first, and relegated to the background Christian tradition and its narrow creeds and doctrines.

Here, then, is a record of the achievements of some

of the men and women who openly declared themselves to be either Agnostics, Deists or Spiritualists. It is confined solely to those who were prominent pioneers in social reform, omitting the heretical scientists, doctors and others who, by their efforts and example, helped to raise the people to a higher level of thought, and bring about an improvement in the health, comfort, well-being and happiness of the community.

David Hume (1711–1776), the outstanding philosopher and historian, guided his readers out of the way of theological ignorance into the path of reasoned thought. Adam Smith (1723–1790), the great economist, was one of the first to advocate that the 90 per cent. illiterate English children should be taught to read and write. Robert Owen (1771–1858), a Manchester cotton spinner, was one of the greatest men of the 19th century.

He was a pioneer in philanthropy, a word hardly known before his time in Christendom. He conducted his mills profitably and with great ability, but on humane lines, his employees working in clean, healthy, sanitary buildings, and for shorter hours than his competitors. He would have no child labour, and paid his workers during periods of depression. These he instructed, and, in an age of drunkenness, taught them to be sober and thrifty. He advocated an improved environment for all employees, but could find no other employer willing to support him. So alone he educated his workers out of their crimes, drunkenness and filth, and raised them to be respected and decent citizens.

The first Factory Act (1819), the Child's Magna Charta, was largely due to his efforts. All the abuse the Christians of his day could invent was hurled at him, to increase in intensity when he declared himself openly to be a Spiritualist and not a Christian. He conceived and carried out as far as possible all that the later Socialists worked for, and can be considered the founder of Fabian Socialism and the Co-operative movement.

He founded a non-theological school at New Lanark, and was the pioneer of all the reforms the workers now enjoy. He was a man of great liberality, and supported the unorthodox Lancaster, when he started his secular schools all over the country. Only then, in order to prevent the children of their flocks from being contaminated by heretical ideas, did the Episcopalians and Roman Catholics start their Church schools.

In his days titles and honours were being freely handed round to all the schemers, intriguers, parasites and sycophants who were in a position to bribe or influence the leading politicians or the King, but none ever came the way of the really great men and women of that age who were raising their fellow creatures to a higher level of life and thought. Owen was too great a man to trouble about such tawdry stuff, and, by his brilliance, the men whom the ignorant then considered great are now picked out as common clay. On the other hand, those who were then looked upon as of no importance, as the cranks and meddlers with the existing order, are today revered and raised to the rank of nobility in the minds of all who can appreciate true greatness.

So much for Robert Owen, and now, if we put aside the many non-Christian scientists, doctors and all such who by their work have added to the health, comfort and happiness of mankind, let us briefly read the records of just a few more of the pioneer philanthropists and reformers who were opposed to, and refused to profess, the Christian faith. Christians declare that such heretical reformers never existed, and that all the benefits we now enjoy came from the devoted work of professing Christians. As this book is written to help to remove the curse of ignorance (for which the Christian Church is solely responsible, because it abolished the widespread highly organised Roman educational system in the 5th century), the truth will now be told.

Francis Place, the brains behind the reform movement, and his non-Christian collaborators, brought forward and secured the right of workers to form trade unions. This genius for organisation, denied a seat in Parliament, devoted his life to improve the lot of the working man, giving his encouragement to the educational work done by the newly founded Mechanics' Institutes after he had seen, with sorrow, the failure of every attempt made to secure state support for education. Richard Carlile, a bookseller, suffered and achieved more for the liberty of the Press than any other Englishman, experiencing imprisonment sixteen times for selling *The Age of Reason*, but every time, on release, he continued to defy the authorities until in the end he was victorious.

John Stuart Mill, the utilitarian philosopher, by his writings, helped to raise humanity to a higher level of thought. Thomas Firmin founded St. Thomas's Hospital in London, Thomas Cogan founded the Royal Humane Society, and Sydney Waterlow gave large donations for purposes which brightened the lives of the poor. John Pounds founded the Ragged Schools, and Joseph Tuckerman established the Domestic Missions for the poor in England and America. John Fielden introduced the Ten Hours Bill, and pleaded in vain that it should be the Eight Hours Bill. Southwood Smith was the pioneer of sanitation and Sir Henry Tate founded the Tate Gallery in London.

No name stands higher in the annals of philanthropy and humanitarianism than that of Jeremy Bentham, the famous legal reformer, moralist and philosophic writer. In a cruel and selfish age this benevolent non-Christian philosopher laid the foundation of British democratic philosophy, his numerous works emphasising that "the aim of government is to secure the greatest happiness for the greatest number". George Grote, the well-known philosopher, politician and Greek historian, wrote and worked for increased education amongst the people, the reform of prisons, the abolition of the gross injustices in the law, and the improvement of social conditions. Lord Brougham also strove for the education and improved welfare of the people, while Charles Dickens, the Unitarian, by his novels, exposed the appalling state in which the poor lived.

Never must we forget the names of Fanny Wright, Harriet Martineau, Mary Wollstonecraft, the authoress of *The Rights of Women*, and George Eliot, who were all so prominent in their endeavours to raise the legal, political, social and educational status of women, bound to their husbands for life no matter how the latter behaved. Divorce could only be obtained through a Church Court, and seldom was it ever granted. In this work they received the help of William Godwin, the author of *Political Justice*, and Leigh Hunt, the poet and essayist, besides that of Shelley, the poet, who, because of his anti-Christian activities, was sent down from Oxford University.

Catherine Wilkinson originated public wash-houses and public baths. S. G. Howe took a leading part in bringing education to the blind and deaf. Mary Carpenter founded the Industrial Reformatory School for Girls. Dorothea Dix brought about better treatment for lunatics. William Rathbone founded the District Nursing Association, and Francis Cobb did much to prevent cruelty to animals. George Jacob Holyoake carried on Robert Owen's co-operative movement amongst the working classes, and has the distinction of being the last man in Britain to be imprisoned (1841) for giving an un-orthodox reply to a question about Christianity at a meeting he was addressing. For this "crime" he was imprisoned for six months. This happened only one hundred years ago, so we need not wonder that the curse of ignorance still casts its sinister shadow over us.

The greatest philosopher of the 18th century, Immanuel Kant, whose book *On Religion Within the Limits of Reason* was banned in Berlin, sided always with the people against tyranny and oppression. Benjamin Franklin, called "the first civilised American", originated the first circulating library and founded the Democratic party. Thomas Jefferson, the most conspicuous apostle of democracy in America, loved liberty and justice as much as he hated Christianity.

Voltaire stopped the Inquisition in France and ushered in an era of greater religious liberty, but space does not permit us to go all over the world to find heretical reformers, the above four, of the many who could be mentioned, being referred to because of the outstanding work they did for the good of mankind.

Passmore Edwards founded institutes and free libraries for working men. Thomas Paine, the notable social reformer, was the first Englishman to advocate pensions for the poor, the rights of man, the abolition of slavery, and that women should receive their rights as citizens. Last, but by no means least, Florence Nightingale, the founder of the sick-nursing profession, devoted her life to healing the sick and wounded.

So much for the leading non-Christians of the age we are now considering, the infidels who helped to raise humanity to a higher level of thought and comfort. Their rejection of the faith of the land in which they were nurtured in no way dimmed their love for humanity, which shone as brightly in their lives as it did in the lives of later Christian philanthropists who followed their example.

The foregoing facts, moreover, make crystal clear that after Britain had been a Christian country for twelve hundred years it required non-Christians to teach the Christians to become humane, but it is likewise a fact that if Christianity be true a terrible fate awaited these great humanists after death, while the bishops, who put "their regard for their bellies" before the welfare of the people, are now in heavenly bliss with their Saviour and Redeemer, thankful that they are not experiencing the tortures of hell inflicted on those who gave their lives to raise their fellow men and women to a higher social and intellectual level.

The pages of this book, devoted to Christian civilisation, reveal the terrible conditions in which the people lived, but where in any history book do we find a finger pointing to the event which brought about this state of affairs? In Chapter VII it was emphasised that the decision reached at the Council of Nicaea in 325, which raised the Christian Church to the position of the State Church of the Roman Empire, was the greatest and most tragic event in history. Instead of the world being guided by the thoughts of the great philosophers of Greece and Rome, its most virile inhabitants fell under the domination of a hierarchy of ignorant priests, which ruled what became Christendom from that date to the time we are now considering. The Greek and Roman educational system was replaced by theology, and consequently ignorance took the place of the pursuit of knowledge.

From the period dealt with in the next section of this book onwards a change, however, occurs, and we begin to see the effect of the rays of the sun of knowledge lighting up the dark valley through which humanity had been plodding. We are now at the beginning of a new era when the priest is pushed aside, and the schoolmaster takes his place. Instead of a divinely guided monarch, influenced by a God-inspired priest, a representative elected Parliament in Britain carries out the wishes of the majority of the people, who altogether are growing ever more intelligent as each year passes.

Today we look back one hundred years on these

evil sordid times, about which this chapter deals, and all good men and women rejoice that Christian principles, Christian culture, Christian morality and Christian ideals, for which Nicaea was responsible, have gone, never again to return. Fortunately we have now reached the time in history when we begin to see the end of the Theological Age, the termination of this long story of oppression, cruelty, intolerance, injustice and everything that is wicked, a time when ignorance was elevated to rank as a virtue, and all knowledge denounced as a sin.

The 19th century witnessed the holy institution responsible for all this crime and wickedness in its old age, tottering to its grave, the 20th century beholding its dying agony, and its life being maintained entirely by false propaganda supported by its vast ill-gotten wealth and ancient tradition. Nevertheless the Church has still life enough to injure gravely all whom its palsied fingers touch, but, to all who think, its claims and assertions are now passed by unnoticed. Its creeds no longer satisfy, its dogmas lack breadth and tenderness, they are too cruel and merciless for our times. They belong to the Theological Age which science superseded last century, and to most well-informed people the Christian Church is now an interesting relic of the past. The faith for which it stands is now but a shadow to most people, and no more a living flame.

Freedom, and the open spaces, now take the place of the dungeon of a fixed belief. The hideous deformed ideas of the past are giving place to greater kindness, increased sympathy with others, and grander nobler deeds. As faith decreased, the works of charity and mercy increased, and the greater love of man for man advanced as intolerance, fanaticism and superstition faded from the mind. To do all the good we can, to help the helpless, to relieve suffering and increase happiness, is now regarded by many as of more importance than belief in narrow creeds and sacred texts, which meant so much to those who lived before us.

Here we have reached the period of history when such thoughts were beginning to be dimly appreciated by our ancestors, and, from now onwards, we shall notice the effect on mind development of education suppressed for fifteen centuries, and the wondrous change it brought about. The curse of ignorance is slowly lifting, the night is passing, and the sun of knowledge is to be seen just above the horizon.

(8) Social Reform in Britain while her Empire Expands.

The Tory party, after the passage of the Reform Bill, was quite discredited because of its opposition to reform, and when Peel became its leader in 1834 he found it necessary to state that opposition to reform was not now part of his party's policy. This pronouncement is all the more remarkable as it was the age of Metternich in Europe, when that reactionary statesman was everywhere putting back the clock of progress. It points, moreover, to the greater wisdom and liberality on the part of British statesmen, qualities which have more than once saved the country from bloody revolution. The Tories, however, did not regain office until 1841, and, in the interval, the Whigs abolished slavery in British possessions, established workhouses for the poor and improved the condition of child labour in factories.

Prior to 1833 young children could be forced to work for more than twelve hours a day, but in that year an Act was passed which made it illegal for children under nine to work in textile factories, and limited the working day of children (9 to 13 years) to nine hours, and of young persons (13 to 18) to twelve hours. This Act, and one of 1840, making illegal, but not stopping, the employment of children as chimney-sweeps, was the work of the great humanist, Lord Shaftesbury, who was much influenced by the humane work done by Robert Owen, the pioneer of all factory reform, education and the improvement of the social conditions of the poor.

Victoria (1837–1901) succeeded her uncle William IV when he died in 1837. Since the time George I ascended the British throne in 1714, the British sovereign had also reigned over Hanover, of which state he was the Elector, but now, as the Hanoverian constitution precluded a woman from occupying the throne, the British monarch ceased to be recognised by the Hanoverians, and Ernest Augustus, the tyrannical Duke of Cumberland, became King of Hanover. In Britain the indolent Lord Melbourne became Prime Minister, he being also the intimate adviser of the young queen, and from now onwards the British sovereign ceased to express publicly any political opinions. Melbourne's ministry passed a Municipal Reform Bill in 1835, giving all male rate-payers in 178 towns the right to vote for members of their Town Council, but agitation continued throughout the country for a wider suffrage and other parliamentary reforms.

In 1838 a party pledged to these reforms drew up a People's Charter demanding (1) manhood suffrage, (2) vote by ballot, (3) annual elections, (4) abolition of property qualification for voters, (5) payment of members, and (6) equal electoral districts. From this document its supporters derived the name of Chartists. Most of these reformers strove to obtain their aims by constitutional means, and meetings were held everywhere throughout the country, but the more unruly section caused riots. These reached their height in 1848, when the French second Republic was established, but nothing was achieved though their programme was taken up by the Liberal party, to become part of its policy. The people were still mostly uneducated, and unable to use the vote wisely, and it was not until 1928, when education had been general for some fifty-eight years (since 1870), that all men and women over twenty-one years of age were granted the franchise.

In England, up to the Reformation, boys destined for monastic life were taught to read and write to enable them to follow the services, study the Bible, and make copies of sacred books, but we have nothing to make us think that any other children besides these ever received any kind of instruction until Winchester College was founded in 1387 and Eton College in 1440. In the reign of Edward VI (1547–1553) this form of theological teaching was abolished, as the monasteries had been dissolved. They were replaced by Grammar Schools for the purpose of teaching Latin and Greek to Episcopalians to enable them to enter

Oxford and Cambridge universities, then, and up to the 19th century, controlled by the Church, their lazy, useless college dons, more like monks than teachers, being priests, appointed by influence, and not permitted to marry. Consequently discipline was lax, professors grossly neglected their duties, serious examinations were unknown, and the only matter about which there was determination was that Nonconformists and non-Christians were for ever to be excluded from these two seats of learning.

Because of this exclusiveness, these unfortunate outcasts started a number of schools for their own children, but the Episcopalians influenced Parliament to pass the Schism Act, which suppressed them, a form of persecution which was not repealed until the reign of George I. The next move by the Episcopalians was to start Charity Schools, here and there, in 1708, to teach children the alphabet and the doctrines of the Church of England, "to train the poor to poverty" as one historian puts it, but this effort never embraced more than 25,000 children, the vast majority of the population remaining both illiterate and uneducated.

Such, then, was the lamentable position of education at the close of the 18th century, and its evolution during the 19th century is a record of the determination of liberal-minded people to overcome the stiff opposition of the orthodox, who put their beliefs before all else. The hero and pioneer of this struggle against religious opposition was Joseph Lancaster (1778–1838), the son of a Chelsea pensioner, who gave his life to the advancement of elementary education, and the breaking of the iron band of theology, which hitherto had confined instruction to the creeds, dogmas and doctrines of the Christian faith. Like nearly all pioneers, he was a heretic, his scheme being to impart knowledge and ignore theology, and from the age of twenty, in the year 1798, he gathered round him in his home the children of the poor, to whom he imparted free of charge the rudiments of instruction.

Soon the accommodation was inadequate, and then 1000 children were gathered in a hall in the Southwark district of London, to obtain for the first time simple instruction for the purpose of releasing their minds to a slight degree from the curse of ignorance. Fortunately some sympathetic friends came to Lancaster's aid, and provided him with money to build a schoolroom and obtain books, pencils and paper. The brightest pupils were then made monitors, and given classes to teach what they had already learned, but it was all very primitive, as in those days there were no school books, much of the teaching being done by means of slates and sand, on which the children scrawled the letters of the alphabet with their fingers, and made figures for their simple arithmetic.

The order and cheerfulness of the school, and the precision of the children in their work, created widespread notice and religious opposition, but, quite undaunted, Lancaster pursued his plan, going from town to town opening new schools and rousing the enthusiasm of both young and old for his noble work. Unfortunately, this lover of children entirely lacked wisdom and judgment, his zeal for education for ever involving him in financial difficulties, to end in his debts being paid by some admirers of his work, who formed the British and Foreign School Society.

He could not, however, work under restraint, and parted from his friends and helpers, to set up a private school at Tooting, only to become bankrupt.

Then he emigrated to America and Canada, where he carried out a course of lectures, but soon his poor health compelled him to find a warmer climate in Venezuela. Again he visited Canada and the United States, but his aim was to return to England, where, he said, he would put into practice a system which would make it possible "to teach 10,000 children in different schools, not knowing their letters, all to read fluently in three weeks to three months" His vision unfortunately was never realised, as he was killed in New York by being run over by a carriage, a tragic end to a life devoted to a noble and sublime mission.

While all this was going on the Christian Church was consumed by fear for its future. Every denomination saw the red light of danger. Theology, so long triumphant, was at last definitely confronted with the problem it had smothered so successfully throughout the Christian era. Only in ignorance could its evil influence survive, and now that knowledge was definitely making headway every devout Christian shivered in fear of the consequences. In 1811, or thirteen years after Lancaster had begun his good work, the Church of England made the first move to thwart his plan to educate on secular lines the children of England, and this was later followed by a similar one on the part of the Roman Catholic Church.

The plan of these two bastions of ignorance was subtle and for a time successful, because it embraced the opening of competitive schools to teach the elements of education in combination with the beliefs of their religion. Under the direction of a priest, named Andrew Bell, "The National Society for the Education of the Poor in the Principles of the Established Church" came into being, its very limited educational objects becoming evident when Bell announced that he did not desire to instruct the lower classes in the art of writing or arithmetic, because it would "elevate above their station those who were doomed to the drudgery of daily labours".

Now began the long-drawn-out religious struggle over the education of the children of Great Britain, a conflict which still goes on in our own times, three different denominations being involved, and much hatred and bitterness engendered. To prevent the Anglican brand being taught to the children of Dissenters, the Nonconformists and the Whigs, who were mostly non-Anglicans, supported the secular British and Foreign School Society, while the Anglicans and the Tories gave their sympathy to the National Society, the Roman Catholics supporting neither, because their children were made to go to their own newly opened schools, where they were free from all Protestant contamination.

Thus it came about that to Joseph Lancaster is due the fame and honour of breaking the hidebound Christian tradition of keeping the people in ignorance, and, if he had lived one hundred years earlier, he would have been banished or imprisoned. When, therefore, we hear the clergy repeat their often-told falsehood that Christianity brought education to the people, we should remember that this is just another of the tales circulated by the wealthy, highly organised, unscrupulous Christian propaganda system, which, throughout the Christian era, has relied on lies to enhance the prestige of the Church and the beliefs on which it thrives. Unfortunately the B.B.C. gives the clergy full scope to spread their many mis-statements, and their congregations are so ignorant that they accept like sheep all they hear from the shepherd of the flock. So the truth will only reach the people slowly, and the majority will continue for years to live on in ignorance, as the facts are generally unknown because so few have the time, opportunity or inclination to delve into the past to discover them.

The seed which Lancaster sowed took many years to grow, as for the next thirty years the education of the people was quite neglected, the Church, after his death, showing no enthusiasm for a cause so contrary to its established custom. If the State had not been forced, when the franchise was extended, to take up the work he had so brilliantly begun, the vast majority would today be as ignorant as their ancestors had been throughout the Christian era.

The science of education even now is still in its infancy, too much time being given to teaching what is unnecessary, and too little to what is really essential. We have yet to discover the best method of instructing and inculcating ethics, in order to raise the mental level to a position from which it can handle aright our recently acquired control over the forces of nature. Only when we learn to practise the virtues, to master our passions, and control our greed will education have reached one of its many goals, and in this chapter we are merely considering the first feeble attempt to raise the people out of the slough of ignorance in which they had so long sprawled and wallowed.

The urge for progress and reform was now growing year by year, so much so that in 1842 an Act was passed prohibiting women and children working underground in mines, and in 1844 another Factory Act was passed to reduce the working hours of children to six and a half hours a day. Women's working time was reduced to twelve hours a day. An Act of 1847 reduced the working day to ten hours for young people and women, and after 1853 women and children could only be employed during the day. In 1800 the population of Great Britain was between 10,000,000 and 11,000,000, and by 1850 it had increased to just over 20,000,000, the large centres of population now being in the great industrial cities.

Machines were raising the standard of living, necessities were becoming cheap and plentiful, and the poorer classes were beginning to enjoy some of the comforts, and even luxuries, which had been beyond the reach of the rich of earlier times. This tendency continued, and in the chapter which follows it will be possible to tell a brighter and more pleasing story. Gradually Christian civilisation was passing, and giving place to Democratic civilisation, to the rule of the people for the good of all the people.

While all this social progress was going on the British Empire was widening its bounds. British interest in Australia commenced after Captain James Cook (1728–1779), the son of a labourer, and one of Britain's greatest maritime explorers, had charted its coasts and also those of New Zealand in 1769–70. His wonderful discoveries began in a strange way. For centuries the belief had been held that a great continent, abounding in precious metals, lay south of the Atlantic and Pacific Oceans. Various popes had claimed it in the name of the Holy Ghost, and previous expeditions, which had gone south with the papal blessing, had instructions to add this great territory and its inhabitants to the realm of Christ on earth.

The British government, anxious to settle the question once and for all, sent Captain Cook to the Antarctic (ostensibly to observe the impending transit of Venus) with instructions to sail south until he came to land. The legendary land was not found, but, on his various voyages in these southern latitudes, he discovered many islands, including the Sandwich Islands. Unfortunately, in a dispute with the natives in Hawaii, this sagacious, humane and brave man was killed.

A place named Botany Bay, on the Australian coast, was first used by the British as a penal settlement, and in one year alone (1787) over 1000 men and women were banished there for life, many being charged with only petty crimes or the zeal for reform. A year later the first settlement was made five miles farther north, at the spot where now is placed the great city of Sydney, the capital of New South Wales, and chief port of Australia.

Gradually adventurers, besides prisoners, found their way to this new-found land, valuable agricultural and pastoral lands being developed. Settlement started in Tasmania in 1803, in Queensland, then part of New South Wales, in 1826, in West Australia in 1829, in South Australia in 1836, and in New Zealand in 1840. What is now called Victoria was originally part of New South Wales, from which it separated in 1851, in which year gold was discovered and the gold rush began. South Africa, likewise, was separated into Cape of Good Hope and Natal in 1844. In Canada, British Columbia was occupied by the Hudson Bay Company in 1858, the same year as the East India Company passed the Straits Settlements over to the British crown.

The British Crown colony of Gambia was occupied in 1817, and in 1841 came the occupation of Hong Kong under disgraceful circumstances. British merchants were shipping opium into China against the wishes of the Chinese government, which had prohibited the use of this dangerous drug. In 1839 the Chinese seized a shipment of opium, and British warships arrived at Canton to protect British property. War followed, when the Chinese were defeated and forced to cede the island of Hong Kong and open five ports to British trade. Further aggressive action was taken by both Britain and France in 1860 to secure increased trade with China, but the story of this second war will be told in the chapter which follows.

In search of raw materials, which were required for the increased demands of industry, explorers from Europe penetrated into the wilds of Africa, David Livingstone (1813–1873) being the most famous. Arriving in Africa in 1841, he was the first medical missionary, the conversion of the heathen being as much his aim as exploration. In 1849 this modest brave man, who was much beloved by the natives, penetrated farther inland, discovering Lake Ngami and the Zambesi river, to arrive eventually at Loanda on the west coast. Then he crossed the continent from west to east, discovering the Victoria Falls on the way. Later he discovered Lakes Nyasa and

Tanganyika, near which he was found by Stanley, but here we must leave Africa, as the story of further discoveries, and its development, will be told in the next chapter.

This chapter has covered one of the most important periods of world history, during which occurred three of the greatest events in man's long upward climb. The first was the discovery of how to control, and use for human purposes, the powers of nature, the second being the long stride forward which was made by the English-speaking people in the art of self-government, and this led to the third, namely improved social conditions for the people. These three events mark the beginning of a new era in civilisation, and one which is rich in future possibilities for all mankind.

The way forward towards the light will twist and turn, and man, in his upward climb, will often stumble and fall on its rocky surface, but, as education advances, and our knowledge increases, the way will become easier and life will become happier. Aided by the torch of knowledge, and the desire for greater righteousness, developing mind will some day rise to a level not yet appreciated. Then justice, mercy and truth will reign, while compassion, service and consideration for others will be found to be the height of wisdom.

CHAPTER XVI.

CHRISTIAN CIVILISATION.
(1791–1901.)

Introduction. (1) A Revolution in Thought Ushers in a New Era for Mankind. (2) France Under the Rule of Napoleon III. (3) Italy and Germany Become United Nations. (4) The Roman Catholic Church Curses all Progress and Reform. (5) Civil War Lacerates the United States. (6) Progress, Discovery and Reform during the 19th Century. (7) The Rise to Independence of the Dominion of Canada. (8) Britain and her Empire during the Victorian Era.

MUCH of what is told in the preceding chapters of this book has been devoted to religion, because it is the historian's duty to produce the reasons for the actions and events he records. Up to now, at least half of mankind's thoughts and deeds have come from his religious beliefs, and consequently his religion has played a great part in history. This chapter, however, records a change in this age-old outlook, supernatural religion from now onwards playing a less prominent part, and knowledge, derived from intelligent observation and experience, a much greater part in the life of civilised people.

Nevertheless the mystery of existence, the extent of the yet unknown, and the lack of knowledge, still produces much unbalanced thinking, which it is the privilege of those who have delved deeper than most to rationalise if possible. Much that has been dark in the past history of mankind may have already been clarified in the preceding chapters, and now that we are at the opening of a new era of thought let us analyse some of those vital problems which continue to perplex and mystify many in our own times. Wrong opinions spring from the lack of a scientific foundation for our thoughts.

Some three thousand years ago, as the unity of nature became evident, the tendency increased towards the belief in one supreme being who ruled over all the gods and goddesses, he being conceived in accordance with the level of development attained by each individual. As man's mind evolved, so did the God idea develop. The more unselfish, kind and just the individual became, so did his god, until today there are millions of good people who are worried and perplexed because God allows so much evil, misery and suffering in the world.

On 31st May, 1943, a hospital nurse broadcast over the B.B.C. a description of all the misery and pain it had been her lot to witness during her forty years of nursing the sick. She told how her faith in the goodness of God had been so often tried and almost broken. "Why did God permit all this pain and suffering to helpless innocent people who had done nothing to deserve it?" she asked. Her only remaining comfort was her belief in the suffering dying Saviour-god of the Christian Church, and in its rites and ceremonies. To find comfort in this way does not solve a difficult problem, which she avoided by thinking of the imagined suffering that a god experienced for a short time some nineteen hundred years ago.

This devout woman, overflowing with sympathy for all in distress, had from early childhood imaged God to be good, kind and loving like herself, and when she came up against evil, pain and misery she was shocked and wondered why all this suffering was allowed by the god of her imagination. Many millions have been similarly dumbfounded, especially in our times, when mind has developed sufficiently to be increasingly sympathetic towards those who suffer. In childhood this woman had produced a beautiful mental image of God which later experience shattered, her mistake of course being that she had imaged something for which there is no scientific basis. She had created her god in her own image, and had expected her creation to conform to her ideals, and because it did not she was bewildered and sorrowful.

Facts must be faced, and logically and rationally arranged, if we are to have mental peace and contentment. This will not come by creating false mental images, and then sorrowing when we discover that they cannot be retained. Only by facing facts bravely and intelligently, and following where nature leads, can our difficulties be overcome. Light can only come to illumine the many dark problems of life if we use our reason, and only form opinions which are based on a solid foundation of knowledge and experience.

Before life came to earth, nature's laws reigned supreme just as they do today. Effect followed cause then just as it does now and always will. Universal law has always been and always will be; everything changes but nothing is ever destroyed. Mind, when it first manifested on earth, did so in harmony with natural law, pain and suffering following from this association when it and its physical habitation did not work smoothly together. Only by adjusting these physical defects to its liking did harmony return, but ages passed, and millions of living creatures suffered and died, before mind developed sufficiently to be able to do this.

This was eventually accomplished by means of memory, because the mind, by remembering the past and observing the present, discovered the necessary remedies to relieve its suffering. Much still remains to be done to free sentient creatures from pain, but we have already travelled far to reach our goal, and some day the means will be found to counteract the effect of disharmony between the mind and its body. Mind, this super-physical substance, alone can cure its ills, and reach the state of harmony it so desires. By rational thought, by observation and by experience, the mind of man will continue to rise superior to its physical surroundings until in time all nature is used to do its will.

This super-physical substance, which we call mind, divides the living from the dead. Matter devoid of mind lacks life; a stone cannot be compared with that which moves and thinks, it being inert, whereas movement depicts thought and life, while memory in every seed produces a replica of its parents. So mind is king, and, as such, the physician of its body which it must order to its desires by finding remedies for the defects which cause it discomfort and pain. Thus it can counteract, by means of natural law, those physical abnormalities which produce disease, and the more it thinks, and the better it thinks, the healthier will be its habitation.

We know not when, or how, or why, mind first entered into association with matter, but we do know that the more it developed the more it wondered as to the why and wherefore of everything, as to where it came from and whence it is going.   Observation and experience taught it to discern the difference between life and death, between growth, movement and inertness, between right and wrong, between good and evil, between justice and injustice, and, as these ideas developed, it imagined a master mind like unto its own.   It personified an invisible creator like unto itself, in thought and appearance, and with superhuman power.   To the cruel and wicked he was both cruel and wicked, and to the good and kind he was both good and kind.   On him this childish mentality relied for sustenance, just as does a child on its father, and, so long as this childlike image was fixed, the mystery of existence, and the many problems surrounding it, remained unsolved.

So the difficulties which beset the hospital nurse came from a wrong idea which must be eliminated, and facts must be put in its place if peace of mind is to be restored.   But trying to explain a problem on a false assumption, and then relying on faith to help her out, leads nowhere, and it is because some have abandoned this method that progress has been made in curing disease and relieving suffering.

Faith is a very present help in trouble, because it gives comfort to the ignorant, but knowledge is the weapon which will prevent the trouble, and obviate the misery which comes from ignorance.   Knowledge of all nature's laws is therefore the solution of our remaining perplexing problems, as on man alone rests his salvation, and the more he discovers, and the more he knows of the universe in which he lives, the happier will life become.

Consequently we reach the conclusion that the suffering and misery, which so troubles all kindly people, comes from ignorance. If we had lived a hundred years earlier we would have found that our afflictions were much worse than they are today, but, because of the changed outlook which occurred during last century, the position is now infinitely better, and every year witnesses an alleviation of our troubles. So, when the nurse exclaimed, "Why does God permit cancer?" we reply that we live in an ordered universe, and when we find the remedy which exists, and will some day be discovered, cancer, like so many other diseases, will be eliminated by knowledge overcoming ignorance.

Man is his own saviour, and, when he finds the cure, disease, and its accompanying pain, vanishes. Nothing of value comes from stretching out our hands and imploring help from heaven, and this misdirected effort deflects our minds from striving to solve our own troubles. To take the childish, easiest way is not the wisest course, because our succour only comes from developing mind, which has raised us to our present level, and will continue to do so in the years to come. Our help comes from ourselves, from mind, which decided for some inscrutable reason, aeons ago, to make its abode in matter so as better to express itself. Because, in ignorance, it has often gone contrary to nature's laws it has suffered, but the more it has conformed to them the happier it has been.

Each individual has a long and interesting journey,

both here and hereafter, to reach perfection and under,
standing, but, when he attains his goal, his mind will
have unfolded the universe and found Reality, and
also the source whence flows the power that sustains
the universe.

To understand and master nature, to use her for
our good, and not be her slave, must therefore be the
purpose of developing mind, and at the time in history
we have now reached, this momentous idea took root
to grow and flourish in the years ahead. The revolution in thought which came from this changed
outlook we shall now consider, as nothing more
eventful ever took place throughout the ages.

(1) A Revolution in Thought Ushers in a New Era for Mankind.

We have now arrived at the opening of a new era.
For thousands of years, since the ape-man became
man by making practical use of his thumb and fore-
finger to grip an implement, the human race has been
dependent on its own strength, or on that of animals,
to obtain from nature its desires, comforts and
nourishment. All that is now past history, because
we have discovered comparatively recently how to
make nature work for us and do our bidding. Surely
this is man's greatest achievement, the prime example
of the power of mind over physical matter, and most
of it has happened within the past hundred years.

At the beginning of the 19th century life continued
much as it had done for thousands of years, and then
came the change. A beam of sunlight broke through
the surrounding gloom, and a new world became

visible for all to see. Man, by relying on himself, by using his reason, had dissipated the mist which had hitherto encompassed him, and, by observation and experiment, brought light to a dark world.

Inventors, who produced the new ideas, and the engineers who made practical use of their inventions, consequently raised the people to a high grade of comfort and happiness. Thus these really great men demonstrated that mind intelligently directed is lord of nature. Knowledge has raised us from the level of the beasts to a state of well-being unimagined by our ancestors in the 18th century. Direction, labour and capital have all played an equal share in this evolutionary process, and the more these three intelligently combine the farther we shall proceed along the road of progress.

Up to one hundred years ago there was much labour, little knowledge, and less capital, and the foregoing chapters of this book have covered an age of ignorance, during which, by strenuous labour, only the prime necessities of life were won from the earth. Ignorance is the root of all evil, not the love of money, as Paul is reported to have told Timothy. The mystical, irrational Paul never studied economics, as, if he had, he would have reached the conclusion ably expounded by Adam Smith in his great book *Inquiry into the Nature and Causes of the Wealth of Nations*, that money[1] brings liberty to the race, and frees it from bondage and slavery.

Just as Adam Smith (1723-1790) produced a mental

[1] The word "money" comes from the Roman goddess Juno Moneta (Juno the Admonisher), at whose statue a silver article was deposited on the birth of each child.

revolution in the political and economic sphere of life, so did Charles Darwin (1809–1882) in that of philosophy, religion and biology. This illustrious man, after many years of thought and research, published in 1859 his famous book *Origin of Species*, in which he traced man's ancestry from the animal kingdom. Since the time when Copernicus declared that the sun did not travel round the earth, no greater shock had been administered to complacent mankind, because it upset the age-old belief, held by every race and every religion, that man was a special and spontaneous creation of God, or the gods, to crown the creation of the earth.

The consternation, anger and antagonism caused by the opinions of Darwin in the average upper- and middle-class families of Christendom can hardly in our time be realised. Anyone showing the slightest sympathy with this famous biologist's theories was immediately regarded as one who was swiftly travelling on the broad road which leads to destruction. All books which in any way cast doubt on the orthodox outlook were regarded with fear and distrust, and to read such a book was considered to be a grievous sin. The clergy vied with each other in their ridicule and abuse of one who had uncovered another of nature's secrets, and for years the principal topic of conversation after church on Sunday was the question of the descent of man from angels or monkeys.

The Christians of the 19th century were quick to see that if Darwin's theory, that man and the apes had a common ancestor, was true, their entire theological edifice was shattered, and, for the next fifty years, they ridiculed and vilified this noble man. If there were no

Adam, then there was no fall or original sin, and, if
this be so, a saviour was irrelevant and all the Christian
beliefs and ceremonies meaningless. Man, argued
Darwin, instead of having fallen, was a developing,
progressive creature, he having reached his present
position after countless years of slow evolution from
primitive protoplasm. Consequently he threw over
his belief in Christianity, but it took seventy years
before his main conclusions were finally accepted and
he was acknowledged as the pioneer of a new age of
thought.

Besides this his theories gave the idea of ordered
progress, one which was quite new to Christendom,
which, so far, had always looked back with admiration
on the glories of the past, and given little thought to
the possibilities ahead of the human race. Another of
nature's secrets had been revealed by means of improved scientific methods of observation and research,
and the 19th century became brilliant with new
discoveries and the advance in knowledge.

Mental development made all this possible, because Darwin, and his contemporary scientists, were
allowed to live peacefully and pursue their investigations without fear of persecution, as was the lot of
so many of their forerunners. The Church, however,
was not so tolerant to those over whom it had the
power, because not only did the clergy debase themselves by their condemnation of the brilliant naturalist,
but theological professors, who accepted his conclusions, were deprived of their Chairs and cast out as
heretics.

In this connection history just repeated itself, as
Sebastian Castellio, a Protestant theological professor

at Geneva in the 16th century, suffered the same fate. He was the first Christian to proclaim the innocence of honest error, and that other people's opinions were worthy of consideration, even if they were not in conformity with our own. Surrounded by inquisitions, prisons, stakes, thumb-screws, intolerance and cruelty, he was brave enough to make what was then a startling and blasphemous declaration. As that was too much for John Calvin to tolerate from one of his followers, he drove Castellio from his professorship and out of Geneva, accompanied by declarations that he was a child of the devil, a limb of Satan, a murderer of souls, a corrupter of the faith, and that he had crucified his saviour for the second time.

The malignity of the Geneva Christians increased to such intensity towards this brave, tolerant man, and they made his life so miserable, that he shortly afterwards died. His own orthodoxy was not in question, as if it had been he would doubtless have been burned at the stake like Servetus, who could not agree with Calvin on the question of the Trinity. Progress, however, continued, and during each succeeding century tolerance increased. The stake and torture were in time replaced by prison and banishment, and then followed ostracism and abuse, Dr. F. D. Maurice, for instance, losing his professorship at King's College, London, in 1853 because he cast doubt on hell being a fiery furnace.

Education, from the end of the 19th century onwards, then began to have its effect, and, though only eighty years separate the publication of *Origin of Species* from our time, what Darwin taught is now generally accepted by many who still call themselves

Christians, they having to make the best case possible for their creeds, whose foundation has been swept away. The Christian era, up to the time of Darwin, was an age of intellectual night lit by a few stars who, by rational thought, discovered some of nature's secrets, but with Darwin came the dawn which ushered in the age of religious liberty and the toleration we now enjoy.

Thus religion is changing to what it would always have been but for ignorance, a personal matter for each individual, and not an affair organised by a Church, with priests acting as its agents to propagate the creed for which it stands. A personal religion, which each one thinks out for himself, brings comfort and happiness, instead of the misery which comes from the intolerance generated by priests, who, for their own advancement, propagate a belief in an angry deity who provided a narrow way for the elect to travel upon, while the great majority are considered to be on the broad road that leads to destruction.

So a new age of thought commences with this chapter, and now it is possible for the inhabitants of all democratic countries to hold and express every shade of opinion. The past eighty years is therefore a period in which great progress has been made, and the happiness and comfort of everyone has correspondingly increased. For this advance developing mind is responsible, this development having been caused by all the things the inventors, engineers, chemists, doctors, explorers and everyone in all branches of science have brought into our lives.

Now the time has come when this more developed mind must apply the same practical methods to abolish war as it has done to abolish disease, and when this comes about future generations will devote their energy only towards constructive and not destructive effort. Raise the mental level and war will cease, because the least intelligent, and the least imaginative, are the best and bravest fighters, ignoring dangers which make the more developed flinch, hesitate and falter. Eliminate by education this aggressive unintelligent bestial mind in man, and put in its place a mind of higher ideals and outlook. This is the only solution to the problem of war and peace, because an intelligent race of men will negotiate and compromise and not fight for what they want.

In the past the art of killing has always received first attention, and the art of healing far too little. The instruments for destruction and slaughter were always more advanced than those employed in production. Craftsmen thought out means of killing, but not of prolonging life. Swords of exquisite workmanship were being manufactured when the plough was in its infancy. Expensive and elaborately wrought armour was worn before there were good and cheap clothes.

The date when gunpowder was invented is unknown, but, when it first came from the Far East to Europe in 1326, it was used only in warfare to propel balls of iron and brass. Its use revolutionised the conduct of war, but not the surface of the roads, which remained dark mud tracks until the end of the 18th century, when Telford and Macadam blasted the rocks with explosives, and used the pieces to make good and hard roads on which vehicles could travel with ease. So the highwayman, who used these mud tracks, preceded the lamps which lit the new roads, and slops were pitched out of the window on to the head of any unfortunate passer-by before anyone thought of drains.

During the past hundred years, by taking reasoned thought, and using our intelligence, the majority of people in civilised countries now live healthier lives, and are surrounded by greater comfort than were kings, queens, princes and nobles of bygone days, besides having secured more control over nature than did ever the famous conquerors of the past. Greater knowledge produced new and better ideas, which attracted capital that bought the raw material, and paid the men to make the tools, which the engineers used to make the machines, which made the things that give us the leisure and comforts we now enjoy.

Some so appreciated the value of money that they denied themselves something to save a portion of their income, which surplus, when used to produce wealth, we call capital. This they gave to the inventors and engineers to employ in such a way as to produce a profit, which process produced more capital, which encouraged more inventions and built more machines, to produce in turn more capital. So, for the last hundred years, wealth has been rapidly accumulating, and, apart from that wasted in war, it has been devoted to the increase of our knowledge, comforts and pleasures. Consequently we now have greater leisure for study and amusement, and, but for the setbacks occasioned by wars, there seems no end to what the intelligent application of discoveries and inventions will do for the increased happiness of the race.

Leisure makes further education possible, and this

increases refinement, ethical conduct and culture as well as knowledge. Mental wealth comes from physical wealth, because the mind cannot develop in a desert. It must have more, and still more, material things on which to react to make mental evolution continuous. When we criticise the past we must remember the limitations of our ancestors, who, lacking education and the knowledge it brings, had not the necessary material things about them to develop their minds. Consequently they were sluggish and dull, as heredity binds us to nature and her fixed laws, whereas environment enables the mind to expand and enlarge its boundaries. Thus only can we become masters of our destiny.

Our ancestors were ignorant, and we are revolted at their crude ideas and deeds, but we are all creatures of our conditions, because we do as our minds direct us, and they develop according to our heredity and environment. The mind thinks exactly according to its image-making capacity, as thinking consists of the making of mental images by means of the mysterious immaterial substance of which the mind consists, each image being determined by the way the mind reacts to stimulations.

Some minds react differently from others, and, although all minds produce the same images, all for instance making the same image of the same table, each one relates in different ways the thousands of images formed every day in one way or another. Consequently some minds accept what others reject, some form different conclusions, and none think alike, each mind being determined by its heredity and the environment in which it has developed.

Thinking is not a question of will-power or desire, because we believe, and we doubt, or we reject, and think, according to the way the mind reacts to what it hears, sees and feels. The mind is the product of our parents, but its development comes from its environment, and it was the new environment that knowledge brought to man which developed his mind and produced the mentality of today.

Only very ignorant and stupid people now imagine that our salvation or damnation hereafter depends upon belief, because belief comes quite naturally if the evidence exists, and, if it does not, belief lacks a foundation. What is evidence to a child is not evidence to an adult with a more developed mind, and so our ancestors, with childish undeveloped minds, believed what an intelligent person today cannot accept. Their god could not be accepted by enlightened people today, a fact which makes it obvious that man makes God in his own image, and that a just and merciful God is the noblest work of man.

The surplus wealth that is used to produce more wealth, that which we call capital, is essential to progress, and, besides producing our everyday needs, part of the surplus saved is also used to build schools and teach teachers how to teach. From the same source come our colleges, universities, books and instruments, all of which are the means of attaining greater knowledge. As this increases, greater leisure follows, and this in turn gives to future generations still more time to devote to mental development.

In the past, much of the people's surplus wealth, time and leisure were devoted to building pagodas, temples, mosques, churches, monasteries and theological institutions, because they thought that one or more gods controlled the universe, and that, by united prayer, all human desires could be obtained. They relied on one or more divine beings and not on themselves, the consequence being that these edifices were not used to impart knowledge, and there was no progress. That age is passing. Schools instead of churches, colleges and not cathedrals, are now filled each year with more intelligent minds which spread throughout the world the learning they have acquired. A snowball of intelligence has started, which will grow and reach dimensions we can scarcely envisage, because its prospects are as yet too vast to be fully grasped by our generation.

When it was believed that gods, spirits, angels, saints and devils ruled this world, we can well understand why so much labour was expended on sacred buildings. They were the control stations, in which the people, through the priest, made contact with the power that determined the welfare of the people. Likewise it was natural that priests, parsons, ministers, pongyis, mullahs, or whatever other name these representatives of the gods took to distinguish themselves from the common run of humanity, were considered holy and sacred, because they were regarded as the agents of the deities who controlled the universe.

They only had the privilege to be on intimate terms with the powers which caused good health or disease, rain or drought, plenty or famine, victories or defeats, and whose actions touched every angle of human existence. Consequently religion entered into every phase of life, and what science is to us now,

theology was to the people up to last century. Theology, then termed "the Queen of Science", was
such a vital matter that to deny its assertions was as
great a crime as treason.

Religion is still a state affair, and every monarch
is first anointed as priest and then crowned as king,
and this relic of the past still persists at the coronation
of every British sovereign. In Britain the King is still
put forward by the Archbishop of Canterbury as the
representative of God to British Protestants, he taking
the position given by Roman Catholics to the Pope,
and this division of opinion amongst Christians
has been the cause of endless trouble since the
Reformation.

The change over was very slow from belief in the
power of the priest to order nature, to the recognition
that nature's laws are fixed and only require understanding, when they can be used for our benefit.
The fight by rising intelligence against the powers of
ignorance was long and bitter, and only now have we
arrived at the time in history when theology is becoming discredited and science appreciated, the benefit of this change of outlook becoming more and more
noticeable as the 19th century advanced.[1]

More and more we are finding that knowledge,
and not theology, is the remedy for disease and its
accompanying pain and suffering. Gradually we are
learning that ethical education, and not creeds and
doctrines, is the remedy for crime, wickedness and all
our faults and failings. History proves that there is

[1] As mental development proceeds the standard books on psychic
philosophy and psychical research, recording the great discoveries this
science has made within the last fifty years, will reveal better than any orthodox religion the psychic part of man and his destiny after death.

less chance of illness when the people are under the care of the Medical Officer of Health than when they rely on the prayers of the clergy. Only when doctors, clinics and hospitals became plentiful were diseases cured and was suffering relieved. Only when schools became numerous did crime and drunkenness decrease, and we now realise that there is less chance of crime, and the need of prisons, in a town with schools and teachers than in one with only churches and priests, a fact which proves that keeping the people in superstitious ignorance leads to moral disaster.

Every intelligent person today would rather have a certificate about his drains from a sanitary inspector, than rely on the Prayer Book method of imploring Jehovah not to smite us with plague as he did three score and ten thousand in the time of David. When rain is wanted a priest prays for it, and to avert famine a priest prays for good crops, but now we know that intelligent forethought and planning are the best ways to avoid both drought and a poor harvest. Great Britain, however, still officially believes that priests, by their prayers, can assure victory in war, bring rain, cure disease, and make crops to grow, all the landowners being taxed many millions annually to sustain in being an army of black-robed men for the purpose of keeping contact with the imaginary powers in heaven. If this money were devoted instead to research for greater knowledge, and to the inculcation everywhere of the virtues, what a difference it would make to the happiness of everyone!

Ignorance still occupies at times the throne of reason, and this is especially the case in the time of war. God is always considered by each side to be fighting for and sympathising with each combatant, few public declarations on both sides during the last war omitting the acknowledgment that divine help was being given. Nevertheless the strongest, and most intelligently guided, side won then as it has always done in the past. It is as futile to expect God to bring peace as to send rain, and this stupid idea comes about through our ignorance of nature.

God is Mind, and when mind changes its outlook war will cease. When that happens this eternal and sustaining power will have won its greatest victory over matter. So let us all be rationalists, because that is wise, but not materialists, as we now know that there is life and substance beyond physical matter and what we normally experience by our limited sense perceptions.

The story of mind struggling to find increased expression confronts us from the time of primitive life up to our own day. Progress is, however, not a law of nature, and comes only from mind conquering and making use of nature. Progress is the effect of developing mind, which is superior to nature's laws because it can comprehend them and harness them to do its bidding. So there are always two forces at work—one we might term negative, or fixed natural law, and the other positive mental action, which is unchained and roams about at will. These two are for ever interacting through matter, there being a continual struggle between them, the positive endeavouring to get to better grips with the negative.

This being so, a thinking mental substance is overcoming the more primitive unthinking force which never deviates from its set course, and it would seem as if part of the original fundamental eternal mind of the universe broke away from its fixed method in order to produce thinking life on earth. Just as the mind, which produced the being we call man, rose superior to the animal mind, so part of the universal mind evolved sufficiently in primeval times to act independently and produce individual life which acts according to its own desires.

Mind must therefore be an evolving substance, and, having broken through the limits of natural law, is set on a career which may have a boundless future. The first protoplasm, which moved of its own effort against the attraction of gravity, displayed the first spark on earth of this vital directing thinking substance, this psychic part of every living creature which directs its movements and raises it superior to inert matter.

Consequently everything that has life is related to mind, which is outside and beyond the realm of physical matter. So we arrive at the Trinity of Nature—mind, etheric substance and physical matter, the two latter being the vehicles through which mind manifests, the individual mind passing from the physical to the etheric at death, when it discards its grosser covering but retains its finer envelope. A comparison can be made with our wireless set, which can be adjusted to the grosser long ether waves, the medium waves and the short waves. All nature is but a series of vibrations, some of whose longer frequencies we call physical matter, the shorter ones etheric substance, and the shortest of all mind, the latter being the most intense of all the vibrations that make up the universe.

So the ancient Indian mystics imagined Mind, or God, entering matter and then returning to the etheric, from which metaphysical process the theologians produced the saviour-god religions, all the same in essentials, of which Christianity is the one best known to most of the readers of this book. They are all figurative stories, because only in this form came comfort to the majority who had childish minds. These people the mystics called the uninitiated, the initiated, or those of deeper perception, grasping their allegorical meaning, which, with the passage of time, was forgotten, when everyone accepted them as literally true just as did the ancient Greeks their mythology.

From the days of early life to our own times is the story of the unfolding universe, as man came slowly to appreciate better his position in it. It is the story of the ever greater conquest of mind over matter, a fight which will not be won until he attains complete control over his bodily infirmities and his carnal passions.

To secure control over nature is not enough, as unless the mind develops ethically, and increased wisdom accompanies our physical discoveries, we will continue to use them for evil and not only for the sake of our greater comfort and happiness. We have certainly made progress, but it is unbalanced progress, and we of the human race must now devote ourselves to ethical development in order to catch up with the great advance we have made in the understanding of nature's laws.

Nature changes the form of all she produces, to reproduce it in some other form, decay being as natural as growth, but, as man is now mastering the forces of nature, he must also master his inherent tendency to destroy what he produces. Peace brings construction, war only destruction, and until man controls himself there can be no lasting happiness. It is as necessary for him to rule himself as to dominate nature. Without self-mastery his power over nature becomes a terrible danger to the human race, because he now knows enough to bring about its virtual extinction. So it becomes ever more necessary for him to set about his own mastery before he proceeds further to conquer more of nature's secrets.

Animals use for fighting the weapons with which they are born: the tusk, the fang, the claw and the beak. Man, however, employs weapons which he manufactures, and the more inventive he is the more deadly becomes his means of destruction. From a stone thrown by a sling to a bomb discharged from an airplane is a long road in the art of invention, but whereas the stone may kill the one it hits, a bomb can kill thousands, and destroy property it has taken much labour and many years to construct.

So the mechanical age into which we have now entered is one of possibilities of much good and great evil, a fact which enforces the argument used throughout these pages that education must not be confined to material things, but also be devoted to the development of the virtues, as otherwise the race will destroy itself by feasting on the things that are evil—lust, greed, hatred, malice and all that is wicked.

The men and women of kind, unselfish disposition are much to be preferred to those of selfish sterner mould, as they produce happiness, whereas the others create misery through their determination to achieve their own selfish desires, no matter who it is they trample upon in the process. The former are a great asset to the world, and their presence brings peace and goodwill. They have the secret of real and enduring happiness, which is something that comes from unselfishness, but this philosophy is not yet taught anywhere as part of our education. When it is taught everywhere, and all follow it, a great transformation will come to all mankind. Likewise when politicians become philosophers and philosophers become politicians we shall enter a new age of international peace and concord.

One important change came from man's greater command of the forces of nature. Before the industrial age labour was despised and confined to the poor, the rich looking upon it with disdain. To be distinguished a man had to be either a priest or a soldier. Theology and war were the principal occupations of the upper classes, there being then little commerce. Ethical conduct scarcely existed, and honest dealings one with another were as often the exception as the rule. What one wanted he took, if he were strong enough, and to keep a promise was too often subject to expediency.

It is strange to think that Francis Bacon (1561–1626), who became Lord Verulam and Viscount St. Albans, was the first Christian of any standing to maintain that a Christian, or a Christian government, was morally bound to keep an agreement with a non-Christian individual or state. Up to his time the damned heathen were looked upon as only fit for hell, and could be treated accordingly.

Many in our own times were dismayed at the systematic fiendish cruelty of the Germans before and during the Second World War, because we had become unaccustomed to deeds which were practised in Christendom up to a hundred years ago. Many of us were evolving out of the age of ignorance, cruelty, vice, intolerance and wickedness. Even the slight education of the past two generations was beginning to have its beneficent effect upon our treatment of each other, and of animals. The Christian age of wickedness was passing out of our recollection, and only the study of the past could bring it back in some faint degree. Even the more enlightened in these past times were cruel and intolerant when they obtained power, and both Luther and Calvin, who had defied the Pope, denied to others the right to think for themselves.

Now we may fairly claim that in democratically minded countries, all enlightened people accord to others the same freedom as they claim for themselves. Intolerance has now largely vanished, and the greater liberty we now enjoy will still further enlarge the mind, increase wisdom and improve conduct. The 19th century therefore laid the foundation for an improved way of life, and, though ethical progress has been patchy, some nations reverting to the depraved methods of the Middle Ages, a greater number of people lead more righteous lives today than was ever the case in the past.

Unfortunately the course of progress does not run smoothly, and the stream of thought is being continually hindered by rocks, swirls and eddies. To grasp affairs correctly we must therefore return to politics, which produced events so momentous that they have had their repercussions up to our own times.

(2) FRANCE UNDER THE RULE OF NAPOLEON III.

Since the fateful year of revolution (1789) France had experienced every form of government—democratic, autocratic and oligarchic. She had quarrelled with everyone in Europe, enjoyed the glory of brilliant conquests, and the bitter pangs of humiliating defeat. Now, in the year 1853, by a large majority she elects as her emperor Louis Bonaparte (1853-1870), a mysterious, studious and meditative man, the nephew of Napoleon I, who took the title of Napoleon III, fully confident that he was destined to raise to glory once more the royal house of which he was the head. Under his autocratic rule the country prospered, railways were built and industrial and commercial developments proceeded rapidly. Paris was largely rebuilt, and became the centre of the fashionable world.

The Emperor was a good orthodox Christian, and, for a time, he had the support of the Church authorities, who liked him and encouraged his despotic rule. Though the Chamber of Deputies was elected by manhood suffrage, it had no power of government or of initiating legislation, and there was much corruption in its election. The Senate, or upper house, consisted of 150 men who were nominated by the Emperor and completely in his power, the government of the country being in the hands of the Council of State, consisting of his ministers and others whom he appointed. The Emperor was his own Chancellor and Prime Minister, and his ministers were responsible to him alone. All political opponents were punished, and the Press and education were subject to his jurisdiction.

So there was no freedom under his rule, though he retained his popularity with the majority of the people, who were still too ignorant to be able to govern themselves. From time to time he felt it necessary to gratify their love of military conquest, which was one reason why France participated in the Crimean war and the Italian war of liberation, from which latter effort she ultimately secured both Nice and Savoy, acquisitions which the Italians greatly resented. France, naturally, was delighted, but Napoleon's adoption of a free trade policy with Britain, without consulting the commercial interests of France, brought about much anger in the trading and banking sections of French life, where most men were in favour of protection.

In 1863 Napoleon became involved in a strange adventure in Mexico, at the time when the United States was in the throes of civil war. Following a revolution the anti-Roman Catholic party in Mexico, which was led by Benito Juarez, a remarkable Indian, who was honest, patriotic and clear-sighted, secured power, and proceeded to curtail the evil influence of the Christian Church, reduce the power of the priests, and limit their large incomes. This raised the indignation of the Roman Catholics throughout the world, and nowhere was this insult to their religion felt more than in France. Urged on by the Pope and the priests, Napoleon decided on a crusade to re-establish the power and position of the Church in Mexico, another motive being the belief that the country's wealth could be much better exploited under French direction and with French capital.

This mad enterprise therefore had the support of the Vatican and the Bourse, and, to some extent, the Emperor returned to favour with the clerical and financial interests, though the Roman Catholics never forgave him for the help he gave to Italy in her fight for liberation. Whether it was to regain his old popularity, or because he was influenced by the Empress, a zealous Christian, to recover for the Church its old influence and position, the decision was made and a French force was dispatched to Mexico. Then followed the next blunder, when the Mexican National Assembly was forced to accept as their emperor the handsome, kindly and honourable Archduke Maximilian, who was the brother of the reigning Emperor of Austria.

All this interference was possible because Mexico's great northern neighbour was then so busy with her own affairs, but, when the American Civil War ended, the United States, without delay, ordered the French troops out of Mexico, and the Mexicans again rallied round their former republican leader Juarez, a man of their own blood and outlook. The unfortunate Maximilian now found himself alone amongst a people who had no use for him, and he finished his days facing a firing squad. Thus ended this wild adventure, which, by the humiliation it brought to France, reduced still further Napoleon's prestige amongst his people.

The French liberals, who had been from the first

against this venture, were now very bitter, because they considered it contrary to the principles of the Revolution to interfere with other people's religion. The Church likewise remained alienated from the Crown because of the help Napoleon had given to Italy in her fight for freedom, and the commercial classes were still antagonistic to the prevailing system of free trade. So Napoleon, to re-establish his position and meet the growing power of his opponents, made Emile Ollivier, the Liberal leader, his Prime Minister, and promised the people a new constitution which would provide for a new Assembly with power to legislate, control taxation, and appoint its own ministers.

Consequently France, in the year 1870, seemed to be entering on a new era, but, fifteen days after the people had given an overwhelming vote for the new order, war commenced with Germany, and within two months the Second Empire collapsed. Napoleon was taken as a prisoner to Kassel in Germany, to be freed later and live in England, where he died in 1873, the tragic story of how all this came about being told in the next section.

Thus ended the career of a man whose name and family connection gave him a position for seventeen years which he was quite unable to fill. He was a poor administrator, ruthless towards all opposition, and foolish in the choice of his ministers. Intellectually he was superior to the other rulers of his time, but he never chose, or possessed, a minister or a general who could be compared in cunning or ability with those selected by his antagonist William I of Prussia.

(3) ITALY AND GERMANY BECOME UNITED NATIONS.

Since the fall of the Roman Empire the Italians had never been their own masters. The shattering blow they then received divided them up into separate states, which were dominated by either the Christian Church or other foreign rulers, every effort to secure freedom and unity being frustrated by outside interference. We remember how, after their defeat by the Austrians in 1849, the movement for Italian liberation collapsed, but, although it was forced underground, the desire to be an independent nation was never extinguished, and, as every year passed, the strength of this longing increased.

Then, at last, the opportunity came for the long-lost freedom to be recovered, a man with the necessary influence arising to gather around him those who were prepared to fight, suffer and, if need be, die to secure their burning desire. This great patriot and statesman, Count Cavour, is hailed today as the architect of modern Italy, because he planned and worked for a united Italy during the years he was Prime Minister of Piedmont (1851–1859 and 1860–1861), but it was not until 1870 that his dream materialised, when Rome was captured from the Pope.

This ever courteous, courageous and far-seeing man, with the support of his sovereign Victor Emmanuel II, who ruled over the wild and barbarous island of Sardinia and the poor and sturdy people of Piedmont in northern Italy, was determined that all Italy would be ruled by an Italian democratic Parliament framed on British principles.

This great disciple of English liberalism was first a banker and then a manufacturer, but his talent for leadership, and his power of persuasion, carried him into political life, where he set to work to make Piedmont a free democratic state, curb the evil influence of the Church, develop science, trade, railways, and improve agriculture.

Piedmont consequently became the only Italian province which was free to enjoy popular government and liberal representative institutions, Cavour having (1) abolished the age-old iniquitous Church laws, (2) the privileged position of the clergy, (3) reduced their large incomes, (4) abolished their civil powers, (5) closed 300 monasteries, (6) enacted civil marriage, (7) abolished the Inquisition and established liberty of speech.

From this small land of freedom radiated the rays which warmed the many Italian patriots ardently working for unity, liberty and the abolition of the Papal States (occupying all Central Italy), which had kept the country weak and divided for almost eleven hundred years. Thus Piedmont became the base of operations for the long struggle ahead, one with many disappointments, which Cavour, its guiding genius, did not live to see gloriously successful after the lapse of twenty years, as he died in 1861, nine years before the capitulation of Rome.

As was always the way during the era of Christian civilisation, the Church was the enemy of everyone who strove for better and happier conditions for the people. Its policy, in Italy as elsewhere, was to keep the people ignorant, servile and in bondage. So it followed as a matter of course that when Cavour started his campaign of liberation, education and reform, the ecclesiastical leaders declared their intention to fight and oppose him by every means in their power, relying on their tool Austria to work with them to keep the Italian people in their habitual state of degradation.

If the forces working for reaction were strong, so also were those intent on liberation and reform, the scheming ardent patriot Mazzini, the leader of the underground movement, intent on an Italian republic, and the progressive Tuscan baron Benito Ricasoli, being amongst the leaders who directed the people forward until the papal and foreign yoke was severed and Italy was free and united.

Freedom from oppression can never be gained without a struggle, and this will ever be so until the mind of man everywhere rises to a higher level of thought. Consequently Cavour prepared for war, but, with the small number of troops at his command, he was quite unable to secure the Papal States, drive the Austrians out of Lombardy and Venetia, and free southern Italy from the barbarous tyrannical rule of its Bourbon king. He therefore turned to France for help, and to Britain for sympathy and encouragement, both of which he got in full measure.

Napoleon III had kindly feelings for the Italians in their plight, but he also saw his chance to secure increased territory for his country. He therefore made a bargain with Cavour, that in exchange for the support of 200,000 French soldiers the provinces of Nice and Savoy, then within the Piedmont realm, would be handed over to France when victory was won.

When Cavour obtained this promise of help he set about increasing the Piedmontese army, and this brought an ultimatum from Austria demanding its reduction to a peace level. War followed, and Napoleon III, at the head of his army, entered Italy. One blunder after another was made by Austria, who was defeated in 1859 at Magenta, and a few weeks later at Solferino, but the French losses in this last battle were so severe that Napoleon, fearing that Prussia would side with Austria, concluded the Peace of Villafranca without consulting Victor Emmanuel. This gave to Piedmont only the provinces of Lombardy and Parma, and left Venetia still under Austrian rule.

Cavour, who thought that he was on the brink of complete victory, was furious at what he considered to be a treacherous betrayal, and in disgust retired from public life, but he omitted to count on the feelings of the people in Modena, Tuscany, Parma and Romagna, who expelled their rulers, raised an army of 25,000 men and offered to join themselves to the kingdom of Victor Emmanuel.

This new turn of events brought Cavour back, and he succeeded in again bringing in the French with the promise of Savoy and Nice, which they had not yet obtained because of their failure to fulfil the original bargain. When a popular vote was taken, showing an enormous majority in favour of union with Piedmont, France supported the rebel states, and so it came about that France got Savoy and Nice and Victor Emmanuel became king in 1860, his first Parliament meeting at Turin, as Rome and the Papal States were still under the rule of the Pope.

All northern Italy was not yet united, but an important step had been taken to this end. Meanwhile the people living in the Papal States were in misery under the tyrannical rule of the Church, and nowhere else in Europe were social conditions more disgraceful. Only one third of the soil was cultivated, and everyone except the priests was desperately poor. Order did not exist, brigands overran the land, and the numerous monasteries and convents were the abode of vice and corruption. Literature and science were banned, schools did not exist, only one in every thousand could read, and the Press was muzzled.

All enterprise was discouraged, doctors were prevented from using new remedies, and steamships, built to navigate between Rome and coastal towns, were forbidden to operate. Rome was the most dirty, degraded and immoral city in Europe. The use of gas for lighting was forbidden, and the streets at night were in darkness, dogs being the only scavengers. Only priests flourished, there being one priest in every ten of the population, and the blight they cast over everything produced a hopeless and debased community.

Pope Pius IX became more and more reactionary, and, with the support of his Secretary of State Cardinal Antonelli, a notoriously immoral and corrupt man, did all in his power to oppose the Italian longing for freedom. Now that the north had won its liberty, the south of Italy, lying on the other side of the Papal States, and known as the Kingdom of the Two Sicilies, likewise looked for liberation from the oppressive and retrograde rule of the Bourbon

Francis II, but the Pope opposed every attempt made by its inhabitants to secure their freedom, the most ruthless measures being employed.

Now comes into the limelight a prominent personality, Giuseppe Garibaldi (1807–1882), the famous guerilla leader and Italian patriot, an enthusiast for freedom, but a man who was quite lacking in political wisdom. He was the soldier hero of the Italian war of liberation, having already distinguished himself in the fighting which had freed most of the north. Landing at Marsala, in western Sicily (1860), with a thousand or so ardent patriots and adventurers, their only uniform being a red shirt, he marched on Palermo, which surrendered, and within three months all Sicily was in his power.

Next he crossed over to the mainland, won the Battle of Reggio, and triumphantly occupied Naples, which was undefended, as her king had fled. On the Volturno river he routed the Bourbon army and so became master of all southern Italy and Sicily, but Cavour, fearing that Garibaldi would set up a republic, and then proceed to invade Rome, and so anger France, anticipated him by raising an army with which Victor Emmanuel occupied part of the Papal States, and thus kept the holy city free from attack.

The Pope's army of 20,000 men could not stand up to the forces of Victor Emmanuel, and, after they were defeated, the King pressed on to the Teano river to meet Garibaldi, who handed over to his sovereign all southern Italy. Garibaldi was now at the height of his career. If he had been other than a great and noble patriot he would have held for himself the south of Italy he had so brilliantly won, but he had no such ambitions. All he ever asked was recognition and rewards for his volunteer troops, and, as they did not get this, he felt deeply hurt. Differing from the policy pursued by Cavour, and feeling that his task was over, he retired to the island of Caprera, where, with some borrowed money, he set up as a small farmer, preferring poverty and simplicity to the plaudits of the multitude.

There he pondered over how best to free Rome from the curse of priestly rule. Only Rome and Venetia now remained outside the kingdom of Italy, but, when Prussia decided on war against Austria in 1866, she arranged with Italy to attack Venetia, then under Austrian rule, and thus divide the Austrian forces. Italy made a poor effort, and Garibaldi, who again came on the scene, did little with his irregular adventurers when they attacked the Tyrol. With no capable generals, inadequate equipment, no plan of campaign, and undisciplined troops, the Italian army was defeated at Custozza, and a like fate beset her navy. Had Prussia not drawn away a large part of the Austrian army, Italy would again have been overrun by her old enemy, but Prussia defeated Austria and kept her promise to secure Venetia for her ally. Southern Tyrol remained Austrian, but, by an almost unanimous vote, Venetia entered the kingdom of Italy, and only Rome now remained as a state apart.

Rome constituted a difficult problem, as it was considered a holy city by all good Roman Catholics, and the French were determined that it should not become the capital of a united Italy. Their plans, however, miscarried, because, when France became involved in the disasters of the Franco-Prussian War, the

French garrison at Rome was withdrawn, and an Italian army marched in and took possession in 1870, amidst the jubilation of a long-subjected population.

Away back in the year 410, the Christian Visigoths captured this famous city, and from that time for nearly fifteen centuries Italy had been a disunited country, its ancient capital suffering from one degradation after another under ecclesiastical rule. In the keeping of the Church it became a cesspool of iniquity, vice, corruption and depraved superstition. Now, at long last, it was free again to take an honourable place in world history, and become the centre of a united Italy. So the Italian people, with a common culture, history, tradition, outlook, race and language, became one nation under an Italian royal house, with liberal and progressive ideals, instead of being divided into small rival states which were ruled by foreign kings.

Pius IX, the Pope, held out to the last, and refused, in a letter full of curses, oaths and vituperation, all the peaceful overtures made by the King. Only when he heard the roar of the guns did he realise that resistance was in vain. He felt confident to the very last because he had taken what he considered to be all the necessary precautions against capitulation. First of all he had prayed to Saint Peter to preserve the city whose principal church bore his name. Secondly he had visited half the madonnas scattered throughout the city. Thirdly, he had made a pilgrimage to invoke the protection of the wonder-working doll, the Holy Bambino, and lastly, he had climbed on his knees to the chapel on the top of the steps of the Santa Scala, to adore the miraculous relics.

What more could he do? So, when the soldiers entered the Vatican, they found him engrossed in writing a charade. By such warped and irrational minds, the product of theological seminaries, was Europe dominated throughout the age of Christian civilisation, and, because this was so, Christendom is in its present lamentable backward ethical condition, lacking all these years of education, wisdom and progress which were lost through our ancestors being enslaved by superstition.

By a practically unanimous vote (360,000 against 12,000), the citizens of Rome threw off papal rule and joined themselves to the Italian kingdom. The Pope retired to the Vatican, hurling curses and excommunications all round, and repelled all attempts at reconciliation. Thus came to an end the temporal rule of Christ's Vicar on earth, a position which had been secured by blatant fraud and forgery in the 9th century, a story which has already been told. His kingdom, now reduced to the Vatican, was symbolic of the mental change which had come over the people of Christendom, rising intelligence having discovered that the universe is governed by natural law, and not by the dictates of the Holy Trinity and a host of saints whom the Pope professed to represent. Rome now became the capital of a free united Italy, the King took up his residence at the Quirinal, a papal palace, and the dreams of a long line of Italian patriots were at last realised.

While the Italians, under the leadership of Piedmont, were forging their different provinces into one united kingdom, the Germans were pursuing the same process under the guidance of Prussia. When we left Prussia in the previous chapter (1849), Austria had become the dominant Germanic power, but, though Prussia had reluctantly to accept this humiliation, she by no means forgot, and steadily pursued a policy which was eventually to place her at the head of all the German states. Her king, Frederick William IV, suffered from insanity, and from 1857 Prince William reigned as regent until he succeeded to the throne in 1861 as William I.

William I (1861–1888) was a reactionary, and against any form of constitutional rule or parliamentary government. The crown, he declared, had come to him from God, and to God only was he responsible. So here we are again faced with this age-old problem, and it is remarkable that the Prussians eventually accepted him at his own valuation. To his war minister, Albert von Roon, and later to Count von Moltke and Otto von Bismarck is the credit due for Prussia's gradual rise to be the foremost military power in Europe. Military service was made com pulsory for three years, service in the reserve, or Land-wehr, for another four years, and new weapons were perfected. The art of war was diligently studied, and Clausewitz, the greatest of all her theoretical writers, who wrote on total war as the only means to secure results, became the idol of the military caste. Thus Prussia began her era of crime, which, during the next eighty years, was to drench Europe and much of the world in blood and desolation.

The King did not have things all his own way at first, because there was a strong progressive party which wished to have a Parliament modelled on

British lines, and, when he refused to consider such a proposal (1862), a majority in the Assembly declined to pass the Bill providing money for the army. When matters had reached this stage a new figure came on the scene who was to alter once again the map of Europe, unite the German states, and make Germany the dominant power in Europe.

The tragedies, the suffering, the loss of lives and wealth from which the world has suffered over the past thirty years from German aggression, can all be traced back to that fateful year of 1862 when the King of Prussia called into public life a powerfully built Pomeranian squire who, in later years, became known as Prince Bismarck (1862–1890), a man of great energy, courage and eloquence of speech, an accomplished linguist, and well versed in all the diplomatic arts. This remarkable man, who always knew exactly what he wanted, and was prepared to stoop to any debased method to secure his aims, was now, on the advice of Roon, appointed Minister-President and Foreign Minister, he being entrusted with the duty of carrying on the government against the wishes of the majority of the Assembly, so as to enable the King to complete and maintain the reorganised army.

The majority opposition in the Assembly had the support of the country, and Bismarck's appointment caused intense indignation, because he was known as a violent reactionary. This he made clear in his first speech, in which he said that the problems of the time could only be settled by blood and iron. For four years he ruled without a budget, and matters became so strained that in 1863 the other ministers of the

Crown refused to attend the sittings of the Assembly because of the abuse they received.

So long as Bismarck had the King's confidence he had complete control, and the Assembly was helpless. So he jeered at their votes, and told the representatives that God was directing this fight for power, and "will cast his iron dice" sooner or later. Charles I of Britain and Louis XVI of France had faced the representatives of the people with this ancient claim of divine right to rule, to lose their heads for their presumption, and now William I of Germany was following boldly in their steps. His end, however, was different, for which there is only one reason—the dense stupidity of the German people, who, like the French with Napoleon I, were dazzled by military victories, and when thus blinded accepted the chains their master put upon them.

Bismarck's ultimate aim was to unite all the German states under the leadership of Prussia. He was the creator of modern Germany, just as Cavour was the architect of modern Italy, the difference between them being that Italy was first liberated from foreign rule, and then united under a king who reigned over a nation ruled by a democratic parliament. Bismarck united Germany by means of foreign conquests, and refused the Prussian people their desire for parliamentary government. Only Bismarck ruled Prussia, only he was the master planner, looking far ahead to his goal, and waiting for each opportunity, as it came his way, to forge another link in the chain which would bind all the German states to Prussia.

None of the German states wanted to be wedded to Prussia, but in the end he gained his ambition by means of cunning, fraud, wise diplomacy and war. First of all he stifled so thoroughly the strong claim for a Parliament on British lines that it was never revived, a tragedy for Germany and all mankind, as he reversed the clock of progress and made possible the horrors of German aggression. Having successfully overcome the Democrats by ignoring their demands, the stage was set for conquest, and the German people embarked on that long and dangerous road which, after eighty-two years, was to end in their capital being devastated, their towns and factories destroyed, their army and navy routed, the flower of their manhood maimed or killed, and in those who remained, poor, miserable and dejected, being hated with a bitter loathing.

The attempt made by Austria to improve the German Federal Constitution, the worst in the world, was next frustrated. Prussia, and not Austria, in future was to be supreme, and an insurrection in Russian Poland made this plain to everyone when Austria requested Prussia to support her endeavour to secure Home Rule for Poland. This was met by Prussia supporting Russia's oppressive rule over these lawless but gallant people struggling for liberation.

The Poles, Bismarck thought, should be turned into Prussians, their traditions forgotten, and their language and culture obliterated, but that was not part of his present plan, which was to secure Russia's friendship and military alliance. When this materialised he felt that Prussia's eastern frontier was secure, and that he could now safely commence his preparations to knock out Austria, this being necessary to enable him to complete the first stage in his plan for German unification. Then, when that was done, France would be the next to receive attention.

Bismarck's first great triumph came when he secured Schleswig-Holstein for Prussia. Frederick III, King of Denmark, was also duke of these two provinces, but he was childless. Bismarck was determined that they should come to Prussia, and he started the now familiar German story that the Germans living there were oppressed by the Danes. So he blatantly stole these provinces, after a joint Prussian and Austrian army had without difficulty defeated the Danes. Then Prussia and Austria fell out, the latter declaring that the rightful heir to these provinces was the Duke of Augustenburg.

Bismarck made this the excuse for a war against Austria, who was joined by Bavaria, Saxony and Hanover. On the other hand, Italy, as we will remember, so as to get Venetia, allied herself with Prussia, and thus retained a large body of Austrian troops south of the Alps. Bismarck perpetrated this crime deliberately to make Prussia the dominant power, and his policy of blood and iron, on which "the God of Battles would throw his iron dice", was now put to the test of war.

The Prussian-Austrian War of 1866, conducted by Moltke, was short, lasting only two months, but it was one of the most fateful in history. The Hanoverians were defeated before they joined up with the Bavarians and Austrians, the Austrians being next defeated at Sadowa, in Bohemia, and finally, a few days later, the Bavarians were routed at Kissingen. The Peace of Prague gave Schleswig, Holstein,

Hanover, Hesse-Kassel, Nassau and Frankfurt to Prussia, and Venetia to Italy, while Austria was excluded from all future participation in matters concerning Germany. Bismarck treated Bavaria, Württemberg and Baden kindly, and left them their independence, as he feared that they might, in self-protection, join up with France, a scheme which Napoleon III was eagerly encouraging.

This defeat of Austria was a terrible blow to the Austrians, as they realised that Prussia and not Austria was now the head of the Germanic states. Her centuries-old leadership passed over to the statesmen in Berlin, but it had other far-reaching effects. In our time it gave Hitler, the Austrian, the burning desire of uniting Austria with Germany, and creating a powerful Germanic federation of all the German-speaking people of Europe. His earlier dream had been dissolved by the defeat of the Germans and Austrians in the First World War, and he set to work to accomplish what others had attempted, but failed, to do. That was the long-term effect of the Battle of Sadowa, its immediate one being the desire for unity which it brought about in Germany herself.

Bismarck's policy proved successful, as, by encouraging Bavaria, Württemberg and Baden to feel themselves to be blood relations to Prussia, he secured from them their promise to aid her in any future war. Next he formed a separate confederation of the north German states, of which he became the sole responsible minister, with the new title of Reichs-Kanzler, a position which gave him almost autocratic power. Lastly he gave the people manhood suffrage which elected representatives to the Reichstag, a very different assembly from the British Parliament, because it had no control over the ministers of the Crown, and could not interfere with the government of the country, which was carried on by ministers over whom was Bismarck, the Chancellor.

Dazzled by his diplomatic and military triumphs, the German people placed themselves body and soul in the hands of this cold, calculating, pitiless creature, whose one and only ambition was the unification of Germany as the first step to the Germanic race becoming the predominant power in Europe. Hitler was not the first modern German dictator, and history proves that the Germans, to achieve plunder and military glory, willingly give up their liberties and put the State before the individual, in order that their thirst for conquest can be quenched. Bismarck succeeded to the end, and therein lies the difference between the careers of these two evil fanatics.

Besides the consolidation of the north German states under one Chancellor, the defeat of Austria enabled Hungary to secure a separate Parliament, and the Austrian emperor, from now onwards, was the recognised head of two separate states. The defeat of Austria certainly established Prussia as the leading German power, but more was still to be done before Bismarck's plan for a united Germany was realised. Still another war was necessary before the new Germany, under Prussian leadership, was well and truly built. Neither the French nor the German people at that time desired a conflict, but Bismarck, Moltke and Roon did. Napoleon III felt that a successful war would re-establish his waning popularity, but he did not plan for it, as did Bismarck and his military advisers. An excuse to plunge Europe again into war was now awaited, and an opportunity presented itself in 1870.

Spain was the cause of the trouble. A revolution there had caused the Queen, Isabella, to take refuge in France, when Leopold of Hohenzollern, a Roman Catholic, and distant relative of the King of Prussia, became the candidate for the vacant throne. This was planned by Bismarck to anger the French, and give an excuse for war. Napoleon III objected to a German occupying the Spanish throne, and William I of Prussia verbally acquiesced, both monarchs being anxious not to have a repetition of the upheaval which was caused by the Spanish Succession War in the time of Louis XIV.

There the matter would probably have ended had not Gramont foolishly pressed the matter further. He was the French Foreign Minister, and conducted the negotiations because Napoleon was now a sick man and lacked his former grip on affairs. Not satisfied with a verbal acquiescence, this temperamental man demanded a definite promise from William to oppose the candidature of Leopold if ever it was raised on a subsequent occasion. William was annoyed at this persistence, and declined to meet the French demand, but repeated his approval of the withdrawal of Leopold as a candidate for the Spanish throne. So the incident passed off, and could easily have been forgotten if the influence who had planned it all had not been at work behind the scenes.

Bismarck was disappointed at the result, because he had hoped that this incident would give him the excuse he wanted to declare war on France. Not to be thwarted in his plan, he, with the approval of Moltke and Roon, altered the wording of the telegram he received from William announcing what had happened, and made it read to give the impression that Napoleon had sent an insolent demand to William, who, in consequence, had refused to have any further dealing with the French ambassador. This he published, and it had the desired effect. The French completely lost all self-control, Gramont being the leading influence against moderation at a time when wisdom and reticence, and not flamboyant speeches, should have prevailed.

Thus this foolish man, wildly gesticulating, inflamed French passions, his complete loss of balance infecting his mercurial countrymen, as the Emperor, the Chamber of Deputies, the Press and the people all quickly decided that only by war could France's honour and prestige be restored. Nothing could have better pleased the master schemer in Berlin, who thus secured German unity, and France delivered herself over to his evil designs by being the first to issue the declaration of war, the decision being come to on 14th July, 1870, at a midnight sitting of the Emperor's Council, only ten days having passed since the entire affair had started.

The disgraceful incident, which was the cause of this fateful decision, became known as "The Ems telegram affair", because Napoleon's ambassador had met William at Ems, near Coblenz, and it stamps Bismarck as one of the greatest of the many scoundrels Germany has produced in modern times. Why should the fate of millions of innocent people everywhere be in the hands of political blackguards, who, to attain their own selfish ends, either break treaties, publish bogus telegrams, or attack while negotiations are proceeding, and, in every possible way, flout the moral code?   Bismarck was the chief criminal in the bloody wasteful tragedy which followed, but much blame also attaches to Gramont, who inflamed French passions by his bellicose attitude, but neither he nor the Emperor planned for war, they and their people, during a period of momentary excitement, blindly walking into the cunning trap which had been set for them.

Bismarck alone deliberately lit the flames of war, and thus became the unquestioned murderer of many thousands of innocent men who were involved in the conflict.   Half a million Germans were smoothly mobilised, and, for the first time in history, quickly moved to the frontier in railway trains, everything having been thoroughly prepared and the entire campaign carefully thought out beforehand, whereas the French army was quite unprepared, everything being in confusion and disorder.

The Germans were superior in numbers, generalship and artillery, and they conducted the campaign with great speed.   At Saarbrücken, Wörth, Weissenburg, Spicheren, and then at Gravelotte the French were defeated, suffering heavy casualties, the flower of the French army, consisting of 170,000 men, seeking refuge behind the fortifications of Metz, where they were besieged, finally to surrender.   In attempting to relieve them 100,000 Frenchmen were trapped at Sedan, to lose 17,000 men before the rest, including Napoleon, surrendered.

The Prussian successes against Denmark and

Austria were due to the invention by a Prussian, John Nicholas Dreyse, of the breach-loading needle rifle in 1835. Prussian troops were armed with this new deadly weapon, but not so her enemies, who still used the ancient muzzle-loading musket, which was slow and ponderous to load. When, therefore, she went to war against them, her killing power so greatly surpassed that of her opponents that they could not stand up to the rapid fire of the new weapon. It mowed down the opposing ranks so fast that both their attack and defence became impossible, entire battalions being completely wiped out. In 1866 France adopted the new rifle, and the Franco-Prussian War was the first occasion when it was used by both sides with deadly effect.

The disaster at Sedan brought the French Empire to an end, when a Republic was formed, but it would not part with Strassburg and Metz, which the Germans now claimed. So the war went on, the people being urged to further efforts by Léon Gambetta, the outstanding republican orator, a man of amazing energy and resource, who, escaping from Paris in a balloon, raised a new army of 180,000 men within six weeks. In its first contact with the Germans near Orleans it gained for the French their first and only victory in the war, but the fall of Metz, which released the investing army, brought defeat after defeat on those half-trained, ill-equipped men, who were finally overwhelmed at Le Mans and St. Quentin, the remainder of the French army being pushed into Switzerland, where it was disarmed.

While this was happening Paris was closely besieged, its inhabitants, short of food, and bombarded by the enemy's guns, making a heroic resistance, but without avail, as in January 1871 the city capitulated. The Treaty of Frankfurt (1871), which followed, gave Alsace and Lorraine, including Metz and Strassburg, to Germany, besides an indemnity of £200,000,000. This large sum was duly paid, but never did the French forget the loss of their two provinces, the deep resentment which this caused raising a barrier of hatred between the two nations, never to die down. Nevertheless, it is well to remember that Alsace, which was taken from the Germans and given to the French by the Treaty of Westphalia in 1648 after the Thirty Years' War, was largely a German province. Lorraine, on the other hand, was French, but in neither case were the people given a choice, and they had just to accept their fate.

The satisfaction, pride and enthusiasm which this great victory produced in Germany fructified the seed already sown, and paved the way for the terrible tragedies which were to come to the human race in our time. Originally a small outpost on the frontier of a multitude of Slavs, the Prussians had, after centuries of internal conflict and external theft, produced a great Germanic nation which was the most formidable military power in Europe. God, they believed, had indeed blessed them, his chosen people, and just as they had shown their prowess in first defeating the Baltic Slavs, next the once powerful Austria, and now the France that had so humiliated them when the century opened, so they must brace themselves for further effort until all Europe, and then Britain and her empire, bowed down and worshipped them.

Such was the teaching of their most eminent and influential historian, a bitter enemy of Great Britain, Heinrich von Treitschke (1834–1896). This evil-minded man, a devout Christian, as were most of the warmongers in Germany, not satisfied with his own arguments in favour of war, made the god of his own imagination equally anxious for his chosen people, the Germans, to fight their way onwards until they dominated the earth, and all human creation lay at their feet. So he appealed to *The Holy Bible* for support, and found Jehovah a ready ally of the conquering German people, the following being what he wrote:—

Only a few timorous visionaries have closed their eyes to the splendour with which the Old Testament celebrates the sovereign beauty of a just and holy war.

So, by making the German people believe that God was with them, Treitschke, and others like him, poisoned the minds of their fellow countrymen from that day to this, to bring about a prodigious amount of misplaced effort, which was directed on two successive occasions to the devastation of a great part of Europe, and the slaughter of millions of innocent victims.

The result of this teaching embraces much of the story this book has still to tell, but, looking back on it all, how hollow, how false, how wicked and how foolish it all appears! Taking the everlasting touch-stone, namely happiness, as our guide, this insane ambition has added nothing to the contentment, harmony, comfort and prosperity of the German people. It has done quite the reverse, as they have lived all these years cursed by ignorance of the right way to behave, they having been led far off the path of righteousness where only happiness is to be found. Well may we wonder if the time will ever come when the bright light of wisdom, the fruit of knowledge, will guide the race along the right road without it having to experience the misery and suffering which, for countless centuries, has been its lot, because some were for ever straying into the dark wilderness of thorns, to return torn and bleeding without ever being wiser for their dire experience.

In these stirring days of 1871 the dark future was not appreciated, because all that was then obvious to everyone was the plain fact that Bismarck had marvellously triumphed. Pomp and ceremony created the desired emotion fitting for the occasion, when, in the Hall of Mirrors at Versailles, the scene of many past splendours, William I, with Bismarck and Moltke by his side, was proclaimed German Emperor. At long last the German states were all united, to become a curse to the entire human race.

Bismarck spent many months in Versailles, occupied chiefly with the arrangements for admitting the southern German states to the confederation, and the establishment of the Empire. Thus came into being the Second Reich. As Chancellor he was responsible for the whole internal policy of the Empire, and his influence was noticeable in every department of state. He instituted important commercial reforms, but hated bitterly the Social Democrats, whom he tried to crush by exceptional penal laws.

For nineteen years after the Franco-Prussian War had ended, Bismarck ruled Germany with a strong hand, during which time her industry and commerce increased at a rapid pace. A country which had been mostly agricultural quickly moved forward to take the first place in the industrial life of Europe. Her population rapidly increased, and the towns became great centres of production, especially in everything pertaining to chemistry and electricity. Between 1871 and 1913 Germany's annual coal output rose from 30,000,000 to 190,000,000 tons, and her iron and steel output doubled in ten years.

As her ships now sailed to every port in the world, her tonnage within twenty years having increased seven times, the demand arose for colonies, and a feeling of bitterness followed when it was realised that the world was now fully discovered, the other nations having picked up nearly everything there was to secure while she was a land of small states which took no interest in affairs beyond their borders.

Though Bismarck was the first statesman in Europe to introduce insurance legislation for the workers, he became ever more reactionary as he advanced in age, and his tyrannical and unjust legislation against all forms of liberal thought could only have been possible in a land devoid of independent thinking. Liberalism, as understood in democratic countries, ceased to be a factor in politics, and the German people quietly resigned themselves to be ruled by a dictator, permitting both home and foreign policy to be directed by the Chancellor. So Bismarck, as the head of the most powerful state in Europe, dominated the stage of European politics, feared and distrusted, but never defied.

For two reasons his policy was sympathetic

towards France increasing her colonial empire, the first being to take her thoughts off the loss of Alsace and Lorraine, and secondly to antagonise Italy and Britain, his aim being to leave France without a friend in Europe. He feared an arisen hostile France, and, to isolate her further, he formed in 1873 an alliance with Russia and Austria-Hungary, known as the "Dreikaiserbund". His object by this move was to preserve the status quo in Europe, especially in the Balkans, and prevent the spread of Socialism, but he lost Russian friendship when, in 1879, he made a secret treaty with Austria without consulting his Russian ally. From that time Russia has been Germany's enemy, as this treaty with Austria-Hungary was to prevent the expansion of Russian influence in the Balkans. So Russia was dropped, and this dual alliance between Germany and Austria-Hungary became the Triple Alliance by the inclusion of Italy, about which more will be said later on.

This fateful event now made the Balkans the powder magazine of Europe, because Austria's position there had been strengthened and Russia's weakened by the formation in 1867 of the dual monarchy of Austria-Hungary. This arrangement secured the recognition of the supremacy of the German race in Austria and the Magyars in Hungary, each country retaining its own language and Parliament, the shallow but diligent Emperor Francis Joseph (1848–1916) being recognised by both as king. Thus, bound together with a common sovereign, these two separate autonomous states pursued their own independent policy until forced apart by their defeat in the First World War. Politically they looked for expansion southwards towards the Balkans, and socially they freed themselves of Church domination by providing state secular education and permitting religious toleration.

Thus the Germans and Magyars settled down to live peacefully and independently, and Deak, the Magyar leader, who proved himself a statesman in the negotiations, succeeded in removing the long-standing grievances felt by the people of his race. The Slavs, however, felt very differently—the Czechs in Bohemia, and the minority of Serbs, Croats and Slovaks in Hungary, now looking upon themselves as subservient to the two predominant races. The Pan-Slavonic movement consequently increased in importance, and, assured of Russian friendship, it gave to those people, distant from the main body of their kindred, and planted like islands in a sea of Germans and Magyars, a sense of the power and might of their race. By this new alignment the Balkans were divided into two camps, the one looking to Germany for leadership and the other to Russia, to bring about eventually the tragedy of the First World War, as we shall later discover.

Such, then, is the picture of Europe as drawn by that master political artist Prince Bismarck, whose policy had slowly but surely ranged Europe into two camps—Germany, Austria-Hungary and Italy in one, and the Slavonic races in the other, to be joined later by France and then by Britain. He did not live to experience the evil which followed from his deeds, and he left to mediocre men the task of steering Europe through the dangers he, by his ability, had been able to avoid. His overmastering power was not, however, to last much beyond the lifetime of the man he had been the means of making the first German emperor, and, when his great supporter, William I, died in 1888, Bismarck's power and influence rapidly declined.

Finally, after twenty-eight years of undisputed rule (1862–1890), the new Emperor, William II, dismissed the "Iron Chancellor" from office in 1890, and his death followed in 1898. The man to whom destiny had now handed the care of 45,000,000 people was young, only thirty-one years old, erratic, impulsive and inexperienced. He was born with a withered arm and this undoubtedly preyed on his mind, but nevertheless he was endowed with supreme self-confidence, so much so that he announced: "There is only one master in this country, and I am he." As he believed there was a special providence watching over the House of Hohenzollern, he next declared that "It is so ordained for me by God" and "We Hohenzollerns accept our mission only from heaven, and to heaven only are we answerable."

Nevertheless, the god with whom he was on such intimate terms—so intimate indeed that it was difficult to distinguish whether he or his god was the more important—did nothing to save him when he had to seek refuge as an exile in Holland, where he spent the last twenty-three years of his life.[1] Such, then, was the end of this egotistical fanatic, about whom more will be told in the next chapter.

[1] In the Memoirs of the Crown Prince of Germany, a graphic description is given of the mental agony of the Kaiser as he contemplated abdication:— "The Kaiser was alone. Not one of all the men of the General Higher Command hastened to his assistance. Here, as at home, disruption and demoralization. . . . Hoarse, strange and unreal was my father's voice as he instructed Hintze to telephone the Imperial Chancellor that he was prepared to renounce the Imperial Crown if only in this way civil war in Germany could be avoided."

(4) THE ROMAN CATHOLIC CHURCH CURSES ALL PROGRESS AND REFORM.

Many monarchs during the Christian era have either worked hand in hand with the Pope or fought him to secure for themselves his despotic authority. All reformers, those who had the good of humanity in mind, have been in conflict with the Papacy, their aim being to overthrow this tyranny so that they could secure the rights due to all mankind, but nothing could dethrone this King of Ignorance because his subjects worshipped superstition and feared to question his authority.

He, they believed, had the keys of heaven and hell, and the fear of death has been the most potent factor in history. Voltaire in France, and the other illustrious reformers who were his contemporaries, or who followed after him, were loud in their condemnation of the Roman Catholic Church. In Spain, Austria, Hungary, Bohemia, Portugal, Italy and Germany, the reformers likewise hated papal tyranny, and they had their hatred returned to them in full measure by the Church authorities.

Napoleon I, in his youthful zeal for reform, routed the papal army and contemplated the overthrow of the Pope's temporal authority. French troops entered Rome, plundered the sacred places, captured the fatuous Pius VI and brought him to France. Napoleon in his later years, then the despot of Europe, used the Papacy to help forward his ambitious schemes, only to quarrel with Pius VII because he, Napoleon, would not give over additional lands to the Holy See in exchange for the support given. Rome was again occupied by French troops, and the Papal States annexed to France. Then followed a Bull cursing and excommunicating this ravisher of spiritual lands, to which Napoleon replied by capturing His Holiness and bringing him a prisoner to Paris.

Under French control the Papal States immediately benefited. All the infamous tyrannical Church laws were abolished, and juster legislation was put in their place. Property was protected, lawlessness stamped out, and large tracts of uncultivated land brought under the plough. Assassinations, which had been of frequent occurrence, came to an end, and the filthy houses and streets were cleaned up. Rome, from being a dunghill, became, during the French occupation, a city wherein it was possible to live in some degree of comfort. Meantime Pius VII occupied his time in Paris with needlework, and was not able to resume his despotic rule in Rome until Napoleon abdicated, when he returned, to overthrow all the good work done by the French and reinstate the old debased administration.

For many years the subjects of the Papal States bore in silence the evils of papal government, but gradually the more liberal spirit of the age gained strength, and secret organisations plotted the downfall of this devilish tyranny. To protect his régime, and secure their downfall, the Pope "studded the country with gibbets, crowded the galleys with prisoners, filled Europe with exiles, and almost every home in the Papal States with mourning". Nevertheless insurrections continued to occupy the energies of the papal police and gestapo, to end in a general uprising

(1831) which brought the insurgents up to the doors of St. Peter's. Here they decreed the temporal authority of the Holy Father abolished, but these reformers were like sheep surrounded by wolves, because Austria immediately sent an army to his aid and brought the revolt to an end.

Gregory XVI, a self-indulgent sensualist, became Pope on the day the insurrection broke out, and, when it was quelled, both Russia and Austria made strong representations to him to abolish the evils against which the people were struggling in vain. Gregory flatly refused to improve his subjects' intolerable conditions, declaring that all reform was hateful to God and to all good men. Consequently much of the land remained uncultivated, wages continued at starvation levels, the Press had no freedom, literature and science were banned, vaccination, inoculation and modern methods of treating disease forbidden, torture being inflicted on all who rebelled. The death rate in the Papal States was the highest in Europe, priests swarmed everywhere, and the people, uneducated and dejected, lived their hopeless lives in filth and misery from the cradle to the grave.

The retrograde Pius IX followed Gregory in 1846, and, instead of improving the lot of his people, when all the rest of Italy was in revolt against oppression and tyranny, he occupied his time preparing the ground for the general acceptance by all good Catholics of the absolute sinlessness of the Virgin Mary. He was determined to make it a sin against Christ for anyone to doubt his mother's spotless life. He had no documentary proof for this wonderful idea, and accordingly he enquired of all the bishops throughout the world in order that he might know their opinions. Encouraged by the replies he received, he issued a Bull to the effect that the Holy Spirit had revealed to him the important news that the Mother of God had never once committed a sin, and that the Saviour had been born of an immaculate woman, free from the taint of original sin.

To celebrate the reception of this marvellous news, which had arrived nearly nineteen hundred years late, a multitude of ecclesiastics assembled in Rome (1854) to attend the coronation of the Madonna. Here they witnessed her being crowned by the Pope with a diadem, and then heard his solemn pronouncement that from the first instant of her conception she had been preserved immaculate from all stain of original sin, everyone disbelieving this to incur the penalties reserved for the damned. Does this mean that all Christians who had died prior to this pronouncement are in hell? But here we have not space to follow up the meaning of what comes from minds twisted in theological colleges.

Ten years later (1864), when this new weighty dogma had been duly absorbed by the Roman Catholic section of the Christian fold, Pius IX published, with much ceremony, an encyclical letter for the guidance and encouragement of the faithful, in which were defined eighty separate and distinct damnable heresies over which he pronounced his solemn curse.[1] This he called *Syllabus of the Principal Errors of our Age*, which opened with the declaration that it was

---

[1] Other similar encyclical letters were issued by Pope Leo XIII in 1878, 1881, 1888 and in the years which followed up to 1903.

false for anyone to believe "that the Pope can or ought to be reconciled to progress, or liberalism, or the modern state". Then followed his holy curse on education, and many of the things which have to do with the happiness and welfare of the human race, but here it is only possible to summarise briefly this extraordinary document.

His Holiness pronounced his curse and damnation on all:—

(1) Progress, liberalism, modern civilisation, liberty of speech, liberty of worship, and the freedom of the Press.

(2) Who read or circulate *The Holy Bible*, and who believe that they can reach heaven outside of the Holy Catholic Church.

(3) Who criticise the Holy Church, or say "it is not a true or perfect Society having the fullest liberty".

(4) Who declare that liberty belongs to the individual, and that all are entitled to have a say in the government of the country in which they live.

(5) Who say that the State is above the Church, that the Popes have erred, and that the Church must not use force (torture, imprisonment and burning at the stake) to have its authority upheld.

(6) Who say that the ruler is outside the jurisdiction of the Church.

(7) Who believe that the clergy come within the civil law.

(8) Who think that the Church is not free to do

whatever it thinks right irrespective of the law of the land.

(9) Who say that there is liberty allowed to any-one to profess other than the orthodox Catholic faith.

(10) Who think that the Church can be reconciled to the more tolerant attitude adopted by modern civilisation.

(11) Who do not acknowledge the Pope as head of the Christian Church, and who think that civil law supersedes Church law.
And lastly

(12) On all who think that there should be state schools, that the priest should not interfere with education, that knowledge comes before faith, that marriage can be contracted without a Roman Catholic priest, that divorce can be justified, that the Pope must act in the spirit of the age, and not follow the way laid down by the Christian revelation.

Church law, the foundation of Christian civili-sation, which it will be noticed the Pope puts before the laws of the State, is the most cruel and outrageous legal code in Christendom, it having been built up by successive Popes since the 4th century. It is the same today as it was when the Inquisition flourished, and includes amongst other provisions that (1) The Pope is above all rulers. (2) The Church can give to anyone as it pleases, or take from anyone all they possess. (3) The Pope has the right to reduce all non-Catholic nations to slavery. (4) Church law has been received by inspiration from God. (5) The Pope can make slaves of all the subjects of an excommunicated ruler. (6) The Church has a right to censure books, annul state laws, treaties, constitutions, and absolve all who disobey their rulers. (7) The Church has the right to punish rulers and release those who have taken vows or obligations. (8) No tax can be levied on priests. (9) All who persecute heretics have their sins pardoned, and he who kills one who is excommunicated is no murderer. (10) The Pope has full and unlimited power everywhere in the world, can make slaves of whom he likes, and can deal as he pleases with the life, body, property and liberty of heretics. (11) The Pope can command all Christian monarchs to wage war as he pleases, which conflict will be according to the will of God, and lastly (12) No ruler can allow his subjects to have their own religious beliefs, as these must be defined by the State in conformity with the Christian faith.

As these enactments run into thousands, and occupy numerous volumes, no more need be said than that the following decree embraces every one: "The limit of papal almightiness on earth consists therefore solely in their own will." Moreover, the oath that all Roman Catholic archbishops and bishops have to swear at their ordination declares that they will persecute to the utmost of their power, with the help of God, all who have opinions not in keeping with those held by the Holy Catholic Church.[1]

Nevertheless the men who take this oath are allowed to broadcast their opinions and sermons, and

[1] The exact wording of this section of the oath reads as follows: "Heretics, schismatics, and rebels against the same our Lord (the Pope) and his successors, I will persecute, and fight against, to the utmost of my power. So help me God and these his holy gospels."

if a pope, a cardinal, an archbishop or a bishop makes a public statement the B.B.C. passes it on at great length, but will not allow anyone to express opinions which, according to its own words, "do not come within the mainstream of Christian tradition". Britain is not yet a free country, and is still under the yoke of the Christian Church, which controls the B.B.C. so far as religion is concerned. (*See footnote, page* 1109, *Vol. I.*)

Protestantism has been only one degree less antagonistic than Roman Catholicism to liberty, progress and reform, and we remember the attitude of the Protestant bishops in the House of Lords to all measures brought forward for the improvement of British social conditions, and the reform of Parliament. The real difference between these two branches of the Christian faith is that the Roman Catholics recognise the authority of the Pope, and the Protestants do not. Otherwise their fundamental beliefs are identical. Protestants, like Roman Catholics, have opposed everything for the good of humanity at one time or another, their opposition to many things now considered right and proper having been referred to in previous chapters.

Protestants were no distance behind Roman Catholics in their cursing and damnation of heretics. They damned and cursed the Roman Catholics just as heartily as the Roman Catholics damned them. During the 19th century few, if any, Protestant priests omitted to damn all unbelievers in their sermons, but none reached the poetic heights attained by the famous Charles Haddon Spurgeon (1834–1892). This fanatic, addressing a large and fashionable congregation on the subject of the future of unbelievers (all who were not true Protestant believers), described their fate in the following words:—

In fire, exactly like that which we have on earth today, will they lie, asbestos-like, for ever unconsumed, every nerve a string on which the devil shall for ever play his diabolical tune of hell's unutterable lament. Look up there on the throne of God, and it shall be written "For Ever!" When the damned jingle the burning irons of their torment they shall say, "For Ever!" When they howl, echo cries "For Ever!"

That was preached and accepted within the lives of many living today,[1] and for cold calculated cruelty there is nothing between Protestantism and Roman Catholicism, but we must return to the Pope Pius IX. During the decade prior to his holy curses on all progress and reform, Christendom, in spite of the priests, had been awaking from the deadly sleep into which Christians had been put by the leaders of their faith. A steady improvement had taken place in human affairs. Everywhere, except in the lessening of warfare, progress was noticeable. In most countries there was less persecution, and greater freedom of expression. Schools were increasing and prisons becoming less crowded. Houses were becoming more comfortable, and railways, the telegraph, books and correspondence were enlarging life. There was less cruelty and more kindness, more happiness and less misery, better health and less suffering and sickness. Still, in spite of all this progress in human development, the leaders of the Christian Church condemned it all as evil and the work of the devil.

[1] In the year 1902 the author heard the minister in a Presbyterian church in Polmont, Stirlingshire, tell the children present: "If you do not sit still you will go to hell when you die, and burn, and burn, and burn for all eternity."

The Christian Church flourished when the people were most ignorant, and the faithful supported it most liberally when they were in mental and bodily slavery. They gave to the Church their all in exchange for its promise of pardon for sins committed, and a safe entry into heaven. Such a bargain was only possible with those who were fearful, superstitious and ignorant, but, as the light of intelligence increased, the Church authorities took alarm, fearing that increased happiness on earth, and greater intelligence, would weaken their power, and, most important of all, reduce their ill-gotten revenue. Organised religion always flourishes in the slough of ignorance and misery, the faithful receiving from its promises the comfort they would not require if they were intelligent, happy and knew that there was nothing to fear after death.

So the Pope, finding that the time had passed when he could employ the enlightened rulers to carry out repressive measures, imprisonment, torture, banishment and death, resorted to cursing all who disagreed with his selfish outlook. As that did not succeed in stopping the clock of progress, he propounded a new dogma to the effect that he was infallible. When despots find the ground slipping from under their feet they usually proclaim their divinity to impress the waverers and doubters. Hitler adopted this idea when affairs went against him in Russia, and he had to take over military control. Then he called on the German people to trust him, as his divine intuition would ensure his success.

The Pope, relying on the Christian dogma that man is a fallen being, and can only rise through belief in Christ, whom he represented on earth, stood on the road of progress, with his arms outstretched, calling to all who passed by: "Stop! this road leads to hell, and only by being guided by me, God's representative on earth, can you find the way to salvation." After fifteen hundred years of Church domination, during which time it had kept Christendom in ignorance, we need not be surprised that 200,000,000 orthodox Catholics accepted his claim to infallibility with hardly a word of protest. Likewise, for the same reason, we need not be astonished at the loose way the word "Christian" is used today to denote everything good. Surely no more inappropriate word can be used in this connection, as to do so flagrantly violates the history of Christian civilisation.

Attention has already been drawn to the confusion between Christianity and the reported moralisings of Jesus, but we are not so bankrupt in adjectives that we have to use a name with such evil associations to describe our meaning. Christian principles, Christian ideals, Christian culture, and the Christian way of life stand for everything wicked and reactionary to everyone who knows past history, and only those who do not know, or do not think, will ever use this word to describe something good, just and kind.

A name which is dyed red in the blood of the innocent is freely used today for just the opposite to that with which it has always been associated. Why not use the adjective "ethical", and talk about ethical principles, ethical ideals, and so on, and then all the world will understand us, instead of using the word "Christian" which conveys quite a wrong impression, and is distasteful to two thirds of the human race.

By 1868 Italy had become free and united, with the exception of Rome, where tyranny and misrule were rampant. On either side of this island of despotism, in a sea of liberty, was freedom and progress, which it was becoming increasingly evident would some day spread to the Church possessions, because the Italian liberators had no intention of leaving their work half done. Even in Austria, always in the past the Church's most devoted slave, reform and progress were under way. Her defeat by Prussia had opened the way for a more liberal government which had withdrawn her schools from Church control, and allowed freedom of worship and a free Press. Such deeds His Holiness described as "abominable", and they gave him much grief. "A horrible tempest," he declared, was threatening society, and "Satan, his satellites, and his sons, did not cease to let loose in the most horrible manner their fury against our divine religion."

So the grief of the Holy Father at the progress of the times reached such an intensity that he felt that something very impressive must be done. The idea which had been occupying the mind of Pius IX became known when he called together in Rome the 20th Œcumenical Council,[1] which was attended by 800 priests, mostly patriarchs, archbishops and bishops. From all over the world they came, over deserts and oceans, from the slow-moving East, and the fast-moving West, from London, where "Satan has his seat", and the cities once Christian but now in the hands of the infidel Turk.

[1] Meaning the Council representing the entire Christian community throughout the world.

Thirty nations were represented by these saintly men who had come to the holy city to save supernatural religion from the effects of progress, reform and liberty of thought. Clothed in white, the Holy Father, crowned with a mitre of gold, sat upon his throne in the great hall of St. Peter's, while each one of the assembled elderly gentlemen knelt down to kiss one of his knees. Three times he blessed them, and then got down to business.

The principal item on the agenda was the passing of the resolution to the effect that the Pope was infallible, and the only inspired revealer of God's will to mankind. This was no new claim, because the more evident the vices and errors of the occupants of the Papal throne became, as the centuries rolled on, the louder came the demand from all orthodox Catholics that it should be proclaimed from the house-tops that His Holiness could not err. Now, in 1870, the time had come to carry this into effect, as only blind obedience to God's representative on earth could save the Church from collapse.

Cardinal Manning, a recent convert from Protestantism, was a prominent supporter of the motion, which had the approval of an overwhelming majority of the assembled priests, but there was a small minority against, and their opinions caused considerable uproar from time to time, one dissentient being arrested on the authority of His Holiness for too freely expressing his opposition.

Then, after numerous fatuous speeches, much prayer, many public processions, and the frequent celebration of the Eucharist to obtain divine guidance in their decision, the motion was put to the meeting, but not before most of the minority had left the assembly in disgust. By a majority of 535 for, and two against, the Pope was declared to be infallible, and, as this was proclaimed, a flash of lightning and a clap of thunder announced to the majority that divine authority had been thus brilliantly proclaimed, but to the minority it was taken as a sign of divine anger.

The next day the official papal journal announced the decision of the princes of the Holy Catholic Church, to end with a curse from the infallible Pope on all who dared henceforth to deny this latest Christian dogma. Two hundred million Roman Catholic Christians now knew that the God-inspired Pope, who had denounced all progress and reform, could not have erred, and this imposture can be looked upon as the last desperate effort of a well-organised religious community to preserve Christian civilisation and the Christian way of life.

Protestant Christians had already broken away from this insane despotism, and relied instead on the infallible *Holy Bible* as their guide, but this bulwark was likewise proving to be inadequate for the changing times. Increased knowledge was revealing its many errors and failings, and it was becoming more and more a broken crutch. Consequently, as intelligence advanced, its past powerful reactionary influence decreased, to the greater happiness of all concerned.

Since the famous Council of Nicaea, Christendom had experienced 1545 years of priestly rule, which had kept countless millions, who feared to die, in bondage, misery and poverty. The same narrow theological minds which in 325 had clamped down the curse of ignorance on the most virile portion of the human race were still at work, and the centre of ignorance was in Rome. During these fifteen centuries the priestly mind had remained stagnant, and the same theology which had deadened the minds of the Christian priests at Nicaea was responsible for their insensibility to reality in the 19th century.

With such happenings so close to our own times we can better realise the calamity which came to the world when Constantine gave to their predecessors complete ecclesiastical power, which became full political power with the fall of Rome. Need we wonder that education and philosophy, which before that time were making the people kinder, tolerant and more intelligent, were suppressed, to be replaced by intolerance and superstition of the most debased order. What a terrible power is the fear of death, when used for their own ends by ignorant and unscrupulous men who acquire domination over the great majority of simple-minded people.

Organised religion in Protestant lands is now fortunately dying fast, and education is slowly weakening the authority of the infallible Church. Nothing can now stop the decay, and all the threats and curses of Pius IX, and his successors, vanish into thin air. These execrations increased from his time onwards in company with increasing progress, but the defeat of France by Germany in 1871, and the overthrow of Napoleon III, was a terrible blow to the Church. Then France, her "eldest son", proclaimed a Republic, and on this new democratic order Pius IX, and his successor Leo XIII, poured all the curses and abuse at their command.

With the help of French troops the Church had

retained the last of her territorial possessions, but, on the outbreak of war in 1870, the soldiers were withdrawn, when Rome, after a light bombardment, surrendered to the Italians. The following year, after a practically unanimous vote by her inhabitants, in favour of the acceptance of Victor Emmanuel as their ruler in place of the Pope, this historic city became the capital of Italy.

The Pope was given the Vatican, consisting of 11,000 apartments, as his residence, from which he was able each year, on the anniversary of his downfall, to witness the joy of the people of Rome celebrating their great deliverance. On the roof of the Quirinal, his former palace, he saw the flag of united Italy flying from the residence of the man who had dethroned him, and, in a street nearby, a shop sold openly Protestant literature, whose sale and reading he had prohibited under the threat of excommunication.

When he turned his eyes farther from home the scene was equally depressing. Germany, in 1872, withdrew from the Church, and transferred to the State the supervision of all schools which the Church was using to teach theological dogma and not for educational purposes. The German Roman Catholic priests, led by the Jesuits, rose in rebellion against this withdrawal of their special privilege, a revolt which ended in the Jesuits being banished. Ecclesiastical laws were now passed endowing both the German Protestant and Roman Catholic Churches, and defining the status of the priests of both sects.

Special precautions were taken against the crimes to which priests are prone, and from now onwards they could be imprisoned, and deprived of their incomes, if they were discovered intimidating or persecuting heretics. The Pope described this law as "impious and satanic", but his opinion did not prevent Prussia, Italy, Austria and France, a few years later, making marriage a civil contract, to which the Church could attach any religious ceremonial she desired.

Pius IX, after the loss of his temporal sovereignty, never left the Vatican, and always spoke of himself as a prisoner. After lingering into extreme old age, he passed away in 1878, having lived to experience the downfall of the temporal side of the great organisation which Augustine, in his book *The City of God*, had pictured would rule the world, and whose popes would receive the submission of everyone from the highest to the lowest.

What a power for good the Christian Church might have become, if the aim of its leaders had been the mental and ethical development of the people, instead of the ingathering of their offerings in exchange for the gratification of their ignorant superstitions. The Church leaders never rose above the level of their times, and carried their watchword "Semper Idem" (always the same) through the centuries, clinging obstinately to their claim of a special revelation from heaven which was to serve mankind for all time.

They saw, with rising anger, some amongst the human race growing out of the nursery stage to manhood, but they never adapted their teaching to the changing times. To do so would have destroyed their claim to have received the only revelation from God to man, which was their main prop for public support, and on this they decided to stand or fall.

From a wealth-producing point of view the idea has worked with marvellous effect over the long period of sixteen hundred years, and most of the popes, cardinals and bishops became very wealthy men. After the Reformation this applied also to the Protestant hierarchy, because both the leading Roman Catholic and Protestant clergy, as well as their Greek Orthodox brethren, received high positions and great riches through promising believers that heaven and not hell would be their destination hereafter. This diabolical fraud filled the Church Treasury to overflowing, besides making it the owner of a large part of Europe and South America, and, if it had succeeded in its aim to keep the people ignorant, it might some day have owned all the land in Christendom. As it is, the present wealth of the Christian Church throughout the world reaches very many thousands of million pounds, most of its income being exacted from the ignorant poor.

It is possible to fool all the people part of the time, and part of the people all the time, but not all the people all the time, and so the time came when the more intelligent saw through the fraud. When paper and printing came into use the gigantic priestly swindle became ever more evident, to end in the Pope losing the sovereign power which had enabled him, down the centuries, to rule as a despotic and tyrannical monarch.

Popes, patriarchs, cardinals, archbishops and bishops are the products of their theological training, they all being saturated with the superstition and narrow outlook which it produces, many being also greedy for wealth and power. Wherever theology reigns supreme there is no progress and only retro-gression. Consequently the clergy, in such circum-stances, are wolves in sheep's clothing, the enemies and not the friends of the people they claim to comfort, because they deny them the means of happiness secured by personal effort. They pander to the weakness of the individual, and, unlike the school-master, they make no attempt to raise the people to a higher intellectual or ethical range of thought. They belong to the childhood age of the race, and, where education exists, their need is passing, their day is ending, but their work and influence will be looked back upon by future generations with neither approval nor respect.

(5) Civil War Lacerates the United States.

We will remember having read in the last chapter about the bitterness which existed in the United States towards anyone who took the part of the un-fortunate negro slave. As the years went by this feeling became ever more acrid, ultimately to divide the country roughly into north and south, the former generally favouring the abolition of slavery and the south determined that it must remain. The negro had split this great English-speaking community into two camps. For a time many Americans soothed any troubled conscience they had by favourably comparing the lot of the slaves with that of the labourers in Britain and Europe, but gradually, as moral intelligence developed, the revolt against this form of labour increased.

Like so much of what has happened in the past,

religion largely entered into the question, because the slave owners, brought up in the belief that *The Holy Bible* was every word inspired by God, honestly thought that to enslave negroes had divine sanction. What could be clearer or more definite than this:—

Both thy bondmen, and thy bondmaids, which thou shalt have, shall be of the heathen that are round about you; of them shall ye buy bondmen and bondmaids. Moreover, of the children of the strangers that do sojourn among you, of them shall ye buy, and of their families that are with you, which they begat in your land: and they shall be your possession. And ye shall take them as an inheritance for your children after you, to inherit them for a possession; they shall be your bondmen for ever. (*Leviticus* xxv, 44–46.)

After this comes instructions on the rigorous treatment to be adopted towards slaves, but it was only very slowly that opinion changed in the 19th century, and then only amongst those not financially interested, the argument they put forward being that what received the approval of God in the past need not necessarily be right in the 19th Christian century. Those who held this view were considered by the great majority to be outcasts, blasphemers, atheists, infidels and servants of the devil, an opinion which was based on the Bible's affirmation that God never changes.

This being so, the mentality of our ancestors can be understood, because they were as much mesmerised by the Bible as were the Nazi fanatics by their god Hitler and his effusion *Mein Kampf*. Every word, from the first in Genesis to the last in Revelation, was to them God-inspired, and to doubt, question or make light of any passage in the Scriptures was the greatest of religious crimes, one which would bring about the eternal damnation in hell of the unbeliever.

The slave owners had therefore a strong case, because Jehovah, the Hebrew god, who evolved in time into the Father-god of the Christian Trinity, had commanded his chosen people to make slaves of the heathen, and had further laid down a code of cruel and savage laws to be applied to them. The orthodox, therefore, saw nothing wrong in slavery; in fact to them it was a divinely appointed means for Christians, who were likewise Jehovah's chosen people, to obtain the necessary labour to till the soil and obtain their livelihood. Jehovah, to Christians, was the unchanging supreme being, "the same yesterday, today and for ever", and, if he approved of slave labour in the past, he must equally approve of it in the present, his laws about slavery being just as binding on the Christians as they were on the Hebrews.

Fortunately for the slaves, increasing intelligence amongst some of the more unorthodox enabled them to imagine an improved god, because God is just as we imagine him to be. So these more enlightened ones became the heretics and outcasts in a vast community of cruel, ignorant, bigoted Christians, and, as the years passed, the rift between the abolitionists and the non-abolitionists widened. Feeling between the two camps consequently became more and more bitter.

Many of the slaves who escaped were caught by the use of bloodhounds and dragged back, to endure even greater misery, some to be tortured and others to die by being burned alive at the stake. A few, however, escaped, and were fortunate to receive the aid of friends, who pitied their terrible plight. To help a slave to escape was a grave legal offence, the offender being liable to a heavy fine or long imprisonment, but still the risk was taken, an illegal organisation passing them on from friend to friend until they eventually reached Canada.

By 1860 the atmosphere had become so tense that the slave owners made it impossible for anyone holding anti-slavery opinions to remain in the south, brutal violence and murder being quite usual. Within one year 800 people suspected of sympathy with the slaves were the victims of violent aggression, the possession of a book, or a newspaper, favouring abolition being sufficient to implicate anyone and warrant his banishment from the state he had so gravely insulted.

The founder and leader of the movement for the abolition of slavery in the United States was William Lloyd Garrison (1805–1879), and the story of his life of service is that of 19th-century slavery and its final abolition. He had neither money nor influence, and yet, from a garret in Boston, he published *The Liberator*, which was to lead the abolitionists to victory. The hatred he aroused, the dangers he encountered, his imprisonment for "libelling" the slave owners, and the friends he made in his own country and Britain, make up a thrilling story. He advocated immediate liberation, while many abolitionists were in favour of the slaves being liberated by degrees, and on this point there was a sharp division of opinion.

A settlement was attempted by Henry Clay of Kentucky, who advocated a slow emancipation and the gradual return of all the negroes to Africa, but the slave owners would not modify by a jot their legal rights. They became even bolder, and restarted the capturing of negroes in Africa, thousands being brought across the Atlantic. Prizes were given to the dealers who secured the best specimens, and the clergy vied with one another in preaching the most uncompromising sermons against abolition. In the north, by 1860, the position had changed to equally violent opinion in favour of abolition, the captain of a slave ship who brought his living cargo to New York being promptly hanged.

Amidst the clanging of opposite opinions came a startling diversion when John Brown (1800–1859), a wool dealer in Ohio, and some friends, went boldly into the southern states of Kansas and Virginia to aid the escape of slaves to Canada. He, and his twenty-two followers, seized arms from the military, which were stored at Harper's Ferry arsenal, their intention being to arm the slaves. Soon they were surrounded by a force of 1500 soldiers, and after a stiff fight, in which nearly all his followers were killed or wounded, Brown, badly wounded, was captured. He was tried and put to death, to become to the abolitionists a martyr whose "soul goes marching on", but to the slave owners he was nothing but a hated rebel.

Such, then, was the condition of the United States of America in the momentous year of 1860. Wealth was certainly increasing, and her people now had millions of cows, sheep and pigs, the cotton crop having reached 1,000,000 tons annually, and the grain and tobacco crops were each year breaking past records. Her inhabitants numbered over 31,000,000, and received theological instruction in 54,000 churches capable of accommodating more than half the population. Only a fifth of the land fit for cultivation was tilled, and before them stretched a future beyond the imagination of the greatest optimists. The Americans had everything that nature could provide except harmony of mind, the people being under the curse of ignorance, which bred bitter hatred one towards the other.

One day during this period of frenzied feeling Charles Sumner, a senator from Massachusetts, was writing at his desk in the Senate House at Washington. He was a great orator and he used his gift to denounce slavery which he hated intensely. Behind him came Senator Brooks, an ardent upholder of slavery, carrying a heavy stick, with which he mercilessly beat the helpless Sumner until he lay bleeding senseless on the floor. For this grave outrage Brooks was fined a trifling sum, but to his admiring constituents he became a hero.

So they paid his fine, entertained him sumptuously, and loaded him with souvenir sticks to commemorate the occasion. The south, in a most unmistakable manner, recorded its approval of the crime.

When such conditions arise in any country something must happen to break the strain, because it is impossible for a nation so sharply divided in thought to survive. Then it was that a book appeared which profoundly stirred the imagination of the north, where the need of slaves was less, and their conditions in the south not so well understood. This book was called *Uncle Tom's Cabin*, and it was published in 1852, the author being Harriet Beecher Stowe (1811–1896), a woman who knew well the terrible conditions prevailing in the slave-owning states. She had lived on the borders of one, and from those who escaped she learned of their suffering and misery.

She was a woman of keen intellect, and had deep sympathy with the oppressed. She was quite un-orthodox, and consequently right conduct appealed to her more than belief in the dictates of an ancient savage tribal god. Her book owes its success to the air of simple narration which pervades it, and to it having the aggressive strength of a political pamphlet, which appeared at the right time, as it was in harmony with the feeling then prevailing amongst many people in the north. Both in the north and the south it was so denounced by the clergy, the Pope also placing a ban on it, that, especially in the south, it became impossible to buy a copy.

During the eight years which followed the publi-cation of this book, it became ever more clearly realised that the time for argument and discussion was passing. The presidential election of 1860 was the most momentous ever so far held, each party putting forth its greatest strength, to conquer or die, on the issue whether slavery everywhere, and in every state, was, or was not, to be. In the south there was a solid block in favour of its continuance, while in the north opinion was divided. Abraham Lincoln, one of the four candidates nominated, was elected as president, the votes of those in favour of the continua-tion of slavery being mostly divided amongst the other three. Still the fact remained that up to the end of his first term of office Congress would always have contained a majority against him but for the absence of the members of the states which decided to secede from the union. The interests of the south, and of the slave owners, were thus safe, had the south remained in the union, whatever opinion the President possessed on this vexed question.

Abraham Lincoln (1860–1865), born in a log hut, and the son of a small farmer, was fifty-one years old when he reached the highest position a man can occupy in the United States. He had received little education, work from early childhood being his portion, but he had a great thirst for knowledge and borrowed every book in his neighbourhood. He started his career as a clerk in a small store, after which he went to Illinois to study law, entering politics in 1834 as a member of the Illinois legislature.

In looks he was very tall, slender, and awkwardly set up, a born leader, sagacious, resourceful, honest, kind, conciliatory, a king amongst his fellows, besides being endowed with a mind which had been sharpened by adversity. For twenty-six years Lincoln practised law, and took part in all the political controversies of the time, gradually coming round to the opinion that slavery was an evil which must some day be brought to an end, but he took no decided stand as an abolitionist. Such, then, was the man who was elected President of the United States, and who was to shoulder a burden few have been called upon to bear.

South Carolina was the most disloyal of all the states of the union, and considered herself more in the light of a sovereign state. She had previously shown her desire to secede, but the election of Lincoln brought matters again to a head, as to her he was "a man whose opinions and purposes are hostile to slavery". A convention of her people was called (1860) which declared South Carolina a free and independent republic, a declaration which caused much joy and gladness to her inhabitants. Today we would say that she had every right to be so, because the people had a right to their independence and the government they desired, but in those days minorities were not permitted to break away from the nation to which they were attached.

Other southern states hastened to follow the example of South Carolina, as Georgia, Alabama, Mississippi, Louisiana and Florida next announced their independence and the formation of a Confederation to embrace them all. This union adopted a new constitution, which abolished protective duties and strengthened the rights of the slave owners to own and extend the number of their slaves. Jefferson Davis (1861–1865) was elected their president, and when it was evident that war was imminent the other slave states, Virginia, North Carolina, Tennessee, Arkansas and Texas joined in, thus raising the number of states forming the confederation to eleven, with a total population of 9,000,000, of whom 3,000,000 were slaves.

Large minorities were against secession, but persuasion and intrigue overcame all opposition. Twenty-three states, with a population of 22,000,000, remained outside the confederation, and loyal to the old union and President Lincoln. Thus the question of the right or wrong of slavery divided the United States into two separate nations, though the problem had not yet reached the stage of legislation being proposed for its abolition; in fact Lincoln promised the south that he would bring in a measure to the effect that slavery would not be made illegal, and that all fugitive slaves would be returned to their owners. The seceding states, however, feared that sooner or later legislation would be passed at Washington which would adversely affect their interests, and they considered that they had every right to vote themselves out of the union because they could not see eye to eye with the others on this vital issue.

The war which followed was therefore caused by the seceding states breaking up the union, a policy they would not have adopted had there not been this difference of opinion about slavery. The north did not decide to fight the south to free the slaves, but to maintain the solidarity of the United States, and keep it as one nation under one president. When the war began certain northern generals declared that the conflict was one to liberate the slaves, but they were reprimanded for misrepresenting the cause, and when northern generals declared the slaves to be free in the area of their command their proclamations were revoked by Lincoln and declared to be void. Moreover, all slaves captured by the north were termed contraband of war, not prisoners, and they still remained in bondage.

It was in defence of their right to secede, to have their independence, that the south took up arms against the northern states, and they had justice on their side, because they entered the union on the understanding that they could withdraw from it at will. No one in the south doubted the right of any state to secede, not even those who opposed the decision to break away from the union, and President Buchanan (1857–1860), who preceded Lincoln, declared that he was unable to see how secession could be prevented if an individual state wished it.

What had been the United States had now two presidents, and, when the south sent ambassadors to Washington with instructions to settle peacefully all outstanding problems, Lincoln refused to see, or communicate with, them. Already the southern states had been told by him that nothing would be done to alter their legal rights to own slaves, but that no state could secede from the union. In his opinion the status quo continued, and his authority still functioned in their midst, even if force were needed to maintain it, but no aggressive action was contemplated, and the question of war or peace now lay with the seceding states.

Jefferson Davis declared in reply that the discontented states would do as they pleased, and remain in or quit the union as they thought best. Lincoln waited, determined to maintain the union by friendly discussion and to compromise if necessary, but to fight rather than have it broken. Consequently he would not receive ambassadors from the south as from a foreign power, an action which greatly angered the seceding states. On such occasions a conflagration is lit by an incident, trifling in itself, but momentous in its consequences, and this is what now happened.

Fort Sumter, in Charleston Bay, South Carolina, manned by United States troops, was summoned by the southerners to surrender, as, being on their soil, it was their property. The commander refused and its bombardment began. The south was therefore the first to break the peace, and by this act one of the worst civil wars in history began in 1861. Short of munitions and food, the fort surrendered without a man being killed or wounded on either side, but its surrender gave the south the confidence that it could secure a quick triumph against the north. Moreover, this incident brought all the slave states into the Confederation under one leader. Two days after the fall of Fort Sumter, Lincoln mobilised 75,000 men, and war preparations were rushed forward to quell what the north termed a gigantic rebellion.

Four days after the fall of Fort Sumter, Lincoln announced the blockade of all ports held by the rebels, and in a few weeks this became effective. The first battle between the north and south, now termed Federals and Confederates, was at Bull Run (1861), when the Federals were routed and fled to Washington. The Confederates, after this important victory, expected the Federals to recognise the Confederacy, but the latter, stiffened by their defeat, raised their army to 500,000 men. Chastened, but undismayed, the Federals set to work to prepare for a conflict, the size of which they now realised they had underestimated.

After six months of preparation General McClellan moved the Federal forces against Richmond, the Confederate capital, but, though greatly outnumbering the enemy, he turned by his timidity what might have been a great victory into a defeat. Elsewhere General Grant was leading his Federal forces with success, and driving the Confederates out of Kentucky and Tennessee. At sea, after early disasters, due to the Confederates arming an iron ship which destroyed successfully three of the Federal wooden ships, the

Federals set to work to build iron warships with gun turrets, and by so doing they opened up a new era in naval warfare. When this fleet of iron warships was complete it moved south, silenced all the enemy coastal forts, cleared a large area bordering the sea, and in 1862 reached New Orleans.

The Federal Government, believing more strongly than ever that the Confederates were rebels, now (1862) passed a law freeing the 3,000,000 slaves held in bondage in the rebel states. This step was taken because it was considered that all rebels had forfeited their rights as citizens, and that the law permitting a citizen of the United States to own slaves no longer applied to them. By this measure 3,000,000 slaves were nominally freed, but only in the rebel states, because it did not apply to the loyal states, where slavery continued as before. This evoked scornful comment from abroad, the British Foreign Secretary remarking that this measure "professes to emancipate slaves where the United States cannot make emancipation a reality, but emancipates no one where the decree can be carried into effect".

The Confederates were successful whenever they met the forces of the incompetent General McClellan, until at last Lincoln removed him and gave the command to General Burnside, whose first battle was a bloody defeat, 12,000 Federals being sacrificed in vain. Though the loyalist army now numbered 1,250,000 men, the rebellion had not been crushed, and, by superior generalship, the Confederates had been successful in most of the major engagements. The almost complete blockade of the southern ports was all that had been successful in the Federal plan of campaign. Nevertheless, in spite of their series of brilliant victories, the Confederate position was quickly becoming desperate, as economic conditions in the southern states were rapidly deteriorating—food, clothing and munitions becoming ever more scarce.

The first important victory the Federals secured was at Vicksburg, which surrendered to General Grant with its garrison of 2,300 men. This victory cut the Confederate states in two, as this town gave the Federals control of the Mississippi river, but matters still went badly for the Federals under General Hooker in a new attempt to capture Richmond. Before he reached his goal General Lee defeated him at Chancellorsville with a force half the size, and never before did Lee's superior generalship show itself to better advantage than on this occasion, because he had everything against him.

In this battle died the Confederate general known as "Stonewall" Jackson, who was typical of the men fighting on both sides in this pitiless war between kith and kin. They all seemed imbued with the belief that God was fighting for them, both sides claiming him as an ally. Jackson was a devout Christian, rising early each morning to pray and read the Bible. Before he performed the most trifling act he prayed that it would be blessed, or quoted some appropriate text, and yet this pious man was a pitiless fiend. He flogged his slaves unmercifully, and advocated the massacring of all prisoners of war, being guided by the fact that these measures had the sanction of God, because they were in accordance with Jehovah's instructions to the Hebrews on their treatment of both slaves and enemies. When he died he was acclaimed by both sides as "a noble, true-hearted, Christian man", which was the way our ancestors referred to such ruffians after their death.

After his great victory at Chancellorsville, Lee marched with 75,000 men into Pennsylvania, intending to reach Baltimore and Philadelphia, when New York would be at his mercy. While the advance continued the people in the flourishing northern cities trembled, because so far he had been successful in every battle, and his reputation was becoming Napoleonic. At Gettysburg (1863) he was met by an oft-defeated Federal army of about the same size under General Meade. The battle lasted for three days, and, during the first two, success crowned the efforts of the Confederates, but on the last day fortune favoured the Federals, because they broke up all attempts to pierce their centre. The slaughter was terrible, but, though the Confederates stormed time and time again, they could not capture the Federal position. Once they pierced it, only to be thrown out, and when the day ended the assailants were in flight.

The attack had failed, and Lee had been defeated for the first time. The Federals lost over 20,000 men, and the Confederates double that number in this conflict which was one of the most desperate battles of the war. The tidings of victory filled the north with great joy, and everyone was down on his knees thanking Jehovah for deserting the south and giving the north the victory. What a ridiculous situation, because these devout northerners quite failed to appreciate the fact that their defeated enemies were fighting in order to be free to carry out Jehovah's instructions on the keeping and treatment of slaves.

Such is the absurd position stupid humanity reaches when it abandons reason, and accepts an irrational, supernatural religion based on faith and not on rational thinking.

The human race is, however, guided by its emotions as much as by reason. If this were not so it would make fewer mistakes and suffer less. With no justification for their belief that Jehovah was fighting their battles, the imagination of the Federals nevertheless rose to poetic heights, and a hymn which became famous was the result. Everywhere it was sung in the north, to the tune of "John Brown's Body", the opening verse being as follows:

Mine eyes have seen the glory of the coming of the Lord,
He is trampling out the vintage where the grapes of wrath are
    stored.
He hath loosed the fateful lightning of his terrible swift sword.
His truth is marching on.

If these words are read carefully, line by line, and not sung, without thinking, to a popular tune, it will be realised that to the Federal Christians, as to the Hebrews, their god was the Lord of Hosts and God of Battles. So long as religion and war are married, with the imagined blessing of the highest name people can find, there is little hope of peace replacing conflict, and of happiness taking the place of misery. Warriors, pillagers and devastators have always claimed God as their ally, but the time has now come to sweep away all this ignorant theological ignorance, and face facts which are plain enough for all intelligent people to see. Man is his own saviour, and only through reasoned thinking can the world's sores be healed.

At a memorial service held on the Gettysburg battlefield, Lincoln spoke these now famous words. Those men have fought "that this nation under God shall have a new birth of freedom, and that government of the people, by the people, and for the people, shall not perish from this earth". Noble sentiments, to be sure, but they are hardly applicable to a war which was fought to prevent the southern states from securing their independence.

True, the outcome of the war was the liberation and enfranchisement of the negroes, but that came later, and it was not for that reason the war was fought. Neither was it a fight for democracy, but one to prevent the southern states exercising their right to withdraw from the union at their will and pleasure, a right which the northern states denied to the people of the south. This being so, these noble sentiments uttered by the President were political humbug and quite irrelevant.

Only indirectly had slavery anything to do with this bloody conflict, because when the war began the north had no intention of stopping slavery in either the north or south. The south had slaves just as the north then had slaves, and in both north and south they were considered legal property to hold and do with as one pleased. If the north had first of all abolished slavery, and then fought the south to force the southerners to abolish it also, the conflict would then have been a holy war to liberate the slaves, but the struggle was to preserve the union and prevent the southern states from forming an independent nation.

It was to preserve the United Kingdom of Great

Britain and Ireland that Ireland was devastated for centuries. It was to preserve the unity of the British Empire that the British fought the American colonists. So as to preserve the unity of the Spanish Empire, Spain fought the Netherlanders and her colonists in South America. It was to preserve the unity of the Austrian Empire that all the bloody battles in Italy were fought. With the object of bringing about the unification of Europe, Napoleon I, the Kaiser William II and Hitler ravaged helpless independent nations. The tragic story, which many of the foregoing pages of this book reveal, centres round this insane desire for unity and conformity, ignorance blinding zealots to the fact that communities of individuals, like individuals, desire to live their own way of life free of outside domination.

Groups of people, if they wish, have the right to band together and govern themselves, but, beyond all that, the sovereignty and dignity of man comes first and foremost all the world over, and nothing should ever be done to endanger his liberty, life, comfort, health, happiness and possessions. Black, white or yellow races have each the same right to have these vital essentials safeguarded as have the Jews, Christians, Moslems and those of any other faith or nationality. All men and women everywhere have the right, which none should deny them, of happiness, security, peace and freedom during their pilgrimage from the cradle to the grave. These are broad principles on which future statesmanship must base its policy, and, though majorities and minorities complicate the problem, wise consideration, and reasoned planning, will solve most of the difficulties if there be goodwill all round.

The victory at Gettysburg lifted a great load off the minds of the people in the north, but much was still to be done before complete victory was reached and the union made secure. As the north grew in strength the south weakened, because here suffering was now acute and poverty reigned where once there had been plenty. Stocks of everything were running low, and even clothing was insufficient to keep the army clad. By now the north had over 2,000,000 men under arms, and 600 warships, besides enormous resources. Desertion and defeats had greatly reduced the Confederate army, inflation was rampant in the south, and it now took sixty southern dollars to buy what one northern dollar would purchase. In this plight the south had to meet the second Federal attack on their capital, because the north was determined to go on to Richmond and finish the war by giving a death-blow to the enemy's heart.

For ten months there was continuous fighting, and men toiled at the grim task of slaughtering one another. General Grant, in charge of the Federal troops, was strong enough to outflank all positions, and, though the losses on both sides were appalling, he gradually hemmed in his opponents at Petersburg, which protected Richmond. Meantime General Sherman led a large force of Federal troops towards Atlanta, the capital of Georgia, devastating the land on all sides. Reaching there, he destroyed by fire all the public buildings, and then marched on to Savannah (1864), destroying as he went, his advance through a broad belt of fertile country being like a forest fire, everything perishable being destroyed, and the people were left in complete destitution and misery. Many perished from hunger, some became insane, and none who survived ever forgot the suffering and misery they endured from the devastation caused by the army of this pitiless creature.

During the winter of 1864-5 it became plain that the Confederacy was tottering, but Petersburg still held out against Grant's investing armies, now joined by the forces under Sherman. In the spring of 1865 a general assault by the Federal troops carried the enemy positions, and the road was open to Richmond.

Jefferson Davis, when kneeling at prayer in St. Paul's Episcopal Church in Richmond, received the message that the city's defences were pierced. Quickly he fled from the doomed city, which was set on fire by the Confederates rather than let it fall intact into the hands of their enemies. Next morning the city was in the hands of the Federal troops, but not before all the Confederate leaders had escaped, as they thought that they would receive little mercy. Meanwhile Lee fought on, and only when his supplies ran out did he surrender. Then followed the capitulation of all the other Confederate armies (1865) after four years of one of the bloodiest wars in history.

The terms of the armistice permitted all the Confederates to return home, with the promise that they would not be punished for their share in the conflict. Thus this bitter and agonising struggle came to an end after terrible slaughter and destruction, but, as the United States had been preserved, and the "rebels" defeated, the Federals were thankful, and gave thanks on many occasions to God for his great help in fighting on their side. The Great Rebellion, as it was called, had caused the death of about 450,000 men, and the wounded numbered very many more, large tracts of country were devastated, and the cost in money reached £1,800,000,000.

Still, in spite of all this waste of life and property, the fact remained that since 1787, when the United States was established, each state of the union considered itself a sovereign state which had originally entered the Republic of the United States on the understanding that it could withdraw at will. The war changed all this, and from now onwards each state became a unit within a nation. War does not determine justice, but it settles issues, and this great question was now finally settled.

Like Germany and Italy, during this same period of history, the United States became a nation, because it found unity through war, the conflict having taught the people to think as a nation and not only of their individual states. Nevertheless if all these independent states had been allowed their individual liberty, had they wished it, no one would have been any the worse, many lives would have been saved, and much suffering avoided. Are frontiers for ever to be the cause of bloodshed?

Slavery would have come to an end in both the northern and southern states sooner or later, just as it came to an end in British colonies some years earlier. Increased intelligence was gradually breaking down the belief that God approved of slavery, and had made laws which were binding on all captives. As this happened, American Christians would have been forced by world opinion to free their slaves, if their own mental development had not first produced a change of outlook. The war certainly hastened emancipation, as just before it ended the north amended the constitution of the United States, making slavery illegal, and when the war ended this likewise applied to the southern states.

One more tragedy was still to fall upon the now united nation, before the effects of the curse of ignorance had gone their full round. On the evening of Lee's surrender Lincoln returned from General Grant's headquarters to Washington, to find the capital beflagged and rejoicing. A week later he attended the theatre, where he was killed by a shot from a southern fanatic, who, after the deed, leapt from the President's box on to the stage shouting, "The South is avenged!" William Seward, the Secretary of State, was likewise attacked in his own home, the assailant almost stabbing him to death, but he recovered. The grief of the northerners over the loss of their greatly beloved President was intense, as to them he was the symbol of a united nation.

Lincoln was no aggressor, out for loot and power, and he hated war, bloodshed and suffering. Whatever mistakes he made he followed the course which he thought was right. He was a fine and noble product of his time, with the limitations of the age in which he lived, and to those who followed him he left a sterling example of a man who always did his utmost to live up to the light that was within him.

The negro who, up to the present, had had no rights whatever, was now accepted as a citizen of the United States with all the legal privileges of a white man, the successor of Jefferson Davis in the Senate being a negro. Besides making amends for past wrongs, much had to be done to bind up the country's bleeding wounds. Little feeling of resentment remained in the north, and everything possible was done to help the south, which was short of everything. The high price of cotton helped gradually to restore prosperity, and it was found that the negro worked better as a wage-earner than under the lash. Five years after the war was over a complete change had taken place on the question of slavery, and quite as many were now against it as in former times had been for it.

The war had interrupted progress, but now that it was over the wheels began to move again. The first Atlantic cable was laid in 1866, and Alaska was purchased from Russia in 1867. Gold, silver, petroleum and coal were discovered in many parts of the country. Mills of all descriptions arose everywhere, and railroads branched out in all directions until they covered the vast continent. As wealth increased, so did the population, which, by the end of the 19th century, was 76,000,000, or more than double what it was when the war commenced. Politically peace reigned under the guidance of a series of generally wise and good presidents: Grant (1869–1877), Hayes (1877–1881), Garfield (1881—assassinated), Arthur (1881–1885), Cleveland (1885–1889), Harrison (1889–1893), Cleveland (1893–1897) and McKinley, who was elected in 1897 and assassinated in 1901 while still in office.

The United States during the 19th century was blessed by men who led the people to a higher level of thought. Washington Irving (1783–1859), William Prescott (1796–1859), George Bancroft (1800–1891), Richard Hildreth (1807–1865), John Motley (1814–1877) and John Fiske (1842–1901) were amongst her great historians. Further outstanding names occur in other branches of literature, such as Ralph Waldo Emerson (1803–1882), Henry Longfellow (1807–1882), Oliver Wendell Holmes (1809–1894), Walt Whitman (1819–1892), Samuel Clemens (Mark Twain) 1835–1910), but no one had a greater influence, wherever the English language is spoken, than had Robert Green Ingersoll (1833–1899) in lifting the curse of ignorance from Christian minds.

We have seen how ignorance gave the people an entirely wrong idea of the series of ancient manuscripts brought together under the name of *The Holy Bible*. Ingersoll, by his lectures and writings, brought knowledge where hitherto there had been ignorance. A lawyer by profession, he was one of the greatest orators and liberators of last century, but his fellow countrymen so fiercely resented the exposure of their ignorance and mistakes that he had to abandon all idea of obtaining any political office. Repeatedly he refused to give up his self-set task of educating and humanising his Christian countrymen, though he knew that it ruined his chance of a great political career. In 1868 he would have been made Governor of the State of Illinois had he been a Christian, but to this noble high-principled man truth came before all else, and consequently he had to endure the abuse and malicious slander of the clergy who were quite unable to appreciate honest rational thinking.

Primitive man, when he reached the stage of realising that he continued to exist after death, feared the unknown and the gods whom he thought had power to punish him if he angered them. So he instituted taboos and reverenced images and sacred objects, clinging to them as a lame man leans on his crutch. All down the ages such things have helped and comforted frail humanity, just as the image of the suffering Saviour on the cross has helped many a Christian to die in peace.

Then came printing and paper, when some learned to read the only book then available, which they called *The Holy Bible*. Knowing nothing of history, and the similar beliefs of all the other world supernatural religions, it became to them what charms and amulets are to more backward people, and, as men arose to lead them to higher and more advanced levels of thought, they looked upon these reformers and liberators as blasphemers and heretics. Ingersoll, fifty years ago, was such a man, the Voltaire and Thomas Paine of his time, and to him we owe much of the tolerance and religious liberty we, in this generation, enjoy.

Now we must leave this great nation, made up of men and women, both white and black, representing in miniature the people of Europe and Africa. Apart from the negroes the United States is just another Europe across the Atlantic, all its people joined together under one elected leader. If this is possible in America why should it not be also possible for all in Europe to join together on equal terms, voluntarily, without compulsion, and so avoid the never-ending question of boundaries and attempted domination, first by one nation and then by another? Perhaps, as the curse of ignorance gradually lifts, this idea, which in the past has been no more than a dream, may be realised.

(6) PROGRESS, DISCOVERY AND REFORM DURING THE 19TH CENTURY.

In Chapter XV we reached the point in British history when Victoria, at the age of eighteen, succeeded to the British throne on the death of her uncle William IV in 1837. Ascending the throne at this early age, she and her people had every reason to expect a long reign, and they were not disappointed in its length, its peace, and its prosperity. Britain, during the Victorian era, was blessed by many years of peace, all branches of science advanced, trade and wealth increased, and the education of the people commenced. Consequently their morals improved, crime decreased, knowledge increased, and humanitarianism replaced the idea that poverty and suffering were part of the divine plan.

We have already read of the constant unrest of, and the agitation by, the people to have a greater share in their own government, and this continued until the Second Reform Act was passed in 1867, which extended the right of voting in the boroughs to all householders, and to lodgers paying a rent of £10 a year. In the counties, only those paying a rent of £12 a year had the power to vote, an injustice which was removed in 1884, when all householders everywhere obtained the franchise. For the first time in British history the aristocracy and landed gentry could now be outvoted by the artisans, and this meant that politicians, if they wished to keep their seats in Parliament, had to take their instructions from new masters who were determined to have a greater share in the country's increasing comforts and wealth.

Wrongs and injustices of the first magnitude were the earliest to yield to the growing power of the people, and as each decade of the Victorian era passed there was less obvious evil to remedy. Sanitary conditions improved, while land drainage increased productivity and reduced the tendency to fever from stagnant water. Vaccination almost abolished smallpox, a scourge which had taken a toll of 9 per cent. of the population. Improved houses and better food increased the health and stamina of the people. Fresh clean water was brought to the cities to replace the impure liquid impregnated with dangerous bacteria.

Gradually the 8 per cent. of the population living in unlighted, unventilated and undrained cellars in towns in 1850 were moved into better dwellings. Filth and bad ventilation, which were causing more deaths annually than any war, were now being replaced by improved sanitary conditions. Scientists were discovering what hitherto had not been fully realised—that filth breeds disease, and an inadequate air circulation reduces vitality. Ignorance was slowly giving place to knowledge, but it was not until the century drew to a close that every child was educated.

Instead of prisons being filthy damp dark dens, wherein hardened criminals and first offenders, men, women and children, were all herded together in the same place, without beds, with vermin everywhere, new prisons were built with separate apartments. Instead of men fighting duels to the death over some trifling difference, they came to settle matters by an apology or in the law courts. Most of the leading men of the early Victorian era at one time or another killed, or tried to kill, someone because of a dispute. Passions then rose to great heights over what to us would be trifles not worth bothering about, but our ancestors, as a rule, were such uncontrolled children that they acted just as naughty children do.

Both soap and newspapers were very dear, and the people could neither keep their bodies clean nor their minds informed, but, as the century drew on, soap became cheaper as more was used when education made it evident that filth brought disease. The heavy tax on newspapers, fourpence a copy, was withdrawn, and as education advanced their circulation increased. Letters in 1837 cost, according to distance, up to one shilling and fourpence each, but that year Sir Rowland Hill (1795–1879), against great opposition, introduced the penny postage.

Filthy streets—the sewage being thrown out of the windows on to the road—filthy bodies and filthy homes gradually gave place to greater cleanliness. Medical science won one victory after another against disease and epidemics. Anaesthetics relieved pain, and surgery became a practical science now that the patient could be put to sleep. Women found that there was much they could do to help doctors, and so they trained as nurses. As the century drew on, new and better hospitals sprang up all over the land, to end, at the close of the century, with doctors and nurses in towns and villages working together in conjunction with these healing centres. So health has improved and happiness has increased, thanks to the great trail which the doctors and scientists have blazed round the world.

Whom have we especially to thank for the welcome change which has come over our social conditions? Now we are in the age of the really great men, those who by their thoughts and deeds left this earth better than they found it. Smallpox was the scourge of the human race, many victims falling to its ravages, and to Edward Jenner (1749–1823) we are grateful for discovering a vaccine for its prevention. Let us also thank Sir William Jenner (1815–1898), whose work and discoveries greatly reduced fevers, especially typhus and typhoid. Let us thank Louis Pasteur (1822–1895), who, by his genius, discovered antiseptic methods which have saved millions of lives. Let us be grateful to Lord Lister (1827–1912) for developing the aseptic method of surgery, and to Sir James Simpson (1811–1870) for bringing chloroform into general use, the beneficent effect of which has greatly reduced the pain of operations, now made so much safer by Lister's discoveries.

These men, and many others, lived to relieve humanity from the calamities which beset mankind. To save a single life was more to them than a hundred victories in battle. Millions have perished to satisfy the ambitions of individuals, but their aspiration was to save the lives of millions. Science has been too often used to destroy, but, in their hands, it was used to heal and enlarge the frontiers of life. So let us thank the physicians who have laid the hand of healing on the sick and suffering, and at the same time we must remember all the good men and women whose efforts have relieved pain, prolonged life and removed the cause of sickness and disease.

Besides the doctors there are many others who

lived in this age whom we ought to thank.   Let us be grateful to Lord Kelvin (1824–1907) for all his many useful inventions, and for perfecting the compass; to Alfred Russel Wallace (1823–1913) for anticipating Darwin in his discoveries about the ancestry of the race, and to Thomas Huxley (1825–1895) for his efforts to bring the knowledge of scientific discoveries to within the range of the people.   Let us thank Michael Faraday (1791–1867) for introducing the age of modern scientific thought, and for being the pioneer of applied electricity, his work being carried to practical effect by Graham Bell (1847–1922), who invented the telephone, and Thomas Edison (1847–1931), who greatly improved telegraphy and made many other electrical inventions.   Clerk-Maxwell (1831–1879) should also be remembered for discovering the ether waves which led to the invention of wireless telegraphy by Marconi and then the radio.

Let us also remember John Dalton (1766–1844), Sir William Crookes (1832–1919), Sir Joseph Thomson (1856–1940), Sir William Ramsay (1852–1916) and Lord Rayleigh (1842–1919) for their discoveries relating to the constitution of the physical universe, efforts which were crowned by the finding of radium, the outcome of the painstaking work bravely done by Pierre (1859–1906) and Marie Curie (1867–1934). Besides the tasks accomplished by these illustrious researchers, the discoveries made by Wilhelm Röntgen (1845–1923) and Lord Rutherford (1871–1937) revealed to us the wonders of radio-activity.   Sir Charles Lyell (1797–1875), by his patient labours, told us the story of the earth from his examination of fossils, rocks and strata, and thus proved its great age, the story of the creation in *Genesis* from now onwards being disbelieved by all thinking people.

Let us thank the great poet of this age, Lord Tennyson (1809–1892), and the men and women who wrote to instruct and charm, Lord Lytton (1803–1873), Charles Reade (1814–1884), George Eliot (1819–1880), George Meredith (1828–1909), William Morris (1834–1896), Robert Louis Stevenson (1850–1894) and Thomas Hardy (1840–1928), who was the last of the famous Victorian novelists. Let us also acknowledge with gratitude those who exposed ignorance, and advocated knowledge in place of superstition—men like Herbert Spencer (1820–1903), who tried to weave the knowledge of his time into harmony with universal law, and William Lecky (1838–1903), who shed light on the prevailing darkness by his histories on the development of ethics and rational thought.

David Ricardo (1772–1823) and later Walter Bagehot (1826–1877), both famous economists, helped to complete and round off the work so ably done by Adam Smith in the 18th century, while John Stuart Mill (1806–1873) quickened thought upon every problem on which he wrote. His influence on political and philosophic opinion was profound, and never did he tire in his efforts to discover improved ways to raise the standard of life of the people, the emancipation of women being the subject of one of his many books on philosophy, progress, justice and reform.

Sir Henry Rawlinson (1810–1895), by his painstaking efforts, unravelled the ancient language of Babylon, and Sir Henry Layard (1817–1894) made many discoveries at Nineveh, including an immense library of books of brick which had been written upon when they were soft. Champollion (1790-1832), the distinguished French Egyptologist, and Thomas Young (1773-1829) discovered how to read the Egyptian hieroglyphics. These four men were amongst the pioneers who opened a closed page in human history, and, by their discoveries, revealed whence Christianity obtained its dogmas and doctrines.

Let us also remember with gratitude the explorers who risked all to discover new lands. We have already read of Livingstone's work in opening up Africa, but let us also thank those explorers of this period who penetrated up rivers, and through jungles, in their search for new territory. At the opening of the 19th century only the coastal fringe of Africa was known, but in the last quarter of the century the broad outlines of its geography were nearly completed. This was due to the work of John Hanning Speke (1827-1864), Verney Lovett Cameron (1844-1894), Sir Henry Morton Stanley (1841-1904), Joseph Thomson (1858-1895), Sir Samuel Baker (1821-1893), Sir Richard Burton (1821-1890), James Grant (1827-1892) and many other explorers of different nationalities, especially Belgians, Portuguese, Germans, Italians and French, who shared in the honour of opening up this vast hitherto unknown continent.

Let us thank all the great men of this period, those who lived to find improved means of healing the sick, the great inventors, constructors, discoverers and mental liberators, as well as those who used these discoveries to make this earth a happier, easier and more pleasant place in which to live, a world in which the people are healthier, better fed, better clothed, cleaner and more intelligent than were their ancestors of a hundred years earlier. Many of these benefits and comforts could have come to Europe from the Moslems a thousand years earlier if Christianity had not put a ban on education, and replaced knowledge by an infallible Church and a God-inspired book. Consequently the lack of learning maintained an autocratic caste in power which, for its own benefit, kept the people in ignorance and serfdom, but, with the coming of education, progress commenced, and now we are beginning to witness its effects.

When the people obtained the vote the Anglican Church was forced to abandon its exclusive attitude towards all other Christian sects in the country, while those professing no religion received their rights as citizens. Dissenting ministers were now permitted to perform marriages, and the parish burial ground was opened to receive the bodies of those who had not conformed to the State Church. Likewise it became unnecessary for the Anglican burial service to be read at funerals. Jews in 1858 were allowed to become members of Parliament without taking the oath "on the true faith of a Christian", and in 1871 the Universities, hitherto closed to dissenters and unbelievers, opened their doors, the students' religious beliefs ceasing to be questioned, while compulsory attendance at Church services was also abolished. Eventually the deadly stranglehold of Christianity was broken when Charles Bradlaugh, an avowed atheist, was permitted in 1886, after a long and bitter struggle, to occupy his seat in Parliament without declaring that he was a Christian.

During the age of Christian civilisation, all who

believed in only one God were bitterly persecuted. These people, now called Unitarians, whose religion contains neither creed nor dogma, were originally the early Jesuians of the Apostolic Church, later to become known as Arians. Their non-trinitarian beliefs brought about the calling of the Council of Nicaea, which established the Christian Church as the State Church of Rome, and set it off on its career of world domination. From that time onwards this sect was so persecuted that it had no chance of self-expression, but, after the Reformation, some faced the hatred of the Christians, and formed themselves into bodies which assembled together for public worship.

Only in Poland, Transylvania, Britain and America was this possible, but even there they had to face many years of persecution, during which time they were put to death, imprisoned and banished. Not until 1813 was it possible to profess openly in Britain the beliefs of the early followers of Jesus without punishment, and only after 1844 were Unitarians able to possess legally their own places of worship. As late as 1855 fines were imposed, up to twenty pounds, on those of all denominations who met for religious worship in buildings other than churches if the number exceeded twenty, the bishops in the House of Lords always opposing the repeal of this law.

The most famous Unitarians in England were Sir Isaac Newton, Joseph Priestley, Sir Charles Lyell, Charles Darwin, John Milton, John Locke, Charles Lamb and Florence Nightingale, its most outstanding ministers being Lindsey, Channing, Martineau and Stopford Brooke, though many other famous names, such as Emerson, Longfellow, Oliver Wendell Holmes and Theodore Parker, in both America and Britain, could be mentioned if space permitted.

Because the Arians lost the amendment, and the motion was carried at the Council of Nicaea to incorporate into the Jesuian religion the Egyptian idea of a trinity of gods, they, and all who thought like them over the past fifteen hundred years, had to suffer from bitter persecution. No decision, no battle, no edict ever had such an effect on history as had the majority decision at the Council of Nicaea in 325, the most famous date in world history, because from it grew Christian civilisation, which eventually embraced a third of mankind.

At the close of the 19th century, if we look back to the beginning of the reign of Victoria, there is everywhere progress to be seen in the intervening years, and the disdainful contemptuous way the upper classes spoke to and treated the lower classes gave way to increased courtesy. Education and knowledge were making people more humane, kinder and happier.

Animals were better looked after, and much unnecessary cruelty was made illegal, though much still remains to be done by abolishing all blood sports, such as hunting the fox, hare, otter, deer and other animals which are made to suffer to give pleasure to a small number of sportsmen and women who lack both pity and compassion. Flogging of men and women with the lash slowly decreased from being a common occurrence to become a rare event, but in the early part of the century 500 lashes would be inflicted for slight offences, and these at times killed the victim.

On one occasion (1811), when a newspaper protested against an offender being given 1000 lashes, the editor was sent to prison for eighteen months.

Hanging likewise became less common, executions at the end of the century being few compared with 500 a year when the century opened, even though the population had doubled in size. Banishment for life likewise declined from nearly 900 in 1834 to become negligible. For this greater mercy towards offenders thanks is due to the heretical Sir Samuel Romilly (1757–1818), a kindly, much beloved, upright humanitarian who laboured strenuously for many years to try and make Christians more humane, and get them away from their attachment to the cruel Mosaic code of laws. But he only managed to exempt from hanging the pickpocket and the thief who stole linen from a bleach field. By 1820 Parliament became more merciful, and excluded poaching from the death penalty, if the poacher had not blackened his face, but many years were to pass before the sheep and cattle thief got off without being hanged for his crime.

All this is certainly much more cheering reading than we have been accustomed to in the preceding pages, and, as education increases, confinement in prison may become as rare as hanging is today. This, and all our other problems, depend on mental development—that alone, because with mental development comes enlightenment. Going back to the beginning of history, we find progress ever followed by reaction. After centuries of stagnation came advance, then again stagnation, then progress, and so on one after the other until we come to the present day, when we have only to use the golden key, namely education, to find the remedy for most of our miseries, troubles and tribulations. Education unlocks the book of knowledge, which is our only sure guide to increased comfort and happiness.

Enlightenment first came to mankind when he found that the gods did not help him, and that he must solve his troubles by his own exertions, by reaching the heights of knowledge and freedom through the development of his own mind, which alone makes each one of us independent rational individuals. When man discovered that he, and he only, was his own saviour, and that he need neither fear nor implore the gods, real advancement commenced, and now we are in the period of history when the hitherto slow-moving river of progress begins to swell into a flood. Progress, however, is only progress if it improves the health of the people, increases their comforts and adds to their happiness. All else which does not do so is retrogression and the misuse of knowledge, another of the many evils which comes from ignorance.

(7) THE RISE TO INDEPENDENCE OF THE DOMINION OF CANADA.

Progress comes from the people themselves, because they only can determine their destiny. Not only in Britain were the effects of developing mind noticeable, but also in her English-speaking colonies, where the colonists were claiming more independence, less interference by the mother country, and a more representative electoral system.

Canada, however, has a history peculiarly her own. Because of her situation and mixed population, her people had problems to face which did not confront the other British possessions inhabited by purely British stock, such as Australia and New Zealand. Up to 1791 the Canadians had no say in their own affairs, they being ruled by a governor appointed by the British Crown. After that date the country was divided into Upper and Lower Canada, the former containing mostly British settlers, and the latter the much larger and older established French colony. Each colony had its own governor, who was appointed by the King, an Executive and Legislative Council, and a Legislative Assembly elected on a restricted suffrage, but, as the Governor had dictatorial power, the people had to do his will and pleasure.

This mistaken policy of dividing Canada into two parts, to prevent it becoming too strong, and some day following the road of independence adopted by the Americans across the border, was much resented by the British colonists, and it led to great trouble in the years ahead. Upper Canada wanted the establishment of free schools everywhere, but the clergy of Lower Canada firmly refused to agree to their people being educated. This attitude, together with trade differences which were inevitable between two separate provinces using the same waterways for communication, created a spirit of antagonism, and this developed into one of social hatred. The British wished to have a united Canada in which all would be educated and loyal to the Crown, whereas the French were quite content to remain illiterate, and looked forward to the day when they would become independent and free from all British restraint.

This internal antagonism was only quelled for a

few years, when bad feeling developed between the Canadians and Americans during the British-American war (1812–1814), which, we remember, came about by Britain seizing and searching American ships during her war with Napoleon. Then America took the opportunity to try and conquer Canada. At first the British drove out the invaders, but a year later the British were heavily defeated, when towns and villages, including Buffalo, on both sides of the frontier were burned down. During 1814 many fierce and bloody battles were fought, thousands were killed and wounded though nothing decisive was accomplished, and then Britain and America made peace in this wicked needless conflict in which Canada had no special interest.

Besides disturbances caused by war, religion created much unrest in Upper Canada, the Episcopalians adopting an exclusive attitude towards all who had different religious ideas from those they held. The Episcopalian Church was the State Church, and, with its political power, it denied to the dissenters all religious rights. It regarded itself as the only Protestant Church under the Act of 1791, and all who dissented from it were considered to be neither Protestants nor true Christians.

Consequently the opinions of dissenting clergy did not count, as such people had no rights or position. This being so, the seventh part of all the Crown Land set apart by the Act, now amounting to 3,000,000 acres, and known as the "Clergy Reserve", belonged to the Episcopalian Church. For fifty years this was a burning question, and the cause of endless discord and bitter hatred, the dissenters never abandoning their claim to a participation in this wealth of which they considered they should have their share.

Both religion and politics, therefore, kept in being acrid domestic strife, and laid Canada wide open to all the reformers and agitators who found their way to her shores. Robert Gourlay, a Scotsman, a passionate democrat, raised the standard of revolt in 1817, only to be imprisoned and then banished, an action which widened the cleavage of opinion in the country still more. Three years later he was followed by another Scotsman, William Lyon Mackenzie, whose love of reform, and hatred of the prevailing political and religious abuses, were genuine and deep. He roused the people to rebel against their many grievances, and declared that there was neither justice nor tolerance in the land, it being rotten with corruption and intrigue, because those in power conducted its legislation solely for their own ends. He demanded that the people should get the power to put matters right, and, though he was elected five times to the Parliament of Upper Canada, he was expelled as often.

Numerous petitions were sent by the Canadians to the home government, but nothing was done to meet the wishes of the colonists. Then Lower Canada revolted in 1837, under the lead of an eloquent Frenchman named Papineau, and the people began to drill and arm themselves with a view to overthrowing British tyranny. Bands of armed peasantry roamed the country around Montreal, and riots were frequent. The British government, remembering how easily the American colonies were lost, now took alarm and sent out Lord Durham, who used his powers unwisely, but his report on existing conditions, and their remedy, became the text-book of his successors and the basis of Britain's future policy towards the English-speaking colonies. From now onwards it was accepted that they must be free to manage their own affairs.

Firm action in Canada brought peace after six weeks of disorder, but not for long, because Mackenzie declared war on the government unless the people secured full say in the conduct of their country's affairs. Fifteen hundred men attacked Toronto, only to be defeated, when Mackenzie fled to the United States to raise a band of marauders who invaded Canada. They too were defeated, and this brought the Canadian Revolution to an end. Three years later a Bill was passed in Britain uniting the two provinces, and rectifying the most pressing injustices and grievances.

Canada, from 1840 onwards, was ruled by a governor, and a reconstituted Legislative Council and Legislative Assembly, the latter being chosen by the people, the Council, like the British Cabinet, holding office so long as it had a majority in the Assembly. At long last Britain accepted the fact that a colony had its rights, and was not just a part of Britain across the seas to be ruled only according to the dictates of the Crown. How tragic it is that this more enlightened outlook was not adopted by the British ruling class in the previous century, as, if it had been, all North America would probably be still within the British Commonwealth. Incalculable wealth, countless lives, and untold misery might have been saved over the past two centuries, had the British people of the 18th century not been so blind to the great opportunities which were then within their grasp.

Right up to the middle of the 19th century Canada was involved in political and religious difficulties, so much so that a mob burned down the Parliament House in Montreal. This was not rebuilt, as the capital was moved to a small town, the name of which was changed to Ottawa. The State Episcopalian Church was disestablished immediately the people obtained the power, because of its intolerant arrogant attitude and the disgraceful way it had misused its power.

It had become an abomination to the people, who now deprived it of any legal claim to justify its contention that it was the only Church in the land. This exclusive organisation had suffered the same ignominy in America, and was to experience the same curtailment of its power in all the British colonies and Ireland. The same fate would have overtaken it in England had it not yielded somewhat to public opinion, but ultimately it must be disestablished as such an institution is an anachronism in a democratic country.

Gradually, as time went on, the racial antagonisms lessened, and the steady flow of immigration from Britain soon removed the feeling of numerical inferiority which had prevailed so long amongst those of British lineage. The French retained their language and customs, and were regarded as equals and fellow citizens. Both sides forgot their old grievances and became friends. All the restrictions on Canadian trade were removed, the St. Lawrence was opened to the ships of all nations, and Canada was free to trade as and where she pleased. Great cities arose, canals, roads, and then railways were built which ultimately joined the two oceans. The new Canada took the name of Dominion of Canada in 1867, when British Columbia united with the other provinces. The reason the word dominion was adopted was because of *Psalm* lxxii, 8. "He shall have dominion also from sea to sea, and from the river (St. Lawrence) unto the ends of the earth", Canada stretching farther north than any other country.

Such then is an outline of the rise to independence and greatness of this vast territory. By unusual wisdom for these days the government of Lord Melbourne surmounted a dangerous crisis in the Empire's history, and retained in its attachment to the Crown a great and loyal nation, which became a source of wealth to its inhabitants, and a tower of strength to the Empire in the strenuous years which lay ahead.

(8) BRITAIN AND HER EMPIRE DURING THE VICTORIAN ERA.

Viscount Melbourne (1835–1841) was Prime Minister when the young Queen Victoria came to the throne in 1837, at the time when the people were demanding their proper place in the administration of their own country. In the previous chapter particulars were given of these demands, but even if the aristocratic caste, which then ruled Britain, had wished to have manhood suffrage, an idea which was repugnant to it, such an advance was impossible because the vast majority of the people were illiterate, and education must precede the vote.

Nevertheless we are here at the threshold of better

times, the awakening conscience of a more advanced age bringing to an end many abuses, and the introduction of numerous reforms. It was during Melbourne's administration that slavery was abolished throughout the British Empire, and Lord Shaftesbury secured better treatment in mines and factories for children who received only a penny a day for working a twelve-hour day six days a week. This great reformer, and friend of the oppressed children, who, though tender in years, were treated as slaves, devoted his life to making their lives tolerable, but he received little help from his Christian contemporaries, the clergy especially being his particular enemies, opposing him in all his schemes for improving their conditions. In his diary of 6th April, 1849, less than one hundred years ago, Lord Shaftesbury wrote:

I trace much of our evil to the moral condition of our ecclesiastical rulers and ministers. It is possible that they may be improved in comparison of former days; they are wholly insufficient in reference to the present. Look at the metropolis! Why so frightful a state of spiritual desolation? Why so many wretched, forsaken, naked vagrants? I have said this and received in reply, "The clergy are unequal to the task." Well, then, why do they discountenance and almost insult those who toil to collect the outcasts into the Ragged Schools?

Elsewhere he wrote "They (the clergy) have exhibited great ignorance, bigotry and opposition to evangelical life and action, and have seriously injured their character, influence and position." Again he wrote of "a collision of the clergy and the mass of the people. The Church will destroy itself." At that time it was considered to be a religious sin to criticise the priesthood, and, when this is remembered, we shall better realise how evil was their influence when this noble man was forced to write as he did.

What Shaftesbury did for the poor, Richard Martin did for animals. He succeeded, after years of work and discouragement, in getting the first laws passed in Britain for the purpose of protecting animals against cruelty, and he was one of the founders of the Royal Society for the Prevention of Cruelty to Animals.

So that correct knowledge of what took place in Parliament was available to the public, there was issued for the first time during Melbourne's ministry authorised reports (Hansard) of parliamentary proceedings. In 1837 the first electric telegraph was invented, and the next year a regular steamship service began with America.

Britain, unlike so many other lands, has been fortunate in not experiencing many revolutions, evolution being more noticeable. In the first half of the 19th century social conditions were so terrible that an upheaval might easily have taken place, the supporters of the People's Charter, the Chartists, being the cause of widespread riots, while throughout the manufacturing districts great discontent prevailed. Fortunately some of her politicians had more flexible minds than the one possessed by the cast-iron Duke of Wellington, and in Sir Robert Peel (1841–1846), who now became Prime Minister, we have an instance of the type of man whose mind was sufficiently supple to change with the changing times.

Peel was nurtured in the Tory tradition, and throughout his forty years of parliamentary life (1809–1850) he proved himself to be a strong, honest and courageous man. He did not move quickly, but quick enough to keep pace with the changing thought of his time. Like Gladstone, at a later date, he was prepared to go back on his earlier reactionary opinions, most of the progressive measures he fought for in his later life having been previously denounced by him in unmeasured terms. So it came about that Roman Catholic emancipation, Free Trade, Church reform[1] and the extension of the franchise ultimately received his support, and when his career ended he was able to look back on a series of legislative measures which laid the foundation for the improved social conditions Britain now enjoys.

The mental urge which in those days was gathering increasing momentum could not be stopped by a body of exclusive theologians, and, as they would not agree to students who were not Anglicans attending Oxford and Cambridge Universities, while also reserving the leading schools for those of their own denomination only, other ways had to be found to overcome the difficulty. So an influential band of Nonconformists and Secularists founded London University in 1827, devoted only to the pursuit of knowledge, all theology and religion being excluded. All ancient tradition was ignored, and, for the first time, Britain had a seat of learning freed from the reactionary influence of the priest. This indeed was a great event, because it established a principle which it is hoped will some day be followed by every school and university throughout the world.

Surveying these years of slow but steady progress,

[1] Several Acts of Parliament were passed removing the worst abuses and scandals relating to the Church of England. Plurality of livings (several livings belonging to one priest) were abolished, and a reduction was made in the number and wealth of the Cathedral clergy.

we observe the outstanding omission on the part of British legislators to realise the necessity for legislation directed towards the education of the people. Those who did appreciate the need, had all their efforts blocked and thwarted by the Church of England hierarchy demanding that if there was to be education of the people it could only be theological, on the basis of Episcopalian doctrines, to which requirement the Nonconformists would not agree. Moreover, both the Whigs and Tories feared an educated working class, and it was this fear of a multitude of ignorant people that held up social progress.

Far wiser would it have been to have first raised the people mentally, and made them able to take their place as intelligent citizens, after which social legislation would have followed naturally. Instead of this being done, the uneducated masses were for years rioting and clamouring for education and reforms. These were denied them because they were regarded as a class apart, their illiteracy and ignorance making them a despised community that God had decreed was to perform the labour and drudgery for the benefit of the more fortunate educated upper classes.

Against this orthodox outlook the heretical Lord Brougham (1778–1868) expressed his strong dissent, his book *Observations on the Education of the People* leading to the formation of the Society for the Diffusion of Useful Knowledge, but religious opposition prevented his Education Bill from passing through the House of Commons in 1820. Again he tried in 1839, to meet with no better success. This brilliant Scottish advocate, scientist, orator and statesman, who became Lord High Chancellor of England, was interested in every branch of knowledge, and carried on the campaign inaugurated by Joseph Lancaster to have all the people educated.

During a great portion of his life of ninety years he played a conspicuous part in promoting legislation for the good of the people. His indomitable energy, his vehement eloquence and his enthusiastic attachment to the cause of freedom, reform, progress and humanity certainly entitle him to be regarded as one of the most illustrious men of his age.

Nevertheless even he, with all his ability and brilliance, was unable to break down the prevailing belief that humanity was divided into two sections and separated by an impassable gulf, the gentry on the one side, and on the other the toilers, who had few rights and no privileges, whose duty it was to obey those whom God had set over them. If the people themselves had not risen mentally to a higher level they would certainly have remained as serfs for all time, but now we find a quickening of their intelligence. In the year 1844, at Rochdale, began in a humble way the Co-operative movement, when twenty-eight poor weavers (the Rochdale pioneers) joined together to purchase their daily necessities at wholesale prices. From this small beginning sprang the now immense world-wide organisation, employing millions of capital, which has proved such a boon to the poorer classes, besides encouraging the habit of thrift, and being the means of their cultural advancement by lectures and discussion meetings.

Because of the number of Episcopalian and Roman Catholic landlords, patronage, or the right of landowners to appoint the parish minister, was abolished in Scotland in the year 1690, but in 1712 one of the early Acts of Parliament after the Union restored this privilege. In the years which followed an increasing number of democratically minded Scottish Presbyterians had grown ever more resentful at this withdrawal of their once much-prized right, which enabled each congregation to elect the minister of its own choice, so much so that the country's religious and social history was largely influenced by this Act of 1712. It brought about a long series of secessions from the established Presbyterian Church. It separated families and friends, and maintained religious disharmony until the end of the 19th century.

The greatest explosion came in 1843, when this smouldering grievance burst into flame, to become known as the Disruption. From a total of 1200 ministers, 451 left the Church of Scotland under the leadership of Dr. Thomas Chalmers, and formed the Free Church of Scotland, each congregation electing its own minister. This meant new churches and manses and no state grant, but their congregations enthusiastically supported them. Though there was much distress and hardship, the new Church was soon placed by Chalmers on a sound financial basis by each member contributing a penny a week to what was called the Sustentation Fund. In 1874 the grievance was legally abolished, but it was not until 1929 that the two churches reunited.

It is strange that this ancient privilege of the patron having the power to appoint the parish priest should still prevail in England, the members of the Church of England being quite content to accept the priest appointed by the patron without in any way being consulted beforehand. Scotland overthrew this relic of the days when the people, like children, did what their masters the landlords told them, but, in other respects, the members of the Scottish Presbyterian Church were equally childlike in their religious outlook.

The minister was the dominant influence in the parish, each Kirk Session, before which the ungodly parishioners were brought, being an Inquisition in miniature, the ministers and elders being equivalent to the Inquisitors of the Faith, who, throughout the Christian era, deprived the people of all liberty of thought. Scotland, since the Reformation, until towards the end of the 19th century, was as minister-ridden as ever Europe was priest-ridden, and the catalogue of sins for which the offender had to come before the Kirk Session grew to such a length that it covered almost every human activity, from the "sinful" acts of kissing one's wife and children on the Sabbath, or having the window blinds up on that holy day, to other more grievous offences.

This gestapo was particularly active in the days when witchcraft was accepted, but, in the years which followed, increased unbelief gave it many an opportunity to exercise its functions. These consisted of forcing the delinquent to make public his humiliation and repentance in the stocks, besides branding, imprisonment or public admonition, the harshness of the punishment being as pitiless as it was cruel. All the sunshine of life was squeezed out of the Scottish people to an even greater extent, and for a much longer time, than happened in England, as

Calvinism in the raw took a grip of the people's lives in a way that never happened under Episcopacy south of the border.

Like the clergy everywhere, the Scottish ministers were great worshippers of titles and wealth, and did nothing to promote social welfare. They approved and supported the most abominable cruelties towards those who sought to improve their conditions in life, and when two men were hanged, drawn and quartered for agitating for something better, the General Assembly, in 1822, informed George IV that all such people were impious traitors who undermined the Christian religion.

Leaving Scotland, we again take up our story when Lord John Russell (1846–1852), filled with reforming zeal, succeeded Peel as Prime Minister under the shadow of a serious famine in Ireland. Already over-populated, her 8,000,000 inhabitants at the best always lived under the shadow of want, and when a blight killed the potato crop thousands died of starvation. Britain had experienced a bad harvest and could do little to help the distress. This famine made obvious the need to repeal the corn laws, which were preventing cheap grain from coming into the country. It not only brought to a head this burning question of long standing but reduced the population of Ireland by* half, some 4,000,000 Irish peasants crossing the Atlantic, only, as too often happened, to die of typhus contracted on the voyage because of the terrible conditions under which they lived.

Britain in those days was governed by two powerful interests—the landowners and the industrialists.

Gone was the time when the landowners alone monopolised the wealth of the country, as they had now
against them a strong political body of wealthy
industrialists, whose interests were to secure cheap
food and living conditions, to enable them to sell
their wares cheaply abroad. Interesting results followed from this state of affairs, the first being the
repeal of the corn laws, due largely to the unsparing
efforts of Richard Cobden (1804–1865) and John
Bright (1811–1889). Cobden, a Manchester calico
printer, impoverished himself by his exertions, and
Bright, a Rochdale manufacturer, stirred the country
and Parliament by his powerful vigorous speeches on
the iniquity of taxing corn imports. Bright wanted
free trade and cheap living, and the landowners wanted
good prices for their harvests.

The industrialists won, the corn laws were repealed
in 1846, and the landowners did not forget the
bitterness of their defeat. Consequently, when public
opinion forced Parliament to improve the conditions
of factory workers, we find the landowners helping
forward these measures in order to get even with the
industrialists. John Bright, who wanted cheap living
so as to produce cheap goods, fiercely opposed
legislation to reduce the long hours of labour in the
factories, and so we find the landowner Shaftesbury
advocating better factory conditions, and Bright,
the industrialist, in favour of cheap grain.

This, when it came pouring in from America from
1875 onwards, ruined many a landlord and farmer,
2,000,000 acres of corn land slowly going out of
cultivation, and the exodus of farm labourers to the
towns and overseas increased, but the town-dwellers

ultimately benefited by being able to obtain cheap food. The day of the landowners, as a political power in the country, was gone, and they had to bow to their fate. Politically, this controversy over cheap food caused a split in the Tory party, the members who had voted for the repeal of the corn laws joining the Whigs, and from this time onwards the Whigs were termed Liberals and the Tories Conservatives. The term Liberal, strangely enough, came from Spain, where those who called themselves Liberales unsuccessfully attempted to establish parliamentary government, universal suffrage, political and personal liberty and abolish the Holy Inquisition.

While these two groups in Britain were each working for their own ends, four separate Bills were introduced into Parliament between 1850 and 1855 for the purpose of establishing State education for the people, but on every occasion they were defeated because of religious opposition. Though the Church managed to keep the people ignorant, it had not, however, the power it once had to prevent progress in other directions. So we find at this time, when the squires and clergy on the one hand were ranged against the industrialists on the other, there commenced in 1843 vast railway developments which covered the land with a network of iron roads.

Thus much traffic was taken from the canals and roads, causing widespread distress amongst bargees and innkeepers, the old coaching inns losing their age-old function of servicing both travellers and horses. Enthusiasm, however, outdistanced discretion, and within a few years much distress and loss were caused by the collapse in the value of railway securities, which, by over-optimism, had been forced up far above their intrinsic values. When the slump came financial panic and widespread ruin followed.

The Earl of Derby formed a new administration in 1852, but it did not last throughout the year, and then came a coalition under the Earl of Aberdeen (1852-1855). During this ministry was fought the terrible Crimean War, about which something must now be said.

If we turn back to the first section of Chapter X we can there refresh our memory about an amazing action, or rather series of actions, by the leaders of the Christian Church. Then, at the Council of Toledo, in 589, the decision was made to alter the Nicene Creed, and later, after different Church councils had debated on this weighty problem, the change was finally adopted by the Western Church in 1054. From that time onwards Christendom was split in two because the Eastern Church refused to recognise this tampering with Christian belief.

Knowing as we now do how the life and teaching of Jesus has been misrepresented to us in the Gospels and Epistles, he personally cannot be regarded as responsible for all the suffering which followed. Neither can he be blamed for the 25,000,000 victims who perished from the persecution of the Church which claims him as its founder. Those who distorted his teaching, and falsely claimed to follow him, were the men who were responsible for this crime, and also for all Christendom after the Reformation being divided into three hostile camps. Nevertheless the fact remains that if Jesus had not been born all the trouble which ensued would not have arisen.

This being so, it seems strange that he should be called the Prince of Peace.

The chief actor in the great human tragedy, entitled "Christian Civilisation", which has occupied the stage of the Western world for sixteen hundred years, was Paul of Tarsus, who was the first cause of all the disharmony which followed. In consequence of his mistaken zeal in transforming Jesus into another Pagan Christ, this sincere fanatic, cursed by ignorance, set the stage for this prolonged era of misery and suffering—by misrepresenting the life and teaching of Jesus, by the distortion of facts, by false claims, and by being guided by mystical emotionalism instead of his reason. No other man, not even Hitler, has been responsible for more human anguish than has this man, now known to us as Saint Paul, though of course this was never his intention.

Paul involved Jesus in all the tragedies which have surrounded his name since the Council of Nicaea in 325. One calamity after another followed from Paul's departure from the truth, the consequence being that the civilised world before his advent was a better place in which to live than during the centuries which followed. Most of the great thinkers of Greece, Egypt and Rome lived before his time, during an age when we read little about religious intolerance. The Holy Inquisition was entirely a Christian invention, as in Pagan times the gods, under different names, were the common heritage of everyone everywhere throughout the Roman Empire, where, in the time of the Republic, there existed a tolerance towards religion only to be compared with that which exists in our own time.

When, however, a fixed creed was adopted, defining the Pauline Christ, which all must believe or perish, social conditions changed for the worse, and intolerance took the place of tolerance. Since its production in the year 325 the Nicene Creed has been the cause of continual strife and suffering, and now, once again, this blood-stained theological formula was the reason for a bloody war and terrible suffering because of Europe being divided over its interpretation.

The devastating Crimean War arose from a dispute between Western Roman Catholic Christians and Eastern Orthodox Christians over the custody of certain sacred shrines in Jerusalem, France taking the side of the former and Russia of the latter. A settlement was reached which the Tzar Nicholas I (1825–1855) so deeply resented that he mobilised his army (1853) and demanded immediate satisfaction, besides Russian protection over all Orthodox Christians within the Ottoman Empire. These proposals Turkey rejected, well knowing that in the event of war Britain would stand by her, and when Russia moved her troops into the Danubian provinces belonging to Turkey, Britain and France declared war in 1854.

From the time Britain occupied India she feared Russia, her great northern neighbour, and when the opportunity came to strike at her she did, the excuse France made for joining in the struggle being that her interests in Syria were threatened. Russia then withdrew her forces from Turkish territory, and this tragic war might have ended without a shot being fired, but both Britain and France were anxious to humiliate Russia. French democrats disliked her form of government, the Roman Catholics especially hating the Russians because they were Orthodox Christians and did not accept the addition of the word "Filioque" (= and from the son) which the Catholics added to the Creed in 1054. In fact this one word was the primary cause of the disastrous Crimean War, and again emphasises the truth of the statement attributed to Jesus that he had not come to bring peace but the sword, and to set the people at variance one with another.

Once the fire of war was lit both France and Britain rushed into the blaze, determined to mortify Russia, each country providing forces of about equal size, no one being clad or equipped for a campaign during a rigorous Russian winter. They, in company with their Turkish ally, now moved against Russia, though it should be remembered that the danger of Russian aggression had passed when she withdrew her troops from Turkish soil. Ignorance, and all the crimes and follies which come from it, was now rampant, as will be realised when we recollect that Tennyson a year earlier had written his *Ode*, a fulsome panegyric, on the death of the Duke of Wellington, whose imposing military obsequies influenced the poet to glorify war and its great exponent just dead.

Sevastopol, the famous city and fortress in the Crimea, must first be captured before peace can be discussed, said the warmongers in London and Paris, led by Lord Palmerston, then the Home Secretary, and Napoleon III. So an allied force was landed in the Crimea, in September 1854, without the necessary food, clothing, tents or hospital appliances. After defeating the Russians on the River Alma the allies delayed their advance, and so gave the enemy time to strengthen Sevastopol, and protect it from the sea by sinking ships at the entrance to the harbour. Its siege was then begun. Elsewhere the Russians attacked Balaclava, the allied base, but were repulsed. after which followed the Battle of Inkerman in which they were likewise defeated.

Then came the fierce Russian winter, when illness and disease caused havoc amongst the ill-equipped allied troops, and not until Spring came was fighting resumed. Sevastopol was then attacked and captured, to bring the war to an end. The Treaty of Paris restored this city, and all else captured, to the Russians, on the understanding that Turkey's integrity be respected, and that she no longer oppressed her Christian subjects, but Russia failed to secure her protection over the Orthodox Christians living under Turkish rule. The Black Sea was declared neutral waters on which no warship was to sail, and on whose shores no fort was to be built.

This treaty was broken in 1871, and Britain's legacy from this senseless war was 20,656 dead soldiers, many thousands of widows, orphans, and mutilated men who had now to live out their lives with broken health, while the National Debt was increased by £50,000,000. France likewise suffered, but besides the casualties in the Russian army, which were heavy, many thousands of her peasants died from exposure and famine. For every one man killed in this war seven died of wounds or disease, a number which would have been much larger had not Florence Nightingale, after much opposition from the military authorities, organised a nursing service, and, by her efforts, reduced the death rate in the military hospitals by half.

This heroic woman stands out alone as great in an age of mediocrity and selfishness. Moved by the reports of suffering which were coming from the Russian front, she, a fully trained nurse, along with thirty-seven helpers, went out to Scutari, where hospital conditions were deplorable, to try and ease the sufferings of the wounded, who in those days received little consideration. By her example and energy she brought about a transformation in the conditions prevailing in the military hospitals and the sanitary needs of the troops, but her fame rests on more than this, as her exposures of the nursing conditions of those days brought about the raising of the nursing profession to the position it has now attained. She, more than any other woman, elevated the position of women, who, from now onwards, were permitted to enter public occupations for their own good and the lasting benefit of the human race.

Viscount Palmerston (1855–1858) succeeded Lord Aberdeen when he resigned because of popular dissatisfaction with the conduct of the war, and, by his vigour and determination, brought it to a successful conclusion before the year 1855 ended. This energetic, laborious, patriotic but tempestuous man, who, as much as anyone, was responsible for the war, was very dictatorial in his dealings with foreign nations. At times he alarmed his colleagues by his aggressiveness, but he was sympathetic with liberal movements abroad, and encouraged Victor Emmanuel II and Garibaldi in their struggle for Italian independence.

He looked upon the Chinese with contempt, and when a pirate ship, the *Arrow*, flying the British flag, was seized by them (1857) he described the mandarin who arrested the pirates as "an insolent barbarian", being evidently quite unaware of the fact that this Chinese gentleman could claim an ancestry which was cultured and civilised hundreds of years before Palmerston's ancestors had emerged out of savagery. Britain avenged this "outrage" of the Chinese by bombarding and capturing Canton. Meanwhile the French, not wishing the British to get all the Chinese trade into their own hands, had joined the British as allies, and the war continued until 1860, when China was forced to give increased trading facilities.

While the British were mixed up in this conflict with China, news arrived (1857) of a mutiny of the sepoys in Bengal. They resented (1) the British annexation of Oudh, from which many of them came, (2) the British attempt to westernise them, and (3) their cartridges being greased. The Hindus considered that grease came from the cow, which they reverenced, while the Moslems said that it came from pigs, which to them were taboo.

So the cartridge grease offended their religious scruples, and they revolted, murdered their officers, and seized Delhi, where, after setting up as their leader a descendant of the Great Mogul, they tried to raise a national rebellion. By besieging, and eventually capturing, Delhi, the British, under Sir John Lawrence, the Punjab Commissioner, prevented the mutiny from spreading, but the rebels captured Cawnpore and a terrible massacre followed. Luck-

now, the capital of Oudh, held out until it was reinforced by General Havelock, to be finally relieved by
Sir Colin Campbell, who arrived from Britain with
reinforcements.

The British generally were hated by the natives,
as, since the occupation of India, they had been
arrogant, contemptuous and overbearing towards
them, and, when it seemed that their overlords had
lost control, pitiless cruelties were inflicted on the
helpless British men, women and children now at
their mercy. When the mutiny was quelled merciless
retribution followed, all offenders being severely
punished, and everyone suspected of cruelty was
tortured and hanged without trial. Landowners, who
had sympathised with, or helped, the rebels forfeited
their lands, and Britain made it clear that never again
was her power to be questioned. The uprising had,
however, made obvious that something was radically
wrong with the government of India, and Parliament
now brought to an end the long rule of the East India
Company, a Bill being passed transferring its powers
to the British Crown, which from now onwards was
represented in India by a Viceroy.

Palmerston's administration resigned in 1858,
when Lord Derby again became Prime Minister, and
during his brief spell of office Lord Canning was the
first Viceroy of India. The following year Palmerston
again returned to power, and it was his ministry
(1859–1865) which so angered the Federals, during
the American Civil War, for its sympathy with the
southern Confederates. When a dispute arose with
the Federals because they seized two Confederate
envoys from a British steamer, Palmerston prepared a

fierce protest, which the Prince Consort softened down and so prevented a trifling incident becoming the cause of war. As it was, Britain herself was guilty of a breach of neutrality by allowing the warship *Alabama*, built for the Confederates, to sail from Birkenhead, in spite of the Federal request that it be detained. After the war was over the United States demanded reparation from the British for the damage this ship had done to Federal vessels and cargoes, and the sum of £3,000,000 was eventually paid over as compensation.

In 1861 the Prince Consort died, and thus the Queen lost her best and chief adviser. For the country his death was a great loss, as he was a man of noble character, wise, tactful and progressive, the arts, science and industry receiving his constant aid, and social problems his active sympathy. Palmerston died in 1865 after a long parliamentary career of nearly sixty years, during which time he held important offices and was twice Prime Minister. His chief interest was in foreign affairs, and for twenty-five years he controlled British foreign policy.

In his long life he saw many valuable measures passed, many reforms instituted, and such innovations as railways, steamships, the electric telegraph, the penny post, increased education, and a great broadening in the franchise. He lived to see Britain struggle out of darkness into the dawn, he beheld a gleam of light appearing after a black night of ignorance, and the sun of knowledge rising above the horizon to illumine the heights with her beneficent rays.

Earl Russell, formerly Lord John Russell, succeeded Palmerston in 1865, but, although he attempted to reform the franchise, he was unsuccessful, and, after only seven months in office, he resigned in favour of the Earl of Derby (1866–1868), who again became Prime Minister. His government at last succeeded in passing an electoral Reform Bill (1867), which satisfied the people in the towns, as all town house-holders obtained the vote, but those living in the country, paying less than £12 a year rent, remained disfranchised. Ireland again became a source of anxiety; insurrection, conspiracies and riots filling the news, a new Irish Republican brotherhood, which came to be known as the Fenians, being responsible. A general election was held in 1868, when the Con-servatives were defeated, and the Liberals took office, but here let us pause for a moment and reflect, because three men had now arisen whose deeds were to reshape Britain and Europe, and greatly affect our lives today.

In the year 1862 the King of Prussia appointed Bismarck as his Chief Minister of State, with in-structions to break the power of the large majority in the Prussian Parliament which was demanding that the ministers of the Crown should be responsible to the people through their parliamentary representatives. The King was just on the point of meeting this demand for democratic government; in fact, if he had not then discovered Bismarck, he would have either done so or resigned. What a tragedy for mankind that at this fateful cross-roads in human affairs the wrong road was taken! How the German people and all Europe have suffered from this terrible mistake! What a calamitous and catastrophic discovery was this finding of Bismarck!

Fortunately for Britain, the Crown had by now lost the power to flout the wishes of the people's representatives, but not so in Germany, the consequence being that the Germans laboriously plodded farther and ever farther along the dangerous road of political servitude, while Britain, taking the opposite way, pursued the road which brought her into the land of freedom and political liberty. When the Germans were giving themselves over to the keeping of a tyrant, Britain, by her parliamentary system, was preparing two illustrious men to lead her into this land of intellectual freedom where all have a say in the country's government, and can express themselves freely on everything which appertains to their welfare and happiness.

The most remarkable of these two great leaders was William Ewart Gladstone (1809–1898), the son of a produce merchant of good social lineage, who, with his wife, left Scotland, their native land, to live and prosper exceedingly in Liverpool. William, their fourth son, was educated at Eton and Oxford, to enter politics in 1833 as a Tory diehard and strong opponent to reform. He was just a product of his time, his parents being devout Christians who accepted the prevailing squalor and misery as coming within the divine order.

Consequently slavery, which had been approved by their god, was right, and his father saw nothing wrong in deriving much of his wealth from plantations in Demerara, where he owned large numbers of slaves. These he treated so badly that William's maiden speech in Parliament was devoted to defending his father when a member gave instances of cruelty on the

Gladstone estates. "Slavery," declared William, "has the sanction of the Holy Scriptures."

Brought up in this mental darkness, William Ewart Gladstone lived and thought as a Tory reactionary, and, as his parents had nurtured him well in Episcopalian doctrines, he was naturally a vehement opponent of the entry of Nonconformists to the Universities, to the removal of all Jewish disabilities, and to an extension of the franchise. For nearly twenty years this brilliant young man was looked upon as the coming Tory leader—"a man has uprisen in Israel" one peer declared—and, if he had not paid a visit to Naples in 1851, his great gifts might always have been employed against, and not in favour of, progress and reform.

His visit to that beautifully situated city, then the centre of papal and regal iniquity, removed from his mind the curse of political ignorance, as there he discovered that 20,000 honest decent men were imprisoned, and being cruelly tortured, or had been exiled, because they had expressed their wish for democratic government. He arrived in Italy a Tory, and left it with entirely changed ideas, to become the most famous of all British political reformers.

Gladstone became a tremendous force for justice and reform. Eleven elections did he fight, four times was he Prime Minister, and his fiery eloquence, which gripped his audiences both outside and inside Parliament, where he was a master strategist, made him the most powerful figure in British politics in the latter half of the 19th century. During this time were fought the historic political duels between him and his great antagonist Benjamin Disraeli

(1804-1881). For twenty-eight years (1852-1880) these two warriors confronted each other, and their wordy wars produced the Britain we know today, because Disraeli, though a strong imperialist, was by no means a reactionary. He was a humanitarian at a time when Gladstone was not, in fact it was he who democratised the Tory Party, which came to be known under its present unfortunate name of Conservative.

For a generation this eminent Hebrew led the Conservative party, trusting the people and admitting the better-paid artisan to the suffrage. He was a friend of Turkey, as he feared and distrusted Russia, because to him India was the brightest jewel in the imperial crown. Gladstone, who disliked imperialism, extended the suffrage, broke the tyranny of the Irish Protestant Church, and would probably have settled the Irish question satisfactorily if the Conservatives and reactionary peers and bishops in the House of Lords had not thwarted him. The greatest blessing Gladstone gave to Britain was general education, a matter which had been quite neglected during the Christian era. We shall be reading more about these two stalwarts, the practical Gladstone, who was the champion of progress, but quite uninterested in philosophy or science, and the romantic Disraeli, who, by means of his widely read novels, exposing the social evils of the times, spun his political ideas into story form for the people to digest at their ease and leisure.

Gladstone became Prime Minister in 1868, his ministry lasting for six years. He at once set about to try and settle the grievances from which the Irish still suffered. These had been many and real, as during the 18th century the Irish Parliament, composed only of Protestants, imposed on the Roman Catholics some of the most repressive laws ever formulated in the English language.

This legislation was on the same lines as that of Louis XIV against the Huguenots in France, and no Roman Catholic could (1) sit in Parliament, (2) hold office under the Crown, (3) vote in an election, (4) be a lawyer, physician, sheriff or gamekeeper, (5) own a horse worth over £5, and, if he did, a Protestant could take it from him for that amount, (6) inherit money if his brother became a Protestant; instead it went to the Protestant brother, (7) inherit property as next of kin if no will had been left, (8) marry a Protestant in a Roman Catholic Church, the penalty being the hanging of the priest, or (9) enter the Strangers' Gallery of Parliament House in Dublin.

When the British and Irish Parliaments were joined in 1801, 6,000,000 Roman Catholics in Ireland lay prostrate under Protestant domination, and it required the greater part of the British army to maintain order. Not until 1829 were Roman Catholic disabilities removed, and then only after strong and bitter opposition. Along with Britain, social conditions improved in Ireland, and considerable progress took place in the development of her resources, but she was still dissatisfied, and rightly so, as she continued to suffer from real grievances. Four fifths of the population were Roman Catholics and only one tenth Episcopalians, but still the Episcopalians enjoyed the tithe revenue they took from the Roman Catholic Church in the time of Henry VIII. While the Roman Catholics had to suffer every possible indignity from the Protestants, they had also to witness their money going into the pockets of a Church they detested for all its past cruelties.

In 1868, when Gladstone became Prime Minister, he disestablished and disendowed the Irish Episcopal Church, and severed it from the Church of England, greatly to the anger of the Episcopalians in Britain and Ireland. However, by doubling the number of its clergy, and increasing their salaries before the Bill became law, the Episcopalians managed to retain much of the revenue which the Act had allocated for the good of Ireland. Gladstone likewise abolished the scandalous land laws, which ground down the peasant for the benefit of the owner, who could eject any tenant at his pleasure. The only reply the tenant could make was to kill his landlord, and this he frequently did.

The wrongs and cruelties inflicted on the Irish by the English, over many centuries, created a hereditary hatred of everything to do with England. The removal of the old land laws was only one grievance less, but they had many more which, because they went unheeded in London, raised the demand for Home Rule. Charles Stewart Parnell (1846–1891) the proud, aristocratic, inscrutable uncrowned King of Ireland, the bitter enemy of England, and the friend of all her enemies, led the Irish members in Parliament in their fight for a free Parliament in Dublin. Because of his systematic obstruction of legislation, and open defiance of the law in Ireland, Gladstone was forced to pass a new Land Act guaranteeing tenants fair rents and fixity of tenure. The extremists next resorted to bloodshed, and, after the murder of Lord Frederick Cavendish, the newly appointed Chief Secretary for

Ireland, and his Under-Secretary Burke, in Phoenix Park, Dublin, in 1882, which was followed by dynamite outrages in London, Gladstone became convinced that Home Rule was the only solution of the long-standing Irish problem. From this time onwards he devoted much of his political life to bring it about.

Now followed some pressing measures for Britain which were already long overdue, the most important being that of education. Christian civilisation commenced in the year 381, and now we are in the year 1870, a span of some fifteen hundred years, when, for the first time since the fall of the Roman Empire, a minister of the Crown was given the duty of furthering education. War, religion and foreign affairs had in the past occupied most of the time of legislators everywhere, but seldom had a thought been given to removing the curse of ignorance.

For the past seventy years the education of the people had been the aim of the reformers and the desire of the working classes. Feeling as they did their own lack of knowledge, and wishing their children to have a better chance in life, they had supported petition after petition to the government and every other effort to secure national education. They had neither the means nor the opportunity to send their children to the private schools, and consequently they grew up as ignorant as their parents.

The Church had done its utmost to prevent the extension of the franchise, because, so long as the people had not the power, education could be denied them. Now this was no longer possible, as the various Reform Bills, which the bishops had done their utmost to keep from passing through the House of Lords, had largely extended the representation of the people. Consequently, after all the heated controversy and repeated failures throughout the century, Gladstone's government now succeeded in passing an Education Act, and to William Edward Forster, the son of a Dorset Quaker, was assigned the novelty and high honour in 1870 of planning the education of British children. The State thus made itself responsible for the education of the people, and he was given authority to build schools with the money which came from local taxation and government grants.

This noble idea that the State should be responsible for education was first put forward by Plato, and then by the Roman educationalist Quintilian, but although these pioneer schoolmasters had proved by the results obtained that supernatural religion was unnecessary to produce good men and women, the idea still prevailed in the 19th century that Christianity was necessary to create a good citizen. Although there were ample churches everywhere for everyone, and the black army had a priest in every parish, the schoolmaster was nevertheless brought in as an additional propagator of the superstition which had been such a hindrance to progress and reform. Orthodox religious teaching was consequently given to all children unless the parents objected.

Education at school became compulsory in 1876, but lack of school buildings meant that many remained illiterate, and fifteen years had still to pass before it became free, after which it was possible for every child to attend regularly. This was a great step forward, but ignorance will not be banished until supernatural religion takes no part in school education, because the mind of the schoolmaster and that of the priest work on entirely different planes of thought.

To the priest the tenets of his religion come before truth and facts, and to him theology comes before knowledge. He is taught at his theological college the necessity of moulding the young mind, when it is pliable, into line with his theological beliefs, as only thus can a Christian, or any other type of orthodox religious believer, be produced. To the schoolmaster truth must always come first, and only facts be the jewels worth seeking. Consequently evidence, enquiry, doubt, wonder and criticism must be open and free, while every road to further knowledge is explored. Every fact must be welcomed, because the doubting, wondering, enquiring scholar, who wants facts and evidence, is the future scientist who will increase our range of vision and bring more comforts, besides greater happiness, to the human race.

The main purpose of education (a Latin word which means to lead out) is to train the mind to think rationally and logically, and create a desire for knowledge. The logic of Euclid is therefore as important to learn as is the acquiring of facts. Correct thinking makes people wise and virtuous. The well-developed, well-balanced mind cannot be cruel, unjust, untruthful, pitiless, revengeful or unkind, and consequently the object of education is not only to teach facts but to train the mind in virtue and wisdom, so that it thinks straight, weighing up every situation correctly. By correct education the virtues come to be accepted as something natural, and part of oneself, which is hurt, and put out of harmony, by doing some wrong deed.

So it will some day come about, when the mind is educated aright, that to do what is wrong will be so mentally painful that we shall do what is right quite naturally. Children are taught not to fall out of windows, or downstairs, or to go too close to the fire, and so on. That represents the beginning of instruction, which in time will be so systematically developed that the young people of the future will learn the value of justice, truth, kindness, pity and mercy as part of their everyday experience. Missionaries abroad in time will cease to propagate supernatural religion, which raises no one, and instead confine their efforts to an endeavour to raise the more backward races to a higher ethical standard everywhere throughout the world.

If only education had been allowed to develop during the Christian era, a solution would have been found by now for many pressing problems, including that of war, and because that did not happen is the greatest of all human tragedies. Just as Christianity extinguished the lamp of learning in the Roman Empire from the 5th century onwards, so did it repeat the process in 1212 (See Chapter IX, Section 5) when it smothered, with its superstitions, the advanced knowledge accumulated by the Arabs. Thus, for the second time, it denied to the Western world the benefits which come from knowledge.

Only during the last seventy years has education occupied the attention of the British administration.

Fifteen hundred years earlier flourished the great academies of the Roman Empire which lit Europe, Asia and North Africa with intellectual light, and they attained their highest development and efficiency in Gaul. With the coming of Christian civilisation went all learning; one by one the schools were closed, and the teachers murdered or banished. Christianity and knowledge could not live together, and so the Greek and Roman attempt to enlighten mankind was extinguished. Need we wonder that the great majority everywhere are still children, some, like the Germans, believing what their rabid politicians tell them, while others, like the Spanish, are still in the deadening grip of the priests. Need we be surprised that everywhere these grown-up children produce guns, airplanes and explosives to destroy what has been constructed, in just the same irresponsible way as a child destroys the sand-castle he has spent hours in erecting?

Ninety-five per cent. of the population of Germany are professing Christians, according to a census taken prior to the Second World War, and their lack of honest education is the cause of their moral backwardness and simplicity. Consequently they gave full power into the hands of the world's greatest criminal, whom they elevated to the level of a god, believing his lies and that they would secure increased happiness by plundering their neighbours. What they did this century, France did last century, and every leading country in Europe has done from time to time.

The development of character must become the first aim in education, because what we are mentally, as expressed by the mind which does not die, is what we carry over to the next order of existence at death, where we shall be either good or bad inhabitants. We came into this world naturally, and we enter the other world according to natural law, and not according to the religious beliefs we hold. The problem of another existence is one about which most people have very mixed and hazy opinions, but growing scientific evidence points to this earth being but the nursery stage in our career, and that each of us has a future hereafter which will be determined by our character.

As we sow we reap, both here and hereafter, but, as we develop mentally, the sowing will be better and more wisely done, while the reaping is not confined to this earth. Hence the vital importance of education based on sound scientific lines, as the more truth we learn the less we shall have to unlearn here in after years, and in the hereafter.

Education in the future must therefore embrace the development of the mind from every possible aspect, operating quite apart from organised supernatural religion, and not in partnership with it. Knowledge, derived from facts, must always come first. Relying on priests for fifteen hundred years to educate and develop the minds of the young in Christendom explains why in 1818 three quarters of the inhabitants of Britain were quite illiterate, only one in every seventeen being able to both read and write, and why in 1870 nearly 3,000,000 children of school age were unable to read or write. Millions of public money were spent to support the clergy in luxury, and to keep up churches, but nothing on schools.

From 1870 onwards more and more schools have

been built, and the years given to education have been extended. Just as the schools filled so did the churches empty, a fact which explains the bitter opposition on the part of the Church leaders towards all attempts to educate the people, they having always realised the baneful effect which learning would have on church attendance. The people, at long last, had secured a weapon with which to slay the theological monster which had kept them ignorant, poor, servile and in subjection down the ages. Already, in our own time, they have mortally wounded it, but not until it is finally destroyed will intelligence arise sufficiently to overcome all the evils which follow from ignorance.

Wherever there is progress to record there is likewise recession in Church influence, because the light of knowledge destroys one by one its false claims, and removes its diverse tyrannies. The Church stood for ignorance, but, just as this was replaced by knowledge, the people in democratic lands have substituted kindness, mercy and justice for the age-old cruelty, injustice and tyranny which had hitherto prevailed, while improved conduct followed from the increase in more reasoned thinking.

Soon the results of education became apparent, reading and literature increased, the mind developed, and greater knowledge dissipated the fear of hell which had so tormented and terrified the people down the ages. Consequently it now became possible for a child not to be baptised, and fines and imprisonment for not attending church were not enforced. Clerical tyranny slowly faded away, and everyone was free to think, to wonder, to doubt and allow his mind to roam at will in all directions. One could now safely question the contents of the Bible without the fear of imprisonment for blasphemy, and marriage ceased to be a religious to become a state affair.

The Sacrament became less and less desired by those about to die, the priest became a less frequent visitor to the deathbed, and burial without clerical assistance was also permitted. Church burial grounds became available to all, and the dead were no longer divided up into the damned and the saved, the distinction between consecrated and non-consecrated ground ceasing to interest intelligent people. The laws against Sunday pleasures and amusements fell into disuse one by one, and in all directions greater happiness, better health and increased prosperity followed the lightening of the curse of ignorance.

Amongst the reforms passed by the first Gladstone government was the University Test Act (1871), which allowed Roman Catholics and Nonconformists to take their degrees at Cambridge and Oxford Universities. A Ballot Act (1872) was passed securing secret voting at elections, and the Supreme Court of Judicature was established in 1873. The buying and selling of commissions in the army by officers was abolished. Other measures improved previous Acts relating to poor relief, Trades Unions, and crime, and when Gladstone had finished (1874) all the good work he could induce Parliament to accept for the time being he advised a dissolution and resigned.

Benjamin Disraeli (1874–1880), who later became the Earl of Beaconsfield, now took over the office of

Prime Minister and continued to pass measures for the good of the people. His Public Health Bill (1875) compelled local authorities to make adequate medical and sanitary provision for the health of the people; the Artisans' Dwelling Act empowered local authorities to destroy slums, and the Merchant Shipping Act prevented unseaworthy vessels from sailing, and ships from being overloaded.

This latter Act was the outcome of the labour of the great humanist Samuel Plimsoll (1824–1898), who gave over much of his life to improving the lot of seamen, who up to now had been sent to sea in ships quite unseaworthy. These were known as "coffin ships", and, to prevent vessels being overloaded, a "Plimsoll Line" was marked on every ship to denote the limit to which each could be loaded.

Foreign affairs occupied much of Disraeli's attention. Conditions in the Christian provinces of Turkey, namely Herzegovina, Bulgaria and Serbia, were so bad that revolt and open war broke out. Again the fear of Russia developed, because it was thought that this trouble would act as an excuse for her to invade Turkey, seize Constantinople, and threaten Britain's new route to India by the recently completed Suez Canal. Turkish cruelties were denounced openly by Gladstone, but these did not prevent the British from sending their fleet to protect Constantinople when Russia invaded Turkey, and her troops neared this vital centre which Disraeli made clear would never be allowed to fall into Russian hands.

A dangerous situation ended by Turkey giving up her control of these Christian lands, and so Rumania,

Bulgaria, Serbia and Montenegro became independent, both Bosnia and Herzegovina passing under Austrian control. This enabled Disraeli to turn his attention to affairs in Afghanistan, where Russia was intriguing with the Amir. British troops were sent to Kabul in 1878, and a new Amir was forced to accept a British agent to control foreign policy, and give over to Britain certain frontier posts which greatly strengthened India's northern defences. The following year the British agent and his staff were murdered by a band of Afghan soldiers, and General Roberts, who became Lord Roberts, was sent to occupy Kabul. He next made a spectacular march from Kabul to Kandahar, to relieve a British force besieged there, and when this was successfully accomplished in 1880 peace reigned once more.

To strengthen further the authority of British rule in India, Disraeli arranged in 1877 for the Queen to take the title of Empress of India, and this gave her the same position in the eyes of the Indians as that claimed before the Mutiny by the Great Mogul. Disraeli next carried out his boldest deed by purchasing for Britain half the shares in the Suez Canal Company from the Khedive of Egypt. His policy met with strong opposition from the Cabinet, but it proved a wise and profitable transaction, and strengthened British control over this neck of land so vital to British communication with India. Finally he annexed the Transvaal (1877), for reasons to be explained later on, an act which was to bring much trouble in its train.

Disraeli now resigned, his aggressive foreign policy having met with much opposition from Gladstone and the Liberals. Gladstone, in 1880, again became Prime Minister, his administration (1880–1885) restoring to the Boers in South Africa their independence so unjustly taken from them by Disraeli. He also withdrew the British troops from Kandahar.

For long Egypt had suffered from Turkish misrule, to end in a revolt under the leadership of Mahomet Ali. This remarkable man was the creator of modern Egypt. With French help he remodelled the army and navy, reorganised the government, encouraged trade, industry and education, and commenced the barrage of the Nile. To his firm government, Egypt was indebted for the tranquillity which it enjoyed under his enlightened rule. The well-equipped, well-disciplined Egyptian army, led by French officers, took Syria (1832) from the Turks, and, if Britain had not then intervened, both Egypt and Syria would have ceased being Turkish provinces.

After his death his voluptuous nephew, a religious bigot, brought the country back to its old disordered condition, and by 1876 interest payments on foreign loans were suspended, when Britain and France established a dual control over the country's finances. Moreover they persuaded the Sultan to depose the Khedive in favour of his son, which interference produced a nationalist rising under Arabi Pasha. France withdrew from further interference in Egyptian affairs, but the British bombarded the forts at Alexandria held by Arabi, defeated the Nationalist army at Tel-el-Kebir (1882), occupied Egypt and established a form of protectorate.

In the Sudan, farther south (1881), a revolt against Egyptian rule, led by one who styled himself the Mahdi (Messiah), had reduced the country to anarchy. There the Egyptian army was defeated, and Gladstone, not wishing to be mixed up further in the trouble, sent General Gordon to Khartoum to withdraw the garrison. Gordon was an unfortunate choice, as he was a soldier only, with a soldier's mentality, a Christian crusader and no diplomatist. So, against orders, he stayed on, and vowed that he would smash the Mahdi, but before this was done the enemy closed in on the town, where he, one other British officer, and a small native force were besieged by a wild mob of dervishes. Gladstone would not send out a relief force until compelled to do so by public opinion, but it arrived too late, as Khartoum a few days before its arrival was captured, when Gordon was killed. All Egyptian troops were now withdrawn, Gladstone was bitterly criticised, unjustly, because the fault primarily lay with Gordon exceeding his instructions, and the Sudan was left to the mercy of the dervishes for thirteen years.

Meanwhile Egypt prospered under the wise administration of Lord Cromer, during which time Lord Kitchener, as he became, built up a well-disciplined Egyptian army which he led into the Sudan, to destroy finally the dervish hordes with his machine-guns at Omdurman in 1898. Then the Sudan became an Anglo-Egyptian dependency, its importance to Egypt being that it controls the Upper Nile. At home the most important measure passed by Gladstone's second ministry (1880–1885) was the Third Reform Act (1884), which abolished the previous distinction in the franchise between the town and country dwellers, and gave the vote to every adult householder. The

country labourer was now for the first time enfran
chised, and had his say in the affairs of the land of
which he was the backbone.

The Marquis of Salisbury (1885–1886) succeeded
Gladstone, but the next year a general election
returned Gladstone to power, though his term of
office lasted for only six months. Gladstone's short
reign during the year 1886 was distinguished by his
attempt to deal with Ireland. The main proposal was
to alter the Act of Union of 1800, and give the Irish
their own Parliament in Dublin to legislate on all
local affairs. Ireland was, however, to remain as part
of the United Kingdom. This Bill split the Liberal
party in two, some of Gladstone's leading supporters,
including Joseph Chamberlain and John Bright, forming a new party which they called Liberal Unionists.
A general election followed; Gladstone was defeated,
and Salisbury again became Prime Minister (1886–
1892) with the support of the Conservatives and the
Liberal Unionists.

Various measures dealing with Ireland were passed
by this administration, but its most important work
was the Local Government Act (1888), which created
County Councils in Great Britain. This Act placed
the management of county affairs in the hands of the
people living in each county, and so relieved the
Justices of the Peace of this administrative work
which they had carried on gratuitously for the previous
three hundred years. Their patriarchal care of the
people was now withdrawn, and they retained only
their judicial powers. The cities and boroughs, since
1835, had managed their own local affairs by means of
elected representatives, and now the counties were

given the same responsibility. All of London outside the old city boundaries was likewise put in charge of a new county council, which knitted a widespread area into one unit. In 1891 education became free and the responsibility of the State in all elementary schools.

Just as the people of Britain were becoming better educated, more sober in their habits, and consequently better able to determine the conditions under which they intended to live, so likewise were the people in the British dominions, and this enabled them to obtain increased self-government. Many in Britain feared that each self-governing colony would soon declare its independence, but Lord Rosebery and William Edward Forster developed the idea of self-government for all under one throne, a policy which has been fully justified by events. In 1887 the first London conference was held of all the self-governing colonies, and each year since then London has been looked upon as the centre of every question of interest to the Empire, now developing more into a British Commonwealth of Nations than an empire in the old sense of the word.

During the century Britain had been steadily adding to her wealth, the production of coal and iron, and then steel, having progressively increased. In 1848 she was producing about half the pig-iron of the world, her trade far exceeded that of any other country, and this supremacy was followed in the production of steel. Then came the discoveries of gold in California and Australia, and this brought about a period of rising prices and increased purchasing power, just as happened in Stuart times, when the new silver mines in

South America had the same depressing effect on the silver currency as the increased gold supplies now had on the sovereign.

For the past hundred years Britain had been adding to her already vast possessions in Asia, and one by one the territories bordering her original Indian Empire were absorbed into it, a strip of Nepal, inhabited by the Gurkhas, being added in 1813. In 1819 she acquired Singapore, in 1824 she took Rangoon and Lower Burmah from the Burmese, and in 1826 she took Assam. Now, in 1885, her troops advanced inland from Rangoon, up the Irrawaddy river, and captured Upper Burmah, a valuable seizure because it was believed to contain rich supplies of oil, and this turned out to be the case.

The Burmese in these parts had proved troublesome to the ever-encroaching invaders, and their king had defied all British protests, but when the imperial forces approached Mandalay, his capital, he surrendered. Thus this huge tract of valuable rice-bearing land, extending for many miles on either side of a great navigable river, besides vast teak forests and rich oil deposits, became part of the Empire.

Gladstone, now aged eighty-three, again returned to power in 1892, and the following year he brought forward a second Home Rule Bill, which passed the House of Commons but was rejected by the House of Lords. Religion was behind this never-ending question, the Protestant minority in the north fearing domination by the Roman Catholic·south, which, for three centuries, had been nurtured in bitter hatred towards the Protestants. Protestant Britain largely shared these fears, thus making Ireland a seemingly insoluble problem, and one which was not to be solved finally for another twenty-nine years.

Gladstone did not go to the country when the House of Lords threw out the Bill, and confined his attention to passing the Parish Councils Act, by which the management of local affairs in each parish was put in the hands of the members elected by the parishioners. After this he retired (1894) in his eighty-fifth year, and so brought to an end the political career of one of Britain's greatest statesmen, a man of sterling honesty and noble character, whose life was entirely devoted to the advance of the welfare of the people, their well-being, education and prosperity always being his first consideration. The Earl of Rosebery carried on as Prime Minister into the next year, after which the Liberal Government resigned.

Lord Salisbury (1895-1902) then took office for the third time, and immediately appealed to the country, to receive a large majority, which meant that the question of Home Rule for Ireland was indefinitely postponed, though measures continued to be passed for the improved well-being of her people. The Irish Local Government Act created County Councils, and the Land Purchase Act set aside £10,000,000 for the purpose of enabling tenants to become freeholders. Ireland's wrongs had now been removed one by one, but independence was still the aim of the majority, and how this came about will be told later on.

Meanwhile the British Empire was being over-hauled by the vigorous imperialist Joseph Chamberlain, who, as Colonial Secretary, advocated preferential trade within the Empire. He arranged loans to build railways where required and to carry out development works in the West Indies and the dependencies in Africa and the Far East. His schemes for the study of tropical diseases made habitable those lands which hitherto had been the white man's grave, and large tracts became civilised which in the past had been so isolated that all the abominations which come from ignorance flourished.

Turkey now gave concern, because in Armenia the Turks massacred thousands of Armenian Christians on the charge of rebellion against the Sultan, while in Crete an attempt was made to throw off Turkish rule. In 1897 the Greeks declared war on Turkey, to be defeated and have Thessaly overrun. Nothing was done for the Armenians, but the principal European powers forced Turkey to make a peace favourable to Greece, and withdraw her troops from Crete, which finally came under Greek rule.

The boundary between Venezuela and British Guiana caused a dispute in 1895 which nearly led to war with the United States, as she held that under the Monroe doctrine, "America for the Americans", the British should not dispute Venezuela's claims for additional territory. This caused anger in Britain, but good sense ultimately prevailed and the question was put to arbitration, when Venezuela lost her claim. Again the Sudan caused trouble. After the battle of Omdurman a French officer, Major Marchand, attempted to claim part of the Upper Nile, known as Fashoda, for France. The British Government insisted on his withdrawal, and there was much indignation and talk of war in France, but peaceful counsel in the end prevailed when France made a treaty with

Britain which left the entire valley of the Nile in British possession.

Since the Crimean War Britain had prospered exceedingly, her few wars being frontier conflicts calling for little expenditure in lives or money, but this peaceful state of affairs was not to last. We remember how Holland founded a colony in the 17th century in the extreme south of Africa. It was populated by farmers from Holland, but, after the defeat of Napoleon, it was retained by Britain who had occupied it in 1806 when Holland was forced to become an ally of France. Finally, in 1815, it was ceded by the King of the Netherlands to Britain for the sum of £3,000,000.

Cape Colony proved to be a very convenient place of call for vessels on their passage to India, and, after 1820, both Dutch and British settlers found their way out there in increasing numbers. The Dutch, or Boers (the Dutch word for farmers), were deeply religious, and fervent believers that the Bible was a God-inspired book. So, like most other people of those days, they regarded slavery as a divinely approved institution, and when the natives were caught they were enslaved. The Boers were often cruel, intolerant and ignorant, whereas the British were just beginning to wonder whether slavery was really all that the Hebrews had said about it. In 1833 Britain decided to free the slaves in Cape Colony, but the compensation she gave to the Boers was so inadequate and difficult to obtain that they decided to move farther north, to get away from British influence, and so be free to enslave the natives as they pleased. Consequently in 1833 the Great Trek northwards began, to end in the founding of the Transvaal and Orange Free State, each a republic under a president.

Britain recognised the independence of these two new states, but refused to agree to the Boers establishing themselves in Natal, which was claimed as British territory. When, however, the Zulus became a menace in 1877, Britain annexed the Transvaal so as to protect her possessions, because she considered that the Boers were not strong enough tó keep back this rising tide of savage invasion. A less drastic policy would have met the danger equally well, and Disraeli angered the Liberals by his action.

A few months later Britain defeated the Zulus, when the Boers expected to have the Transvaal returned to them. As this was not done they arose to drive out the invaders, defeating a small British force in 1881 at Laing's Nek, and a month later routing the British at Majuba Hill. Gladstone had come into office during the previous year, and, as he had never approved of Disraeli's aggressive policy, he restored to the Boers the independence which should never have been taken from them. After victory it is wise to be generous, but after defeat magnanimity is regarded as weakness, and from this time onwards the Boers looked upon the British with contempt, the consequence being that bitter feeling arose between the two nations.

This development was only the beginning of a very difficult period in British history, as in 1886 gold in enormous quantities was discovered underneath the land on which these simple Boer farmers were grazing their herds and growing their crops. Some of their land thus became fabulously valuable, but only because people with money in Britain were prepared to sink shafts and erect the necessary buildings and machinery. Without these the gold would have lain for ever where nature placed it. So money and labour flowed into the Transvaal, mines were sunk, expensive machinery installed, and many British took up their residence amongst the Boers, who never showed them any friendship or goodwill. Had wisdom reigned a harmonious partnership could have been arranged between the landowners and the capitalists, but the Boers did not want foreigners, their wish being to live their own lives as farmers in their own Dutch environment.

Soon the "Uitlanders", as the Boers called the foreigners, outnumbered the original Boer inhabitants, and were paying the largest share of the Republic's taxes, but they had no political rights and no share in the country's government. When they complained, Paul Kruger (1883–1900), the President, a pious, crafty and ignorant man, took no notice, because he hated the British. Moreover, he personified the bigoted Puritanism of his fellow countrymen. Against his policy stood Cecil Rhodes (1853–1902), the son of the Vicar of Bishop's Stortford, who had made a fortune in diamond and gold mining, and was anxious to bring all South Africa under British rule, his dream being an Africa which was British from the Cape to Cairo. He it was who established the British South Africa Company, which received a charter from the British government to develop a large territory north of the Transvaal, to become known as Rhodesia.

Rhodes encouraged the Uitlanders to agitate for equal treatment with the Boers, and sympathised with their attempt to gain by force what they could not get by persuasion, his judgment being affected by the exasperating attitude of Kruger. At length matters reached a crisis when his friend Dr. Jameson, the Administrator of Rhodesia, crossed into the Transvaal (1895) at the head of an armed force to lead an insurrection. His plan failed because the Boers trapped his expedition, and he had to surrender. The home government was not responsible for this rash act, but anti-British feeling naturally increased. Rhodes resigned his office of Premier of Cape Colony, and Kruger became ever more determined to deny the Uitlanders the rights they demanded.

The next four years did nothing to improve relations between Britain and the Transvaal, and both sides prepared for war which commenced in the Autumn of 1899, the Boers, believing that their independence was threatened, making the declaration of hostilities. The British underestimated the strength and preparations of the enemy, who was joined by the Orange Free State, and soon Kimberley, Mafeking and Ladysmith were besieged. Sir Redvers Buller was defeated at Colenso in his attempt to relieve Ladysmith, and elsewhere the Boers, fighting skilfully and courageously, were successful at Magersfontein and Stormberg, much to the delight of all Europe. If there had been no powerful British navy anything might have happened, as the British Empire stood alone without a friend.

Feeling deeply the fact that she was powerless to take advantage overseas of the opportunity offered by Britain's troubles abroad, Germany now set about building up a powerful navy under the direction of a young determined officer who later became famous in the First World War as Admiral von Tirpitz. Far-reaching effects follow from widely remote events, and the South African War set in being repercussions which have gone on vibrating up to our own times.

Disasters on the field made apparent certain weaknesses in the British army, which were rectified before the great clash came in Europe fourteen years later. Many lessons in modern warfare were learned, and, after the replacement of Buller by Lord Roberts, who had Kitchener as his Chief of Staff, the military situation changed in Britain's favour from that time onwards. A new army of 200,000 men was sent from Britain, Kimberley was relieved, and at Paardeberg the Boer army, which had besieged Kimberley, was defeated and surrendered. Bloemfontein and Pretoria, the two capitals, were occupied, and at Diamond Hill the last organised resistance was crushed and broken.

These successes relieved Mafeking and Ladysmith, when Kruger, realising that the war was lost, left for Europe. Though the Boers could not now hope to win, they stubbornly resisted for nineteen months by means of guerilla warfare, but, by the erection of block-houses and wire fences, each part of the country was slowly cleared. The methods adopted were drastic, all livestock and non-combatants being removed before each area was cut off, when it was then cleared up. The civilians were placed in concentration camps, which were so mismanaged that many died of disease, and this caused much criticism in Britain and great indignation throughout the world.

Gradually the guerillas were rounded up, and

finally Generals Botha and De Wet sued for peace.
The Treaty of Vereeniging (1902) brought to an end a
war which had cost Britain £200,000,000, and both
the Transvaal and the Orange Free State became part
of the British Empire. Britain provided £3,000,000
to rebuild and restock the Boer farms, and promised
early self-government, a pledge which she kept in
1906. Three years later Cape Colony, Natal, the
Orange Free State and the Transvaal united to become
the Union of South Africa, a self-governing dominion.

If this war had occurred a hundred years earlier
everyone would have supported the government in
its active prosecution, but a hundred years of mental
development had worked a wondrous change, and
quite a number of British people disapproved of it in
spite of the exasperating circumstances which brought
it about. Even victory did not remove their doubts
as to the righteousness of the conflict, a very interesting mental development which was quite new in
history, because on this occasion the Lord of Hosts
and the God of Battles did not get unanimous support
from the conquerors. Though the people in the
churches prayed to him for victory, as heretofore,
many dethroned him in their own minds, and thought
instead of the cruelty, the suffering, the loss and the
misery the war had caused.

A notable feature of the latter half of the 19th
century was the development of humanitarianism.
Since the time of the Council of Nicaea, Christians
had devoted their thoughts mostly to themselves here
on earth, and to their salvation hereafter. The Father-
hood of God, which was clearly defined at that
momentous assembly of priests, was vastly more

important to them than the Brotherhood of Man. Now, by education, they began to realise that it was much more important to give succour to those who needed their help than to devote their thoughts and offerings exclusively to an invisible being who was quite unaffected by the gifts they made to churches, theological colleges and the clergy. Consequently philanthropy, a new word for Christendom, was born, to grow and develop as the years passed.

Philanthropy, which means the practical love of mankind, now made it possible for steps to be taken to meet the rising surge of feeling that the outcasts, the poor, the suffering, and all who needed help, should have it. Neglected, ill-used children were the first to benefit from this improved mental outlook, and the scandal of the boy chimney-sweep was brought to an end in 1875, the cruel flogging of boys by their masters likewise declining. Then came the formation of the Society for the Prevention of Cruelty to Children in 1884, about which time also began the foundation of orphan homes when men like Barnardo, Müller, Quarrier, John Galloway and others, with the financial support of many thousands of sympathisers, took pity on the multitude of ragged, half-starved, neglected children who swarmed the city streets, and gathered them into homes, where they were clothed, fed, educated and trained to be worthy citizens.

John Ruskin, the patron of art and beauty, by his writings and his work, which covered a wide range of subjects, devoted his talents and money to social problems, financing Octavia Hill in her schemes for renovating, cleaning and modernising some of

London's filthy insanitary slums. Many others did their part in different ways, until the time came when the people, by their votes, decided that the State should be responsible for social welfare, thus ending the dreadful contrast between luxury and the abject poverty which was such a feature of the 19th century.

Victoria did not live to see the end of the South African War, as she died in 1901, having reigned longer than any other British monarch. On her accession she found the influence of the throne weak and discredited, and she left it strong and respected, her court maintaining a high moral standard. In 1897 she celebrated the sixtieth year of her reign, and this occasion was marked by loyal and enthusiastic rejoicings in which all parts of the Empire participated. The war, and the suffering it entailed, caused her much sorrow, and this is probably the first occasion on record of a victorious monarch remarking that "my heart bleeds" for all who have suffered. Monarchs in the past have too often regarded war as an event which regularly occurred, and they have been generally insensible to the misery it caused, particularly so if they were successful.

Queen Victoria was specially fortunate in her Prime Ministers, and also because she was destined to live during a time of great progress and reform, though she herself did little to promote the social well-being of her people. She seemed quite indifferent to the terrible social conditions which prevailed at the opening of her reign, and these were only partially improved when it closed. Moreover, she was antagonistic to many of the remarkable reform movements by which her era was so enriched.

To others, but not to her, the improvement was due, and it was what was done by the reformers, the humanitarians, the scientists, the inventors, the doctors, and many others that raised her reign to a pinnacle ever to be remembered in world history. At long last the war against ignorance had begun in earnest, and its victories were becoming evident before she passed away.

CHAPTER XVII.

CHRISTIAN CIVILISATION.
(1842–1939.)

Introduction. (1) *The Petrol Engine Revolutionises Life and Warfare.* (2) *The Rise, Development and Appeal of Socialism.* (3) *United Nations Arise in North and South America.* (4) *The Rumbling Before the First World War.* (5) *Germany Involves the World in War.*

THE drift of man away from the beast has been slow but sure. First of all sub-man discovered how to hold and then to use a broken-off tree branch, primarily as a weapon of defence and attack, and then as a tool. By accident primitive man discovered that by rubbing two sticks together he produced fire by friction. A log gave him the idea of a wheel, and a fire of sticks, situated where there was copper ore, brought about the discovery of copper, to be followed later by him smelting it with tin to produce bronze. In like manner the other metals were discovered one by one and put to everyday use.

One discovery followed another; a shadow which he outlined started him off as an artist, and then the time came when he invented signs, which he carved on wood and clay to represent ideas. This was a most important discovery, because it had a greater effect on mind development than any other. From this time onwards he could record his thoughts, and pass them on, in a way he could not do by speech alone. As his mind developed he harnessed the forces of nature one by one and made them do his bidding, because nature works as if by instinct, whereas the mind displays reasoned thought. By experiment and rational thinking, besides a capacity to remember past failures and successes, he has made nature his servant, its power being intelligently used to increase his comfort and improve his health.

All this advance, and much more, is comprised in the word "progress", and here we ask a profound question. Why has it been possible for a being, seemingly composed of only flesh, bones and blood, to accomplish this great conquest of the forces of nature, and turn the earth on which he lives, and the laws which rule the universe, to his own advantage? The Greek philosophers pondered long over this problem, even though in their days the conquest of nature was not so marked as it is in our time, and they arrived at the conclusion that thought belongs to an order superior to the material, which latter is governed by the mechanical rule of cause and effect.

Consequently they placed the mind, which produces thought, in the divine order, as appertaining to the gods, and gave to this super-material order the name "etheric", to denote the region composed of a subtle elastic fluid permeating space, which they called "aither", the dwelling-place of the mind after death. From there it came unindividualised, and there it returns individualised. The coming of Christianity, however, swept away all these profound thoughts, and when the time came last century, and science overthrew this superstition, many scientists, disgusted with what had been taught in the name of religion, became materialists and denied the existence of mind, which foolish attitude persists amongst some even in our own times.

The capacity for thinking comes from the mind, a super-physical substance, which must not be confused with its earth instrument the physical brain, a material creation which decomposes with the physical body and is quite incapable of thought. The brain is an extension and expansion of the spinal cord, and parts of the brain can be removed without the mind being affected, its capacity for thought showing no appreciable diminution. Mind is king, and, by development, it has the power to learn the ways of nature and bend them to its will. Nature's laws are fixed, but they have only to be understood and used aright to make life happy, comfortable and pleasant. Because this has not been done in the past is the reason for much of the misery which history reveals.

Our future task is to learn and remember ever more clearly the mistakes of the past, and profit by them. History, heretofore, has been taught as a record of cause and effect, and not as it should have been—as a lesson to enable us by greater knowledge to direct events into the effects we desire. Mind can direct most events as it wishes, if it learns the way to do so. Nature puts no obstacle in the way, and there is no divine decree that man should always walk in the mist and shadows, seeing no purpose or direction, and asking questions to which he thinks there is no answer.

The value of history lies in its storehouse of past experiences, from which we can learn from the achievements and mistakes of our ancestors the right way to live. Poverty can be abolished by thought and intelligent planning, and increased research will conquer all diseases. War can be abolished if we learn to govern the world as a single unit, and not as separate nations, each striving only after its own selfish desires. The interest of man should be in mankind, and not in one particular group of people, but that, and much else, will only be generally accepted when ethical development becomes part of education everywhere throughout the world.

The study of the mind is a quite neglected science. The reason for this neglect has been because of the difficulty of studying an immaterial substance, but the means are available and are ignored solely from ignorant prejudice. For some thirty years the author has studied the make-up and working of the mind, his many opportunities to experience psychic phenomena having given him an abundance of material from which to form his conclusions. This is the only practical way of discovering the composition, the qualities, and the method of operation of the mind. As the mind of man has made the history of mankind, we are here at the source of all we have read so far, and all we have still to read in this book. So we realise how important to future generations is the scientific study of the mind, for the purpose of its future development along right lines.

Mind is the individual, the ego, the real person, the reality of the body to the individual coming from the images made of it by the mind. Everything on earth is different from what it seems to be. We think that the body is the individual, and that when it decomposes the person has ceased to exist. We also think that the sun goes round the earth, that space is empty, and that matter is solid. All these, and much more, are illusions. Matter, for instance, is an open network of vibrations, caused by the motion of electrons and protons, separated from one another by distances which are relatively as great as those which separate the planets from the earth.

As we read in Chapter III, these invisible electric charges revolve at immense and different speeds, and thus create the vibrations which produce the mental images that give us the sensation of touch, smell and sight. Light, for instance, coming as radiation, or ether vibrations, from the sun is reflected to our eyes according to the frequency of the vibrations of the object it strikes. Thus, through the vibrations this sets up in the nerves of the eyes and brain, we get the mental image and the colour, because every object vibrates at a different frequency, and sends the corresponding light vibrations to the eye, at the frequency at which the object struck by the light is vibrating. Consequently we perceive the different colours, because colour is determined by the vibrations of the object.

Everything we sense is thus imaged, and can be re-imaged, just as a film can be run through the cine-camera time and time again. This faculty we term memory, the mind having the capacity to re-form past images whenever it is stimulated to do so by a nerve impulse which relates to one that has gone before. These mental images are what are real to us, because they are the individual, as each one of us is mind, the body being the unthinking camera. The mind, which is ourselves, is the film which senses its environment by means of mental pictures that can be recalled, and this constitutes life.[1]

[1] The mental process which makes up life is fully explained in *The Unfolding Universe*, diagrams being used to make the subject clear and explicit.

Mind is the only enduring reality, and this being so it deserves much more care and cultivation than it has ever received in the past. Mind is the eternal vital substance of the universe, and, when it becomes individualised, it remains so after death, its stimulation then coming through our etheric eyes and etheric brain from etheric substance vibrating beyond our present physical sense perceptions. Each one of us is a part of this universal mind, individualised, and our life on earth consists of the images the individual mind makes while housed in a physical body. This body is only the outer garment, as each mind constructs from conception an etheric duplicate body in which it functions after it leaves the physical body, and one which is in harmony with the vibrations of a higher frequency than those it experiences on earth.

Immediately after death each one is the same person as he was before this experience occurred, and nothing of any value is lost by the change. Life indeed would be a tragic farce, and contrary to all we know of nature, which changes but never annihilates, if death ended everything to us and all our memories and experiences were lost in the grave. Consequently it is quite wrong to talk or think of someone who has died as being buried, because only the discarded physical body returns to earth, the Christian belief that it will arise again being due to ignorance, the idea having been copied by the early Christians from the Egyptians.

Our time on earth is for the development of our mind, our personality and our own character being the result, and only by natural death should our connection with the earth be severed. To force the mind out of the physical body by suicide, or by violent death, prevents it from obtaining the earth experience for which it has individualised on earth. Its development comes about best in harmonious conditions, and everyone should cultivate the means of producing comfort and happiness, as mind development is our purpose on earth.

The pages of history reveal the disastrous consequences which followed from mankind's ignorance of his purpose on earth, and from his lack of knowledge of what followed after death. His deeper thoughts consisted of finding a way out of the thicket and thorns into which his ignorance had led him. Because of ignorance he did wicked deeds and thought evil thoughts, and he gave overmuch of his time to religious observances to adjust the debit balance. If man had only known that instead of all this wasted effort he should have been developing his mind, both ethically and educationally, how much higher would have been his aspirations and how much nobler would have been his life here on earth.

Had he known the truth and followed the path of reason instead of that of folly, he would thus have fitted himself for the life hereafter, to which he devoted so much of his time and energy. Had he been possessed of greater knowledge, religious persecution would have been unknown, and the sacrifice of millions of men and animals as food for the gods would never have taken place. Priests would never have imposed on the people, tyrannised over them, or kept them ignorant and relieved them of their hard-won earnings. The dread of death would have been overcome by knowledge, and the fear of the gods, which has for ever haunted humanity, would never have been the dominant influence down the ages. Truly death has had a profound effect on history, man's ignorance of its meaning casting a black shadow on every page of the human story from primitive times to the present day.

Now, however, we know that death is only a change of environment, like turning a corner on a road. We are out of sight to those who are behind us, but we continue just as we were before we reached the bend. We find ourselves to be the same as we were on earth, in a world which will appear to us to be as solid and substantial as does this earth, because there the vibrations of our etheric bodies will correspond to those of our new surroundings. The image-maker, the mind, does not die when the physical body decomposes, death being an illusion, because what we call death is only physical decomposition, due to the departure of the mind, which takes with it its instrument, the duplicate etheric body.

When this etheric structure is severed from the physical body decomposition follows, but, as each one of us is mind, we shall still think of and remember our experiences on earth until they are eventually forgotten. All that has happened is that we commence to function in another aspect surrounding and interpenetrating this world, which new environment is composed of substance at a higher frequency of vibrations than the one in which we now live.

If these vital facts are always remembered we shall better appreciate the importance of mind development, besides the strengthening and ennobling of our characters, and never countenance anything which will cramp or hinder our natural evolution. In this new endeavour bodily health is important, because the body reacts on the mind which cannot act perfectly on an imperfect instrument. Consequently the body and brain must be healthy to obtain the best mental effects.

When the facts contained in this philosophy, which the author in his other books has tried to make simple and clear, become absorbed, we shall look at life from a new angle, and realise that war, cruelty, injustice, and all that is evil, retard our mental development. The task of everyone is to dethrone ignorance and enthrone knowledge and wisdom, which is just another way of saying that we must dethrone evil and enthrone righteousness. Consequently, if our children and succeeding generations are educated along the lines laid down by this ethical philosophy, we shall come to realise that everyone has an object in life, namely to reach as near perfection as possible in all we do or think. By so doing we lay the foundation of happiness here and hereafter, by cultivating that part of us which survives death, the imperishable mind, and thus we do not waste our time on earth.

Individuality, not uniformity, must be the future aim of each individual, all regimentation by Church or State being resisted and defeated. The striving for uniformity has been the great mistake which history reveals our ancestors to have made. Every influence which turns the mind into a machine, and makes it function only as a master mind directs, is contrary to the best interests of the individual. So dictatorships must go, including industrial bondage and the domination of the priest. Men and women everywhere must cease sinking their individuality, and resist any attempt to drill them like puppets in the art of mass murder.

Education on right lines will develop individuality, and that in time will bring to an end the tragedy in the story of the human race. Education can defeat dictatorships, and enable communities and nations to live together in harmony with their neighbours, as, while claiming complete liberty of thought, the individual will appreciate the need to grant to others all the rights and privileges he expects for himself. Consequently, some day, different groups of people, living as enlightened democratic nations, will be able to dwell in harmony because increased knowledge will enable everyone to understand and appreciate the outlook of everyone else.

The martyrdom of man has come from the curbing by tyrants of the free development of the mind, and the pages of history reveal how great were the agonies of the past which followed from this despotic thwarting of the natural evolutionary urge to secure complete individuality. To prevent the achievement of this innate desire, millions have been outstretched on crosses, bound to stakes, clamped on racks, or have faced death, suffering and loss of liberty in countless ways, including hunger, poverty and misery. Untold millions have been sacrificed on the altar of tyranny, some to support it on the battlefield, and others to prevent it reaching those they died to save. Education on right lines can put an end to this terrible ignorance of man's duty to man, and give the reason for his sojourn on earth.

Tyrants, who have guided these persecutions, are but human products. They arose because of a combination of events which were brought about by the ignorant multitude, comprising a nation, merging its will-power in one man or body of men, who swayed the masses this way and that because the people had left their thinking to these more forceful minds. This in future will be impossible if all are educated to think as individuals, and taught to realise the disaster which the lack of individuality always brings about.

This sheep-like attitude must be ended by education and then each nation will become an assembly of individual thinkers, not a congregation or flock of worshippers who repeat a formula in unison. We must not be puppets to be moved by the pulling of strings, because each one must be master of his own thoughts. Each one is an individual thinking unit here on earth, for the purpose of developing his personality, and destined for something hereafter which is beyond our comprehension so long as we are limited to the vibrations of physical matter.

Progress, which means the increase of comfort and happiness, comes from the aspirations of the mind, which, by memory, remembers that which is good and thus avoids that which is evil. On earth we are bound by physical laws, but we can learn to use them for our advantage. Disease, for instance, is natural, but, by study and thought, an equally natural way can be found for it to be cured. War, likewise, is natural, and can be cured by the same method. It is all a question of mental concentration on the aim desired, and it is false to claim that we need the stimulus of war to develop our minds. It would be just as sensible to assert that we require disease and pain for that purpose, but who would be so foolish as to endure needless suffering to strengthen his character?

Unfortunately the fifteen hundred years of education lost through going down the wrong road in the year 325 has prevented us from discovering by now how to control the population problem, the international economic problem and the national boundary problem, which are the chief causes of war. Besides this, the complete lack of systematic ethical teaching throughout the Christian era has retarded our cultivation of the love and respect for mankind which is essential for future peace and happiness.

The development of self-control is equally important, as to be able to rule one's passion and emotions is to win a victory over our animal ancestry. Increased mental development will enable us to conquer our inheritance from our jungle ancestors, who acted on the impulse without rational thought. So far, instead of conquering these impulses, we have prostituted them by furthering our animal passions which developed in the forests when our ancestors had to fight for the food they required in order to exist. Now we know enough to get all we need by peaceful means, but still we are cursed by this jungle legacy, and we use our inventions for destructive and not only for constructive and productive purposes.

Being ignorant of the reason for our time on earth, we are unaware how best to live, and, instead of keeping to the straight road to which knowledge, wisely applied, directs us, we go down by-lanes and get lost. We become fearful and miserable, and yet all the time the high road of righteousness lies before us, but we will not keep to it. Such is the revelation of history, and all the follies of the past are repeated in our own times because the vast majority is ignorant of the past, and of the mistakes made by our ancestors. These should have been driven into our minds when they were young and plastic, and, if this had been done everywhere, the tragedies history records would not have been so often repeated.

We have applied our minds only recently to material progress, but have quite neglected ethical progress. We have advanced further materially than ethically, and, until our ethics overtake our material progress, knowledge will bring us misery as well as happiness. This ethical evolution is not to be confused with what is called "spiritual development" or "spiritual life", which are orthodox expressions relating to a mental state which gives to some emotional minds a peculiar satisfaction. This attitude of mind produces a purely selfish outlook and is quite unrelated to ethical conduct. Such expressions are never used in this book, because the word "spiritual" has been so debased by Christianity, the priests and people using it when referring to Church possessions, such as spiritual lands, spiritual princes, spiritual vestments; in fact it is a word which Christians have monopolised and only applied to those who think along the Christian way. This being so, they are welcome to keep the word to themselves.

Spirituality has not led us far on the road to righteousness, or to greater social harmony and peace, and we are now in this chapter entering the age when Christendom, lacking fifteen hundred years of ethical teaching, becomes involved in two of the most destructive wars in history. Invention misapplied creates havoc to life and property, and no new discovery is more responsible for this than the petrol engine, which, wisely applied on land, on sea and in the air, could have brought the people of earth into closer contact, to their lasting benefit. Instead of this it has been also used for the mass murder of both combatants and non-combatants, and it has made war today a total affair in which everyone becomes involved.

So we now enter the age of mechanised war, when all the inventions which could have been employed only for the good of mankind are turned to his destruction. The events recorded in this chapter reveal in a more striking degree than ever before the danger which comes from our not realising the purpose of life, and consequently applying our discoveries to cut short the time each individual mind should be on earth. As no new discovery has been more misapplied than the one which produced the petrol engine, let us now give some consideration to this great invention.

(1) The Petrol Engine Revolutionises Life and Warfare.

During the 19th century coal was the only mineral employed to produce the power which turned the wheels of travel and industry. In the 20th century, which we have now entered, a new substance came more and more into everyday use to transform the lives of everyone. Coal, formerly king, has now to compete with petroleum, a rival which in many respects is its superior, because it has made possible machines which could not conveniently be operated by coal. Last century coal enormously increased both power and speed, while this century petroleum has augmented them still more.

Millions of years ago vegetation died, and was covered over with water in the form of lakes and seas, in which floated silt brought down by the rivers. This silt sank to the bottom to form, over ages of time, a hard rock covering, which pressed ever harder on the vegetation below until it in turn became hard and brittle. This substance we call coal, which has been known to mankind for thousands of years, as it protrudes in places from the earth's surface, and its use increased as invention created machines to enable it to be raised from greater depths.

Petroleum was probably produced from the bodies of fish and animals which settled on the sea bed millions of years ago, to become covered, as was coal, by floating sediment that sank to the bottom. Over aeons of years a deep layer of rock formed over these animal remains which, unlike the vegetation, remained liquid, to be forced out by the gas it produced in those places where the original covering of rock had been broken by earth convulsions. This released liquid, by atmospheric action, was transformed into bitumen which we use to spread on our roads to give them a smooth surface.

Petroleum has been known by civilised man from the dawn of history. Herodotus wrote about it, and, to come to more recent times, British representatives to the King of Burmah referred to it in 1765 as oozing out of springs and wells near Mandalay. In 1814 it was observed in Ohio, and fifteen years later in Kentucky, when a well was sunk to obtain brine. Instead of brine it yielded sufficient oil over the next thirty years to fill 50,000 barrels, most of which was allowed to run to waste. The small quantity saved was bottled and sold as an embrocation!

That was all that was known in America in 1860 about this great power-giving substance. James Young, a Glasgow chemist, the pioneer in Britain of this new fuel, knew more about it than did the Americans, because in 1848 he commenced to refine illuminating oil from deposits discovered in Derbyshire. His success attracted the attention of the United States, where wells were sunk, deeper and deeper, with ever-growing success, and from that time to this there has been a never-ending hunt to secure land under which it was thought oil deposits lay.

Coal had for long been known as a means of producing heat, but no use was made of the gas it gave off until last century, when this was used for lighting purposes. Then it was discovered that gas in a confined space, when in contact with a light, exploded. This led Lenoir in 1860 to construct a cylinder into which air and gas were led by a pipe and exploded by an electric spark. Next, a piston was inserted which was driven out by the explosion, and then it was only a matter of cogs, wheels and timing to get the explosion to occur at the right second to drive out the piston, which, on its return journey, forced out the fumes.

Petroleum was found to become gaseous much more easily than coal, and so the next step was made by Julius Hock of Vienna (1870), who drove a gas engine by spraying petroleum mixed with air into the cylinder. Brayton, an American engineer, followed with an improved type in 1873, and then Otto, in 1876, produced his gas engine which became known all over the world. The next advance came when Daimler invented (1885) a small petroleum-gas-driven engine which he attached to a bicycle. He sold his patents to the French firm of Panhard and Levassor, but it was Karl Benz who invented the motor car.

Then the brothers Orville and Wilbur Wright attached to a glider a petroleum engine which turned a propeller, giving sufficient forward speed for the pressure of air on the inclined wings to exert a lift which enabled the glider to fly off the ground for a distance of 852 feet. The petroleum-driven engine had made it possible to cover distance in the air, independent of land and sea, because petroleum could be easily vaporised, whereas to obtain gas from coal requires an elaborate plant.

Petroleum, being liquid, could be carried much more easily than coal, and, in consequence, a fuel supply could be stored in the vehicle to move it long distances. This made possible the construction of a ship to sail underneath the surface of the water, to become known as the submarine. Thus it came about that by experiment and rational thought the engineer produced the motor-car, the airplane and the submarine, which, if we had been ethically developed beings instead of just thinking animals, we would have used for improving our conditions without a thought of putting them to destructive purposes. Unfortunately we are not ethically developed beyond our own national boundaries, and consequently it was not long before someone thought of turning the motor-car into an armoured tank, the airplane into a bomber to carry bombs which explode as they touch the ground, and the submarine into a torpedo-carrying vessel which can carry on its deadly work without being seen.

Airplanes can be so swiftly moved that the next step was not to declare war, but, under the cloak of negotiations, to send squadrons of bombers to attack the fleet of the country singled out for attack, as the Japanese did (1941) before they were at war with the United States. The airplane has taken away all security from life. Before its advent, sufficient time was given for the victim of attack to make preparations for defence, but not now, as overnight the British fleet could be attacked, damaged, sunk, or seriously crippled by a nation with which the British were at peace. A lightning stroke can defeat, or seriously weaken, an unsuspecting victim, and this can be previously camouflaged by all the wiles which cunning can imagine. Bombs of ever greater destructiveness are being produced, the latest, which release atomic energy, being capable of causing such terrific blast and heat that nothing can stand up to them.

Every nation is free to produce bombers and bombs at will, and we have yet to devise a method of protection. One atomic bomb can devastate a great city and destroy its inhabitants. One single bomber can carry enough atomic bombs to cause widespread havoc and kill millions. A new and deadly machine has been perfected, which is a much more terrible enemy to the human race than was once the plague. The plague was conquered, and this new terror must likewise be defeated if the human family is to live free from the fear of falling bombs, against which there is no protection.

The tractor and the motor plough have greatly increased our power of cultivation, and the motor-car has given much pleasure besides having added considerably to our range and ease of movement. Nevertheless, as it uses the roads originally intended for horse traffic, death and injury have come to many thousands. If only a fraction of the money spent on war since the petrol engine was invented had been used to build new roads, with all the necessary safety devices, such as bridges, subways and footpaths for pedestrians, the death toll on the roads would have been greatly curtailed.

The airplane is quite a different problem, as it adds nothing to our happiness or comfort, and its drone disturbs the peace which made the country once a paradise. Moreover, it has added enormously to the cost of national defence, and put out of productive use many thousands of acres of agricultural land now used as airdromes. Of all the achievements of man its invention so far is the greatest tragedy which has befallen the human race.

Its constant menace is obvious, but there is another aspect to be remembered. The only hope of avoiding future wars is to bring the human race under one single control, and the airplane may make this possible, though how the unified control is to be worked is the problem still to be solved. If such can be done, this tremendous striking force can be used to police the world and keep the peace, and a further advantage will be the fact that the airplane enormously reduces distance, which will enable the world family to get to know one another better, and, by travel, to increase in knowledge and understanding. The airplane opens the door to greatly increased and quicker travel and intercommunication, but this does not necessarily mean increased comfort or happiness, and its obvious dangers, for the present, greatly outweigh its possible advantages.

(2) THE RISE, DEVELOPMENT AND APPEAL OF SOCIALISM.

After thousands of years as an inhabitant of this earth, after centuries of toil and struggle, individualised mind, which we call "man", developed sufficiently to reach the stage recorded in the previous chapter. Certain groups of mankind, which we term nations, had become the masters of their own destiny, while others were groping towards the same goal. Now·we come to a new stage to which thought has advanced, and this again was caused by a book.

We remember how, so far, six books had produced a profound effect on the Western world: Augustine's *City of God*, Copernicus's *Revolution of the Heavenly Bodies*, Darwin's *Origin of Species*, Paine's *Rights of Man* and *The Age of Reason*, the latter written to correct some of the mistakes in the most popular of them all, *The Holy Bible*, the book which has fundamentally moulded the religious outlook of the Western world. The Eastern world has been equally influenced by literature, as there also six books were deeply reverenced by two thirds of the human race: Mahomet's *Koran*, the teachings of Confucius as contained in *The Great Learning* and *The Doctrine of the Mean*, the Indian *Vedas*, the Hindu *Bhagavad-gita*, and the Buddhist *Suttantas*. Now we come to another book which greatly influenced the period we have reached, and the years which followed up to our own times, but first of all something must be said of its author.

Heinrich Karl Marx (1818–1883), by his works and writings, did for society what Paine did in the realm of politics and religion. Both men made the people think about their everyday affairs and beliefs, in a way they had never thought before. Marx, born into a German-Jewish legal family, and educated at the universities of Bonn and Berlin, after studying law, history and philosophy, in which he took his degree, became the greatest theorist of modern Socialism.

He intended to settle at Bonn as a lecturer, but, as his radical ideas made a university career impossible, he became editor (1842) of a German radical newspaper which was suppressed the following year. Then he moved to Paris, where the Socialist movement was at its zenith, to contribute articles to those newspapers advanced enough to publish them. There he met Friedrich Engels, who had been converted to Socialism by Robert Owen, and together they worked as close friends to the last. Marx died in London before he had completed his best-known work, *Das Kapital*, but, from the notes he left, Engels finished it.

Marx, if he had lived longer, and had not suffered from ill-health, would have given the world a much greater amount of scientific work of a high order than is to be found in *Das Kapital*, wherein he attempted to make clear historically and critically the whole mechanism of capitalist economy. Here is not the place to proclaim the strength or weakness of his arguments, as what interests us is the effect they had on the wage-earners, with minds lacking knowledge, simple, fresh and ready to accept ideas from an educated man, an outstanding economist, and one who had given his life to try to prove that labour should get a greater share in the wealth it helped to produce.

His theories and opinions were the natural outcome of the centuries of serfdom and slavery which had been the lot of the common man, and his contribution focussed attention on the evils of the past. His prophecy that the rich would get richer and the poor always remain poor on a subsistence wage has not, however, been realised, because he forgot two important factors.

One was the growing power of organised labour, under the name of Trade Unions, which broke the vicious rule of low wages, and secured an increased reward for labour and better working conditions. The other was the advance made by invention, discovery and improved means of production and distribution. These two factors, more than polemics, have raised the standard of living four times higher than ever before, and, let us hope, now that the people have political power, that there lies before them a future of dignity, security, freedom, comfort and increased leisure for everyone.

Marx, though his writings are unnecessarily bitter and extreme, besides being involved, which makes his meaning sometimes difficult to grasp, was probably the greatest single dynamic intellectual force of the 19th century. As a thinker on economic questions, in their relation to everyday life, he towered above all who lived before him. Some hate his ideas, some admire them, some agree and some disagree, but, no matter what view is taken, they cannot be ignored, because they split the world into two different aspects of economic thought, the Communist and the Anti-Communist. They stimulated the Russian Revolution, brought into being the Nazi and Fascist tyrannies, fed the flames of the Spanish Civil War, and were a contributing cause of the last world war.

From the first, *Das Kapital,* and the other publications of Marx and Engels, have been subjected to all kinds of criticism, but no one can deny that he broke new ground and opened up new ways which enlarged the social outlook. Nobody before him had shown so clearly the role of the agencies of production, and nobody so masterfully exhibited their great determining influence on the social structure.

Besides expounding economic theories, he was the great force behind the International Working Men's Association, in leading which he displayed political sagacity and toleration which compare favourably with the spirit of some of the publications of the Communist League. He was more a teacher than an agitator, and his expositions on such subjects as education, Trade Unions, working hours and co-operation are highly instructive.

Nevertheless this educative process was not permitted to continue, because anarchist agitations, the Franco-Prussian War and the doings of the Paris Commune in 1871 raised passions to such a height that it proved impossible to maintain any kind of centralised labour federation, so much so that in 1876 the International collapsed. Subsequently other international congresses took its place, and much of the ideology which animated them was absorbed into the programmes of the Socialist and Labour parties as they gradually became prominent political forces.

These have mostly founded their policy on the basis of its principles, but not always in accordance with Marx's theories. His argument in favour of state, as opposed to individual ownership of the means of production, has already influenced legislation in most countries, while the Soviet Republics of Russia have carried his ideas farther than any other country, her constitution being based on the communist principles enunciated by Marx.

More conservative Britain, adopting her traditional policy of evolution in place of revolution, made use of her parliamentary system to pass laws which largely mitigated the evils of uncontrolled capitalism. The formation of the Labour Party in 1893 by a Scottish miner, James Keir Hardie (1856–1915), gave the artisan the representation he desired, each election returning an increased number of Labour members to Parliament, until finally they secured control in 1945 with a large majority.

Keir Hardie was the first elected Labour member and John Burns (1858–1943) was the first Labour member to hold office. They, and many of their comrades, were intelligent, just and honest men, who, by self-education, had raised themselves well above the position into which they were born. Books by now were plentiful at reasonable prices, and the free libraries endowed by Andrew Carnegie and other philanthropists enabled the working man to continue the meagre education he had received at school. So the position the Labour Party has attained today is due to the ability and intelligence of its leaders, who have fitted themselves for the responsible offices they are now called upon to fill.

Organised labour, by means of Trade Unions, Co-operative societies and the Labour Party in Parliament, kept the rights of man before the public, and, as the years passed, and intelligence increased, compassionate legislation followed, many readers being influenced by two outstanding books, *Looking Backward* by Edward Bellamy and *Merrie England* by Robert Blatchford. All parties, Conservative, Liberal and Labour, urged forward by the growing power of the people, shared in this effort to raise the standard of living and increase the joy and gladness in life, but behind them all were strong intellectual forces, such as came from William Morris, Herbert· Spencer, Bernard Shaw, Sidney and Beatrice Webb, who stirred the social conscience by publishing many striking facts and figures. Likewise the Fabian Society relied on the increase of knowledge to bring about reform and the development of both state and municipal enterprise, its policy being not to incite revolution and embitterment between the different classes of society.

Elsewhere, in the English-speaking world, evolution and not revolution was the policy adopted, and the self-governing British colonies furnished valuable experiments in the direction of State Socialism. Similarly, in the United States, moderation in the adoption of new political methods was evident, and her attitude to the new outlook resembled the one adopted by Great Britain, so much so that Socialism acted more as an incentive to progress than to revolution in those lands where the people were free and had a say in their own legislation. On the other hand, where the people lacked their rights as citizens,

Socialism was hailed as the way by which liberty would be won and the rule of the people achieved.

From the time of the suppression of the Commune in Paris (1871) Socialism became most pronounced in Germany, where it excited considerable alarm amongst the capitalist and ruling classes. Here its aim was to establish by all legal means a socialistic society, and prove the falsity of the so-called Iron Law of Wages, which denied the possibility of wages rising above subsistence level. As labour, it was argued, is the means by which all wealth and culture is secured, then to society, meaning everyone, belongs the entire product of labour by an equal right, to each one according to his reasonable wants, all being bound to work for the common good. The Social Democrats, who supported this programme, had two members in the Reichstag in 1871, but in 1877 the number rose to twelve, and, as the years passed, their strength grew until, in 1884, twenty-four members were returned to that assembly.

In Spain, Italy, France and Russia this fallacious fundamental principle of Socialism, that labour is the only means by which wealth is secured, made headway under different names. In Russia, under the name of Nihilism, it took its most aggressive form, and only the reverence of the peasantry for the person and office of the Tzar prevented revolution. As these Russian radicals received no mercy from their government, they gave none, and in 1878 began the conflict between them and the autocratic state which culminated in the violent death of Alexander II in 1881.

So it came about that as the 19th century drew to a close, the liberated workers throughout a great part of Europe, and also in Britain, looked forward to the day, soon to come, when they, in the name of all society, would seize political power, take over the control of production, and bring to an end the rule of the capitalists. Affairs, however, have not gone just as they expected, but, all the same, economic progress, under wise direction, has still much to achieve in its beneficent aim to raise the standard and well-being of society everywhere.

The present economic order, in which industry is carried on by private competitive capital, may some day pass away, but, if a new system is to take its place, it must come slowly, and the constitutional methods adopted by the majority of British Socialists have won for them the respect of the community. When the majority wish the experiment, it will then be possible to make the change with the least disruption, but only on the basis of liberty and justice to all concerned, and not by bloody revolution. New ideas have certainly been created, and the end of the 19th century saw these taking shape in more practical and wiser form, which, when the 20th century opened, gave promise of happier and fairer conditions for those who have been looked upon down the centuries as born only for toil and hardship.

When the 20th century commenced, Sociology, or the Science of Society, was receiving careful and considered attention from men and women in all grades of society. University students were becoming as interested in the subject as the artisan. The improvement of social conditions, the abolition of poverty, and the finding of means to settle international disputes peacefully instead of by war, were the ideals of those who were leading the race to a higher plane of thought and action. Developing mind was mapping out a new era for mankind, which was to make the people happy and comfortable here and now, the great discovery having been made that increased leisure, happiness and comfort were in their own hands, and not something only to be longed for in another world after death.

The previous fifty years had been a period of great material progress. Science was making man master of his fate. Birth control was preventing unwanted babies, and women were becoming the mistresses of their own bodies. Organised labour was becoming strong, and now had the power to bargain.[1] Machines were doing the work hitherto performed by those little better than slaves. Consequently the artisans were living lives of greater comfort, and the most intelligent were beginning to have only the number of children they desired. Science was reducing illness, suffering and early death, while life was being prolonged into healthy old age. Travel was becoming simple and comfortable, and electricity was employed to light both streets and houses as well as to move the street trams. Motor-cars and buses were steadily increasing in numbers, isolated villages being linked up with the larger towns, and the airplane had reached the stage of being an object of wonder and interest.

New and hitherto rare fruits, cereals and spices were filling the counters of the provision shops at prices which more people could afford to pay. Invention was producing new and beautiful clothes at

[1] The Trade Union Acts of 1871 and 1876, and the Conspiracy Act of 1875, gave labour combinations the position they hold today.

moderate prices, and all kinds of new articles were coming into everyday use in our homes. The hitherto poor were beginning to live and dress well, by education their manners had improved, and they were now treated by the well-to-do with more respect. Doctors and nurses were ever at call, and our hospitals were becoming great national institutions radiating healing in all directions.

Everywhere the tendency was for the people to take a greater share in their own government, and the question was generally debated as to whether the State should become the universal provider, or only the protector of the people. Two extremes of thought prevailed, the one held by the Anarchist that all forms of government were evil, and the other that it was the government's duty to plan for everyone from birth to death. Now it is quite evident that to obtain the full benefits of civilisation, and all that invention produces, the people must work together, because education, state insurance, electricity, drainage, roads, water, railways, posts, telephones, telegraphs, radio and other public utilities are only possible in a community working as one unit.

No one can be free to do only as he wishes and completely ignore his neighbour, as, unlike the animals, we are all interdependent. Consequently the rule of law must prevail. We sacrifice our liberty in one direction so as to secure a wider, fuller life in another, as to obtain complete unrestrained freedom would mean that we lose all the benefits of civilisation. No one is prepared to do this, because we are all willing to regulate our lives for the good of the entire community, in order to enjoy the benefits which come from a combination of effort. So long as freedom of thought and liberty of expression remain, and we can live our own lives as we desire, without infringing on the rights of others, no one need complain. Mental development thus proceeds unhindered, in fact more rapidly when we are able to give less and less thought to obtain those necessities and comforts which are needed to create the conditions in which the mind best thrives.

In primitive civilisation how little mankind had, and what a drudgery life was! To take a journey, to cook a meal, to secure clothes to keep out the cold, to protect the feet, to keep out rain and wind, to secure a sheltered warm home, and to produce the things required to sustain life, were all much more difficult than they are today. So our ancestors toiled from early morning to late at night, and from early childhood to old age, and then only managed to secure the bare necessities of life in a very primitive form. Planning, discovery, invention and reasoned thought have changed all that, so much so that we now have time for relaxation and mental development as never before. Life is now fuller, happier and freer, the restriction which civilisation imposes really producing greater leisure and freedom than when man lived his life alone, and thought of none but himself and his family.

Scientific planning, for the purpose of dividing amongst a greater number the good things of life, was becoming more and more prevalent in the early years of the 20th century, the government making itself responsible for education, health, working conditions, minimum wages, drainage, water, roads and many other things. Fifty years earlier no government would have considered such matters as part of its duties, the welfare of the people not being considered as coming within the range of State economy, as that was a Church affair only.

Another feature of the times was the growth of internationalism, and the growing feeling that all men are brothers. Improved travel facilities, and the development of commerce, were helping the people in different countries to know one another better. Labour everywhere had a common aim, the improved conditions of the people, and Trade Unionists from all over the world met each other periodically in different capitals to exchange views on the problems of the times. Science, Art and Literature had also broken down the national barriers, the leading scientists, artists and writers spreading their influence everywhere untrammelled by boundaries. Books, in ever-increasing numbers, were being translated into different languages. So much was internationalism developing that an international language, Esperanto, was invented, to take the place which Latin had once held when it was the international language of Europe.

The two world wars have retarded the progress which was so evident in the early years of the 20th century, and the destruction and hatred they have occasioned will prevent its universal return for many years. Meantime let everyone everywhere study closely the causes which have brought about this social disaster, and vow that a new order must be created to prevent the repetition of the catastrophies it has been the fate of the past two generations to experience.

(3) UNITED NATIONS ARISE IN NORTH AND SOUTH AMERICA.

We have by now a general idea of the history of mankind from primitive times to the latter half of the 19th century of the Christian era. The outstanding events in the story of man's long upward climb have been recorded in the preceding pages, and now we are coming close to our own times. In the previous chapter we reached the end of the Franco-Prussian War (1871), the close of the American Civil War (1865), and British history was brought up to the end of the South African War (1902). Now we must take up the important events which happened between these dates and the time when all the world, in one way or another, became involved in the greatest conflict of all times.

So let us start with the United States, united as never before. With the slaves now free, all friction between those in favour of and those against slavery passed away, and thus ceased this fountain out of which only strife had flowed. The abolition of slavery was accompanied by the recognition of the negro as an equal citizen, and this meant that he had now the right to sit in the state legislatures, and exercise his vote in framing laws for those who had lately owned him as they did their cattle. Several states withheld for a time their concurrence in a franchise which humiliated them so deeply, and thus they denied themselves representation, having to accept instead the governors appointed by the President.

Time unfortunately has not yet eased the problem

of two distinctly different races, of different colour, habits, intellect and outlook, living together. Outwardly the United States is made up of a united people, but inwardly there is such a distinction between the white and the black races that they live their lives apart. In the South, in every town and village, there are two sets of schools, on the railways there are two sets of carriages, and at the stations two separate waiting-rooms, one for white and one for the coloured people.

Amongst the whites there is always the inward sense that the negro is a millstone around the neck of the southern states, one which cannot be removed, and this causes the race riots and lynchings which are sometimes such a shocking feature of life in Georgia. The question of race and colour is still a problem, not only in America but in many parts of the world, and only time, which will bring education, culture and a higher ethical standard to everyone, both white and black, will solve it.

Abraham Lincoln's successor to the presidency was Andrew Johnson (1865–1869), a poorly educated, unwise and obstinate man who was quite unfitted for the position, a most unfortunate choice for a time when the nation's wounds required healing after the long and bloody strife. He so opposed the plans of reconstruction, as laid down by Congress, that he was impeached and tried before the Senate, with a view to his forcible removal from office. He managed, however, to retain office by only one vote. His term expired in 1869, when he was succeeded by General Grant, who remained president until 1877, during which time the new president had the mortification of discovering several members of his cabinet involved in corrupt practices. At this time financial morality was at a low ebb, and many millions of dollars were embezzled one way and another by state and city officials.

These unfortunate affairs were incidents in a period of great prosperity. New factories arose, villages became towns, and immigrants, at the rate of 350,000 a year, exchanged the poverty of Europe for the plenty of this new land of promise. The population increased by a million a year, and European capitalists found many new opportunities for the employment of their surplus wealth, to receive large, but sometimes uncertain, returns in the way of interest. New railways were constructed at the rate of 6000 miles annually, and all seemed to be set fair until a financial panic developed in 1873, when all business came to a standstill. America had been prospering on a wave of inflation, and, when it broke, six years elapsed before confidence returned.

Education in the United States at this time was still far from embracing everyone, as, when the census of 1870 was taken, 17 adult males and 23 adult females in every 100 were quite illiterate. The position in reality was not so bad as it was in Britain, as many of these illiterates were negroes whose masters had deliberately kept them ignorant, and others were immigrants from Europe who had never been educated. The percentage of white-born educated Americans was larger than the percentage in Britain at that time, as the common school, giving free education, had been maintained by most of the northern states from before the War of Independence. The youth of the United States had indeed many advantages over the young people in Europe, because their country spent a larger amount on education than was spent on it in all Europe, and they had no military service to perform.

With slavery abolished the United States could again take her stand for freedom and righteousness, as was intended by her founders, and she has exerted a profound influence on the struggle for freedom in Europe since the time of the French Revolution. This is an important fact to remember, and one which might never have materialised had the American colonies remained under British domination. What is now the United States certainly led Europe and South America on to the road of greater freedom which these two continents now enjoy. Since her break with tyranny she has been looked upon by freedom-loving people as an organisation of free people, intent on protecting their individual rights and liberties, besides being freed from the age-old tradition in Europe that someone had been divinely appointed to rule, quite irrespective of the wishes and aspirations of the people.

The American idea spread throughout Europe, and helped considerably in the growth of liberal ideas and the overthrow of despotism. The sustained exhibition, upon so vast a scale, of freedom in thought and deed, with its happy results in contentment, peace and prosperity, could not fail to impress deeply the oppressed nations of Europe. Here was a nation of men and women who made their own laws, appointed their own rulers, and to whom decrees and ukases, and all that is hateful in despotism, were unknown. Gratefully we record the inestimable service the United States has thus rendered to mankind.

As the 19th century drew to a close, the happy spectacle was presented of national prosperity, harmony and peace. The southern states were once more contented within the union, while capital poured in to exploit its mineral resources, and develop new industries. As the national public revenue far exceeded all reasonable demands for the efficient support of the government, past debts were paid off, and the treasury became full to overflowing. The surplus revenue in 1887 was over 100,000,000 dollars, and no one was owed anything. President Cleveland consequently attempted to reduce the import tariffs, now that all the revenue they were bringing in was not required, but he was defeated by a narrow margin.

Six new states were now (1889–1890) admitted into the union: North and South Dakota, Wyoming, Montana, Idaho and Washington. A general Pension Bill, giving generous benefits, became law, and, in other ways, the surplus revenue was spent, but the country's great prosperity was not to continue without a set back, which came in 1892.

Following the great World's Fair at Chicago, which drew enormous crowds from the entire continent, dark clouds began to close upon the financial horizon. Slowing down of trade, wage reductions, strikes and distress increased. Investment companies, which had placed loans in the west, and railway companies, which had pushed far into the wilderness, were severely affected. The cycle of prosperity had gone its round, and now had come the reaction, bringing bankruptcy and liquidation in its train.

This state of affairs brought about the defeat of the Democrats in 1896, the Republicans obtaining power with a large majority, when William McKinley (1897–1901) became the President in the following year. The new Congress was responsible for involving the country in war with Spain over Cuba. In 1898 the U.S. battleship *Maine*, when on a friendly visit, was blown up in Havana harbour, probably by a mine. Spain denied all responsibility, but the Americans did not believe this, and such was the popular outburst of indignation that intervention in Cuba followed two months later, the excuse being to secure to the Cubans a stable government of their own. War followed, despite Spain's efforts to meet all objections short of relinquishing her sovereignty over the island.

This conflict, arising out of an incident in Havana in the West Indies, commenced at Manila in the Philippines in the Pacific, as it so happened that an American fleet was at Hong Kong, and Commodore Dewey was instructed to attack the Philippines, another Spanish possession. He found the Spanish fleet in Manila Bay, where, in a few hours, he succeeded in destroying all the enemy's vessels, and disabling all the shore batteries, without the loss of an American seaman. A considerable Spanish fleet had by now gathered in the narrow harbour of Santiago in Cuba, only to be bottled up by an American blockading force. An American military force landed, and, when nearing Santiago, the Spanish admiral made a bolt, only to lose all his fleet by capture or destruction. In this campaign, lasting four months, the United States did not lose a single vessel and only about a dozen men.

America demanded from Spain, as the price of

peace, the secession of the Philippines and Porto Rico, and the relinquishment of her sovereignty in Cuba. Spain could only agree, but she was somewhat appeased by the present of 20,000,000 dollars from the United States, which asked for no war indemnity. By now the victor had become fully possessed with the idea of colonial acquisitions, and of commercial expansion in China and the Pacific. Accordingly, in 1897, the United States annexed Hawaii, an independent kingdom, giving as the reason that it was essential to naval operations. Here it was, in Pearl Harbour, that she suffered such a treacherous blow prior to the outbreak of war with Japan in 1941.

America treated the Filipinos as if she had bought them from Spain along with the islands, and a struggle for independence followed. The native leader was captured and imprisoned, and it was not until 1902 that most of the American troops were withdrawn. Towards Cuba the pledge of autonomy was renewed, and a constitutional convention called, but the United States remained in military control until 1902, when Cuba became a republic. Then it was that the American troops and governor were withdrawn. Porto Rico, on the other hand, became a colony.

An anti-foreign uprising in China (1896) led to a joint military relief movement towards Peking, in which the United States took part with the chief European powers. Since then her policy has been to maintain the "Open Door" attitude in Chinese commerce without interfering with Chinese autonomy. In 1901 the completion of the Panama Canal was first discussed, and after many difficulties were overcome this wonderful waterway was finished in 1914. Now the largest ship can pass through it, and so save the long voyage round by Cape Horn.

President McKinley, to whom the United States was indebted for her territorial expansion in the Pacific and Atlantic oceans, met a tragic death. When visiting the Pan-American Exposition at Buffalo (1901), he was shot by an anarchist, who was captured and executed. Theodore Roosevelt (1901–1909), the Vice-President, became the President, and proved himself to be a leader of remarkable ability. He was a man of many parts, having seen all sides of life, a Republican, passionately interested in reform, and a strenuous worker for civic righteousness.

He came on the scene when financial affairs had reached such a crisis that something had to be done to curb the power of the great trade combines which had come into being over the past thirty years. No other country had grown more rapidly in population and wealth within this period. Its railways now exceeded in length those of Europe, and five great systems stretched from east to west. Mass production was in full blast in the leading industries, while improved communication was now making it possible for the great combines to sell their wares all over the country, and compete with industries which, prior to the railways, had supplied the local markets.

So Chicago became the centre of a continental meat industry of colossal dimensions, Minneapolis the focus of the flour trade, Massachusetts of boots and shoes, Rhode Island of textiles, and Pittsburg of iron and steel. As the separate industries congregated, so competition gave place to combination, until the time came when gigantic trusts or combines controlled the mass production of the principal essentials of life. Many economies in production were possible by mass production, and at the Chicago packing plants every part of the pig was claimed to be used except the squeal! Combination thus led to monopoly, and so we find the trade dictator arising to become more powerful, and amass greater wealth, than the great plundering warriors of the past.

Men like Rockefeller, the oil king, Carnegie, the steel king, Duke, the tobacco king, and Guggenheim, the copper king, arose from poverty to control the oil, steel, tobacco and copper production and distribution far and wide. When Rockefeller, the son of a pedlar, could not buy up a rival he squeezed him out until he had control of the home petroleum market, and was in active competition with other producers and distributors in all parts of the world.

All this became possible, primarily, because in the United States enormous deposits of oil, iron ore and copper were discovered, and tobacco could be grown to advantage over great tracts of country. This was likewise the age of the great financiers when there arose to power Pierpont Morgan, and others like him, men of wide vision, great business capacity and tireless energy, whose love of power and wealth urged them on to create one gigantic combine after another until they had the industrial life of the people in their hands.

In 1904 what had been 5300 independent businesses were now under the control of 320 combines, a state of affairs which came about quite naturally by the merging of capital and mass production. Production became more efficient, and many savings were effected, but along with much that was good came much that was bad. Their power reached into the state legislatures and swayed Congress, as what a combine wanted it could get by the necessary bribery and corruption. Steel, for instance, was protected by a high import tariff which enabled it to defy British competition, and the oil monopoly enabled prices to be charged far above cost of production and distribution. When laws were passed to protect the public a way was generally found to get round them.

The Republican party was allied with the large manufacturers, who demanded high tariffs to protect their goods from external competition, and, in exchange for its help, ample funds were forthcoming for the party treasury. When Theodore Roosevelt became president, he was determined to clean up the political abuses so prevalent, and prove to the people, insistent on reform, that the government, and not the trusts, governed the country. Before he had been nine months in office he broke up the railway monopoly controlled by Morgan, Hill and Harriman, and then followed the successful injunctions against the oil and tobacco trusts. This "trust-busting", as it was called, distinguished between the good and bad combinations, because it destroyed the worst and curbed the power of the rest.

So, when Roosevelt retired from office, he had the satisfaction of knowing that he had purged the country of some of the worst abuses arising from trade monopolies, and had brought in various measures of social reform. His successor, William Howard Taft (1909–1913), accomplished nothing spectacular, as he lacked his predecessor's energy and drive, and, when the Republican Party split in 1912, the Democrats succeeded in securing the election of Woodrow Wilson (1913–1921) who pursued an active and successful progressive policy. The high tariffs were reduced, the banking and currency system was reformed, the powers of the trusts were severely limited and labour conditions were improved, but all further reforms were halted by the outbreak of the First World War.

For over two years Wilson was able to keep his country neutral, but in the end the task was impossible, the sheer ruthless barbarities of the Germans having prepared the way for the United States siding with the forces fighting against aggression. So, when Germany recommenced unrestricted submarine warfare in 1917, sinking eight American vessels, and then told Mexico that when the war ended she would help her to regain the lands taken from her by the United States, Congress, in April of that year, declared war on the enemy of civilisation. American industry had already supplied much war material to France and Britain, but now it geared itself to greater efforts, and an army of 2,000,000 men under General Pershing was transported to France. A great shipbuilding programme was successfully carried through, and her three hundred warships greatly eased the strain on the allied navies.

Likewise eight of the South American republics joined in against the common enemy, seven broke off diplomatic relations, while Argentine, Chile, Colombia and Mexico remained neutral, the latter being in the throes of civil war. All over the South American continent the people showed their sympathy for the allied cause, whether or not their governments declared their belligerency or adopted the policy of neutrality, but it was Brazil, more than any other, which displayed the greatest hostility to the enemy of freedom, her proximity to the West African coast being doubtless the reason.

Nineteen independent republics were by now situated south of the United States, in full agreement with the Monroe Doctrine, first propounded though not originated by President Monroe (1817–1825), when the Holy Alliance of European powers in 1823 seemed about to use force to restore to Spain her lost colonies. This doctrine declared that the lands of the Americas were no longer open to invaders from across the sea, and that any attempt by a European, or other power, to interfere with the independence of the American republics would be regarded by the United States as an unfriendly act. This developed later into Pan-Americanism, the object of which is to maintain peace over the entire northern and southern continents, and expand inter-American trade on a mutually profitable basis.

In 1889 all the South American republics sent delegates to Washington, when plans for closer co-operation were discussed, and, though little was then achieved, this conference is regarded as the starting point of Pan-Americanism in a practical form. Out of this came the Pan-American Union, for the purpose of fostering American internationalism and friendly relations between all the American republics. For many years the southern continent feared its powerful northern neighbour, and not until Franklin Roosevelt propounded the policy of the "Good Neighbour" were the fears of the South calmed down. Now Pan-Americanism is a vast democratic movement for continental solidarity, every year tending more towards a common understanding amongst all the American republics on a basis of equality and complete independence, with a view to ensuring peace and prosperity amongst all the people of America.

The achievements of the Spanish and Portuguese in South America, during their century of independence, is one of the outstanding events in modern history. Lacking coal, their countries may never become great industrially, and, for that reason, until other means are found to protect them, they will always be open to attack by powerful nations able to produce heavy armaments. Their other resources are great, and their future prospects bright, because the broad band of culture and civilisation which they have established from the coast inland increases in size every year over forests, high mountains, deserts and plains to new and pleasant lands. Almost everywhere more land remains to be developed and made productive, and no one can doubt the immense possibilities awaiting these vast territories, as large as the United States and Canada combined, but with as yet only half their population.

(4) THE RUMBLING BEFORE THE FIRST WORLD WAR.

During the opening years of the 20th century, slight political tremors were being felt in Europe, which increased in force until they produced in 1914 the greatest social convulsion so far recorded in history.

Europe, that volcano of diverse passions, then experienced her greatest and most violent eruption, but before this poisonous discharge belched forth to cover much of the earth, let us see how Britain has fared since we left her at the end of the South African War.

The amiable, diplomatic and sociable Edward VII (1901–1910) succeeded to the British throne on the death of his mother Victoria, his wish being to pursue a policy of goodwill to all mankind, and one of friendship towards France, Russia and Germany. Lord Salisbury remained Prime Minister for seventeen months of the new reign, to be succeeded by Arthur James Balfour (1902–1905), a man of culture and philosophic mind, who was called upon to deal with a particularly difficult problem. Since the adoption by Sir Robert Peel of the policy of free trade, Britain had prospered exceedingly, but new and powerful competitors abroad had arisen, and Joseph Chamberlain, an ardent Imperialist, now declared himself in favour of protective tariffs, to include the whole British Empire.

By this proposal he split the Conservative Party for and against protection, just as he had split the Liberal Party in Gladstone's time by leading a revolt against Home Rule for Ireland. Many who believed in free trade left the Conservative Party, and Balfour had to resign office in 1905, quite unable to decide whether to support Chamberlain or not. Apart from this controversy important improvements were made in education, as the result of Sir Robert Morant's Education Act of 1902, and Labour Exchanges were set up to help the unemployed to find work, a scheme which only became really effective in 1909, when further legislation was passed.

The Education Act of 1902 transferred the local administration of education from the School Boards to special county and borough committees, thus bringing the cost of the instruction of the young on the rates and under the direct control of elected bodies. Moreover, it provided for secondary education, but, in spite of its beneficent object, the Nonconformists were aroused to bitter hostility because denominational schools were from now onwards to be supported by the ratepayers. Why, they declared, should they be called upon to support the teaching of Anglican and Roman Catholic doctrines in the Church schools, and why, because of the lack of schools, should some require to send their children to Church schools to be taught doctrines which to them were abhorrent?

During the past 350 years there has been resistance by the Nonconformists to Church of England tyranny and exclusiveness, the Church and Chapel have been in constant open conflict, all the hatred and bitterness which comes from organised supernatural religion rising to the surface in every town and village in England. During the 19th century this was focussed on the question of theological education, because English Christians could not agree as to what was true and what was false, and a number of zealous dissenters preferred to go to prison rather than pay rates which were used for teaching children what they believed was untrue.

Besides the religious controversy which then raged, the question of tariffs divided the country into two camps, to end in putting the free trade Liberals into office for the next ten years, Sir Henry Campbell-Bannerman (1905–1908) now becoming

Prime Minister. Complete self-government was immediately granted to the Transvaal and the Orange Free State, and shortly afterwards they were joined by the Cape of Good Hope and Natal, to form the Union of South Africa, with General Botha, who had led the Boers a few years earlier against Britain, as the first Prime Minister.

Here indeed are justice, toleration and liberty exemplified, as never before in history. A new chapter in world history had opened which entitled Britain, in the years to come, to stand for justice and liberty in Europe, a course she could never have pursued had Campbell-Bannerman not taken this wise decision within her own dominions. Lord Haldane, a man of great ability, reorganized the British regular and territorial army, and to him was due the efficient but small force which Britain was able to land in France at the outbreak of war in 1914. To strengthen her position in the Far East Britain made an alliance with Japan in 1902, and this gave her an ally in the First World War who safeguarded her possessions in the Pacific Ocean.

When Campbell-Bannerman resigned in 1908, because of ill-health, Herbert Asquith (1908–1915), likewise a Liberal, and a man blessed with a well-balanced mind, became Prime Minister. He was determined to carry through many overdue reforms, and to this end he appointed David Lloyd George his Chancellor of the Exchequer, a man who was to prove himself a tough fighter for the improvement of the social life of the people. Asquith's government introduced the Old Age Pension Act, giving a pension of ten shillings a week to old people, and a National

Insurance Act, which was sponsored by Lloyd George, to insure workers against unemployment and illness.

Moreover, this administration set itself earnestly to improve the lot of the poor, to care for the health of the people, and attend to the welfare of the children. Much good and greatly needed legislation was passed, and Britain began seriously to make up for all the past centuries of neglect of social progress. This was especially noticeable in the new youth movements. The pioneer of them all, Sir William Smith, founded the Boys' Brigade in Glasgow in 1883, but this was largely overshadowed from 1908 onwards by Lord Baden-Powell's Boy Scout and Girl Guide organisations, all of which have done so much to improve and develop the characters of the rising generation. Though the social conscience was developing, reforms by Parliament did not come about without much opposition being encountered, and the House of Lords unwisely rejected the 1909 Budget because of certain new land taxes. It was during the bitter controversy which followed that Edward VII died in 1910.

George V (1910–1936), his son, succeeded, to find himself involved in the dispute caused by a Bill which Asquith brought forward to restrict the power of the House of Lords, a body of non-elected men who, in the majority, had angered all liberal-minded people by their reactionary methods. This Bill, which became the Parliament Act (1911), passed the House of Commons, and was only passed by the House of Lords after the King had agreed to create, if necessary, a sufficient number of Liberal peers to secure its passage.

Following the passing of this Act, the Upper House

could not reject money Bills, nor any Bill passed by the Commons in three successive sessions, and the life of a single Parliament was reduced from seven to five years. Only then did Britain become a democracy, because up to now the veto of the unelected House of Lords prevented the elected House of Commons from effectively ruling the country.

Now the Liberals had a weapon with which to secure the passage of the Irish Home Rule Bill. One was passed through the House of Commons (1912), and, by means of the Parliament Act, it passed eventually (1914) through the Upper House. Ulster, led by Lord Carson, was determined not to be ruled by a Roman Catholic majority in Dublin, and months of unrest and controversy followed.

John Redmond, the Irish Nationalist leader, promised any safeguards Ulster demanded, but all efforts to compromise failed. A general revolt was in progress, both sides were arming and ready to fight, when swiftly the rebellion collapsed in the autumn of 1914, everyone being faced with a far graver problem. War with Germany had commenced, and, although the Home Rule Bill had become law, its provisions were suspended until the war came to an end.

Let us now cross over the Channel, and see how France has fared since her humiliating defeat in 1870. When that year ended all France was conquered and only Paris held out, to capitulate in January 1871. The following month, elections took place for the National Assembly which was to meet at Bordeaux to arrange terms of peace. After a prolonged discussion the members who were returned favoured a republic, when Louis Thiers became chief of the executive.

A fierce outbreak by the extreme Socialists and Republicans of Paris interfered greatly with the peaceful labours of the more moderate Bordeaux Government, and finally these extremists set up the Commune in Paris which declared itself in opposition to the new Republic. Then followed, with its accompanying horrors, the second siege of Paris by the Bordeaux Republicans, the gloomy spectacle of street fighting, and the burning and destruction of public buildings by the Communists, lasting for nearly two months, during which time Thiers concluded the peace terms with Germany as recorded in the previous chapter. With these settled he next attacked and captured Paris, overthrew the Commune, and moved his administration from Bordeaux to the capital.

Since the year 1870 France has been a republic, based on manhood suffrage and the freedom of the Press, the constitution providing for two chambers, a Senate and House of Deputies, which together elect the President for a term of seven years. The first President was Louis Thiers (1870–1873), who was the only one to exercise a controlling influence, his firm handling of the Communists adding greatly to his prestige. He was a strong and gifted man, and by his wisdom and energy did much to rehabilitate the nation suffering from defeat. Few of the presidents, or their premiers who followed, have left lasting impressions, the men chosen securing office because of their solidity, character and ability, the President's duty being to preserve stability, and do nothing spectacular, France having had enough of this in the past. She was now a democratic parliamentary governed country, because the Cabinet ruled the country under the direction of the elected deputies, to whom it was responsible.

The weakness of French republican politics lay in the fact that France lacked the stabilisation of large and highly organised powerful parties as in Britain, her parties consisting of small weakly-held-together groups, combining kaleidoscopically to produce one government after another in bewildering rapidity. The Cabinet, therefore, had not the respect or power possessed by its British equivalent, its chief, deprived of the influence wielded by the British Prime Minister and burdened by trivial details, being often uncertain how long his government would last.

Consequently the maintenance of a long-term policy was always difficult, and the state of flux in which many issues became involved alienated public interest, the people often losing respect for their rulers in spite of the eloquence and brilliance of the debates. Nevertheless continuous administration was maintained, and the Republic survived the attempt made in 1887 by the handsome gallant General Boulanger (then the popular hero for his work in pacifying Tunis), to revise the constitution, curtail its democratic basis, and restore the old privileges of the Church.

One of the most outstanding figures of republican France was Jules Ferry (1832–1893), a great man and an outstanding statesman. As Minister of Education, as Prime Minister and as President of the Senate he left an enduring mark on French politics. This ardent courageous man, endowed with great administrative ability, was one of the most criticised and abused of all French politicians, his passionate desire for French expansion abroad, particularly in Africa, angering the Liberals, while his determination to introduce popular education brought upon him the bitter hatred of the Church, whose hierarchy was anxious to have the people remaining simple and ignorant.

His detestation of priestcraft, and all it stands for, sustained him in pursuing his fixed course, to dissolve the Jesuit religious associations and reduce the power of the priests. Consequently he broke the power of the Church in France, legalised Trade Unions, added Madagascar and Tunis to the colonial empire, and won his great educational conflict when Church theological schools were abolished in 1882, to be replaced by state secular schools, when education became free and compulsory.

Most of France was illiterate in 1870, but from 1882 onwards French children received education instead of theological instruction, fourteen hundred years having elapsed since the great Roman academies had last spread their intellectual light over all Gaul. In the 5th century they had been closed down by the Christian Church, and only now, after France had been brought to the verge of civil war by the opposition of the priests, did the reformers' battle-cry "Clericalism is the enemy of mankind" achieve its purpose. The great development in education during the next fifty years is certainly one of the most outstanding achievements of the Third Republic.

However, Ferry's colonial policy over Tunis lost to France the friendship of Italy, and its continuance after his time over Morocco strained relations with Germany and Spain, nearly to involve France in war with Britain over Fashoda. Nevertheless France has been the most powerful factor in bringing peace and civilisation to a vast area of North-West Africa, her large empire there standing her in good stead during the two world conflicts. It was saved for her by the heroism of General de Gaulle, when the French government made the fatal mistake in 1940 of not quitting Bordeaux and making Algiers the French capital until Paris was free of enemy occupation.

In 1894 one of the most deplorable religious and racial tragedies shook all France, the rest of the world looking on in wonder and amazement. Few, who did not live through these years (1894–1903), can appreciate the passions which were aroused when Captain Alfred Dreyfus, a young Jewish artillery officer, was found guilty of betraying military secrets to Germany. After being degraded he was sent to Devil's Island, off the coast of French Guiana, where he would probably have ended his days had not Colonel Picquart, a Protestant, and an officer of the general staff, obtained, at the risk of his military career, the necessary evidence to secure his release.

A heated controversy followed in which all France was divided, the Church, the Monarchists and the Imperialists being ranged against him. Emile Zola (1840–1902), the eminent novelist, formulated a case against the general staff of the army, composed of rabid Roman Catholics, of complicity in an anti-Semitic plot, and eventually Colonel Henri and Major Ester-hazy were discovered to be the real culprits, but not before Dreyfus was brought home and retried.

The military authorities fought hard to maintain the first verdict, and succeeded in doing so for a second time, as Drefyus was again found to be guilty. Then

he was immediately pardoned (1903) and set free!
Evidence accumulated that behind it all were the leading priests and religious orders, whose hatred of the
Jews and the Republic had caused them to take a
prominent part against an innocent man, so as to
discredit both the Jews and the Republic. Many of
the religious orders were eventually proscribed, none
were allowed to teach, and their members left France
for Britain and other lands, where they commenced an
insidious campaign to proselytise Protestant children
by means of cheap education, only possible in consequence of their wealth. Thus were many children
drawn into the Roman Catholic fold, to their lasting
mental deterioration.

A complete separation now took place between
the Church of France and the State, money payments
were stopped and Associations for Worship were
formed to take over all the Roman Catholic churches.
The Pope protested, but in vain, and France, once the
darling "eldest son of the Church", obtained her hard-
won liberty after fourteen centuries of theological
bondage, men of all classes and beliefs now rising to
the highest positions in the land.

In Germany, on the other hand, there was no place
for liberal thought, her people, who are so backward
politically, bending their great talents for organisation
to the development of trade and commerce throughout
the world. Consequently, after her victory against
France (1871), she prospered exceedingly. No longer
a people thinking of the interests of their own states,
the Germans became one united nation compactly
organised and disciplined. The army from that time
took first place, and the military caste became the

dominant power. Things might have been very different had Frederick III lived, as he was a man of liberal and progressive outlook, but he died of cancer after a reign of only three months (1888), to be succeeded by his son William, which brings us to the point where we left Germany in the previous chapter.

William II (1888-1918), a deeply religious man, believed that he was the Emperor of Germany by divine right, and as this was so Bismarck was now unnecessary. So the Iron Chancellor, who acted as a check to the realisation of his divine mission, was dismissed (1890), and the young emperor took the reins of government into his own hands. Bismarck's policy had been to fit Germany into the place she was entitled to occupy because of her situation and capacity, and, by his unswerving determination, he raised her to be the leading power in Europe. He was not interested in colonial development, or the expansion of her sea power, but the young emperor had visions of a vast colonial empire supported by a mighty navy.

Besides making Germany materially great, Bismarck had, by his policy and his triumphs, put her on the broad road which was to lead her to destruction. Might now took the place of right, and German policy was based on the ruthless doctrine of the strong trampling down the weak, as propounded by the twisted mind of Nietzsche (1844-1900), her famous reactionary philosopher, who very appropriately ended the last twelve years of his life hopelessly insane.

International law and justice were passed aside in contempt, blatant selfishness reigned supreme, and only that which benefited Germany obtained unqualified approval. The Lord of Hosts and the God of Battles, the Emperor believed, was now on the side of Germany, whose inhabitants had been singled out as his chosen people. When such ideas obsess the mind of a man wielding great power there is little hope of a future of peaceful progress. Especially so as he accepted the Bible as his divinely inspired guide from beginning to end, a book which contains some three hundred passages recording the brutal way the Hebrews, who were in some respects little better than savages, treated their enemies.

So began a policy which was to end in a fierce, determined and powerful attempt at European domination, but this idea only developed slowly as the steps were taken, one by one, on the road of ambition. A quite unnecessarily powerful fleet of warships was constructed, and Heligoland, ceded by Britain in 1890, became an important naval base. Then the Kiel Canal was constructed (1895) to join the North Sea and the Baltic, and make it unnecessary for ships to pass round the Danish peninsula. By 1897 Britain began to take alarm, as an attempt was evidently being made to challenge her position on the sea, one which was vital to her existence.

Already Germany had secured her share in the dividing up of Africa, and the Emperor, taking advantage of the unsettled state of China, took possession of Kiaochow in 1897, a district which became a trading centre of great value. By cultivating the friendship of the Sultan of Turkey, Germany obtained entry into Asia Minor and Mesopotamia, but her projected railway to Baghdad was never completed owing to her defeat in the First World War.

The Emperor's autocratic rule drove many moder-

ates into the ranks of the Socialists, to be first con-
ciliated by progressive legislation and then denounced
as traitors, but still their number increased until they
formed the largest single party in the Reichstag.
Strong indeed was the opposition of the progressive
parties to the Emperor's ambitious designs, and to the
increasing power of the reactionary military clique who
had his ear. Germany, however, is a land where the
people are children politically, and the Emperor's
glamour overawed the multitude, who left their fate
in his hands and followed blindly, but eagerly, where
he led.

Down south, in Hungary, the land which was
occupied by the Huns in the 4th century, the Hungarians had obtained Home Rule and manhood suffrage. The Magyars, whose ancestors had wandered
thither from the Ural mountains in the 9th century,
dominated all the other minority races, but there was
both intellectual and industrial freedom and progress.
In Austria all men over twenty-four received the vote,
while the Czechs in Bohemia, and the Poles in Galicia,
realised some of their aspirations. Over all this mixed
company of different races and religions reigned the
Emperor Francis Joseph (1848–1916), during whose
long reign the Empire's old divisions and antagonisms
were in many respects healed.

Farther north in Russia 50,000,000 serfs were
liberated during the reign of Alexander II (1855–1881),
and this was followed by the spread of Nihilism, a
name which came from its adherents finding nothing
to approve of in the constitutional order of their
country. The only difference between a Russian serf
and an American slave in those days lay in the fact

that a serf could not be bought or sold, but, in exchange for their land, they gave their overlord forced service. He only was their judge in all civil matters, and could inflict corporal punishment on all who displeased him. In 1858 the serfs obtained their freedom, and this power of punishment was withdrawn, the law courts taking its place. They were also able to purchase their own land by instalments, but the price was too high, and this caused much dissatisfaction and discontent.

This injustice, combined with the fact that they were excluded from any share in their own government, and that liberty of thought and expression were ruthlessly suppressed, produced Nihilism, whose adherents, while condemning the entire existing order, demanded a clean sweep of the old régime and a new one set up in its place. With no Parliament or representation, as in some Western lands, the people were unable to express themselves in any other way, and revolution was consequently the only one open for them to attain their desires.

Violence, insurrection and terror increased, and assassinations were frequent, to end in Alexander II, a man anxious for progress and reform, being murdered in 1881 when he was making arrangements to grant a representative assembly, or Duma, the Russian word for Parliament. His reign is noteworthy, not only because of the reforms instituted, and the growing demand for greater liberty, but also because Russia expanded her frontiers eastwards, first of all bringing Central Asia under her rule, and then all Siberia as far east as the Pacific Ocean.

The new Tzar, Alexander III (1881-1894), had no liberal ideas, and, instead of making concessions, he waged a bitter conflict against everyone holding advanced opinions, all having unorthodox political or religious ideas being persecuted. Consequently many Jews, Protestants and Roman Catholics shared the same fate as was prescribed for all other offenders, and, by sheer ruthlessness, he stifled all opposition until his death in 1894. His son Nicholas II (1894–1917) followed him, and did his best to promote industry and trade. Then came the war with Japan (1904), which ended in Russia's humiliating defeat, a catastrophe which exposed the corruption and incompetence of the ruling caste, and made it impossible for the aristocracy to retain the power they had wielded so long. Finally the army and navy mutinied, and revolutionary disturbances occurred in the large cities.

In 1905 the Tzar summoned a Duma, based on a wide franchise, with power over legislation and taxation, but there were so many extreme opinions, and such violent quarrelling, that it was dissolved. The people had been given the power, but not the education to fit them to govern themselves, and the Tzar, fearing that extreme measures would be carried, took this drastic action, to repeat it during the session which followed. Agitation became violent, numerous arrests were made, while executions and exile to Siberia removed many of the reformers and extremists. Finally a Duma, which assembled by rather unconstitutional methods, proved sufficiently loyal and moderate to satisfy the Tsar, but, by 1914, the opening year of the First World War, much still remained to be done to put this quite uneducated priestridden country on to a democratic basis, and satisfy the subject races such as the Finns and Poles.

If we now cross over to the other side of Europe we find in Spain only reaction. In a country dominated by the Roman Catholic Church, representative government and freedom are impossible. A body of liberal opinion was battened down, the Press was controlled, and there was neither religious toleration nor freedom of speech. The Church directed what education there was, and dominated the entire government by its vast wealth in land and property.

During the long reign of Isabella II (1833–1868) there was a series of military dictatorships, to be followed in 1873 by a republic, which lasted for only a year, as it received no popular support. Absence of education, and the political sense, made government by the people impossible, and so the Bourbons returned in 1874.

Not until 1910 was representative government introduced by means of manhood suffrage, but, as 60 per cent. of the population was quite illiterate, parliamentary government was a mockery. Owing to the Church's control over the minds of the people, it is estimated that there were not more than 6000 of the 20,000,000 inhabitants of Spain who had the faintest idea how to use the vote. No government lasted long enough to frame any measures for the good of the people, and so Spain remained the most devout and the most backward country in Europe.

Italy prospered after its unification, though the new monarchy had to face the bitter opposition of the Vatican. This bitterness did not soften with time, and all orthodox Catholics were forbidden to take any share or interest in their country's government. In Rome the violence of the hatred of the Holy See towards the monarchy was plainly apparent, and the two courts were in open hostility. Victor Emanuel II was fortunate in his ministers, who carried on parliamentary government successfully on the British model, in strange contrast to Germany as the unity she had achieved did nothing to destroy her ancient form of autocratic rule.

Unfortunately Italy was too weak and exposed to stand alone, and she again tied herself to a wheel of the German juggernaut, Austria lashing herself to the other one. Counting on their fear of Russia, Bismarck brought the three countries together by the treaty known as the Triple Alliance (1882). From that moment Russia became their accepted enemy, and the three powers agreed that should she attack one the remaining two would come to the assistance of the country attacked.

This treaty was quite inconsistent with Germany's previous undertakings towards Russia, and was just the type of dirty work which Bismarck commenced, and Hitler, even more blatantly, continued. So Austria and Italy remained the satellites of Germany until 1914, when the latter broke away, as she would not support allies who had been the aggressors.

In Italy, as elsewhere in Europe, the influence of Karl Marx spread fast, his doctrines captivating the Italian imagination. By 1890 Marx was the recognised authority on the cure of all the ills from which the wage-earner suffered. As in France, extremists attempted the overthrow of the entire capitalist system by a revolutionary strike (1904). but with no greater success.

Besides these social problems, which each European

state was tackling in its own way, Italy cast her eyes across the Mediterranean, with thoughts of Rome and her once mighty empire. Imperial ideas began to form in minds which hitherto had been occupied in bringing about unity at home, to grow in intensity as the years passed. Without a pretext, Italy attacked Turkey in the same treacherous way as she attacked Greece in 1940, sending an army in 1911 to the Turkish north African province of Libya. The adventure was more difficult than she expected, but she managed to hold on until she eventually forced the Turks to cede to her Cyrenaica and Tripolitania. This war brings us to a consideration of the state of affairs then prevailing in the Balkans, and in Turkey, a country which within the past thirty years had lost so many of her possessions.

We remember how the Turkish Empire in 1566, at the time of the death of Suleyman the Magnificent, comprised Libya, Egypt, Palestine, Syria, Asia Minor and in Europe reached nearly to Venice, Vienna and the Polish border. Greece first of all obtained her independence in 1829, and then, half a century later, Britain took control of Egypt in 1883, at a time when the Turkish Balkan possessions were straining to secure their independence. Montenegro and Rumania had secured self-government, though they remained nominally within the Turkish Empire. Bosnia, Herzegovina, Serbia and Bulgaria were still kept in subjection by terrorist methods, the first two having tried and failed in 1875 to throw off their overlords by means of an insurrection. Bulgaria next made the attempt, only to be crushed down in such a brutal fashion that a thrill of horror spread through Europe.

We have now come to the time when by conflict

these Balkan lands secured their freedom, but first of
all let us appreciate the position from both the political
and religious aspect. When this diversity of races,
huddled together within the Balkan peninsula,
obtained their independence from Turkish rule they
were for ever pulling against each other, and one or
other was made use of by Austria, Germany or Russia
for their own ends. The Slavs looked to Russia for
protection, the Magyars to Austria, and besides these
and other races, with their own particular political
outlook, there was the German element which was
always a disturbing and unsettling influence.

Moreover, these Balkan races were Christians, and
this was one reason why they wanted to throw off the
Moslem yoke, but that is only half the story. As
already explained, they were composed of different
kinds of Christians, some believing that the "Holy
Ghost proceeded from the Father" and others that
"The Holy Ghost proceeded from the Father and the
Son". The addition of the Latin word *Filioque* (and from
the son) to the Creed in 1054 made all the difference to
these Balkan Christians. So the former were known
as Orthodox Greek Church Christians, while the others
remained Catholics and accepted what the others
rejected as an innovation.

This little Latin word was a contributing cause of
the trouble which now developed in the Balkans, to
end in the conflagration of the First World War. The
story of how this addition was made to the Creed in
the 11th century, and how the Christian Church split
in two because of it, has already been told. It divided
Europe from that time onwards into two separate
flocks of Christian sheep, which bleated at each other

until the Reformation produced the Protestant flock, who also left the papal fold.

Thus was created a third flock, to increase the disharmony, though the Protestants remained Catholic Christians, but they did not recognise the Pope as the head of the Church. Other minor beliefs were discarded by the Protestant Catholics, who ever afterwards designated their co-religionists as Roman Catholics. The majority of the people in the Balkan Christian lands were adherents of the Orthodox Greek Church, the same one to which Russia was attached, and this meant that they looked to Russia for liberation, and she in turn considered them as co-religionists coming under her wing.

Germany and Austria did not want Russia to interfere in the Balkans, and Britain did not wish Russia in Constantinople, as one day she might cut the British route to India through the Mediterranean. So, when a revolt against Turkish misrule broke out in Bosnia and Herzegovina in 1875, and spread to Montenegro, Serbia and Bulgaria, Europe shivered in fear of what was going to happen. The Turks crushed this rebellion and massacred 12,000 Bulgarian Orthodox Christians, and Russia, feeling that the time had come to interfere, declared war on Turkey in 1877. Russia defeated the Turks, who were forced to sign the Treaty of San Stefano, its principal feature being the creation of a vast autonomous Bulgaria, to be administered under Russian tutelage, and garrisoned by Russian troops for two years.

Britain was so greatly alarmed at Russia's growing strength towards the Mediterranean that she sent her fleet to the Dardanelles, and it seemed as if Europe was

on the eve of a second Crimean War. Peace was
fortunately preserved by Bismarck calling the interested
powers to Berlin, where the Treaty of Berlin (1878)
was signed providing for Rumania, Montenegro and
Serbia becoming sovereign states, and Bosnia and
Herzegovina, though nominally remaining under
Turkish rule, coming under the administration of
Austria.

Bulgaria retained her independence, but was
reduced in size by the creation of a new state, called
Roumelia, which was situated just west of Constantinople and placed under Turkish rule, to become again
united to Bulgaria in 1885. Britain obtained Cyprus
from Turkey as her reward for having supported
Turkey in the negotiations, and Russia was given
Bessarabia, a province which sixty-two years later was
to be the cause of war between Rumania and Russia.

Russia was bitterly disappointed with the outcome
of the Treaty of Berlin, and felt that Germany, Austria
and Britain had secured a diplomatic victory at her
expense. Consequently her attitude towards Germany
underwent a marked change, as Bismarck, she felt, had
been the moving spirit in bringing about her humiliation. Roman Catholic Austria now felt that she
and Orthodox Russia were definite rivals in the
Balkans, and because of this she aligned herself with
Germany.

France meantime was making aggressive conquests
in North Africa, Tunis having just been occupied,
and Italy, feeling all alone, with none to turn to for
help in time of trouble, saw no other way for self-
protection than to become again tied up with her
former enemies north of the Alps. So that was how

the Triple Alliance came to be formed, consisting of Germany, Austria and Italy, a combination which created a solid block in Central Europe against Russia in the east and France in the west.

France now felt herself isolated and in peril from this powerful Central European combination, and, just as Italy felt compelled to join with people with whom she had no interests or sympathy, so France was forced into an alliance with Russia, whose form of government and culture was quite different from her own. All that they had in common was their hostility towards Germany, the hatred of the French being sustained by the loss of Alsace and Lorraine following the 1870 war.

Britain, disturbed by the unfriendly attitude of Germany during the Boer War, and her increasing navy, now in turn felt isolated, and, though there was no real friendship with France, her loneliness forced her into concluding the *Entente Cordiale* of 1903, a treaty which placed her on the side of France and Russia. Thus two political blocks were formed in Europe, a development which had its origin in the two opposing racial and religious factions in the Balkans.

Many hoped that with Europe now paired off into two groups of much the same strength, peace would prevail, and this desire was strengthened by the fact that Western Europe had maintained peace since 1871, a longer period than ever before since the 2nd century. The love of peace was growing, just as the hatred of war, and the realisation of its futility, were increasing. Education was, for the first time, lifting aside, to some slight degree, the curse of ignorance, and if it had been permitted everywhere to continue its righteous mission, on right lines, what a difference it would have made to millions who were to suffer grievously over the next two generations. Germany alone thought and spoke of war, its glories and its triumphs, and her leaders poisoned the minds of their people by promises of rich plunder at small cost.

An attempt was made by the Tzar in 1898 to counteract the gathering storm, as in that year he invited all the great European powers to meet at the Hague to discuss a plan for general disarmament. His intentions were noble and sincere, but no agreement was reached, though an international tribunal was established at the Hague for the settlement by arbitration of international disputes brought before it. Again, in 1907, a conference met there, but nothing was arranged, and so Europe settled down to wait and see whether Germany would continue her warlike preparations, or become a good and peaceful neighbour.

The disastrous defeat of Russia in her war with Japan (1905) increased Germany's defiance of the existing order in Europe, Count Schlieffen, the German Chief of Staff, bluntly declaring that now the time had come to attack France. Similar bellicose remarks, made by other responsible Germans, had the effect of drawing France and Britain more closely together, when the opportunity was taken to prepare military plans to meet the threatened conflict. Consequently a race began in naval construction, Britain's aim being to maintain a two-power standard, because only by so doing could she feel safe, as on her navy she depended for her existence.

The defeat of Russia by Japan removed any fear

Germany may have had of the safety of her eastern frontier. So the German Emperor set out on his magnificent triumphal march through the Holy Land, passing on to Tangier, where he assured the Sultan of Morocco that he could count on German help against French aggression. Next he interfered in French politics by forcing, under threat of war, the dismissal of Delcassé, her Foreign Minister, who was planning the French occupation of Morocco. Then he encouraged Austria in 1908 to annex Bosnia and Herzegovina after a revolution in Constantinople had deposed the Sultan.

This aggressive move by Austria angered not only Russia but also Italy, who had no wish to see Austria becoming the predominant power in the Balkans. France, however, secured a protectorate over Morocco, though Germany sent a warship to Agadir, on the Moroccan coast, as a protest, an incident which caused immediate reactions in Paris, London and Rome. Britain warned Germany that her action might provoke war, and Italy, fearing that all the North African coast would be snapped up before her eyes, declared war on Turkey (1911) and occupied Tripoli and Libya, as we read a few pages farther back.

Germany greatly resented her failure to prevent Morocco coming under French influence, but other events followed which further threatened the peace of Europe. A secret Balkan League was formed by Serbia, Montenegro, Bulgaria and Greece which had for its object the driving of Turkey out of Europe. This was the preliminary of the Balkan-Turkish War of 1912, which ended in Turkey being completely defeated, and the Bulgarians capturing Adrianople, the city which guards Constantinople. The peace terms did not, however, satisfy Bulgaria, who thought that, as she had done most of the fighting, she should have a larger share of the plunder, including the port of Salonika.

A new war now (1913) started between Bulgaria and her former allies, in which she was heavily defeated. The Turks reoccupied Adrianople, and the struggle became a massacre, producing horrors which rank amongst the worst in history, to end in Bulgaria suing for peace. When 1914 opened Bulgaria had gained access to the sea, but had lost much of the territory which was once within her grasp. Serbia had enlarged her boundaries, but was dissatisfied because millions of her race in Bosnia and Herzegovina were under Austrian domination, and she wanted them within her domains. Greece gained increased territory, including Crete and Salonika, and, if Serbia had not had ambitions which conflicted with Austrian policy, the Balkans might now have settled down to a period of peaceful progress.

Serbia, unable to get her desires, now wanted to have Albania so as to obtain access to the sea, but Austria, who feared this growing warlike power, now the centre of Slavonic nationalism throughout her empire and the Balkans, would not agree, and Albania was made into a separate kingdom. Then, in June 1914, the bad feeling between the two countries became acute when the Archduke Francis Ferdinand, the heir to the throne of Austria-Hungary, was assassinated at Serajevo, the capital of Bosnia.

The Austrians accused the Serbian government of complicity in the crime, and sent it a drastic ultimatum to be accepted within forty-eight hours. Serbia accepted all but two of the Austrian demands, and asked that these should be submitted to arbitration. Austria, knowing that she had Germany behind her, refused and declared war in July 1914. This was the spark which produced a conflagration that spread to more than three quarters of the land surface of the earth.

(5) GERMANY INVOLVES THE WORLD IN WAR.

It is now well known that Austria's attitude towards Serbia was approved, if not instigated, by Germany, who, of all the countries in Europe, was prepared for war. Germany knew that France would stand ·by Russia, and that Russia would side with Serbia, as the Serbs, like the Russians, are Orthodox Christians and Slavs. Race, however, counts as much as religion in determining thoughts and actions in times of crisis, and these two well-tested bonds again proved to be irresistible.

If the murder of the Archduke had not occurred, some other reason would have been found sooner or later, because Germany, then the richest and most powerful nation in Europe, had all her plans prepared for a swift and heavy blow at France in the west. When France was knocked out she intended to turn with all her remaining strength and smash Russia in the east. So, when Russia supported Serbia, and mobilised her army, Germany declared war on her three days after the Austrian declaration to Serbia, and then followed this up two days later with a declaration of war on France.

The peace-loving British Foreign Secretary, Sir Edward Grey, did his utmost to confine the war to the Balkans, but all his efforts were in vain, as Germany, whose mouthpiece was the blustering irresponsible William II, was fully prepared and determined to strike quickly and heavily, first at France and then at Russia.

On 4th August, 1914, German troops invaded Belgium, thus taking the easiest way into France, though this meant her breaking the 1839 treaty which Prussia had made with Belgium to respect her neutrality. On the same day as this happened Britain declared war on Germany, because she considered that the neutrality of the Netherlands was vital to her safety. This was followed by similar declarations by the dominions of the British Empire. What a cost in lives and wealth these low countries have been to Britain, who, since the beginning of the 18th century, has feared their occupation by a power intent on dominating Europe.

Britain lives by having command of the sea. Whenever she loses that she can be starved into surrender by the power which does command the sea. Her policy, since she became industrialized, and dependent on foreign imports of food, has been to prevent any one European nation from securing sufficient ports to enable it to outbuild her in war vessels. Either France, Germany, Russia, or any other country dominating Europe, would create this danger. Consequently it was in Britain's interest to keep Belgium neutral, because that was the principal highway between France and Germany, and the main road from the east to the Channel ports.

Britain did not want Germany, intent as she was

on conquering Europe, any closer than Bremen and Hamburg, or in possession of the Dutch, Belgian and French dockyards. That was why Britain joined in this struggle, so as to protect her sea power and her coasts from invasion.

It may well be asked why, if this be so, Britain did not participate with France in the Franco-Prussian War, one of the few major wars on the Continent in which she has not taken part, but the position then was far different from what it was in 1914. Then Germany was not a united nation, and had no thought of dominating Europe. She had no sea power, and was planning no great navy. The quarrel between France and Prussia did not endanger Britain, and so she left them to fight it out alone, after vigorously warning both sides that Belgian neutrality must be observed.

The Belgians, when attacked in 1914, fiercely, and for a time successfully, resisted the German invasion, a check which surprised the invaders and gave the allies time to concentrate their forces. French troops moved into Belgium, to be joined by a British expeditionary force of 90,000 men under Sir John French. Nevertheless, the Germans were greatly superior in numbers, with everything ready for the fray, and, after a month of delaying actions at Charleroi, Mons, Le Cateau, and elsewhere, the allies found themselves forced back to within only twenty-five miles of Paris, from which the government had moved to Bordeaux.

Nevertheless, in spite of the long and arduous retreat, the allied forces were intact, under complete control, and, when they reached the River Marne, they turned against the enemy and drove him back as far as the River Aisne. The excellent timing of this master counter-stroke was the work of General Joffre, the imperturbable French Commander-in-Chief, who thus saved Paris, completely upset the German plan of campaign to crush France at a blow, and made possible Germany's ultimate defeat.

The Battle of the Marne (1914) was one of the great decisive battles of history, because it produced a war of position, in place of one of movement, and so gave the allies time to mobilise their vast resources and secure victory. Following their defeat, the Germans unsuccessfully tried to outflank the allies by working round from the north, the effect being that as each new attempt was made it reached farther and farther north, to be stopped finally by the sea.

With Paris thus barred to them a desperate attempt was next made by the invaders to reach the Channel ports, and cut off the help coming from Britain. At the Battle of Ypres, in October and November 1914, and again in April 1915, when the Germans first used poison gas, they were held, the Channel ports were saved, and Germany had to be content with Zeebrugge and Ostend.

When 1914 ended, the two sides were facing each other on a twisting line, extending from Ostend in the north through Arras, Soissons, Rheims, Verdun and Nancy to the Swiss frontier. Trenches were dug, and all manner of fortifications erected by each side to prevent a break-through. Thus began a long conflict, with each side intent on piercing the other's defences, so as to get at the rear of the enemy and behind his ramparts.

Many and bloody were the battles fought, and terrible was the suffering endured, with this end in view, over the next four years, each side straining to the utmost to secure sufficient local superiority to achieve its object, while the factories on both sides were ever extending to produce more, and still more, guns and shells to break down resistance.

Fortunately for the French and British, the Germans could not bring their entire weight of men and material to bear on the western front, because the Russians had so far met with little resistance and were devastating East Prussia. This thrust from the east probably saved Paris and the allies in the west, as the Germans, confident that they had the capital within their grasp, detached some divisions before a decision in France was reached, and hurried them to the east, where they, under Marshal Hindenburg, inflicted at Tannenberg (1914) a disastrous defeat on the invaders.

Russia thus saved her western allies from defeat, but at a terrible cost to herself. Still, she was able to strike deep into Galicia and capture Lemberg and Przemysl (1915), besides over 100,000 Austrian prisoners, but this was only a temporary triumph, as a few months later the Germans, under Mackensen, drove her out and occupied Poland, Lithuania and Courland.

Austria was making no headway with her war against Serbia. Twice she was defeated, and Germany had to weaken her main front in the west to support her ally, while in Britain, Lord Kitchener, on whom the nation cast its cares and anxieties, was busy enlarging the British army, into which hundreds of thousands of volunteers were enlisting. It was a fight for time, as Germany and Austria still greatly outnumbered the fighting forces so far mobilised by the allies.

Kitchener soon realised that, at the best, the allies could only hold up the enemy until he was slowly worn down, when the French, Russians and British, with sufficient trained men, could then eventually overwhelm him. Consequently, in spite of the Russian defeat at Tannenberg, the allies met the year 1915 with greater confidence, now that the enemy in the west was pinned down to trench warfare, but they were to suffer many reverses, defeats and disappointments before the tide began to turn.

Italy, so far, had remained neutral, but the entry of Turkey into the war (October 1914), on the side of Germany, still further increased the balance against the allied powers. This meant the dispersal of the allied effort, which they ardently desired to concentrate in France, where the war would be either won or lost. Nevertheless, in spite of this unfavourable development, it was now clear that Germany's plans for a quick war had failed, and this being so new ones had to be adopted which 1915 saw put into effect.

The Germans now decided that, as an immediate decision could not be obtained in the west, they would hold what they had won there, and swing all their available men over to the east and crush Russia finally and completely. Then, with the eastern danger removed, they would throw everything they had on to the west to secure, if possible, a decisive victory. The allies, for their part, never lost sight of the fact that it was vital to maintain their line intact in the west, but they nevertheless decided on a bold attempt against

Turkey, their object being to force the Dardanelles. With this accomplished the Turkish danger would be reduced, the Balkans perhaps brought in on the side of the allies, and help could be sent to Russia now in great need of increased supplies.

The plan was good but its execution was bad. The Turks discovered what was intended, and the British fleet ran into an unsuspected mine-field which it could not penetrate. This gave the Turks time to strongly fortify and make impregnable their positions overlooking the Dardanelles, which defences could have been easily taken by a surprise attack had troops accompanied the fleet.

So it came about that when an allied army, mostly composed of British, Australian and New Zealand troops, landed at Gallipoli a month later, in April 1915, it was met by a withering fire, and only held the positions secured with difficulty and at great cost. When it was discovered that no headway could be made, and that to hold on meant further heavy losses, the expedition, which had endured much suffering, 120,000 casualties, and had fought with great determination and courage, was withdrawn at the end of 1915.

Though unsuccessful, this abortive effort had been the means of keeping Russia in the war by the promise that, if successful, she would receive Constantinople, and, moreover, it had pinned down the Turkish army during a critical phase of the war. These two factors should be remembered on the credit side when considering the Gallipoli balance sheet, as then was the time when attempt after attempt was being made by the Germans to break down the allied defences in

France. Both sides, in fact, were doing their utmost to overcome the elaborate fortification system each had erected, and, though some ground was gained here and there, nothing decisive was achieved.

At Neuve-Chapelle, Festubert and Loos the British lost heavily in these endeavours, being baffled by not having a sufficient weight of shells to blow the enemy out of his strongly fortified positions. At the end of 1915 Sir Douglas Haig replaced Sir John French as Commander-in-Chief, and David Lloyd George became Minister of Munitions for the purpose of producing enough shells to blast a way through the enemy lines. Next year, on the resignation of Asquith, Lloyd George became Prime Minister of a coalition government (1916-1918) which was to see the allies through to victory.

Lloyd George was a man of remarkable administrative and constructive ability, being also endowed with untiring energy. He proved himself to be a courageous and resourceful war leader, his zeal for complete victory being as great as that for social reform. His life was one long continuous conflict against vested interests and reaction, his pity and compassion for the poor and needy urging him forward in his various schemes, including Health Insurance and Old Age Pensions, designed to improve the social betterment and security of the people. His powerful fiery oratory, at times unnecessarily provocative, embroiled him in constant conflict with his antagonists and made him the greatest political force of his time. He goes down to history as the most gifted and renowned of all the sons of Wales over the past four centuries, while the seed he planted will grow and multiply to the lasting good of not only the present generation but of all who come after us.

During the year 1915 the Germans again pushed the Russians out of Galicia, this time to a line stretching from Riga to the north of the Rumanian frontier. Being badly organised, and lacking both equipment and munitions, the Russians, who had sustained enormous losses, remained on the defensive, an attitude which enabled the Germans and Austrians, now joined by the Bulgarians, to inflict a decisive defeat on Serbia. By this attack from the north and east the Serbian army was completely routed, the country was overrun by the enemy, and the plight of the population was pitiful. Though Britain, France and Russia thus lost an ally, they gained one when Italy, tempted by the promise of the Trentino and Trieste, entered the war on their side in May 1915, and formed a new front on the Austrian-Italian border.

From the day Britain entered the war a blockade of Germany was maintained, and on the high seas both sides destroyed by mines and surface raiders all the shipping within reach. Several enemy cruisers, especially the *Emden,* did much damage to allied shipping before they were eventually rounded up and destroyed. Meanwhile the main battle fleets kept their stations, the British navy ready to attack should the enemy fleet of half its strength venture into the North Sea, but it could not prevent the enemy from sending out raiding cruisers, which bombarded some British east coast towns, and then hurriedly returned home.

Minor naval engagements were fought up to the end of 1915, the British scoring three victories, one off the Falkland Islands, another in the Bight of

Heligoland, and the third near the Dogger Bank, the Germans gaining a victory off Coronel in Chile. The same year the Germans started submarine warfare, sinking all allied ships at sight, and this increased in intensity to include every ship, enemy and neutral.

The only engagement in which the Grand Fleets took part was in 1916 when they met off Jutland. The battle commenced with an action between British cruisers, under Admiral Beatty, and a German squadron, this being followed by another when British battleships, under Admiral Jellicoe, made contact with the enemy's heavy ships. A general action ensued, lasting twenty minutes, in which the British lost twice the tonnage and personnel as the enemy, but, before accounts could be squared, the Germans bolted and reached home in the fading light. Never again did the German ships risk another encounter, and consequently they remained bottled up in port until, by the terms of the Armistice, they were delivered over to the British at Scapa Flow, where they were treacherously scuttled by their crews.

When 1916 opened, the two foes were still facing each other in Europe, in much the same positions as they had occupied during the previous year. Soldiers lived like rabbits, in dug-outs, well below the surface, and defended trenches often deep in mud. They suffered incredible discomfort from both mud and water, and, when not trying to rush the enemy trench opposite them, their time was occupied in throwing grenades and sniping at any one of the enemy who unwittingly exposed himself. Thus both sides lived lives little better than is experienced by foxes, badgers and rabbits, so as to be better protected from high explosives and bullets. Invention had driven warriors underground until a new weapon was invented by the British, the tank, which was first used by them, rather ineffectively, at the long-drawn-out Battle of the Somme.

Farther south the Germans, in the first six months of 1916, attempted to capture the powerful fortress of Verdun so as to turn the right flank of the French army, their losses in dead alone being 350,000 men. This tremendous effort was extremely costly for both sides, but the Germans failed to achieve their object. Likewise the British failed to break through on the River Somme, a battle which was a veritable carnage, the total casualties on both sides exceeding 1,000,000, the British share being 400,000.

By now it had become clearly evident, in consequence of the heavy losses on both sides, that victory would ultimately rest with the side which had the largest reserve of men. The conflict had become a war of attrition. So conscription was introduced in Britain (1916), and both sides combed out their men up to middle age, to train them for the slaughter.

During 1916 Russia reorganized her armies, and secured large supplies of arms from her allies by way of Archangel. In consequence, she, under the direction of General Brussilof, the ablest of all her generals, achieved some striking successes against Austria, conquering the entire Bukovina, and taking 400,000 prisoners besides much booty. Because of this, Rumania decided to throw in her lot with the allies, but she experienced results far different from those expected. In a short but well conceived campaign the Germanic powers utterly crushed

Rumania, and entered her capital, Bucharest, in the last month of 1916. Henceforward her wealth in oil and corn was at their disposal, though the surface workings of her oil wells had been destroyed.

When Italy became a combatant she attacked Austria, fighting taking place at times at great heights in the mountains amidst the perpetual snow. Nothing decisive was reached, but, by the end of 1916, the advantage lay with Italy. The Austrians, who had pushed down through the Trentino, were driven back, and farther east they had lost Gorizia. Italy, so far, had kept occupied a part of the German and Austrian forces, which valuable help relieved the strain on the west, and so gave Britain time to train and equip her millions of conscripts who were now flowing into the ranks.

Besides maintaining an ever-increasing army in France, Britain had troops in the East to protect India and Egypt from the well-equipped Turkish army, now under German direction, and it was there in Mesopotamia that she suffered a disaster in 1916, when 10,000 men were forced to surrender at Kut-el-Amara. The following year it was retaken, and the British pressed on and captured Baghdad.

Then came the revolt of the Arabs against the Turks, a cleverly conceived affair which was organised by Colonel T. E. Lawrence, and this greatly helped in their ultimate defeat. Next followed the Palestine campaign, under the command of General Allenby, when Jerusalem was captured (1917), and the British pushed on to Damascus. Thus the whirligig of time had brought about startling changes, because Damascus, Baghdad, and the ruins of Babylon and Nineveh, famous as centres of early civilisation, fell one by one into the hands of a people whose ancestors were unknown half-naked barbarians at the time when these cities were at the height of their glory.

Early in 1917 the Germans on the Somme retreated to a strong line of defence which they had been building in their rear, to become known as the Hindenburg Line, but nothing spectacular occurred until the winter was over. Then in April the French, under General Nivelle, who had succeeded Joffre as the French commander, made a carefully prepared heavy attack on the River Aisne, only to be repulsed with such grievous loss that for a time their morale was broken, and there was widespread insubordination.

The British were now left to carry on the offensive alone for the remainder of the year, attacking at Messines, and again at Ypres, in an effort to recover the Belgian ports which were being used by the enemy as submarine bases. This was the third great battle before the once beautiful medieval city of Ypres, now a heap of ruins, and it came to be known as the Battle of Paschendaele, one of the most terrible of all the conflicts in what had been up till then the bloodiest and fiercest of all wars. Here the British suffered 300,000 casualties and gained nothing strategically.

As the year 1917 advanced it became clear that al was not well with Russia. Lord Kitchener had attempted to reach her in the previous year, but was drowned not long after he started, the warship on which he was travelling sinking by striking a mine or by an enemy torpedo. Whether his presence in Russia would have made any difference no one can say, but in March 1917 came the revolution, when the estimable but weak, priest-ridden Tzar, Nicholas II, abdicated, and was removed to Siberia. Somewhere, sometime later, he, his wife and his family met a tragic end.

The sufferings of the Russian people during the war had been terrible, and their losses in battle were very heavy. If the people had had confidence in, and respect for, their rulers all this might have been borne, but, for years, there had been revolt against injustice and tyranny, and the sufferings of the war gave opportunities for the extremists to influence the people as never before. This was a revolution caused by misery, hunger and war weariness, and it came at a time when feelings and resentment against the old order ran high.

Four million casualties, the belief that corruption in high places was rife, and the strong suspicion that the foolish and superstitious Tzarina, under the influence of a profligate priest, Rasputin, was working for the enemy, embittered the people against their rulers. Finally the reactionary and oppressive methods of Protopopoff, the Minister of State, brought matters to a head. A riot occurred in Petrograd (now Leningrad) in March 1917, to be followed by strikes and mutinies in the army. The movement, led by the extremists, spread rapidly everywhere, and the moderate reformers were regarded with no greater favour than the old gang of reactionaries.

A committee of the Duma, led by Prince Lvov, did their best to govern the country and conduct the war, but nothing could prevail against the fiery eloquence of those who advocated Soviets, or workmen's and soldier's councils, being set up. Their plan was food for all, immediate peace, the land for the people, and a dictatorship of the proletariat. Kerensky formed a provisional government and led the more moderate section. He endeavoured to reorganise and revitalise the army, and also the people, over whom had settled a pall of inertia. All they now wanted was peace, no annexations and no indemnities, but, as Kerensky was not strong enough to retain control of affairs, he was driven out of office. Then the extremists, in November 1917, entered the Winter Palace at Moscow and took over the reins of government, which they based on Communist principles.

The organisers of the revolution were two humble exiles who had recently returned to Russia, Ulianoff, who took the name of Lenin, and a Jew, Braunstein, who adopted the name of Trotsky. Two more audacious and resolute men never before secured control over such a vast multitude, but, before their exile, they had laid the foundation on which they now set to work to build up a new Communistic Society.[1]

Within three months Russia had made peace with Germany and Austria, the Duma, which, prior to their accession to power, had been preparing a parliamentary constitution, was abolished, and all wealth and lands

---

[1] At the Russian Social Democratic Party Congress held in 1903, opinion on the most essential questions concerning the structure of the party, and on various important political questions, was divided, which led to a majority and a minority. The majority was led by Lenin, and the minority by Plekhanov. This cleavage of opinion developed in subsequent years into an open split, and eventually to the formation of two parties. The word for "majority" in Russian is "bolshinstvo" and for "minority" is "menshinstvo". The adherents of the majority of 1903 called themselves "Bolsheviki" and those of the minority "Mensheviki". Consequently, in later years, the party led by Lenin was known in common usage as the Party of the "Bolsheviks", and its members also used the same term. The members of the minority, and the party which they formed, called themselves "Mensheviks".

were confiscated from the rich and middle classes. In March 1918 the Treaty of Brest-Litovsk imposed on Russia the payment to Germany of a large indemnity, and the abandonment of Finland, Russian Poland, Estonia, Lithuania, Livonia and Courland, now called Latvia. That was the price the people of Russia paid, to receive in exchange the rule of the Soviets, but the story of this interesting experiment will be told in the next chapter.

This blow to the allied cause was softened by new allies joining their ranks. After hesitating for long, Greece, the United States, and then most of the republics of South America, declared war in 1917 on the Germanic powers, but the allies faced a dangerous year until reinforcements arrived from across the Atlantic. The Germans were now able to concentrate their forces against Italy and France, and Italy was the first to feel the effect of the Russian collapse.

At Caporetto (1917) she was decisively defeated, losing in prisoners alone 250,000 men, and then the enemy overran the plains of northern Italy. With the help of reinforcements sent by Britain and France this advance was halted on the River Piave, and now came the turn of the allied troops in France to parry the fierce thrusts of a still powerful but desperate enemy. Under the direction of Hindenburg and Ludendorff extensive preparations to break through were completed, the aim being to secure a decisive victory before the American reinforcements had time to arrive.

Their first attack began in March 1918 at St. Quentin against the British, who were forced back, and unable to rally for five days after the terrific onslaught. The German aim was to reach Amiens, and cut the railway running from the Channel ports to Paris, but, in spite of their initial success, they failed to achieve their object. Marshal Foch now became Commander-in-Chief of all the allied forces, so as to co-ordinate better both the defence and attack, because it was now realised that unity of command was essential if the allies were to achieve victory.

In April the Germans delivered with success a second blow in Flanders, but again they failed to reach their objective, the Channel ports. This was followed in May by a third attack on the French along the River Aisne, in the neighbourhood of Rheims, when the French were taken completely by surprise and swept back to the Marne, to within only forty miles of Paris, but Rheims still stood firm and unshaken. Later, in July, the Germans crossed the Marne and attempted to reach Paris, but this time without achieving any success. Their three previous desperate attacks had so weakened them that from now onwards the initiative passed to the allies, who were receiving a regular supply of American reinforcements which were taking over sections of the line from the hard-pressed and weary troops.

In July the allied counter-offensive opened and this forced the Germans back from the Marne, after which an attack by the British drove them from their positions near Amiens. Allied tanks now became prominent in a succession of important engagements which were continued all along the line, and these were so successful that by September the Hindenburg Line was broken by British troops. This was a great victory, but it was secured at a terrible sacrifice of life. Nevertheless it brought the end in sight, as

Ludendorff, now realising that a German victory was impossible, resigned his command. In October, Austria, with all her subject races in revolt, was decisively defeated by Italy at Vittorio Veneto. Bulgaria, without German support, collapsed to an allied attack from Salonika, and Turkey was decisively defeated in Palestine. This remarkable series of successes brought their reward as first Bulgaria, and next Turkey and then Austria sued for peace.

By November 1918 all Germany's allies had surrendered, the German army was in disorganised flight across the Rhine, and her sailors, instead of obeying an order to attack the British fleet, mutinied. Revolution broke out in Berlin, and the Kaiser, William II, after a period of intense mental strain and indecision, decided to abdicate and find refuge in Holland, a flight which his people never forgave. The kings and princes of all the different German states likewise abdicated. All resistance now came to an end, and the German army surrendered unconditionally when an armistice was signed on 11th November, 1918.

In this way terminated the most devastating war mankind had ever experienced, its four years of destruction and slaughter leaving Europe shattered and bleeding. The only important European countries which escaped being drawn into the vortex were Holland, Denmark, Norway, Sweden, Switzerland and Spain, and those who remained neutral outside of Europe were hardly more numerous. Fighting also occurred in Africa, where the allies attacked and captured the German colonies, and Japan took the German possessions in China without difficulty.

Though Britain was never invaded, damage and loss of life occurred from bombs dropped by airships and airplanes. Civilians were also drowned at sea, the greatest single disaster being when the *Lusitania* was sunk by a torpedo from an enemy submarine, 1200 passengers being drowned. The United States vigorously protested, as amongst these were about 100 of her citizens, but it was not until Germany commenced unrestricted submarine warfare, when she sank ships of every nationality, that the United States entered the war as a combatant.

On the success of the submarine campaign Germany placed her highest hopes of victory after her failure to secure a decision on land, and, if it had continued as successfully as it began, Britain, sooner or later, would have been starved into surrender. It reached its height in April 1917, and, if the loss of tonnage experienced that month had continued, the end of the year would have found Britain in great straits. Fortunately for the allied cause, counter-measures were instituted, the convoying of merchant ships by destroyers being found to be the most efficacious. By the end of 1917 the danger had been largely overcome, and Germany's hope of starving Britain into surrender had gone.

The devastation caused by this war was due to it being mostly fought by machines. Science allied itself with destruction, and the men in the workshops and laboratories were as much involved as the soldiers. Previous wars had been fought by cannon and musket, but, in this one, invention had perfected machines for killing and destruction to such a degree that the loss of life and material damage were on a far greater scale. The submarine did enormous destruction to shipping; the airplane dropped bombs far distant from the scene of actual fighting; the destructiveness of the high explosives used in bombs and shells shattered everything within a wide area; the tank, which came into increasing use, battered down all on its path, and the machine-gun, with its devastating fire, mowed men down as a scythe does standing corn.

Vast areas, where the fighting occurred, were devastated and left desolate, towns and villages becoming only heaps of rubble, and vegetation everywhere was non-existent. Fifty million men were engaged in this tremendous struggle, and the loss of life and the number of wounded was appalling. Owing to the unnatural conditions under which the soldiers had to live, the deaths and suffering from disease were very heavy. The British Empire lost nearly 1,000,000 men killed, 2,000,000 being wounded. On this basis the total casualties, not counting the deaths by disease, must have approached 8,000,000 killed and 16,000,000 wounded, a gigantic price for innocent men to pay in satisfaction of the murder of an Austrian Archduke.

Besides all these victims it is estimated by competent authorities that 17,000,000 civilians perished by disease, starvation and malnutrition. No words can describe the misery and suffering the war occasioned. Marriage became impossible to millions of women, while millions more became widows and their children orphans. Many men lost their sight for life, others their reason, while a multitude had their lungs destroyed by poison gas, and others degenerated into nervous wrecks. Many of the wounded dragged out a miserable existence until relieved by death.

All this long-drawn-out agony, which affected millions who were entitled to a life of happiness, came about primarily from the aggressive policy adopted by the divinely guided William II, to whom "The Lord is a man of war" (*Exodus* xv, 3.) Yet this monstrous criminal was allowed to retire to Holland and spend the remaining twenty-three years of his life in comfort and luxury, occupying himself chopping down trees on his estate, and, like Napoleon, writing his memoirs, to impress the world with the idea that he was innocent of all his crimes.

If a man murders another he is convicted as a criminal and hanged, but one who is responsible for the murder and disablement of millions in war is not legally considered a criminal, there being no law against such a person, and there cannot be until international law makes war a crime, and backs this up by international force. If the All Highest War Lord had been imprisoned for life, and treated as a criminal, which is the fate he deserved and should have had, it would have acted as a deterrent to other would-be world conquerors, and Hitler might not have repeated another similar crime against mankind.

Ignorant and stupid humanity has suffered terribly down the ages from the lack of knowledge and wisdom, and the First World War is only another and a tragic reminder of how essential it is to bring the people together economically and nationally, as human beings, under an All-humanity Federation, having one international law for all. This is essential to world peace and prosperity. Each national group would have home rule and its own laws as at present, but all would be bound together by international law, supported by a single world police force, to maintain its observance. This must some day take the place of nationalism and all the evils which follow in its train.

If our present suffering does not bring this about, war will recur time and time again until ethical knowledge and wisdom take the place of ignorance. Only then, when this knowledge is put into daily practice, will the human race have learned the right way to live, its protection against the evil-doer being a universally accepted ethical code, backed by the necessary force which would be strong enough to enforce the will of the majority of peace-loving people. Only thus will mankind be able to realize the true purpose of life, as set out in the introduction to this chapter.

If only the opinions expressed by the Greek philosophers and moralists had prevailed, and education had continued to develop during the Christian era instead of being banned, if only the philosophers and educationalists of Greece and Rome had been allowed to teach instead of being liquidated or exiled, what a high standard of thought and life we would now have reached! Instead of this happening Europe and the Middle East were perverted by the opinions of an assembly of ignorant, superstitious Christian priests who met at Nicaea in 325. Their decisions spread a black curtain of intolerance and ignorance over what became Christendom, so much so that only now, in our own day and generation, have our minds developed sufficiently to stimulate the aspirations of all good men and women for international peace. Only now have we reached a point when something is being attempted to bring law and order to an age-long distracted world.

Peace negotiations commenced in Paris in January 1919, delegates from thirty-two different nations being present. Georges Clemenceau, whose energy and strength of character kept France from collapsing during her darkest days, represented France and was chosen to preside over the deliberations. President Woodrow Wilson represented the United States, Orlando represented Italy, and Lloyd George Great Britain.

The French were particularly bitter against their defeated enemy, who, after humiliating them in 1871, had now ravished their land without cause or reason. Much of North-eastern France was devastated, the French casualties had been very severe, and it was natural that the terms they insisted upon were drastic, principally for the purpose of ensuring that such a blow would not be struck at them again.

President Wilson, an idealist, worked for moderation, based on a settlement which contained fourteen clauses, of which the following is a summary.

Open diplomacy and no secret treaties in the future.

Freedom of the seas.

The removal of economic barriers.

The settlement of colonial claims, with consideration for the interests of European powers and native races.

The reduction of armaments.

The evacuation of all territory overrun by the invaders.

Alsace and Lorraine to be returned to France.

The establishment of an independent Poland.

The readjustment of boundaries according to nationality,

Austria and Turkey to give autonomy to races within their domains.

The setting up of a League of Nations, at which all nations would be represented, to guarantee boundaries and to settle all future disputes amicably without recourse to war.

This, however, was not the time for moderation and balanced wisdom, because the wounds were too deep, and they still hurt intensely. Paris, moreover, after experiencing the shadow of the German army for four years, was too close to the devastation for other than hard and bitter facts to be considered. Germany's guilt was too flagrant to be lightly forgiven. She had devastated much of Europe without the slightest justification, and only by her own miscalculations, and the unbounded efforts of her victims, had she been thrown back, defeated in her object of dominating Europe. If Germany were pardoned too easily, it was argued, she would prepare again, even more thoroughly, and make sure that the next time her evil designs were accomplished. Considering the enormity of her crime, the peace terms she was eventually forced to accept were relatively light, especially when we remember how she had treated France in 1871, and Russia as recently as 1918 at Brest-Litovsk.

Each of the allies had some objection to make to one or other of President Wilson's fourteen clauses. In the end it was decided that Germany must return to France the provinces of Alsace and Lorraine, and adjust her boundaries in favour of Belgium, Denmark and Poland. East Prussia was cut off from the rest of Germany by a strip of land, to become known as the Polish Corridor, which gave the new Poland access to the sea. Germany surrendered her colonies, which were divided between Britain, France, Japan and the Union of South Africa, under a mandate from the League of Nations. The Saar, with its rich coal-fields, was given to France for fifteen years in recompense for the damage which had been done to the northern French coal-fields. Germany handed over most of her merchant ships to replace some of those she had destroyed, and delivered to France supplies of coal, cattle, etc., to make up for what she had stolen.

Unfortunately the French were not given the permanent bridgeheads on the Rhine which Foch and Clemenceau so earnestly desired, because Lloyd George and Wilson feared that this would lead to another war for their recovery by Germany. This disastrous mistake made possible the Second World War, as France was again left exposed to attack, and bad feeling was created between her and her former allies.

Germany had to pay a heavy indemnity to France and Belgium, but this was considerably reduced when she pleaded inability to do so. She surrendered her fleet of warships, and agreed to have no air force, to limit her navy, and reduce her army to 100,000 men, who were not to be conscripted. A zone, thirty-two miles east of the Rhine, was not to be fortified, she was not to unite with Austria, and finally she was forced to admit that she was responsible for the war. To ensure that these terms were kept, the Rhineland was to be occupied by the allies for fifteen years.

The old Austrian Empire was divided into separate states, namely Austria, Hungary, Yugo-Slavia (including Serbia and Montenegro) and Czecho-Slovakia, better known up to then as Bohemia and Moravia. The latter obtained Slovakia from Hungary, who had also to give up Transylvania to Rumania and Croatia to Yugo-Slavia. Greece enlarged her frontiers, and Turkey, once master of the Balkans, was nearly pushed out of Europe, losing Syria, which went as a mandate to France, while Palestine, Transjordan and Iraq were mandated to Britain. Italy, much to her annoyance, received only the Trentino, Trieste and Zara, but she helped herself to Fiume, the Hungarian port at the head of the Adriatic.

A howl of indignation went up in Germany at such severe impositions, but, except for her colonies, she only lost in land what she had previously stolen from her neighbours. The indemnity payments were only partially met, but she more than balanced what she did pay by borrowing £2,000,000,000[1] from America and Britain for reconstruction purposes and never repaying it. The coal, etc., which she sent to France only made up for what she had destroyed and stolen.

The ships which she handed over replaced only to a small degree those she had sunk. Otherwise the terms were not vindictive, and were imposed principally for the purpose of preventing a recurrence of her crime. When, however, the fifteen years of occupation elapsed (1934) Germany broke the treaty, and set to work to build up again her army and air force. Within the next five years she worked to such effect that she produced a military machine which in 1939 again

[1] This figure was given to Parliament by Winston Churchill on 3rd October, 1944.

struck at Europe without the least justification, and in the same ruthless fashion.

The First World War was fought by the allies to maintain the balance of power in Europe, a policy which came into being at the beginning of the 16th century when nationalism began to develop. The last four centuries record a long series of conflicts caused by one state after another attempting to dominate the Continent. First Spain, then Austria, France, Prussia, and now Germany, have in turn assumed the role of master of Europe. The weaker states have always combined against this absolutism, to break it in the end after long and bitter struggles.

The Austrian-Spanish combination struggled for more than a century to maintain its mastery. France, in the time of Louis XIV, maintained it for only forty years, and Napoleon for eighteen years. Prussia, and then Germany, overawed Europe for fifty years, to be overthrown in 1918, but not finally, because she rose again within a generation, unrepentant, and as determined as ever on the realisation of her evil designs.

Britain, for her own safety, has generally sided with the weaker nations, because a dominant power in Europe was always to her a danger. Being close enough to Europe to be invaded, and depending entirely on the sea for her existence, she has, since losing her possessions in France, become involved in European conflicts in which she generally had no direct quarrel. She might have stood aside in the First World War, but, if she had, Germany would have spread herself all over Europe and built up a navy which would some day have destroyed her. So she continued her traditional policy of throwing her weight against the aggressor, but the success attained in 1918 was purchased at a great price in lives and wealth, the National Debt being increased by £7,000,000,000.

The war, as it developed, became a long siege of the Central Powers, the beleaguered enemy endeavouring to break out and destroy the forces that were hemming him in on land and sea. In this he failed, and, when weakened, the besiegers broke down the defences of the besieged, to become the victors.

Thus was demonstrated the supreme importance of sea power, as without this weapon the allies would have been defeated. Further, it brought to light how science, through lack of ethical wisdom, was perverted for evil purposes, the toll of death and suffering being thus raised far beyond that experienced in any previous war. Science has brought countless blessings to mankind in relieving pain, prolonging life, and increasing comfort and happiness, but it has also caused the wounds of conflict which it helped to heal.

This great tragedy, which engulfed the human family, set men and women thinking as they never thought before. They stood aghast at the horror of it all, the slaughter, the suffering and the misery. Not one of the combatant nations benefited, and all lost heavily in lives, wealth and happiness. For four years millions of men and women toiled to produce the weapons of destruction. For four years millions of men used them one against the other. Every thinking, reasoning being resolved that this war was to be the last, a decision which indicated a decided mental advance, and pointed to the time, which must come, when mankind's will-power is definitely set against war as a means to an end.

Only by will-power can the earth be cleansed of this evil. Only by education, with this aim in view, can human will-power be directed to achieve this purpose. Only by the power of the human mind can the method be found to give to everyone his fair share of the world's wealth, and thus eliminate all cause for aggression. Only by a world-equipped force, maintained by the people and for the people, will the aggressor be kept down, and cease to attempt to dominate his fellow creatures. It must be done, and it can be done, but only by means of world-wide mental development, which will raise the ethical conscience of mankind to a higher level than now prevails.

CHINESE AND JAPANESE CIVILISATIONS.
(399–1941.)

THE WESTERN WORLD DISCOVERS THE FAR EAST.

So far our attention has been mostly concerned with that part of the world known as the Western hemisphere. In Chapters IV, IX and X we went farther east and kept ourselves in touch with events in India and China, and we will remember how the Mongols from Mongolia very nearly swept over all Europe. If that had happened, history would indeed have changed its course, but, by some fortunate chance, the Mongol leader Ogdai altered his direction and, after passing through Russia,

Poland and Silesia, turned his face again towards the east to return home by way of Hungary.

After his death in 1241 his successors built up a powerful Chinese Empire which united China under one emperor. Never before was this land more illustrious, and it was at this period that we left China in Chapter X. Then it was that Marco Polo, about whom we have already read, visited China, to return home to Italy with such stories of the glory, greatness and power of Kublai, the Great Khan, that few believed him. Though this ruler undertook public works, patronised literature and relieved distress, he never became popular, to die unregretted, as it was never forgotten that he was an alien and a barbarian. The Khans who followed were not conspicuous for their deeds, and within thirty years of the death of the Great Khan the star of their dynasty was in the descendant. From now onwards each reign was more troublous than the last, and outbreaks of revolt became increasingly frequent and serious. Finally in 1355 the last and worst of the Mongol rulers had to escape by flight from the vengeance of the son of a labourer, Choo Yuen-chang (1368–1398), whose forces met with little opposition.

After capturing the capital, Nanking, he set about the subjugation of the Empire, and, when this was done thirteen years later, he proclaimed himself emperor, taking the name of Hung-woo. Then he won the affection of his people by his generosity towards his enemies, and the regard he showed for the welfare of his subjects. By the end of his reign the Mongols had lost all their earlier conquests, when once again a new Chinese royal house was established and acknowledged all over China, to become known as the Ming dynasty, but not without the usual struggle.

As so often happened, the death of an emperor meant a scramble for the throne, and this again occurred when Yung-Lo (1403–1425) eventually succeeded in fighting his way up to the coveted imperial yellow mantle which in China, on the shoulders of the wearer, was the symbol of power. Two religions then prevailed in China, Buddhism and Taoism, the beliefs of the Emperor determining the state religion, and now it was that the former faith was suppressed in favour of the latter.

For the next hundred years the emperors ruled well, and peace reigned, to be followed by civil war, which encouraged neighbouring rulers to invade the land. The Tartars came down from the north, and a Japanese fleet appeared (1542) off the coast, her soldiers carrying fire and the sword through the littoral provinces. Again in 1592 the Japanese invaded and utterly devastated Korea. The Emperor of Japan was on the point of proclaiming himself emperor when the Koreans soundly defeated them at sea, blockaded their own coast and starved them into surrender. Thus did 250,000 Japanese surrender or perish, and this great victory was all due to the ingenuity of Yi Sun Sin, the Nelson of Korea and the greatest fighting sailor of the East. He turned a wooden junk into an ironclad warship by surrounding it with plates of iron, and across its bow he placed a great turtle shell which he used as a ram. This he operated to such effect that every Japanese junk was quickly sunk and the invaders were stranded.

The Japanese did not profit from experience, as

they broke the peace treaty in 1597 when 1000 ships set off for Korea filled with troops which overran their victim. Again Yi Sun Sin pursued the same tactics, and, by ramming and shooting flaming arrows into the enemy ships, he destroyed them all, only, like Nelson, to die of wounds after he knew his victory was complete. Again the Japanese who had occupied Korea surrendered or perished, and, after this second failure, this boastful nation, which claims never to have suffered defeat, ceased to trouble its neighbours for three hundred years.

Thus was Japan punished for her aggression, but another powerful foe was at the gates of China, and this time there was no brilliant defender to save her. The Manchu Tartars, goaded into war by the injustice they were constantly receiving from the Chinese, advanced into China (1616) and followed up one victory after another, completely defeating their foes. They did not remain, but these disasters brought the Ming dynasty to an end. Again, with the fall of the dynasty, rival forces fought for the throne. Rebel armies roamed over the land plundering, destroying and flooding the countryside. Once more China was divided between the two most powerful bandits. Then followed a time of intense suffering for the people, famine being so acute that human flesh was openly sold in the markets. Cities were left in ruins, and the dykes of the Hwang-ho river were cut, its waters flooding vast areas.

Matters reached such a pitch that the Chinese invited the Manchus to dispel the rebels. This they did, and then occupied Peking, where they settled down to dominate ultimately the entire land, much to the disgust of the Chinese who had expected them to return home to Manchuria when their mission was accomplished.. A new dynasty was established in 1644, known as the Ta-tsing, and the Manchus set about restoring peace and prosperity, which was accomplished by moderation, the Chinese officials being retained in their respective offices.

The new emperor Shun-che (1644–1661) found great difficulty in restoring order, and, to enforce the authority of the new régime, the Chinese were forced to shave their heads and wear pigtails as a symbol of Manchu sovereignty. Now it is that we find China, this land of mystery to Europe, coming ever more into the news. The Russians in 1656 sent an ambassador to Peking, only to have him sent back because he would not kowtow to the Emperor, and the Jesuits greatly influenced the son of Shun-che, who succeeded to the throne. He, Kang-he (1661–1721) was a successful soldier, but he particularly shines as a scholar, a dictionary of the Chinese language being published under his direction. After a brilliant reign of sixty years, during which time Tibet was added to the Empire, he passed into the realm occupied by his ancestors, but the tragedy of this period was the great earthquake at Peking, when 400,000 people perished.

The two emperors who followed were in turn peaceful and warlike, kind and cruel, Keen-lung (1735–1795) being the latter. Twice he, invaded Burmah and once Cochin China. His campaigns provided him, as they did Julius Caesar, with an outlet for his literary gifts. He wrote incessantly both prose and poetry, and did much to encourage literature by collecting and publishing books. His relations with the British in India were far from cordial, and this was largely because of his injustice towards their merchants. So bad did this become that the British sent an envoy to the Emperor to lay their grievances before him, but, though he was well received, his mission was unsuccessful.

Again, in the reign which followed, rebellion followed rebellion, this unrest being due to the Emperor's incompetence. The position of foreign merchants at Canton so deteriorated that the British Government sent Lord Amherst to Peking in 1816, but, as he would not kowtow to the Emperor, he, like the Russian ambassador before him, was sent home without having entered the imperial presence. Lord Napier followed in 1834, but the difficulties and anxieties from which he suffered in Canton so reduced his health that he died.

This period opens a black chapter in British history, as the British were attempting to force on the Chinese the dangerous drug opium, against their determined opposition. Because the Chinese officials seized some imported opium, and burned it, the British declared war on China in 1840, and occupied Hong Kong, which they retained as a British settlement. Then the British captured Canton, Amoy, Ningpo, Tinghai, Chapoo, Shanghai and Chin-Keang Foo, base thefts which show that their ethical standard was still at a low level, and that might took the place of right.

This disgraceful war of unjustified aggression ended in the ports of Amoy, Fuh-chow-Foo, Ningpo and Shanghai becoming open ports to foreign trade, and Britain receiving an indemnity of 21,000,000 dollars. From now onwards British aggression in

China continued, and other European powers, fearing that all the plums would fall to Britain, joined in the game of snatch-and-grab. Again Britain, without justification, declared war on China in 1857, and Japan did likewise in 1894, following a dispute over the chaotic state of affairs in Korea. Politically China at this time was a boiling cauldron, revolt following revolt, and what government she had was rotten to the core.

The country was too large, and its communications were quite inadequate for a central government to exercise its authority. With the death of each emperor the same events happened, ambitious men coming forward to seize the throne. Still the fact remains that China has remained a nation for a longer period than any other, its history going back into the mists of the past, the numerous revolutions in no way diminishing the people's love of their own way of life, and their desire to preserve their land as a nation under their own independent form of government.

This again became pronounced when European countries commenced to interfere in Chinese affairs. A great hatred of Europeans naturally developed, to produce the Boxer[1] national movement for the expulsion of all Europeans. In 1900, under the direction and sympathy of the Empress, the Boxers rose against the intruders, 250 Europeans being murdered, while the rest barricaded themselves within their own legations in Peking until relieved by a mixed European force under a German general. Abominable atrocities

---

[1] The name Boxer is derived from a literal translation of the Chinese designation "The fist of righteous harmony", which was originally a secret society of malcontents.

were committed by the Chinese on the foreigners, and before the rising was quelled a large part of Peking was in ruins. This was followed by the annexation of Manchuria by Russia.

When the Boxer rising subsided, China came under the influence of those Chinese who had broken with past traditions, and received an education in America or Europe. They began to consider an improved constitution, education for the people, and the suppression of the opium traffic. In 1912 the Emperor abdicated, and this great mass of concentrated humanity, under the leadership of Sun Yat Sen (1912–1913), became a republic, he being its first president. This brought the Manchu domination to an end, and the pigtail was abolished.

Likewise a start was made to replace the ancient and involved form of picture-writing, which had made general reading and writing impossible, its place being taken by our form of script. This was followed by the foundation of many new and vigorous universities, to satisfy the growing thirst for knowledge which is one of the most noticeable features of present-day Chinese social life.

Japan, fearing a united prosperous China, just as Germany feared an arisen Russia, worked against Yuan Shih-kai (1913–1916), her great leader in the reform movement. He became the Republic's second president, and in 1915 was proclaimed emperor. After his death in 1916 the old trouble started again, different military leaders fighting for control, each being helped one way or another by intrigues on the part of the United States, Japan and the chief European powers, who were one and all anxious for trading concessions.

On the other hand, these foreign intruders used the heavy indemnities they received from China, following the Boxer rising, for the advancement of the country's education, and towards the establishment of a banking system, new public works, railways, sanitation and suchlike objects.

This enlightened policy did not, however, damp down the fire of Chinese hatred towards the foreigner, which again blazed into fury when a British police official in Shanghai (1925) ordered his men to fire on a Chinese crowd that was demonstrating against the killing of a Chinaman in a Japanese factory. From this followed an anti-European and anti-Japanese movement, which cemented the Chinese into a solid block against the foreigner who, they felt, was out to exploit them and use them for his own enrichment.

This feeling was intensified when Japan in 1932 occupied Manchuria, and made it clear that if China was to be exploited she would be the exploiter. Taking advantage of civil war, she invaded China in 1937, gaining one victory after another, until the government, under the leadership of Chiang Kai-shek, who started his career as a pedlar, was forced far into the interior, making its capital at Chungking, where he directed guerilla warfare which baffled the invader. Both the United States and Britain supplied the Chinese with arms through Burmah, after the Japanese had seized all the ports of China, and this led up to the war between them and Japan, a story which will be told in Chapter XVIII.

The Japanese occupied a large part of China, but contact was always maintained between the Chungking government and the nations which allied themselves to the cause of a free and independent China. Consequently much more friendly relations developed between unoccupied China and Russia, Britain and America, especially the two latter, who renounced their treaty rights in 1943, and thus removed a long-standing grievance.

The aspirations of the Chinese have been directed during the past eight years to freeing their land from the Japanese invader, and adjusting their social conditions in accordance with Western ideas. The former they have now achieved after all these years of terrible suffering and devastation, a prolonged agony during which they have shown great qualities of endurance and sacrifice.

With the coming of education to China, let us hope that the natural intelligence of the Chinese will respond to the wider knowledge which can raise their ancient civilisation to new heights of prosperity, now that they have regained their freedom. Before the Japanese invasion, railroads were opening up the land, a development which is still in its infancy, and Christian missions had become medical hospitals which trained the Chinese in European methods of healing. American culture has taken hold of the Chinese mind, and, from across the Pacific, she is drawing her inspiration for the further great efforts still needed for her future advancement.

The Chinese people as a whole hate war and love peace, but they have been for ever cursed by a powerful, unruly gangster faction, which has brought nothing but devastation on the land for thousands of years. Given peace, and with modern agricultural implements in the hands of her industrious and intelligent peasants, the productivity of her rich and fertile land could be greatly increased, while the incipient industrial co-operative movement could develop internal trade and bring to the people articles hitherto new and strange to them. Some day new schools, and books printed in modern type, which many are now learning to read, will widen a hitherto very restricted outlook, to produce eventually a new China out of the oldest existing civilisation, and one, we hope, which will create conditions that will give the people the peace they have been so long denied.

North-east of China, divided from the mainland by the Korea Straits, lies a long chain of islands in the Pacific Ocean, known to their inhabitants as Dai Nippon, but to English-speaking people as Japan. The ancient history of Japan is enshrouded in mythological legends, their purport being to claim that her people are descended from the gods. Consequently they call their country "The land of the gods", and trace their sovereign's pedigree back to the Sun goddess.

This idea is not peculiar to the Japanese, and is inherent in the human race, it going back to the ancient world-wide belief that at death we enter another order of existence which is just bordering the one we experience on earth. When priests and theologians came on the scene, the venerated ancestors, living in another world, were evolved into supernatural beings and called gods and goddesses, to whom omnipotent power over the affairs of earth was attributed. They ceased to be regarded as men and women in the other world (as they really are, and as was originally accepted), to have draped around them beliefs which received the name of supernatural religion. Different communities evolved different beliefs, but all were anchored to the fact that invisible beings lived in our midst, who could make their presence felt through certain gifted people, who were called by different names, and in our day are known as mediums.

Nevertheless the fact was never forgotten that these beings, now called gods and goddesses, were in reality the ancestors of the earth's inhabitants, and every religion remembers this when recording the early history of mankind. The correct translation of *Genesis* vi, 2-4, tells us of the fertilising activities of "the sons of the gods" on earth, and this ancient idea that the gods produced children by mortal women eventually evolved into the belief that Christians were the "children of God", an expression used ten times in the New Testament. Besides this the Hebrews, and later the Christians, have always believed that they were the chosen people, enjoying a unique relationship with God, they being created only "a little lower than the angels" (*Psalm* viii, 5) and made in their likeness, an idea which came originally from clairvoyants seeing the men and women of the other world whom they called gods.

The Bible mythology of *Genesis* that the gods produced children from mortal women, and the New Testament story that a god impregnated a virgin, was as sincerely believed by all Christians up to within recent times as do the Japanese believe that they are the children of the gods. Moreover, their belief in a divine monarch prevailed throughout Christendom up to last century. So we need not be surprised that the Japanese, a deeply religious people, believe that they are the divinely chosen people descended from the gods.

They believe literally their mythology, which relates how the gods came to Japan and populated the land. Consequently they think that they are made in the image of their gods, that all the other races came from animals, that the Emperor is divine, the representative of the Sun goddess, and that it is their duty to obey his sacred commands as the dictates of heaven, and die for him if need be. This was taught to the children from infancy, no freedom of thought being permitted, all denying the foregoing, in the past, being tortured to death.

Japan, by such beliefs and methods, has for long been a nation of fanatics, because the state religion Shintoism has been drilled into every child, and nearly everyone devoutly accepts it. The Japanese are sunk deeply in the slough of ignorance, they still being at the stage most Christians were at last century, and many are still at today. This being so, we can better appreciate two interesting historical facts, the first being the reaction this fanaticism has on the attitude of all other nations towards them, and secondly how equally hateful Christians made themselves towards all non-Christian nations when, as God's chosen people, they took possession of a large part of the earth's surface.

The first Japanese emperor is supposed to have commenced his reign in 660 B.C., but from this date until 399 A.D. legend takes the place of history, though nothing reliable is known prior to the 10th century A.D., after which the country's history is more reliable The Mikados claimed direct descent from the first emperor, and from the 10th century onwards they have ruled the land with the help of their nobles. The Japanese belong to the Mongolian race, and more closely resemble the Siamese and Malayans than any other, but their culture was derived from China. They were originally barbarians, to become civilised about the same time as did most of Europe, their social system being likewise based on feudalism.

During the Christian Middle Ages the Japanese copied their military system from the Chinese, from which time a complete separation took place between the military class and the trading and agricultural classes, the former becoming the dominant power. Though one civil war followed another, the military caste seldom lost its predominant position, a status which it has retained to our own times. From the Middle Ages the Mikados became merely puppets, swayed by the military faction in power at the time, but in 1868 a revolution shattered its power and restored the Mikado to his ancient traditional place of supreme ruler, a change which was, however, only temporary.

Like China, the country was perpetually devastated by civil war, the small gangster element, as in other countries, keeping the large majority in subjection, but the nobility demanded, and always received, abject obedience and reverence. Japan's first contact with Europe was in the 16th century, when some Portuguese reached her shores from China. Then followed missionaries from Europe to convert them to Christianity.

The old religion of Japan is Shintoism, or veneration of tribal ancestors, but from China came Buddhism and the Confucian philosophy. These three beliefs were too firmly planted to be replaced by Christianity, especially as the Christian missionaries could not agree as to what was the faith they had come to teach. Some of the missionaries were Roman Catholics and some were Protestants, and they hated each other so bitterly that violent quarrels between them were frequent.

The attempt to Christianise Japan failed, and the missionaries were sent home in the 17th century because of their impudence, their intolerance, and the way they robbed and persecuted the Japanese. Moreover, the Japanese were influenced in coming to this decision by the cruelties the Christian missionaries were practising in the neighbouring Philippine Islands, torture being applied to all who would not become Christians. This represents the Christian attitude towards the heathen in those days, and, although it has now changed, a recent remark by a missionary, speaking at a missionary meeting in Glasgow, reveals the same disregard of the rights of the natives, who are still considered as heathen and looked upon as of little account. "We gave the heathen the Bible," he said, "and in exchange we got their country."

The treatment of the Japanese by the Christian missionaries in the 17th century led to Japan closing her doors on all Europeans, and for two hundred years she became a land of mystery, completely cut off from the rest of the world, no ship capable of crossing the ocean being permitted to be built. Sometimes strange ships passed her headlands, and some were wrecked on her shores, but any that approached too close were shot at until 1853, when four American warships refused to be thus driven off. Again, in the following year, ten American warships, propelled by steam, a hitherto unknown sight in Japan, landed their crews and Commodore Perry, who was in charge of the expedition, made Japan open her ports to foreign trade· This was only possible by means of force, and various bombardments by British, French, Dutch and American warships were necessary before the Japanese learned to show the foreigner the respect he expected to receive. How much better for everyone if they had been left alone!

Japan was deeply humiliated, but with humiliation comes repentance, and the Japanese repented of their isolation policy. With great energy, during the long rule of the Mikado Mutzu Hito (1867–1912), they set themselves to copy everything that the West could teach them, to such effect that from 1866 to 1896, a period of thirty years, they turned themselves from mediaevalism into a progressive modern state. With the deadly weapons she received from Christendom she defeated China (1894), Russia (1905), entered the First World War against Germany (1914–1918), overran much of China (1937–1939), and then in 1941 attacked the United States and the British and Dutch possessions in the Pacific. Certainly she had well and truly copied the ways of European and American civilisation, from which she learned much and gave little in return.

Thus she repaid her teachers for their lessons, but she hated her instructors because they prevented her from reaping the fruits of her war in 1894 against China, while they themselves slowly encroached on China by helping themselves to the Chinese land and ports they desired. Russia, Britain, Germany and America were determined that all they could get out of China would come to them and not go to Japan, the consequence being that at the beginning of the 20th century we find Russia in Manchuria and Korea, from which she was ejected by Japan after her defeat in 1905, and the other Western nations occupying the Chinese ports, from which they were finally turned out by Japan in 1941.

Japan, encouraged by her victory over Russia at the Battle of Port Arthur (1904), pursued the policy of self-preservation thrust upon her by the aggressiveness of the above-named intruders, and this safety-first attitude was just what Britain has consistently adopted in Europe. Consequently, when Japan found some of her enemies involved in war in 1941, she took the opportunity to clear them all from her midst, and occupy as much of their territory as was within her power. What Japan took from the British, Dutch, Germans and Americans had previously been taken from former owners, and, if Japan was wrong in what she did, the countries mentioned were equally so by taking what did not belong to them at an earlier date.

CHAPTER XVIII.

CHRISTIAN CIVILISATION.
(1914–1945.)

Introduction. (1) *A World-Wide Attempt is Made to Abolish War.* (2) *The United States Makes a Tragic Blunder.* (3) *Britain Between the Two World Wars.* (4) *The Anglican Bishops Suppress a Vital Document.* (5) *Most of Europe Falls into the Grip of Dictators.* (6) *Germany Again Plunges the World into War.* (7) *The Vatican Favours the Dictators.*

WHEN the greater part of a city is consumed by a fierce conflagration, the citizens, when they rebuild it, make as certain as possible that such a catastrophe will never happen again. They plan that there will always be an ample supply of water available, and that fire alarms are erected within easy reach, so that quick contact can be made with the firemen and their appliances, posted at their respective stations. These protective measures are possible because the inhabitants are each and all interested in securing the future safety of their lives and property. They work in harmony with one end in view—the immediate stamping out of fire before it has had time to spread.

After the great world conflagration, about which we read in the previous chapter, some believed that the time had come to rebuild civilisation on the lines adopted by the citizens when re-erecting their damaged city. A central fire-station was to be ever ready, to put out local fires of passion, which are for ever occurring when nations cannot agree over boundaries, and suchlike disputes which disturb the world's peace. It was a fine and noble idea, and its failure did not come from lack of endeavour, but from neglect to provide the water with which to smother the flames of war. Consequently all the carefully-thought-out scheme was useless when the time came for it to be required. In other words, men, fire-engines and hose-pipes are useless without the force of water to extinguish the flames, just as the League of Nations was found to be useless because it had no force behind it to carry out its decisions.

Imagine a school of a hundred boys. Up to now fights between different boys have been common, and, on occasions, groups of boys have fought other groups, but the time came when nearly every boy was involved on one side or another. A bloody mêlée ensued, causing broken arms and legs, lacerated faces, black eyes and battered heads, and this went on until they all became exhausted. The master comes on the scene, and, to prevent a recurrence of such a disgraceful episode, he appoints six of the strongest boys to keep order and punish any one who disturbs the peace. So long as these six boys work together peace reigns, but they know that the master is watching them and that they can go to him in time of trouble.

The story of the human race, as related up to our own times, is that of men and women with the minds of children, without a master, for ever quarrelling, fighting and snarling at each other. The earth they occupy is limited, but their numbers increase without any thought of where and how the increased population is to live. So, when they form themselves into communities called nations, they set out to grab what they want from one another, the weakest always falling a victim to the strongest. Under this method of existence a nation can only find security by wasting the substance of its toil on weapons of destruction and defence, and, as invention increases, the burden of armaments grows ever more intolerable.

So the time came, after the end of the greatest of all conflicts, when the wise ones of earth's children said amongst themselves that all this waste of life and treasure must stop, and in future all shall get together and amicably settle disputes without recourse to fighting. These wise ones were idealists, and quite ignored the fact that the majority of mankind were still ignorant children. They well knew that amongst individuals no laws could be enforced, and no law court verdicts would be accepted, if there were not a national police force to back up the decisions which the legislators and judges had made. Yet they expected communities of different languages and nationalities, each ignorant of, and living differently from, the others, with diverse traditions, laws and ideals, to accept the decisions of the majority of nations which lacked the force to back up their findings.

In the school, the master used the six boys as a police force, but in everyday affairs there is no master everyone will obey. The people imagine one whom they call God, but his opinions always coincide with the wishes of the individual or nation. Up to now, therefore, this idea has produced trouble instead of alleviating it, because each nation believed, at one time or another, that it had been privileged to hold the place of the divinely chosen people who were destined to dominate all others. The human race is of course too ignorant to realise that the God capable of solving all mankind's troubles resides within each one of us, that man alone is master of his own destiny, and that only by all directing their minds aright can the world's troubles be cured.

What is encouraging about the attempt which was made to outlaw war is the fact that the people of many lands got together for the first time, to try and devise the necessary political and legal machinery to bring about the ardent desire of the great mass of mankind. Hitherto prayer had been the only recourse of the righteous who desired peace amongst men. That had failed, and now something practical was being done which in the end may prove to be the means to cure this chronic running sore, when the method to enforce decisions is discovered.

(1) A WORLD-WIDE ATTEMPT IS MADE TO ABOLISH WAR.

During the First World War the prevailing feeling amongst men and women, who had the future happiness and welfare of the race in mind, was that this great conflict was to be the last, and that its end was to usher in a new and better world, freed from injustice, tyranny and the many social wrongs from which it suffered. The terms of peace made by the allies were as much to secure safety as repayment for some of their losses; in fact, if, by forgoing recompense altogether, future peace could have been definitely assured, most of the victors would have been only too willing to have waived every form of indemnity. All had suffered and were certainly entitled to redress, especially the French, because their country-side had been cruelly devastated, but it was the future security of Europe that concerned the statesmen as much as anything else.

Consequently, in the peace negotiations that followed the Armistice, the establishment of a League of Nations formed an integral part of the Treaty of Versailles, which formulated the terms of peace, and was signed by the representatives of all the powers concerned in June 1919. All nations were invited to join this Assembly, except Russia and the defeated and guilty nations, the intention being to permit the latter to become members after it was seen that they were genuinely attempting to fulfil the terms of the peace treaty.

The idea behind the League of Nations was the formation of an alliance of all the nations of earth to form a unified world state. It was to have its Parliament, known as the Assembly, made up of representatives of each of these nations, who were to meet at Geneva every September. Its Cabinet, known as the League Council, was to be composed of permanent members representing the Great Powers, such as the United States, Britain and France, and temporary members elected by the other states for a period of three years. Its supreme Court, called the Permanent Court of International Justice, was to meet at the Hague, and its Civil Service, or League Secretariat, was to be permanently situated at Geneva.

All nations who became members of the League subscribed to its object, which was "to promote international co-operation and to achieve international peace and security". It provided the necessary Court of Appeal for the settlement by arbitration of all matters in dispute between its members. If any party to a dispute refused to be bound by the findings of the League it would have to face the opposition not only of its original adversary but of the entire League.

This opposition might be nothing more than the expression of disapproval, but, in serious cases, economic sanctions were to be applied, bringing about a partial or complete cessation of trade with the offender. As a last resort combined military measures were to be taken against an aggressor who would not abide by the decision of the League. However, no combination of powers, whose duty it was to keep the peace, ever came into being, and without force the League could not enforce its decisions. An attempt was made in 1924, by means of the Geneva Protocol, or Draft Treaty of Mutual Assistance, to improve the machinery of the League as an instrument to preserve peace and deter aggression, but unanimous agreement could not be obtained and the project was dropped.

If all the nations in the world had eventually become members of the League of Nations, each determined to keep its rules and regulations, and support its decisions by force, all would have been well, and the history of the years which followed would have been very different. Unfortunately the noble idea never materialised, in fact the League never functioned as was intended. In the first place, many of the forty-two states which became members did not give it their full allegiance. They feared to lose their freedom of action, or they did not trust its power to prevent attack, but its doom was really sealed from the first because the United States refused to join. Without her its back was broken, and it could not claim worldwide authority.

France, in consequence, felt bitterly the position in which she was placed, as she had only agreed at the Peace Conference to abandon her plan of keeping the German frontier behind the Rhine, in consideration of an Anglo-American Treaty of Guarantee. This never materialised because America withdrew from participation in European affairs, and Britain alone would not implement the guarantee. France consequently lost faith in both America and Britain, and when defeat came upon her in 1940 she, in desperation, threw herself at the mercy of her conquerors, refused to consider all further offers and promises from Britain, and decided not to continue the fight from North Africa.

Most nations nominally supported the League and sent representatives to Geneva, Germany being accepted in 1926, Turkey in 1932, and Russia in 1934. Lord Cecil and General Smuts did their utmost to make the scheme a success, and everyone hoped that the United States would some day support the institution her president had been the means of creating. Though she held aloof, Kellogg, her Secretary of State, in 1928, originated a treaty to be known as the Kellogg Pact, through which all the great powers renounced war, but these solemn promises were soon forgotten by some of the signatories.

In 1932 the League's real trouble began when Japan occupied Manchuria. As nothing dreadful happened, Italy was encouraged to attack Abyssinia in 1935, and hated Britain for leading the economic blockade against her. Japan and Germany withdrew from the League in 1933, and Italy followed their example in 1937 Russia's membership was brief, as she was not invited to join until 1934, to be expelled in 1939 because of her aggressive attack against Finland.

The attempt to secure disarmament was equally ineffective, as the Disarmament Conference, which met in Geneva in 1932, accomplished nothing. Japan, Italy, Germany, Russia, the United States and other countries did their best to secure the abolition of the bomber from future warfare, but without success. Great Britain insisted on retaining bombers in her air force, as they were required to keep the wild tribesmen on the North-West Indian frontier in order. The ghastly accounts of their shattering effect are available for all to read, though before the attack the villagers were warned and advised to scatter.

France, in fear of Germany, would not consent to reduce her armaments, and opposed the German attempt to increase the German army. Germany, indignant at this treatment, withdrew from both the Conference and the League, and commenced to rearm. A few years later the League was powerless to prevent her from occupying Austria and Czechoslovakia (1938), and equally so when Italy attacked and annexed Albania without any provocation in 1939 and Japan invaded China.

During the years between the two great wars Britain and France dominated the League, and earned for themselves the intense dislike of Germany, Italy and Japan, all of whom had conquests planned ahead which it was the duty of the League to prevent materialising. The League suited Britain and France, and the weaker countries, admirably, they declared, because the former had all they wanted, and now, along with the smaller states, wished security, whereas they, who wanted more, having come late on the scene, found all the fair places of the earth occupied. With this grievance in mind they got together, to become known as the three Axis Powers, or the three late-comers who wanted something from the others, and were prepared to fight for it if necessary.

The League of Nations was the first practical attempt towards righteousness between the nations, and it was the prelude to a further effort at a later date. Much good work came from the gathering together of the representatives of the different nations, and the work done by the International Labour Office still remains in being and deserves special mention. Social, economic and other subjects were discussed for the purpose of raising the standard of health and living everywhere, to result in much being done for the benefit of humanity, such as the League's work against the opium traffic and the white slave trade. Its primary effort, to outlaw war, failed for very obvious reasons, which can best be realised if we go back to the boys at school.

If the master had mustered all the boys into a league, and told them to punish any bully amongst them, his scheme would have failed. Instead he made the six strongest boys responsible for maintaining peace, and the reason he did so was because he understood human nature. A hundred boys out to

maintain peace amongst themselves, without anyone
over them, might secure their aim if all are equally
united in this high purpose. Amongst this company
are, however, some who feel strong enough to go their
own way, and, if they dislike anyone, they cannot
suppress their feelings, while, if they see something
they want from one weaker than themselves, they are
sufficiently undeveloped ethically to take it. The
first one who does this is shunned and not spoken to
by the rest, or the others set upon him and give him a
thrashing.

Smarting from his punishment, he withdraws from
the league, determined to have his revenge some day
in some way. Others, of low ideals, are influenced by
him, and when the next aggression takes place the
league is not unanimous. Fearing a definite split in
the league, the punishment inflicted does not exceed
isolation of the offender for a limited period, but this
is difficult to maintain amongst so many, as few like
to keep up a grievance for long. Those who keep to
the terms of the league ultimately find themselves in
the minority, and disliked by the others for their
resolution to keep the offender at arm's length. Finally,
only those of strong character remain, to discover
themselves isolated and in the position the majority
had originally decreed for the offender.

The master, knowing the weakness of human
nature, did not, therefore, make all the boys responsible for punishing an offender, but put six of the
strongest in charge, as a kind of police force, but, if
he were not there to keep an eye on these six boys,
some day it would be found that one or more became
slack, and would not take the trouble to interfere in a

dispute, or that they fell out amongst themselves, to settle their quarrel finally by a fight. To prevent this he would have to be ever on the watch to keep his wardens up to the mark, and get rid of those who were not maintaining the standard he had set. Thus he kept the peace in his school.

Unfortunately, there is no master, or Chief Constable, over the nations of the world, as each is his own master. There is no comradeship, and they only know each other by name. They speak different languages, live apart, are misrepresented one to the other, and all have different aspirations. Some have land or trade that the others wish, and all want their own force to protect them, while others are prepared to grab, on a favourable opportunity, some land from a neighbour. Some increase rapidly in population, and others decrease. So some want more room to live in, and envy those they think have too much. The boys, if they all had been ethically developed, could have lived in peace without wardens over them, and so also can the different nations, but much must change, and ethics must develop, before this is possible.

Further experiments will be necessary before the right solution is found, but fundamentally the peace of the world rests on complete respect and observance of the virtues, which, up to now, have been almost completely ignored. Ignorance is the root of all evil, and only by knowledge and wisdom will come righteousness. When that happens an international arbitration court should be sufficient to secure justice and keep the peace, but, until the education of the backward nations is complete, peace must be kept by the combined force of the strongest powers, whose first duty is to educate mankind in the practice of the virtues, while they themselves set an example of righteousness, and give no cause for offence to those who put their trust in them and are guided by them.

(2) THE UNITED STATES MAKES A TRAGIC BLUNDER.

When the United States entered the First World War, President Wilson made an eloquent definition of the war aims of the allies. He insisted that the democratic nations were not fighting the German people but their tyrannical autocratic government. This very generous gesture was not borne out by later events, as a few years after the Germans were freed from this tyranny they joyfully put the chains around themselves once again, padlocked them, and handed the key to the keeping of the world's greatest criminal. People who voluntarily return to prison, after being released, can hardly expect others to believe that they do not prefer this state of existence to freedom, and that they are fit to manage their own affairs.

Wilson was a scholar, a kind, thoughtful man, with high ideals, but he lacked political wisdom. He visualised a new and better world, organised under a League of Nations, which would bring peace and justice to war-weary humanity. Early in 1918 he sent to Congress a message in which he outlined the fourteen points already given in Chapter XVII, and when the German armies were rolled back in the following Autumn, and defeat seemed certain, the German government appealed to Wilson, to be told that the allies would only negotiate with a new régime that genuinely represented the German people. When this condition was accepted, and the Armistice terms were arranged, the war came to an end. Then followed a succession of blunders, to terminate in one which was the most tragic of all.

Wilson decided to go to the Peace Conference in person, an act which greatly offended many of his countrymen, as did his unwise decision not to include any prominent Republican in his Peace Commission. Again he offended the Republicans by appealing to the people to elect a Congress composed of Democrats, all of which so lowered his prestige that the League of Nations, which he sponsored, became a secondary matter, and his defeat the first consideration to many who otherwise would have welcomed his scheme. A large number of Americans feared to become further entangled in European conflicts, and advocated a policy of isolation, but to the last there was a possibility of a compromise with his opponents, if only he had agreed to certain changes. He insisted, however, that it was to be his scheme or nothing, and he would not yield.

Little is to be gained by analysing the reasons for the decision to which Congress came, as the fact remains that it turned down the participation of the United States in the League of Nations, and thus committed one of the most tragic blunders of history. What a different story we would have to tell if Congress had supported its president, or if he had been less rigid in his determination to have his own way. What a difference it would have made if the United States, Britain and France had maintained a strong effective striking force to support the decisions of the League, instead of the former standing aloof and Britain trying to show the way to disarmament by curtailing her own army and navy.

Some errors cannot be rectified, and those made within the White House and the Capitol in the years 1919-1920 made possible the tragedies which were to follow, Britain and France alone not being strong enough to enforce the decisions of the League. Such is the curse of ignorance, but, besides this, it must be remembered in Wilson's favour that he was a sick man by now, as he had suffered a paralytic stroke and was quite out of touch with public opinion.

The last opportunity passed in March 1920, when the Senate, by its final vote, rejected the League Covenant, and thus condemned the United States to those years of sterile isolation which she could have used to such advantage to uphold the authority of the League and maintain peace. The great Republic had envisaged a better world order emerging from the crucible of war, but, when the time came to prepare its foundation, she shirked her responsibility, and so wrecked the project for which she had sacrificed so much wealth and so many lives.

Warren Harding (1921-1923) followed Woodrow Wilson, and then came Calvin Coolidge (1923-1929), during which period there was a wave of prosperity. Immigration was restricted, and impoverished Europe found a door half closed to her surplus population, anxious to make a fresh start in this land of promise. Even here Nemesis laid her heavy hand, because in 1929 the soaring stock market was caught in the whirlwind which had produced the distress in Europe that eventually carried Hitler into power in Germany. Inflation had blinded the American people to the fact that the four years of destructive conflict had to be paid for, and now the bill was due to be met. Banks failed, factories closed down, and railroads went bankrupt, until finally 15,000,000 Americans could not find work. This was a world-wide financial *débâcle* which brought tragic losses, immense suffering and terrible privations everywhere.

Such was the critical position which faced the new president Herbert Hoover (1929–1933), and throughout his term of office he was occupied in attempting to cope with the economic disaster. When he failed, the country, in desperation, turned to Franklin Delano Roosevelt[1] (1933–1945). the choice of the Democratic Party, and one who had brilliantly served his term as Governor of New York. The same financial storm which swept Hitler into power in Germany was likewise responsible for Roosevelt becoming president, to become eventually one of his most powerful opponents.

Franklin was a distant relative of Theodore Roosevelt, and proved himself to be a man of great ability and progressive outlook, combined with great energy and drive. Soon he brought courage out of despair, and before his first term had ended he had passed through a docile Congress more legislation than any of his predecessors, arousing in turn greater hatred and admiration than any president since the time of Lincoln.

His reform and relief measures soon amounted to billions of dollars, as he set going great schemes for public works, housing, roads, bridges and electric

---

[1] Franklin Roosevelt was inaugurated President for the fourth successive time on 21st January, 1945.

supply. Then he broke up into smaller units the great utility companies supplying electricity and power, because these had been manipulated for the benefit of a few insiders. After this he turned to agriculture, and, by various measures, improved the productivity of the soil and the farmer's income.

Legislation was also passed to increase the bargaining power of labour, fix minimum wages, and maximum hours of work. A Government insurance scheme was also passed to insure the workers against old age and unemployment, while the banking system was reformed and strengthened. Long-range planning for soil development and enrichment also received his attention, but, just as Woodrow Wilson was interrupted in his schemes by the First World War, so was Roosevelt by the catastrophe of 1939.

Now came the time of reckoning. That which we sow we must reap. If we sow ignorance we reap adversity, and the United States certainly paid in both money and lives for the mistake she made in refusing to participate in the League of Nations. Too late she discovered that the airplane had so conquered distance that her land was no longer isolated from attack, and that in these modern days no one can safely adopt the comfortable policy of looking on while others do the fighting. So this powerful country became involved in the war against Germany, Italy and Japan, and had to spend thousands of millions before the enemies of freedom were defeated. How much wiser it would have been to have thrown her immense weight into the scale against aggression before these countries set out on their reckless journey for world domination, and so prevented the appalling waste of lives and treasure this involved.

Though the Republic had taken some important steps in world co-operation, such as the Kellogg Pact (1928), under which nearly every nation agreed not to resort to war, yet, by Congress passing two Neutrality Acts, one in 1935 and the other in 1937, it tied the hands of the President and State Department in such a way that little help could be given to the democracies when they were faced with totalitarian aggression. Not until Germany attacked Poland did Congress repeal the embargo on armaments, but then it was too late to prevent the conflagration. The fire had started which spread round the world, and, when Britain stood alone after the collapse of France, fear of the fate which might befall them, if Britain was next defeated, entered American minds.

Then it was that the United States stripped herself for the conflict, and right heartily did she enter the fray. Though she could not now prevent the catastrophe, yet, when she woke up to realise what it meant to her and all freedom-loving people, she gave generously and with both hands. By her lavish and liberal help she made victory for freedom possible, as, under the Lease-Lend Act, she supplied at her own expense ships, airplanes, tanks and munitions to all her allies, in such vast quantities that the enemies of mankind were ultimately overwhelmed. Britain pursued the same policy to all in need of help, and the United States ultimately became one of the largest beneficiaries from the mutual aid policy which the war brought into being.

Now that the folly of isolation is realised in

America, the future peace and happiness of the world is unlikely to be again jeopardised by this dangerous policy of standing apart, because the bomber has brought home to all the American republics the startling fact that Europe's danger is their danger. Thus the forces of democracy and freedom have been greatly strengthened, and, with their help, distracted Europe, which has suffered so cruelly from the ravages of war, may now emerge from its long period of travail into a much desired era of peace, prosperity and happiness.

(3) Britain Between the Two World Wars.

The last chapter brought British history up to the outbreak of the First World War in 1914. Immediately on its commencement Asquith, the Prime Minister, appointed Lord Kitchener as Secretary of State for War. His past record had made him one of the most trusted and popular of British soldiers, and this appointment gave the people increased confidence at a time when the enemy was carrying all before him. His greatest work was the raising and organising of about 3,000,000 volunteers into an efficient army, and, although he could not work harmoniously with some of his colleagues, he never lost the affection and admiration of the people. He was one of the outstanding personalities of the war, a man of unbounded energy, fearless integrity and amazing foresight, his direction having a profound effect on its course and the ultimate allied victory which was largely due to the foundation he laid.

The failure of the British at Gallipoli (1915) forced

Asquith to form a coalition government, the chief men of the Conservative Party—Balfour, Bonar Law and Austin Chamberlain—taking office under him, the Labour Party being represented by Arthur Henderson, and Ulster by Lord Carson. His leadership lasted until the end of 1916, when he resigned because of the feeling that the successful prosecution of the war needed a younger man with more energy and driving force. David Lloyd George, who had been so successful as Minister of Munitions, took his place, and became Prime Minister (1916–1922) of the second coalition government. He at once set up a small War Cabinet of five ministers, of which he was the most outstanding member, and, when hostilities ceased, a grateful country recognised in him the man whose energy and direction had contributed in a great degree to secure victory for the allies.

Women had for years demanded inclusion in the franchise. During the reign of Edward VII their agitation had assumed formidable proportions, when they found that their aspirations were being passed over unheeded when only constitutional methods were adopted. Under the name of Suffragettes, and the leadership of Emmeline and Christabel Pankhurst, they threw off all restraint, and committed every conceivable act of violence, assaulting Cabinet Ministers and setting both public and private buildings on fire. Imprisonment only fanned their determination to proceed with their policy to obstruct until their rights were recognised.

On the outbreak of war all this agitation ceased, and they turned their energies to winning the war, becoming nurses, ambulance drivers, motor and lorry drivers, munition workers, besides relieving men on the land and in industry in every possible way. After that their claim to share in the country's government could not be refused, and the Representation of the People Act (1918) gave the vote to women over thirty and to men over twenty-one years of age.

The same year emancipated the child worker by the passage of the Education Act (1918), which extended the school-leaving age to fourteen years, and put an end to children spending half their day at work and the other half at school. It also provided for nursery schools and medical inspection of the children, its comprehensive aim being to empower the State to look after the welfare of all children and young people from the age of two to eighteen. Provision was also made for Continuation Schools which would ensure, under compulsion, the part-time instruction of all from the age of fourteen to eighteen, but lack of the necessary money after the war made it impossible to carry this praiseworthy intention into effect.

Four years of intensive destruction of wealth seriously crippled this, and other pressing social reforms, but, as the country recovered, social problems again received attention, so much so that much of Britain was largely rebuilt, and the artisans were able to live in houses furnished with many of the amenities scientific discovery had provided.

In the interval between the two world wars the standard of living advanced more quickly than ever before, and by increased medical attention the health of the people improved. Shorter working hours enabled them to spend some of their leisure in sports and amusements, which quickly developed as the demand increased. The most popular was undoubtedly the cinema, which was soon to be seen in every place of any size, while the radio found its way into nearly every home. The finest and the worst music became available to everyone for the small charge of ten shillings a year, while the popular penny newspapers ran serial stories, football competitions, and employed astrologers to foretell the future with little success.

We remember the terrible description of a working-class home at the beginning of the 19th century, before the artisan obtained a vote, and when he was little better than an uneducated serf. Though slums still exist, and many country districts still lack water, sanitation, gas and electric light, the intervening century had produced a vast change in his position, education and culture, and nowhere was this more noticeable than in his home. The modern working man's house is no longer contained in a tenement in a dismal street, but is set apart from other houses and surrounded by a garden. Its rooms are airy and comfortable, with large windows. Different shades of curtains and carpets give each room a warm and cosy appearance, while arm-chairs, pictures, ornaments, tablecloths and chinaware add to their comfort and attractiveness.

By gas, or electricity, the rooms are lit and the cooking is done, while gas or electric fires heat the house and maintain a constant supply of hot water. Well-tested drains prevent smells and keep the family well and healthy. The radio gives the world's news, and both educates and entertains. Buses pass nearby, connecting shops, railways, cinemas and school, while a bicycle stands ever ready in an outside shed.   The children are well dressed, with good boots and stockings, their knowledge being greater than that of most kings and queens of not so very long ago, and, if they are clever enough, they can continue their education to fit themselves for positions their grandfathers rarely ever thought of attaining.

By putting aside a small part of their weekly wage, the workers are now insured against the expense, and loss of wages, caused by sickness and accident, while both husband and wife can be sure of a weekly pension when increasing age makes work a burden. Besides this, all can now lend their savings to the State, and receive interest and their money back when they want it.   His own, and his wife's, municipal and political votes carry as much weight as those of a millionaire or titled aristocrat, and everyone can say, believe, read and do what he likes, provided no one is harmed.

Surely this is a triumph for education, and, if all this can come about after only fifty years of instruction, to what heights may the race not rise in the centuries to come?   Reason and knowledge are now replacing blind superstition and the acceptance of degraded conditions as part of the divine plan.   Ahead there are almost unlimited possibilities, so long as liberty of thought and expression march hand in hand with increasing knowledge and wisdom.

Though all this has been accomplished there is still a black side to the social picture, and this is clearly emphasised in the report made in 1943 by the Hygienic Committee of the Women's Group on Public Welfare.

This is based on what transpired as the result of children being evacuated from British cities in 1939 prior to the heavy air raids. Too many of these children were found to be verminous, ill-clothed, undernourished and untrained in decent habits. An investigation of their homes revealed the terrible conditions in which they had been brought up, and the ignorance and stupidity of their mothers.

The hard crust of urban destitution and degradation, the Committee reported, has as yet been hardly dented, and the effect of evacuation has been "to flood the dark places with light and bring home to the national conscience that the submerged tenth still exists in our towns like a hidden sore, poor, dirty and crude in its habits, an intolerable and degrading burden to decent people forced by poverty to neighbour with it." A mighty effort in education and improved environment is the Committee's remedy, but it emphasises that education must begin from the age of five in nursery schools if this squalor is to be conquered eventually.

Andrew Bonar Law (1922–1923) succeeded Lloyd George as Prime Minister when the coalition government came to an end in 1922. He led the Conservative Party which secured power after a General Election, only to be faced with the slump in trade following the inflationary boom which developed after the war. The unemployed, numbering 2,500,000, were a heavy burden on the country because of the amount also required for pensions for widows, orphans and the wounded, besides the additional interest required for the National Debt, now ten times as large as in 1914. The new premier was in failing health, and, greatly to the regret of his supporters, who admired him for his party loyalty and integrity, he resigned after being only eighteen months in office.

Now it was that Britain, who had proclaimed a protectorate over Egypt, when Turkey, her overlord, entered the war on the side of Germany, acknowledged the independence of this ancient civilisation, to follow this up in 1936 with the Anglo-Egyptian Treaty of Friendship and Alliance which permitted British troops to protect the Suez Canal. This treaty proved of vital use to the British during the Second World War. Likewise, in 1932, Britain acknowledged the independence of Iraq. In Palestine the situation was more difficult, as both Jews and Arabs looked upon it as their national home.

Lord Balfour's declaration in 1917 that "His Majesty's Government views with favour the establishment in Palestine of a national home for the Jewish people, and will use its best endeavours to facilitate the achievement of this object" aroused the indignation of both the Arabs and Syrians. This policy was certainly in direct opposition to the wishes of 90 per cent. of the inhabitants of these parts, and fortunately no attempt was made to put it into effect. Greater wisdom carefully restricted Jewish immigration, and Sir Herbert Samuel (now Lord Samuel), the first High Commissioner, by his strictly impartial administration, brought a measure of peace and prosperity to the land.

The conciliatory intentions of the British government towards the Arabs were demonstrated in 1923 by the grant of autonomy to Transjordan, but the irreconcilable antagonisms of Jew and Arab in

Palestine still remained a permanent source of anxiety, the non-co-operative attitude of the Arabs rendering impossible the creation of the Legislative Council originally contemplated. This means the continuance of semi-autocratic control by the British until the time comes when a peaceful settlement is secured or, failing that, Britain returns her mandate to the United Nations and gives up the attempt to reconcile the Jews and Arabs.

The Arabs feel towards the Jews much as the English today would feel towards the Welsh, whose ancestors were driven out of England at the time of the Saxon invasions, if they now claimed England as their home, and wanted to return to it and dominate the English. If only the Emperor Julian (361–363) had had a longer reign everything would have been quite different, and it is one of the great tragedies of history that this tolerant Pagan was killed before he completed his work of restoring philosophic thought to the place it had so long occupied. Had he enjoyed a long reign the blight of Christianity would not have settled on a third of mankind, because he would have undone Constantine's mistake of making it the state religion of Rome.

Likewise the Jews would not have been homeless all these centuries, as he planned their return to their native land. When Julian died, the Christians, guided by the text that Palestine was to remain desolate (*Matthew* xxiii, 38), influenced the Roman policy in the opposite way to that intended by Julian, so much so that the influx of Jews to Palestine was stopped, and never again allowed to proceed. Thus they lost their last chance to recover their country, and ever since then they have been wanderers in strange lands.[1]

Another age-old problem facing the British was how to pacify the Roman Catholic Irish. The war had loosened the links between Britain and the Dominions, which latter now secured the status of "autonomous communities within the British Empire, equal in status, and united by a common allegiance to the Crown". Ireland was a much more complicated question, as the people were not united in their demand for home rule, and the Roman Catholics and Protestants disliked and distrusted each other. A rebellion in the south was suppressed in 1916, but two years later Eamon de Valera was elected President of Sinn Fein (We Ourselves), to stimulate this organisation into an active powerful force against all British authority in Ireland. In 1919 he declared Ireland to be a republic, and appointed a government to rule the country. The British employed irregular troops, known as Black and Tans, to suppress the rebellion, and on both sides terrible atrocities were committed.

To solve this century-old problem, caused by two opposing branches of the same religion, and the different political aspirations of the people, a Government of Ireland Bill (1920) was passed by the House of Commons, which established a Parliament in Ulster and another in Dublin, each subordinate to the one at Westminster. This the Sinn Feiners refused to accept, and, with the blessing of the Pope, they continued their fight for complete independence. If the British government had continued its old traditional policy towards Ireland its reconquest would once

[1] This tragic story will be found at greater length in *The Psychic Stream*.

again have been necessary, but, owing to advancing intelligence and greater toleration, the British decided to make southern Ireland into the Irish Free State, a self-governing dominion. This was opposed by de Valera and his party, and not until 1927, when they secured power, did they cease resistance.

For ten years fairly friendly relations existed between William Cosgrave, the first Free State Prime Minister, and Britain, but when the Sinn Fein Party obtained a majority, and de Valera became head of the government, he passed measures making the Free State completely independent, and entirely ignored the British crown. All interest payments on British loans to Irish farmers were stopped, and a trade war followed because Britain imposed tariffs on Free State imports into Britain to compensate her for the loss.

Finally the separation between Britain and what is now known as Eire became complete when Edward VIII abdicated, and de Valera proclaimed Eire a republic, with himself as the first president. An Anglo-Eire agreement acknowledged the sovereignty of Eire, and Britain (1938) withdrew all her forces from the forts and defences on the coast of Eire, a move which uncovered Britain to attack by sea, as was only too clearly realised a year later when the Second World War commenced. Ulster continued loyal to the British crown, because the Protestants there predominate and maintain a majority in the Ulster Parliament, which concerns itself only with local Ulster affairs, her representatives, thirteen in number, still continuing to sit in the British Parliament.

Another difficult problem, also caused by religion,

was the status of India, where a strong nationalist movement had been gathering way since 1885. The difficulty arose from the Hindus being in the majority, while the more virile Moslems, and those of other religions, formed the minorities. In 1919 the Government of India Act gave the elected representatives of the people some share in the country's administration, and paved the way for eventual dominion status. Education and public health were handed over to the control of Indian ministers, the intention being gradually to educate the Indians in the knowledge of government.

The Nationalists, under the leadership of Mahatma Gandhi, refused to co-operate in this division of authority, and adopted a policy of civil disobedience. They refused to obey British laws, or co-operate with British rule, and boycotted British goods, a state of affairs developing which brought about a visit of the Simon Commission to India. A series of conferences ended in an amended Government of India Bill becoming law in 1935. This new legislation abolished all division of authority, and gave self-government to the Indian provinces.

Further, it provided for India being organised on a federal basis, and the granting of responsible government to a Federal Assembly, the Viceroy being responsible only for foreign policy and defence. Then came the entry of Japan into the Second World War, which brought matters to a head, as we shall discover later on. Meanwhile we shall return to affairs in Britain, remembering that during this interval between the two wars the difficulties caused by the growth of nationalism in both Ireland and India were always receiving the earnest attention of the government in power.

Stanley Baldwin (1923–1924) succeeded Bonar Law as Prime Minister, to continue his party's policy of tariff reform. Then followed a General Election, when the Conservatives appealed to the nation for a mandate to carry through a system of tariffs on imported goods as a remedy for the prevailing industrial depression. They lost a considerable number of seats, and this gave the combined Labour and Liberal members a majority. The Labour Party claimed the right to form a government, and, as this was wisely agreed to by the other older organisations, the first Labour Prime Minister took office.

The man who was given this responsible office was James Ramsay MacDonald, who had risen from humble circumstances to be the leader of the Labour Party. He was very unpopular during the First World War because of his pacifist utterances, and his opposition to Britain becoming involved in the conflict, losing his seat in the 1918 election, to regain it in 1922. Though his tenure of office was brief, lasting only throughout the first ten months of 1924, he handled the country's foreign policy with ability and success. When, however, he attempted to re-establish friendly relations, and to reach a trade agreement with Russia, the Liberals withdrew their support, and his short term of office came to an end.

A General Election followed which returned the Conservatives with a majority of two to one, but the most remarkable event was the fact that the Liberals were represented by only forty members. This once powerful political party, whose policy resembled that of the Whigs, had suffered more from the extension of the franchise, and internal disruption, than had been thought possible. The artisan distrusted the representives of the old political organisations and preferred his own party, to which he subscribed, and which chose its representatives from men who came from the working class or had special sympathy with its aims. The progressives now supported Labour, while those who feared Socialism backed the Conservatives, and the consequence was that the once famous Liberal Party fell between two stools.

Stanley Baldwin now became Prime Minister for the second time (1924–1929), and one of the first moves of the Conservatives was to return to the gold bullion standard, which had been abandoned during the war. This meant a free market in bullion, and that the Bank of England was now able to use its discretion in its purchase and sale of bullion, but gold coins did not come freely into circulation. This relaxation of a war-time measure was intended to encourage trade and restore London to its old position as the banking centre of the world. Unfortunately this delicate financial operation was not skilfully performed, as, by raising the value of the pound to its pre-war level, British goods became too dear for foreigners to buy, because, to secure British currency, they had now to exchange more of their own. British export trade declined in consequence, and the coal trade was the first to feel the falling off in demand.

The only remedy open to the mine owners was to reduce wages, and to this proposal the operatives refused to agree. The Trades Union Congress supported the miners, and called for a cessation of work by all workers except those in essential services, such as lighting and sanitation. The General Strike commenced on 4th May, 1926, but, as thousands of volunteers came forward at the request of the government, it only lasted nine days. Much harm was done to the cause of labour, as many who were sympathetic with its political aims for better conditions were determined not to allow it to become a tyranny. The support the government received at this critical time convinced the Labour leaders that they had made a mistake, and they called off the strike, which brought the 2,500,000 who had obeyed their call back to work.

This attempt at such an unconstitutional method of obtaining something for a section of the public—"direct action" it was called—decided the government that it must not happen again. So it passed the Trade Disputes Act (1927), which made sympathetic strikes illegal. It later passed the fifth Franchise Act (1928), which gave the vote to all men and women over twenty-one years of age. Britain had now become a truly democratic country, and had entered the age which we may rightly call Democratic Civilisation. Christian Civilisation had now passed away; the autocratic rule of first the priest, then the divine king, and lastly the aristocracy, was over, and the people, who had for so long remained uneducated, at last came into their own.

As the result of the election which followed, a year after this Act was passed, Labour became the largest party in the House of Commons, but again it had to depend on the small Liberal representation for a working majority. So, for the second time, Ramsay

MacDonald (1929–1935) became Prime Minister, to be faced with one of the worst economic storms Britain has ever had to encounter. The gale blew for two years, to end in the financial crisis of 1931. A big Budget deficit followed, and foreign investors, fearing Britain's ability to pay, hastened to withdraw their money from London.

The Labour Cabinet resigned, and the next day MacDonald formed a National Government, made up of those Labour ministers who still supported him and representatives of the Conservative and Liberal parties. In order to balance the Budget taxation was increased, and cuts were made in the social and other services. Finally Britain abandoned the Gold Standard, and the value of the pound in foreign currency fell to about thirteen shillings.

The National Government, after making this drastic attempt to balance the nation's revenue and expenditure, and encourage foreign trade, then appealed to the country for support. Because of the large number of Conservatives returned, who were pledged to support the coalition, the National Government again found itself in power with Ramsay MacDonald as Prime Minister. The country's trade was at such a low ebb that tariffs were now introduced against certain foreign imports. Consequently the policy of free trade, on which Britain had prospered in the 19th century, was abandoned, owing to the many changed circumstances, the principal one being that foreigners were now able to produce and export goods as cheaply as, and in some cases cheaper than, it was possible to produce them in Britain.

In 1935 MacDonald resigned the premiership in

favour of Baldwin, and in January of the following year George V died after a reign of twenty-six years. During this time both he and Queen Mary were conspicuous for the conscientious way in which they carried out their royal duties.

Edward VIII succeeded his father, and reigned throughout the year 1936. He was a great disappointment to everyone, as he showed neither the wish nor the ability to rise to the responsibilities of his high office. Moreover, his private life caused much adverse criticism. Finally, as the government would not consent to him marrying an American woman whose husband was still alive, he abdicated, and, under much secrecy, left the country one night for France, to the sorrow of a few but to the great relief of the entire empire. He was given the title of Duke of Windsor, and married the woman he loved after she had obtained a divorce.

His brother, the Duke of York, succeeded him as George VI in December 1936, much to the satisfaction of everyone, and shortly after his coronation in the following year Baldwin resigned the premiership, to be succeeded by Neville Chamberlain (1937–1940), the younger son of Joseph Chamberlain. He had previously been Minister of Health and then Chancellor of the Exchequer, which offices he had ably filled. He was now faced by a formidable problem, which he boldly and bravely attempted to solve, but, to understand the difficulties with which he was confronted, we must go back and tell the story from the beginning.

In Britain the feeling had existed after the First World War that Germany must not be kept down for ever, that she had learned her lesson, and would not again plunge Europe into war. So it came about that in 1923, only five years after the termination of the great conflict, Britain would not support France in her right to occupy the Ruhr when Germany defaulted in her reparation payments. French troops alone entered Germany and occupied this vital region for two years, during which time German finances became chaotic. Inflation of the currency began, and the mark, from being worth about a shilling, lost all its purchasing power. Stark ruin came upon all Germans whose savings were in fixed interest securities, and all salaries and pensions became of no account. Finally Germany agreed that a committee should assess her capacity to pay reparations.

New and lighter reparations were now agreed upon, and both Britain and the United States lent large sums to Germany (which were never repaid) to help her to rehabilitate her industry and trade. The world slump, which began in 1929, particularly affected Germany, already suffering from her defeat, and the effects of her currency inflation. There was much unemployment and distress, a state of affairs which encouraged the people to snatch at any straw to find salvation. Later on, when we come to Germany's part in these years between the two world wars, we shall find how this world-wide depression was the reason for the National Socialist Party making the headway it did, because its leader, Adolf Hitler, promised the Germans relief from all their troubles if only they would give him their support.

When, in 1921, Britain's alliance with Japan terminated, a four-power pact was concluded between Japan, the United States, Britain and France, to respect the rights of each in the Pacific Ocean, and to settle all outstanding differences by negotiation. At a further conference, which included the above powers, and also Italy, a naval treaty was signed limiting naval armaments for at least ten years, but they could not agree to limit land armies. Discussions, with the object of reducing the chance of war, continued, and at Locarno in 1925 an international conference drew up a number of agreements to prevent boundary disputes in Europe from developing into war, Britain guaranteeing the existing German, Belgian and French frontiers.

Sir Austin Chamberlain, the elder son of Joseph Chamberlain, as Foreign Secretary, took a leading part in carrying this conference through to a satisfactory conclusion, and then Germany was invited to become a member of the League of Nations. By 1930 all the allied troops placed in Germany as an army of occupation had been withdrawn, five years before the date mentioned in the Treaty of Versailles. Relations between France and Germany now commenced to improve, and great hopes were set on something really practical being done to reduce the chance of war when a Disarmament Conference, at which sixty-four nations were represented, met at Geneva in 1932, to see what could be done to reduce the burden of armaments. Agreement could not be reached, and the conference consequently adjourned indefinitely in 1934.

From the time that the Disarmament Conference broke down, the insane race began to build up armaments. "Once bitten, twice shy", and France was now much more than twice shy, as she had been badly bitten by Germany on two separate occasions.

At the Disarmament Conference Germany had demanded equality in arms with the other great powers, but France refused to agree because no guarantee was' forthcoming that she would be protected against future aggression by her powerful neighbour. Britain was anxious to see Germany again prosperous, and relieved of some of the terms of the treaty which were such a burden on international trade. Consequently at a Conference held at Lausanne in 1932 all further reparation payments by Germany were practically abolished and her indebtedness funded. It had been discovered, just as Germany found out after the Franco-Prussian War, that as reparations can only be paid in goods, these unnatural exports from Germany, for which there were no equivalent imports, were severely affecting the trade of the countries receiving the reparations.

The incapacity of the League of Nations to maintain peace became evident in 1931, when Japan invaded Manchuria, a province largely inhabited by Chinese. Both countries were members of the League, and all it did was to condemn Japan for her aggression, a fact which was noted with satisfaction by both Hitler and Mussolini. No economic boycott, or sanctions, as this is called, was attempted, and Japan consequently broke the Covenant of the League without in any way suffering. Manchuria became known as Manchukuo, and was put under Japanese control. When she got away so well with this flagrant act of aggression and departure from her solemn undertaking, she resumed hostilities against China (1937), to become ultimately involved in war with Britain and the United States.

In 1933 Hitler became Chancellor of Germany, and, by means of the gestapo, quickly bound his subjects to absolute obedience to his will. Gradually he demolished the Treaty of Versailles, introduced compulsory military service, and commenced the building up of a navy, army and air force. German troops next reoccupied the part of the Rhineland which had been demilitarised under the Treaty of Versailles. Italy, which had come under the dictator rule of Benito Mussolini in 1922, defied the League of Nations by invading Abyssinia (1935), another member of the League, and thus broke the solemn covenant she had made when becoming a member. Fifty-one nations, under the lead of Britain, applied sanctions against her (which means ceased to trade with her), but in such a perfunctory way that she was able to continue her campaign, occupying the capital Addis Ababa in 1936, and annexing the country to the Italian Empire.

The League of Nations was now utterly discredited, and Britain became seriously alarmed, because Japan, Germany and Italy had broken their vows to the League, and flagrantly ignored its provisions. Winston Churchill, since 1934, had been warning the government of the danger, to receive the reply from Baldwin:—

This government will see to it that in air strength, and air power, this country shall no longer be in a position inferior to any country within striking distance of our shores.

That was said in March 1934, to be followed a few months later by a flat contradiction to a statement made by Churchill that in twelve months the German

air force would be as strong as that of Britain.
Baldwin again assured the House of Commons that

It is not the case that Germany is rapidly approaching equality
with us. Her real strength is not 50 per cent. of our strength
in Europe today.

That was said in November 1934. In March
1935 Hitler announced that Germany had an air force
equal to that of Britain, and this, be it remembered,
was the boast of the Chancellor of a country which,
under the Treaty of Versailles, was not permitted to
have an air force of any kind or size. Likewise
Germany, contrary to the treaty, built up a large
navy until it reached in battleships 35 per cent. and
in submarines 45 per cent. of the British tonnage.
In June 1935 a naval treaty was signed between
Britain and Germany setting that as the limit of her
building programme, but in April 1939 Hitler
abrogated this, as to him no promise or treaty was
binding after its purpose was served.

Baldwin and MacDonald, up to 1938, had in turn
ruled the country for fifteen years. Nothing had been
done to reduce unemployment, which for years hovered
at well over a million. They gave much of their time
to the affairs of the League of Nations, but entirely
neglected the country's defences, the air force having
declined to the sixth position after being the largest
in the world at the end of the First World War. Likewise the army was quite inadequately provided with
modern weapons.

The people of a democratic country get the government which represents the opinions of the majority,
and the Baldwin and MacDonald governments faith-

fully represented the vast majority of the people of the land, who then had no fear of Germany, and only wanted peace. In those days it was difficult to imagine Germany again challenging Europe, so why, it was asked, build up armaments when no one threatens the world's peace. Nevertheless history will hold both these men blameworthy for not telling the people of the danger which existed, and for lulling them into a false sense of security by soothing speeches.

Events, however, moved swiftly, and, when Baldwin saw the coming storm, well knowing how ill-prepared we were, he handed over the reins of government to Neville Chamberlain (1937). Chamberlain, because of existing circumstances, was forced to attempt conciliation with the two European dictators, Hitler and Mussolini. He secured an agreement with Italy for the maintenance of the status quo in the Mediterranean, but in the Spring of 1939 this was broken when the Italians invaded Albania.

In March 1938 Hitler invaded Austria against the terms of the Versailles Treaty, and in September, when Czecho-Slovakia was likewise threatened, Chamberlain flew to Munich to interview the German dictator. There the Munich Pact was signed, which laid down the terms and conditions for the surrender by Czecho-Slovakia of the Sudetenland to Germany. At the time it was considered fortunate for Britain that this agreement was reached, because she was quite unprepared for war, and it gave her the necessary time to increase her armaments. Then it was thought that this pact had also saved the Czechs themselves from German domination, but six months later, in March 1939, German troops occupied the entire country, a bitter blow to both Britain and France, as this development deprived them of a well-armed ally of more than 1,000,000 men, besides her great armament factories.

Again Hitler had flagrantly broken his promise, and Britain was at last aroused to the seriousness of the European danger. Germany's plan was to annex one country after another. If each submitted tamely, well and good; if not, then force would be employed to bend them to the German will. Chamberlain now abandoned his policy of appeasement, armaments were expedited, and Britain guaranteed the independence of Poland, which was the next victim on the German list to be struck down. Nevertheless, though war by then seemed inevitable, Britain surrendered to the Irish Free State her naval bases at the southern Irish ports. This blunder of blunders cost Britain, when the war came, immense losses in lives and ships, because she lacked these bases for her defence measures against enemy submarines in the Channel and the Atlantic. Eire adopted throughout the war a strictly neutral attitude, and all Britain's appeals to her for the use of these ports were in vain.

Britain had no interest in Poland's independence, which was a thing of recent date, the outcome of the First World War, and for centuries she had placidly seen the Poles the subject people of Russia, Austria and Germany. Ill-governed as the country was, the Poles passionately prized their new-found freedom, and when they were attacked by Germany they fought stubbornly and bravely, with Britain and France as their allies. Once again, within a generation, the time had come to challenge Germany's second attempt to subjugate Europe, as, if she succeeded in her purpose, Britain was doomed. Europe, under German rule, meant that her shipbuilding capacity would be so largely increased that before long the British navy would be outbuilt and at the mercy of its enemy. Then the British Empire would fall to the irresistible power of Germanic might, after which world domination was her purpose.

In August 1939, much to the surprise of everyone, Germany concluded a non-aggression pact with Russia. Confident that Britain and France would not now dare to intervene, Germany at once invaded Poland, but again, as in August 1914, she miscalculated, because, on 3rd September, 1939, Britain and France declared war. So commenced the tragedy of the Second World War. The previous six years had been a record of intrigue, broken promises, intimidation, and increased reliance on force on the part of Germany, Italy and Japan, while international morality, the keeping of treaties, and respect for the rights of other nations, had sunk to as low a point as ever before recorded in history.

With the coming into power of Hitler and Mussolini all semblance of political righteousness in Europe was forced into oblivion, and evil, stark and blatant, ruled in Berlin and Rome. Italy, under the inspiration of the patriotic Mazzini, had freed herself from Austrian tyranny, to become now within seventy years as despotic as her former overlords. Seldom before was the ignorance of the importance of righteousness more marked than it was between the years 1933 and 1939. Because of this ignorance many millions of innocent victims were to suffer and die in the years which followed, and Europe, East Asia and North Africa were to be overrun and dominated by the arch-fiends of rampant militarism, intent on spreading destruction, starvation, suffering, misery and death wherever their evil tentacles could reach.

When Chamberlain stepped out of his airplane on his return from Munich in September 1938 he remarked, "This means peace in our time"; and later, from a window in Downing Street, he shouted: "I bring you peace with honour. Out of this nettle, danger, we pluck this flower, safety." He mistook Hitler for a man as honourable as he was himself, because later he declared in Parliament that "I have no hesitation in saying, after the personal contact I established with Herr Hitler, that I believe he means what he says."

Now we realise the truth of the old saying that when one sups with the devil one requires a very long spoon. Hitler, on his part, had not reached the level of intelligence to know that "Righteousness exalteth a nation, but wickedness is a reproach to any people". (*Proverbs* xiv, 34.) Events have proved the truth of this proverb, but ignorance still reigns, and much of the human race has yet to alter completely its mental outlook if a repetition of the disasters of past years is to be avoided.

(4) THE ANGLICAN BISHOPS SUPPRESS A VITAL DOCUMENT.

We remember the story about the uncanny raps and noises which occurred in 1848 in a farm labourer's cottage at Hydesville in the United States. Mention was made of this incident in Chapter XV because of the effects which followed, as here began what came to be known as Spiritualism.

Spiritualism stands for the fact that life does not die at death, and that the so-called dead are actively alive in another world surrounding and interpene-trating this one. Spiritualists know this because their friends who have died have returned to them, and at times been seen, but more often heard, when certain natural conditions have been observed to make this possible. Not only can they speak to us through the use they make of the medium, but they can also hear what we say to them, and thus make conversation possible. From these conversations Spiritualists know (1) that, to begin with, their friends are still much the same, in form and character, as they were on earth; (2) that everyone reaps what he sows, but progress is open to all; and (3) that our friends are often with us and can know all that takes place on earth. Spiritual-ism is consequently a natural, and in no way a super-natural, religion, because it is based on personally experienced facts which give satisfaction and comfort, besides contributing an urge for increased mental and ethical development. We are mind, and mind never dies; death is a door, or a bend in the road of life, and not a wall or a dead end.

Of course there is nothing fundamentally new in this, as Spiritualism, under the name of Ancestor Worship, was man's first religion, a natural outcome of what he himself experienced, and one which was so general that at one time it was accepted by all the races of mankind everywhere. By ignorance it became theologised, and priests, to their own profit and advancement, became the interpreters of the mystery of death. From these early times a constant conflict has been waged between the priest and the prophet, the old name for the one now called a medium.

Ancient documents, moreover, make it clear that the origin of every new religion came about by one or more people experiencing, in one form or another, what we today call psychic phenomena, a name which embraces the direct voice, clairvoyance, clair-audience, trance utterances, and the movement of objects without physical contact. This old literature is full of these supernormal occurrences, and, in spite of mistranslations and foolish elaboration, the Bible, from the first chapter of *Genesis* to the last of *Revelation*, contains stories of many such incidents crudely recorded, the reappearance of Jesus after death, for instance, giving rise to the Christian religion.

Here is not the place to explain how this experience developed into the belief in his physical resurrection, or why it was that similar psychic incidents produced the many other world religions. That is a study to which *The Psychic Stream* is devoted. It deals with the age when man looked upon the departed, who returned to earth, as gods, angels or devils, but now we are in a new age, the Scientific Age, when natural phenomena are rationally enquired into, and those who return after death are recognised as men and women and not as gods who are responsible for the ordering of the universe. Consequently, when the disturbances occurred at Hydesville, scientific men began to investigate and attempt a rational explanation.

From that date to this, hundreds of thousands of men and women, including many with outstanding

scientific reputations, have experienced psychic phenomena in the presence of mediums, and almost without
exception they have accepted the obvious conclusion
that the phenomena are caused by etheric men, women
and children who once lived here on earth.   A natural
religion, and not a supernatural religion, consequently
developed, based on the actual proof of survival after
death, and not on faith, its ethical teaching being
based on the fact that as we sow we reap, both here
and hereafter.

Natural religion discards theology, mysticism,
rites, ceremonies, creeds, doctrines, dogmas, holy
books and priests, because its adherents realise that
all these arose from the misinterpretation by our
ignorant ancestors of phenomena which, when intelligently understood, make clear that death, like
birth, is a natural biological affair, and not a punishment for sin.   Now we know that we enter a new
environment at death just as naturally as we arrived
here, no theological passport being required.

This, then, is what is called Spiritualism, which to
millions has become the only natural religion, with
thousands of churches throughout the civilised world.
It corresponds more closely to the beliefs and worship
of the early followers of Jesus, before they became
Christians, than any of the other later interpretations
of his mission on earth, as will be discovered from
early Apostolic literature such as *De Anima, The
Teaching of the Twelve Apostles*, and *The Shepherd of
Hermas*.   These three untampered writings are older
than the Gospels and Epistles, as we now have them,
because the original gospels and epistles were mutilated, added to and withdrawn from, for three hundred

years during the age when Christianity was in a state of evolution, so as to keep them in line with the new cult, as it borrowed all it now professes from surrounding Pagan beliefs.

As the priests supplanted the mediums of the early Apostolic Church, as doctrine and dogma took the place of clairvoyance and trance, and as the dictates of the priests superseded the utterances of the "divine spirit", who was believed to speak through the lips of the entranced mediums in church, so the early Apostolic Spiritualism gave place to Pagan Christianity, with all its Pagan dogmas, holy days, ceremonies and ritual which now make up the religion.

Until we came to understand the constitution of physical matter, how it is but a range of vibrations between two fixed points, it seemed incredible that man could be the possessor of two bodies. Now, however, we know that another order of substance, outside the range of our sight and touch, can exist within and without the range of physical matter, as this other substance consists of vibrations at a greater frequency than those which make physical matter appeal to our senses.[1]

Scientists consequently became ever more interested in psychic phenomena. Some, such as Sir William Crookes, Alfred Russel Wallace, Lord Rayleigh, Sir Oliver Lodge, Sir William Barrett, Sir Archibald Geikie and Sir Joseph Thomson in England, Dr. Hyslop and Professor William James of Harvard in America, and Lombroso, Flammarion, Bozzano and Charles Richet in Europe, as well as many others, carried through exhaustive experiments which

[1] This is fully and simply explained in *On the Edge of the Etheric.*

convinced them that the phenomena they experienced were caused by discarnate beings who had once lived on earth.

A fact worthy of mention, and one which is quite unknown to historians, is the interest Queen Victoria took in Spiritualism, and the following is recorded because she was a prominent woman, and not for any other reason, her experience being typical of what hundreds of thousands of people have also discovered. Her deep interest began shortly after the death of her husband, the Prince Consort, and this is how it happened.

Robert James Lees (1849–1931), then a boy of about thirteen years of age, was so mediumistic from early childhood that his family and friends were converted to the belief that discarnate men and women spoke through him when in a state of trance. Soon after the death of the Prince in 1861, while the Lees family was having a private sitting in their own home, Lees was controlled by a man from the other world who gave the name of Albert, the Prince Consort. He then made the request that Queen Victoria be told that he could communicate with her through this boy medium.

The editor of a newspaper, a friend of the Lees family, was present at this séance, and published this request purporting to come from the late Prince Albert through Lees while in trance. This came to the notice of Queen Victoria, who, prior to her husband's death, had been convinced by her experiences with other mediums that such communication was possible. So she sent anonymously two members of her Court to the home of Lees, who requested that they might have a sitting with him. They did not mention who they were, or from whom they came, and gave assumed names, but the boy was not long in trance before the Prince Consort purported to speak, and he greeted these two courtiers as his friends, calling them by their correct names.

Then the boy in trance shook hands with them, and gave them correctly the highest Masonic handshake, which normally he did not know. The Prince, through the boy who was in trance, then told the visitors that he knew they had come from Queen Victoria, and, though at first they denied it, he forced them by the evidence he gave of his identity to admit that this was so. Before the séance ended he had given them such accurate information, which only the Prince Consort could have known (some of it being of a very private nature, known only to the Queen), that when her envoys returned to Windsor she was quite satisfied that these communications could have come only from her husband. She was especially impressed by a letter the boy wrote when controlled by the Prince. This was of a particularly personal nature, and he then signed it by a unique name used only by the Prince in etters to the Queen when he was on earth.

She then sent for Lees, and asked him if he would give her a sitting, which he did, and the Prince again spoke through the medium. The Queen then said to her husband that she wanted Lees to remain permanently at the Court so that he would be available at all times, but the Prince objected, saying that he did not wish this boy to be his medium. He, however, told the Queen that he could speak to her equally well, and just as easily, by using the vocal organs of the son of a gillie on the Balmoral estate whose name was John Brown. The Queen immediately sent for Brown, and thus began the long and strange friendship of Queen Victoria with John Brown, who, up to his death, was used as the medium of the Prince Consort to communicate with his wife, whom he advised on many questions until her death.

Robert James Lees, when he grew up, became a highly respected journalist and author. He wrote several books, of which the best known is *Through the Mists*, it being a record of the communications he believed he had received from the etheric world. Queen Victoria ordered six specially bound copies, which she presented to members of her family. The acquaintance of the Queen with Lees did not end with their first meeting, in fact it continued throughout her life-time, and on five different occasions the Prince Consort spoke through him in the presence of the Queen. Shortly before she died she sent for Lees and thanked him for all he had done for her. From time to time she offered him honours, a comfortable annuity for his life-time, and gifts, all of which he refused. He would take nothing, he said, in return for his services.

The Queen, knowing the prejudice there was at Court, and by the Church, towards everything relating to Spiritualism, never wrote to Lees and always sent her messages by a special courier, but she kept a record of all that transpired at her sittings with both John Brown and Lees. Dr. Davidson, the Dean of Windsor, who afterwards became Archbishop of Canterbury, was always hostile towards the lady who carried the title of "Defender of the Faith" being so unorthodox, but she quite ignored his advice to discontinue her communications with her husband, and brought up the members of her family to believe in the principles of Spiritualism. That is why the Royal Family have had sittings from time to time with the world's leading mediums.

After John Brown's death the Queen wrote a monograph about him and wished to publish it. Dr. Davidson and Sir Henry Ponsonby, her Private Secretary, firmly objected to this proposal, the former threatening to resign his position as Court Chaplain. Moreover, Ponsonby destroyed Brown's private diaries so that what was written therein would never become known. Thus it was that the influence of two Court officials prevented the Queen from publicly testifying to the comfort she had received from the communications she believed she had had with her husband, through the mediumship of her highland gillie.

Lees never spoke to anyone outside his own family about his close contact with Queen Victoria, or of her communications with her husband, and consequently only the members of his family knew what was happening, and this they kept private. The foregoing information was given to the author by his daughter Eva Lees, with permission to incorporate it in this book, and this is the first occasion that all the facts have been made public.

Now we come to the year 1938, when the leaders of Christianity in Britain were becoming alarmed at the decline in church attendance, not more than 5 per cent. of the population of London, and 20 per cent. in the country, attending the numerous orthodox churches. Increased knowledge was making the people disbelieve in Christian doctrines, and Spiritualism was drawing to the Spiritualist churches, and meetings devoted to its exposition, large numbers who hitherto had been regular attenders at the services of the orthodox places of worship. To many people it was more convincing and comforting to receive an evidential message from one who has passed on than to hear from the lips of orthodox ignorance about the blessed dead, and the resurrection morn, when the dead would arise to be paired off as sheep or goats. (*Matthew* xxv, 32.)

So it came about that the Archbishop of Canterbury appointed two committees, one to enquire into Christian doctrine, and the other into Spiritualism, both of which delivered their judgment in 1938. The committee on doctrine had been sitting since away back in 1922, to decide how much of "the only revealed religion" it was still possible to believe, while the other was asked "to investigate the subject of communication with discarnate spirits and the claims of Spiritualism in relation to the Christian faith". From what later transpired it was evidently expected that this latter committee would finally kill this menace to orthodox religion.

When these two committees finished their task they delivered their reports to the Archbishop, who published one, but not the other. The one dealing with doctrine was published, because it went over the old familiar ground, and left no one wiser than he was before, but when Dr. Lang, probably to his great surprise and consternation, found that the committee which had investigated Spiritualism had produced a majority report in favour, and not against, he suppressed it, and it has never been published.

The Committee on Doctrine, composed mostly of High Priests (21 out of 25 being priests), reiterated its belief in the Thirty-Nine Articles of the Church of England, but very few people were interested in its opinions, and the newspapers entirely ignored them, which shows how low the orthodox religion has fallen in public estimation from its heyday, when, even as late as the end of last century, such a report would have received widespread notice and comment.

The committee on Spiritualism, as already mentioned, handed its report to the Archbishop and, as it was not published, several of its members began to talk about their successful investigations, and what they had done and reported. The editor of *Psychic News* printed the story of their experiences and opinions, of how for two years they had sat at séances with medium after medium, had examined numerous reputable witnesses, and how, finally, they had reached their conclusions. The seven signatories of the majority report, covering numerous pages, which supported the claims of Spiritualism, included one bishop, two well-known canons, one prominent dean, a celebrated psychologist, an outstanding K.C. and a lady member.[1] The three who signed the minority report, of not more than two pages, reserved judgment.

When this unexpected position was disclosed to the Archbishop he decided, as already mentioned, not to publish the findings of the committee. Instead of doing so he called together all the diocesan bishops, and they confirmed his decision that the findings

[1] In October 1947 *Psychic News* secured a copy of the conclusions reached in this majority report and published it on 8th November, 1947.

must not be published. Dr. Temple, when he became Archbishop of Canterbury, adopted the same attitude as his predecessor, when urged to publish the committee's report, but we may be sure that if its findings had been unfavourable to Spiritualism there would have been no delay in its publication, as a warning to the faithful.

By this action the Episcopalian bishops have added another page to the disreputable record of their Church since the time of Elizabeth. It is a long and terrible story, of how its priests supported the massacre and persecution of the Irish Roman Catholics, and finally goaded them into such hatred of the English that their descendants parted company from Britain whenever they got the chance. It is a story of the pitiless torture and slaughter of 28,000 Scottish Presbyterians, and the exile of many thousands as slaves; it is a tale of the relentless persecution of the English Puritans, the Quakers, Unitarians and Methodists, 20,000 being exiled, and all not subscribing to Episcopalian doctrines being excluded from Oxford and Cambridge universities and the leading schools.

It is a tale of opposition to all progress and reform, of opposition to scientific research and discovery, to the people being educated and having the right to vote, of support of slavery, child labour and all the horrors the poor endured up to last century, including the murdering and torturing of innocent women they termed witches. Now, in an attempt to save for a little longer their threadbare creeds and dogmas, they withhold from the people this vital truth, because it does not fit in with the religion the early Christian priests produced after they banished the mediums from the Apostolic churches.

We are here faced with the eternal conflict between truth and falsehood, good and evil, liberty and bondage, and the withholding from the people of a report issued by a committee chosen by the Archbishop of Canterbury is in keeping with the principles of the Christian Church since its foundation. This obvious fear of truth being revealed has a deep significance, because it is evident that the bishops realise that Christian beliefs can prevail only so long as the truth is suppressed.

The life of mankind, since the time priestcraft first fastened itself on to the life of the people, has been bound up in the belief in the gods, in supernatural beings, in heaven and hell, in prayer and supplication, in salvation and damnation, in beliefs, forms and ceremonies. The comfort these ideas and performances gave to the people has been counterbalanced by the misery which came from intolerance and persecution, while untold wealth, time and energy have been misdirected. Besides this, millions of victims have been sacrificed on altars, mutilated by torture, murdered by painful death, and untold multitudes have wasted away their lives in prison or in exile.

All this evil has surrounded the false belief in the gods, while the priests have lived in comfort, and often in luxury, on the toil of the people they neglected to educate or elevate. By misinterpreting nature's laws, by turning the men and women of the other world into supernatural beings, and using their invisibility to create mystery, by worshipping falsehood and flouting truth, they have thrived to the detriment of the mental and material wealth of the people. How much of the present evil and wickedness which now prevails on earth is due to the policy pursued by the theologians of the past and present is hard to define, but their systematic opposition to factual education, and their utter disregard of ethical instruction, must have a prominent place amongst the causes which have kept back the mental development of the human race.

Now, for the first time in history, the theologians made a scientific enquiry, only to be so frightened by the results that they smothered them up and refused to make them known. Knowledge and theology are certainly not good companions, and we may well wonder what scientific progress would ever have been made by such methods. The first time the Anglican theologians used their reason, and made enquiry into the facts concerning those they call gods, angels and devils, they became aware of the danger their absentmindedness had led them into. For a brief period they became psychic researchers, and adopted scientific methods which revealed that the mystery on which they thrived was no mystery. For a brief moment the truth was before them that the other world is a natural world in which live, as men and women, the people who had once lived on earth. For this short spell the falsity of their theology appeared before them in all its hideous nakedness.

Fearing to face the truth, they suppressed it, and then began a series of actions by the police against different well-known reputable mediums, in different parts of the country, under the old Witchcraft and

Vagrancy Acts. There may have been no connection between the suppression of the Church report on Spiritualism and this outburst of persecution against mediumship, but, from what we know of ecclesiastical methods, and what transpired at the trials of the mediums arrested, it was evident that the orthodox faith was on guard against its ramparts of superstition being breached.

No evidence of fraud was brought against the different mediums arrested and charged under the Vagrancy Act of 1824 and the Witchcraft Act of 1735, their crime being that they were mediums. Consequently, when one offered to demonstrate in court her supernormal gifts, permission was refused because, according to British law, all mediums only pretend to make contact with the other world. This conclusion is the result of British law being based on Church law, which does not acknowledge the possibility of communication between the two worlds, and consequently all mediums only pretend to do what is impossible and are ipso facto frauds. We have to go back to the time of Jerome to pick up the origin of this absurd legislation, and, if the reader wishes to refresh his memory, the details will be found in Chapter VIII, Section I.

Because we still suffer from Church legislation, and are too ignorant and foolish to repeal its cruel and stupid laws, heavy fines were imposed on these mediums, one being sent to prison for nine months. Obviously there is no justice in this legislation, as jurisdiction is not concerned with what is possible or impossible in nature. Galileo was tried and punished because Church law holds that the sun circles the earth, and the earth is the rigid centre of the universe. To assert, as he did, that the earth circled the sun, and also has a diurnal rotation of its own, was contrary to Holy Scripture and consequently blasphemy.

With the truth or otherwise of scientific questions the law should have no say, as what concerns it, so far as mediumship is related, is fraud, and only if this charge be proved should the question of punishment follow. Neither a judge nor jury should, therefore, be called upon to deliver judgment on the possibility or impossibility of supernormal phenomena, that being quite outside the province of the law of any land.

The evil influence of theology still hangs heavily over progress and discovery, and, so long as Church influence remains, these ancient stupid laws will not be repealed. On Church law they are based, and on Church authority they are enforced, the judges at these recent trials being quite open in their opinion that mediumship is contrary to the Christian religion. Britain, and every Christian country, is still suffering from the evil effects of Church law, and today we are still in the same position legally, so far as mediumship is concerned, as we were at the time of Joan of Arc, and the centuries which preceded and followed, when mediums were termed witches and burned or drowned.

Anyone who thinks will appreciate the strange position which now exists, when mediums, endowed with natural supernormal gifts, are persecuted, while the Anglican Church is in possession of a lengthy and carefully prepared document which recognises that through them other-world people can regain touch and communicate with us here on earth. Moreover, it was due to the phenomena which follow from their supernormal gifts that the Christian religion came into being, and yet the opinions of the people who recognise the importance of these gifted mediums, who held a leading place in the Apostolic Church, are treated by many with derision. Spiritualists in Britain today are legally regarded as outcasts, and are in the same position as were the Nonconformists up to last century.

Spiritualists are today the only people in Britain who have not yet attained religious freedom. The Witchcraft Act places all mediums in the category of criminal frauds, and the Vagrancy Act regards all Spiritualists as rogues and vagabonds, the penalty under both Acts being imprisonment or fine. Moreover, the clergy never lose an opportunity to denounce Spiritualists for their beliefs, although they are carrying out the advice of the Apostles Peter and Paul[1] to make contact with the etheric world by means of mediumship, the writings attributed to Paul encouraging the use of psychic gifts though he surrounded them with his mystic Pagan theology. The law of Britain, as it stands today, convicts Jesus as a criminal, for which crime the punishment up to the 17th century was death at the stake, while today it is a heavy fine or imprisonment.[2] Truly we live in a curious world, surrounded by inconsistencies, deception and dishonesty practised by those who have the hardihood to set themselves up as leaders of the nation's moral conduct.

Nevertheless the fact is as clear as crystal that,

[1] Chapter ii of *Acts* and Chapter xii of 1 *Corinthians* are largely devoted to the importance of spiritual gifts, which should have been translated psychic gifts, this being the meaning of the Greek word charismata.

[2] Since this was written the Fraudulent Mediums Act of 1950 has given religious freedom to Spiritualists.

slowly but surely, the basic truths which have produced half the events of history are now for the first
time becoming recognised and understood in their
true light. Now we know the origin, and understand
the evolution, of every supernatural religion, besides
the reason for every religious belief. Natural psychic
law is behind them all, but what is true was turned
by the theologians into what is false, the error becoming
stereotyped and supported by an ignorant priesthood
which had a valuable vested interest in its continuance.
The consequence was evil instead of good, and
history makes evident the discord and misery which
has come from going contrary to natural law.

While many of our ancestors gained comfort from
believing what was false, this was only possible so
long as they remained ignorant, every attempt by the
minority to depart from the orthodox form of belief
bringing upon it endless persecution. So education
was banned and increased knowledge considered a
sin, and this the people accepted as right and proper,
their minds being quite undeveloped. Consequently
they were ruled like children, both fear and superstition
acting as better deterrents to crime than reasoned
obedience to law. Neither priest nor king knew of
any better way, and it suited the upper and ruling
classes well, they having all the good things of life
supplied to them by the servile masses.

For thousands of years a dull level of ignorance
prevailed, and the people continued to believe that
the divine rights claimed by both priest and monarch
were the gift of powerful supernatural beings, who had
appointed them as their agents on earth. It is
impossible to exaggerate the drag this idea has been

on human progress, because it established a divinely appointed status quo over everything, the ruling class always being Conservative in politics and orthodox in religion.

These divine rulers consequently encouraged their superstitious subjects in their fear of the hereafter, terrible punishments being predicted after death for those who were disobedient on earth, and it was not until the people secured some education, the vote, and the power, that this method of Church government by fear finally ceased. In different times, and different lands, this employment of religion to aid the monarch to rule received different names, in Christendom it being called "government according to Christian principles". That was why both Church and State were so violently opposed to democratic government, but, with the passing of the Theological Age, a momentous change of outlook has brought us to one of the great turning-points in history.

Today we stand at the opening of a new era for mankind, and one which will profoundly alter for the better our outlook on life. In the past, man has lived in a theological dream-world, his mental nourishment being error and not truth. Half the events recorded in this book have come from misunderstanding and misinterpreting natural psychic law, and this has meant that error took the place of truth. Consequently, as always happens when error and not truth is worshipped, ignorance was encouraged and intolerance was rampant. With natural law flouted, violent opinions, caused by error, produced folly which created many of the terrible events this history records.

Fortunately, from now onwards, the prospect is that history will take a new course. Reason, in democratic countries, is slowly taking the place of blind faith, and the important discoveries made by psychic science, which only the minority accept today, will gradually be acknowledged by all who put truth before ancient erroneous tradition. These new ideas are not yet popular, because experience of psychic phenomena is confined to those only who are sufficiently interested to enquire, but some day they will be accepted, as was every new discovery, which was first denounced, then accepted by the thinking few, and finally by the unthinking majority. The theologians, with their minds fixed on the past, will be the last to face the truth, preferring to sink with their old worm-eaten ship rather than abandon it and join one with its timbers sound.

It is clear that organised orthodox religion is doomed, and that in future religion will become a personal matter, dependent on psychic knowledge, and not on mystery based on ignorance. As the Church is founded on theology it is unable to give satisfaction to developing mind, its creeds and doctrines being firmly fixed on the existence of two supernatural worlds, the one being inhabited by fantastic gods, angels and saints, and the other by fiendish beast-like devils. On this false foundation rests supernatural religion, and the cruelties and follies for which it was responsible make up half the story told in the foregoing pages of this book.

If the people had known the truth; if they had been aware that the other world is a natural place, similar to this earth, which all reach irrespective of religious beliefs; if they had realised that their happiness there depended on their characters here; if they had been aware that its inhabitants were men and women who had lived on earth, and were still enjoying a solid, real, full life in all its aspects—half the history of mankind would have been different. By theology the other world has been transformed into an unnatural place, divided off between the saved and the damned, who became unnatural beings after death or resurrection. All these mistakes, and many more, have caused an enormous amount of wasted effort, retarded mental development, and are the cause of half the troubles of mankind.

The other half is due to ignorance of how best to live on earth, to power politics and fanatical nationalism which has wasted immense wealth and energy in war. Corruption follows in the wake of absolute power, and only occasionally does history record that unlimited power has been wielded justly and wisely. With these two evils, superstition on the one hand, and misdirected power on the other, most of the history of man is concerned, a truly shocking record of folly and ignorance. Only when knowledge takes the place of ignorance, and a high ethical standard of conduct replaces the present way of life, will this earth give to all the happiness everyone desires.

(5) Most of Europe Falls into the Grip of Dictators.

One of the most unexpected results of the First World War was the set-back in Europe to the political progress made in the 19th century. The Italians, who fifty years earlier had fought so strenuously against the Austrian tyranny, and won for themselves national liberty and parliamentary government, put themselves again under the yoke of a dictator, and, instead of pursuing a policy of enlightened progress, returned to the old path of conquest and suppression of freedom. Instead of helping Spain to gain her liberty from tyranny, Italy supported Franco, who established a dictatorship. Italy likewise gave to Hitler his inspiration to clamp on Germany the iron collar of subjection, and start her again on the road of aggression. Russia changed one form of autocracy for another, and Portugal and Austria likewise came under the power of autocratic rule.

Britain, France, Scandinavia, Finland, Czecho-Slovakia, Holland, Belgium and some of the Balkan states maintained the political liberties they had won during the previous century, but, with more than half of Europe away back again to the age of decrees, instead of parliamentary laws passed by a free majority, liberty had certainly received a set-back. Europe was now ranged into two camps, each holding diametrically opposite political views. Responsible cabinets, representative assemblies and democratic institutions came to be looked upon by these reactionary nations as suitable only for people who had entered into national old age and decay.

The future, they claimed, rested only with the nation which had passed its thinking and destiny into the hands of an autocratic leader, who took his own decisions, and enforced his will upon his subservient subjects. The life of everyone was now expected to be dedicated to the service of the State, and to the leader who had managed, through intrigue, blood and terror, to secure a safe seat on the national saddle.

According to this totalitarian plan, terror, tyranny and servitude were the highest aspirations of mankind, and all the liberators of the past had been leading the race down the wrong path to its own destruction. The generally-accepted opinion which had evolved throughout the 19th century, that the path of political progress lay through representative government, unbiased education and honest enlightenment, with every citizen having the right to speak, think and vote as he thought right, was cast overboard, treated with contempt, and considered as the sign of degeneracy by all those who preached this gospel of unthinking subjection.

Russia was the cause of this political reaction. There it started, to spread under another guise to Italy, Germany, Austria, Portugal and Spain. It infiltered its poison everywhere on earth, and even those of liberal political ideas found themselves wondering if the days of democratic government were over. The swift decisions made by the dictators appealed to those who were wearied by democratic parliamentary discussions and deliberation, from which sometimes little materialised. Consequently the dictator-governed nations looked upon themselves as the virile master races which were destined, by their new-found efficient machinery of absolute rule, to dominate the slower-moving and more deliberate-thinking people of earth.

To find the cause of this new order which came to Europe, we must start with the Russian Revolution of 1917, organised by the moderate Socialist Kerensky, which dethroned the kind, humane and weak-minded Tzar Nicholas II. This new government lasted for only a few months, as the arrival from Switzerland of Lenin, the fiery revolutionary, was the beginning of the Bolshevik Revolution and the setting up of a Communist state. The establishment of this new order in Russia was the first cause of the political upheaval throughout Europe, because it upset democratic principles which the people were just beginning to understand and appreciate.

As Russia was the first cause of much of the evil that fell on Europe in the years following the First World War, let us start with her from the time of Vladimir Lenin (1917–1924), and pursue the narrative until it ends with the second great world conflagration through which we have recently passed. We remember how, after centuries of tyranny in France, the revolution broke the bands of social discipline, to bring about chaos and renewed tyranny. So likewise in Russia history repeated itself, because there after the revolution the trust in authority was undermined, the fabric of custom was broken, and the people, loosened from their old moorings, looked out across an uncharted sea bewildered and confused.

Then it was that a man arose, a Messiah, to lead the people into the acceptance of a new political and social outlook, based on the teaching of Karl Marx. Lenin, like Mahomet, denounced the old order and proclaimed a new one that was to take its place. Communism was now to replace the old system of individual ownership, which had existed since the first animal used sufficient foresight to collect and store a supply of food for future use. This indeed was putting into practice a theory which had always repelled everyone who had anything, and had always been denounced by the Christian Church as contrary to the will of God. Consequently the cry arose throughout the world, from the lips of property-owners, that Russia had pulled apart the props which supported the structure of society, had denied the existence of God, and shattered the moral standard on which society was based.

Faced with the opposition of the Church and the capitalists, large and small, Lenin denounced religion as "the opium of the people". He exposed the wickedness and corruption of the Church, broke its power, and put himself forward as the prophet of a religion from which the adherents gathered the fruits on earth, a doctrine quite contrary to all the hitherto accepted ideas of religious faith. Like all who bring forward new ideas, he was a visionary, fanatical to the extent that he hated the old order, and an ardent believer that his new system of society would bring peace, happiness and contentment to the Russian people.

Lacking both position and wealth, he had trod the wine-press alone, first in a Siberian prison, because of his advanced opinions, and later in humble lodgings in London and Switzerland. There he had planned for the day he believed must surely come, when he would be able to establish in Russia the dictatorship of the proletariat, and overthrow the existing bourgeois régime. Endowed with great vigour, clear-cut ideas, complete self-confidence and eloquence, he was a powerful force in rousing his countrymen to a realisation of his own ideals.

Such was the man the German General Staff secretly conveyed to Russia from Switzerland in 1917, for the purpose of weakening the morale of the Imperial Russian army, then retaining many valuable German divisions urgently needed for the western front. The plot was entirely successful from a military point of view, but its effects were far different from those expected. A long chain, with its links of cause and effect, leads from that deep-laid plot to Germany's ultimate defeat, with the help of Russia, twenty-eight years later.

Lenin had the welfare of his people always uppermost in his mind, education, better housing and all modern comforts being, he considered, their birthright, but, to him, the people were the downtrodden serfs who had toiled for those which circumstance had set over them. For these latter he had no pity, and he could look on with composure at their wholesale destruction by massacre and starvation. Only by such means, he thought, could a solid foundation be laid for the new order he was determined to establish.

Class war was to him the door through which downtrodden man was to reach Paradise, but he was practical as well as a visionary, and discarded the schemes of Trotsky and Zinovieff that he should carry his revolutionary campaign to the countries abroad. Later, in 1921, he permitted private trading, when he discovered that his theories were in some respects impracticable, and he also concluded commercial agreements with Britain (1921) and with Germany in 1922.

He, and his associates, were frugal in their living, and honest in their handling of public funds. They continued the secret police, which had been such an

evil feature of the old order, because they had many
enemies at home and abroad who were planning and
plotting their downfall. The Red Army, and a well-
organised Communist Party of from 2,000,000 to
3,000,000 men and women, who permitted no opposition, and were zealously bound to the Communist
ideology, were Lenin's reply. With these weapons
he ruled Russia for six years, during which time he
transformed the life and institutions of the Russian
people beyond recognition.

When he died, in 1924, divine honours were paid
to him, as the one who had been responsible for
sweeping away the old hated régime, and putting in
its place an order of society in which all were treated
as equal. Education was general, social welfare took
first place, and the lowest born could rise to whatever
position his or her capacity permitted.

All this was not accomplished without outside
interference, because, at the outset of its career,
Russian Communism was confronted with a civil
war, its opponents receiving help from her former
allies, who, by this means, tried to keep Russia still
engaged in fighting the Germans on the eastern front.
Dreadful atrocities were also perpetrated by the White
Russians, the name given to those who were against
Communism, as they showed neither pity nor mercy
when they overran Siberia under the leadership of
Kolchak and Denikin, and marched on Moscow.

All such attempts were repulsed by Trotsky and
his Red Army, and the fact that the enemies of Communism were backed by foreign money had the effect
of consolidating the great majority behind the new
régime. Its success only heightened the fear of

contamination which was felt by neighbouring states, and in Finland, then occupied by the Germans, and in Hungary, all attempts to follow Russia's example were suppressed with the utmost ruthlessness.

Joseph Stalin,[1] the son of a shoemaker, succeeded Lenin in 1924, and four years later announced the Five-Year Plan for intensive development of the country's resources. This new plan now took first and foremost place in the lives of the people, because it embraced education, farming, transport and industry, all of which were to be developed on a scale hitherto never before attempted. In five years it was expected that Russia would be in the forefront of European nations. Unbelievable changes took place, under the iron rule of the Ogpu (or secret police), all of which were carried through by the sustained enthusiasm of the people, who accomplished in a few years what it had taken other lands a century to perform. Education made rapid progress, and twenty years after the Revolution 90 per cent. of the people could read and write, whereas before then it was the other way about.

Stalin's policy was to advance the standard of living, and to plan for ever greater production. He desired peace so that Russia could develop her vast internal resources, and, with this end in view he concluded through his Foreign Commissar Litvinoff ten non-aggression pacts. When Russia joined the League of Nations she gave its aims and objects her firm support, though she had to leave it because of her

[1] The name given him by Lenin, which means steel, because of his strength of character. His real name is Joseph Vissarionovitch Djougoshvili.

attack on Finland in 1939. Now it is realised that this aggression would never have happened had Russia not then foreseen that soon she would have to face an attack from this direction, the safety of Leningrad requiring that the Finnish border be removed farther to the west.

Such briefly is the story of Russia in the years following the Revolution, and now we go back to Italy in the year 1922, where the First World War had produced a general feeling of disillusionment and lassitude. Much had been suffered and little gained; in fact, with high taxation, dear food, and scanty fuel, the people doubted if anything whatever had been won from these years of blood and toil.

Communism took hold of the poor, and Lenin became an idol to many. Parliament debated, but great leaders were few. The people, after years of servitude to the Church, the Bourbons and the Hapsburgs, were ignorant, and did not know how to use their power for their common upliftment. They had complete freedom and democratic government, but they could not rightly use their power, and allowed it to slip from them so as to secure peace from continual labour upheavals.

When the Italian will-power was at its lowest, a political zealot, named Mussolini, appeared on the scene and copied the methods of Al Capone, a fellow countryman in America, who, by bribery, corruption and terror, had succeeded in capturing the municipal government of Chicago for his unlawful trade in alcoholic liquor. Mussolini improved upon this thug's methods, and employed them on a national scale so successfully that another gangster in Germany,

Hitler by name, formed a gang of lawless ruffians which by degrees chained the majority of gullible Germans to his will and pleasure.

The major events which happened during the interval between the two world wars largely centre round these two super-criminals, the rest of Europe being at times aghast at their braggings, deceptions and terrorist methods. The first tyranny to appear was Fascism,[1] which fastened itself on the neck of the Italian people, by promising to save them from the destructive influence of Bolshevism, if only they would forgo their liberties and place their destiny in the hands of one who had arisen to be their Saviour.

The Italians made their choice, and put manacles on their wrists to keep their hands from shaking. They could not stand alone, having for centuries been accustomed to tyrannical popes and despotic rulers. They feared their future when left to themselves. All the property classes, especially the Church, the greatest property-owner, dreaded Communism, and by their united influence they swept the people into the net of Fascism, the enemy of Communism.

The Fascist Party, with Benito Mussolini (1922–1943) as its leader, gradually became a powerful influence in the State, but let us start at the beginning of its development by learning something of its founder, and how he gathered strength and power. Mussolini was the son of a blacksmith, and prior to the First World War was the editor of a Swiss Socialist newspaper. His extreme opinions did not prevent him from urging Italy to declare war on Germany in

---

[1] The name is derived from *fasces*, a bundle of rods bound round an axe, which in Roman times was a sign of authority.

1915, because of her open aggression, he himself becoming a soldier to suffer the wounds of battle. On his return to civil life he conceived the idea of a new political party to rule Italy, and restore her ancient greatness.

Burning fiercely with the heat of extreme patriotism and ambition, this fiery, clear-headed, forceful man gathered round him, from amongst the neglected discharged soldiers, a body of strictly disciplined gangsters who controlled, first the streets of Milan, and then those of other towns, killing, beating and torturing all who opposed them. They would enter houses of political opponents and ransack them from roof to cellar. By such terrorist methods his organisation grew to such strength that he felt strong enough to force the King to give him political power.

On 30th October, 1922, when the government resigned, this army of ruffians marched on Rome, and forced the King, Victor Emanuel III, under threat of civil war, to give Mussolini control of the State. Whenever he obtained power he ruthlessly stamped. out all opposition, in accordance with the party motto "No discussion, only obedience", his power coming from his secret police, who soon discovered all opponents, and these were swiftly removed to concentration camps. The rigorous discipline he imposed on his supporters made him the dictator of Italy, and when this was achieved he set about completely reorganising both the central and local governments, besides industry and transport, all of which were put under Fascist control.

The newspapers, the professors, and all authors, were compelled to conform to the new political doctrine, and because some would not do so thousands were exiled to Sardinia and elsewhere, while others were murdered. The leader of the parliamentary opposition, Matteotti, was assassinated, and a new form of political representation was introduced. A terrorist election followed in 1923, which returned a majority of Fascists, composed of fanatical Roman Catholics and those who had resented the liberalism introduced since the country had been united. These were arbitrarily given two thirds of the seats in Parliament, and from that day onwards they became the "yes men" to everything the Duce (leader) decided was to be done, this being the only way totalitarian government can be conducted.

The new tyrant, the arisen Caesar, certainly worked for the unity and prosperity of Italy. He succeeded in dissipating the fatigue and despondency which had come over the people, besides firing the nation with his own fierce vitality. Strikes were prohibited, and every industry was directed towards useful productive work which permitted the proprietors and the workers to have their due reward. A new high standard of efficiency prevailed everywhere, the trains were clean and ran to time, and all public graft was severely punished. Great public utility works were started, malaria-infested marshes were drained and cultivated, and Rome was largely rebuilt.

The Fascist Party set itself fiercely against Communism, and, with the willing help of the Church, banned all free political discussion. The crucifix returned to a prominent position in every school, and the priests again took control of education. In 1929 the State became reconciled to the Church, which was given the Vatican City, comprising an area of about a square mile around St. Peter's and the Vatican, and then began the ridiculous performance of receiving ambassadors from, and appointing papal ambassadors to, foreign countries, to represent this remnant of what had once been the Papal States.

All liberty vanished in Italy, but the people accepted this as the price they had to pay for the return to the days of the glorious Roman Empire, with Caesar once more the divine monarch receiving their obedience and homage. Imperialism followed, and maps of the old Roman Empire appeared everywhere in public places as a pointer to what Italy intended some-day to accomplish. The long-subjected nation had arisen, phoenix-like, from its ashes, intent on inflicting on others that from which it had suffered from the Germans, French and Spaniards over the past fifteen centuries.

Abyssinia was the first to be singled out for conquest, Italian troops in 1935 invading this semi-barbarous Christian nation. By the free use of poison gas and bombs, dropped by airplanes on the unprotected natives, and in spite of the sanctions imposed by the League of Nations, the capital Addis Ababa was occupied the following year. Then the King of Italy was proclaimed Emperor in place of her legitimate sovereign, who had fled with his family and all the wealth he could carry with him. In this wanton aggression Mussolini received the support of the Pope, who blessed the Italian soldiers when leaving Italy for Abyssinia, and ordered services of praise and thanksgiving in all Italian churches after every victory. The Duce was sprinkled with holy water by His Holiness, who decorated him with the Order of the Golden Spur, and described him as "The man of God"

Next came the Italian conquest of Albania (1939), likewise blessed by the Church. When that was completed the Fascists set greedy eyes on Tunis in North Africa, on the French island of Corsica, and on the department of Nice, which latter had been given to France for the help Napoleon III had rendered to Piedmont in her fight against Austria at the time of the war of liberation. When France collapsed in 1940, and Italy became the ally of Germany, these were to be part of her reward, but events turned out differently from what Mussolini expected.

It was unfortunate for the Italian people that they were not ready for representative government, because if they had been, affairs in Europe, and in Italy, might have been very different. Democratic government is an art which develops out of century-long tradition, and requires for its smooth working a people with not only the critical faculty well developed but also the necessary patience and character to make progress slowly. It failed in Italy, as in Russia, because the education and temperament of the people had not reached the stage to make it workable, and, for the same reason, the attempt made by Germany to establish a republic was equally unsuccessful.

The German Republic was founded in the dark hour of Germany's defeat. It was republican Germany that signed the Armistice and the Treaty of Versailles, its representatives meeting at Weimar in February 1919 to draft a new constitution. It was elected by the great majority of the German people, but from the first it had to weather severe storms, Communists, Reactionaries and Royalists all working for its downfall. President Friedrich Ebert, a good and honest man, esteemed by all, by forceful and timely measures, rode through the storm, heightened as it was by a gale of fierce pamphlets from the pen of the violent Communist Rosa Luxembourg. Then, in 1920, Dr. Kapp, royalist, seized Berlin with a naval brigade, and the scared government fled to Stuttgart, but the rising had no popular support and the usurper was defeated.

Fulfilling the terms of the Versailles Treaty was its next difficulty. France, under Poincaré, demanded her reparations and security, the former to be paid immediately, and the security to last for all time. The Germans pleaded poverty, and, as they were behind in their deliveries, the French settled black colonial troops in the Rhineland. Even that did not quicken payments. So the French and Belgians, after determining that the least they would accept was £6,600,000,000, occupied the Ruhr, an act which did not meet with the approval of the British government. Then followed the inflation of the German currency, probably deliberately engineered so as to evade this heavy obligation, but it had far-reaching and calamitous effects on the German people. Within a year the mark was worthless, and everyone receiving salaries, wages and fixed interest was reduced to poverty.

With German industry strangled by the French occupation of the Ruhr, where the workers adopted a policy of passive resistance and limitation of output, the plight of the country went from bad to worse. France had gained nothing, French currency had depreciated by half, and Poincaré was forced to resign and give place to Herriot. This more liberal-minded statesman set the stage for something more practical, and in 1924 the proposals of the Dawes Committee, which investigated Germany's capacity to pay, met with acceptance, only to be modified later.

French troops were withdrawn from Germany, after which followed the Treaty of Locarno (1925), brought about by the happy combination of three statesmen: Briand, representing France; Stresemann, representing Germany; and Austin Chamberlain, the British representative, all intent on securing the peace of Europe. The treaty embodied an undertaking to the effect that if one of the three was attacked by Britain or France or Germany the others would go to the help of the victim. Germany, moreover, pledged herself to accept both her eastern and western frontiers, and not try to alter them by armed force.

Next came the question of disarmament, or, in place of this, the right of Germany to rearm, her claim being that either all disarmed or that she be allowed weapons for her own protection. The German Press became militant, and it was becoming common knowledge that what she could not do openly she had been carrying out in secret since 1921. France accordingly refused to consider disarmament, and in 1929 Stresemann, the German Foreign Minister, died without having secured the aims of the German Republic. His death was a great loss to his country and all Europe, as he had wisely carried his country through a very difficult period, and had been the mainstay of the Social Democrats.

For seven years Germany had put forward her claim for general disarmament, or to have the right herself to arm, but all in vain. France could not trust her, as her wickedness had been too great for that generation ever to forgive or forget. This failure to achieve the right to rearm undermined the prestige of the German Republic in the eyes of the German people, and, as the poor, who were many, were becoming infected by the propaganda of the Communists the country slowly drifted towards revolution. To crown all, an economic blizzard in 1929 swept over the world, and struck heavily at poverty-stricken Germany, levelling the Republic to the ground.

Not only did the republic vanish in this whirlwind, but also the £2,000,000,000 which had been lent to Germany by Britain and America for her rehabilitation. Her industries had been extended by foreign aid, new factories built, and many workers' houses and fine buildings had been erected. These loans were now recalled, only to accentuate the crisis, and little was ever recovered. Banks closed their doors, trade fell away, the unemployed became numerous, 6,000,000 being out of work, and the Budget could not be balanced. Bereft of her strong leader Stresemann, with the bitter cry of poverty and misery rising from every street, the red flag of Communism was unfurled and proudly floated in the poorer quarters throughout the land.

Such, then, was the position in 1933, when a Messiah arose with the promise that all would be well if only the people would put their trust in him. To understand better the origin and development of the movement which the Saviour represented, we must go back to the close of the First World War, to a German hospital on Armistice Day. There lay, blinded by gas, Lance-Corporal Adolf Hitler, of the 16th Bavarian Infantry Division, whose father, a minor Austrian customs official, had changed his name from Schickelgruber to Hitler. History might have been far different if this change of name had never taken place, but, like the arrow that killed Harold at Hastings, small causes produce momentous results. Adolf Hitler, a house-painter by trade, would have found it difficult with the name of Schickelgruber to arouse the emotions of the German people, and "Heil Schickelgruber" would have been too much of a mouthful for even them to utter.

Adolf recovered from his blindness, and left the hospital heavily weighted in mind by the defeat of the German army. So he resolved to give over his life to make Germany again great and powerful. When Mussolini formed the Fascist Party he decided (1920) to follow his example, and formed one in Germany on the same lines. His enthusiasm infected others, and, like a snowball, the membership grew in numbers and influence. This freak of nature, this audacious scoundrel, with his unbalanced mind and warped visions of the future, dominated all with whom he came in contact. He was physically tough, and mentally resentful towards everyone who differed from him, his high-pitched, hysterical oratory lashing his hearers into irrational emotion and subjection to his will. Violently anti-Semitic, ardently patriotic, and filled with Nordic pride, this fanatic denounced the Social Democrats for their weakness in the face of their country's defeat, all Jews, Liberals and

Communists being blamed for the disasters which had befallen the people.

The pages of history overflow with the savageries of despots, but Hitler far outdistanced them all, his political career being steeped in murder and destruction for which there is no previous equal. To assess his iniquities would exhaust the resources of accusation, as his wickedness was too deep for words. Instead of devoting himself to healing the wounds of the First World War, and leading his country back to peace and prosperity, he dedicated his life to the further destruction of everything non-Germanic. He chose the road of ruin, misery and bloodshed, and set himself to destroy everything good and noble which mankind had striven to attain in his long climb from savagery.

Hitler's every action was destructive, every move he made being for war and conquest; he lived for, and dreamed of, war, which in the end destroyed both him and the Third Reich. Lacking decency, culture and education, this supreme demagogue never tired his devoted subjects with his repetitive long-winded effusions, and, under his evil spell, they returned to their primeval savagery, following him to the depths of hell. Only amongst Germans was this frightening fact possible, only Germans would have worshipped such a monstrosity, and to many he has become a hero and a legend.

His party took the name of National Socialists, which was abbreviated to Nazi. When its aims were consolidated they were found to conform to the doctrines of Hegel, which were discussed in an earlier chapter, and to the already recorded opinions of

Treitschke, the most influential of all German professors and publicists. These were (1) to make the State all-powerful and the people mere cogs in its machinery, and (2) to abolish the separate states and unite all into one nation with one national army. Its future aims were (1) to repudiate the Versailles Treaty, (2) secure the return of the German colonies, and (3) the disfranchisement of the Jews, its distant aim being the complete domination of Europe by Germany, after which would follow the German domination of the world. All its members burned with a fierce patriotism, attacking pacificism as a sign of degeneration, cosmopolitanism because the Germans were the chosen race, and the practice of the virtues as a sign of weakness.

Hitler, after an abortive attempt to secure power, was arrested and put in prison (1923-4), where, like John Bunyan, he wrote an account of his progress under the title of *Mein Kampf* (My Fight). This badly written, and clumsily put together effusion, depicted the Nazi heaven on earth that all true Nazi pilgrims would reach, if only they followed his teaching. This is another book to be added to the thirteen already mentioned, all of which have exerted a great influence on mankind; not that this one was much read outside of Germany, but because of its effect on the German people, and what it roused them to do towards their neighbours. Its advocacy of force and domination over other nations was diametrically contrary to that expressed in *Rights of Man*, on which Britain, the Dominions and the United States have developed their form of government, and produced free and enlightened communities.

"The whole character and education of the true National State," Hitler wrote, "must find its apex in racial instruction, and brand the feeling of race and purity of blood into the minds of the youth, so that they will maintain a race of men on the road by which they will sweep away all those of non-Aryan nationality." This is typical of the ravings which fill this Nazi Bible, it being everywhere uncompromising, selfish, national, and lacking in all humanitarianism. Narrow nationalism, and utter contempt for all but those of German blood, cover its pages from first to last, while every virtue is flung aside, and all that experience teaches us produces righteousness and happiness is scorned and derided.

Mein Kampf faithfully represents the German mentality of the past eighty years. Never did a nation get a leader whose outlook better suited its introspective, egotistical attitude to life. This blood-stained treacherous tyrant was just typical of the race which, when it bludgeons its way into neighbouring lands, is selfish, cruel and overbearing towards its victims, but ever servile to its own rulers, whom the people in general have always followed blindly, no matter how deep they wallowed in crime.

Put a German in uniform and he becomes a brute; consider the Germans in the mass and they are a repulsive degraded race, however agreeable they may be as individuals. All the evil which comes from the curse of ignorance has found expression in Germany over the past thirty years, to end in them being the most miserable, the most despised and the most abhorred people on earth.

Democracy, which has been the aim of all the

enlightened nations of the past, with its maxim that the State should secure the happiness of the greatest number, was rejected by an overwhelming majority in Germany. In its place was set the ideal that the duty of the individual is to devote himself body and mind to the State, without question, as a slave obeys his master. Women were reduced to the level of breeding machines for the purpose of producing men to fight and plunder. Nothing was considered to be nobler than to fall in battle, as conflict created the great heroes of the race, virtue consisting of facing the rigours of warfare, out of which emerges everything that is noble and sublime.

Such was the gospel of hate and violence that the majority of the German people accepted without protest, they having learned nothing from the misery and poverty which followed their defeat in the First World War. Such were the ideas of the man whom the President of the Republic, Marshal von Hindenburg, made State Chancellor in 1933, when scared by the fear of a Communist régime taking the place of the discredited Republican government. Hitler's brilliant propaganda, and the able way he had prepared the ground beforehand, though not winning for him on the first occasion a majority of votes at the election, placed his party in a commanding position as the only one with a policy which appealed to the people.[1] It expressed all their pent-up resentment, their fear of Russia, and it voiced all their hopes, giving them

[1] In 1930 nearly 7,000,000 votes put 107 Nazis into Parliament, and in 1932 14,000,000 votes returned 230 Nazis, thus making them the largest single party Germany has ever had. The 1933 election increased the number to 288, and, with the support of the Socialist and Catholic parties, Hitler was made Chancellor and Dictator for four years.

the courage, which hitherto had been lacking, to face the future.

No sooner did Hitler become master of the State (1933–1945) than he made himself master of the people by putting their minds in chains. Around him he gathered a host of criminal ruffians to whom he gave positions of authority. He followed the example of the Christian Church when it came into power, and destroyed everything that stood for liberty and freedom. All books in Germany not conforming to the new ideology were seized and burned, and from that day onwards Germans were forbidden to read any literature which had not the sanction of the Nazi Party. The Socialists had expected Hitler to establish a Socialist state, and the Monarchists looked for the return of the Kaiser, but such promises as he had made were now flung to the winds.

Instead of implementing these pledges his Storm Troops and Black Guards, which the Republic had been too weak to put down, were at once organised into an army of terrorists directed by a secret police, the gestapo. All liberty of thought and action vanished overnight, and the majority of the people meekly accepted their fate, submitting to gangs of Nazi ruffians in uniform parading every street and entering any house suspected to contain someone whose opinions did not conform to those of the new régime.

All such victims were sent to concentration camps, to be tortured, bullied and driven to death or desperation. Such was the fate of a people lacking in all political sense and direction, who, for centuries, had meekly obeyed all they had been instructed to do, and were no better able than are children to govern themselves by the parliamentary methods of democratic government. Like whipped spaniels they grovelled at their master's feet, licked his outstretched hand and called him "Our beloved Führer".

Nations get the rulers they deserve, and the Germans were shackled with the Hitler despotism because they were quite unfitted mentally for anything better. Instead of valuing the freedom they had so recently secured, and instead of setting themselves to learn the democratic way of government, they almost unanimously voted themselves to become the slaves of a tyrant to whom they gave unlimited power. In place of liberty they chose servitude to an untried, uncultured, uneducated fanatic, and overthrew the Republic which had secured the entrance of Germany into the League of Nations as a first-class power. Moreover the Republic had stabilised the German currency after the collapse of the mark, secured a reduction in the amounts due as indemnities, and had greatly improved conditions of labour, besides taking the first difficult step towards eventual recovery. All that was forgotten, and the Reichstag, in which had vapoured the opinions of inexperienced and quarrelsome representatives, became a charred ruin and the symbol of the nation's political incompetence.

Short cuts are often dangerous, but a nation, brought up to believe that might is right, lacked the intelligence and the patience to continue laboriously working out its own salvation by constitutional means. Its people in the past had worshipped force, and now they themselves became a nation in chains, a nation of stupid infatuated slaves, who worshipped their master because he hypnotised them into the belief that he only could save them from being eventually dominated by Russia. When his devilish work was ended he had left his victim a corpse without a soul, everything but the putrifying flesh being destroyed.

Consequently it came about that the Press, the universities, the schools, and eventually the army, fell under the Nazi yoke. Decrees took the place of laws, concentration camps and prisons became the abode of the enlightened, of all who were brave enough to speak their honest thoughts, and Germany settled down to build up a mighty army which, when the opportunity came, would be powerful enough to sweep everything before it. All Trade Unions, political parties, and the petty German states within the Reich were abolished, one centralised organisation taking their place. Everything was unified and regimented, as all were now expected to think politically the same thoughts. "Heil Hitler", and the outstretched arm, symbolised a nation of automatons, ready and eager to obey the will of the drill sergeant whenever he appeared. So the melancholy spectacle was witnessed of the great majority of the German people delivering themselves over gladly to their "beloved Führer", and bowing in reverence before his undisputed will.

When Hindenburg died in August 1934 an overwhelming majority (98.79 per cent.) pronounced by their votes their acceptance of Hitler as their Führer (= leader), and gave into his hands full power to do with them as he liked. Probably the votes in this election were tampered with, and this is not a true figure, but what is true is that nearly all Germans hilariously acclaimed the Nazi Party when it took over the government, and it moreover received the blessing of the Protestant and Roman Catholic bishops. If it had not represented the will of the majority, a sullen defiant people could have made its administration impossible, but only a small fraction showed their displeasure. Consequently, with the consent of the vast majority of the German people, the Third Reich came into being, comprising a population of nearly 70,000,000 industrious and virile people, who proclaimed before the world their entire lack of balance and moderation, and their desire for servitude instead of freedom.

The greatest enemy of humanity, the greatest antagonist to civilisation, in fact evil, naked and unashamed, now ruled Germany by the free choice of the people themselves, and no nation in history ever so completely "sold themselves to the devil" as did the Germans to Hitler. Like attracts like, and, for all the wickedness and misery which followed, the German people are entirely to blame, because they were well aware what this monster of iniquity was like before they elected him and made him their national hero.

Had he not burned down the Reichstag (1933) in order to put the blame on the Communists, so as to increase his power over the people and abolish for ever the chance of democratic government coming again to Germany? Moreover, he had put his aggressive warlike plans in his book, which most Germans had read, as therein he forecast his territorial ambitions "with the help of God" and "by the might of the sword" when God will "allow the blood of the people to be shed once more". Therein was his attack on Russia clearly foreshadowed, after Britain had been lulled to sleep by a friendly treaty.

Besides this, all his terrorism of the previous ten years, his numerous murders, his intolerance, his treachery and deceit, were meekly accepted, including the "Blood Bath" of June 1934, when Roehm, one of his earliest supporters, and some 1200 others, were foully murdered. Likewise was condoned his treacherous and brutal murder of Dr. Dollfuss, the Chancellor of the Austrian Republic. So long as he represented a strong, defiant, proud, uncompromising Germany he received the support of the German people; the fact that he had degraded the name "German" to the lowest depths, and brought their civilisation back to the worst period of the Middle Ages, mattered nothing.

The German mentality puzzles many people, because, as individuals, they are decent and agreeable, but in the mass so hateful. To solve this enigma one has to live with them and discover their inmost thoughts, as only thus can we understand why it was that they were prepared to put "guns before butter". Since their defeat in 1918 they were haunted by fear, that strong emotion which everyone experiences from time to time. For the twenty years following their defeat this fear was never absent, because the German people were always looking eastwards in apprehension towards Russia, only to become tenfold more fearful when she became reorganised and industrialised.

Germany was a close neighbour of this vast

continent of some 8000 miles wide, embracing over 8,000,000 square miles of territory, and supporting a population of over 150,000,000, which was rapidly increasing each year. Russia, under the Tzars, was always a menace to Germany, but Russia educated and industrialised, under the capable and energetic Stalin, was a positive danger, and Hitler's constant fulminations against him came from fear.

The ever-present fear of Russia was primarily responsible for the Second World War, just as it was fear that made Lydia attack the growing Persian Empire in 550 B.C., and kept the Romans for ever attacking the German tribes in the west and the Parthians in the east. Fear caused the Romans to attack Carthage, just as it caused Japan two thousand years later, in our own time, to attack China, which was becoming modern in her outlook and united in her politics.

The Bolshevik creed certainly worried the German capitalists, but it was the Bolsheviks, as Russians, that frightened the German people as a whole to a very great degree, and it was by working on this latent fear that Hitler enslaved his people and bent them to his will. He and his gang had all their plans arranged for the domination of Europe, but what interested the average German was the confidence he gave them that by their blood and sweat he would secure Germany for a thousand years against the hordes they imagined were gathering in the east, intent on her destruction.

That was the scheme Hitler set out to carry through after he had succeeded in consolidating the Reich by the renunciation of the hated Versailles Treaty. To strengthen his frontiers he first incorporated Austria, and a year later Czecho-Slovakia, within the German boundaries, but when he found that Britain, instead of going to sleep after the Munich Pact, became very much awake, he decided that the time had come to strike before all his potential enemies became too strong.

The next section contains a summary of the German programme, which began with Russia and hoped to end with Russia deprived of Ukrainia and its immense wheatfields and granaries. Besides this the Donetz, rich in coal and iron, and the Caucasus from which flowed the oil, the life-blood of mechanized Russia, were likewise to be seized. Thus Hitler would paralyse his enemy and secure her riches, but to be able to hold them he would have to push the Russian army beyond the Urals and keep it there.

At the back of every German mind lay the hope of some day accomplishing this grandiose plan, and this aspiration explains why the German people followed Hitler submissively in peace and in war. Likewise it explains the meaning of Hitler's cryptic remark to the British ambassador on the outbreak of war that he would rather have a war in 1939 than five years later. What he meant was that Germany intended to be on top before it was too late, because if he waited for another five years Russia would be too strong to defeat. It moreover explains the Lavals and the Quislings who came under his domination, as they, and their followers in Europe, also feared what they called another Mongol invasion of Europe when the Russians became strong enough, and sufficiently eager, for territorial conquests.

If the Germans had been led by a wise and good

man, and if Germany had not contained such a large number of utter scoundrels, willing and eager to pursue evil instead of righteousness, the fears of the German people could have been removed by a defensive alliance with Poland, Czecho-Slovakia, Rumania and Bulgaria, which in itself would have created a strong barrier against Russian aggression. Instead of this statesmanlike way of meeting a danger Hitler aggravated it by withdrawing from the League of Nations, and using the ever-present fear of Russia to further the plans he and his inner clique had made for world domination.

On this fear he built up his scheme of European conquest, and eventual world conquest, and when he discovered the sympathy accorded by some Germans to Neville Chamberlain's peaceful aims, after the British Prime Minister's visit to Munich, he turned on once more at full blast the theme which had worked so well in the past. The Russian bogey was brought out again, the simple uncritical Germans again began to shiver, and their Press commenced an abusive campaign against Britain for interfering in Europe, where she had no business. Hitler and his gang did not want peace, the leading iron and steel manufacturers wanted war, and his simple dupes believed his lies, which twisted everything to suit his own evil designs.

Hitler, and he alone, was the first and foremost influence responsible for the war, but if he had not ruled over a nation of sheep he would never have got away with it. Consequently the Germans themselves were to blame for the terrible tragedy which was to follow their giving full power into the hands of an unbalanced, abnormal, sadistic creature, suffering from hysteria, paranoia-persecutoria and megalomania, as any sensible person was able to realise by his deeds and speeches, his writings and his conversation.

Hitler's first act, when he became Chancellor, was to withdraw Germany from the League of Nations and the Disarmament Conference, and when, two years later, conscription was restored and rearmament commenced, the hysterical pleasure of the German people knew no bounds. By now only teachers permeated with the Nazi doctrine could teach in schools, and all who expressed anti-Nazi opinions eventually found themselves in concentration camps, the consequence being that Germany lost to Britain, Russia and the United States the foremost position she had previously held in the world of science.

Instead of being famous for her scientists she became a nation of political fanatics, who were kept at fever heat by the radio, which, with wearisome reiteration, blazoned forth the Nazi doctrines. These embraced day by day a bitter denunciation of the Jews and the danger of Bolshevism, none but the Nazis being permitted to approach the microphone. So the vast majority of Germans were transformed into Nazis, a name which will carry contempt and hatred so long as a decent man and woman survives on earth.

Hitler was well served by his principal officers. Joachim von Ribbentrop ably conducted his tortuous foreign policy, and Schacht manipulated the country's finances, while Joseph Goebbels proved himself a competent and unscrupulous propaganda minister. Hermann Göring built up a formidable air force, and

Heinrich Himmler (the most powerful of them all, and the greatest terrorist since Torquemada, the Christian priest, directed the Inquisition) organised a secret police force which permitted no critic to escape detection. Every evil device was invented to catch unawares all who were opposed to the Nazi régime, and on them was inflicted, without previous trial, whatever punishment the Nazi officials decided.

The Jews suffered from the most outrageous brutalities, their standard of living being reduced to the level of outcasts, and much of their wealth was confiscated to enrich the chief gangsters. Hitler himself, who never lost a chance to denounce both the Jews and plutocrats, benefited greatly financially from this persecution, to become the richest plutocrat in Europe. The other leading gangsters enriched themselves according to their positions, and amassed enormous fortunes, some of which was invested abroad as a precaution against a turn in their fortunes.

Hitler, with borrowed money, became the sole owner in 1921 of the Zentral Verlag, the great German publishing combine, whose net profits rose to nearly £10,000,000 a year, all of which went into his own private purse. At first its profits were small and its development was slow, but, after he became Chancellor, they grew quickly by him confiscating the properties and goodwill of all competitors. In 1935 it took over, by confiscation, a large Jewish publishing business and two other important concerns, after which followed, likewise by confiscation, the Wulf News Agency, which had a complete monopoly of the distribution of news in Germany. Then came the taking over of practically all the advertising agencies.

The Zentral Verlag published all the Nazi Party books and all the technical and professional periodicals, including *Mein Kampf*, a copy of which everyone was expected to have in his home. It owned, moreover, two thirds of all the German newspapers, with a daily circulation of 16,000,000 copies. No other newspaper and publishing magnate had ever before obtained such control over what the people read, but when a man becomes the chief gangster over a nation of slaves, and is unscrupulous enough, he can of course do anything he likes, as there is no one to raise a word of protest. This was only one means he used to increase his wealth, as in other ways, by a secret tax on industry, he secured an additional income of £3,000,000 a year, much of which went in bribery and corruption.

While thus enriching himself, and living in the greatest luxury, he was sufficiently wise to make his slaves feel that he was their great benefactor, and to do so he planned to keep Germany ahead of other countries in social progress. Germany, we must remember, was a pioneer in insurance, because Bismarck first instituted insurance against sickness (1883), then against accidents (1884), and finally in 1889 for old age. Nothing was done against unemployment, but by 1914 much had been done that had been left undone, and Germany compared favourably with the social progress of any other European country.

The social policy of the National Socialist Party was in part a continuance of past tradition, the only difference being that the Party developed it to its own advantage. Elementary education had been compulsory in Prussia and Saxony since 1815, and this was supplemented by a highly developed system of continuation and technical schools. The Republic developed this mixture of paternalism and humanitarianism, going the length of giving labour a legal status such as existed in no other country, the maintenance of anyone who could not find employment being the direct obligation of the State. In social progress Germany has to her credit many past achievements which blossomed and bore increased fruit under the Nazi régime.

There was much to admire in Nazi social legislation, its methods of accomplishment being what revolted every freedom-loving democratic individual. In Britain, for instance, the people themselves, through their representatives, produced the social conditions they now enjoy, but in Germany the people accepted what they were given. Holidays with pay, combined with the cheap travel, entertainment and the sporting service of Kraft durch Freude (Strength through Joy), though not new, was extended by the Nazis and greatly appreciated. In like manner was Schönheit der Arbeit (Beauty of Work), which was concerned with improving the amenities of the life of the workers. Inspectors visited factories to see that they were clean and well ventilated, and that all canteens were airy, clean and attractive.

The labour movement, or Labour Front, as it was called, became an organ of the Nazi Party, its main function being to reconcile the vast body of German workers of every grade to the social and political aims of the Nazi régime. It took over all the Trade Unions' funds, its membership became 25,000,000 and all employers and employees, except Jews, were expected to join. It had no independence, no bargaining power, its officials were appointed by the Party, and it had no power over wages or hours of labour, which was the function of the Trustees of Labour. This latter organisation took the place of the Trade Unions, and the right to strike and bargain over hours and wages was made illegal.

When Hitler became Chancellor in 1933 there were 6,000,000 unemployed, the result of the economic depression of the three previous years, and this was the main cause of the fall of the Republic and one of the reasons for his spectacular rise to power. Vast schemes for new roads, canals, houses, land improvement, railways, public works, etc., were at once put in hand. This was named the First Four-Year Plan, and it had the effect of reducing the unemployed to well under three million within a year. Then followed the rearming of Germany in 1935, and the Second Four-Year Plan to render Germany independent of essential materials and foodstuffs from abroad, all of which, as the pace quickened year by year, with war drawing nearer, reduced unemployment to negligible proportions.

For the return of employment, and the improvement in social conditions, Hitler received the unbounded gratitude of his devoted subjects, who now looked on in grateful amazement to see him tear up the last shreds of the detested Versailles Treaty by the threat of the powerful armaments they had produced.

In 1936 Germany repudiated the Treaty of Locarno and occupied the demilitarised zone of the Rhineland, thus breaking her plighted word given at Locarno and Versailles. By now secret rearmament on a large scale was in full swing, so much so that by 1938 she felt strong enough to invade and annex Austria, likewise contrary to these treaties. Czecho-Slovakia was next annexed to Germany (1939), contrary to Hitler's pledged word as given in the Munich Pact, and this was followed in the Autumn by the breaking of his country's peace treaty with Poland, a friendly nation which the Germans invaded without any provocation.

The other nations of Europe looked on in growing alarm as year by year Germany's power and aggression increased. Poland, now her victim, was only recovering from the First World War, as on her soil the principal battles of the eastern campaign had been fought. During that time she was drenched in blood, her towns blasted by explosives and her people exposed to indescribable barbarities. Out of this hell of suffering a new Poland had arisen when the war ended, and the Poles, after more than a century of servitude, again found themselves free, though impoverished and battered.

Under their great patriot Joseph Pilsudski (1867–1935), who for years had been organising a national Polish army, they, with their new-found liberty, attempted to take Kiev (1920), only to be driven back by the Russians, who again overran their country. Then the tide turned with the help of General Weygand and his staff of French officers, when the Polish army, under the command of Pilsudski, won a complete victory over the invaders, who were driven across the border into their own country. Though quite inexperienced in self-government, the Poles adopted a modern democratic parliamentary system, but efficient government became impossible as fourteen separate parties were formed, and ministry after ministry took and relinquished office in bewildering rapidity.

Matters went from bad to worse, and Pilsudski felt compelled to return from his retirement, as only he could produce order out of chaos. He refused to be President but became Minister of War, and secured the election of a respected professor as President, under whom sat a permanent council to direct the business of state. Parliament was not abolished, but it was only expected to meet and discuss affairs until the time came when the people were sufficiently educated to govern themselves. As Minister of War, with a devoted army behind him, Pilsudski was dictator of Poland until his death in 1935. He secured non-aggression pacts with both Russia and Germany, and brought a feeling of security to his people, who for centuries had been ravaged by war.

Much of what became eastern Poland was taken from Russia after the First World War, and this she lost to Russia in 1939. Here, during the time it was occupied by the Poles, their Catholic hatred towards the Russian Orthodox Christians was pronounced, and for twenty years a continuous effort was made to transform them into both Poles and Roman Catholics. To carry this into effect the Russian Christians in Poland were tortured and imprisoned by the methods adopted by the Inquisition.

Under the rule of the devout Pilsudski persecution reached its height when priests, acting as Inquisitors

of the Faith, went from place to place, accompanied
by armed soldiers, to close the Orthodox churches,
apply their tortures, or arrest those who would not
subscribe to the Catholic faith. In the part of Silesia
which Poland secured from Germany in 1919, Roman
Catholic persecution of the German Protestants was
also grievous, and this was happening in Poland when
the Vatican was flooding the world with its false
propaganda about religious persecution in Russia,
a subject which is further considered at the end of this
chapter.

Fear of Communism produced legislation in
Poland, Czecho-Slovakia, Rumania and the Baltic
States, which satisfied the peasantry by the division
for their benefit of the larger properties. The large
landowners disappeared, and their place was taken
by a bastion of contented peasant owners who separated Russia from the rest of Central Europe. This
bulwark the self-styled enemy of Communism, Hitler,
broke down when he attacked Poland in 1939,
because, under the treaty concluded with Russia a
month before the German invasion of Poland, he
gave Russia the opportunity to occupy again part
of Poland and the Baltic States.

So as to be able to strike swiftly at Russia, when
the time came, Hitler crushed all western Poland,
and thus avoided the necessity of fighting through
it before he reached his real enemy Russia. This
savage treachery, carefully prepared a year beforehand,
was only to be expected from one who had a few
years earlier, in company with his fellow thug Mussolini, sent soldiers to Spain who perpetrated the most
atrocious cruelties upon thousands of innocent men,

women and children. This came about in 1936, when General Franco, a devout Roman Catholic, with a priest always by his side, raised a revolt against the Spanish Republican government, and this brought to a climax the increasing bitterness between the Fascist and Communist factions. Moreover, the Republican government was unfriendly towards the Church, which hitherto had dominated Spain in much the same way as the Anglican Church had tyrannised over England a century earlier.

All the reactionaries in Spain joined, or supported, his force of rebels, and a cruel and devastating civil war followed, during which an attempt was made by Britain and France to prevent outside help from reaching either side. Foreign volunteers, however, hastened to Spain to support both sides, and while France, Britain and Russia, in some measure, helped the Liberals, Italy and Germany gave open and material aid to Franco, Mussolini stating that he was determined Franco would win. Troops, technical experts, airplanes and armaments, in ever-growing quantities, poured into Spain from Germany and Italy, until the Liberals were overwhelmed after a desperate and prolonged struggle which lasted for three years.

During this time of fratricidal strife, terrible outrages were committed by both sides on a helpless people. Unprotected towns and villages were subjected to a pitiless bombardment by German and Italian airplanes, and thousands who were taking no part in the conflict were thus wiped out or mutilated. In 1939 Madrid was captured by the rebels, when Franco became dictator of a totalitarian Fascist state with the Church restored to its old position, while the people had again to accept the loss of their liberty, which the majority had fought so gallantly to retain.

The Jesuits returned from exile and were given back their lands and wealth, the annual state payment to the Church was restored, the burial grounds, which under the Republic had been transferred to municipal ownership, were returned to the Church, and the priest again became supreme in the schools. Consequently religious pictures and emblems are now plastered on the walls of both the schools and squalid prisons, which latter, for the treatment accorded the prisoners, resemble those of the Middle Ages. Vindictive vengeance, terror and torture are now general, and everywhere the shadow of the priest is to be seen. Verily the Church won this, its latest, holy war, "this veritable crusade for the Christian religion" as Cardinal Goma of Toledo put it.

In the interval between the two world wars four great European states became totalitarian in their method of government, and the 19th-century dream of democracy coming into its own was shattered. Ignorance was behind the reaction, just as it was the cause of the incompetence displayed by France, who permitted her democratic system to be undermined and sapped by her too numerous unscrupulous politicians prostituting their positions for their own immediate gain.

Between 1918 and 1934 the average duration of an administration in France was a little over eight months, which discontinuity of rule made firm and consecutive government impossible. Responsible ministers had their hands tied by standing committees which usurped their functions and impaired their authority. Reforms beneficial to the people were consequently difficult to secure owing to vested interests, corruption and intrigue. French democratic government collapsed in 1940 under defeat, but, with France again arisen, a thorough overhaul and remodelling of her government has come about to enable her to take her place as a leading democratic power in Europe.

The period in European history between the two great wars was one of slow financial recovery from the First World War, but it was also a time of many individual and racial tragedies which were directly due to that great upheaval. Greece was severed by a deadly feud between the Venizelists and the Monarchists, to end in the return of King George to the throne in 1935. From Asia Minor, Greeks fled to escape Turkish tyranny, and from Germany streamed the persecuted Jews. Russian aristocrats fled from the wrath of their own countrymen, and Europe was nearly everywhere, first here, and then there, a seething cauldron of unrest, with poor humanity earnestly desiring peace and prosperity, only to see it steadily slipping from its grasp.

All might have been so different had ignorance not reigned supreme. Educated, intelligent and enlightened communities of human beings would never have permitted affairs to develop as they did, but the First World War seemed to produce a kind of mental paralysis which enfeebled the will, and allowed to be lost all that the fight for liberty had gained during the previous fifty years. Europe's suffering was unfortunately not yet over, as only an interregnum had been permitted by destiny to allow her to breathe before the stranglehold of war once again overtook her. Again the time had come for the lash to be applied once more to the flesh, still deeply scarred and not yet healed.

When this ghastly story has been told our history ends, the final chapter being devoted to a consideration of what we have read. The value of history is not in its record of events, but in the lessons to be drawn from them, as only by learning from the past can we make our upward climb to perfection less difficult. Practical steps must certainly be taken in the years to come for the increased security and happiness of the people, and past experience is our only guide. So we must ponder deeply over the lessons the past has to teach, honestly resolved that, by our increased knowledge and wisdom, measures will be taken to ensure that those who come after us will not be the victims of the trials and sufferings we have experienced.

(6) Germany Again Plunges the World into War.

We have now arrived at the beginning of the greatest war, the greatest slaughter and the greatest tragedy in all history, when a tornado of unparalleled destruction swept over the earth. This fierce hurricane produced more suffering, and greater misery to a greater number, than has ever before been experienced in the past. It was because of the appalling extent and severity of the calamity which had engulfed humanity that the author devoted his spare time during this period of devastation and desolation to write this history of mankind from a completely new angle of thought, in the hope that by his labour he would contribute something to guide the people everywhere into a better and wiser way of living.

This tragedy, which overtook the human race, caused him to think deeply in order to find the cause which has produced all the suffering and misery that has befallen mankind from primitive times to the present day. These afflictions can be traced back every time to ignorance and all the evil it produces. So, with this as his theme, he set to work to write a history of the past from a new aspect, in the hope that his unorthodox, but nevertheless truthful, record may help to lead those who come after us out of the dark forest of ignorance and folly into the light of knowledge and wisdom.

By revealing the waste of effort, the quite unnecessary loss of life and wealth, besides the suffering which ignorance always brings in its train, and by exposing the cause, and propounding the remedy, future generations have now something to guide them which was not possessed by our ancestors. Let us hope that with this increased knowledge a brighter future opens for mankind, who, up to now, has been ignorant of the right way to live and attain security, comfort and happiness.

Our long journey through historic time has now brought us to the year 1939, which opened in a lull after a violent diplomatic storm which the Munich agreement three months earlier had prevented from developing into war. This pact was hardly concluded before it was broken by Germany invading Czecho-Slovakia. President Roosevelt then asked Germany for a pledge of non-aggression against the remaining states of Europe, only to be met by an evasive reply.

Germany's bad faith was now so apparent that both France and Britain prepared for the coming inevitable clash of arms, and she was given unmistakable warning that her next act of aggression would be resisted, on their part, by force. Poland, Turkey, Rumania and Greece now received their promise of help in the event of any interference in their sovereign rights, and the British Parliament passed an Act making military service compulsory for men reaching the age of twenty.

Poland was the next country the Germans now prepared to attack, and this was preceded by a demand for the return of the Polish Corridor leading to the sea, and also the port of Danzig. Meantime Germany and Italy concluded a military alliance, and Britain and France attempted to bring Russia on to their side. Much to the surprise of everyone, Russia concluded a non-aggression pact with Germany, thus putting Poland at the aggressor's mercy, because neither France nor Britain could send her effective aid.

On September 1st, 1939, the Germans stated that the Poles had rejected her terms of peace, but it is now known that no such terms had been presented. Simultaneously, with this false declaration, they sent their air force over Warsaw, and other Polish towns, which were bombed unmercifully. Hitler, by this act, not only broke his country's non-aggression treaty with Poland, but also broke his undertaking to his own people that he would never lead them into war without their consent by means of a plebiscite. That, however, was now forgotten, and the German people entered this new war, as they did every other over the past seventy-five years, by giving their leaders their wholehearted support and confidence.

A few days before the invasion of Poland, Hitler made a speech (found amongst secret documents after the war) to his generals and Nazi chiefs, who enthusiastically cheered when he said:

I have sent to the east my Death's Head units, with the order to kill without pity or mercy all men, women and children of the Polish race or language. Poland will be depopulated and colonised with Germans; in Russia there will happen just what is practised in Poland. If Chamberlain, or such another dirty swine, comes with peace propositions he will be thrown downstairs even if I must personally kick him in the belly. Glory and honour are beckoning you, gentlemen. Act now quickly and brutally. The citizens of western Europe must quiver in horror. Now on to the enemy! In Warsaw we will celebrate again.

Such a creature will be ranked by history on an even lower level than Joshua, Jengis Khan, his son Ogdai, and Timurlane, and we are therefore not surprised that Britain and France, realising that their turn would come next, declared war on 3rd September, 1939, to be followed by the British Dominions, and so began the Second World War. Eire adopted a policy of neutrality, and took no part in the war. To find the first cause of this great catastrophe we must go back twenty-two years to the Russian Revolution, from which followed the sequence of events tabulated hereunder:

(1) The Russian Revolution finally ended serfdom and general education commenced. An educated, virile Russia was a greater danger to

Germany than the effete, mismanaged, ignorant Russia of the Tzars.

(2) Education encouraged industry, and the machine took the place of hand labour.

(3) The machine developed Russia's vast mineral resources.

(4) Russia became a strong, efficient, mechanised industrial state with a growing well-equipped army.

(5) Germany was then poorly armed, and deprived of the Saar with its rich coal-fields, which had been given to France for fifteen years.

(6) Hitler promised to get back all that Germany had lost in the last war, and to build up a strong army to protect her eastern frontier.

(7) The German people almost unanimously gave him unbridled power, and then he began to rearm in earnest.

(8) When Germany became strong and powerful the inner Nazi clique prepared for war to secure the domination of Europe step by step, the principal aim being the final removal of Russia as a military power.

(9) All their scheming was directed to this culminating goal, the elimination of Russia, but it had to be accomplished in a round-about way.

(10) Peacefully Hitler managed to strengthen Germany by incorporating Austria and Czecho-Slovakia within the Reich, the Saar by now having been returned to Germany.

(11) Poland was next to be conquered, but the British and French guarantee to preserve her sovereign rights caused an alteration in Hitler's plans.

(12) Germany had no wish in 1939 to go to war with Britain and France, as that was to come later, but Poland had to be eliminated to enable her to get at Russia. Consequently war with Britain and France became necessary because of their guarantee to Poland, and Russia was in the meantime to be kept quiet by means of a non-aggression treaty until Britain and France were defeated. It is difficult to explain why Russia agreed to this, as at the time it was so evidently contrary to her ultimate interests, and events proved that she made a colossal blunder for which she paid right dearly.

(13) When the Russian pact was signed Germany attacked Poland, and then Britain and France declared war on Germany. France was conquered but Britain was not. Then Germany made her fatal blunder, as she gave up her attempt to conquer Britain and broke her treaty with Russia, hoping now to smash Russia and so overcome the British blockade by obtaining all she needed in the east. With this accomplished all her vast shipbuilding and other resources would be applied against Britain. who was to become her final victim in Europe.

(14) Russia, however, was not conquered. The produce expected from Russia was not

obtained, the blockade remained, and Germany was faced with Britain, Russia and the United States, all determined to defeat her.

The pages which follow will tell the story of how the German plans developed and were foiled, and of how the tragedy she brought on Europe ended. So we now go back to September 1939, when the German army, systematically trained to be cruel and brutal, was battering its way through Poland towards Warsaw. Italy and Japan, aggrieved that their ally had made a pact with Communism, held aloof, and Germany alone was at war with the British Empire and France until the collapse of France the following year.

The onward rush eastwards of German mechanised troops, supported by an overwhelming air force, proceeded at great speed, because Poland could do little to stem this ferocious aggression, and before the month ended Warsaw surrendered. To prevent Germany getting all Poland, and in order to put as much territory as possible between her and her potential enemy, Russia now swept in from the east, and the Poles, caught between two fires, surrendered, the two invaders dividing the country between them.

France was protected against invasion, up to the Belgian frontier, by an elaborate system of defence known as the Maginot Line, while Germany, on her side, had the equally strong Siegfried Line, against which neither France nor Britain attempted to attack. Part of the Belgian frontier was protected by British troops under General Lord Gort, who had landed in France within a week of the outbreak of war, and over both the French and British forces was placed the French General Gamelin. Germany, however, made no attempt to attack in the west, a state of affairs which lasted into the middle of 1940.

Meantime the British navy blockaded German ports, and German shipping was sunk or forced to seek shelter in home or foreign harbours. German submarines were active against allied shipping, and many good ships, precious cargoes and valuable lives were lost by sudden unseen torpedo attack. This, however, did not go unchallenged, as forty German submarines were destroyed within the first three months of warfare. Later much destruction of shipping was caused by bombs and mines, the German magnetic mine causing havoc until means were discovered to neutralise its effects. Against the British navy Germany was less fortunate, three British cruisers, collectively much inferior in gun power, forcing the commerce raiding battleship *Graf Spee* into Montevideo, where she was scuttled by her own crew to avoid internment.

In Britain many children were evacuated from the large towns to the country to lessen their danger from bombing. Winston Churchill took over charge of the Admiralty, and Parliament passed much emergency legislation, besides setting up new ministries to co-ordinate more efficiently the war effort. Conscription was extended to men of forty-one, and the income tax was raised to 7s. 6d. and then to 10s. in the pound.

In Europe the end of 1939 found Russia in possession of the Baltic States (which was the price Hitler had paid for her neutrality), and at war with Finland for the purpose of pushing the Finns farther from Leningrad. Their frontier was so close to this city that it would be in danger should the Germans later land forces in Finland to attack Russia. This war could have been avoided if the Finns had accepted the generous compensation Russia offered for this land which was so vital for her safety, but throughout the Finns were stupid and uncompromising, to suffer grievously for their folly in the end.

During the first two months of 1940 the Russian-Finnish conflict continued, the numerically superior Russian forces only with difficulty beating down the Finnish spirited resistance, but by March the Finns were compelled to make peace and remove their frontier farther west. No sooner was this conflict ended than the German forces were again on the march, this time striking at Denmark and Norway. The former made only trifling resistance, but the Norwegians put up a stout defence under the leadership of their king, who was later forced to leave his people and find refuge in Britain. By dropping soldiers from parachutes behind the Norwegian defence lines, by heavy bombing and the help of traitors, of whom the most notorious was Major Quisling, who gave his name to the sinister breed, the Germans occupied the principal towns and controlled the land.

Britain sent help to the hard-pressed Norwegians, but the men who succeeded in landing were quickly driven out. Even isolated Narvik in the north, where the British landed after a successful destroyer engagement, could not be held and had to be evacuated after one month of occupation. The failure of this expedition had its effect in London, as it raised to a head the feeling in Parliament that the Neville Chamberlain government was lacking in drive. Chamberlain was forced to resign, and Winston Churchill became Prime Minister of a government in which the Labour and Liberal leaders now agreed to participate, thus making the administration representative of the entire country. A similar reorganisation, for the same reason, had taken place seven weeks earlier in France when Paul Reynaud had replaced Daladier as Prime Minister, and now both governments worked together through a supreme War Council after concluding an agreement not to sign a separate peace.

Winston Churchill (1940–1945) succeeded Neville Chamberlain as Prime Minister in May 1940, and Chamberlain accepted the office of Lord President of the Council. He did not long survive his relinquishment of the premiership, as he died in November 1940 following an abdominal operation. Shortly before his death Churchill wrote to him, "You did all you could for peace, you did all you could for victory". His ashes were buried in Westminster Abbey, but the deeds and example of this great and noble man will long be treasured by the British people. He represented everything that is upright and honourable in present-day British political life, his aim always being to increase and further the welfare of the people, to whom he devoted his long life of public service.

Winston Churchill took over the helm of state when the storm was near its height, and before long had to suffer the shock and disappointment of the loss of France as an ally. His strength, wisdom, courage and calm at that critical period of British history will never be forgotten. It forms an epic which will never die, so long as men and women live to cherish liberty and hate bondage and servitude. He gave Britain, her Dominions, her colonies, enslaved Europe, the Americans, and all lovers of freedom, both hope and courage in civilisation's darkest hour. By his strength and determination he made us all strong and resolved to resist, to work, to overcome and conquer, or perish. In Britain's midnight hour he was the light to which everyone turned for guidance and deliverance.

He could only promise that, through blood and sweat and tears, victory would finally crown the British effort; he kept to facts and always spoke the truth, never making the position to be better or worse than it was. On his shoulders rested a burden of responsibility and care during those anxious years which few can realise, and yet he never wavered nor faltered, leading the people ever onwards on their rough and dangerous climb to the heights called victory.

History will place him for his courage on a level with William Pitt, for his foresight alongside of Kitchener, for his energy and devotion to duty beside Lloyd George, and for his policy and strategy in the company of his illustrious ancestor John Churchill, 1st Duke of Marlborough. Fortunate it was for Britain and the Empire, providential it was for all humanity, to have such a leader during this, one of civilisation's most dangerous periods, and historians of the future will regard Winston Churchill as amongst the greatest and grandest figures of all time. Never before did so many owe so much to one single man.

During the war Parliament confined its energies to passing legislation concerned with the conduct of the war, numerous measures being adopted to secure the safety of the realm. As victory came closer, attention was given to post-war problems, rebuilding, town and country planning, trade at home and abroad, shipping and civil aviation. The most discussed of all the proposals centred round the report of Sir William Beveridge, who was commissioned to draw up an improved scheme of social insurance and workmen's compensation. He put forward an ambitious plan for social security, aimed at the abolition of poverty, by providing all citizens with a subsistence income during old age, unemployment, disability, ill-health, maternity, widowhood, and a grant for funeral expenses.

Parliament gave general approval to these proposals at the end of 1944, and set up a Ministry of National Insurance to administer all present and future insurance legislation. Besides these much-needed social measures the Minister of Education, R. A. Butler, introduced and carried through Parliament a new Education Bill in 1944, which superseded all previous Acts, and involved a complete recasting of the national system of education into primary, secondary and further stages.

The County Councils and County Borough Councils became the only education authorities, and it became necessary for every school to be registered and open to inspection. Nursery schools, well designed primary schools, and secondary schools of various types became available to all children free of charge. Compulsory part-time education for all young people up to eighteen years of age was provided, besides adequate facilities for technical and adult instruction, but the Bill was marred by the concessions made to religious scruples, much heated discussion being aroused by the provision that on the teachers devolved the duty of instructing the children in the Christian religion and the contents of the Bible.

Churchill was fortunate in his choice of ministers, who one and all helped him loyally to bring the ship of state safely into harbour. Anthony Eden proved himself an able and far-sighted Foreign Secretary, and Sir Kingsley Wood, as Chancellor of the Exchequer, a sound financier. On his death Sir John Anderson took over this office and maintained his predecessor's reputation. Lord Woolton, as Minister of Food, was a great success, and kept the food supply justly and evenly distributed. Ernest Bevin mobilised the country's labour, and Herbert Morrison, as Home Secretary and Minister of Home Security, had an arduous task in organising the country's fight against bombs which blasted and set fire to towns and villages.

Often were the relations between the House of Commons and the government sorely strained, following the long and dismal series of disasters due to Britain's lack of weapons. The fall of Singapore and the loss of Tobruk were two outstanding occasions when the Prime Minister had to face his hostile critics. Churchill successfully parried the thrusts, in spite of being bound to secrecy in regard to the great and promising enterprises that were then on the way, and when success followed defeat he was heartily accorded the gratitude of a much relieved Parliament and people.

On the day Churchill became Prime Minister the Germans made another, and this time the most violent, of their lightning attacks. Without previous warning, and lacking justification, the full fury of the German onslaught was unloosed against Holland and Belgium for the purpose of forcing a passage into France round the north of the Maginot Line. The Dutch had relied for their safety on the opening of the dykes, and the consequent flooding of the land, but this proved inadequate against the high speed of the attack, accompanied as it was by intense bombing and the dropping of parachutists. After the havoc and slaughter caused by bombs dropped on Rotterdam, which obliterated a large part of the city, the Dutch army surrendered only five days after the attack began.

Meanwhile British and French forces stationed on the frontier quickly moved into Belgium, but here again the rapidity and concentration of the invading army's movements quickly broke down the allied strategic plan. At a critical point of the allied line, near Sedan, two French divisions broke under the attack, leaving a gap through which the German tanks poured into France. The advancing invaders quickly widened the breach, and, swinging to the right, advanced on the Channel ports. Thus the Belgian army found its right flank fatally exposed, and, by the time the Germans reached Boulogne at the end of May 1940, King Leopold was forced to surrender.

France was now open to the invader, as the left wing of the French army was threatened by encirclement, and the British forces were cut off from the

French with only Dunkirk to which to retreat. No other course was now open to the British commanders, and hurried arrangements were made for the re-embarkation of their forces in the face of heavy enemy pressure and intense attacks from the air. One of the most hazardous of operations was carried through successfully by a remarkable feat of co-operation between the three fighting services, helped as they were by volunteers who manned every available craft, down to rowing-boats, which were hurried over to Dunkirk to pick up and bring to England the men waiting on the beaches. A desperate rear-guard action kept the Germans off long enough to enable the greater part of the British army to be evacuated, 300,000 out of 330,000 returning home safely, but many lacked everything but their clothes.

Britain, already short of arms, was now further crippled by the loss of the entire equipment of the Expeditionary Force, and only by intense effort was this made good, but not before the enemy commenced violent air raids preparatory to invasion. France meantime was experiencing the horrors of invasion. General Weygand replaced Gamelin, who was dismissed, but it was now too late for him to stem the headlong rush of the German mechanised columns. These swept onwards, driving before them not only the French army but a host of civilian refugees, who were mercilessly bombed and machine-gunned from the air.

Paris was captured without resistance, and the French Government fled to Bordeaux. In fear and panic the Cabinet decided on complete surrender, thus breaking the treaty with Britain not to make a separate peace. Alone of all the countries overrun by Germany, France, the largest, was the only one to work treacherously with her former enemy against her friends, the governments of all the others, except Denmark, leaving their lands, taking up residence in London, and continuing to fight and defy the enemy.

Marshal Pétain, the hero of the successful defence of Verdun in the First World War, became Prime Minister of the southern part of France unoccupied by the Germans, his appointment being made by the National Assembly at Bordeaux, after Reynaud resigned when he could get no support for his plan to continue the fight from North Africa. Pétain, a super-pessimist and defeatist, and the other advocates of surrender, who now had the upper hand, further turned down the British offer to unite the two states, France and Britain, under a system of common citizenship, if only France would carry on the fight. Churchill, who made this proposal, was told in reply that "Germany would next wring Britain's neck as easily as that of a chicken".

Italy, who had so far done no fighting, now entered the war on the side that appeared to be already victorious, hopeful that she would share in the pickings when the French Empire was divided up, and France came under the influence of Pierre Laval. This unscrupulous quisling (who, with others like him throughout Europe, met a traitor's death when the war ended) was mainly responsible for the fatal blunder made by the National Assembly when it agreed to unconditional surrender. He was ready to subject his country to any humiliation for the sake of peace, concluding an Armistice with Germany on

22nd June, 1940, to become later her willing agent when he obtained supreme control. Northern and western France were occupied by the Germans, and the French government moved to Vichy to reorganise, as best it could, the southern provinces with which it had been left.

Britain was now in extreme peril, as she stood alone, poorly armed, against the might of both Germany and Italy. A small but good air force, and the navy, were all she could rely upon to save her from invasion. Her outer defences on the Continent had collapsed, and now she had to guard alone an immense coastline. In North Africa her position was equally serious, as, with the entry of Italy into the war, and the withdrawal of the French fleet, her forces in Egypt, now faced by a superior Italian army based in Libya, could no longer be supplied by way of the Mediterranean, the long sea route via the Cape being necessary.

Fortunately neither Germany nor Italy was quite prepared to pursue immediately their advantage, but, by August, intense daylight air raids began on Britain. These were intended to prepare the way for invasion, the enemy's endeavour being to destroy the British air force and airdromes, so as to secure command of the air over the Channel, and isolate the ports on both sides from British attack by air or sea.

The German attempt to secure complete mastery of the air failed, though the Battle of Britain, fought in the air, was long and bitter. From the beginning of August, for two months, large forces of German bombers, accompanied by fighters, flew across the Channel and subjected southern England and London to a heavy bombardment by day, but the British fighters, under the direction of Air Chief Marshal Lord Dowding, gradually wore them down by destroying three for every one they lost. In September the R.A.F. destroyed 1064 enemy aircraft, a number the Germans could not replace. Heavy daylight bombing now ceased, and this, the greatest air battle so far ever fought, terminated with Britain victorious.

The Battle of Britain was one of the great decisive battles of history, and when it was won the Royal Air Force turned on the French Channel ports, and smashed the barges which had been assembled for invasion. Never before did the British people owe so much to so few, that small company of fearless airmen who, during these two critical months, beat off the vanguard of the invading army.

Britain's confidence now returned with the knowledge that though still outnumbered in both machines and men, she was, from the point of view of quality, superior in the air. A "Home Guard" had by now been formed, her army was again becoming equipped, and, as the enemy realised his defeat, he commenced intense night bombing of London and other cities. Much destruction was caused, and many civilians were killed and wounded, but these new tactics brought no military decision, and only stiffened the British determination to resist and produce the required enormous quantity of weapons and munitions. British fortitude, under the most devastating attack a civilian population had hitherto been called upon to experience, defeated the German attempt to break the nation's morale, and prepared the way for ultimate victory.

Likewise in the Mediterranean the situation changed to Britain's advantage. Some of the principal French warships which seemed to be on the point of being handed over to the Germans by the Vichy government were put out of action by the British Navy. Vichy broke off diplomatic relations with Britain, but the French colonies of Chad, the Cameroons and Equatorial Africa declared their adherence to the cause of Free France, and against the policy adopted by Vichy of collaboration with Germany. An attempt was made by General de Gaulle, the heroic leader of the small French forces fighting by the side of Britain, to capture Dakar on the coast of French West Africa for what was called Free France, but it failed because Vichy, already aware of the intention, strongly reinforced the garrison with her own sympathisers.

The Italians, in October 1940, now launched a treacherous attack on Greece through Albania, without any justification, to meet first with stiff resistance, and then be driven back. British bombers then attacked Taranto harbour, and delivered a crippling blow at the main Italian fleet lying there, an action which swung the balance of sea power in the Mediterranean over to Britain's favour. General Wavell, the British commander in Egypt, now struck at the Italian army in Libya, and swept it into Tripolitania, taking as prisoners most of those who survived, and great quantities of ammunition and equipment. By the beginning of 1941 Britain was supreme in Egypt and Libya, while Eritrea, Italian Somaliland and Abyssinia were being successfully invaded, and the British navy, under Admiral Cunningham, dominated the eastern Mediterranean.

The year 1940 closed with Britain's position definitely better than it was when France collapsed six months earlier, and her bombers were causing great havoc to German and Italian cities. Nevertheless her position was by no means comfortable, because she likewise was suffering from very heavy bombing raids each night, and these caused great havoc, principally to dwelling-houses. Germany, moreover, dominated all central Europe as well as Italy and France, and Japan had become her ally awaiting a favourable opportunity to pounce on the unprotected east. Both Hungary and Rumania had been swept into the German net, and Spain seemed likely to be the next to be caught. Turkey proclaimed her neutrality and friendship with Britain, but Russia remained an enigma, professing friendship for Germany, but still retaining large forces on her frontiers.

On the other hand the United States, realising her danger in the event of a German victory, drew ever closer to Britain, and sent her large supplies of arms and food. President Roosevelt was returned at the presidential election pledged to support the British Empire to the utmost of his country's power. Fifty American destroyers were given in exchange for air bases in the British West Indies, but the greatest help came from the passage, early in 1941, of the Lease-Lend Act.

This very timely piece of legislation enabled the American Government to deliver, without limit, both weapons and foodstuffs, without payment, to all fighting against Germany and Italy. Britain's credit in the United States was now exhausted, and, by this generous help, she was relieved of all future anxiety about payment for the large quantities of war material she still required before she would be in a position to reach equality with her Continental enemies, who now had all the conquered countries in Europe working for them.

The year 1941 opened with the fires of the great incendiary raid on London of 29th December still smouldering, when many buildings were destroyed. Fire-watching in all cities became compulsory, and, by a reorganisation of the fire services, such wholesale destruction was nowhere repeated. The Royal Air Force raised night fighting to a high degree of efficiency, and, as the months passed, the night raiding of Britain decreased. By now the position was reversed, as Britain's air force had greatly increased, and Germany suffered much material damage by British night raids over her principal factories and munition centres, while British daylight raids were frequent against German-held positions in occupied France.

The Germans were now coming to realise that their lightning war of destruction had failed, and that they and most of Europe were beleaguered. Though they fortified the coast of Europe from the Pyrenees to the North Cape, to prevent a British landing, they could not break the British blockade until they had conquered Britain, which had now become an island fortress. Germany had taken all she could remove from her conquered territories, and her victims were on the verge of starvation, but the fact remained that until she could break out of the encirclement her future was uncertain, as the plunder would not last for ever.

Her position could be compared with that of a boy who had put out his hand to grab an apple from a tree growing by a wall, only to find a strong hand from over the wall grasping his before he could remove his spoil. Until the hand was beaten off his apple was useless to him. So he slashed away, but, though the hand holding his was severely lacerated, it still held him in its grip. Germany, like the boy, had now to do something desperate to defeat her enemy. Moreover, she required vital supplies, especially oil, to keep her population well fed and her vast factories and mechanised army moving. As an invasion of Britain was too hazardous an adventure, she struck south to Greece, hoping to get the air control of the Mediterranean, and thence move on to Syria, Palestine, Egypt, Mesopotamia and farther east. Her entire original plan of campaign had gone wrong, and now she was floundering but still very dangerous.

By the Spring of 1941 large German forces were massed in the Danube valley, and fresh troops had been landed in Tripoli. In a few weeks all that the British had gained in Libya had been lost, because they had withdrawn too many troops to send to the help of threatened Greece. A British naval victory, a few weeks earlier, over the Italian fleet, at Cape Matapan, had improved the position at sea, but on land, first Yugoslavia, then Greece, and finally Crete, were overrun and occupied by the enemy, the latter by means of parachute troops and gliders. The British navy, in spite of considerable loss from air attack, prevented a landing by sea.

Germany did not follow up her victory; in fact this attack southwards turned out to be a great strategic blunder, as little was gained. She had suffered heavy casualties, and, when she next turned on Russia, not enough good fighting weather remained before the winter to enable her to achieve her object—the capture of Moscow and Leningrad. Britain then conquered Syria, to protect the east from invasion, having to fight France, her former ally, to do so, and she also occupied Iraq, which probably explains why Germany did not carry out her drive to the east. By midsummer (1941) the area under German control had been increased to include the whole of the Balkans, but she was still encircled by sea, and on land by Russia, Turkey, Syria, Palestine and Egypt, while Iraq farther east, and in the south Eritrea and Abyssinia, were by this time in British possession.

Germany had now to do something drastic, as her hope of reducing Britain to starvation by sinking her shipping was rapidly waning. She even sent her newest battleship, the *Bismarck*, to sea without adequate protection for the purpose of destroying all the shipping she came across. After sinking the *Hood* off Iceland she herself was sunk, and her accompanying cruisers driven into Brest. American naval forces were now established in Iceland to help to guard the convoys to and from America, and later they received instructions to shoot at sight any enemy submarines they saw. America, moreover, armed her merchant ships and permitted them to sail across the Atlantic.

With this increasing co-operation from the United States, and the ceaseless watch of the British navy, the sinkings of allied cargo ships, which had grown to an alarming height in the early summer, fell off steadily, and by the end of 1941 it seemed as if the Battle of the Atlantic was well in hand. The British blockade of German-occupied Europe therefore controlled the entire strategic situation, while the attempted German blockade of Britain by submarines and bombers, dangerous as it was, never became a decisive factor in the war, because new ships helped to replace those that were lost.

Baffled in the Atlantic, and unable to force her way through into Asia by her southward thrust into the Balkans, Germany now decided to break the 1939 pact with Russia. This was a move always intended, but not until Britain was conquered, and her failure to accomplish this was the cause of Germany's ultimate defeat. She now based her last remaining hope of victory on the chance of forcing the Russian army back to the Ural Mountains, and, if this was successfully accomplished, an attempt would be made to break through the Caucasus Mountains to Baku and Persia. There the prize was the rich Russian and Persian oilfields, and after that she hoped to secure the riches of India. Moreover, with the rich agricultural, industrial and mineral resources of Russia under her control, she expected to counteract the effect of the blockade. Then, with the Russian menace on her eastern flank removed, she hoped to throw successfully an overwhelming force against Britain, defeat her, and so end the war.

On 22nd June, 1941, Germany made her most fatal blunder. With all Europe, outside of Russia, now working for her she felt sufficiently strong to meet and defeat her greatest enemy. So she attacked Russia, in company with Finland, Rumania, Hungary and Italy, quite underestimating the force she thus brought against her. The impetus of the German onslaught, and her immense initial superiority, did indeed compel the Russian armies to fall back everywhere. A great expanse of devastated territory was occupied, but the Russian armies were not conquered, nor even broken.

Slowly they fell back, both sides losing heavily, but the farther they retreated the stronger became their resistance, until, finally, winter set in. Then, at the end of November, the Russians, under Marshal Timoshenko, turned on the invaders and drove them out of Rostov, a victory which was followed by another farther north which pushed the Germans from the gates of Moscow. The time lost by attacking the Balkans could not now be recovered, and the German armies were forced to endure in the open one of the earliest and worst Russian winters within living memory.

Thus the year 1941 ended with the once unconquerable German army lacking the necessary winter clothing, suffering terrible hardships, and losing by frost-bite, death in battle, wounds and illness a large proportion of the men who six months earlier had so confidently advanced into the unknown. During the winter the Russians gradually freed more and more of their territory, until the intense cold brought the offensive to a halt.

Russia had, however, lost in her retreat many men killed, wounded and captured, much equipment and many important manufacturing districts, but from the beginning of the conflict both Britain and America supplied her with all the armament they could spare by way of the Arctic port of Murmansk and Persia, which latter was occupied by British and Russian forces.

To co-ordinate better both policy and strategy Roosevelt and Churchill, accompanied by their advisers, met at sea. There they also drew up a joint statement containing the principles on which they hoped to see the world reconstructed after the war. This came to be known as The Atlantic Charter, to which Russia and the representatives of all the exiled governments later subscribed. All the United Nations therefore became bound to its conditions, and these they accepted as a fundamental basis on which the world after the war was to be established. Its eight principles read as follows:—

The President of the United States and the Prime Minister, Mr. Churchill, representing His Majesty's Government in the United Kingdom, being met together, deem it right to make known certain common principles in the national policies of their respective countries on which they base their hopes for a better future of the world.

FIRST, their countries seek no aggrandisement, territorial or other.

SECOND, they desire to see no territorial changes that do not accord with the freely expressed wishes of the people concerned.

THIRD, they respect the right of all peoples to choose the form of Government under which they will live; and they wish to see sovereign rights and self-government restored to those who have been forcibly deprived of them.

FOURTH, they will endeavour, with due respect for their existing obligations, to further the enjoyment by all States, great or small, victor or vanquished, of access, on equal terms, to the trade and to the raw materials of the world which are needed for their economic prosperity.

FIFTH, they desire to bring about the fullest collaboration between all nations in the economic field, with the object of securing for all improved labour standards, economic adjustment, and social security.

SIXTH, after the final destruction of the Nazi tyranny, they hope to see established a peace which will afford to all nations the means of dwelling in safety within their own boundaries, and which will afford assurance that all the men in all the lands may live out their lives in freedom from fear and want.

SEVENTH, such a peace should enable all men to traverse the high seas and oceans without hindrance.

EIGHTH, they believe all of the nations of the world, for realistic as well as spiritual reasons, must come to the abandonment of the use of force. Since no future peace can be maintained if land, sea, or air armaments continue to be employed by nations which threaten, or may threaten, aggression outside of their frontiers, they believe, pending the establishment of a wider and permanent system of general security, that the disarmament of such nations is essential. They will likewise aid and encourage all other practicable measures which will lighten for peace-loving peoples the crushing burden of armament.

It seemed, as the year progressed, that 1941 would end with the allied position distinctly improved, but Japan, when General Tojo became head of the government, upset all such calculations. Throughout most of the year the Japanese had been attempting without success to destroy the Chinese forces under General Chiang Kai-shek, and so bring to an end this long drawn-out struggle which she had started to prevent China becoming a modern state and a danger to Japan. Resentful at the embargo America had placed on war materials to Japan, and of the help she was giving to

China, the Japanese, on 7th December, under cover of negotiations, and without first declaring war, attacked in great force, by seaborne aircraft, the American fleet and air force stationed at Pearl Harbour in Hawaii. Much damage was done, and, while America was temporarily paralysed, the treacherous foe attacked the Philippine Islands after declaring war on America and Britain.

Meanwhile in Europe both Germany and Italy declared war on the United States, to receive in return a declaration of war from most of the countries in South America. Thus it was that the world, for the second time within a generation, was again at war. Russia, the United States, China, the British Empire, the Dutch Empire, and most of South America were now lined up against Germany, Italy and Japan. Certainly this was a state of affairs Hitler never envisaged when he made his treacherous attack against Poland two years earlier. So it came about that the close of 1941 found Winston Churchill in Washington, and Anthony Eden, the British Foreign Secretary, in Moscow for the purpose of combining both strategy and policy with only one object in view, namely the utter defeat of the three Axis powers.

The initiative which the Japanese had obtained by such foul means was exploited to the full. The British battleships *Prince of Wales* and *Repulse*, which had been sent to Singapore, were sunk by Japanese dive-bombers, and their elimination gave the enemy full use of the sea between Japan and Siam, a country which became her ally. Siam was made her base for attacking Malaya, which, besides Sumatra, Java, Sarawak, Borneo and other adjacent islands, were conquered early in 1942 after bitter fighting against the comparatively small and ill-equipped garrisons. The loss of Singapore, with its elaborate and costly naval base, was a bitter blow to the British, whose army, after an uneven series of battles down the entire length of the Malay peninsula, had to surrender.

With the Japanese supreme along the entire coast of China, and in command of the sea, Hong Kong was quickly isolated and captured, the Philippine Islands likewise sharing the same fate. Next the invaders crossed from Siam into Burmah, captured Rangoon, and cut the road which was carrying the supplies destined for China. While this operation was proceeding the Japanese landed on New Guinea, and commenced their preparations to attack Australia. There all the man-power available was hastily mobilised, and, with the help of armaments from America, preparations for defence were swiftly made.

This state of affairs came about by Japan having a temporary command of the sea, part of the American navy being under repair after the damage done at Pearl Harbour, another part being engaged in convoying troops to Australia, while the remainder was helping to convoy munitions and troops across the Atlantic. The British navy was fully engaged in the Atlantic, the Arctic and the Mediterranean, in which latter sphere British hopes had again been disappointed. By December 1941 the Axis forces for a second time had been driven out of Cyrenaica, but supply difficulties made it impossible for the British to reach Tripoli for the purpose of cutting the enemy's supply base from Italy. While awaiting further supplies, the enemy, now reinforced, was able to reoccupy some of the territory just lost, and so the attempt to reach Tripoli was frustrated.

During the early months of 1942 thoughts were mostly turned to the Far East, where the Japanese were carrying all before them, and by May the last of their conquests was completed when they occupied Mandalay. The British army had consequently to find its way to India over mountains and rivers, and through jungles and swamps. Naval battles were fought in the Pacific in which both sides lost heavily, and, with strong Japanese forces now firmly based in New Guinea, great alarm was felt for Australia, not only for her own safety but for the future of the war against Japan, because Australia was being prepared as the base for future action against the enemy.

The threats to the United Nations were manifold, and, with the coming of Spring, anxious thoughts turned not only to Australia, but also to India and Ceylon, menaced by the Japanese; to Egypt, threatened by the Italians; and also to Russia, where the Germans were preparing for a great drive into the Caucasus. American troops and weapons poured into Australia, while India was reinforced by an army from Britain, and Madagascar was occupied by the British to protect their sea route to the east.

The uneasy political situation in India next became a source of anxiety, and Sir Stafford Cripps went out there on a special mission to the Indian leaders, hoping that by the promise of self-government after the war he might win their full co-operation in the effort now being made to protect their land from invasion. His

mission, however, failed, and he had to return home
with nothing accomplished.

By now the Axis plan of campaign for 1942 was
clear. Japan intended to drive through India to the
west, Germany through the Caucasus, and Italy, with
German help, through Egypt, the meeting-ground of
all three being Persia. It was an ambitious scheme
which fortunately failed. Malta, in spite of intense
air bombardment, still gravely interfered with Axis
supplies reaching North Africa, where in Egypt
British power was rapidly growing. An expanding
British army in Bengal protected India, Ceylon became
an island fortress, and Russia, through her Arctic
ports and Persia, was receiving increasing quantities
of supplies for her expanding armies. Time was still
on the side of the United Nations, whose production
of weapons was rapidly increasing, and would continue to do so provided none of the props collapsed.

Both sides during this period prior to the renewed
German offensive in Russia were active under the sea
and in the air, but the Russian and North African
campaigns had severely stretched the German air
force. Britain consequently experienced relief by a
reduction in the number and size of the air raids. On
the other hand, German industrial targets were heavily
bombed night after night, and daylight raids were
made over northern France. British submarines took
a heavy toll of Italian shipping in the Mediterranean,
but the enemy was equally successful in the Atlantic,
where British and American ships were lost in large
numbers, especially oil-tankers, which were the particular target of the enemy.

In spite of this heavy loss of United Nations ships,

cargoes and lives, the end of 1942 found them with well over 1,000,000 tons more shipping than they had when the year began, the great increase in ship-building, especially in America, more than making up for the losses. In the Pacific, America administered the first severe check to Japanese aggression, as, in the Battle of the Coral Sea, seaborne aircraft inflicted heavy damage on Japanese warships, and this victory was repeated at Midway Island. These two heavy blows against the Japanese navy was the beginning of the decline in her sea power, and from now onwards her weakness at sea became ever more evident.

By now the snow had melted in Russia, and the German forces were massed for a great onslaught, which was forestalled in May 1942 by a Russian attack against Kharkov. Though this did not secure its objective, the enemy's plans were disorganised and his offensive was delayed. When at last the German attack began it was first of all limited to the Crimea, during which the great fortress of Sevastopol, after a heroic resistance, surrendered. Now the Germans felt free for their drive to the east, their plan being to (1) capture Voronezh, Stalingrad and Rostov, (2) penetrate the passes of the Caucasus to the Caspian Sea and reach Baku to obtain much-needed oil, and (3) deprive Russia of the use of the Volga, the productive Kuban and the industrial Donetz coal and iron district. Rostov fell, and the foothills of the Caucasus were reached, but the German failure at Voronezh and Stalingrad prevented them from turning north, enveloping Moscow and driving the Russian armies beyond the Ural Mountains.

While all this was taking place in Russia, the

British in Cyrenaica were fighting a desperate battle to prevent Marshal Rommel from forcing his German and Italian troops through their defences and capturing Egypt. The battle, which lasted a fortnight, ended in the British being driven back by superior armament to El Alamein, only some sixty miles from Alexandria. Tobruk was captured, and for a time it seemed as if nothing could save Egypt and the Middle East. Mussolini arrived on the scene, all prepared for a state entry into Cairo, but nothing is certain in war, and he had to return home disappointed because the British held the enemy at the gates of Egypt, to keep him there until they were ready for their counter-attack.

Meantime the Germans in the Caucasus had reached the Black Sea, and as far east as Mozdok, but they were still battering away at Voronezh and Stalingrad. As Rostov had fallen, these two cities alone stood between them and the fulfilment of their plan. Fortunately they both withstood all attacks, though for months the enemy threw masses of men against them to secure their capture, the fighting around Stalingrad being particularly fierce and bloody. At this dark hour Winston Churchill visited Stalin in Moscow, his purpose being to improve still further Anglo-Russian relations, and increase the co-operation established by the earlier visit of Molotov, the Soviet Foreign Commissar, to London, when a far-reaching twenty-years' alliance had been concluded between Great Britain and Russia.

Churchill's visit took place in August 1942, and from that time onwards the danger which threatened the United Nations slowly lifted as each month passed, the increased armaments, for which their people had worked so strenuously, now having their effect upon the enemy. As Summer turned into Autumn the heroic defenders of Stalingrad gradually fought the invaders to a standstill, and the defences of Voronezh still held. The success of the epoch-making defence of Stalingrad, entailing as it did the defeat of the enemy's main strategic plan, marked the turning-point in the war. Henceforth the initiative, which had rested with the Axis over the previous three years, passed to the United Nations.

In October the British, under Generals Alexander and Montgomery (the two men who were to become, as time went on, the most outstanding British military leaders), won their first decisive land victory, when they drove through the Axis positions at El Alamein, capturing or destroying a large part of the enemy's army and the bulk of his tanks and equipment. What remained dashed for Tripoli, closely followed by their triumphant victors. Close touch was kept with this fleeing army, in spite of thousands of land-mines which had to be removed all the way along the barren and waterless coast road. Soon all Cyrenaica was cleared, and by the end of 1942 the Germans and Italians were falling back on Tripoli, which was evacuated early in 1943, the enemy retreating into Tunisia. From El Alamein to Tripoli is nearly 1200 miles, and the journey was accomplished in three months in spite of heavy rearguard actions, land-mines, and every obstruction which could be put in the way.

While this was going on in the east, the western coast of North Africa suddenly blazed up into activity, when in November the largest sea convoy so far known landed an army of British and American troops at the principal ports of Algeria and Morocco. The French resisted, but quickly submitted, to throw in their lot with the United Nations. An attempt to capture Bizerta and Tunis failed, as the Germans swiftly landed troops and foiled the attempt. This gave them the necessary bridgehead, and from now onwards both sides poured in troops for the coming battle, the Axis being determined to hold this vital strip of land, and thus deny the passage of the Sicilian Straits to the vessels of the United Nations, who required it to enable them to increase their supplies to the Far East.

Events now moved swiftly, the Germans occupying all unoccupied France, including Toulon, where the French blew up their fleet to prevent it falling into the enemy's hands. Hitler, realising that France, Italy and Greece were now open to attack, declared Europe a fortress, and set to work to fortify all the northern coast of the Mediterranean. Italy was now heavily bombed from both England and North Africa, and while all this was proceeding a dramatic change came over the entire Russian position.

North of Stalingrad a powerful Russian army had been secretly assembled, and in the last week of November 1942 it struck swiftly and surely. So effectively was the blow struck that the German and Rumanian armies investing Stalingrad, originally numbering 330,000 men, were cut off from their base, surrounded, and eventually captured or wiped out by death from battle, wounds, cold, disease or starvation. Southwards drove this powerful Russian force, and when the year 1942 closed it was rapidly clearing all the Germans out of Caucasia, besides menacing their great bastion fortresses, Briansk, Orel, Kursk, Kharkov and Rostov, which held together their entire southern front. Farther north the Russians captured Velikiye Luki, and when 1943 opened the long-besieged Leningrad was entered by the Russians, who thus finally shattered the German plan to turn the Russian right flank, and, by an enveloping movement, capture Moscow.

The beginning of 1943 witnessed the German defence line in Russia quickly crumbling, while the British were in occupation of Tripoli and firmly established, along with American troops, in Algeria and Morocco. The Japanese had been driven out of Papua in New Guinea, from the Solomon Islands, and the British were penetrating northern Burmah from India.

Throughout the war the cruelties the Germans inflicted on the people of the occupied countries were brutal to a degree. No mercy was shown to millions of men, women and children—Jews, Poles, Russians, Czechs and Yugo-Slavs especially being treated in the most savage fashion. As the Axis military position deteriorated German cruelty increased, especially towards the Poles and Jews, which latter they endeavoured to obliterate from Europe.

The ghastly story of German enslavement, persecution, torture, imprisonment and murder of the people of the Slavonic and Semitic races has yet to be told in full, and not until all the facts are gathered together can it be estimated in its entirety. Millions thus suffered from German savagery, and the United Nations pledged themselves to punish all found guilty from the highest to the lowest. The Germans were the pioneers of total war, but this was not enough to satisfy their sadistic lusts, and their record of mass murder and persecution will stain the German name for centuries to come.

This account of the greatest war in history, the greatest wholesale massacre in human annals, the greatest tragedy from which mankind has ever suffered, is being written as it proceeds, but words cannot express the heights and depths of the people's emotions as the ghastly holocaust developed. One has to live through such years of organised murder, suffering, mutilation and devastation to realise the meaning of what is called total war. With gunfire and bombing raised to a fine art, the nerves of both soldiers and civilians were often strained to breaking-point. With alternating hope of victory and fear of defeat, with only necessities available to the fortunate, and less than that to the unfortunate, with the streets of every town and village in complete darkness at night, with money, hitherto available for pleasures and luxuries, being devoted to wholesale destruction, life, during modern warfare, was hard and nerve-racking. If future generations keep this in mind, they will never permit the repetition of such a calamity to overtake the race.

Until the end of 1942 the German and Italian people had been sustained by solid gains of territory, and the people of the United Nations by faith and hope that some day the tide would turn. With the opening of 1943 the Central Powers commenced to experience defeat, the United Nations then beginning to reap the reward of their courage, steadfastness and strenuous labour. Only now did the dim light of victory begin to glow for them, to brighten as every month passed until the day came when final victory was achieved. For their enemies the outlook became ever more dismal, and only by fear of death, or confinement in concentration camps, were many kept from expressing themselves, while their pent-up feelings, as lie after lie told them by their leaders was uncovered by the march of time, can be better imagined than expressed.

From now onwards, those who had been promised domination over Europe and the British Empire had to suffer from the intense bombardment of their towns and cities, much of industrial Germany and Italy being devastated, millions rendered homeless, and many thousands of civilians killed and wounded. What these two countries had inflicted on their enemies from the air in the first three years of the war was now returned to them in tenfold measure, while, at the same time, the casualties suffered by their fighting men mounted to millions, losses such as only Russia amongst the United Nations experienced.

When the year 1943 began it was evident that the time had come to co-ordinate further the offensive policy of the United Nations. Consequently Churchill and Roosevelt met at Casablanca in January to complete their plans, and announce that only by the "unconditional surrender" of all the Axis powers would the United Nations cease the conflict. The immediate strategy then determined for the Far East was to deprive the Japanese of their most advanced outposts, and convert these into allied bases, a policy which made steady progress throughout the year. While Russia held the main German armies, measures were completed to force Italy out of the war, a plan which was brilliantly successful, thanks to the remarkable achievements of the Russian army, which attracted most of the German strength.

The record of Russian progress during 1943 is an epic story, and one that will take a foremost place in the annals of war. After inflicting on the Germans and Rumanians a shattering defeat at Stalingrad, the Russian armies drove on, with only occasional setbacks, to clear the lower Don valley in January, and capture Rostov in February. From now onwards town after town in the Donetz region and Ukrainia fell week by week to the irresistible Russian pressure, to end in the capture of Kharkov, which was lost again for a time by a German counter-attack.

Meantime, while the victorious Russians paused to bring up supplies and reorganise their tired and depleted divisions before resuming their drive westwards, both Britain and America were engaged in freeing all North Africa from the grip of the enemy. By March the troops of General Montgomery, based on Alexandria in Egypt, had overcome all obstacles, captured Libya and joined up with the other allied forces under the American General Eisenhower in Tunisia, the plan being to bring about the destruction or surrender of the enemy intent on holding the important harbours of Tunis and Bizerta. This plan was accomplished in May, when all North Africa fell into allied possession, a prize which enabled immediate preparations to be made for the conquest of Italy. Chile and Iraq had by now joined in with the cause of the United Nations, whose ascendant star they, and other neutrals, now realised was shining ever more brightly.

After heavy attacks from aircraft based on Africa and Malta, which heroic island was now free from her three years of blockade and constant air raids, Sicily was invaded in July with unexpected ease, the landing forces, which required 3000 ships of one kind and another, making good their footholds according to plan. Syracuse and Catania were quickly subdued, and, after determined resistance around the base of Mount Etna was broken, Messina was captured, a victory which led to the capitulation of Italy and the downfall of Mussolini. Germany now had the additional burden of defending Italy, which was already definitely hostile to her and Fascism, and it was against German troops that the allies fought their way up the peninsula.

In September British and American forces crossed the Straits of Messina to occupy Calabria on the mainland, and then, with the help of the new Italian government under Marshal Badoglio, which placed all available Italian resources at their disposal, the northward advance began in company with an allied force which landed near Salerno south of Naples. A critical situation there developed for a time owing to the lack of sufficient protection from the air, to be resolved by the timely arrival of the army making its way to Naples from the south. Naples was occupied in October, but the road to Rome proved difficult and costly, because the Germans, firmly based in northern Italy, now under their complete control, disputed every mile of the difficult mountainous country which intervened.

Meanwhile the enemy was expelled from Corsica and Sardinia, and, by the withdrawal of Italian troops from the Balkans, the forces of resistance in Yugo-slavia, under Marshal Tito, made headway. Mussolini, who had brought such disaster and devastation on his country, was now a prisoner of the new Italian government, but, by a daring coup, he was rescued by a party of German airmen and taken to the north. Here he set up a Fascist Republic, but it came to little, and the fallen Duce, once the idol of his people, and now under German protection, faded into oblivion.

The Mediterranean was by this time open along its entire length to allied shipping, much of which had hitherto been going round the Cape to Egypt and India. With the consequent saving in tonnage, and the great reduction of the number of ships lost by submarine attack, the year 1943 ended with ample ships available to the United Nations, all their losses of merchant shipping having been made good by new vessels, mostly all of which were built in America.[1] Germany had already experienced crippling losses to her capital warships, but just as important was the fact that her submarines from now onwards were mastered, Portugal rendering the allies useful service in this direction by handing over to them the use of the Azores as a base for light naval vessels and aircraft, which worked together for their destruction.

Germany's only hope of victory now lay in completely defeating Russia, before Britain and America

[1] By the end of 1943 Britain had lost 2921 merchant ships and coastal vessels, which was nearly half the number afloat when the war commenced.

had finished their preparations to land an army in France, and so force their enemy to fight on three fronts. So far the English Channel had prevented the millions of trained British and American soldiers from participating in the struggle, and Germany was well aware that once they obtained a foothold on the Continent her doom was sealed, she not having sufficient men to protect all her frontiers. Consequently, while she built up strong defences along the French, Belgian and Dutch coasts, she again struck with tremendous force at Russia, this time against their salient before Kursk. The city withstood the onslaught, and, after it was absorbed, the Russians struck back with even greater force.

The months of August and September 1943 stand out as two of the most momentous in military history. Week by week, Russian cities, towns and villages over a front of 1000 miles were freed from the deadly grip of the invader, Orel, Kharkov, Taganrog, Briansk, Smolensk and Taman being the principal places to be set free. No decisive break-through occurred, no large enemy forces were cut off, but steady pressure forced him back mile by mile until he reached prepared positions on the River Dnieper, a distance of 450 miles from Stalingrad, his most easterly point of penetration Even this natural barrier failed to hold the Russian forces, all the German defences collapsed, and the Crimea, in which large German forces were lodged, was cut off.

The end of the year consequently witnessed the enemy fighting desperately to retain his last foothold in western Ukrainia, but all his efforts were in vain and the historic city of Kiev was captured by the Russians in November. A counter-attack to recapture the city failed, and when winter came the Russians continued their drive, which was to free Odessa and take them into Rumania. Farther north, at Nevel, they commenced their onslaught which in 1944 was to develop into a mighty avalanche and carry them forward into Poland, East Prussia, the Baltic States, and finally into Germany.

As the year 1943 wore on the air bombardment of Britain slackened, the depleted German air force being sufficiently occupied in the battle areas. As this once-powerful destructive machine declined, the Royal Air Force struck deep into Germany every night when the weather was favourable, with ever-increasing bomb loads, city after city being devastated, to the great curtailment of her production. After Essen, Hamburg, and much of the Ruhr area, had been laid waste, with large tracts of western Germany reduced to ruins, and important dams destroyed, the air attacks on Berlin began in earnest in November, and continued during 1944 until much of the capital was a mass of rubble.

From the newly captured airfields in southern Italy, British and American bombers now commenced their almost daily attacks on all centres of production in those lands hitherto mostly free from air attack, all northern Italy, southern Germany, Austria, Czecho-Slovakia, the Balkans, and the Rumanian oil refineries being now open to destruction from the air. These raids increased in intensity month by month from both Britain and Italy until the conclusion of hostilities, special attention being given to aircraft factories and oil refineries.

While many cities and towns of Europe were being laid waste, with wealth squandered like water, and lives sacrificed by the million, the war against Japan continued to yield valuable results. With the allies established in the Solomon Islands and eastern New Guinea, preparations were now well advanced for further operations. These embraced the capture of the numerous islands which are studded throughout the Pacific Ocean between New Guinea and Japan, the plan being ultimately to cut off Japan from all her new conquests by sea. On the Indian frontier the British offensive in Arakan achieved nothing decisive, but farther east in China the Japanese were equally unsuccessful in their drive up the Yangtze River. Now that Australia and New Zealand were safe, and there was no immediate danger to India, the United Nations devoted most of their strength to the defeat of Germany, believing that until this was accomplished, Japan, so vulnerable at sea, and now so inferior in warships, could wait, the interval being occupied in securing the bases from which to strike at her when the time came.

With increased confidence on the part of the United Nations the year 1943 closed with preparations being made to re-establish Europe when victory was achieved. The problems of reconstruction were both varied and numerous, but the question of feeding her poverty-stricken inhabitants was one of the most pressing. To pave the way for this immense task an inter-allied conference opened at Hot Springs in the United States, to consider the means of securing the future food supply of the world, as the demand from Europe was expected to create a shortage everywhere.

To the United Nations Relief and Rehabilitation Administration was given the task of feeding, clothing and housing the people of liberated Europe and China, and besides this a corps of officials was formed, under military supervision, to provide for the civil administration of hostile territory when conquered.

When 1944 began the belief was general that before the year closed victory would be achieved by the United Nations, all plans for this having been completed at Tehran, the capital of Iran (Persia), where Churchill, Roosevelt, Stalin and Chiang Kai-shek had met together in the previous November. Closer co-ordination between Britain, America and Russia, who would be responsible for the rehabilitation of the world, was there achieved, and the decisions reached embraced not only the strategy to be employed to bring about a speedy victory, but also the policy to be pursued towards a defeated Germany, Japan and their allies, and the help required for the victims of their aggression.

With the collapse of the German defences on the Dnieper, the southern half of the 1000-mile Russian front surged forward during the winter months of 1944, crossing one river barrier after another, until Rumania was entered, the important Black Sea port of Odessa being recaptured in April, and the Crimea also cleared of the enemy. Meanwhile General Alexander's stiff fight up Italy had been held by the Germans at Cassino, and, to get round this obstacle, he landed troops by sea at Anzio, thirty miles south of Rome, the intention being to turn the enemy's flank. This

venture did not succeed, and four months passed
before the German defences at Cassino were broken.
Then the two allied armies joined up, and marched on
Rome, which was captured in June with little resistance. King Victor Emmanuel, who had been so
closely associated with the Fascist régime, now
resigned in favour of his son Umberto, who became
Lieutenant of the Realm.

On 6th June, 1944, came the most staggering blow
Germany had yet received, as on that now famous day
a British and American army landed in Normandy,
the most formidable of the land fortifications, declared
to be impenetrable, having been smashed during
previous weeks by incessant bombing from the air.
This immense and hazardous operation, after years of
careful planning, met with immediate success, and,
when the German outer defences were broken, troops
poured ashore from the thousands of transports con-
voyed by the British navy, now busily engaged ferrying
men and armaments across the Channel from ports in
the south of England. Quickly a large harbour and
breakwater were erected, composed of huge concrete
structures each of which was towed across from
England and sunk in the appointed place, quite the
most outstanding engineering feat of all time.

General Eisenhower, the supreme commander,
and General Montgomery who landed with the army,
now set their plans in motion. British and Canadian
troops drove for Caen, and the Americans, placed
farther west, pushed inland across the base of the
Cherbourg peninsula. Still, in spite of the severe
bombing of the enemy's communications, resistance
was everywhere stiff, and the outcome of this vital

battle for a time hung in the balance. Against the British and Canadians the Germans placed the bulk of their heavy armour, and, though they prevented the immediate capture of Caen, a vitally important road centre, the Americans on the right, with less opposition, penetrated inland, captured the Cherbourg peninsula, and swung south to the Loire. Then they turned east out of Brittany in the direction of Paris, and thus enveloped the enemy's left flank.

Now followed a rapid and dramatic transformation of the entire campaign, a large enemy armoured force being trapped at Falaise, while other enemy detachments were pushed behind the fortifications of St. Nazaire, Lorient and Brest. Most of what remained of the once powerful German army fled for the Pas de Calais, hammered all the way by the British and American air forces as the enemy struggled across the Seine, over which every bridge had been destroyed by air attack. This historic campaign liberated Paris with the help of the French partisans, and, by the time most of France was cleared, the Germans had lost in dead, wounded or prisoners more than 1,000,000 men.

This great victory, the outcome of the Battle of Normandy, simplified the next allied landing in the south of France, where British and American forces, based on Italy, captured Toulon and Marseilles. Northwards they marched, fighting all the way into the Savoy Alps, and up the Rhone Valley, to wheel east round the northern frontier of Switzerland, and fall into line with the victorious army from Normandy, now in possession of Belgium, part of Holland and all Luxemburg. French partisans cleared up much of what remained of German-occupied France, and by

September it seemed as if the Siegfried Line would be turned at Arnhem in Holland, where allied parachute troops were landed by air to hold the crossings of the Lek. Unfortunately they were overwhelmed before the British, who had reached Nijmegen, could arrive; the last Rhine delta river was not crossed, and this easy way into the heart of Germany was barred, much to the disappointment of everyone who had hoped that a victory here would finish the war before the end of 1944.

Headlong as had been the enemy's flight from France, he had left garrisons in the northern ports now urgently required by the allies. All of these, except Dunkirk, were soon captured, including Antwerp, but bitter fighting followed to clear the Scheldt estuary before this important port could be used. Still, the fortifications of the Siegfried Line and the Rhine barred the way to complete allied victory, and a slow but steady pounding of the Siegfried defences commenced. Aachen was captured, the River Saar was crossed, while the piercing of the Belfort Gap and the capture of Metz and Nancy gave Alsace and Lorraine, including Strassburg, back to France.

Together with the disaster which overtook the Germans in Normandy came the news that an important section of the German military clique, disgusted with his handling of the German strategy, had attempted to kill Hitler by placing a bomb near him. This exploded but it failed to kill him, and all suspected of complicity were hanged, including many high-ranking officers. Hitler now went into retirement, and Himmler became the master of Germany, the army coming under his control, while the last reserves of

German man-power were forced into the ranks to become known as the Volksturm.

Secret weapons, known as V1 and V2, in the form of flying bombs and rocket bombs, had by now been launched against London and neighbourhood. This form of attack had no military value, but it caused much damage and loss of life, though its ferocity was reduced by all the launching sites on the French coast falling into allied hands two months after it commenced.

When midsummer came, the eastern front blazed up anew, a powerful Russian offensive travelling fast and far. All eastern Poland was overrun, and it semed as if Warsaw would soon be in Russian hands, but it was halted just outside the city. There the Poles, expecting immediate liberation, rose against their German oppressors, only to be liquidated in an uneven contest because they could get no help from the Russians. This incident unfortunately further embittered the Poles against the Russians, who were already mistrusted because of their claim to Poland's eastern provinces.

In the north the Russians forced their way into Lithuania, Latvia and Estonia, capturing Riga, but their attempt to enter East Prussia was checked on the frontier. Farther north their offensive against Finland succeeded in bringing this misguided country to terms, and getting her to co-operate in driving the Germans from her soil into Norway, a move which brought the Russians so close to where the German super-battleship *Tirpitz* was sheltering that it was moved farther south, to be finally sunk by air attack.

We have already read that in the south the Russians

had entered Rumania. After a temporary hold-up events moved fast. Bucharest, the capital, and the oilfields at Ploesti were captured, and Rumania sued for peace, to join the allies in their struggle. Bulgaria followed next, and this forced the Germans to leave Greece, when the British occupied Athens. The victorious Russian army now drove on up the Danube to Budapest, aided by Marshal Tito's Yugoslav partisans, and by the end of the year nearly all Hungary was cleared, a provisional Hungarian government suing for peace and siding with the allies.

We last left the British and allied forces in Italy at Rome, with the formidable Apennines still to cross before northern Italy, and her broad plains, could be reached. Slow but steady progress continued throughout 1944, Leghorn and Florence being captured, and then the piercing of this grim mountain range commenced. By Autumn the worst was passed, Ravenna and the Po valley being reached, but Winter prevented an exploitation of these gains.

It seemed as if the entire western front, from Italy to Holland, would not now stir much until the Spring, but Rundstedt, the commander of the German Rhine army, sprang a sharp and unpleasant surprise, when in December he broke the American line south of Aachen in an attempt to work round to Antwerp and cut off the northern allied army. If this had succeeded, he had hoped to be able to transfer forces from the west to the east, to meet the coming Russian Winter offensive, but it failed, though a month passed before the salient he had created was straightened out.

In the Far East the war against Japan proceeded favourably, though the Chinese were pushed farther up the Hwang-Ho (or Yellow) River. In Burmah the British forces, based on India, after first repulsing an attempt by the Japanese to invade India, pushed over seemingly impassable mountains, and through impenetrable jungles, to reach, first the Chindwin and then the Irrawaddy rivers. Kalewa and Bhamo were captured, and then the British drove south to Mandalay, while on the coast Akyab was occupied.

In the Pacific the Americans secured more bases nearer Japan, first the Marshall Islands, and then the Marianas, to land finally on Leyte, one of the Philippine islands, from which they moved farther north to land on Luzon, the largest island of the group nearest Japan. Bitter opposition was encountered, but before the Americans were secure on Leyte they had to meet and engage the Japanese fleet, to inflict upon it a devastating defeat, a victory which gave the American fleet, now joined by a large part of the British navy, an overwhelming superiority.

The European countries, liberated by the allies, were found to be in a pitiable condition, much of what they ever had, besides many of their male population, having been removed to Germany. Tracts of northern France was devastated, but it was in Greece, Holland and Belgium where destitution and starvation were worst. Rival political parties in Greece made matters more difficult, disharmony becoming civil war, which was only quelled after a personal visit by Churchill, and a strong British force had landed in Athens.

With Europe bled white, and everyone eager for permanent peace and prosperity, the time was now ripe for international discussion on this vital question.

Consequently a conference of allied representatives met at Dumbarton Oaks in the United States, in the Summer of 1944, to draw up a basis for a lasting peace and collective security against future aggression. It recommended the establishment of an international organisation, under the title of The United Nations Organisation (U.N.O.), comprising administrative bodies similar to the moribund League of Nations, whose principles were to be reinforced, and, if necessary, effective measures taken against any nation threatening to disturb the future peace of the world. What these measures were to be, and how to apply them unanimously, was the problem which came up for consideration at San Francisco the following year.

The allies, at the beginning of 1945, entered the year of complete victory over all their enemies. In Europe their armies closed in on Germany from east, south and west, East Prussia falling to the Russians after bitter resistance, while in the west the Germans, exhausted by their abortive attempt to break through south of Aachen, could not withstand the American counter-attack. Weakened and outnumbered, Germany fought and lost the last decisive battle west of the Rhine, which was crossed by the British and Americans in February, when Cologne and the other Rhineland cities fell one after the other.

This victory enabled Holland to be cleared of the enemy, while the Russians in the east had reached the River Oder, and in the south had entered Budapest and were closing in on Vienna. Three weeks of difficult fighting during April broke the German resistance

in Italy, when the River Po was crossed, and unconditional surrender followed on the day after the
lynching near Milan of the fugitive Mussolini, now
heartily cursed and hated by the people he had so
misled.

The Russians were now in the suburbs of Berlin,
and had crossed the Elbe while the British and
Canadians were sweeping towards Hanover, Bremen
and Hamburg. The Americans, well across the
Rhine, were forcing their way deep into central
Germany to join up with the Russians. The once all-
conquering German army was now in rags and tatters,
the troops surrendering daily by thousands, during
which time Berlin was being shattered by a pitiless
bombardment and Vienna had surrendered.

The great cities and strongholds of both east and
west had now been captured one after the other, and
on 2nd May the flaming ruins of Berlin surrendered
after both Hitler and Goebbels had committed
suicide in a deep shelter in the Chancellery, their
last refuge in the doomed city. One by one the other
leading Nazi mass murderers did likewise, or were
rounded up, to be tried at Nuremberg for their crimes
against humanity and put to death, leaving their
miserable dupes to drink to the dregs the cup of
misery and hatred they had been responsible for
brewing.

On the other side of the world the same fate was
quickly approaching the Japanese, already in extremis.
Sea power had given the allies a stranglehold over
them, and their grip had been loosened on those lands
they had overrun when the going was good. By May
they had been forced out of Burmah by the capture of

Mandalay and then of Rangoon. In the south the Australians had overcome stubborn resistance in New Guinea, while island after island in the Pacific was occupied by the Americans, the Japanese in many of them being stranded, to die of starvation. Next the Philippines were cleared of the enemy, and then the islands of Iwojima and Okinawa. This development cut off the Japanese in China from their base, and brought the allies so close to Japan that what remained of her navy was either destroyed at sea or by bombs when sheltering in home waters.

An ultimatum to surrender was ignored, and then followed the use for the first time of two bombs which released the tremendous energy contained in the nucleus of the atom, one on Hiroshima, the arsenal of Japan, and the other on the port of Nagasaki. The Japanese had no defence, and the destruction of life and property was so widespread that they surrendered unconditionally a few days later (14th August) to avoid complete annihilation, when followed the landing of American troops, who took over complete control of Japan.

The United Nations now stood masters over an impoverished and stricken world, Russia having just entered the eastern fray to overrun Manchuria, and their immediate task was to prevent complete chaos, as the bonds of society were everywhere straining to breaking-point. In February, Churchill, Roosevelt and Stalin had met in the Crimea to co-ordinate the lines of allied policy and administration when victory was attained, and their decisions were now being applied in Germany with all possible speed. Everything was therefore ready when Japan surrendered, but long-term plans had also been carefully considered, to be again reviewed and expanded at Potsdam after Germany capitulated.

Under the shadow caused by the untimely death of Franklin D. Roosevelt in April, delegates of all the United Nations met at San Francisco to draw up the Charter of a permanent organisation of collective security. Forty-eight nations ratified this historic document, pregnant with hope for the years to come, as it rectified the mistake of the former League of Nations by having a place for a decisive military force to stop aggression. The rule of law in international relations, backed by a powerful police force, is now emerging. Moreover, the Security Council of the United Nations was given the onerous responsibility of controlling the use of atomic energy, which, from now onwards, must be the principal factor in either preserving world peace or the destruction of everything we cherish.

The discovery in 1945 of the way to release the terrific energy within the atom must rank as mankind's greatest achievement, and it is one which, if wisely handled, will increase enormously our wealth and comfort. With the decline of the world's greatest coalfields and oil supplies, this new-found energy, dependent on uranium, will some day supply power to an extent so far unimagined. It is one of the effects of the war, and if, from fear on the one hand, it preserves peace, and, on the other, the power necessary for production is increased, much good will have come out of evil. The American, British and Canadian governments combined to organise the scientific development which led to this great discovery, and the cost of the necessary equipment, which was erected in the United States, reached the enormous figure of $2,000,000,000.

It now lies with the people themselves to determine whether civilisation will be immeasurably enriched or severely crippled by the use that is made of the basic power of the universe. In Chapter III we read how ethical conduct had developed as the result of experience, because man, a selfish creature, discovered by degrees that by treating others as he himself liked to be treated his own comfort and happiness increased. Fear was one of the causes which brought about the civilised way of life, it created a national police force and it may bring into being an international police organisation which will prevent war. As fear has played a large part so far in ethical development, then increased fear should now stimulate still further a desire for greater righteousness amongst nations, and bring about a standard of international conduct hitherto only practised within each nation.

Important political changes occurred during the year, the presidency of the United States, on the death of Roosevelt, being taken by Vice-President Truman. In Britain, and other European countries where elections were held, Socialism gained increased representation, the one exception being Austria, the Communists also in some lands becoming much stronger. Churchill, much to the regret of many, lost the premiership to Clement Attlee, who became head of a Labour Government, supported by a large majority, which at once set in motion legislation for the nationalisation of the Bank of England, the coal industry and other monopolistic utility undertakings, compensation being provided to existing proprietors. This new economic outlook promises further similar changes in other countries, the principal exception so far being the United States, which remains wedded to individual effort as distinct from state control.

Volumes would be required to encompass the evidence produced at the various trials of the Nazi mass murderers, besides the terrible discoveries of unimagined horror made at the different concentration camps in Germany, and those of what was once German-occupied Europe. Likewise countless books would be needed to record the deeds which produced the misery to millions of victims, the death by mass murder of millions more and the displacement of millions from their homes to work in Germany. Never before in history have so many perished in actual warfare, by exposure, disease, starvation and calculated murder, and this was followed by famine in Europe, India and China when the fighting ceased.

No correct estimate will ever be made of the money value of the property destroyed, or the amount of wealth uselessly dissipated. Britain alone sacrificed a quarter of her national wealth in the struggle, but we must leave it to the future historian to provide the details of the suffering, and the destruction of life and property, which followed from the wickedness of the German hierarchy, backed up by the vast majority of the German people.

So we now leave Germany divided into four zones, the east being occupied by the Russians and the west by the British, American and French. When the time comes for the occupation forces to leave Germany, let us make sure that the rich Ruhr coal area, and

Rhineland, which supplied Germany with the sinews of war, and without which she would cease to be a menace to the world, will be retained under some form of international control. Otherwise she may again bring an even greater catastrophe upon civilisation, because many Germans are still savages with only a veneer of culture, and the people generally are easily led by anyone who appeals to their debased mentality.

Japan was likewise occupied, the American forces predominating, and she, like Germany, will learn through suffering that the way of transgressors, when defeated, can be very hard. Her abominations were no less flagrant than those of her Western ally, millions in China being homeless, millions having died by war, neglect and starvation, and her responsible leaders likewise paid the price of their crimes.

As 1945 closed, the many formidable problems facing the victors were being energetically mastered. Here indeed was a task of herculean dimensions, increased by the multitude rendered homeless by the destruction caused by bombing, by the vast surge of millions of displaced persons seeking their old homes, and the mass migration into central Germany of Germans from the lands in the east which were theirs no longer. The Germans greatly pitied themselves after their defeat, but showed little appreciation of their guilt and no capacity to think politically. Many years of education will be necessary to change the mentality of the younger people, some of whom remain imbued with the Nazi doctrines, while their elders seem quite incapable of grasping the democratic way of life, the rudimentary ideas of self-government having been obliterated by twelve years of National Socialism.

When we contemplate the background of destruction and widespread destitution over large parts of Europe and Asia, the United Nations have before them a tremendous task, not only to lift Germany out of the morass into which the Nazis led her, but to help in the social and political reconstruction of the more backward countries she and Japan devastated. The affairs of the allies, moreover, call for serious concern, the British National Debt, for instance, having increased more than threefold, her credit abroad being exhausted, while shortages of nearly everything have necessitated drastic control to prevent inflation.

Only by toil and deprivation can the tremendous losses be replaced, and a generation will pass away before the serious man-power shortage is made good. It will take many years before the repercussions of this tremendous cataclysm will cease to affect the lives of the people concerned in some way or another. They will continue to suffer from shortages of many things hitherto plentiful, and all because part of the human race was ignorant of the right way to live.

(7) THE VATICAN FAVOURS THE DICTATORS.

Throughout the fateful years preceding the Second World War, and during the time this conflict was being waged, one important fact, which everyone should remember, stands out clear and vivid. At a time when evil stark and rampant had to be resisted or accepted, we had either to follow the Christian maxim "Resist not evil" (*Matthew* v, 39), or be guided by our reason and fight against the powers of darkness. That problem was faced by every country involved, and, with the exception of Denmark, each decided that the only course open was to fight when attacked. Where, however, theology reigned supreme, where ignorance was enthroned, where supernatural religion was most venerated—in a word, at Rome, the centre of Christendom—the desire of the Church hierarchy was for the forces of freedom and justice to be defeated, and those of tyranny and bondage to be victorious.

Those who have read this book so far will not be surprised that this was so, especially when we remember that the Vatican refused to co-operate, or be associated in any way, with the League of Nations. A Church whose motto is "Semper Idem" cannot change, and must be left behind by all who are intent on righteousness and the well-being of mankind. Nevertheless its power for evil is immense, as, with its vast wealth, its estimated annual income of £150,000,000, its army of a million priests, monks and nuns, and its multitude of 180,000,000 subscribing members, it is the greatest organisation in the world today, even though about half of its supporters are illiterate South Americans of the lowest type. No Balance Sheet, or Income and Expenditure account, are published, and how the money is spent is only known at the Vatican, but we do know that when money is required it is always available, to further the interests of the Church in whatever way is thought most desirable.

As its existence depends on its subscribers remaining ignorant, the Church is against all free expression, and its members are forbidden to read books critical of its beliefs and deeds. Moreover, it has such a grip over the World Press, and it indirectly controls so many newspapers, that it can influence world opinion largely as it desires, the consequence being that the doings of the Holy See are always presented in the most favourable light. Nevertheless, though it can camouflage its political activities, it cannot hide them from those who know where to look, and always we find the same age-old sordid tale of intrigue and reaction, a policy which has done so much to make up the tragic history of Christian civilisation.

After bitter conflict, covering the past five centuries, between the Church and the reformers, the people in our time secured a greater say in their own affairs than ever before. Education was spreading, and the hitherto downtrodden masses were, at long last, shaping their own lives in a way never before experienced. For sixteen hundred years the Church had kept them ignorant and servile, but now they were expressing themselves politically, the vast majority being good peaceful citizens, in favour of evolution and not revolution. They were anxious, by means of democratic elections, to pursue a policy which they believed would increase their knowledge, improve their comfort, reduce their drudgery and advance their happiness. This, however, was contrary to the policy and interests of the Vatican, and consequently the Pope issued an encyclical in 1931 strongly condemning Socialism, it being anti-Christ and of the devil.

The coming to power of Mussolini gave the Church new life and vigour, because it has always flourished in partnership with autocrats. A new chance to reimpose its authority came, when, in return for its promises to support Fascism, and influence the people to do likewise, it received from the new Fascist state £19,000,000 in cash and bonds, besides the recognition of the political independence of the Vatican.

The reason given for this palpable bribe was compensation for the Papal States, whose inhabitants, sixty years earlier, had almost unanimously voted themselves away from papal administration into that of a united Italy. A further bribe to secure clerical support for the Fascist régime was contained in a Concordat, which affirmed the supremacy of the Vatican over the religious life of the people, and made the Church a state institution in receipt of a large annual revenue free of taxation. Besides this all monasteries and convents were legalised, marriage by priests was reinforced, and they were given control over education, no criticism of the orthodox faith being permitted. All that the 19th-century Italian liberators had worked for evaporated into thin air, and the Pope was once more the master of the mental life of Italy.

Consequently all liberty vanished, and when Mussolini attacked Abysinnia the Pope gave him and the Italian soldiers his blessing, besides the promise of the support of the Church. No ecclesiastical voice was ever raised in condemnation of the massacres and abominations of that campaign. Instead, the priests, from the highest to the lowest, were enthusiastic, and regarded it as a holy war, the Pope's pronouncements making it evident that he wanted to control the Christian Coptic Church of Abysinnia, as much as

Mussolini wanted the country's mineral wealth. When next Albania was attacked by Italy, and then Greece, the same clerical support was given to this unprovoked aggression, and all the cruelty which followed. Here again it was evident that the Pope wanted to secure control over the Greek Orthodox Church in the Balkans. Moreover, when 70,000 Jews were callously and brutally banished from Italy, no voice of protest came from the Vatican.

When Hitler secured power in Germany, with the help of the large Roman Catholic vote, a Concordat was reached between the Vatican and the Nazi government in 1933. Although Hitler throughout maintained a contemptuous attitude towards the Church, it never denounced this treaty of friendship, and never did it utter a word of condemnation about the numerous abominations perpetrated by the Germans in the lands they invaded and despoiled. On the other hand, the Vatican was quick to notice and condemn any unfriendly attitude of the Nazis towards the faithful in Germany. Much was said about the closing of some monasteries, but the world Press carefully refrained from mentioning that this was because they were riddled with corruption, and sodomy was rife.[1]

This vice has always been rampant in these places where men are herded together and denied family life, and one German monastery was closed in 1936 because 326 Franciscan monks out of its 400 inmates were found to be guilty of this unnatural practice.

---

[1] *The World Almanac*, which is cautious in its statements, reported that "Up to October 1938 more than eight thousand Catholic monks and lay brothers have been arrested" for sodomy and seducing young girls.

The closing of some Bavarian Church schools came about by a vote of the people, who voted in favour of National schools, because, not only was education in the Church schools bad, but the parents refused to leave their children in the charge of priests, monks and friars after these scandals became known.

Whatever grievances the Church had in Germany, the fact is clear that the Vatican supported Hitler to the last, and tried to protect the Nazi criminals when their doom approached. To the Vatican, any state which denounced Democracy, Socialism and Communism, and denied the people their liberty, was worthy of support, and every country where liberty was valued was considered to be an enemy of the Church. Consequently, for this reason, when Norway was invaded, the Pope refused to make a protest.

When Pius XI died in 1939, Cardinal Pacelli became Pius XII, to welcome to the Vatican, from time to time, the infamous Ribbentrop, and hear from him the plans Germany had made for the conquest of Europe. This fact has now been revealed in the impartial *Annual Register.* Another visitor was the fanatical Christian, Matsuoka, the Japanese envoy, who told His Holiness what Japan proposed to do, to be rewarded with a high Papal decoration. Thus the unholy alliance, Germany, Italy and the Vatican, was now increased by yet another anti-democratic state, Japan, who received the blessing of the Vicar of Christ on the foul work she was doing in China, and proposed to do until all Asia was in her power.

While these interchanges of confidence were taking place, the German Roman Catholic bishops met in 1940 at Fulda, in Prussia, to resolve that "after the completion of the final German victory, special ceremonies of gratitude to the German troops and loyalty to Hitler will be announced". So there was no doubt about the attitude of the Roman Catholic Church in Germany towards the Nazi Party, and, when the attempt was made on Hitler's life in 1944, the Pope, Pius XII, was so relieved at his escape that he sent him a telegram of congratulation, although he well knew that this greatest mass murderer of all times was prolonging a hopeless bloody struggle.

The friendly attitude of the Vatican towards the scoundrels, who wrecked the peace and happiness of Europe during the last decade, was evident long before the world war commenced, and this was clear by the help it gave them through its repeated denunciations of Russia. From the time the Church was re-established by Mussolini as a temporal power, there poured from its official Press and radio a torrent of vile abuse about Russia which was accepted as true, not only by Roman Catholics, but in Protestant lands.

These lies had the unfortunate effect of isolating Russia from France and Britain, and this gave Germany and Italy the opportunity they were awaiting, to knock out France without having also to fight Russia at the same time. The hatred of Russia, which the Vatican inspired in the minds of the faithful, brought over to the side of Hitler all the quislings, mostly all Roman Catholics, who were such a help to Germany in every country she conquered. To them it was either German or Russian domination, and the fear of Russia, engendered by the Vatican, made them choose the former as the lesser of two evils.

The friendship of the Vatican for the Nazis and Fascists, however, took even more practical shape some years before the world war began, when, for the ninth time in little more than a century, the Liberals in Spain were overthrown and crushed in the most brutal manner. For years past Spain had been ruled by autocrats, inspired by a corrupt aristocracy, and an equally debased Church. Discontent increased to fever heat, so much so that in the General Election of 1931 the Republican Socialist Party secured a majority of nearly three to one, when the Cortes disestablished and disendowed the Church, expelled the Jesuits, secularised education, marriage and divorce, and enlarged the franchise.

The Church, facing loss of power, with more than half the people against it, and complaining that Christ had been crucified for the second time, plotted and planned. Finally it succeeded in securing General Franco to lead a revolt against the government, the papal banner being the first to be unfurled over the rebel headquarters at Burgos, while Franco's flag flew from the roof of the Vatican. Thus began a holy war (1936–1938) against the Spanish democrats, the Pope announcing his support of the rebels against the majority of Spaniards who remained loyal to democracy.

Only foreign imported armies could overcome the people's resistance, and, after the Pope had made a world-wide call for help, men from Italy, Portugal, Germany, Ireland and elsewhere, joined the rebel standard, to be opposed by those who came from Russia, and elsewhere, who were equally zealous to fight on the other side. So Spain became the battle-ground between Communists, Socialists, Liberals and Democrats, on the one hand, and Fascists, Nazis and Roman Catholics on the other.

The account of this bloody struggle has been given in a previous section, and, after Franco triumphed, all political and religious liberty vanished, the prisons filling to overflowing with untried prisoners, who wasted away, if they escaped being tortured or shot, while in Portugal, where another equally devout dictator, Salazar, is supported by the Church, the same conditions prevail. Here, as in Spain, every priest is a Fascist, and their fulsome eulogies of Hitler were a feature of their sermons.

From Spain reaction spread to Austria, where the ground was prepared for this priest-ridden land being annexed by Germany. There the Christian Socialist Party, led by a priest, Seipel, under orders from the Vatican, worked against the Social Democrats, whose enlightened policy was gradually leading the more intelligent away from the Church into the fresher air of liberty. Then followed Dollfuss, a pious Roman Catholic, whose dictatorship did not please Germany because he was against union with that country, though his rule was as tyrannical as that in any totalitarian state. So he was murdered by the Nazis, and the equally orthodox Schuschnigg took his place, to follow the same anti-German policy which Seyss-Inquart, the real power in the country, opposed.

It was Seyss-Inquart, the first of the quislings, who, with the help of Cardinal Innitzer, acting for the Vatican, delivered Austria over to Germany, and, when the invading army arrived in 1938, the bishops instructed the people to be loyal to Hitler, while every church bell pealed as the Swastika flag was unfurled from the cathedral tower of Vienna.

Next followed the German occupation of Czecho-Slovakia, likewise aided by the Church, which had always hated the Czechs since the day the papal army, after devastating Bohemia, was defeated by them away back in 1431. Under the leadership of the non-Christian Masaryk, the Czechs had become free, democratic and prosperous, but the Roman Catholic Slovaks, under the lead of a priest Hlinka, were dissatisfied and wished to separate from their heretical countrymen. Hlinka died, to be followed by the more extreme zealot, another priest, Tiszo, who became the tool of the Vatican, which was set upon splitting Czecho-Slovakia in two, just at the time when Hitler was threatening the very existence of the State.

The Czechs consequently expelled the Papal Nuncio from Prague, because of the aid the Vatican was giving to Hitler, and then followed a mass demonstration against the government, which was organised by the Church, and presided over by a cardinal. Next followed the demand by the Sudeten Germans, led by the Roman Catholic Henlein, who was Hitler's agent, to be incorporated within the Reich. This engineered revolt became the excuse Germany made to take over Bohemia and Moravia, while Slovakia became an independent state and fought against Russia with the blessing of the Pope.

When France collapsed in 1940 she broke her agreement with Britain not to make a separate peace with Germany, a dastardly act which greatly prolonged the war, and for a time made its outcome uncertain. This inglorious page in French history also records the end of the Republic, against which the Church had fulminated for seventy years. Now the French priests openly expressed their sympathy with the brutal hordes of German invaders who had swept through their land, driving millions of civilians before them. Thus they mingled their satisfaction with that of all their brother clergy throughout Roman Catholic Europe, because they believed that now the end of democracy had come. Roman Catholic quislings secured power, not only in France but also in Holland and Belgium, while anti-churchmen were persecuted and liquidated, most of the collaborationists everywhere being churchmen.

The intrigues of the Roman Catholics in France before the war were largely responsible for the rottenness which prevailed in French politics, as they caused bitter antagonisms and disunity amongst the people. France's unfriendly attitude towards Russia, the great buttress on which lay her safety, came from false Vatican propaganda; in fact this falsification of news by the Holy See prepared the way for Hitler to carry through his plan to conquer Europe, a policy he so clearly set out in *Mein Kampf*. To Germany and Italy the Vatican was a most welcome and useful ally, and the work it did all over Europe and America, in isolating Russia, was invaluable to them both in preparing the way for the conquest of each European country in turn.

So much had the Church's propaganda influenced Laval, an intimate friend of the Pope and zealous churchman, that to him peace at any price was imperative, to enable Germany to deal a deadly blow at Russia, and knock her out for all time. To him a prostrate France was worth while if it also meant a vanquished Russia. No man exerted himself more to take France out of the war, and break her word to Britain, and by his ceaseless efforts he persuaded the French Assembly to nominate Pétain with authority to end the war as best he could. Then all who opposed this policy, and wished to continue the war from North Africa, were arrested.

The Vatican, on the other hand, gloried in the great victory secured by the Church from the fall of the Republic, the official Vatican daily newspaper *Osservatore Romano* describing this tragic event as "the dawn of a new and radiant day, not only for France but for Europe and the world", while the English *Catholic Herald* wrote that "France, purified and glorified in heroic suffering, can look out once more upon Europe with a clear Christian purpose". To the Vatican the fall of the Republic, and the imminent collapse of Britain, to be followed by the end of Russia, was the salvation of Christian civilisation, when autocracy would return and rule Europe, as it had done before such devilish inventions as republics and democracies had been produced.

Britain, in those days, stood alone as the guardian of Democratic Civilisation, while four devout Roman Catholics—Pétain, Laval, Weygand and Bonnet—ruled unoccupied France in the interests of Germany. All Frenchmen now received instructions from the Vatican to support this Vichy quartet, and Laval, for his services to the Church in overthrowing the Republic, was blessed by the Pope and rewarded with two high papal decorations, his daughter receiving a gold and coral rosary.

We may well wonder why the Vatican conceived such a hatred of Russia, and pursued such fanatical, unscrupulous false propaganda against her. Why did the Pope each year issue a strident appeal for Bolshevism to be destroyed by war, when Communism, like Socialism, is an economic and not a religious affair? Socially the Russian people were better cared for than were the masses in many Roman Catholic countries. In Russia all were free to believe what religion they wished, and there was no religious persecution, the Roman Catholics being free to worship as they pleased, so long as they did not use their churches for political purposes.[1]

As this was not the cause, we might well imagine that, as the head of the largest capitalist corporation in the world, the Vatican was afraid that Communism would some day despoil it of its possessions. All-powerful Russia will in the years to come be either a great force for good or evil; who can yet say which course she will take, but this we know, that the Christian Church is still in being in this totalitarian police-ridden despotic land. The Western and Eastern Churches have always been bitter enemies, and the Vatican radio has given an opportunity to the Western Church to express openly a long-standing hostility towards an old rival. When thinking of these things we must never forget the age-old quarrel between the Western and Eastern churches over the word "Filioque", which the Western Church added to the Creed in 1054, to cause this long-standing disruption.

[1] In 1929 the Foreign Secretary stated in the House of Commons that he had heard from the British Ambassador in Moscow that there was no religious persecution in Russia.

Having read this book so far we will remember the hatred of the Church of Rome towards the Eastern Christians, because they would not accept this unwarranted interpolation to the Creed, and how Christian Europe was in consequence split in two, wars and bitterness between these two branches of the Christian Church continuing up to our own times.

Moscow, to the Eastern Christians, occupies the same place as does Rome to Western Christians, and the Patriarch of Moscow and all Russia takes the place of the Pope. Patriarchs and popes have reviled and abused each other unmercifully for the past nine hundred years, and the aim of the Vatican has always been the subjection of the Eastern Church to its domination. Every pope has wanted to recover the authority once wielded by Rome over all Christendom, and, with Hitler set on crushing Russia, the long-wished-for opportunity had come. Great must have been the hopes the invasion of Russia raised in the Vatican, great must have been the disappointment at its failure, and to Pius XII this event must have been as severe a blow as was the defeat of the Spanish Armada to his predecessor Sixtus V.

The majority of the people in the Balkans (75 per cent. to be exact) belong to the Orthodox Eastern Church, and the Italian attack on Greece was regarded as paving the way for them also to fall under the control of the Holy See. Except in the most backward countries, the Roman Catholic Church has been steadily losing members, it being estimated by Joseph McCabe (the greatest living authority on the subject, to whom the author is indebted for many of the facts and figures given in this section) that over

70,000,000 have severed their connection since the beginning of the 20th century. Other fields must be opened up to maintain revenue, and the bringing of Russia and the Balkans into the Catholic fold has not only been the prayer of every pope for past centuries, but today would be a valuable additional support in maintaining the splendour of the Vatican Court, and the princely incomes of its hierarchy throughout the world.

In the Far East there was also profitable ground awaiting cultivation, which would still further increase the Church's wealth, "the docile and naturally submissive people of the East", as the Vatican terms them, being expected to give forth a rich harvest. A new and profitable vista was opened up to the Roman Catholic Church when Japan promised the Pope protection, and possibly a monopoly of this field outside Japan. The Japanese intended to keep their own gods for their own people, but the Christian gods were good enough for her conquered subjects.

Though the world's Press has passed over very lightly the political intrigues of the Vatican during the past ten years, the historian must emphasise an influence which helped so potently to produce some of the events recorded in this chapter. Once again the bane of supernatural religion has helped to destroy the wealth, life and happiness of a great part of mankind, the curse of ignorance being behind it all, ignorance which the Church, in its own interests, ardently desires to continue.

The leader of this reactionary policy is the Pope at Rome, the representative on earth of a humble Jew who, we are told, lived a short life of poverty and hardship, sustained by the alms he received from his friends. From this simple basis, because of a series of unusual occurrences, this otherwise unknown man was transformed into the second person of a trinity of gods, and claimed as the Christ, the Creator, Mediator and Redeemer of mankind.

Then the claim was made, and has been always sustained, that he had appointed the Pope at Rome as his vicar and representative on earth, with full authority to do as he pleased, this position, moreover, making His Holiness infallible. Besides representing God on earth, the Vicar of Christ also inherited the glory and tradition of the Imperial Caesars, he claiming to be both the spiritual and temporal ruler of mankind. All three claims have been both useful and profitable, because, on some occasions, he claims the meekness and humility of Jesus, on others the divine power of God, besides the material power of a Roman Emperor, who could inflict death, banishment or persecution on any disloyal subject.

Under this blatant imposture a large part of mankind has lived for sixteen centuries, and, if this is not the most fantastic event in history, which one is more so? To the continued propagation of this chimera the Roman Catholic Church is committed, and consequently ignorance, under autocratic rule, is necessary if it is to be believed. Here indeed we are faced with the eternal problem of knowledge and ignorance, liberty and tyranny, truth and falsehood, good and evil, which can only be rightly solved by increased education. This only will advance the knowledge that will dissipate the clouds in which so many still wander.

CHAPTER XIX.

DEMOCRATIC CIVILISATION.

Introduction. (1) *Ethics Must Take the Place of Supersti-*
tion. (2) *The Democratic State of the Future.* (3) *Justice,*
Peace and Security Must Be Our Aim. (4) *The Curse of*
Ignorance Will Some Day Pass Away.

THE preceding pages reveal how most of mankind's
troubles have come from ignorance. He was ignorant
of the art of government, of the method of organising
society so as to get the best out of humanity, and of the
right and proper way to live in comfort and harmony.
He was ignorant of the origin and meaning of religion,
transforming the natural into the supernatural. He
was ignorant of astronomy, having but a faint idea of
his place in the universe; ignorant of geology, not
realising the great age of the earth on which he lived;
ignorant of biology, knowing little of his make-up, his
origin and his destiny; ignorant of economics, and
consequently unable to trade to the best advantage;
ignorant of chemistry and the powers latent within
matter, and ignorant of how to make the forces of
nature work for him and relieve him of the toil and
burden of production and distribution.

As the panorama of history opened up before us, as
we passed from chapter to chapter, we saw the effect of
developing mind—a little here and there was learned
and remembered. From the age when the only thing
to distinguish man from an animal was the club he
wielded, on to the present day, is a long period in

history, but a very short one when compared with the time life has been on earth. Our perspective is limited, and history takes us only a comparatively short way back on the course of time. Compared with the time life has been on earth, history represents no more than what a second is to a day, and for that fraction only have we any written guide of the past.

Clothed as we are in physical matter, our interests are concerned with the affairs of earth, but our consciousness is not confined to our present surroundings, each one having a destiny elsewhere which, in duration and activity, will some day and somewhere enable us to realise that our earth experiences can be compared to the time when, as children, our outlook did not far exceed the walls of our nursery.

This history therefore relates to the nursery stage of the human race, and it contains much of the ignorance and folly associated with childhood. In spite of all the wealth in food, comforts and luxuries that this earth can provide, about 150,000,000 of its some 2,000,000,000 inhabitants are still on the border-line of starvation, two-thirds of mankind lack a properly balanced diet, and this will become more pronounced if soil erosion and the increase of population are not checked.

Only the history of a portion of the human race is known, that of those living during the past six thousand years in the coastal regions and in the temperate belt encircling the earth. What happened to earlier human beings and to those countless millions who have lived and died in the vast spaces of Asia, Africa and America is unknown, because they have left no record to guide us.

Much is now known of the early civilisations of

Mesopotamia and Egypt but not so much about China and India. The thoughts and deeds of their inhabitants were reviewed in the earlier chapters when we found that they laid the basis of our present-day knowledge and way of life. Most of our history, however, has had to do with Europe because here developed the greatest virility, and here mind was stimulated to greater activity than elsewhere, so much so that it produced a people which dominated the greater part of the human race. Only for four centuries did western Europe enjoy the benefit of a single government, when Rome dominated that part of the Continent and the lands surrounding the Mediterranean. This age, when men lived in peace, and when culture and learning spread, was destroyed by the Frankish-Germanic hordes, which ever since have been the cause of strife and unrest throughout Europe.

Under their hammer blows the Empire vanished, leaving, in place of the culture of Virgil, Cicero, Seneca and Horace, the Christian Church, built upon the Pagan superstitions of the age and the impressive fabric of Roman law. On its teaching and outlook Christian civilisation was built up, to develop into the barbarism of the Dark Ages, which was followed by wars for religion, for dynasties and territory, all of which have left their stain upon the culture of the present day. Justice was then unknown, ignorance was glorified, intolerance and cruelty were rampant, and only within the last hundred years has Western civilisation slowly emerged from the dark shadow which theology has cast over a great part of the earth.

Ethics and supernatural religion have nothing in common. Religious beliefs have changed down the ages, but not ethical conduct, which embraces all time and all mankind. The substance of what is good in the Sermon on the Mount can still be read on the walls of the temples of Egypt, where it was written over four thousand years ago. The wise of all the lands and faiths, for thousands of years, have advocated righteousness, but only the few have appreciated its importance or tried to follow their advice. The average mind today, in every land, does not yet realise the importance of ethical development as a cure for most of the world's political and economic troubles, and, though some know more than others, they are too limited in number to influence the judgment and actions of the majority.

The human race can be likened to a family of different ages, without a father or mother to guide and control the children's thoughts and actions. Like children, the people of earth have shown a childish mental instability, and been guided by leaders who were likewise children mentally with similar faults and failings as those they guided. The people formed themselves into groups, each leader speaking and acting for the one he represented. He was generally more pugnacious and masterful than the rest, but seldom as wise or as learned as some of those who were passed over. The leaders, as a rule, were not selected because of their knowledge or wisdom, but because they could influence the multitude in a more dramatic way, appealing to their emotions as a wiser and more experienced man would never do.

So long as this mentality prevails throughout the human race, which is selfish by nature, though limited in living space and unlimited in its desires, quarrels and conflicts will continue. If all the nations had elected as their leaders men renowned for their wisdom, honesty, knowledge and prudence, what a difference it would have made to world history !

Instead of so doing, the people have allowed their rulers to reign by what is called divine right, their sons to succeed them, or they have acclaimed others who appealed to their childish minds. There was no standard of ethics, wisdom or knowledge set for these leaders to live up to, and all that was necessary to secure their subjects' obedience and devotion was their lineage or military prowess. So suffering consequently followed from bad and foolish leadership, a forceful adventurer, or his less capable successor, sooner or later bringing calamity to his deluded people.

Much of past history has been darkened by bad leadership, and the hope of the human race rests on the people themselves rising in intelligence and determining the policy to be pursued. Until knowledge, wisdom and righteousness are enthroned, no league or treaties will ensure world peace, prosperity and contentment, and now that some have left behind the Theological Age and entered the Democratic Age this must be remembered. Only by thinking and doing what is right and avoiding what is wrong will peace and happiness come to mankind.

(1) Ethics Must Take the Place of Superstition.

Now we have come to the kernel and source of all the troubles that affect mankind, so far as they concern our conduct one with another. This can be appreciated better, now that we have covered in outline the whole course of recorded human history. Now we can clearly realise that what has been absent in the past is a sense of justice, kindness and tolerance between man and man, as individuals, tribes or nations.

> So many prayers, so many creeds,
> So much of self we keep in mind,
> And yet forget that this world needs
> The simple art of being kind.

By planned systematic training a child's character can be so moulded in early life that it will become just as it has been taught. The mind is a very plastic substance when in course of development, and, up to the end of last century, when general education begun, the mind of the child had received no scientific consideration, its development having been left to its ignorant parents and equally ignorant priests. To the latter the child was a future supporter of their debased superstitions, and their only interest lay in developing its mind along this line of thought so as to make it a loyal and devoted subject of their organisation. "Give us a child from the age of five until it is ten," said the religious leaders of all the world's faiths, "and it will be our staunch follower until old age."

That was the outcome of ignorance during the Theological Age, because it was found to be the simplest way of managing childlike people. The priests were the pioneers of this form of mental development, which was later adopted by the politicians. We remember how the Turks took the boys of subject Christian races and taught them to hate their religion and all of the Christian faith, the result being that they produced a host of Moslem fanatics eager to fight against the Christians. Thus they reared a disciplined body of zealots who respected only Moslem beliefs, and hated all other faiths with such ferocity that they became splendid soldiers, being both fearless, pitiless and cruel. Hitler carried on this method and produced a ruthless, brave, fanatical youth who hated and despised all who did not belong to the Germanic race.

What the priests, the Turks and Hitler did in an evil direction can be equally well done for the cause of righteousness. The power of influencing the young has been demonstrated by ignorant and cruel men, but the time has now come for enlightened teachers and leaders to take the power for evil away from those politicians and priests who wish to mould the childish mind in a way that will further their own fanatical beliefs. The ambitious priest and politician, the one intent on the advancement of his Church and faith, and the other on the aggrandisement of his country, are the two great dangers which future generations must avoid. Both are fanatics who wish the minds of the coming generation to think as they think, to the glory of the Church or the expansion of their country.

The clergy represent the Theological Age which has passed and is discredited by all thoughtful people, and the question that now arises is whether they should continue to have any further part in the intellectual instruction of the people. For fifteen hundred years they controlled the mental and social life of Christendom, and if they had had their way we would all be still living in the Dark Ages. This fact history makes crystal clear by their opposition to every reform and all progress, as to them theology was everything and knowledge nothing. On theology only they relied to make and keep the people good, the reason for the poor results achieved being obvious from what they taught, and still teach, to those who put their trust in them.

This, then, is the substance of what is told to every Christian congregation when a child is baptised, the extracts being taken from the Episcopalian Prayer Book: (1) "All men are conceived and born in sin . . ."; (2) "We beseech thee . . . that thou wilt mercifully look upon this child; wash him and sanctify him with the Holy Ghost; that he, being delivered from thy wrath . . . may come to the land of everlasting life"; (3) "that he, coming to thy Holy Baptism, may receive remission of his sins by spiritual regeneration"; (4) "that this infant may enjoy the everlasting benediction of thy heavenly washing"; (5) "Doubt ye not therefore, but earnestly believe, that he will . . . give unto him the blessing of eternal life, and make him partaker of his everlasting kingdom"; (6) "Ye have brought this child here to be baptised; ye have prayed that our Lord Jesus Christ would vouchsafe to receive him, to release him of his sins, to sanctify him with the Holy Ghost, to give him the Kingdom of Heaven and everlasting life"; (7) "This infant must also faithfully, for his part, promise by you that are his sureties (until he come of age to take it upon himself), that he will renounce the devil and all his works, and constantly believe God's holy Word, and obediently keep his commandments".

Then the god-parents are asked in the child's name to renounce the devil and all his works, after which they are told that Jesus Christ has taken the punishment, so as to secure the forgiveness of our sins, and how the mystical effect of sprinkling water on the child's face has washed away his sins. This is nothing less than belief in magic, the pretended art of influencing events, the occultism which runs through all religions, and the clergy of our time still perform the functions allotted to the tribe's witch doctor or medicine man. After the sprinkling takes place the congregation is told that the child is now regenerate, being dead unto sin and living unto righteousness. Furthermore, they are informed that he is now numbered with the saved and the inheritor of the everlasting kingdom.

The infant, fortunately, is unconscious of all this palaver, but, from the Church point of view, it is the first step to secure him as a member and future supporter of the organisation. The next step is the Confirmation service, when the door is opened wide for him to walk right in with the least possible inconvenience to his conscience, but, as he has been regenerated and saved since baptism, his moral character does not give the Church any concern.[1] Anyone, good, bad or indifferent, who has been baptised can go through this formality, as the applicant for Church membership is only asked if he "can say the Creed, the Lord's Prayer, the Ten Commandments, and if he can also answer to such other questions as in the short Catechism are contained". Then he is asked to renew the promise made by his god-parents, after which follows a few prayers, an address and a blessing, which brings the ceremony to an end.

The effect of all this, in the days when it was taken seriously, was to produce a religious snob, who, accepting the word of the priest magician that he was

[1] On 8th January, 1949, Margaret Allen was confirmed and received into the Anglican Church, after being sentenced to death by hanging for deliberately murdering an old woman.

regenerated and cleansed of all sin, looked upon himself as one of the elect because he had been sprinkled by water and had the sign of the cross made over him. All who had not received a Christian baptism he considered as damned inferior creatures who were destined for hell, while he had a valid passport for heaven. Being asked to renounce the devil and all his works is much too indefinite to have any effect on one's character, and the fact that the youth could repeat the Creed, the Lord's Prayer, the Ten Commandments, and answer the theological questions in the Catechism, added nothing to his ethical development

Much has been said and written about the high ethical standard of what is called the Sermon on the Mount, but how few have ever read the entire sermon, covering three chapters, and given intelligent thought to what they contain? A few verses have a high ethical value, but more than that cannot be said when the entire three chapters, containing 111 verses, are carefully considered. Much that remains is stupid and lacking in all practical sense; much is cruel, some so much so that it can only be described as abominably wicked. On the teaching contained in this so-called sermon the Inquisition was established, the Inquisitors of the Faith flourished, and our fanatical ancestors based their arguments in favour of torture, imprisonment, banishment and death for all unbelievers.

Do unto others as we would that they do to us is not the foundation of Christianity, as some have so boldly asserted in our day. This wise ethical remark by Confucius requires no priesthood, no Church, no creeds, no dogmas, doctrines, ritual, ceremonies, holy book, holy days, or mystical scheme of salvation for its propagation. In fact the reported sayings of Jesus about righteousness are only a repetition of similar remarks on the subject which were said by wise men from the time of the ancient Egyptians, Assyrians and Indians away back three thousand years ago. For Christianity, after its past black record, to claim a monopoly of these opinions is plagiarism and reveals not only Christian ignorance but a complete lack of honesty and respect for the truth.

The theological Christ will some day take the same place as that now occupied by the other saviour-gods of the past, and Krishna, the only other saviour-god still to be worshipped, will likewise join company with the other mythological creations who at the height of their glory received the reverence and adoration of the human race. With mystical theology outgrown, the supernatural religion which grew round the original human figures will vanish into the mists, but natural religion will always remain, it being a personal matter for everyone, but not something to be systematically taught as a lesson in church or school.

Prayer is a personal emotional expression, and not something to hear from other lips, or as set phrases to be repeated on appointed occasions, because its value lies in the relief it gives to pent-up emotions in time of excessive sorrow or jubilation. Man is an etheric being, and, as this is so, one's personal religion can no more be obliterated than can the individual mind, which is something beyond the material. Religion is not a legendary affair about an event which happened in the distant past. To Christians this occurred some nineteen hundred years ago; to the Hindus, some three thousand years ago, when their saviour Krishna is believed to have died to save humanity, and to those of other faiths there is some past traditional event from which sprang their beliefs.

All supernatural religions had their saviours, or other forms of sacrifice which secured salvation. Each saviour god religion had its saviour, about whom similar claims were made as centred round Christ, and all had, and those which have survived still have, their holy books, sacred dogmas, divine doctrines, holy days and holy men who supervise their teaching, their spiritual lands, buildings and vestments. All that, however, has nothing to do with natural religion, and it only displays the ignorance of humanity wandering through life with the instinctive feeling that each one has a destiny, while burdened with the false idea that he must believe something to secure happiness hereafter. Much nonsense has consequently been imagined, and this has been encouraged by the priesthood, which has commercialised life's mysteries, and produced creeds and dogmas to comfort and frighten the ignorant who could not think for themselves.

The author is old enough to remember the misery he endured as a child when orthodoxy flourished fifty years ago. All who then experienced militant Christianity will remember how children were terrorised by fear of the Christian hell, and how they were forced to endure at least two long bouts of being preached to every Sunday. We remember that everything science has now proved to be true was denounced as coming from the devil, and how Sunday was a day of religious gloom and misery. All who by thought and effort have emerged from this mental prison, all who have exchanged the chains of bondage for the unbounded freedom of knowledge, have no wish to inflict on coming generations what they endured.

Then it was that foolish and ignorant men, who made God in their own image, devoted their lives to preaching from the privileged platform, known as the pulpit, their devilish doctrines which depicted God as a monster waiting to torture at death for all eternity the souls of all who could not believe their narrow stupid creed. Against their evil teaching no reply was allowed, no one could answer back to defend the character of the deity, and the mental torture they inflicted on minds young, sensitive and virile, had to be experienced to be understood. Democratic civilisation will surely never allow this state of affairs to return as, now that the people have thrown off the tyranny of the Church and obtained the education it denied to them for fifteen hundred years, they must retain their freedom and never again allow this wickedness to blight the childish mind.

Today, in countries where books are plentiful, all can discover, if they take the trouble, everything that is known of man's psychic make-up and destiny. Far better to seek the truth from those who do not make a living from purveying superstition, and keep to the results so far discovered by honest men and women who have made psychic investigation their study. This they have not done for the purpose of enriching themselves, or obtaining an improved social position, but solely for the sake of following in the train of facts and evidence. These they have recorded so that everyone might benefit from their experiences.

As the child grows into youth he should, if

sufficiently interested, be given the elementary books available on psychic investigation, and, as he grows older, he can then study more deeply a subject which has produced a vast literature, some of which will always remain classic of this new branch of science. Then the student should pass on to study the recent works on the origin and beliefs of the different world religions, written by scholars who devoted their lives to this research, remembering always that the gods and goddesses were just names given to men and women who once lived on earth, and returned to be seen as apparitions, which were then believed to be divine creations.

By this study he will discover that religion is something based on an etheric foundation, which to each one of us when we die will be as real and solid as is this earth. To our ancestors, who knew little, but imagined much, the after-life was pictured in many strange and weird aspects, and fear caused them to think and do many cruel and curious deeds. Their religious speculations entered into almost every phase of life, to cause comfort to many, but the symbolic meaning behind all the world's religious beliefs received little consideration.

Every religion has the same basis, namely the fact that man is a triune being composed of mind, etheric and physical body, and on this foundation the superstructure of supernatural religion has been reared. Those who preach the dogma of the different world religions have never been taught in their theological colleges the meaning of, or the symbolism behind, their beliefs, and only those who have made this branch of science a study can realise how all the

world's different religious beliefs can be traced back
to man himself as a triune being.

So Religion, in its many and varied aspects, is a
fascinating subject for study and investigation. Its
correct interpretation will bring comfort as well as
intellectual satisfaction, and remove doubt and despondency. Misinterpreted, misunderstood and debased by supernatural superstition, it has produced
much that is evil, as where ignorance reigns there also
will be found wickedness. Thus supernatural Religion
has been closely associated with intolerance, the outcome of which has been war and persecution. It has
been woven into tyranny and injustice, to bring about
much misery when handled by evil men who traded on
the natural ignorance and fear of what happens after
death.

Natural religion, like so much else that is true,
has been overshadowed by supernatural religion, which
is false. Consequently supernatural religion and
wickedness have always kept partnership, and the
people in their ignorance have had to suffer. So,
when supernatural religion became a state affair, it was
used to keep the people submissive, and, as it was not
based on truth, increased knowledge was discouraged.
The result was disastrous, because wherever organised
religion reigned supreme, so likewise did ignorance,
and this is a feature of all religious civilisations, such
as Christian, Moslem, Hindu and all the others, until
we come to our own times, when more enlightened
communities have prepared the way for Democratic
civilisation.

This, it is hoped, will some day sweep away most
of the evils connected with the old religious civilisa-

tions, which are based on ecclesiastical organisations intent on keeping the people in childlike obedience. Then, in democratic Britain, there will be no State Church, as in a democracy the people who go to church should support the type of organisation they themselves prefer, and not cast the burden on the taxpayers, landowners and farmers, most of whom have no sympathy with the propagation of the theological opinions contained in the Thirty-Nine Articles of Religion.

Today we live under different conditions, and more developed intelligence looks on life from a new aspect. Not by fear, but by the increase of knowledge, does a democratic community rely on good behaviour. We are still in the early stage of this development, and are still largely ruled by our desires, hopes, fears and emotions instead of by our reason. Conduct has not yet advanced into the position of becoming a science which all will some day learn from childhood upwards.

When this advance comes about every child, everywhere, will be taught to analyse and develop his character, and continue to do so throughout his life. He will learn which qualities produce happiness and those which produce misery. He will be taught how to subdue and conquer the evil within him, and develop what is good. Self-analysis, correctly conducted, will produce good men and women, and, when everyone is trained to subject his thoughts and deeds to a high ethical standard, happiness and contentment will spread throughout the whole human race. Social progress is primarily an individual effort, and, as the individual mind advances, so likewise will the state to which the individuals belong.

In Section 3 of this chapter are tabulated some of the qualities with which we are born. Some inherit more good qualities than others, while evil predominates in some who are less fortunate. Some live in good, and others in bad surroundings, and this influences our heredity, but much, if not all, of the disabilities of both heredity and environment can be overcome by education. Our schoolmasters and schoolmistresses should come from the very best that the nation can produce, and their profession should be considered as ranking as the first in the land. Their ethical standard must be the highest to which the individual can attain, so that their pupils will set them up as examples on which they base their conduct through life. The boy and girl produce the man and woman, and their correct upbringing will scme day make the home a fit dwelling-place for the child of the coming more enlightened age.

The great majority, given the comforts and necessities of civilisation, have no desire to rob or kill their neighbours, whether they belong to their own nation or not. They are quite content to live and let live. Likewise the majority do not wish to be unjust, cruel, intolerant, domineering, untruthful, pitiless and unmerciful, faults which come from ignorance and can be eliminated by education. Some, however, have warped minds intent on plunder, savagery and all that is wicked. These must be kept down by the majority who prefer righteousness to unrighteousness, and this can be done if the greater number is sufficiently determined that good will prevail.

Now that machines can produce cheaply all that we need, our desires are more easily satisfied, and so

recedes the urge to take that which belongs to someone else. Crime, therefore, within the nation should
decrease, and if the people everywhere will only
concentrate on improving their own lot by invention
and improved methods of production and distribution,
they will find that they will get all they need without
plundering their neighbours. Increased intelligence
should, moreover, bring about a reduction in the
production of children who cannot be properly
supported, and education, with the help of science,
can make woman the mistress of human creation.
On her own forethought of the future much of the
peace, happiness and prosperity of the human race
depends.

Every child should learn that happiness, but not
selfish happiness, is the goal for which all should
strive. If we are happy we are in harmony with our
surroundings, to attain which should be the aim of
ethical education. Ethical teaching should take the
child back to the time of primitive man, and, from this
period onwards to the present day, the mistakes made
by our ancestors and their consequences should be
emphasised. The child should be taught why and
how he did what was wrong, and how it was some
discovered that doing what was right, or righteousness, is always the best policy because it brings
happiness, whereas wrong-doing causes unhappiness
and misery. Thus the way the entire moral code was
built up from experience should be made known to
the child, who will then realise how wrong-doing and
selfishness eventually convinced the moralists, of the
past and present, that happiness can come only from
righteousness. Not a sentimental kind of righteous-

ness, but one which relates to practical, everyday affairs for the well-being of oneself and every other person.

Ethical science can be made so simple, interesting and convincing that the child, when he has absorbed what it has to teach, will do right quite naturally, as right thinking and right acting will become a habit, Happiness can be secured by correct teaching, and each one of the virtues which brings it about should be explained and stressed to the child from an early age. Then he will do what is right, and avoid wrong-doing, because he knows that it is within his own self-interest to do what is right and avoid what is wrong.

If this is taught in the schools of every nation for the purpose of producing happiness in the world, in the nation and in the family, then, within a generation, disharmony and crime will decline, the fear of war will decrease, and within a hundred years the danger of war will vanish. To put it another way: if everyone would intelligently read and study history honestly recorded with the devotion and zeal that our ancestors gave to the Bible, what a transformation it would make in family life, in society and in world affairs!

Within the nation's family life happiness will some day take the place of the unhappiness caused by selfishness due to ignorance, and the nation, composed of ethically trained individuals, will seek peace and concord with other nations whose people are similarly trained. An international language which all could learn would greatly simplify this process. As some nations are more advanced than others, it will, however, be necessary to prevent the less developed from spoiling the happiness of those who have learned the art of right living, and consequently co-ordinated force must be used for the purpose of restraining them until they reach a higher ethical outlook on life.

It is important to appeal to the self-interest within everyone, as ethical development comes from intelligent self-interest. We are all highly individualised beings, which means that our thoughts are naturally centred on ourselves. Ignorance produces selfishness, which causes unhappiness, whereas intelligence causes our self-interest to be directed aright, and this creates happiness. This can be better understood if we take each virtue separately, analyse the cause which produces it, and observe the effect its practice has on ourselves and others.

Love is the greatest force in the world. The love of self and the love of others dominate most of our actions. If this force is directed intelligently it causes happiness, but unintelligent love creates misery. As our mind develops we are hurt if we injure, neglect or cause pain and suffering to those we love. Primitive man loved only himself, and then his mate and her offspring. Then he loved others of his tribe to a lesser degree, until we arrive at the time when the love of humanity now makes doctors and nurses dedicate themselves for the good of the entire race, irrespective of nationality or creed. Missionaries of all religions now live amongst those they think of as heathen, for the purpose of bringing them the blessings they believe accompanies the acceptance of their religion.

The cause of this increase in the power of love is the telepathic understanding which developing mind now has for other minds. More developed mind can now image the thoughts and feelings of other minds in a way undeveloped mind cannot do. This increases the power of love, which now extends in our day to the animals, many of which we now realise have feelings akin to our own. Nevertheless we have a long way to go before they are all kindly treated, much unnecessary cruelty still existing, especially for the purpose of giving pleasure, as otter hunting, hare coursing, fox and deer hunting are particularly objectionable forms of amusement. Cruelty to animals, as to humans, was quite in keeping with the times up to last century, but now our sympathy towards animals is increasing, and some day blood sports and their debasing effect will come to an end.

Sympathy, patience, mercy and pity for human weakness and suffering are likewise increasing, because more developed mind can now image the feelings of others, which was something our ancestors could not do. They were selfish, cruel and unjust because they were incapable of thinking outside themselves. We are more sympathetic because we are hurt mentally when others suffer, as we now realise that they have feelings like ourselves, and our increased imagination enables us to appreciate what they feel. It now upsets us mentally to know that others are in distress, and so we are all kinder than were our less intelligent ancestors.

From this feeling of pity comes charity and consideration of others less fortunate than ourselves. Kindness thus increases and cruelty decreases. We are kind because we know that it is welcomed and appreciated by others, just as we ourselves appreciate kindness. Further, we now realise that kindness produces kindness in return, and that the harmony of the human family increases in consequence. This harmony enlarges our happiness, because our more developed and more sensitive minds dislike disharmony. So we are not rude, uncouth or unkind to others because of the reaction this conduct brings upon ourselves. Thus the practice of the virtues is increasing in consequence of intelligent self-interest, the happiness of others bringing about increased happiness to ourselves. This is what follows from mental development, which is the only method of removing the unhappiness which comes from the curse of ignorance.

Justice now prevails as never before, because we ourselves realise how we are hurt by injustice. A well developed mind is now hurt nearly as much by an act of injustice towards others as it would be if it were directed towards oneself. We now try to be just in our dealings with others because we are ashamed of ourselves if we are unjust. We feel that we have fallen to a lower mental level. Our pride is consequently hurt, and we think that we have demonstrated that our mind is not so well developed as we had imagined. To be just, therefore, causes us happiness and mental harmony, whereas injustice causes the reverse.

Honesty can be considered from the same angle. We know that we like to be treated fairly and honestly, and we realise how much we resent our possessions being taken from us. To make others suffer what we would suffer from dishonesty arouses our sympathy for their feelings, and makes us unhappy at their sorrow. Therefore we try to be fair in our dealings one with another, and to take what does not belong to us causes the developed mind more suffering than the pleasure it receives from the possession of the stolen goods.

Mind seems now to be reaching out more and more to other minds, and, when one mind suffers, it affects other minds hitherto beyond its orbit. As this orbit widens the human family will become more closely knit together mentally, and this will have the effect of increasing its harmony and peace. The development of this form of telepathy will increase the melody and decrease the disharmony of life.

Prudence comes from increased experience. Prudence demands that war should cease, because, apart from its wickedness, it is imprudent to risk our fate on the uneven balance which conflict creates. Victory is never certain, so why deliberately, as does the aggressor, take such a risk on such a gambler's chance? Prudence should make us always weigh up possibilities, and not rush into a venture without care and thought. Our ancestors showed little prudence in their actions because their minds were ill balanced and undeveloped, but a well-trained mind should make few mistakes. Courage, combined with caution, always produces the best results and the fewest regrets, because pangs of remorse generally follow hasty actions.

Temperance and self-control in all things are wise, because disharmony follows from lack of restraint and excess. One can love overmuch as one can drink and eat too much. Here self-interest should produce temperance in all things, and thus enable each one to live a healthy and normal life. Intemperance debases the mind, and excess in everything should always be avoided. The importance of a healthy mind must be

instilled into the young, who will learn to avoid in-
temperate practices as they would shun an infectious
disease.

Finally, it is important that all should be trained in
the importance of truth. What is true can only come
from the knowledge of facts, and developing intelligence will learn to sift the true from the false. Children should be taught the importance of truth in their
own self interest, and for the sake of their own and
everyone's happiness. To be surrounded with untruthful people makes life unreal and unstable. We
know not what to believe, and this causes conflicting
emotions which produce disharmony. We expect
to be told the truth at all times, and it follows that we
in turn must always be truthful. If we are not we
cannot expect others to be honest to us. This applies
to the affairs of everyday life, but it does not follow
that we should be lacking in tact and consideration of
the feelings of others in what we say. We can still
be truthful and tactful.

Many people say what is untrue in ignorance, and
children should learn to say only what they know to
be true. This requires the cultivation of their critical
faculty, which is a quality that should receive a prominent place in mental development. To be critical, but
not over-critical, about what we hear and read shows
intelligence, and every child should be taught how to
be intelligently critical of all things. Many people
accept as true something they read or are told without giving the question proper consideration. They
should be taught that if they are so simple they will be
considered stupid by their fellows, and that they must
take thought before they speak. Loose thinking leads

to loose talking, and, as the mind becomes better trained in the future, this should decrease. A happy society can only be maintained on mutual trust, and one of the principal supports of happiness is truthfulness and honesty in all things.

Such, then, is a brief summary of how children everywhere should be taught how to mould their characters. They should not be told only that they must be good, but the reason why they must be good, stress being laid on the fact that goodness will make others, and also themselves, happier. The aim of everyone must be to secure happiness through righteousness. Only by doing what is right can we reach real and lasting happiness, and it must be impressed upon everyone that they will be unhappy by doing what is wrong. Appeal should be made to their own self-interests, because righteousness brings its own reward, or, as Plutarch put it:

> Every condition of life, if attended with virtue, is undisturbed and delightful, but, when vice is intermixed, it renders even things that appear sumptuous and magnificent distasteful and uneasy to the possessor.

That was how this noble Pagan looked on life, and Plato thought likewise, but he added the warning that "the most virtuous of men is he that contents himself with being virtuous without seeking to appear so". Unfortunately, the advice of the really great and wise men of the past has received little consideration, because they have been ignored by all the supernatural religions, which put belief and ceremonials before virtuous living. Consequently the people have been guided by ignorant, and often evil, men who led them down the wrong road because they either knew no better or it was in their interests to do so. By ignoring the moralists, and following the theologians, past history is a tragic story. We can, however, profit by it if we learn what to avoid, and, by so doing, the new structure of society which we build on the ruins produced by the latest exhibition of mass wickedness will be more solid and enduring.

(2) The Democratic State of the Future.

The aim of democracy is to secure the greatest happiness of the greatest number. In a democratic state the people guide their own affairs by means of a majority, who, so long as they remain in the majority, legislate for the people as a whole and not for their party alone. Periodical elections ensure that the majority does not outstay its welcome, and that changing opinion can always produce a majority which is in keeping with the opinion of the greatest number. The people elect their representatives, to whom the ministers selected for the different state departments are responsible, and the man chosen as Prime Minister leads the party which is in office.

Over all is one who represents no party but the entire nation, a king or a president, whose duty it is to preserve majority rule, and from whom the ministers receive, and to whom they return, their insignia of office. This method always preserves a head, and prevents chaos between the time a government goes out of office and a new one is elected. It preserves a permanent head, with no power to legislate, but with the authority to accept the resignation of ministers and confirm the appointment of those who take their place.

This is what we mean by democratic government. It is eminently fair and just; in fact it is difficult to imagine a fairer or juster way of governing a large community made up of many different opinions. It has taken thousands of years to reach this point in our political development, and, though it is not perfect, it is as near perfection as we have yet achieved. Its imperfections come from the failings within each human being, but with increased ethical development the troubles from which democratic government suffers should be smoothed out.

The democratic system is right, but its method of working is often wrong. Its worst feature is caused by lack of method, which at times deprives the majority of their right to rule. This comes about by allowing an unlimited number of representatives to appeal for election to Parliament. Parties can be formed without number, and there is nothing to prevent more than two candidates coming forward at an election, each of whom appeals to a proportion of the voters. If three representatives ask for election, the one elected may not be the one the majority would have voted for if there had been only two candidates. This can happen in every constituency, with the result that Parliament could be composed of perhaps half a dozen or more different cliques. Those who get together to form the majority of members to make up a government thus do not necessarily represent the opinion of the majority in the country, and yet, when they elect their ministers and leader, the king or president must give these ministers office.

This all leads to intrigue and bribery, because the strongest cliques bribe by promises the smaller cliques, whose support they require to secure office. The parties and cliques, which between them can secure by combination the majority of votes, elect the ministers and rule the country. This combination is generally obtained by promises which often degenerate into bribery and corruption, as the smaller cliques give their support to the side which promises to vote as they wish it to vote. Thus one small minority can secure legislation which is contrary to the wishes of the majority of the electors.

This has been the cause of the discredit into which democratic government has so often fallen. It has happened often in France and from time to time in Britain, but past tradition and moderation have maintained in Britain two predominant parties, and so prevented the chaotic conditions which have so often prevailed in other less advanced democratic countries. Consequently some, who are less developed politically, abandoned in despair the parliamentary system and returned to despotic rule, because they could not produce two strong groups of politicians who would share alternately the responsibility of government. The best way to preserve this essential feature is to limit the number of parties to two, the electors having the choice between two policies, as this is quite sufficient to secure a fair representation of opinion.

Democratic government does not mean that representatives must be elected to Parliament to support every shade of opinion in the country. If every member of Parliament went to Westminster to secure only his own limited form of legislation the wheels of government would stop, as a majority could rarely ever be secured. Fortunately this state of affairs can only happen to a limited extent, as each constituency contains so many different individual opinions that a representative for each is impossible. Consequently voters have to choose the candidate who represents most nearly their opinions, but the occasion happens too often of a minority securing the election of their candidate by the vote being split between three or more candidates for election, the one getting the most securing election.

Another danger in a democracy is the fact that constituencies increase and decrease in population, and that some members therefore represent fewer electors than do others. This means that the size of every constituency must be kept the same as much as possible. Other anomalies and difficulties exist in democratic countries, but all can be overcome as they arise. Given all-round goodwill the method works well, and this has now been amply proved. Its best feature is that there is always an alternative government, thus ensuring liberty of expression and the impossibility of a dictatorship, with its accompanying tyranny in the form of concentration camps and control of the Press.

The democratic system is good, but its success must always remain with the people themselves. If they sink into a condition of political coma, Parliament might be overthrown by some powerful individual who has caught the imagination. Then a dictator will be in command, and the secret police will be everywhere. The people will again become as children, and be made to do the bidding of their master.

Democracy means freedom, but only if the people keep it alive, because if they become indifferent to their liberty, tyranny will surely take its place.

Democratic government which has not an enlightened and active body of opinion behind it can also lead to another kind of disaster. Since France became a democracy, many elected representatives have been men who were intent on their own interests and not on those of their country. They used their positions to enrich themselves by placing public money amongst those who paid them best. Graft, corruption and intrigue are dangers in every form of government, and a democracy is no exception, though its real strength will come when in every country the integrity of its public men rises to the level reached in Great Britain, where corruption is now ruthlessly stamped out.

The machine has so increased production that where the raw materials are plentiful there is little we now need that cannot easily be increased far beyond our requirements. By a scientific expansion of output, and the efficient handling of labour, we can today produce and distribute all we require from a productive effort much less than was required in the past. This opens up great possibilities for the future, provided we discover the way to abolish war and the waste it causes. If we could be relieved of the burden of armaments, it is not too much to claim that it will become possible to obtain all the production and distribution required from the six hours' daily work of each man and unmarried woman between twenty and fifty years of age.

This reduction of the years and hours of labour

should increase the time that future generations will have for culture and leisure. Now it is possible to envisage the time when every one will continue his education up to the age of twenty, and live half his life free from the burden of toil. Then we shall have reached the time when we can talk about the leisured masses and not only of the leisured classes.

The increase of wealth which the machine now makes possible opens up many vistas to the imagination. Our earth, if scientifically exploited, can yield sufficient for all our comforts and necessities. The forces of nature are now sufficiently under control to be directed in an ever-increasing degree to the increased comfort of mankind, and now that we have found the way to release the tremendous power within the atom, endless possibilities lie before us of both good and evil.

If this revolutionary discovery is wisely handled it will be possible to produce power, light and heat at the minimum of cost, and eliminate all drudgery from work. Moreover, science now enables us to make ever-increasing use of the minerals and the soil, and, by the skill of the chemist and engineer, matter can be fashioned or directed in an ever-increasing degree to produce the requirements of developing mind. Consequently we are already surrounded by comforts and luxuries undreamed of by our ancestors; increased knowledge, moreover, having reduced pain and suffering, improved our health, and prolonged and enlarged the scope of life.

We have everything we need to' make this earth a very pleasant place, and when we learn the art of harmony, happiness and peace, much quite unnecessary suffering and trouble will have been left behind. Then our great discoveries will be used for construction but never for destruction, and science will no longer be a partner in the business of first increasing and then decreasing our wealth, of both healing our infirmities and inflicting wounds and death. This past misuse of knowledge makes clear that though we have learned to harness the forces of nature and fashion matter to our desires, we have not yet learned to control our jungle heredity, and treat each other in the only way which will secure lasting happiness.

Some nations, which have all they need, still desire the satisfaction of dominating others to secure a higher standard of living at the expense of their neighbours. So as to get these additional pleasures they burden themselves with increased work and taxation to secure the means to achieve their ambitions. Thus they reduce their own standard of life and that of their neighbours, who must follow in their lead from self-protection. Consequently they not only decrease their own comforts, but their young men court death, privations and suffering for the uncertain chance of living to obtain the fruits of victory.

Individual thinking is much more rational than mass thinking. One has only to know the technique of how to appeal to the mob, as Hitler and Mussolini did, and an emotional unthinking nation will accept what is told them without question. For sixteen centuries Christians throughout Christendom have been preached to, and accepted all the clergy told them, rarely giving critical or rational thought to what they heard, and when last century they obtained the vote their critical faculties had largely ceased to exist, because they had never been developed. Consequently politicians and mob orators in many countries have led the people like sheep, and more often than not on the road to disillusionment, misery and suffering.

This mass thinking, let us hope, will decrease as education increases. Then facts, and not emotional rhetoric, will appeal, and the day of the mob orator will have passed. Children in the mass, like a herd of animals, think and act without considered thought, and most of the human race has never outgrown its childish ways. Consequently progress has been very slow, every new idea being denounced by the Church as contrary to the will of God, because it alone had the truth, while everything outside its knowledge pertained to the devil. Almost everything we now enjoy was at one time or another attributed by this institution to the devil, who seems to have always been foremost in his desire to increase human happiness and comfort; in fact, on this assumption, he is the world's greatest inventor and reformer.

No greater benefit ever came to mankind than that which developed from the conception of mutual assistance in the form of insurance against all the mischances of life. One would think that there could be nothing wicked in this proposal, and yet many years passed before it was put into general practice because it amounted to want of trust in God and the efficacy of prayer—"Take therefore no thought for the morrow" (*Matthew* vi, 34) being quoted against the idea. Not until the 17th century, after the great fire of London, was a system of insurance designed and put into practice, only to meet with strong religious opposition, which contended that God would always provide, and that not a sparrow suffered from divine neglect. Owing to this ignorant opposition, it was not until within our own times that it was realised how great was the benefit which insurance can bring to everyone.

Only now are we at the beginning of the insurance era, when, by taking thought for the morrow, we can prevent all the poverty and want which come from unemployment, sickness, accident, old age and death. The consequences of fire, earthquake, storm and the other forces of nature which do us harm can now likewise be insured against; all of which evils in the insurance policies are termed "Acts of God". Our ancestors attributed to God all the evils which befall us, and blamed the devil for inventing a sensible way to avoid the consequences of these disasters by everyone sharing in the danger. These calamities; death excepted, only come to a few and not to the many, but no one knows who will be the victim, and so, by each one contributing a little, all can be protected.

By means of insurance much misery and individual loss have been avoided in the past, and when the possibilities of mutual assistance are exploited to the full, most of the terrors, calamities, mishaps and hardships which befall mankind can be reduced to a minimum. By insurance, a provident, far-seeing community can be relieved of most of the hardships suffered by our ancestors. It makes possible the maintenance of an efficient medical and hygienic organisation, devoted to the health and welfare of the entire community from birth to death, but, besides the safeguards which come from foresight and intelligence, the State is now making itself ever more the protector of the child.

Though the output of the machine is almost limitless the raw material is not always so, and the acreage available for food has its limitations. Consequently the danger of over-populating the world must never be overlooked. Having smaller families has certainly helped to increase the standard of living, and we have to go back to the time when the people were wretched and poor to find a high birth rate. As they become more intelligent, most women wisely prefer to limit the numbers of their children so as to have fewer cares and increased leisure. In the past they were mere child producing machines, which were worn out by the time they had reached middle age, as we discover from the old tombstones. The mother generally died about forty, having been preceded by several children who had died in infancy or childhood, largely through want of sufficient care and nourishment. These bad old days, we hope, are now passed, never to return.

Much has been written, and much more will be said, about the future of the human race. Developing mind, as it harnesses nature more and more to its requirements, has endless possibilities ahead. What atomic energy will accomplish can only be imagined at this early stage of its development. Like electricity a hundred years ago, it is just in its infancy, but what a sturdy and robust creation electricity has become within that short time! Already electric power and heat have done much to save labour, and to an increasing extent this will be applied to the wheels of industry to generate power, and relieve the housewife of household drudgery. Plastics are now being used in the manufacture of an unlimited number of different articles, so much so that much of what we require is being fashioned in numerous designs of plastic material at prices within everyone's reach.

We must, however, curb our imagination of what the future has in store for humanity, because we could go on envisaging the many ways in which the life of the people will be enriched by new discoveries and inventions. The effect of the war has been to retard progress, and burden nearly every country with greatly increased debt. On the other hand it has increased our knowledge of healing, and taught us improved methods of production and distribution which will now be applied to peaceful purposes. Many old traditional ideas have been abandoned, and the minds of most people have been stimulated to reach out towards new and better methods unimagined by our ancestors.

The war has brought about a revolution in our social and industrial outlook. Now we realise how, by more scientific planning, we can put our knowledge to much greater practical use. Far too little planning has been done in the past, and we have been content to accept conditions and not make the conditions which would greatly increase our prosperity and comfort. Sufficient money has not been spent in Great Britain on scientific research for the purpose of increasing the welfare of the people. Russia spends eight times and the United States six times more than does Britain with this end in view. Though much has still to be discovered, we now know the most nourishing foods to eat, how best to cultivate the land, the best and quickest way to make and move things, and if we apply our increased knowledge wisely the next generation will benefit from the trials and tribulations which forced us to think and improve our methods.

So long as we do not lose our individuality, which must never be affected by the idea that we exist for the good of the State, better and quicker methods of production and distribution will make life fuller and happier. Always it must be accepted that the State exists for the good of each individual, and no official-dom must ever be allowed to reduce the individual to a cipher in the State. The individual is a very wonderful and precious creation, and provided that this is not forgotten there seems to be an era of increased comfort, leisure and happiness before the human race, if only it can avoid the ever-recurring plague of war. So let us now see if this deadly thing can be conquered.

(3) JUSTICE, PEACE AND SECURITY MUST BE OUR AIM.

We are now nearing the end of our story of man's upward climb from savagery to present-day civilisation. First of all we read of roving nomadic tribes, and how some settled down in the deltas of rivers to secure their livelihood by means of agriculture. Conflict waged between the nomads and settlers, which in the end produced the nation because the settlers combined for mutual protection. Agriculture caused the building of villages which grew into towns, and thus commenced civilisation (Latin, *civis* = citizen). Wherever the land was suitable nations grew up and developed, and the struggle for existence continued as nation fought against nation, the weak being either obliterated, absorbed or dominated by the strong.

This way of life was similar to what happens amongst wild animals, as, for example, gorillas, chimpanzees, orang-outangs and gibbons, which behave very much as does man himself. They live in groups, each having its own territory, and they are kind to one another within these groups but show no friendliness to their neighbours. Here we find the amity and enmity complexes fully developed, and when we come to tribes of human beings we discover the same friendliness within the tribe and the same hatred towards everyone outside.

When tribes grew into nations the same attitude of mind prevailed, there being constant ruthless struggle one with another. Each national unit was held together by a nucleus of amity and co-operation within, and an outer crust of enmity towards everyone beyond its frontiers. Mind only, and nothing else, erects the barriers between nations, and within these separate and independent groups the laws of natural selection and survival of the fittest prevail, present-day man being the result.

These natural laws proceeded, but not unhindered, as civilisation in one way is anti-evolutionary because it helps to develop the mind to become free from the domination of savage instinct. On the other hand, it aids evolution because it makes possible intensive competition between individuals within the nation, and this develops intelligence. Within the nation natural passions are held in check, and evolution takes a path contrary to that observed in either jungle or tribal life. In civilised life, force is used to protect and encourage the amity or ethical side of man's dual nature, whereas amongst the uncivilised the enmity or non-ethical aspect prevails.

Civilisation has consequently prepared the ground for better times to come, and made it possible for all that is latent in the mind to come to the surface. It made possible ethical mental development, and turned man from a selfish brute, thinking only of himself, into one whose sympathy goes out to others. First his understanding overflowed to his wife and family, then it reached the tribal boundary, and has today widened to encompass the nation. He therefore has the capacity to increase his sympathy and friendship towards others, and no reason exists why some day his mind should not develop to the point of including all the people on earth within his range of compassion.

Aristotle could not believe that the brotherhood of man could embrace more than 100,000, the most in those days who could live at peace together. Now nations of over 100,000,000 evolve together in peace and happiness. Russia and the United States comprise numerous races and languages, so why could not Europe some day live as one homogeneous federal state? The Roman Empire laid the basis for this union, but mankind was not then ready, and after four hundred years the attempt dismally failed. Ruthless evolution, as applied by natural law, took full control to produce the ever-warring Europe this history has recorded.

To abolish war means the changing of the course that evolution has so far taken, but it is well worth doing provided a better way of life is achieved. Mind is king and can direct nature into the way she must go. So far, nature has been the master and man her servant, but, with the coming of education and the passing of ignorance, a revolution is taking place which will ultimately transform the life of mankind. The hitherto unthinking impulses, the desires, hopes and fears which led to evolution, must be submerged, and reasoned thought take the place of blind subservience to nature's ruthless ways.

Reason has played a small part in evolution, and we have reached our present status by blindly groping along a rough and stony road with little light to guide us. Natural law must now be harnessed to reason and man become master of his own destiny, though the many problems which still confront him will involve him in constant trouble until his mental development has reached a much higher level. To produce a united contented world will be just as difficult as it was to produce the first united nation of people who lived together in peace, a task which was accomplished successfully to bear good fruit down the ages.

Evolution has always proceeded without rational thought, to produce what is both good and bad in us today. One side of our character developed towards righteousness and the other towards unrighteousness, the one showing kindness and friendship towards some and hostility towards others. The analysis set out on the next page makes clear that man is a dual creation having within him the capacity for both good and evil. Some have the good qualities more pronounced than the bad, but to a greater or less degree man is made up of both good and bad. In primitive times the bad predominated, but amongst civilized communities the good predominates. Stress and strain produce varied effects, sometimes bringing

ANALYSIS OF MAN

History and experience teach us that man is a composite being, composed of qualities which are both good and evil. Here the outstanding ones are analysed, those which produce good on the left, and those causing evil on the right:

His own individuality is to him his most precious possession. He resents outside interference with his personal ideas and actions.	1	He tries to deprive others of their individuality, and make them subject to his will.
He is prepared to suffer and die to retain his personal freedom.	2	He is prepared to suffer and die to dominate others to his will.
He thinks and works to clothe and feed himself and those he loves.	3	He will take from others what they have and love.
He will fight, suffer and die to retain his lawful possessions.	4	He will risk suffering and death to take what others own and love.
He is fond of children and home life, going without things to increase their happiness.	5	He produces children he cannot adequately support.
He wishes to live and work in peace and comfort, and allow others to do the same.	6	He will risk suffering and death to invade other lands, and kill their inhabitants so as to secure his needs.
He loves, and is prepared to work and even die for those he loves. He is capable of sincere sympathy, kindness and understanding.	7	He hates and despises some so intensely that he is prepared to suffer and die to secure their misery or death.
He thinks of the feelings of others, and says and does nothing to make them unhappy.	8	He thinks only of himself, and is indifferent to what he says or does so long as he obtains his desires.
He is tolerant, unselfish, forbearing, patient, reasonable, just, kind and gentle.	9	He is intolerant, cruel, unkind and overbearing, and cares only for himself.
He loves truth and justice, and prefers knowledge to ignorance.	10	He cares nothing for truth and justice, and prefers ignorance to knowledge.

out the best and sometimes the worst in humanity. Briefly we can describe the good man as unselfish and the bad man as selfish, but, as the mind determines both, mental development is the only means of producing the enlightened unselfish man who is as near perfection as we can imagine.

Civilisation and Society are necessary to this end, not for themselves but to give the r'ght conditions for personal evolution. They are a means to an end, namely mental development which produces human happiness. Here on earth mental growth is still in its nursery stage amongst the vast majority, and the human race has only made halting progress on the road which passes after death through the etheric realms to some far-off distant goal. This being our destiny, the development of personality is consequently the purpose of existence both here and hereafter.

Nature has evolved our minds to their present level, and consequently ethical development is not contrary to evolu ion, which by stress and strain, by good and evil thoughts and deeds, has made us what we are. By ruthless methods she has fitted us for something better, and it now rests with us to say whether or not we make progress along the lines of men al evolution, and part for ever with the harsh methods she used to forge the being we now call civilised man. We must choose between evolution in the raw, jungle evolution, or peaceful evolution, based on an ethical standard, which both family and national life have proved profitable and possible.

Jungle evolution has raised us to the summit of the organic scale, but, if reasoned thought does not now take command, mental evolution will be stunted and warped by forces which make further mental development difficult. Tyranny, aggression and domination destroy mental evolution. Aggressive people have no free institutions, and no liberty in which thoughts can grow. Freedom and liberty are hated by tyrants, and must be fought for until aggression and domination are no more.

Tyrants are possessed of the jungle mind, whereas developed mind seeks to suppress the animal within us, and fashion a new species which is controlled by reason and wisdom, not by thoughtless instinct. The past dual mind of man, friendly to his own people and at enmity with the rest of mankind, must therefore evolve into one which harbours friendship and kindness for all. This taming of man will eliminate the hateful, ferocious, intolerant side of his character, and develop the domestic or friendly side, thus making this earth what the homeland has become.

Civilisation for many centuries favoured the tyrant, because with it came slavery and serfdom, both being possible only within a civilised country. It made use of slaves and serfs to form a useful basis to support the more intelligent classes. Civilisation is based on toil, and the least intelligent have always had the drudgery to perform. Tyranny and bodily slavery went together, and in non-democratic lands the form it now takes is mental, but, as we evolved out of the former, so will come some day the end of the latter. A free democracy favours the individual who has courage, enterprise and advanced opinions, just the opposite to what happens under a dictatorship which produces the slave mentality and thwarts evolution.

Civilisation transformed man's way of life, and made possible the life we now experience. It produced a leisured class which thought and wondered, invented an alphabet, writing, arithmetic, and then came books which contributed much to the world's knowledge. Through civilisation came justice, security, wealth and comfort, a state of affairs within each nation which has prepared the way for these blessings being applied internationally. Civilisation raised man's standard of living, as the settled man is able to plan and organise his life in a way the wandering nomad cannot do.

Civilisation, however, made war fiercer because it could be fought, financed and planned in a much more thorough manner. As the tribes amalgamated into nations, small wars ceased and large wars commenced. War forged the civilisations of the past and present, and so far it has occupied a large part of history. Therefore war cannot destroy civilisation, though it can cause a temporary setback to progress. No defensive war is fought to save civilisation, but to preserve a way of life the people understand and appreciate. Domination is detested because a conquered people feel that they alone can work out their own evolutionary destiny, and their younger men sacrifice themselves for this end. Preservation of one's own society still takes the place of the natural desire of self-preservation, and a feeling of national exaltation prevails over personal desires.

The waste of life, wealth and effort this has entailed can best be exemplified by the history of Europe. If we look at a map of Europe, in the year 1066 for example, the time of the Norman conquest of England, we find the frontiers much the same as they are today, with the ancestors of the present European nations living on the same soil. If there never had been a war from that day to this, Europe would have changed little in race or characteristics, and yet what have the preceding pages disclosed?

One invasion after another, one conquest following the other, one dominant power declining to give place to another. The frontiers, notwithstanding some five hundred conflicts and all their consequent bloodshed, destruction and misery, only swayed backwards and forwards like a pendulum. If the boundaries of one country bulged outwards for a time, they were sooner or later pushed back again. Spain, France, Austria, Germany, Turkey and Sweden dominated Europe to a greater or less degree, though never for very long, but each was the cause of strife, destruction and suffering, all because there was no supreme authority to keep order.

To continue this state of affairs would reveal that the mind of man cannot develop out of doing what is wrong into doing what is right. It would thus be as much chained to custom as is nature, which destroys and creates without thought. War, and undeveloped mind, are inseparable, the consequent result being nations armed to the teeth, and wasting their substance on unproductive effort. History is largely made up of war, which has made and destroyed nations. So far that has been the destiny of the race, but more developed mind now foresees something better for mankind. War, tyranny, slavery and superstition are now seen to be evil things, which have retarded progress, created suffering and lowered the dignity of man. Consequently, with the advent of education, the time is now coming, provided much greater attention is given to ethical development, when intelligent direction, intelligent control, intelligent planning and intelligent forethought can spare the race many of the troubles it has endured in the past.

Now that the world has become so small, as the result of our new-found power of rapid travel, what happened locally in the past is occurring in a world-wide sense. Asia, Africa, Europe and America had their own wars in the past, but now most of the inhabitants of earth take sides and fight on one side or the other at the same time. War has ceased to be an evolutionary affair, as the same races fight one another with the same fierceness as those of different breed. War has become a total affair and everyone becomes involved, every nation and continent, so much so that we now realise that if there is to be peace instead of war all the nations must unite to this end and act together under one recognised authority.

The people must now be educated in world government, just as they are being educated in national government. As they have found a way to keep peace within the nation, they will have to find an international method to control unruly nations. Ignorance, which breeds selfishness and greed, has so far prevented the human race from agreeing on a workable solution of the problem, but perhaps, after the latest holocaust, reason will take the place of folly. When all the nations agree to work together for the good of all, and not against each other for the temporary enrichment of individual groups, there will then be a distinct prospect of international peace throughout the world.

The conclusions reached in this book are that developing mind can determine its own destiny, and if mankind wills to live at peace he can do so. Only the curse of ignorance has directed evolution into the channel it has taken, and now it rests with mankind, by planning and forethought, to submerge the enmity evolutionary urge and replace it permanently with an amity or ethical urge. Search the writings of biologists and anthropologists as we may, and nowhere do we find the belief that we must bow to the fate prescribed by irrational evolution and direct our ways only along its hard uneven road. They all agree that the beast within us can be tamed out of us, that man can rise superior to his animal heredity, and that war serves no useful or evolutionary purpose. Nature's haphazard way of doing things, they believe, should now be replaced by planned and reasoned forethought, and evolution directed in the way that developing mind decides it must go.

We have found in education the way to solve many of our problems. We have found that guiding mind, by taking reasoned thought, can be trained to direct the human species along the right and not the wrong road. We must leave the old rutted and heavy roads behind, and travel on the one which reason has smoothed out and made pleasant for all.

Up to our own time evolution was given full play in our social life, everyone striving for himself, only the fittest surviving and the weakest going under. The poor, who could work and could find work, obtained a bare existence, and those who could not had to live on charity from hand to mouth as best they could. Natural law of supply and demand flourished, and free competition had the field to itself. These were the days of grinding poverty, sweated industry and ruthless competition. The national conscience has now risen against nature's way of doing things in industry, and it has also risen against nature's way of doing things socially. Just as developing mind has humanised industry and our social life, so must it humanise world politics and eliminate the desire to regard the small and weak state as the vassal of the stronger.

With the spread of education there must come everywhere in time the government of the people by the people. Enlightened and educated people hate tyranny and all forms of despotism, and if Germany had remained a republic the Second World War would probably never have occurred. Democratic nations are less war-minded than dictatorships, and, if the people are wisely led and have a free say in their affairs, the chance of war is greatly reduced. To avoid war in the future it is therefore essential that the people everywhere be educated to the point that they can govern themselves wisely, and work harmoniously with other nations, all being intent on the common good and not on one nation scoring over another.

Man has made great material progress, especially during the past two hundred years. Now the time has come to progress in another direction, because material progress matters little if his mind does not think aright. By research, experiment and invention he has harnessed a great natural force, which is called electricity, and made it work for him. By the same methods he has produced the bomber and explosives which he uses in war-time to destroy the power stations producing the electricity. To build with one hand and destroy with the other is just childish folly, and yet no one knows how to prevent this from happening.

We have trained our minds to think in one direction only, namely how to apply natural resources for the benefit of groups of people and not for all humanity. Our motto has been "The nation is my country and to further its prosperity is my purpose in life", instead of "The world is my country, and to help to make humanity prosperous and happy is my aim in life". At an earlier stage in man's sojourn on earth he first of all thought only of himself, then of his family, then of his tribe, and now he thinks of the nation.

The time has now come for us to take the next step and think of humanity as a whole, as we are all one family with the same desires, feelings and destiny. It is all a matter of mental development, and, as the capacity of the mind has enlarged, so have we made the advances already achieved. Each one must now train his mind to think of the earth as a unit, without boundaries, the most distant part being more accessible than Edinburgh was from London at the beginning of last century. Consequently all nations must get away from the idea that one or more may impose its will on another by force, and this means that each nation must relinquish that part of its sovereignty hitherto devoted to power politics.

First of all the simple trilobite could envisage only its very immediate muddy surroundings, but, as mind developed, it took in a larger range until the time came when our ancestors could think of the forest in which they lived. Then they moved out into the open and obtained a wider vision, which was increased by travel when they discovered how to make a wheel on which to move their belongings. This greatly extended their range of movement, but for thousands of years they were pinned down to the neighbourhood in which they were born. Movement increased and mind developed as, by land, the horse, or mule, or ox, became the motive power, while on sea it was the wind, but not until the power of steam was discovered did travel become general. Now the petrol engine has brought every land within easy distance, because it has enabled us to fly.

The mind can only develop by contact with things material, and its thoughts, until it learned by experience, were naturally confined to its immediate surroundings. Now it is just learning to think of the earth, and its inhabitants, as one and indivisible, and when this important addition to its range of knowledge comes to be appreciated we will be able to think in world-wide terms, and not only from the limited angle of our own nation. From now onwards let us think as world citizens, and not as inhabitants of the particular patch on which we were born. Let us cease from thinking that only the people with whom we mix, and to whom we speak our particular form of language, are always right and everyone else is wrong, because, if we had been born on the other side of a frontier, perhaps only a few miles north, south, east or west of our birthplace, our outlook would probably be different.

Every individual thinks differently, and so do groups of individuals. This being so, all must learn to be as tolerant internationally as we are one towards the other within each national group. When each country can conduct its foreign policy in the same benevolent way as it does that relating to home affairs, we can all become world citizens, thinking as world citizens and not merely as members of one particular section of the world's family.

When all reach this level of thought, we shall cease producing machines to destroy the products of each other's labour. When the mind so develops to encompass this vision, we shall never think of killing someone living across an imaginary line, called a frontier, just because he happened to be born on the other side. Frontiers should not increase our will to kill and destroy, because killing is still murder, no matter where a person is born. What is now a nation, not so very long ago was composed of separate tribes which fought one another. Now they are united as one people, who live at peace and work for the common good of the nation. This being possible, it is equally conceivable that those who live on different sides of an imaginary line will some day live peacefully one with another, and this much-desired achievement would be hastened if each country formed a League for the Promotion of International Goodwill.

Each nation has its own force to prevent disorder, but some nations are now reaching the stage when their police force and their prisons are not fulfilling to the same extent their old-time functions. Some localities in these nations have even now reached the stage when both police and prisons have become almost unnecessary for the purpose of law and order. The magistrates in the local courts now deal mostly with motorists exceeding the speed limit, or who have not attended to their lights, but much less with theft, cruelty, disorder, drunkenness and many other crimes and misdemeanours which were common only fifty years ago. Education has brought about this advance, and, if some districts can reach this enviable position, all can. It likewise follows that if education can reduce crime to this extent within fifty years, it can some day eliminate it altogether.

Likewise education can eliminate war, but it must have time and peace in which to pursue its sacred mission. No state exists today which can contemplate the abolition of force for the maintenance of law and order. Force must remain until education makes it unnecessary, but how to apply that force internationally is the great difficulty. The first League of Nations failed because it lacked the necessary force to prevent the aggressor flouting its decisions. It was a noble but quite impracticable ideal, and, so long as some nations are criminally minded, and led by criminals, all efforts to prevent aggression by means of conferences are stupid and a waste of time.

The future endeavour of all good men and women must be twofold: first, the firm establishment of a world organisation as an international court of justice, backed up by a force which all must obey, and second, the adoption of an international code of ethics which will be taught to children everywhere, not as a lesson, but as something each must absorb when young so as to secure his own individual happiness and comfort. When we come to realise that our own individual comfort and happiness is closely linked with that of our neighbour across the road, and across the frontier, most of the world's economic and political troubles will vanish. Systematic ethical instruction will some day achieve the desire of the vast majority of mankind, namely world peace and prosperity. That is our plan for world peace, but it will fail unless there is justice to every nation and no cause for complaint.

By conquest the world's inhabitants have spread themselves over the world, and the Second World War was just a repetition of the age-old game of snatch and grab, this time played and lost by the aggressors. Moreover, by pursuing this policy, the world so far has been developed, each nation whose inhabitants were prepared to risk money on foreign enterprises obtaining concessions from poorer countries, or just occupying them and making the natives their subjects. If this had not been done most of the gold, the oil, the copper, the silver and much else would have remained where nature placed them. All this, however, has caused bad feeling and jealousy both amongst the natives and amongst those who were not first on the scene, and the preceding pages have recorded the conflicts which have occurred for the purpose of securing wealth possessed by some, and desired by others who felt themselves strong enough to take what they wanted.

This ever-present danger to the future peace of the world is obvious, so long as there is no recognised authority all will respect. Property must always be respected or otherwise there will be chaos. In a self-contained state this has been done through centuries of evolution. Britain a thousand years ago was as chaotic as much of the world is today, but bit by bit a system of laws and protection produced law and order, and now the different counties and towns do not fight one another. Likewise a world order must be developed, though the difficulties ahead are much more formidable than those which produced peaceful Britain.

Nevertheless events are moving towards world unification. Russia now dominates Europe and Asia, just as the United States does the Americas. If this domination is wisely used, both these great nations can maintain peace throughout the world. Nations are today striving for greater unity of policy than ever before, and it is unity of purpose that will bring about peace, the numerous different sovereign states in the past, each with its own policy, having been the cause of so much turmoil. Instead of diversity of power, to be the cause of war, we now have it concentrated between two great groups, both of which declare their desire for world peace. That, if sincere, is a great advance towards a better world, but the question is whether the ethical cement is yet strong enough to bind the people everywhere together for one purpose only—the peace and happiness of mankind.

Only gradually did the blessings of peace come to individual nations, because it was possible to establish one unified control. Only slowly were the fifteen different kings and chiefs in England merged by war into one throne, under which the parliamentary system developed. Each nation is sufficiently self-contained to develop law and order under one authority, but when we come to deal with world affairs the position is quite different. First of all there is as yet no firmly established world authority wielding the necessary force that all are willing to obey, there is no international law that all will accept, each nation doing internationally what it wishes and defying others if it is strong enough to do so.

Secondly, each nation, with few exceptions, speaks a different language, and is consequently mentally separated from all the others. Thirdly, nations are made up of people·having a different ancestry, tradition, religion, culture and outlook, the geographical situation of each producing a different mentality. Fourthly, some are richer than others, some have more and better ports, some have no access to the sea, and some have possessions abroad in which they invest their wealth and receive in return produce on which they can always depend.

Consequently, those who have less than others envy their richer neighbours, but their love of country, and their own independence and way of life, is so intense that they prefer to remain as they are, and be burdened with defence, rather than come within the protection of a federal organisation whose united members would have common interests to the benefit of all concerned.

The right to independence is now recognised by democratic people, but until all are prepared to give to others what they demand for themselves there is no prospect of permanent world peace. Some countries which have all they require are always greedy for more, and so the plundering of the weak by the strong will continue until the time comes when an effective world force is organised to preserve law and order everywhere, just as do the police in civilised lands.

One essential to future peace is the abolition of national armies, an international police force taking their place for the sole purpose of keeping order and peace. So long as armies remain, and men are trained as professional soldiers in the science of war, in how best to attack and conquer an enemy, the danger to peace will be ever present. These men have little to do in times of peace, and fret if they see no chance of ever putting their knowledge to practical use. So they are for ever scheming, and thinking of the battles they will fight with some possible enemy. To teach men the art of war is just playing with fire, and to give them the opportunities for which they have worked means war. So professional soldiering must everywhere be abolished, and they must instead become policemen, not trained to fight battles but to keep order between the different nations of the world.

The earth is becoming so populated, that when the population of one country grows beyond its capacity to support, more territory is required for its sustenance. A limitation of the size of each country's population to its capacity is essential, and birth control should be encouraged to prevent an undue increase. If a country will not adopt birth control, its people should be told that its further expansion will not be permitted.

Otherwise the most backward and prolific nations may cover the face of the earth, and push out the more enlightened ones who realise the folly of bringing children into the world if there is not enough land to support them. Those people who breed like rabbits think only of their own immediate satisfaction, and ignore the fact that if they have children, whom they cannot support, their offspring must either die of starvation, or be killed or maimed in war, fighting for more living-space. This subject must form part of the world's ethical code which all countries will adopt.

When we have an international police force, instead of standing armies of professional soldiers, the past disreputable methods adopted by armament firms of encouraging governments to be for ever increasing and improving their armaments will cease. Likewise will be removed the traffic in arms with countries on the verge of war, as has happened in past times when the world's great armament firms competed with one another to sell them war material. On the occasion of the war between Bolivia and Paraguay (1932-34), while the League of Nations was endeavouring to end it, millions of pounds worth of armaments were supplied to both sides by the armament firms of Britain, America and Europe, and by means of much graft and intrigue they were successful in preventing an embargo being put on arms to both the belligerents.

Until all the nations disarm they will continue to add to their armaments new and better weapons in time of peace, and this means that companies making weapons of war compete with one another to get the business. So they advertise, and have their own travellers and methods of securing orders. One outstanding sinister character, who made it his business to sell arms, was Sir Basil Zaharoff, the greatest universal armament provider of all time. On one occasion Zaharoff, who made millions from selling weapons of destruction, remarked, "I made my first hundreds gun-running for savages. I made wars so that I could sell arms to both sides. I must have sold more arms than anyone else in the world."

So highly did the British government esteem this

outstanding pedlar of death, that it made him a Knight Grand Cross of the British Empire and a Knight Commander of the Bath, while Oxford University honoured him with the degree of Doctor of Civil Law. Honours were given him by France and Greece, while the King of Spain made him a duke. "Cabinet Ministers", wrote his private secretary after his death, "were his puppets, kings were his pawns", and British titles were bestowed on those who helped him "through his external instrumentality". "Sometimes the purchase price went to party funds. Sometimes it went by rather more devious methods to private funds."

On another occasion Zaharoff sold a submarine to his native country, Greece, and then went on to Turkey, whose government he induced to buy two submarines because Greece had made this addition to her navy. The story of the graft, intrigue and crime surrounding this man is one of the most disgraceful records in human history, and emphasises that so long as armaments are produced one war will follow another.

Vickers in Britain, Krupps of Germany, Schneider-Creusot of France, Dupont of America, Mitsui of Japan, and all the other armament firms of the world have employed agents who sell the weapons of destruction they produce. These agents often secured for themselves a profit of 100 per cent., part of which they used to bribe the politicians of different countries. By this means these countries increase their armaments at the expense of the people who will be the sufferers when they come to be used.

Let us not forget the Shearer scandal of 1927, when the American warship builders employed Shearer to prevent the success of the Naval Disarmament Conference. His activities consisted of (1) violent anti-British propaganda to keep the United States in fear of Britain, (2) influencing votes in Congress against reducing warship building, (3) preparing articles for the newspapers, (4) lecturing to patriotic societies, and (5) lavishly entertaining naval officers and newspaper correspondents. He claimed from his employers 255,655 dollars commission for his successful work, and because he was not paid in full he took them to law. The evidence which was given in court caused such a sensation in America that a public enquiry was held, and this brought to light the graft and propaganda that had been at work to prevent the Naval Disarmament Conference from being successful.

Even the weapons produced in one country have been turned against its own people, as, for instance, when the Turks in the First World War used against the British, Australian and New Zealand troops, when they landed at Gallipoli in 1915, the guns and shells supplied to them by Vickers. Moreover, the Boers used machine-guns against the British which were made by Vickers. Krupps exported half the guns they manufactured in their vast slaughter-machine factories, 27,000 having been exported to fifty-two different countries from its foundation up to the opening of the Second World War. The Bavarians and Austrians in 1866 used Krupps' guns against the Prussians. Some of the guns used by the French against the Germans in the Franco-Prussian War of 1870 were manufactured by Krupps, and, with some of the money made by this evil traffic over nearly a century, Krupps financed Hitler at the outset of his political career, and reaped from armament orders a rich reward for this expenditure.

Prior to Japan's attack on China, both Britain and America supplied China and Japan with large quantities of munitions of war, but, as these instruments of death are traded in like any other merchandise, further examples are unnecessary. Wherever the weapons are made the fact is now evident that war in our time means that everyone suffers. Gone are the days when adventurers, out for loot and excitement, made war on their neighbours. They could not settle down to honest toil, and so became soldiers of fortune. From such men the armies of the past were recruited, but this has quite changed because all the fit young men are now forced to fight.

The future of the world is in the hands of the people themselves everywhere, not just in some countries but in all. So long as backward nations exist, those who love peace and hate war must combine to protect themselves as allies, and not remain as single nations. Union is strength, whereas separate defences can be overcome one by one. All the peace-loving nations must therefore unite to ensure their combined safety, and do their utmost to educate the barbarians into a wiser and better outlook on life.

When this task is accomplished, when ignorance is dethroned and knowledge and wisdom reign supreme, a new era will have dawned for the human race. At some distant period, for which we all should work and strive, the world will be governed by humanity for humanity as one unit, and not as many separate nations, each striving for its own selfish ends. Unification will bring peace and concord out of the chaos and discord of nationalism, the nation in future confining its administration to the internal affairs of its own country.

If we could only be sure that the United Nations Organisation would become firmly established, and receive the sustained support of all the great powers of the world, how different would be our outlook! To-day we are just at the opening of a new era, fraught with tremendous possibilities of good or evil. Will the human race this time take the right road and follow where reason and wisdom lead, or will it again make another tragic mistake and go down the road to destruction? Only the future can tell whether mental development has yet reached the stage when nations will co-operate for the good of the human race, or work along their own separate selfish paths. Have the world's leaders yet reached the level of thinking as world's citizens, and not for their own countries alone? That will come in time, but whether it has now come it would be hazardous to predict, because both the leaders and the people still lack the knowledge and ethical development which automatically lead to wisdom and righteousness.

One of the first duties of the United Nations Organisation should be to promote knowledge, increase culture, stimulate ethical conduct and improve the people's health everywhere. In its capital should gather all who lead the people to a higher standard of life, and these leaders should evolve themselves out of narrow nationalism and be intent on leading the world to realise the folly of frontiers as barriers studded with guns and bayonets. Some day, let us hope, such boundaries will be as undefended as those dividing the counties of England, or the states of North America, and the people on each side of them will be as safe from attack as those living on the frontier between the United States and Canada.

Internationalism will some day take the place of nationalism, and love of, and service to, all humanity will replace the past aggressive glorification of the particular patch on which each one was born without will or choice. The world will then become one's country, and humanity one's fellow countrymen, who will all learn an international language, freed from the unnecessary difficulties surrounding present-day speech. When this time comes, knowledge will have largely replaced ignorance, wisdom will have superseded folly, and most of our troubles will have faded away like the morning mist. Then the sun of righteousness will shine forth on a world at peace, harmoniously knit together with one aim, the good of all mankind.

(4) THE CURSE OF IGNORANCE WILL SOME DAY PASS AWAY.

Some day the curse of ignorance will pass away. Some day wisdom and not folly will rule the world, because folly comes from ignorance and wisdom from knowledge. We can judge the future from the past, and, by looking back, foretell its course. If we look back we find that over countless ages mind has more and more dominated matter. This mysterious substance, with its wondrous power of development, has, over aeons of time, moulded physical matter into its own design, first in the form of a body suitable to its requirements, and then surrounding matter. What a contrast between the earliest form of life, the amoeba, and ourselves of the present day, and yet countless causes and effects have produced us from this our primitive ancestor, each one being a link in a long, long chain extending from that far-off age to the present time.

If this has been possible what is impossible? If mind can so develop this increasing power of expression, is there any limit to its advancement? This thought gives us renewed hope for the human race, which already has accomplished so much. History's record of life on earth is equivalent to less than a minute in our lives, but pre-history, which takes us back into the depths of time, gives hope and encouragement that there is a purpose in our lives which developing mind will progressively make clearer.

Developing mind, in one form or another, has continued its slow spiral course, ever towards greater appreciation of its environment, and ever towards greater expression. That is what we gather from the past, but it is only a fraction of the story. To limit mind only to the physical is to regard it solely from one angle, whereas its power of expression must be regarded from many angles, because it pertains not to the physical order which is limited by fixed and rigid laws.

Mind seems to be boundless in its power of expression, and its earth experience is only one phase in its seeming eternal career. So we must not consider the history of mankind as a record of the beginning and end of its power of development, but rather as we would the life of a child which has its future stretching far out before it. Past history is but the story of the nursery stage of human development, which continues, after the change we call death, to reach out to heights we on earth cannot imagine. The temporary passage of mind through physical matter is only a stage in its evolution, and geology, biology and history record the progress it has already made in its power of expression during this period of its development.

We are each part of this universal, developing, thinking substance, and each one can further help in hastening its power of greater expression. By training, and the accumulation of greater knowledge, we know from past experience that its development can increase, and it now behoves us to mould our own plastic thinking substance into an ever-higher range of thought. No better way can be found than by learning the past achievements and mistakes of the human race, its past outlook on life, and the reasons which directed its thoughts into formulating the numerous ideas history records.

For this reason *The Psychic Stream* was written, to put on record the development of man's religious ideas, and now *The Curse of Ignorance* tells his political and social history from primitive times, embracing in outline most of what we know of the past. The knowledge we can derive from these two branches of history—religious and political—now enables us to judge both the wisdom and folly of our ancestors, but it is on their mistakes that we should chiefly dwell if we are to avoid them in the future.

There are two ways in life, the right and the wrong way. By knowledge, which brings wisdom, we can be led to take the right way in the future more often than did those who went before us, and this way leads to greater happiness, which must always be our destination. The broad way leads to happiness and the narrow way to misery. So we must make certain that future generations place their feet on the broad road, and are not directed by ignorance into the narrow one which leads to dejection and despair.

The broad way is the road whose foundation is based on all that makes life bright, comfortable, healthy and happy, its borders being planted with trees from which can be gathered the fruits of intelligent effort. Those who travel this way make the best of the world, and take advantage of all that science can offer, while those who take the narrow way rely on the supernatural to supply their desires. Instead of applying intelligent labour and direction to their affairs, they employ their time appealing to heaven for protection and sustenance. Only within recent years has a portion of humanity intelligently applied itself to improving its conditions on earth, and wisely left to nature its destiny hereafter.

There are these two ways of life into which the young can be led, the broad way on which travel the righteous whose minds are great enough to keep company with all the good of every land and clime, no matter what political or religious faith they have adopted. On the narrow way we find the bigots of every shade of thought, who are tolerant only of those who think as they do. Their companions are so few that they all march along in single file, because their principal occupation consists in saving their own individual souls, humanity to them being divided up between the few who are saved and the many who are damned.

These two roads lead either to freedom or tyranny. The broad tolerant way recognises that all should be educated into the way of self-government. This way leads to mental freedom, greater self-expression, and its destination is mental harmony and peace. Those who adopt this way are freed from fear, as the knowledge, which comes from liberty, breaks their prison chains. They fear not the political party in power because they are its master, and it their servant, whereas the narrow way leads to bondage, the people being in terror of their despotic master, their ruler, who governs them, not as they wish, but as he thinks they should be ruled. He instructs and they obey. He thinks and they do as they are told. He can lead them to disaster and they must follow, while all who resent this treatment are persecuted or imprisoned.

The broad way leads to investigation, to reasoned thought, and to observation which bring comfort, things of beauty and happiness to life, while the narrow way contains those who fear to use their minds in case they offend the god of their own creation. They prefer to be subservient, to cringe and crawl, rather than allow their minds to roam at large and gather in the wonders which make life so rich and pleasant. So the heretics took to the broad road, and gave us all we now enjoy, while the orthodox kept to the narrow road, and denounced all progress and reform, which, they said, were contrary to the will of God.

These two ways of life lead in different directions: one, the broad way, to all that earth supplies, music, the arts, industry, invention, free, happy and comfortable homes, while the other way leads to the monk's cell where love is despised, and music, gaiety and laughter, and all the joys of life, fail to pierce the surrounding gloom. Happiness hereafter, to those treading this narrow way, can only be purchased by misery here on earth. "Sell whatsoever that thou hast and follow me", we are told, was the substance of the teaching of Gautama the Buddha, Krishna the Saviour, and Jesus the Christ. This idea haunted the minds of our ancestors, and, instead of making a heaven here on earth, some preferred misery so that one day they might reach heaven above. Gradually the findings of psychic science will remove the fear of death. Then, ever fearful humanity will realise that the hereafter is a place so natural that all this unnatural effort is quite unnecessary, and only a waste of valuable time.

There are two ways of life, one leading to righteousness, which brings happiness, and the other to unrighteousness, which produces misery. One leads to kindness, mercy and sympathy, the other to hatred and cruelty; one to tolerance and the other to intolerance; one to justice and the other to injustice; one to truth and the other to error; one to peace and concord and the other to quarrelling and war; one to mental development and the other to mental contraction. One is the Secular way and the other is the Theological; one is the Democratic and the other the Despotic; one is the sane and the other the insane. One leads to the gathering of all the fruits of the earth into an abundant harvest for the good of all mankind, while the other leads through a parched desert, the route chosen by lone travellers seeking their own salvation in some distant heavenly oasis, where they hope to revitalise their parched and shrivelled souls.

One way is to consider the individual as a cog in the wheel of state or industry, as one who has no personal rights and must obey the dictates of some political or industrial dictator. The other way is to recognise in everyone the divine spark which can by freedom, tolerance and education produce the nobility of character all should aim to achieve. The only nobleman is the one whose character is noble; all other made by kings, if lacking this, are but tinselled figures who shine from borrowed rays of royal sunlight. Only character, and one's own individuality, count both here and hereafter, and the aim of all good men and women must be to secure justice, freedom, and equal rights for everyone everywhere. The policy of the democratic state must be to banish fear—fear of illness, fear of want, fear of oppression, fear of unemployment, fear of war and fear of all the terrors which have for ever haunted humanity in the past.

One way is the broad road leading to happiness, contentment, tolerance and understanding, while the narrow way leads to misery, on which our ancestors have wearily toiled, too ignorant and stupid to be more than cattle to their masters who lorded over them. The broad way secures social equality for everyone, and abolishes privileges and selfish interests. Those who walk thereon regard all men and women as having the same rights to education and happiness, besides all the pleasures this life can give, and not as slaves to some dominant power which takes all it can out of them, to cast them aside in the end to finish their days in poverty.

One way leads to the scientific prevention and cure of disease, while the other relies on prayers, consecrated bread and wine, the crucifix, relics and charms to drive out the devil. One is the rational and the other the theological way of curing disease. One way leads to radiant health, and the other to a life of suffering and misery. The way of knowledge leads to peace, the road of ignorance to war, the former being planted on either side with all that the virtues can produce, while the latter has growing along its borders lust, cruelty, hatred, mistrust, greed, intolerance and all that vice can propagate. One way leads to freedom, and the other to domination by those who falsely claim divine authority for keeping their slaves in mental chains.

For thousands of years there was only one way to think, namely the theological way, when all feared or worshipped the men and women of the other world, and called them gods or goddesses, saints or devils, attributing to them supernatural powers over earth and mankind. Then it was believed that every phenomenon of nature was the direct result of an act of a god or a devil, and that the divine monarch, and his nation's priests, could, by prayer, influence the gods to do their will. By rational thinking, observation and experience some wise men developed the scientific outlook. Consequently there are today two ways of thought—the one which believes that the universe is governed by the supernatural which can be influenced by ceremonials, rites and prayers, and the other which accepts nature's laws and works within their framework for the development of the human mind, realising that the same cause invariably produces the same effect.

One way finds in man the source of what is good and bad, which means that man himself must save himself, must right his evil ways and find salvation for himself, there being no lifeboat waiting by to save all who seek its aid. The other way is to think that individual and national conduct is determined by God, who allows this and forbids that, a substitute being provided to take the punishment due to the evil-doer. The first way comes from observation and reasoned thought, and the other from theological speculation, devoid of facts or reason, the former being the friend of liberty and knowledge, while the latter keeps company with ignorance and tyranny.

To depart from the ethical code means one thing, to depart from the theological is another; the one who does the former is a wrong-doer, while the latter is a sinner. The former does that which is evil against himself or his neighbour, whom he can harm, while the other is assumed to sin against God, whom he cannot hurt.

So there are two roads which man can take—the broad road leading to harmony or the narrow one to disharmony; the one to knowledge, and the other to ignorance. For thousands of years the narrow road was crowded by a dense mass, seeking to find happiness by supplications to a higher power, while, on the broad road, a few solitary figures travelled, who relied upon their own thoughts and deeds to bring them the happiness they desired. As the centuries passed, and the mind developed, more and more crossed over to the broad road and the narrow way became less crowded. Now, as we look ahead, we can see that the narrow way fades into a faint streak until it finally disappears into a mist of obscurity.

On the other hand the broad road widens the farther we look, there being ample room upon it for all the growing throng of intelligent, industrious, happy, contented people who now realise that as they sow they shall reap. The schools, from which they come, have so developed their minds that they quite naturally accept the fact that here and now is the place to be happy, and that service to others is the height of wisdom, because happiness comes from making others happy. Moreover, they have learned that, by following a certain world-wide accepted code of ethics, harmony takes the place of disharmony and happiness replaces misery.

Those travellers on the broad road leading to wisdom and knowledge have come to realise that if they sow selfishness, greed, cruelty, injustice and all that is evil they will reap what they have sown. So they have cast aside their evil ways and now sow unselfishness, charity, kindness, justice, mercy, truth and all that brings happiness, harmony and concord.

Here we must leave our fellow travellers on both roads. Our history has brought us in contact with those who have taken one or the other. From them let us learn our lesson as to which is best. We have just emerged from a conflict which has been caused by the complete disregard of all that experience teaches us produces happiness. It came primarily as the result of ignorance, against which the forces which preferred liberty to tyranny had to mobilise once again to prevent the destruction of all they felt made life worth living.

We have now once more emerged from the darkness of war into the sunshine of peace, and, if night again settles down on mankind, it will mean that broken, bleeding and suffering humanity has once again been sacrificed on the altar of war without the god of cruelty, lust and hatred being satisfied. Once again some future generation will experience all the horrors of modern mechanised atomic warfare, from which the guilty and the guiltless suffer equally.

Now we know the only remedy which will remove the curse. Now we know that by education, increased wisdom and ethical instruction, the demon of war can be slain, and that the slaughterhouse in which the youth of each generation has been sacrificed can be closed for ever. Education for everyone is still a tender plant, not more than two generations old, but, if it is now nurtured and well watered, it will grow and spread its leaves until they cover the earth. Until then, the nations, which have learned their lesson, must protect this tender plant by maintaining peace until the developed cultured mind produces not only increased comfort and happiness, but also the will and the means for securing enduring peace and goodwill amongst men.

From knowledge comes wisdom, which produces righteousness, whence flows happiness. Ignorance is the fount of wickedness, from which pours all the forces that produce suffering and misery. Everyone must therefore develop the habit of righteousness, of always doing, saying and thinking that which is right, until it becomes so much a part of ourselves that we cannot do otherwise. Each one must cultivate this habit until we reach the position that to do what is wrong makes us miserable. If we sow righteousness we shall reap righteousness; if we cultivate our character in the right way we shall reap the happiness which comes from right thinking. As we foster, nourish and train the mind, so shall be the harvest.

Here we now leave the vast human throng moving on to a destiny of its own making, forever composing a story which future historians will have to tell. We can go no farther, but let us ponder deeply over what has already happened, and contribute, in the years to come, all that is within our power to

> Ring out the grief that saps the mind,
>   For those that here we see no more;
> Ring out the feud of rich and poor,
>   Ring in redress to all mankind.
>
> Ring out a slowly dying cause,
>   And ancient forms of party strife,
> Ring in the nobler modes of life,
>   With sweeter manners, purer laws.
>
> Ring out false pride in place and blood,
>   The civic slander and the spite,
> Ring in the love of truth and right,
>   Ring in the common love of good.
>
> Ring out old shapes of foul disease,
>   Ring out the narrowing lust of gold;
> Ring out the thousand wars of old,
>   Ring in the thousand years of peace.[1]

END OF VOLUME II.

---

[1] Alfred Tennyson in "In Memoriam".

INDEX

The page numbers in light type refer to Volume I, those in heavy type to Volume II

At a time when newspapers and periodicals were greatly reduced in size, because of the shortage of newsprint after the Second World War, and few were publishing reviews, "The Curse of Ignorance" received considerable prominence. The following are extracts from some of the many reviews it received.

"Mr. Arthur Findlay spared no trouble to make his history accurate. Into his narrative, ranging from primitive times to the end of the Second World War, he has packed a life-time of learning. To this wealth of knowledge he gave the title *The Curse of Ignorance*, because this was a history with a purpose, a monumental work, a monument, in fact, to mankind's folly—and mankind's hope."—*Daily Mail*.

"Arthur Findlay's *The Curse of Ignorance* is monumental in that it ranks him as a first-class historian, to be compared with Gibbon and other great writers. In one respect it puts him ahead of them—his lucidity. He not only gives a more enlightened interpretation of the past, but deals excellently with modern events and trends. If you will get these two volumes and spend delightful hours absorbing them, you will have promoted yourself to the level of a well-informed person, and will consider them worth many times their price."—*Educational Guide*.

"Mr. Arthur Findlay, who ranks among the leading historians of our day, has now given us *The Curse of Ignorance*, a lucid history of mankind from primitive times to the end of the Second World War—a truly monumental task. Throughout this competent and very readable work he strives, in vividly written pages, to show how ignorance and selfishness have led to wars, resulting in untold misery. All will agree with him as to the need for increased knowledge and an advance in our ethical standards."—*Staffordshire Advertiser*.

"Mr. Findlay is a brilliantly clever man and a most able advocate. . . . There is a tremendous amount of good, solid and dexterous historical analysis in his stupendous world history."—*Essex Chronicle*.

"Mr. Arthur Findlay (for many years a magistrate of Ayrshire and Essex, and a partner in one of the leading firms of Chartered Accountants and Stockbrokers in Glasgow; Chairman of several companies; a member of the Order of the British Empire and who farms 400 acres of his estate in Essex) writes history with a skilful pen, and tells his story in a way that both fascinates and captivates the reader. *The Curse of Ignorance* is destined to make its mark in historical literature and will undoubtedly become a classic."—*Psychic News*.

"*The Curse of Ignorance* is a very remarkable book. Mr. Arthur Findlay gave seven years' devoted labour, six hours a day, every day of the week, to writing this compendious history of mankind."—*Liverpool Daily Post*.

"Mr. Arthur Findlay has given us a compendious and most lucid work. Any writer who can creditably complete such a task has achieved no mean feat, and this Mr. Findlay has certainly performed. We cannot withhold a feeling of gratitude from a writer who has the monumental energy to give us 2,328 vivid pages marked by almost Gibbonian role but less verbosity. Here we have history of quality."— *Wolverhampton Express and Star*.

"The author is well known all over the world for his books on psychic phenomena, and this his latest work—a fascinating record of human activity throughout the ages— deals with the history of the human race from the psychic aspect. This book is a work of erudition and a mine of historical information and fact, written in a clear and lucid style. It is of absorbing interest. I recommend it to all thinking men and women, as much can be learned from a perusal of its pages. Its two volumes will be an asset to the home library."—*Essex County Telegraph*.

"This massive work is history presented from a new and wider aspect, and this more modern approach clarifies the many difficulties with which historians have been faced in the past. It is certainly a stimulating and thought-provoking analysis of the development of mankind, written from the psychic angle of thought."—*Northampton Chronicle*.

"Mr. Findlay, in telling mankind's story—religious, political and social—from primitive times to the present day, has addressed himself to this important problem with great knowledge, discernment, wisdom and a conviction born of unquestionable sincerity."—*Cambridge Daily News*.

"The condensation, even in two such large books, of this vast subject is in itself a commendable feat, but even more interesting than the author's summarizing of historical events is the angle from which he approaches them."—*Leicester Mail*.

"The deep wide sweep of his human survey gives the book, which is profound and sincere, a strong general appeal, and enables the author to bring out, time and time again, his main theme that ignorance is the root of most evil and unhappiness, particularly so in the case of war."
—*Carlisle Journal*.

"This is a history, a labour of love, written with a purpose. These two volumes may well find a place on the busy man's bookshelves, for they afford an opportunity for the easy study of the history of the world in the light of current events. They avoid religious prejudice which has so often represented the Christian era in a too favourable light."—*Stock Exchange Gazette*.

"These two stupendous volumes bridge the whole history of mankind on this earth. The contribution of the Hebrew, Greek, Roman and Christian civilizations is most carefully assessed. To say that *The Curse of Ignorance* will stimulate thought and provoke discussion is a gross understatement."—*Head Teachers' Review*.

"Here are two volumes, a veritable cyclopaedia of world history, a perfect library of themselves. Mr. Findlay has written a challenging and widely informative book for which we cannot but be grateful."—*Paisley Express*.

"Arthur Findlay marshalls facts clearly and vigorously in his two-volume world history."—*Northern Echo*.

"In this history of mankind the past follies of the race are recorded with painstaking research."—*Newcastle Journal*.

"Mr. Findlay has accomplished his task with outstanding success, and his work will live in the annals of history as one of the greatest contributions to our literature."—*The Two Worlds*.

"*The Curse of Ignorance* appeals to the mind that is seeking, not for theological inexactitudes, but for a reasoned scientific formula of life . . . it is a book far more formidable and imposing than his previous works, both in size and content."—*Hertfordshire Mercury*.

"*The Curse of Ignorance* has been a labour of years and a labour of love, a vast monument of industry. None can deny that if we were to follow its positive principles the sword might be sheathed in England's green and pleasant land."—*Belfast Northern Whig*.

"Mr. Findlay's new book is a monumental work. Those who come to this book with open minds will find a light shone into many dark places."—*Kilmarnock Standard*.

"The author has accomplished a tremendous task and makes his plea with lucidity and skill. He is fearless in his exposition. On the historical side it is obvious there has been much research work."—*Public Opinion*.

"Mr. Findlay, in interesting and readable style, shows how so often the folly of ignoring events of the past has brought tragedy and misery to countless numbers of the human race. His work will repay most careful study and thought."—*Essex Weekly News*.

"Mr. Arthur Findlay has written a truly monumental history of mankind. Taking the widest sweep as a world citizen he traces the long story of man's upward climb and spot lights the mistakes that led to oppression and war through ignorance."—*East Anglican Daily Times*.